HOMOSEXUALITY

PSYCHOANALYSIS

HOMOSEXUALITY

&

PSYCHOANALYSIS

Edited by Tim Dean and Christopher Lane

The University of Chicago Press
Chicago & London

TIM DEAN is associate professor of English and Interpretive Theory at the University of Illinois, Urbana-Champaign. He is the author of *Gary Snyder and the American Unconscious* (1991) and *Beyond Sexuality* (2000).

CHRISTOPHER LANE is associate professor of English and director of Psychoanalytic Studies at Emory University. He is the author of *The Ruling Passion: British Colonial Allegory and the Paradox of Homosexual Desire* (1995) and *The Burdens of Intimacy: Psychoanalysis and Victorian Masculinity* (1999), as well as editor of *The Psychoanalysis of Race* (1998).

The University of Chicago Press, Chicago 60637
The University of Chicago Press, Ltd., London
© 2001 by The University of Chicago
All rights reserved. Published 2001
Printed in the United States of America

00 09 08 07 06 05 04 03 02 01   1 2 3 4 5
ISBN: 0–226-13936–0 (cloth)
ISBN: 0–226-13937–9 (paper)

Library of Congress Cataloging-in-Publication Data

Homosexuality and psychoanalysis / edited by Tim Dean and Christopher Lane.
     p.   cm.
   Includes bibliographical references and index.
   ISBN 0-226-13936-0 (cloth : alk. paper) — ISBN 0-226-13937-9 (pbk. : alk. paper)
   1. Psychoanalysis and homosexuality. I. Dean, Tim, 1964– II. Lane, Christopher, 1966–
   RC506 .H66   2001
   616.89'17'08664—dc21

                                                              00-046713

IN MEMORIAM

Andreas Bjørnerud

APRIL 11, 1965–DECEMBER 15, 1992

Lynda Hart

AUGUST 23, 1953–DECEMBER 31, 2000

CONTENTS

ACKNOWLEDGMENTS

So many people contributed to the making of this book that we feel a debt of profound gratitude. We acknowledge, first, our appreciation of the contributors to this volume, who made working on the book so stimulating and pleasurable. We are especially grateful to Arnold I. Davidson for helping us prepare the Foucault essays for publication. Daniel W. Smith translated Foucault's pieces within a tight deadline, and Sébastien Dubreil provided welcome assistance in negotiating the Parisian publishing world.

At a decisive moment in the life of this project, Joan Copjec invited us to present versions of our work on homosexuality and psychoanalysis at the Center for the Study of Psychoanalysis and Culture, SUNY-Buffalo, and we are grateful to Joan and to Sue Feldman for arranging our visit. For support and encouragement over the course of this book's making, we'd also like to thank Parveen Adams, Judith Butler, Teresa de Lauretis, Cynthia Dyess, Didier Eribon, John Fletcher, Randall Halle, Langdon Hammer, Alice A. Jones, Armando Maggi, Karol Marshall, Ellen Lee McCallum, Bethany Ogdon, Jacqueline Rose, Stuart Schneiderman, Charles Shepherdson, Kaja Silverman, John David Smith, James Swenson, and Michael Warner. Jason K. Friedman's copyediting expertise was invaluable on many occasions, and his support of this project kept us going. We also thank Jason B. Jones for research assistance.

At the University of Chicago Press, Doug Mitchell and Robert Devens went beyond the call of duty in shepherding our manuscript through the review process. We thank them both for supporting this project (and us) so generously and enthusiastically. Two anonymous readers for the Press made many helpful suggestions, which contributed to the book's final shape. Thanks are due to Erin DeWitt, who copyedited the entire manuscript with such care. Emory's Research Council provided funds to cover the cost of permissions, as well as a semester's leave to complete the book. The graduate school and the dean of Emory College supplied a generous subvention to defray the cost of the cover art. The University of Illinois's Campus Research Board also provided a semester's leave, which helped during the book's copyediting and proofreading stages.

For assistance with the permissions, we thank Ted Gurney at Cambridge University Press, Nicholas Royle at the *Oxford Literary Review*, Véronique Héron at Librairie Arthème Fayard, and Florence Giry and Anne-Solange Nobel at Éditions Gallimard.

· · · · · ·

"The West and the Truth of Sex," by Michel Foucault, first appeared in *Le Monde* (November 1976), as "L'Occident et la vérité du sexe." It was subsequently reprinted in *Dits et écrits, par Michel Foucault, Vol. 3 (1976–79)* (1994). Copyright © Gallimard, 1994. Translated and reprinted with the permission of Éditions Gallimard.

"The Death of Lacan," by Michel Foucault, first appeared as "Appendice: La Dépendance du sujet (Foucault et Lacan)," in *Michel Foucault et ses contemporains*, by Didier Eribon (1994). Translated and reprinted with the permission of Librairie Arthème Fayard. Copyright © Librairie Arthème Fayard.

"Closing Up the Corpses: Diseases of Sexuality and the Emergence of the Psychiatric Style of Reasoning," by Arnold I. Davidson, first appeared in *Meaning and Method: Essays in Honor of Hilary Putnam*, ed. George Boolos (1990). Reprinted with the permission of Cambridge University Press. Copyright © Cambridge University Press.

"Freud and Homosexuality," by Paul Robinson, first appeared in *Constellations* 6 (1999). Copyright © 1999 Blackwell Publishers Ltd. Reprinted with the permission of Blackwell Publishers Ltd.

"The Eroticism of Desolation," by Catherine Millot, appeared as "L'érotisme de la désolation," in *Gide, Genet, Mishima: Intelligence de la perversion* (1996). Copyright © Gallimard, 1996. Translated and reprinted with the permission of Éditions Gallimard.

An earlier version of Jonathan Dollimore's essay appeared in "Beyond Redemption: The Work of Leo Bersani," a special issue of the *Oxford Literary Review* 20 (1998). Copyright © OLR. Reprinted with permission.

THEORIZING

SEXUALITY

HOMOSEXUALITY AND PSYCHOANALYSIS: AN INTRODUCTION

Tim Dean and Christopher Lane

. . . .

1. Overview of the Problem

Until quite recently, the relationship between homosexuality and psychoanalysis was wholly adversarial. Although in 1973 the American Psychiatric Association decided to remove homosexuality from its list of mental disorders, the legacy of that pathologizing view still lingers. Conservative campaigns touting the myth that homosexuality can be "cured," combined with the proliferation of numerous reparative therapies, have revived that legacy with a vengeance.[1] Neither psychoanalysts nor lesbian, gay, and queer people have forgotten that the mental health establishment routinely used to consider same-sex desire as a form of illness. Freud, however, did not think of same-sex desire as in any way pathological. Despite all his biases and shortcomings, the founder of psychoanalysis conceived of homosexuality as part of everybody's sexual constitution and thus not in itself a problem. "Psycho-analytic research," he maintained in 1915, "has found that all human beings are capable of making a homosexual object-choice and have in fact made one in their unconscious" (*Three* 145n).

The problem is not homosexuality but social attitudes toward it. We might even say that homophobia, rather than homosexuality, makes people ill. If we accept that everybody has made a homosexual object-choice in his or her unconscious, then it is homophobia, the irrational fear of same-sex desire—including one's *own* same-sex desire—that generates internal strife and thus neurosis. From this perspective, psychoanalysts' business would be to analyze homophobia, rather than perpetuating it by treating homosexuality as a problem. And, indeed, substantial attention recently has been devoted to demystifying negative attitudes toward same-sex desire, using psychoanalytic conceptual tools. For example, in the important collection *Disorienting Sexuality: Psychoanalytic Reappraisals of Sexual Identities* (1995), a number of New York analysts, most of them lesbian or gay, join forces to investigate their profession's heterosexism and to challenge the normalizing impulses in contemporary clinical theory and practice.[2]

In the present volume, psychoanalyst Joanna Ryan continues this investigation, asking why clinicians in Britain and North America have resisted critiques of heterosexism and continue to rely on more orthodox assumptions about gender and sexual development. And, in a related discussion, psychoanalyst Daniel L. Buccino argues persuasively that a Lacanian clinical approach differs even from classical Freudian analysis in its viewing object-choice as merely one way of elaborating deeper questions about self-knowledge. Unfortunately, however, these explicitly anti-heterosexist clinical voices remain in the minority.

Sometimes it is tempting to imagine that the problem lies entirely with social attitudes toward homosexuality, as if the difficulties could be treated as wholly external. Were this the case, we would need nothing more than a social critique of homophobia and a program for social change. However, Freud's universalizing of same-sex desire points in a different direction. Rather than simply revealing homosexuality as a normal and natural expression of human erotic potential, Freud's connecting sexuality to the unconscious instead makes all sexuality perverse: "The disposition to perversions is itself of no great rarity but must form a part of what passes as the normal constitution" (*Three* 171). The idea of the unconscious dramatically changes how we can and should think about human sexuality.

Contrary to Freud, most political efforts to win legal protection and, more broadly, social sanction for nonheterosexual forms of erotic expression have been based on the claim that those alternative forms are neither deviant nor pathological, but instead represent normal variations of human sexuality. Attempting to adjudicate the question—as pressing in his time as in ours—whether homosexuality is innate or acquired, Freud continues, "The conclusion now presents itself to us that there is indeed something innate lying behind the perversions but that it is something innate in *everyone*" (171; original emphasis). From this Freud was led to argue that human sexuality is constituted as perverse because it emerges in the drive's separation from natural functions. By defining the drive as unnatural, as operating *contra naturem*, Freud effectively "queers" all sexuality.[3]

This view of Freud still tends to generate surprise; it does not represent the standard view of psychoanalysis. We have put together this volume in order to explore ideas that remain new and unfamiliar. Even psychoanalysts sympathetic to lesbian and gay political movements have not always appreciated the radical nature of Freud's position on homosexuality, finding it politically progressive to move beyond classical psychoanalytic theory. We think Freud's ideas deserve more attention and that his theory of the unconscious has not been fully appreciated. By articulating homosexuality with psychoanalysis, we mean to encourage psychoanalysts and psychoanalytically oriented critics to think harder about the work that the category *homosexuality* performs. In doing so, this volume aims to challenge the heterosexism that is explicit and implicit in much psychoanalytic writing. Our aim is not to exempt Freud—or psychoanalysis—from critique, but to reconsider Freud's most basic ideas about sexuality and the unconscious from the perspective of same-sex desire.

This enterprise is made possible by work in lesbian and gay studies, as well as by recent developments in queer theory. For complex historical reasons that we elaborate below, lesbian and gay thinkers have been, at best, ambivalent concerning psychoanalysis. Although some of the most advanced psychoanalytic theorizing has come from gay and lesbian critics such as Leo Bersani and Teresa de Lauretis, most people working in the burgeoning field of lesbian and gay studies tend to avoid much engagement with Freud. This volume aims to encourage lesbian and gay critics, as well as queer theorists, to take more seriously the conceptual tools that psychoanalytic theory makes available.

One of the greatest paradoxes in the history of psychoanalysis is that psychoanalytic institutions have developed in directions antithetical to psychoanalytic concepts. Lesbian, gay, and queer people have felt the impact of clinical institutions, with their normalizing moralism and discriminatory practices, more readily than we have encountered psychoanalytic ideas that offer a firm grounding for nonheterosexist accounts of erotic desire. This distinction between psychoanalytic institutions and Freudian concepts already suggests that the term *psychoanalysis* is neither unified nor monolithic. In this volume we present work from various psychoanalytic schools and orientations—Freudian, Kleinian, Lacanian, Laplanchean—but we also want to emphasize a broader disjunction between institutions and concepts. While others labor to reform the actual practices of treating patients, training analysts, and administering clinical institutions, this volume tries to provide theoretical tools for that reformist enterprise.

If the term *psychoanalysis* in our collection's title thus represents a far from unified entity, the term *homosexuality* likewise should be viewed as designating multiple formations, practices, and desires. We want to acknowledge at the outset that, in fact, plural homosexualities and psychoanalyses are at stake. The diversity of homosexual practices and desires cannot be conveyed in a book title. Psychoanalysis has had much more to say about same-sex desire in men than in women, and, as Paul Robinson points out in his contribution to this volume, "Freud's failure to extend to lesbians the same dispassion he lavishes on his male homosexuals [is] a reflection of his larger problem with women." Part of this problem lies in the masculinist tendency to theorize women's sexuality in terms of, or by analogy with, men's. We would like to emphasize that same-sex desire in men and in women should not be treated according to a single conceptual model, as if male and female homosexualities were symmetrical, analogous, or complementary. In their important study *Wild Desires and Mistaken Identities: Lesbianism and Psychoanalysis* (1993), psychoanalysts Noreen O'Connor and Joanna Ryan have traced the consequences of doing so, showing how different clinical schools persistently misunderstand lesbianism. Without rejecting psychoanalytic concepts, O'Connor and Ryan aim to create a nonpathologizing framework capable of accommodating what remains most diverse and unpredictable about women's fantasies and desires.

Given the differences between lesbian and gay sexuality—as well as multiple differences within these two categories—we can begin to appreciate the considerable difficulties of doing justice to lesbian and gay concerns under a single rubric. These difficulties are exacerbated by multiplying nonnormative sexual identities, as lesbian and gay organizations now routinely acknowledge at least three other groups of nonheterosexual people: bisexuals, the transgendered, and queers. Rather than a lesbian and gay movement, we now have an LGBTQ movement, a coalition unified somewhat precariously by its distance from and resistance to the heterosexual norm. Sometimes the category *queer* is used as an umbrella term—a kind of shorthand—for these disparate sexual identities, though that usage remains inconsistent and, indeed, controversial. No small part of the controversy surrounding the term *queer* stems from the sense that a single term cannot describe everyone's sexual identity. And, of course, throughout the last century, gay and homophile movements have been motivated by a fundamental desire to acknowledge and do justice to sexual identities that diverge from the heterosexual norm. Quite apart from the obstacles imposed by reactionary forces, this is difficult to accomplish because the proliferation of alternative sexual identities makes it that much harder to acknowledge everybody's particular erotic sense of him- or herself.

As we explain in more detail below, the term *queer* responds to this difficulty by conceptualizing sexuality in terms other than those of individual identity or selfhood. Rather than trying to acknowledge and honor everybody's sexual identity, one strand of queer theory suggests that the commitment to identity is itself part of the problem, and that sexuality should be understood differently. Building on feminist critiques of identity politics (most notably Judith Butler's), these theorists argue that sexual identities such as *lesbian* and *gay* are themselves potentially normalizing, because they entail definitions of desire and conduct that require subjective conformity. Rather than offering a politics based on individual identity, this school of thought advocates a politics based on resistance to all norms—a politics that connects gender and sexual oppression to racial discrimination, class inequities, ethnic hierarchies, and national chauvinism. Espousing a far-reaching politics suspicious of all norms, this strand of queer theory divorces sexuality from identity.

A certain tradition of Freudian thought also divorces sexuality from identity formations, seeing in the displacements of unconscious desire a mechanism that undermines the ego and calls into question any secure sense of sexual selfhood. By taking the unconscious into account, Freudian psychoanalysis recasts ego identities—including those of lesbians and gays—as illusory. Further, in Lacanian terms, the ego is created through "misrecognition" and is based on a fundamental perceptual error; it therefore cannot provide a reliable basis for any politics concerned with sexual desire. This tradition of psychoanalytic thought, in its skepticism toward a political movement committed to reinforcing lesbian and gay egos, finds a potential ally in queer theory. The resistance of the unconscious to all norms makes this psychoanalytic concept—and others—very helpful to queer theorists. Part of the present volume's purpose lies in showing how useful psychoanalysis can be for antinormative politics and alternative ways of thinking about sexuality.

2. Foucault and the History of Sexuality

As we have indicated, nonheterosexuals have found it difficult to see psychoanalysis as an ally. When they have looked for intellectual reinforce-
ment in recent years, lesbians and gays more often than not have turned
to Michel Foucault, the French philosopher whose books on medicine,
psychiatry, madness, and sexuality contributed so much to our understanding of the historical variability of erotic identities. Indeed, because
queer theorists have canonized the first volume of Foucault's *History of
Sexuality* (1976; trans. 1978), any effort to articulate homosexuality with
psychoanalysis necessarily must engage with Foucault's critique of psychiatric and psychological modes of conceiving sexuality.

Our claim that psychoanalytic institutions developed in directions antithetical to Freudian concepts finds support in Foucault's histories of institutions, as well as in his methodological critique of how histories of
ideas tend to be conceived and narrated. This is one reason we decided
to translate into English for the first time Foucault's précis of *The History
of Sexuality*, "L'Occident et la vérité du sexe," which *Le Monde* published
in November 1976. Foucault's greatest contribution was to make us aware
that the way we see ourselves as sexual beings is a comparatively recent
historical development. Not only did the affirmative identities *lesbian* and
gay become available only lately, but also, more significant, our tendency
to consider sexual desire as expressing an interior truth is a historically
produced phenomenon, albeit one that it is difficult to think without.
According to Foucault, although there has been same-sex erotic activity
throughout history, sex was not understood as self-definitional until the
last century: It was not seen as an integral part of a person's identity. For
example, the common notion of "coming out" as lesbian and gay—the
familiar idea that one organizes his or her life narrative in terms of a
trajectory leading to the discovery of sexual orientation—would have
been an utterly foreign concept to, say, participants in the Greek institution of pederasty.

Hence sexuality has a history, and psychoanalysis is part of that history. But the role psychoanalysis played in that history—and has yet to
play—is sufficiently complex to warrant careful attention. In *The History
of Sexuality*, Foucault even characterizes his historical narrative as "an
archaeology of psychoanalysis," as if his book were really all about psychoanalysis (130). Although Foucault rarely wrote directly about psychoanalysis, his work makes clear just how difficult it is today for us to contemplate sex without thinking in loosely psychoanalytic categories. From

the late nineteenth century, we inherit ways of understanding sexuality that came into being around the same time as psychoanalysis did. This is especially the case with homosexuality. Foucault provides the best summary of this shift in thinking, and the most famous passage in his *History of Sexuality* bears repeating:

> This new persecution of the peripheral sexualities entailed an *incorporation of perversions* and a new *specification of individuals*. As defined by the ancient civil or canonical codes, sodomy was a category of forbidden acts; their perpetrator was nothing more than the juridical subject of them. The nineteenth-century homosexual became a personage, a past, a case history, and a childhood, in addition to being a type of life, a life form, and a morphology, with an indiscreet anatomy and possibly a mysterious physiology. Nothing that went into his total composition was unaffected by his sexuality. It was everywhere present in him: at the root of all his actions because it was their insidious and indefinitely active principle; written immodestly on his face and body because it was a secret that always gave itself away. It was consubstantial with him, less as a habitual sin than as a singular nature. We must not forget that the psychological, psychiatric, medical category of homosexuality was constituted from the moment it was characterized—Westphal's famous article of 1870 on "contrary sexual sensations" can stand as its date of birth—less by a type of sexual relations than by a certain quality of sexual sensibility, a certain way of inverting the masculine and feminine in oneself. Homosexuality appeared as one of the forms of sexuality when it was transposed from the practice of sodomy onto a kind of interior androgyny, a hermaphrodism of the soul. The sodomite had been a temporary aberration; the homosexual was now a species. (42–43; original emphases)

Since space prevents us from doing full justice to this rich passage, we'd like to emphasize here Foucault's double perspective on psychoanalysis: On the one hand, his reference to "a past, a case history, and a childhood" clearly implicates psychoanalysis in the late-nineteenth-century invention of homosexuality as a species category; on the other hand, his reference to "the psychological, psychiatric, medical category of homosexuality" pointedly omits psychoanalysis from this process of invention.

Foucault acknowledges this apparent ambiguity when he states that the idea of homosexuality as a species category remained foreign to psychoanalysis. At the historical moment when nearly everyone around him was thinking about homosexuality in evolutionary or racial terms, Freud insisted that same-sex desire was a universal human potential, and therefore that "psycho-analytic research is most decidedly opposed to any attempt at separating off homosexuals from the rest of mankind as a group of a special character" (*Three* 145n). By refusing to grant homosexuality the status of an identity, Freudian theory resisted the racializing perspective on sexuality—a resistance that, according to Foucault, earns psychoanalysis a unique place in the history of sexuality.

Unfortunately, Foucault's crucial distinction between Freudian ideas and psychoanalytic institutions has remained obscure to his Anglophone audience; this is the result, in part, of a significant mistranslation in *The History of Sexuality,* when Robert Hurley renders *psychanalyse* as *psychiatry.* The passage in which Foucault specifies the unique place of psychoanalysis should read as follows:

> And the strange position of [psychoanalysis] at the end of the nineteenth century would be hard to comprehend if one did not see the rupture it brought about in the great system of degenerescence: it resumed the project of a medical technology appropriate for dealing with the sexual instinct; but it sought to free it from its ties with heredity, and hence from eugenics and the various racisms. It is very well to look back from our vantage point and remark upon the normalizing impulse in Freud; one can go on to denounce the role played for many years by the psychoanalytic institution; but the fact remains that in the great family of technologies of sex, which goes so far back into the history of the Christian West, of all those institutions that set out in the nineteenth century to medicalize sex, it was the one that, up to the decade of the forties, rigorously opposed the political and institutional effects of the perversion-heredity-degenerescence system. (119)

Foucault viewed psychoanalytic concepts as conflicting not only with psychiatry, psychology, and medicine, but also with its own institutions and practices. In other words, Freud's best ideas remained hard to translate into practice and to institutionalize successfully—even for Freud himself.

This difficulty is explained in wonderful historical detail by philosopher Arnold I. Davidson, whose contributions to this volume are part of his larger project on the nineteenth-century concept of perversion. He shows that Freud inherited the concept of perversion and destroyed its embedded assumptions, without ever fully grasping his own innovation. Davidson's second essay in this volume, "Closing Up the Corpses," should be read in conjunction with his "Sex and the Emergence of Sexuality," as well as his classic account of Freud's *Three Essays on the Theory of Sexuality* (1905), "How to Do the History of Psychoanalysis." In all three essays, Davidson shows how the contradictions in Freud's theory of sexuality derive not from Freud's personal limitations, but from his participation in the uneven dynamics of large-scale conceptual change. While this process of conceptual mutation remains incomplete, its beginnings can be located in the nineteenth-century shift from pathological anatomy to a reclassification of disease based on function. What Davidson calls the "psychiatric style of reasoning" emerged when perversion could be located in neither genitalia nor brain neuroanatomy, but was instead seen in psychological terms, as a functional disease of the sexual instinct.

As a concept, perversion makes sense only so long as the sexual instinct is conceived in functional terms; Freud broke that conception by divorcing the instinct from natural functions and by claiming that the sexual drive emerges independently of any particular object of satisfaction to which it might subsequently become attached. For Davidson, as for Foucault, psychoanalysis thus holds a unique position in the emergence of our modern understanding of sexuality. However, Freud's originality stems not from his treating sexuality as historical, but paradoxically from his universalizing gestures ("all human beings are capable of making a homosexual object-choice and have in fact made one in their unconscious" [*Three* 145n]). Despite the congruence between Foucauldian and psychoanalytic views of sexuality—and notwithstanding the potential alliance between queer theory and Freudianism—fundamental differences remain between historical and psychoanalytic perspectives on homosexuality.

We can restate this basic incompatibility in terms of queer theorist Eve Kosofsky Sedgwick's helpful distinction between universalizing and minoritizing accounts of sexual identity. In *Epistemology of the Closet* (1990), a landmark study that has become one of queer theory's touchstones, Sedgwick identifies as central to our era the tension between a view that sees homosexuality as defining a distinct group of people, on the one hand, and a claim that homosexuality is relevant to—because inherent in—all people, on the other. Lesbian and gay politics has been based largely on the first view, the minoritizing conception of sexuality that considers it analogous to race or ethnicity as a characteristic by which one defines oneself. If we place sexual minorities on a par with racial minorities, the argument runs, then we can campaign politically on behalf of civil rights for lesbians and gays according to the democratic, rights-based model. By contrast, Freud generally held the second view, a universalizing conception of sexuality that refuses the racial model and, along with it, the homophile movement.

In its most basic assumptions, let alone its treatment of nonheterosexuals, psychoanalysis thus remains incompatible with the general tenets of lesbian and gay politics. This fundamental tension was exacerbated rather than resolved by psychoanalysts' tendency, once Freud had died, to revert to the minoritizing view of homosexuality—a reversion that went hand in hand with renewed efforts to pathologize and then eliminate all manifestations of nonnormative sexuality.

3. Further Tensions between Institutions and Concepts

After Freud's death in 1939, a form of psychoanalysis emerged that bore little, if any, conceptual resemblance to its origins. The consequences for a psychoanalytic account of sexuality were disastrous. Tensions between Freud and his associates had been growing since 1911, when Alfred Adler, one of Freud's prominent Viennese followers, broke with him to advance his own understanding of individual psychology. Adler is perhaps best known for defining the term *inferiority feeling,* a state he attributed more to organic factors than to psychical ones. Adler explained sexual behavior in terms of compensation for inferiority feelings, and, like other ego psychologists, he stressed adaptational imperatives in his clinical theory.[4]

Two years later, after trying to desexualize Freud's theory of the unconscious, Carl Jung also broke with Freud. In the years leading up to their split, Zurich-based Jung had been trying to distance psychoanalysis from the implications of Freud's arguments in *Three Essays,* converting Freud's libido theory into a looser model of indeterminate mental energy. Together, Jung and Adler helped formalize an institutional split between the Freudians who believed that homosexuality was an unconscious possibility in everyone, and those who accepted Jung's and Adler's claims that homosexuality signaled a type of person with a fairly predictable relationship to the world.[5]

When Freud died, many North American analysts sided with Adler, repudiating Freud's arguments about homosexuality and the unconscious. The powerful influence of the medical establishment in the United States also affected psychoanalytic perspectives on clinical treatment. In the 1940s and 1950s, as Russell Jacoby explains in his valuable study *The Repression of Psychoanalysis: Otto Fenichel and the Political Freudians* (1983), many North American analysts followed a growing national trend of seeking professional accreditation. While conferring authority on its allies, the medical establishment spurned lay analysts as quacks and tried to restrict psychoanalytic expertise to medical doctors, who taught it almost exclusively to interns rather than to other analysts. As psychoanalysis in the United States became virtually indistinguishable from the medical establishment, it merged, almost imperceptibly, with the very psychiatric and medical model from which Freud had broken at the end of the nine-teenth century.

The postwar development of psychoanalysis in Britain followed a very different path. In his excellent contribution to this collection, Ramón E. Soto-Crespo analyzes the important debates—known as "The Controver-sial Discussions"—that took place in Britain in the 1940s between the Anna Freudians and the Kleinians concerning the relationship between homosexuality and the oral stage. Even while Sigmund Freud was alive, Klein had challenged his account of the Oedipus complex, arguing for the importance of oral drives and aggressivity that, in Freudianism, were viewed—though never dismissed—as "preoedipal." Klein's strong contri-bution to the object-relations school had an impact on psychoanalytic theory whose influence can be felt today in the coalition of analytic methodologies known as the relational school, which leads the way in progressive, nonpathologizing clinical accounts of nonnormative sexual-ity.[6] Although "The Controversial Discussions" did not focus directly on the question of homosexuality, they amplified the role of unconscious fantasy in structuring all aspects of conscious life.[7] By emphasizing infan-tile sexuality and aggressivity even more than Freud had, Klein paved the way conceptually—if not in practice—for an understanding of human sexuality as originally phantasmatic and baroquely perverse.

Together, these developments in Britain and North America signaled a sea change in psychoanalytic accounts of homosexuality. One year af-ter Freud's death, Sandor Rado, at Columbia University's Psychoanalytic Clinic, published an essay in *Psychosomatic Medicine* entitled "A Critical Examination of the Concept of Bisexuality," that rejected Freud's claims about constitutional bisexuality. In a move that would galvanize many clinicians, he argued that homosexuality derived from a pathological fear of the opposite sex, and that it could—and should—be cured. Rado voiced similar claims eight years later in "An Adaptational View of Sexual Behavior," thus contributing to what Joanna Ryan, in this collection, calls a "widespread psychoanalytic endorsement of heterosexuality as biologi-cally ordained, natural, fitting, mature, the essence of human sexuality and relationships." Because Rado's "Adaptational View of Sexual Behav-ior" aimed to locate heterosexuality in biology, his argument stressed gen-der complementarity; homosexuality, in this model, was by definition unnatural and pathological.

One result of this conceptual shift was that the "negative" Oedipus complex—already downplayed by Freud in the early 1920s—no longer was seen as integral to subjectivity or accounts of sexuality. Freud had argued since at least 1914 (in "From the History of an Infantile Neurosis") that "inverted" and "normal" Oedipus complexes arise concurrently in young children. In part, he wanted to explain the intricacy of gender identification and the consequent unpredictability of these complexes' "dissolution" into conventional heterosexuality. Whereas the "normal" Oedipus complex pictures the father and son as rivals for the mother, the "negative" Oedipus complex in boys represents the father as both an object of desire and an imaginary ideal guiding the boy's "masculine" identification. During the "negative" Oedipus complex, in other words, the mother is viewed as an obstacle to the boy's sexual desire for the father.[8]

Although Freud needed a theory capable of explaining why identification is unpredictable and precarious, he struggled to minimize the homoerotic implications of this theory—a struggle discussed by Christopher Lane in his contribution to this volume. Yet after Freud's death, critics such as Rado reinterpreted the "negative" Oedipus complex "as a regressive defense against a more basic heterosexual proto-oedipal stance toward the mother" (Lewes 107). In a strange about-face, then, the "negative" Oedipus complex came to be viewed not as constitutive of sexuality, but as a radical departure from normalcy, a psychical error producing deviant tendencies of effeminacy in men and excessive masculinity in women. Psychoanalysis in the 1940s—centrally affiliated with the medical establishment in North America—was cast as one of the few agents capable of "correcting" this pathology and returning men and women to the heterosexuality from which they had strayed.

These arguments appeared so frequently in essays by Franz Alexander, Edmund Bergler, Grete Bibring, Ben Karpman, Herman Nunberg, and Fritz Wittels that their emphasis on "curing" homosexuality brought "psychoanalytic" arguments about homosexuality in North America and other parts of the world fully into alignment with psychiatric treatment.[9] They paved the way for increasingly severe clinical techniques in the 1950s and 1960s, including aversion therapy; shock treatment; the use of noxious stimuli, such as emetics, designed to induce nausea and vomiting; hormone injections; behavioral therapy, including hypnosis and forms of visual and auditory suggestion aimed at "the modification of sexual fantasies" (Bancroft 43); castration; and even lobotomy. As recently as 1972, a medical congress held in San Remo, Italy, discussed "cures for homosexuality such as conditioned reflexes, electric shock treatment, drugs, and even surgical operations" (Hocquenghem 53).

In 1956 New York clinician Edmund Bergler solidified this rapport between psychiatry and American psychoanalysis by using psychoanalytic terminology against lesbians and gay men. *"Today,"* he stressed, as if his words announced technological progress rather than conceptual regression, *"psychiatric-psychoanalytic treatment can cure homosexuality"* (9). Bergler subtitled his study of homosexuality "Disease or Way of Life?"—a question that for him was clearly rhetorical. "I have no bias against homosexuality," he assures readers, but "homosexuals are essentially disagreeable people . . . [displaying] a mixture of superciliousness, false aggression, and whimpering. Like all psychic masochists, they are subservient when confronted with a stronger person, merciless when in power, unscrupulous about trampling on a weaker person. The only language their unconscious understands is brute force" (28–29). Working alongside Bergler was Irving Bieber, whose large report *Homosexuality: A Psychoanalytic Study* appeared in 1962. Bieber's "systematic study of 106 male homosexuals and 100 male heterosexuals in psychoanalytic treatment" claimed to provide "convincing support for a fundamental contribution by Rado on the subject of male homosexuality: A homosexual adaptation is a result of 'hidden but incapacitating fears of the opposite sex'" (vii, 303).

Invaluable accounts of these historical developments appear in Henry Abelove's now-classic essay "Freud, Male Homosexuality, and the Americans" (first published in the journal *Dissent* in 1985–86); Kenneth Lewes's *Psychoanalytic Theory of Male Homosexuality* (1988); and Ronald Bayer's *Homosexuality and American Psychiatry: The Politics of Diagnosis* (1981). As all three note, New York psychoanalyst and clinical professor of psychiatry Charles Socarides probably has taken these arguments against homosexuality furthest. In *The Overt Homosexual* (1968), his first book on homosexuality, Socarides insists that homosexual relations generate only "destruction, mutual defeat, exploitation of the partner and the self, oral-sadistic incorporation, aggressive onslaughts, attempts to alleviate anxiety and a pseudo-solution to the aggressive and libidinal urges which dominate and torment the individual" (8). While Socarides is far from representative of North American psychoanalysis, he is institutionally powerful and prolific, and he actively campaigns on behalf of the possibility of curing homosexuality through "psychoanalytic" means.[10]

4. Beyond Freud

Our discussion in the preceding section helps explain why the gay movement, appalled by the psychiatric-psychoanalytic literature on homosexuality and the clinical treatment of lesbians and gay men, targeted the

American Psychiatric Association (APA) with demands that it remove homosexuality from its *Diagnostic and Statistical Manual of Mental Disorders (DSM-II)*. This training guide for professionals in mental health and the mental sciences includes the APA's official list of mental diseases.

When the APA first published *DSM-I*, in 1952, there was disagreement about, but little political mobilization against, the edition's statement that homosexuals were "ill primarily in terms of society and of conformity with the prevailing cultural milieu" (34). By 1968, however, when *DSM-II* appeared, the APA had reclassified homosexuality and placed it among "other non-psychotic mental disorders," including pedophilia and sadism (44). The revision was a result, in part, of strongly contested changes in psychiatric judgments. In 1955 the Wolfenden Report (recommending that Britain's Parliament decriminalize male homosexuality) received international attention when it rejected arguments that homosexuality was a disease.[11] Remarkably, it did so after the British Medical Association submitted a memo not only urging against reform, but also stressing the number of homosexuals who had been "cured" by turning to Christ (see Higgins 34–35). But when psychiatrist Karl Menninger introduced the American edition of the Report in 1963, he ignored this rebuttal and insisted: "From the standpoint of the psychiatrist . . . homosexuality . . . constitutes evidence of immature sexuality and either arrested psychological development or regression. Whatever it may be called by the public, there is no question in the minds of psychiatrists regarding the abnormality of such behavior" (see Committee on Homosexual Offences 7).

Although it had opposed the APA's previous judgments, the gay movement targeted the APA systematically only in 1970. At the APA's annual convention in San Francisco that year, Irving Bieber was denounced and ridiculed, his arguments drowned out by derisive laughter. Elsewhere at the convention, guerrilla theater and shouting matches took place, and at one point the mayhem was so extensive that a physician "called for the police to shoot the protesters" (Bayer 103). Menninger's professional rigidity and disdain for public opinion—including, of course, the judgment of lesbians and gay men—underscores why the ensuing debate became so rancorous; many of his colleagues, including Bieber and Socarides, held opinions almost identical to his.

After three years of bitter wrangling, the APA finally acquiesced in December 1973, deleting homosexuality from *DSM-II*. But to those psychiatrists and psychoanalysts who had vehemently opposed this move (and had been voicing their opposition, in different forums, for many months), the decision was a capitulation to ideological forces, all the more insulting to their expertise because the APA had heeded the words of homosexuals themselves. For lesbians and gay men, the decision—reaching the front pages of the *New York Times* and *Washington Post*—was a breakthrough victory, signaling in part that their influence could alter core psychiatric arguments about sexuality and gender.

However, the victory was weakened by the APA's decision, also in December 1973, to compromise with its most outspoken members—Bieber and Socarides—and to retain as a diagnostic category *sexual orientation disturbance*. The term was Robert Spitzer's (from his essay "Homosexuality as an Irregular Form of Sexual Development and Sexual Orientation Disturbance as a Psychiatric Disorder") and formed part of his attempt to steer a path between liberals and conservatives in the APA.[12] *Sexual orientation disturbance*—referring to patients "who are either disturbed by, in conflict with, or wish to change their homosexuality"—was dropped from later, still unpublished, drafts of *DSM-III*. In 1977 the term was replaced by a new one, *ego-dystonic homosexuality,* which was viewed as a consequence of "negative societal attitudes towards homosexuality which have been internalized" (qtd. in Bayer 137, 177). The term was formally adopted when *DSM-III* was published in 1980.

Although the phrase *ego-dystonic homosexuality* ostensibly rebuked homophobia, it also stressed adaptation and intrapsychic harmony as the most desirable response to social prejudice. In distinguishing between well-adjusted and self-conflicted homosexuals, the term paradoxically continued to eclipse the psychoanalytic insight that sexuality and sexual identity are *constitutively* conflictual because they involve the unconscious. And it aligned the APA with throwbacks, like Adler, who viewed bolstering the ego as the best means of correcting feelings of inferiority. By emphasizing self-adjustment, the new category also contributed to a form of identity politics that found greater social acceptance the more it downplayed discussion of sexual diversity and nonconformity. Relative to North America's broader cultural perspective on sexuality and the ego, then, the removal of homosexuality from the APA's list of medical diseases represented a bid for normalization at the expense of the very sexuality that much of the gay movement sought to defend.

As Henry Abelove makes clear, Freud's Americanization remains a serious obstacle to articulating his theory of sexuality with a radically antihomophobic politics. Because of the cumulative effect of that theory's dilution and normalization, truly psychoanalytic arguments about sexuality have had a very limited audience in the United States. In France, by con-

trast, psychoanalysis has had neither the same ties nor the same complicity with the medical establishment. And so although the European gay
movements in general were strongly influenced by the American Gay Liberation Front (roughly 1970–72), their directions and local debates often
differed from those in North America. Whereas the civil rights and anti-
Vietnam War movements spurred the American gay movement, the most
powerful influence on the British and French gay movements arguably
was the antipsychiatry movement, shaped throughout the 1960s by such
clinicians and philosophers as R. D. Laing, David Cooper, and Michel
Foucault. This liberationist movement reappraised schizophrenia and
madness, denouncing institutionalized psychiatry as an agent of coercion.
Hence the significance of the fact that, in England, the first unit established by the London Gay Liberation Front was an antipsychiatry group.

This context suggests a conceptual distance between Europe and North
America that, though nominal in 1970 through 1972, widened over time.
In the United States, *gay* and *lesbian* eventually became markers for well-
adjusted identity and political campaigns. In countries such as Britain,
France, and Italy, by contrast, much less cultural and political value could
be attached to these identities, and so fewer European gay and lesbian
groups normalized their sexuality for mainstream political gain. For many
prominent gay writers and intellectuals in Britain and Europe, what
Australian-born Dennis Altman later called *The Homosexualization of America: The Americanization of the Homosexual* (1982) remained troubling. The
history of gay liberation in England is narrated best by Jeffrey Weeks,
whose intellectual and political work remains heavily influenced by Juliet
Mitchell's *Psychoanalysis and Feminism* (1974). Mitchell's reappraisal of
psychoanalysis argues that Freud was more relevant to contemporary
feminism than was either antipsychiatrist Laing or liberationist Wilhelm
Reich. Weeks's pioneering work also is informed by Foucault and European gay liberation theorists such as Guy Hocquenghem and Mario
Mieli.[13] When in 1978 Daniella Dangoor translated Hocquenghem's 1972
study, *Homosexual Desire,* Weeks provided an excellent introduction to
this provocative and still timely book.

An associate of Foucault and of gay psychoanalyst Félix Guattari, Hocquenghem was a radical gay activist, intellectual, filmmaker, and prolific
novelist. *Homosexual Desire,* his first book, appeared one year before the
APA revised its conception of homosexuality in North America and four
years after French workers, activists, and students joined forces in May
1968 to transform society and sexual politics. Hocquenghem's book drew
on the energy and inspiration of the May uprising, and was strongly in-

debted to both the antipsychiatry movement in France and the formation, in 1971, of the Front Homosexual d'Action Révolutionnaire (FHAR), a predominantly lesbian liberation group "explicitly modelled on the American Gay Liberation Front" (Weeks, "Preface" 11).[14] More overtly than Guattari, Hocquenghem used psychoanalytic concepts to advance a radical gay critique of the nuclear family and the capitalist state. In *Anti-Oedipus: Capitalism and Schizophrenia*—published the same year as Hocquenghem's study and translated in 1977, the year Lacan's *Écrits* also became available to non-Francophone audiences—Guattari and philosopher Gilles Deleuze argue that classical psychoanalysis was complicit in formulating the Oedipus complex as a way to regulate desire. Hocquenghem followed Deleuze and Guattari in trying to free desire from the Oedipus complex. It is the family, Hocquenghem claims, that establishes public morality, condemns indecency and perversion, and creates "antihomosexual paranoia." And Freudian psychoanalysis is complicit in this, he argues, because it makes desire oedipal, establishing a framework that controls, rather than simply describes, behavior.

Hocquenghem contends that the family creates homosexuality as a category designed to contain its fear and unsublimated desire. In making this claim and arguing that the containment fails, he rejected the liberal civil rights model adopted in the United States by stipulating that any "exclusively homosexual characterization of desire" is "a fallacy of the imaginary" (36–37). It is a mistake, Hocquenghem suggests, to reaffirm the very distance between homosexuality and heterosexuality that nineteenth-century sexology had created and the Victorians had enforced. Recognizing, with psychoanalysis, that sexual desire is inimical to identity, Hocquenghem wanted to break this mold entirely. Therefore he advocated various forms of "protest against the whole Oedipal system" (124–25), including impersonal sex, that would release desire from all existing frameworks.

Hocquenghem's polemic strongly influenced Italian gay liberation theorist Mario Mieli, whose *Homosexuality and Liberation: Elements of a Gay Critique* appeared in 1977 (trans. 1980). Mieli had lived in London at the height of the Gay Liberation Front and returned to Milan in 1972 to help found *FUORI!* ("Come Out!"), a revolutionary collective and magazine. Yet although Mieli followed Hocquenghem in attempting to liberate desire from the nuclear family, his relationship to Freud—and to psychoanalysis more generally—is less antagonistic than Hocquenghem's. Mieli's book is scattered with references to Ferenczi and Reich, as well as to Freud and Norman O. Brown, for many years an American guru on matters erotic.

But while Mieli is less critical of psychoanalysis than Hocquenghem, his account of desire and repression is also in fact less psychoanalytic.

Mieli's book illustrates what Foucault, one year earlier, had critiqued as "the repressive hypothesis." Foucault was alluding to a hydraulic conception of desire, evident in much of Reich's and Marcuse's work, that views society as a pernicious agent suppressing sexual enjoyment, and liberation as unlimited freedom to express oneself sexually. Whereas Hocquenghem arguably avoids falling into this conceptual trap, Mieli does not. Mieli is closest to Reich and Marcuse—the objects of Foucault's critique—in arguing that "the general neurosis that affects everyone in our society is largely a function of the social suppression of the gay desire, its forced repression and its conversion into pathological symptoms" (62). Hocquenghem did not countenance the idea of "gay desire," since the adjective *gay* already presumes too much about desire's aim and implicitly restricts its range.

Nonetheless, Mieli's work represents a significant accomplishment, bringing together gay liberation theory, psychoanalysis, and Italian communism. He wittily rewrites the usual formulation "a feminine brain in a masculine body" as "a healthy mind in a perverse body" (166). While Hocquenghem considered Freud complicit in the normalization of desire through the Oedipus complex, Mieli was concerned with engaging those moments where Freud seemed genuinely baffled by psychic processes and unable to advance a coherent theory of desire. And whereas Mieli writes explicitly as a gay man about specifically gay issues, Hocquenghem refuses to represent himself as a gay writer, focusing instead on impersonal sex and cruising among men, during which "organs look for each other and plug in, unaware of the law of exclusive disjunction" (117). Resisting imperatives to consolidate the shifting sands of erotic desire into identity categories, Hocquenghem reinterprets and politicizes Freud's theory of polymorphous perversity.

5. Queer Theory and Psychoanalysis

Hocquenghem's theoretical polemic in *Homosexual Desire* has had a strong influence on queer theory, an eclectic school of thought developed primarily in the United States during the 1990s, as a result, in part, of political reconfigurations surrounding AIDS activism. In contrast to mainstream lesbian and gay political movements, which seek legal reform through established power structures, queer theorists and activists draw on the radically oppositional and separatist energies that Hocquenghem articulated two decades earlier. Thus while lesbian and gay activists campaign for the right to serve in the military or the priesthood, to get married, and to adopt children—in short, to pursue the same kinds of lives as average heterosexuals—queer activists reject this vision of "normal" social life as desexualizing. And while some lesbian and gay "assimilationists" have argued that homosexuality is innate and thus immutable (it's not our fault and it can't be cured), queer theorists contend that sexuality is more fluid, more dynamic, and potentially revolutionary. The assimilationists say that our homosexuality shouldn't set us apart from normal life, whereas queer theorists view sexuality as a focal point of resistance to all norms. Thus one tension that queer theory throws into relief is that between lesbians and gays who want a respectable, normal existence, and those who want to use their sexuality politically to disrupt normality, with its gender hierarchies, racial discrimination, and conventional expectations about "family life" for all.

Another tension that queer theory highlights is the conflict between viewing sexuality as immutable and seeing it as malleable. In his contribution to this volume, Brad Epps addresses this conflict, arguing that, paradoxically, queer theorists fixate on "fluidity" to an almost fetishistic degree. Lesbian and gay assimilationists, who compose the majority of nonheterosexual North Americans, consider their sexuality something with which they are born, something that is so much a part of them that it can't be changed. The political benefit of this point of view lies in its tacit resistance to the idea that homosexuality is curable. The assimilationists also often see their lesbianism or gayness as incidental—it's an essential part of themselves, but not necessarily the most important aspect of their lives. For instance, a gay doctor may consider his professional identity as a physician more important than his sexual identity as a gay man. By contrast, queer theory views sexuality as socially constructed rather than something essential with which one is born; yet queer theory also views sexuality as more self-defining than do assimilationists. As a result of its definitive opposition to norms, queerness represents that which separates the individual from the rest of society—hence one's queerness becomes the most salient feature of one's life. Above all, *queer* entails understanding sexuality in primarily political terms.

Like Hocquenghem, North American queer theorists have found in psychoanalysis an armory of conceptual tools for describing social processes of normalization and how they might be resisted. The works of theory considered foundational for this school of thought are Butler's

Gender Trouble and Sedgwick's *Epistemology of the Closet,* both published in 1990, though neither advertised themselves as works of queer theory at the time. Butler combines Foucault and French feminism, together with ideas borrowed from Jacques Lacan, to denaturalize gender to the nth degree. She argues that even the most basic gender identities, such as *man* and *woman,* are socially produced ideals that coerce us into thinking in heterosexual terms. It is not merely that social definitions of gender shift over time while remaining calibrated to women's disadvantage, but also, more fundamentally, that these definitions reinforce ideas about complementarity between genders. Gender norms thus oppress not only women but everyone, by scripting us into heterosexuality and marking nonheterosexuals as gender deviants—hence the enduring stereotypes of lesbians as inappropriately masculine and gay men as inappropriately effeminate. By articulating Foucault's concept of regulatory ideals with Lacan's account of the symbolic order, Butler offers far-reaching claims about the constitutive function of gender norms for subjectivity.

In *Epistemology of the Closet,* Sedgwick also develops ideas from Foucault's *History of Sexuality,* particularly the notion that homosexuality as we know it today is a nineteenth-century invention. She argues that the emergence of heterosexuality and homosexuality as discrete ontological identities produced as an important side effect the social institution of the closet. Once homosexuality and heterosexuality became codified as "orientations," something that defines who you are, it was important to be able to distinguish these types of persons. The "closet" names all those ways that deviant desires can be hidden for the purposes of escaping detection and punishment. Sedgwick's most radical claim is that the hetero/homo distinction, and the visible/hidden distinction that overlays it, became intertwined with the larger epistemological opposition between knowledge and ignorance, such that all signs of ignorance, secrecy, or opacity could be traced to homosexuality. This assertion leads Sedgwick to interpret opacity or hiddenness, especially in nineteenth- and early-twentieth-century literature, as signs of the homosexual closet—a reading strategy that draws heavily on psychoanalytic methodology in its assumption that sexuality is both central and pervasive, while remaining disguised and therefore in need of decoding.

Both Butler and Sedgwick use psychoanalytic terminology and concepts in their work, while maintaining a critical distance toward psychoanalysis in a way that often seems incoherent. With regard to psychoanalysis, these critics sometimes want to have their cake and eat it too. Subsequent developments in queer theory have tended to reproduce this contradiction by relying on Butler and Sedgwick unquestioningly, or by accepting at face value their views of psychoanalysis.[15] However, more recently lesbian and gay theorists have engaged psychoanalysis head-on; indeed, the contributors to this collection provide multiple examples of this kind of work, drawing on queer theory while also pointing it in new directions.[16]

If Butler's and Sedgwick's work evidences unresolved conflicts regarding the place of psychoanalysis in queer theory, de Lauretis and Bersani address these issues more directly in their pioneering work. In *The Practice of Love: Lesbian Sexuality and Perverse Desire* (1994), lesbian critic de Lauretis—generally credited with coining the term *queer theory,* in 1991—rehabilitates Freud's theory of perversion for an account of specifically lesbian desire. Like Bersani and other lesbian and gay critics, such as John Fletcher and Mandy Merck, de Lauretis finds particularly useful French psychoanalyst Jean Laplanche's reading of Freud, in which he argues that perversion is a tautology for sexuality (*Life* 23).[17] According to Laplanche, what Freud called *polymorphous perversity* denotes sexuality's original state, prior to its normalization. Given this original perversity, de Lauretis wants to describe, in a nonpathologizing yet psychoanalytic way, how lesbian desire comes into being. Noting that most psychoanalytic theories of lesbianism have recourse to some account of the "masculinity complex," de Lauretis argues that it ought to be possible to conceptualize female desire without reference to masculinity—that lesbianism should be theorized independently of a heterosexual model. *The Practice of Love* shows how hard it has been for psychoanalysis to conceive of lesbianism in terms of female desire, rather than in terms of desire emanating from a masculine subject position (even if a woman occupies that position).

De Lauretis's solution to this problem lies in theorizing the lesbian subject's fantasmatic relation to maternal corporeality—a relation that permits de Lauretis to reinterpret the psychoanalytic idea of castration in terms of losing the mother's body. According to de Lauretis, the girl can be seen as "castrated" not because she lacks a penis (or the phallus), but because she becomes dispossessed of an ideal maternal form. This line of argument also allows de Lauretis to revive for lesbianism the theory of fetishism, since in her reading the fetish substitutes not for the mother's missing penis, but rather for her ideal body in its totality.[18] The significance of this conceptual move lies in its claiming, in contradistinction to Freud, the prerogative of fetishism for women. Following work on this topic by Naomi Schor, Elizabeth Grosz, de Lauretis, and Ellen Lee McCallum, lesbian fetishism has become a substantial issue of debate in feminist psychoanalytic theory.[19] H. N. Lukes takes up this debate in her contribution to this volume and casts it in a new light. She contends that because theorists use psychoanalytic terminology in their critiques of Freud and Lacan, they find it difficult to modify these terms for their own ends, and so remain bound to the very object they wish to reject.

Lukes engages with the "lesbian fetishism" debate by drawing also on Bersani's interest in the "definitional crisis" that sexuality poses for both lesbianism and subjectivity as such. Bersani, one of this volume's contributors, stands apart from the mainstream of queer theory and has remained critical of many of its basic tenets. A distinguished psychoanalytic theorist long before queer theory's emergence, Bersani redescribes his ongoing project in relation to gay sexuality in *Homos* (1995). Bersani's thesis has been repeatedly misunderstood as a result of its being received in precisely the queer theoretical terms it was intended to disable.[20] *Homos* develops the analysis of homophobia and AIDS begun in his classic essay "Is the Rectum a Grave?" (1987), in which Bersani proposes that positive value might yet be found in the homophobic fantasy of gay male sex as an exercise in abjectly humiliating passivity on the part of the man being penetrated. Rather than defending the subjective agency or putative masculinity of the "passive" partner in anal sex, Bersani suggests instead that we see in this partner evidence of the counterintuitive appeal of powerlessness—the appeal, that is, of relinquishing "the sacrosanct value of selfhood" (222). In sexual masochism, argues Bersani, lies a potential for undoing the pretense of inviolate selfhood that makes us relate to others so aggressively and territorially.[21]

Bersani's ongoing critique of the ego is complicated in *Homos* by his theorizing homosexuality as a form of narcissism. On the face of it, this seems a familiar homophobic charge. What makes Bersani's conceptual shift in *Homos* particularly difficult to follow is that he seems to have moved from critiquing the ego to embracing it: Rather than talking about "self-shattering"—as he had in *The Freudian Body* and "Is the Rectum a Grave?"—suddenly he is talking about a positive form of narcissism. For those of us who had viewed Bersani's attack on inviolate selfhood as fundamentally compatible with Lacan's critique of ego psychology (even though Bersani never framed his work in Lacanian terms), *Homos* appeared initially as a conundrum, even a conceptual regression.

Yet Bersani was commencing a project of theorizing desire outside the familiar terms of lack—a project he pursues in "Genital Chastity" (his contribution to this collection), an essay whose title is derived from a coinage of Freud's in "The Psychogenesis of a Case of Homosexuality in a Woman" (1920). Whereas de Lauretis accepts the psychoanalytic premise of lack and transposes it into feminine terms (loss of the mother's body),

Bersani wants to move beyond an understanding of desire centered on lack altogether. This is partly because psychoanalysts, when they pathologize homosexuality, tend to do so in terms of lack, deficiency, developmental arrest, and other similarly negative terms. By contrast, Bersani sees in homosexuality a form of desire based on self-replication—an attraction in which one desires not what one lacks but what one is. Bersani's neologism "homo-ness" points to a desire for sameness that, though it might look superficially like straightforward narcissism, resists both the impulse toward identity and that toward absolute difference.

As Tim Dean elaborates in his contribution to this volume, homo-ness, in defying the familiar lures of identity and difference, offers an alternative model of relationality, a radically different way of connecting with the world outside the self. Bersani finds this alternative mode of relationality exemplified not only in homosexuality, but also in art. Indeed, his account of sexuality becomes fully intelligible only within the context of his theory of aesthetics—a point that many readers of *Homos* have failed to appreciate. *Homo-ness* is the name for what, in their writing on art, Bersani and Ulysse Dutoit call "inaccurate self-replication," a type of identification that, by undermining the very terms *self* and *other*, pushes psychoanalytic theory to its breaking point.[22]

Building on Laplanchean psychoanalytic theory, Bersani thus appropriates a theory of narcissism in a manner somewhat akin to de Lauretis's appropriation of perversion. Both theorists take up psychoanalytic concepts that have been used against lesbians and gay men, and, rather than simply denouncing these ideas as heterosexist, they show their profound usefulness for thinking affirmatively about nonnormative sexualities. It is telling that the most innovative recent psychoanalytic work on sexuality derives not from psychoanalytic institutions but from university departments of language and literature. This strange sociological circumstance confirms the persistent tension between psychoanalytic concepts and clinical institutions. It also testifies to the influence of Jacques Lacan's ideas on literary theory.

6. Lacan and Homosexuality

Since many, though by no means all, of the essays in this collection engage Lacan's ideas, we want to suggest briefly what Lacanian psychoanalysis offers for an account of nonnormative sexuality. We may begin by noting that Lacan has no theory of homosexuality; *homosexuality* as such is not a concept in his work, just as it isn't a term in Laplanche and Pontalis's standard dictionary of psychoanalytic concepts. This absence signals less a homophobic silencing of homosexuality than an acknowledgment that once we conceive of sexuality in terms of the unconscious, our familiar categories of sexual orientation make little sense. Strange though it may sound, *homosexuality* is not a psychoanalytic concept, though the term frequently appears in psychoanalytic writing. The orientation of desire into homosexual and heterosexual is a function of the ego—or, as Hocquenghem puts it, employing Lacanian vocabulary, "a fallacy of the imaginary."

By theorizing sexuality in terms of the unconscious, Lacan divorces desire from anatomical constraints. His emphasis on language makes sexual desire an effect of representation rather than of biology. Thus one of the most obvious advantages of this school of psychoanalytic thought for queer critique is Lacan's denaturalizing of sexuality. Although Lacan is not alone in arguing that human sexuality is an effect of language rather than of nature, we stress that his account of subjectivity begins from this conceptual foundation. In his "return to Freud," Lacan divests his predecessor of the last traces of biologism.

Lacan's emphasis on symbolic mediation—that is, his insistence that all human relations are routed through representation—leads also to his undermining the heterosexist assumption of gender complementarity. "There is no sexual relation," Lacan perversely asserts. By this he means that there is no automatic, unmediated, or untroubled connection between sexual partners, whether of the same or the opposite sex. For Lacan, as for Freud at his most radical, heterosexuality is a problem rather than a given. Because each subject connects with others only through fantasy, no natural coupling of man and woman can take place. Further, Lacan maintains that in sex we couple not so much with our fantasy of the other as with our fantasy of the Other, a nonindividualized zone of alterity. Even in the most intimate moments of bodily intertwining, our relation to other persons is thus doubly mediated. In this way, Lacan discredits any idea of a harmonious heterosexuality to which human subjects might be restored by psychoanalytic therapeutics.

Although Lacan's mockery of the notion of gender complementarity marks his distance from his transatlantic counterparts' emphasis on subjective adaptation to sociosexual norms, we nevertheless want to register the limits of his critique of heterosexism. While Lacan insists that "there is no sexual relation," his various explanations of erotic relationality's failure tend to be couched in terms of man's failure to relate to woman, and vice versa. In other words, he still thinks and operates within a heterosexual framework. This limitation on how far Lacan was able to push his most radical ideas recalls Freud's inability to grasp fully his own conceptual break with the nineteenth-century idea of perversion. Thus while Lacan appears to have been far from homophobic in his own clinical practice, he did not exploit the counterheterosexist implications of his own ideas but instead remained bound by certain normative expectations about erotic relationality—expectations that conflict with his emphasis elsewhere on the inevitable failure of relationality in all its permutations.

Lacan has more to offer, we suggest, on the issue of norms and normalization than on the question of homosexuality as such. His polemic against ego psychology also mounts an argument against the therapeutic imposition of adaptive norms. Lacan saw this brand of therapeutics—and the culture in which it flourished—as profoundly normalizing. "Strengthening the categories of affective normativity produces disturbing results," he stressed in 1960 (*Seminar* 7:133–34). His own account of subjectivity and of desire was far more anarchic, just as his clinical practice was too wild and unorthodox to retain the institutional sanction of established psychoanalytic organizations. As any reader of Lacan quickly realizes, his own writing is abnormal too—unorthodox, elliptical, perversely rococo, and studded with neologisms. His practice, his theory, and the very form in which he presented that theory are all quite bizarre. Part of what makes Lacan so hard to assimilate—and thus perverse or even queer—is his persistent disruption of normative expectations.

If disruptiveness is the hallmark of Lacan's style, it is also how he characterizes the unconscious—as an interruption, impediment, or blockage in the smooth flow of discourse. The unconscious remains a stumbling block both for individual subjects and for theories of subjectivity. Indeed, Lacan locates subjectivity and desire at the level of the unconscious, rather than at the level of consciousness. He sees the ego as inimical to desire, and therefore conceives of sexuality as unaccountable in imaginary terms. By amplifying in his own conceptual vocabulary Freud's radical insights in *Three Essays,* Lacan theorizes sex as an impasse—as something that thwarts conscious understanding. From this perspective, cultural constructions of sexuality are simply responses to a fundamental psychic deadlock that can never be fully interpreted or resolved. All our attempts to make sense of sex—to make sexuality *mean*—remain inadequate compensatory gestures in the face of an unconscious impasse. Sexuality resists social norms, according to Lacan, not so that some pure form of desire can be liberated from cultural constraints, but because unconscious contradictions cannot be eliminated by imaginary or symbolic identifications, whether normative or queer. Owing to the unconscious impasse of sex, sexuality will always be subject to sociocultural constructions, and those constructions will inevitably fail.

Thus while Lacan treats sexuality as a product of representation rather than of nature, his theory really is not part of the methodological school that discusses gender and sexuality as social constructions. Many of this volume's contributors find Lacanian psychoanalysis so fruitful because it represents a genuine alternative to the rather stale options offered by the essentialism-constructionism debate on sexuality (see Stein; Abramson and Pinkerton). Further, the constitutive resistance of the unconscious to all norms makes Lacan's version of psychoanalysis potentially appealing to queer theory's antinormative critique. At the level of the unconscious, sexuality is as immune to education and political domestication as it is to social discipline. Queer theory may yet find in Lacan the kind of intellectual inspiration and disruptive energy that Hocquenghem found in a certain reading of psychoanalysis.[23]

What Lacan adds to Freud's theory of the unconscious is an extra level of mediation, which he calls *the real*. He maintains not merely that we are creatures of language, but that language contains built-in failures. In Lacanian terms, the symbolic order is fissured by the real—that is, by impediments to meaning that circumvent the possibility of harmony and understanding. Thus both the unconscious and what Lacan calls the real impede successful installation of gender and sexual norms. In other words, Lacanian psychoanalysis offers two conceptual points of resistance to social projects of normalization. Several of this volume's contributors—Dean, Lukes, and Povinelli—develop this specifically Lacanian contribution to queer theory's broader enterprise of challenging social conventions surrounding sexuality.

While Lacan often represented himself as the enemy of bourgeois sexual conventions—including those conventions as promulgated by some psychoanalysts—he did not extend his critique to normative heterosexuality as such. However, in 1956, at a rabidly homophobic clinical symposium on perversion, Lacan fell out of line with the majority of his psychoanalytic colleagues: Choosing not to speak on homosexuality, he focused instead on fetishism.[24] Lacan's followers, like Freud's, have often ignored the most radical implications of his theories and devoted themselves to institutionalizing his work and consolidating its cultural authority. Yet at least one Lacanian psychoanalyst has developed an account of women's desire that is close to de Lauretis's in *The Practice of Love*. Refusing to accept heterosexuality as preordained, Marie-Christine Hamon asks: Why do women love men (and not their mothers instead)? Without encountering the same oedipal prohibition as boys, why do girls forfeit maternal love and make men rather than other women their objects of desire?

Hamon's Lacanian account anticipates developments in queer theory, and Lacanians in France recently have expressed interest in Bersani's work. The beginnings of their engagement with North American queer theory may be found in "L'inconscient homosexuel," a special issue of *Revue de psychanalyse*.[25] While the Parisian reception of this radical work on sexuality may seem barely recognizable to its North American authors, we see continuing possibilities for dialogue between those who are committed to the concept of the unconscious and those who are committed to exploring nonnormative sexualities in theory and practice. The present volume is part of that dialogue.

7. The Shape of an Argument

Because the purview of this collection is extensive, we have organized the essays into five sections. These sections are neither exhaustive nor substantively discrete, but in fact show multiple areas of overlap. We argued at the start of this introduction that, in conceptual and political terms, male and female homosexualities are rarely complementary. Suggesting otherwise and merging the sections on "Gay Sexuality" and "Lesbian Sexuality" would have resulted in an immediate loss of specificity. Yet relative to the book's overall argument, the designations "Gay Sexuality" and "Lesbian Sexuality" are provisional—these part titles are to some degree at odds with the essays and arguments they seem to represent. This tension is inevitable if the book is to engage seriously with both psychoanalytic claims about male and female homosexualities, as well as with psychoanalytic arguments about the unconscious.

Part 1, "Theorizing Sexuality," introduces claims and concepts that recur in all the other essays, including Freud's relationship to psychiatry, sexology, and psychology; Foucault's arguments about Western sexuality and the importance of Lacan's claims about sexuality and the unconscious; psychoanalytic arguments about object-choice, narcissism, and otherness; and homosexuality's impact on theories of sublimation, love, groups, and culture. The next sections of *Homosexuality and Psychoanalysis* (parts 2 and 3, "Gay Sexuality" and "Lesbian Sexuality") build on and modify these claims by outlining specific arguments about sexual differ-

ence and gender. The contributors then turn to clinical and cultural arguments about homosexuality, phobia, and AIDS (part 4, "Clinical Perspectives"), before assessing what happens, conceptually and politically, when
sexuality and the unconscious are seen as extending beyond gender and
identity (part 5, "Queer Relations").

The first section begins with two previously untranslated articles by
Foucault, which, as Arnold I. Davidson's prefatory essay on them points
out, subtly revise orthodox understandings of Foucault's views on Freud
and Lacan. His direct remarks about psychoanalysis are so rare that we
thought it worthwhile to draw attention to his thoughts on the unconscious and its significance in the history of thought and of sexuality. The
following four essays composing part 1 are grouped as pairs. Davidson's
and Paul Robinson's essays, in implicit dialogue with each other, address
Freud's relationship to the nineteenth century and the first decades of the
twentieth century, while Ellie Ragland's and Dean's essays combine to
form a powerful introduction to Lacan's subsequent account of language,
sexual difference, and the *objet petit a*—the object of unconscious fantasy,
which is irreducible to gender and persons, and hence resists symbolization and assimilation into consciousness. While remaining attentive to
the historicity of sexuality, Ragland's and Dean's essays join other contributions to this collection in helping us construct new, antihistoricist ways
of formulating this historicity. Additionally, Ragland and Dean demonstrate that Lacanian psychoanalysis is particularly responsive to recent
demands by queer theorists that sexuality be conceived beyond the binary terms of gender difference. Ragland points out that Lacan situated
his own theory where Freud's work reached an impasse.

In some respects, Ragland's distinction forms a basis for many of the
remaining essays. These examine blind spots and aporias in Freud's theory without concluding that psychoanalysis is thereby irrelevant or that
its conceptual enigmas can be explained by recourse to the key players in
psychoanalytic debates. The contributors show instead, as Lane argues in
his essay, that the intellectual value of Freud's theory remains irreducible
to the circumstances that helped spawn it. Rather than adopting a strictly
historical or psychobiographical approach, then, part 2 focuses on conceptual developments shaping psychoanalytic arguments about male homosexuality. Jason B. Jones accounts for how homosexuality oddly became the centerpiece of Wilhelm Reich's attempt to combine the work of
Freud and Marx. As Reich's theories of fascism, sexual emancipation, and
human nature became progressively more eccentric and absurd, he tied
homosexuality conceptually to his apocalyptic pronouncements about

genocide, destructive orgones ("DOR"), and extraterrestrial life. Ramón E. Soto-Crespo assesses how Melanie Klein's combined accounts of phantasy and negativity influenced her arguments about object relations and the superego, on the one hand, and the conceptual relationship between heterosexuality and mourning, on the other. His argument about the psychic mechanisms of reparation corresponds with psychoanalyst Catherine Millot's haunting essay on the Japanese writer Yukio Mishima, which concludes this section. Millot focuses on the intricate beauty of his 1949 autobiographical novel, *Confessions of a Mask,* and the late novel *Sun and Steel* (1968), to explore what she calls "the eroticism of desolation" in Mishima. Millot is interested in the limits of intelligibility and communication in Mishima's writing, arguing that the absence of subjectivity in his work is too easily confused with homosexual narcissism. Like Mishima's fiction, written—its author tells us—on "the verge of noncommunication," Millot's reading extends far beyond commonplace assumptions about narcissism, indicating how Mishima tried to limit that which in subjectivity resists translation, thereby sealing "the rift at the foundation of his subjectivity."

Part 3 puts lesbian desire in dialogue with a range of contemporary issues, including visions of lesbian communities detached from the Law (Judith Roof's essay); lesbianism's vexed relationship to epistemology and psychoanalysis (H. N. Lukes's); the clinical implications of lesbians' relationship to the Law and to psychoanalysis (Daniel L. Buccino's); and presumptions about childhood innocence and lesbianism's relationship to erotic fantasy (Lynda Hart's). The arguments of all four essays concern knowledge and the fantasies that shape and undermine it. For instance, Roof interprets two alternating but fundamentally related visions of lesbian communities. The first is "the community of dolphins," a metaphor Julia Kristeva adopts in "Stabat Mater" (1976–77) when describing lesbianism's unconscious rapport with the preoedipal. The second vision of lesbian communities, the "safe sea of women," appears in Jane Rule's *Lesbian Images* (1982), a book that tries to situate lesbians outside the Law, but that in doing so creates unforeseen legislation of its own. This is so, Roof argues, because Rule's communitarian vision replicates fantasies of inclusion and exclusion, and so, like Kristeva's argument, guarantees the centrality of Law to a realm ostensibly free from it. Hart's and Lukes's essays advance related claims when discussing, on the one hand, the relationship between legislated innocence and supposedly lawless fantasy, and, on the other hand, theories of desire in which lesbianism consistently points up what Lacan calls "'holes' in . . . meaning" ("Subversion" 299).

Hart's essay distinguishes between incest scenes that popular fiction increasingly represents as women's erotic fantasies and the more usual cultural response to sexual abuse, which entails either striving to forget or struggling to remember what was traumatic. Lukes's account of "Intervention on Transference" (1951), Lacan's reading of Freud's Dora case, makes clear not only why lesbians are the aporia of psychoanalysis, but also, paradoxically, why it is possible to represent the "missed relationship between psychoanalysis and the lesbian subject as one concerning love," and thus transference and ethics. Buccino outlines, in turn, how a Lacanian approach to the clinic and to object-choice challenges the precepts of Freudian analysis.

Part 4 addresses clinical conceptions of the relationship between homophobia and homosexuality, explaining why psychoanalytic perspectives on the unconscious require an entirely new approach to treatment. Joanna Ryan focuses on North American psychiatry and its relationship to reparative therapy, assessing the influence of these arguments on psychoanalysts and psychotherapists in Britain. Suzanne Yang considers how psychoanalytic models can illuminate AIDS and the clinical treatment of its subjective impact. Her account of Kaposi's sarcoma describes how KS lesions have troubled diagnostic medical categories as well as the patient's capacity to own or express the experience of illness. Because AIDS represents a recent chapter in the history of sexuality, contemporary theories of homosexuality cannot claim to be completely relevant if they ignore this topic. In addressing this topic, too, we are turning to broader questions about sexuality and culture that permeate the final section of this book.

Part 5, "Queer Relations," reappraises from a number of different perspectives psychoanalytic arguments about desire, object-choice, communities, and being-in-the-world. Taking a radical approach to the issue of relationality, Bersani begins this section with a brilliant reading of Plato's *Symposium*. He proposes that we rethink psychoanalytic arguments about object-love and lack by considering desire in terms of self-extension and "inaccurate self-replication." Bersani is concerned, above all, with what Foucault calls "new ways of being together," and he assesses homosexuality's possible relationship to novel forms of intimacy by redefining what psychoanalysis often describes as a "fundamentally antagonistic distinction between subject and object."

Jonathan Dollimore's witty and thoughtful essay, "Sexual Disgust," views our relationship to objects from a slightly different perspective. Indeed, he makes perspective itself central to disgust, showing how violent feelings of revulsion can puncture our idealizing accounts of desire, forcing us to adopt a more honest perspective on the body and the politics it engenders. Elizabeth A. Povinelli, in discussing homophobia, also addresses the fantasies and violence accompanying social emphases on sexual conformity. She takes off from David Wojnarowicz's opposition to this conformity and its collective price for lesbians and gay men, using his writing to develop a critique of Lacan's theory of language while stressing, nonetheless, why Lacan's theory of subjectivity remains crucial for detailed analyses of ethics and politics.

The final two essays in this section offer related perspectives on the role of love and the rhetoric of boundlessness in queer theory. Brad Epps's essay interprets crucial limits to queer arguments about the fluidity of desire, while Lauren Berlant's assesses how love circulates in Bersani's, Butler's, and de Lauretis's writing. Contrary to those—including some queer theorists—who view love as conducive to self-expression, stability, and reassurance, Berlant unearths what is least comfortable and most distressing about love, forging parallels between that discomfort and the provocative, unconventional expectations informing many queer perspectives on politics. These final essays don't offer a conclusive statement on "queer relations"; readers will in fact find traces of their arguments in preceding essays by Dean, Roof, and Bersani. But they point to a set of issues with which queer theory has only recently begun to engage, and they consequently make clear that psychoanalytic claims about desire and defeat, extension and mobility, will continue to influence for a long time our notion of a queer future.

Notes

1. Reparative therapy groups and "ex-gay" ministries frequently differ in their emphasis on psychological factors and religious faith, but they share a conviction that homosexuality is a sign of immaturity and gender "dysfunction," and that—with sufficient perseverance—a person can "overcome" his or her sexuality and become heterosexual. Founded in 1992, the California-based group NARTH (National Association for Research and Treatment of Homosexuality) declares in its mission statement that it is "dedicated to the research, therapy and prevention of homosexuality, . . . and is composed of psychoanalysts, psychoanalytically-informed psychologists, certified social workers, and other behavioral scientists, as well as laymen in fields such as law, religion, and education." For elaboration on reparative therapy, see Nicolosi 3–6 and Bancroft 32–51.

2. For commentary on this collection, see Ryan. Other recent critiques of homophobia using psychoanalytic conceptual vocabulary include Bohan, *Psychology and*

Sexual Orientation: Coming to Terms; Burch, *Other Women: Lesbian/Bisexual Experience and Psychoanalytic Views of Women;* Ellis, "Lesbians, Gay Men and Psychoanalytic Training"; Frosh, *Sexual Difference: Masculinity and Psychoanalysis;* Hamer, "Significant Others: Lesbianism and Psychoanalytic Theory"; and Schwartz, *Sexual Subjects: Lesbians, Gender, and Psychoanalysis.* Related—though nonpsychoanalytic— collections of essays include Garnets and Kimmel, *Psychological Perspectives on Lesbian and Gay Male Experiences;* and Stein and Cohen, *Contemporary Perspectives on Psychotherapy with Lesbians and Gay Men.*

3. In this respect, Freud clearly distinguished himself even from liberal contemporaries such as Ferenczi, in "On the Part Played by Homosexuality in the Pathogenesis of Paranoia" (1912). For elaboration on the practical repercussions of Freud's argument, see Spiers and Lynch, "The Gay Rights Freud." This article reprints Freud and Otto Rank's December 1921 disagreement with Ernest Jones over whether homosexuality should prevent interested parties from becoming members in the Psychoanalytic Association. Jones "advised against" this inclusion; Freud and Rank replied, "We disagree with you" (qtd. 9).

4. See Adler, *The Individual Psychology of Alfred Adler* 47–49, 111–19; and *Superiority and Social Interest* 53–55.

5. For a more recent, progressive Jungian approach to homosexuality, see Hopcke, *Jung, Jungians, and Homosexuality.*

6. For an example of the relational school's contribution, see Lesser and Schoenberg's collection *That Obscure Subject of Desire: Freud's Female Homosexual Revisited.*

7. However, Anna Freud did discuss male homosexuality in "Studies in Passivity" (1952 [1949–51]), esp. 245–56, and Klein's influence on psychoanalytic accounts of homosexuality registers in some of the presentations at the 23rd International Psycho-Analytical Congress held in Stockholm in July and August 1963. See especially Gillespie's paper; and essays by Pasche; Wiedeman; Greenson; and Stoller.

8. Silverman's brilliant study of masculine self-mastery sounds the importance of this concept; see *Male Subjectivity* 356–73. Focusing on Proust's and T. E. Lawrence's fiction, as well as Fassbinder's films and theoretical texts by Lacan, Althusser, and Bersani, Silverman's book addresses the political consequences of psychoanalytic arguments about desire and identification, and the implications of these arguments for feminism and gay studies.

9. Duberman voices a powerful critique of such psychiatric perspectives in *Cures: A Gay Man's Odyssey.* See also Isay, *Becoming Gay: The Journey to Self-Acceptance.* Regrettably, the legacy of psychiatric orthodoxy appears in studies such as Morgenthaler's and Ovesey's, which ostensibly critique that legacy.

10. Since 1968 Socarides has published a slew of books condemning homosexuality and advancing clinical arguments that ostensibly will "prevent" it: *Beyond Sexual Freedom* (1975); *Homosexuality* (1978); *The Preoedipal Origin and Psychoanalytic Therapy of Sexual Perversions* (1988); *Homosexuality: Psychoanalytic Therapy*

(1989); *The Homosexualities: Reality, Fantasy, and the Arts* (coedited with Vamik D. Volkan, 1990); *The Homosexualities and the Therapeutic Process* (also coedited with Volkan, 1991); and *Homosexuality: A Freedom Too Far: A Psychoanalyst Answers 1000 Questions about Causes and Cure and the Impact of the Gay Rights Movement on American Society* (1995). The books' respective arguments are almost indistinguishable from one another. Socarides cofounded NARTH with Benjamin Kaufman and Joseph Nicolosi in "response to the growing threat of scientific censorship." One irony is that although Socarides crusades against homosexuality and explains it partly as the result of poor parenting, his son, Richard, an openly gay activist working on behalf of mainstream lesbian and gay organizations, was until recently Special Assistant to President Clinton, Senior Adviser for Public Liaison, and Point Person on Gay and Lesbian Issues at the White House.

11. Elements of the report were enacted into law twelve years later, when Britain's Parliament voted, in 1967, partly to decriminalize male homosexuality, setting the legal age of consent for gay sex at twenty-one years. The legal status of lesbianism in Britain is notoriously vague and has remained unclear since the Victorian age.

12. Spitzer later coined the term *homodysphilia* to clarify this diagnosis, but the term was never formally adopted.

13. Weeks's books include *Coming Out: Homosexual Politics in Britain, from the Nineteenth Century to the Present* (1977, 1983); *Sex, Politics and Society* (1981, 1989); *Sexuality and Its Discontents: Meanings, Myths and Modern Sexualities* (1985); and *Against Nature: Essays on History, Sexuality and Identity* (1991). See also his brief essay "Homosexuality and the Problematic Nature of Psychoanalysis, or, Psychoanalysis and the Problematic Nature of Homosexuality" (1983).

14. Hocquenghem was one of the first men to join this group, which published its writings in *Rapport contre la normalité* (1971) and in a special issue of *Recherches* (March 1973), whose nominal editor was Guattari. For elaboration, see Girard 83–84.

15. See, for example, Edelman, *Homographesis;* Fuss, *Identification Papers* and "Pink Freud." Several psychoanalytic critiques of Butler and Sedgwick now exist: see Copjec, "Sex and the Euthanasia of Reason"; Dean, "On the Eve of a Queer Future" and "Bodies That Mutter"; Rothenberg and Valente, "Performative Chic"; Restuccia, "The Subject of Homosexuality: Butler's Elision"; and Dyess and Dean, "Gender: The Impossibility of Meaning."

16. In addition to Lukes's and Dollimore's essays in this volume, material now exists discussing the place and meaning of homosexuality in almost all the principal case histories. See Findlay, "Queer Dora: Hysteria, Sexual Politics, and Lacan's 'Intervention on Transference'"; Santner, *My Own Private Germany: Daniel Paul Schreber's Secret History of Modernity,* esp. 23, 52–55; the essays published in Allison et al., *Psychosis and Sexual Identity: Towards a Post-Analytic View of the Schreber Case;* Enriquez, *Aux carrefours de la haine: paranoïa—masochisme—apathie,* interpreting Schreber's *Memoirs of My Nervous Illness* (1903); Davis, *Drawing the Dream of the Wolves: Homosexuality, Interpretation, and Freud's "Wolf Man";* Merck, "The Train of

Thought in Freud's 'Case of Homosexuality in a Woman'"; Jacobus, "Russian Tactics: Freud's 'Case of Homosexuality in a Woman'"; and the essays included in Lesser and Schoenberg's recent collection, *That Obscure Subject of Desire: Freud's Female Homosexual Revisited.*

17. See Merck, *Perversions: Deviant Readings;* and Fletcher, "Freud and His Uses: Psychoanalysis and Gay Theory."

18. In this respect, de Lauretis's argument differs radically from Deutsch's arguments about lesbianism. See also MacKinnon's eloquent complaint about psychiatry and homophobia; and for an overview of these and related arguments, see Magee and Miller.

19. See Schor, "Female Fetishism"; Grosz, "Lesbian Fetishism?"; and McCallum, *Object Lessons: How to Do Things with Fetishism.*

20. For elaboration on this misunderstanding, see Dean, "Sex and Syncope"; Lane, "Uncertain Terms of Pleasure"; and the essays included in "Beyond Redemption: The Work of Leo Bersani," a special issue of the *Oxford Literary Review* 20.1–2 (1998).

21. Bersani's project is connected with Kaja Silverman's critique of masculine self-mastery in *Male Subjectivity at the Margins.*

22. Bersani and Ulysse Dutoit amplify this argument in relation to both homosexuality and art in their latest books, *Caravaggio's Secrets* (1998) and *Caravaggio* (1999).

23. The arguments presented here concerning the relationship between queer theory and Lacanian psychoanalysis are elaborated in Dean, *Beyond Sexuality,* esp. ch. 6, "Lacan Meets Queer Theory."

24. See his essay with Wladimir Granoff, "Fetishism: The Symbolic, the Imaginary, and the Real," in Lorand's collection, *Perversions,* 265–76.

25. See *Revue de psychanalyse* 37 (October 1997), a publication of École de la cause freudienne.

References

Abelove, Henry. "Freud, Male Homosexuality, and the Americans." In Abelove, Barale, and Halperin 381–93.

Abelove, Henry, Michèle Aina Barale, and David M. Halperin, eds. *The Lesbian and Gay Studies Reader.* New York: Routledge, 1993.

Abramson, Paul R., and Steven D. Pinkerton, eds. *Sexual Nature, Sexual Culture.* Chicago: U of Chicago P, 1995.

Adler, Alfred. *The Individual Psychology of Alfred Adler: A Systematic Presentation in Selections from His Writings.* Ed. Heinz L. Ansbacher and Rowena R. Ansbacher. New York: Basic, 1956.

———. *Superiority and Social Interest: A Collection of Later Writings.* 2nd ed. Ed. Heinz L. Ansbacher and Rowena R. Ansbacher. Evanston, IL: Northwestern UP, 1970.

Alexander, Franz. "A Note on the Theory of Perversions." In Lorand 3–15.

Allison, David B., Prado de Oliveira, Mark S. Roberts, and Allen S. Weiss, eds. *Psychosis and Sexual Identity: Towards a Post-Analytic View of the Schreber Case*. Albany: SUNY P, 1988.

Altman, Dennis. *The Homosexualization of America: The Americanization of the Homosexual*. New York: St. Martin's, 1982.

American Psychiatric Association, Committee on Nomenclature and Statistics. *Diagnostic and Statistical Manual, Mental Disorders*. Washington, DC: American Psychiatric Association, Mental Hospital Service, 1952.

———. *Diagnostic and Statistical Manual of Mental Disorders*. 2nd ed. Washington, DC: American Psychiatric Association, 1968.

———. *Diagnostic and Statistical Manual of Mental Disorders*. 3rd ed. Washington, DC: American Psychiatric Association, 1980.

Bancroft, John. *Deviant Sexual Behaviour: Modification and Assessment*. Oxford: Clarendon, 1974.

Bayer, Ronald. *Homosexuality and American Psychiatry: The Politics of Diagnosis*. New York: Basic, 1981.

Bergler, Edmund. *Homosexuality: Disease or Way of Life?* New York: Hill and Wang, 1956.

Bersani, Leo. *The Freudian Body: Psychoanalysis and Art*. New York: Columbia UP, 1986.

———. *Homos*. Cambridge: Harvard UP, 1995.

———. "Is the Rectum a Grave?" 1987. In *AIDS: Cultural Analysis/Cultural Activism*. Ed. Douglas Crimp. Cambridge: MIT P, 1988, 1993. 197–223.

Bersani, Leo, and Ulysse Dutoit. *Caravaggio*. London: BFI, 1999.

———. *Caravaggio's Secrets*. Cambridge: MIT P, 1998.

Bibring, Grete. "Über eine orale Komponente bei männlicher Inversion." *Internationale Zeitschrift für Psychoanalyse* 25 (1940): 124–30.

Bieber, Irving, et al. *Homosexuality: A Psychoanalytic Study*. New York: Basic, 1962.

Bohan, Janis S. *Psychology and Sexual Orientation: Coming to Terms*. New York: Routledge, 1996.

Burch, Beverly. *Other Women: Lesbian/Bisexual Experience and Psychoanalytic Views of Women*. New York: Columbia UP, 1997.

Butler, Judith. *Gender Trouble: Feminism and the Subversion of Identity*. New York: Routledge, 1990.

Committee on Homosexual Offences and Prostitution (Great Britain). *The Wolfenden Report: Report of the Committee on Homosexual Offences and Prostitution*. 1955. Introd. Karl Menninger. New York: Stein and Day, 1963.

Copjec, Joan. "Sex and the Euthanasia of Reason." *Read My Desire: Lacan against the Historicists*. Cambridge: MIT P, 1994. 201–36.

Davidson, Arnold I. "How to Do the History of Psychoanalysis: A Reading of Freud's *Three Essays on the Theory of Sexuality*." In *The Trial(s) of Psychoanalysis*. Ed. Françoise Meltzer. Chicago: U of Chicago P, 1988. 39–64.

———. "Sex and the Emergence of Sexuality." *Critical Inquiry* 14.1 (1987): 16–48. Reprinted in E. Stein 89–132.

Davis, Whitney. *Drawing the Dream of the Wolves: Homosexuality, Interpretation, and Freud's "Wolf Man."* Bloomington: Indiana UP, 1995.

Dean, Tim. *Beyond Sexuality.* Chicago: U of Chicago P, 2000.

———. "Bodies That Mutter: Rhetoric and Sexuality." *Pre/Text* 15.1–2 (1994): 80–117.

———. "On the Eve of a Queer Future." *Raritan* 15.1 (1995): 116–34.

———. "Sex and Syncope." *Raritan* 15.3 (1996): 64–86.

de Lauretis, Teresa. *The Practice of Love: Lesbian Sexuality and Perverse Desire.* Bloomington: Indiana UP, 1994.

———. "Queer Theory: Lesbian and Gay Sexualities—An Introduction." *differences* 3 (1991): iii–xviii.

Deleuze, Gilles, and Félix Guattari. *Anti-Oedipus: Capitalism and Schizophrenia.* 1972. Trans. Robert Hurley, Mark Seem, and Helen R. Lane. Minneapolis: U of Minnesota P, 1983.

Deutsch, Helene. "Homosexuality in Women." *International Journal of Psycho-Analysis* 14.1 (1933): 34–56.

Domenici, Thomas, and Ronnie C. Lesser, eds. *Disorienting Sexuality: Psychoanalytic Reappraisals of Sexual Identities.* New York: Routledge, 1995.

Duberman, Martin. *Cures: A Gay Man's Odyssey.* New York: Dutton, 1991.

Dyess, Cynthia, and Tim Dean. "Gender: The Impossibility of Meaning." *Psychoanalytic Dialogues: A Journal of Relational Perspectives* 10.5 (2000): 735–56.

Edelman, Lee. *Homographesis: Essays in Gay Literary and Cultural Theory.* New York: Routledge, 1994.

Ellis, Mary Lynne. "Lesbians, Gay Men and Psychoanalytic Training." *Free Associations* 32 (1994): 501–17.

Enriquez, Micheline. *Aux carrefours de la haine: paranoïa—masochisme—apathie.* Paris: Épi, 1984.

Ferenczi, Sándor. "On the Part Played by Homosexuality in the Pathogenesis of Paranoia." 1912. *Sex in Psycho-Analysis: Contributions to Psycho-Analysis.* Boston: Gorham, 1916. 154–84.

Findlay, Heather. "Queer Dora: Hysteria, Sexual Politics, and Lacan's 'Intervention on Transference.'" *GLQ: A Journal of Lesbian and Gay Studies* 1 (1994): 323–47.

Fletcher, John. "Freud and His Uses: Psychoanalysis and Gay Theory." In Shepherd and Wallis 90–118.

Foucault, Michel. *The Birth of the Clinic: An Archaeology of Medical Perception.* 1963. Trans. A. M. Sheridan Smith. London: Tavistock, 1973.

———. *Histoire de la sexualité,* Vol. 1: *La volonté de savoir.* Paris: Gallimard, 1976.

———. *The History of Sexuality, Volume I: An Introduction.* 1976. Trans. Robert Hurley 1978. New York: Vintage, 1980.

———. *Madness and Civilization: A History of Insanity in the Age of Reason.* 1961. Trans. Richard Howard. New York: Random House, 1965.

Freud, Anna. "Studies in Passivity." 1952 (1949–51). *The Writings of Anna Freud*. 8 vols. New York: International UP, 1966–68. 4:245–59.

Freud, Sigmund. "From the History of an Infantile Neurosis." 1918 (1914). *Standard* 17:3–124.

———. "The Psychogenesis of a Case of Homosexuality in a Woman." 1920. *Standard* 18:145–72.

———. *The Standard Edition of the Complete Psychological Works of Sigmund Freud*. Ed. and trans. James Strachey. 24 vols. London: Hogarth, 1953–74.

———. *Three Essays on the Theory of Sexuality*. 1905. *Standard* 7:123–245.

Frosh, Stephen. *Sexual Difference: Masculinity and Psychoanalysis*. New York: Routledge, 1994.

Fuss, Diana. *Identification Papers*. New York: Routledge, 1995.

———. "Pink Freud." GLQ: *A Journal of Lesbian and Gay Studies* 2.1–2 (1995): 1–9.

Garnets, Linda D., and Douglas C. Kimmel, eds. *Psychological Perspectives on Lesbian and Gay Male Experiences*. New York: Columbia UP, 1993.

Gillespie, W. H. "Symposium on Homosexuality (I)." *International Journal of Psycho-Analysis* 45 (1964): 203–9.

Girard, Jacques. *Le mouvement homosexuel en France 1945–1980*. Paris: Éditions Syros, 1981.

Greenson, Ralph R. "On Homosexuality and Gender Identity." *International Journal of Psycho-Analysis* 45 (1964): 217–19.

Grosz, Elizabeth. "Lesbian Fetishism?" *differences* 3.2 (1991): 39–54.

Hamer, Diane. "Significant Others: Lesbianism and Psychoanalytic Theory." *Feminist Review* 34 (1990): 134–51.

Hamon, Marie-Christine. *Why Do Women Love Men (and Not Their Mothers Instead)?* 1992. Trans. Susan Fairfield. New York: Other P, 2000.

Higgins, Patrick. *Heterosexual Dictatorship: Male Homosexuality in Postwar Britain*. London: Fourth Estate, 1996.

Hocquenghem, Guy. *Homosexual Desire*. 1972. Trans. Daniella Dangoor. Preface by Jeffrey Weeks. London: Allison and Busby, 1978. Reprint, Durham: Duke UP, 1993.

Hopcke, Robert H. *Jung, Jungians, and Homosexuality*. Boston: Shambhala, 1989.

Isay, Richard A. *Becoming Gay: The Journey to Self-Acceptance*. New York: Pantheon, 1996.

Jacobus, Mary. "Russian Tactics: Freud's 'Case of Homosexuality in a Woman.'" GLQ: *A Journal of Lesbian and Gay Studies* 2.1–2 (1995): 65–79.

Jacoby, Russell. *The Repression of Psychoanalysis: Otto Fenichel and the Political Freudians*. 1983. Chicago: U of Chicago P, 1986.

Karpman, Ben. "The Kreutzer Sonata: A Problem in Latent Homosexuality and Castration." *Psychoanalytic Review* 25 (1938): 20–48.

King, Pearl, and Riccardo Steiner, eds. *The Freud-Klein Controversies in the British Psycho-Analytical Society, 1941–45*. London: Routledge, 1991.

Kristeva, Julia. "Stabat Mater." 1976–77. *Tales of Love*. Trans. Leon Roudiez. New York: Columbia UP, 1987. 234–63.

Lacan, Jacques. *Écrits: A Selection*. Trans. Alan Sheridan. New York: Norton, 1977.

———. "Intervention on Transference." 1951. *Feminine Sexuality: Jacques Lacan and the école freudienne*. Ed. Juliet Mitchell and Jacqueline Rose. Trans. Rose. New York: Norton, 1982. 62–73.

———. *The Seminar of Jacques Lacan, Book 7: The Ethics of Psychoanalysis, 1959–1960*. Ed. Jacques-Alain Miller. Trans. Dennis Porter. New York: Norton, 1992.

———. "The Subversion of the Subject and the Dialectic of Desire in the Freudian Unconscious." 1960. *Écrits* 292–325.

Lacan, Jacques, and Wladimir Granoff. "Fetishism: The Symbolic, the Imaginary, and the Real." In Lorand 265–76.

Lane, Christopher. "Uncertain Terms of Pleasure." *Modern Fiction Studies* 43.4 (1996): 807–26.

Laplanche, Jean. *Life and Death in Psychoanalysis*. 1970. Trans. Jeffrey Mehlman. Baltimore: Johns Hopkins UP, 1976, 1990.

Laplanche, Jean, and Jean-Bertrand Pontalis. *The Language of Psychoanalysis*. 1967. Trans. Donald Nicholson-Smith. New York: Norton, 1973.

Lesser, Ronnie C., and Erica Schoenberg, eds. *That Obscure Subject of Desire: Freud's Female Homosexual Revisited*. New York: Routledge, 1999.

Lewes, Kenneth. *The Psychoanalytic Theory of Male Homosexuality*. New York: New American Library, 1988.

Lorand, Sandor, with Michael Balint, eds. *Perversions: Psychodynamics and Therapy*. New York: Gramercy, 1956.

MacKinnon, Jane. "The Homosexual Woman." *American Journal of Psychiatry* 103 (1947): 661–64.

Magee, Maggie, and Diana C. Miller. "'She Foreswore Her Womanhood': Psycho-analytic Views of Female Homosexuality." *Clinical Social Work Journal* 20.1 (1992): 67–87.

Marcuse, Herbert. *Eros and Civilization: A Philosophical Inquiry into Freud*. New York: Random House, 1955.

McCallum, E. L. *Object Lessons: How to Do Things with Fetishism*. Albany: SUNY P, 1999.

McIntosh, Mary. "The Homosexual Role." In E. Stein 25–42.

Merck, Mandy. *Perversions: Deviant Readings*. New York: Routledge, 1993.

———. "The Train of Thought in Freud's 'Case of Homosexuality in a Woman.'" *m/f* 11/12 (1986): 35–46.

Mieli, Mario. *Homosexuality and Liberation: Elements of a Gay Critique*. 1977. Trans. David Fernbach. London: Gay Men's, 1980.

Mitchell, Juliet. *Psychoanalysis and Feminism*. 1974. Harmondsworth: Pelican, 1982.

Morgenthaler, Fritz. *Homosexuality, Heterosexuality, Perversion*. Ed. Paul Moor. Trans. Andreas Aebi. Hillsdale, NJ: Analytic, 1988.

NARTH (National Association for Research and Treatment of Homosexuality): www.narth.com/index.html

Nicolosi, Joseph. *Reparative Therapy of Male Homosexuality: A New Clinical Approach*. Northvale, NJ: Jason Aronson, 1991.

Nunberg, Herman. "Homosexuality, Magic and Aggression." *International Journal of Psycho-Analysis* 19.1 (1938): 1–16.

O'Connor, Noreen, and Joanna Ryan. *Wild Desires and Mistaken Identities: Lesbianism and Psychoanalysis.* New York: Columbia UP, 1993.

Ovesey, Lionel. *Homosexuality and Pseudohomosexuality.* New York: Science House, 1969.

Oxford Literary Review 20.1–2 (1998). Spec. issue: "Beyond Redemption: The Work of Leo Bersani."

Pasche, Francis. "Symposium on Homosexuality (II)." *International Journal of Psycho-Analysis* 45 (1964): 210–13.

Rado, Sandor. "An Adaptational View of Sexual Behavior." In *Psychosexual Development in Health and Disease: The Proceedings of the Thirty-eighth Annual Meeting of the American Psychopathological Association, Held in New York City, June 1948.* Ed. Paul H. Hoch and Joseph Zubin. New York: Grune and Stratton, 1949. 159–89.

———. "A Critical Examination of the Concept of Bisexuality." *Psychosomatic Medicine* 2.4 (1940): 459–67.

Rapport contre la normalité. Paris: Éditions Champs Libres, 1971.

Reich, Wilhelm. *The Mass Psychology of Fascism.* 1933. 3rd ed. Ed. Mary Higgins and Chester M. Raphael. Trans. Vincent R. Carfagno. New York: Farrar, Straus and Giroux, 1970.

Restuccia, Frances. "The Subject of Homosexuality: Butler's Elision." *Clinical Studies* 5.1 (1999): 19–37.

Revue de psychanalyse 37 (October 1997). Spec. issue: "L'inconscient homosexuel."

Rothenberg, Molly Anne, and Joseph Valente. "Performative Chic: The Fantasy of a Performative Politics." *College Literature* 24 (1997): 295–304.

Rule, Jane. *Lesbian Images.* Trumansburg, NY: Crossing, 1982.

Ryan, Joanna. "Reflections on *Disorienting Sexuality.*" *Gender and Psychoanalysis* 2 (1997): 177–84.

Santner, Eric L. *My Own Private Germany: Daniel Paul Schreber's Secret History of Modernity.* Princeton: Princeton UP, 1996.

Schor, Naomi. "Female Fetishism: The Case of George Sand." *Poetics Today* 6.1–2 (1985): 301–10.

Schreber, Daniel Paul. *Memoirs of My Nervous Illness.* 1903. Ed. and trans. Ida Macalpine and Richard A. Hunter. New York: New York Review Books, 2000.

Schwartz, Adria E. *Sexual Subjects: Lesbians, Gender, and Psychoanalysis.* New York: Routledge, 1998.

Sedgwick, Eve Kosofsky. *Epistemology of the Closet.* Berkeley: U of California P, 1990.

Shepherd, Simon, and Mick Wallis, eds. *Coming on Strong: Gay Politics and Culture.* London: Unwin Hyman, 1989.

Silverman, Kaja. *Male Subjectivity at the Margins.* New York: Routledge, 1992.

Socarides, Charles W. *Beyond Sexual Freedom.* New York: Quadrangle/New York Times Books, 1975.

———. *Homosexuality.* New York: Jason Aronson, 1978.

———. *Homosexuality: A Freedom Too Far: A Psychoanalyst Answers 1000 Questions about Causes and Cure and the Impact of the Gay Rights Movement on American Society.* Phoenix: Adam Margrave, 1995.

———. *Homosexuality: Psychoanalytic Therapy.* Northvale, NJ: Jason Aronson, 1989.

———. *The Overt Homosexual.* New York: Grune and Stratton, 1968.

———. *The Preoedipal Origin and Psychoanalytic Therapy of Sexual Perversions.* Madison, CT: International UP, 1988.

Socarides, Charles W., and Vamik D. Volkan, eds. *The Homosexualities: Reality, Fantasy, and the Arts.* Madison, CT: International UP, 1990.

———, eds. *The Homosexualities and the Therapeutic Process.* Madison, CT: International UP, 1991.

Spiers, Herb, and Michael Lynch. "The Gay Rights Freud." *Body Politic* (Toronto; May 1977): 8–10, 25.

Spitzer, Robert. "A Proposal about Homosexuality and the APA Nomenclature: Homosexuality as an Irregular Form of Sexual Development and Sexual Orientation Disturbance as a Psychiatric Disorder." *American Journal of Psychiatry* 132 (1973): 1214–16.

Stein, Edward, ed. *Forms of Desire: Sexual Orientation and the Social Constructionist Controversy.* New York: Routledge, 1992.

Stein, Terry S., and Carol J. Cohen, eds. *Contemporary Perspectives on Psychotherapy with Lesbians and Gay Men.* New York: Plenum, 1986.

Stoller, Robert J. "A Contribution to the Study of Gender Identity." *International Journal of Psycho-Analysis* 45 (1964): 220–26.

Weeks, Jeffrey. *Against Nature: Essays on History, Sexuality and Identity.* London: Rivers Oram, 1991.

———. *Coming Out: Homosexual Politics in Britain, from the Nineteenth Century to the Present.* London: Quartet, 1977, 1983.

———. "Homosexuality and the Problematic Nature of Psychoanalysis, or, Psychoanalysis and the Problematic Nature of Homosexuality." *Among Men, Among Women.* Conference Papers. Amsterdam: U of Amsterdam P, 1983. 4–15.

———. Preface to Hocquenghem, *Homosexual Desire* 9–33.

———. *Sex, Politics and Society: The Regulation of Sexuality Since 1800.* London: Longman, 1981, 1989.

———. *Sexuality and Its Discontents: Meanings, Myths and Modern Sexualities.* London: Routledge and Kegan Paul, 1985.

Wiedeman, George H. "Symposium on Homosexuality: Some Remarks on the Aetiology of Homosexuality." *International Journal of Psycho-Analysis* 45 (1964): 214–16.

Wittels, Fritz. "Collective Defense Mechanisms against Homosexuality." *Psychoanalytic Review* 31 (1944): 19–33.

1

FOUCAULT, PSYCHOANALYSIS, AND PLEASURE

Arnold I. Davidson

. . . .

Despite the genuine complexities and real ambiguities that characterize Michel Foucault's attitude toward psychoanalysis, one can at least say with confidence that the Freudian discovery of the unconscious represented for him a decisive epistemological achievement with respect to the philosophy with which he was surrounded, that is to say, with respect to phenomenology and existentialism. It was the psychoanalytic discovery of the unconscious that, as Foucault emphasizes in "The Death of Lacan," allowed one to question the old theory of the subject; whether described in Cartesian or phenomenological terms, this theory of the subject was incompatible with the concept of the unconscious, an incompatibility that Sartre embraced and carried to its ultimate conclusion in *Being and Nothingness*. Thus, for Foucault, in spite of their overlapping philosophical formation, Lacan and Sartre appeared as "alternate contemporaries," unable to inhabit the same epistemological space. Foucault would therefore see as one of the defining features of existentialism the attempt "to show how human consciousness or the subject or human freedom came to penetrate everything that Freudianism had described or designated as unconscious mechanisms" ("Interview avec Michel Foucault" [1968] 654).

Since Foucault, in consonance with Lacan, understood the unconscious as a system of logico-linguistic structures, he could oppose the primacy of the subject, of psychological forms, to the search for logical structures, structures that could not be understood or explained in psychological terms and whose existence could not be reconciled with the Sartrean sovereignty of the subject. Structuralism could be understood as "the search for logical structures everywhere that they could occur" and if they could be located within the subject, then the epistemological primacy of consciousness would be overthrown ("Interview" 653; for elaboration, see Davidson, "Structures"). Such were the fundamental stakes in the philosophical debate between existentialism and structuralism, as Foucault conceived it. However odd it may sound, the existence of the unconscious was a decisive component in Foucault's *antipsychologism*. Moreover, Foucault's interest in linguistics and in the search for linguistic structures played the same kind of epistemological role in his thought, since the existence of these structures would show that language could not be understood by reference to the intentionality of consciousness, thus further limiting the powers of the subject. The space of the psyche was threatened by this alternative space—the space of logic, of logical and linguistic structures, rules, operations—and this threat was one that Foucault was committed to pursuing. He took Lacan to be committed to a similar pursuit. In another brief interview about Lacan, Foucault says that reading Lacan's first texts in the fifties helped him to discover that one "had to try to free everything that hides itself behind the apparently simple use of the pronoun 'I'" ("Lacan" 205). If the structures of the unconscious helped one to realize this aim, so too did Foucault's archaeological histories. And thus Foucault could only have been grateful for Lacan's intervention at the very end of the discussion period following his presentation of "What Is an Author?" to the Société française de philosophie, when Lacan remarked:

> Structuralism or not, it seems to me that, in the field vaguely determined by this label, it is nowhere a question of the negation of the subject. It is a matter of the subordination (*dépendence*) of the subject, which is extremely different; and quite particularly, at the level of the return to Freud, of the subordination of the subject with respect to something truly elementary, and which we have attempted to isolate under the term "signifier." ("Qu'est-ce qu'un auteur?" 820)

The same general kind of subordination is a theme that pervades Foucault's *The Archaeology of Knowledge,* and, in both Lacan's case and Foucault's, a certain form of humanism—exemplified by but hardly limited to Sartre—is a constant target of attack.

It should come as no surprise, then, that even after the publication of the first volume of *The History of Sexuality*, often misinterpreted as a full-scale rejection of psychoanalysis, Foucault always insisted on the significance of the psychoanalytic theory of the unconscious and wanted, in effect, to detach its significance from the much more suspect psychoanalytic theory of sexuality. As he said,

> What is important is not the *Three Essays on the Theory of Sexuality*, but the *Traumdeutung*. . . . It is not the theory of development, it is not the sexual secret behind the neuroses and psychoses, it is a *logic of the unconscious*. . . . ("Le jeu de Michel Foucault" 315; my emphasis)

This brings me to "The West and the Truth of Sex," Foucault's brief sketch of some of the main themes of the first volume of *The History of Sexuality*. We know that Foucault had originally intended to entitle this volume *Sex and Truth*, and that he thought of its central problems as revolving around the question of how the domain of sex came to be placed within the field of true discourse, that is to say, how in the West sexual behaviors became the objects of a science of sexuality, and how these true discourses were linked to different mechanisms of power (see "Le jeu de Michel Foucault" 312 and "Sexualité et vérité" 137). Without trying to take up these general questions, I want to underline the distinction, highlighted by Foucault in this brief essay, between an erotic art and a science of sexuality, a distinction that raises a series of issues that most commentators on *The Will to Know* have failed to develop. One underlying, fundamental motivation for this distinction is precisely to undermine, from a new angle, the old theory of the subject as it had come to be incorporated into psychoanalytic and other related types of psychological theory. Although Foucault is not everywhere consistent in his terminology, I would claim that we should draw the conclusion from his discussions, here and elsewhere, that while *ars erotica* is organized around the framework of body-pleasure-intensification, *scientia sexualis* is organized around the axis of subject-desire-truth. It is as if one could say that the imposition of true discourses on the subject of sexuality leads to the centrality of a theory of sexual desire, while the discourse of pleasure and the search for its intensification is exterior to a science of sexual desire. Just as Foucault wanted to divorce the psychoanalytic theory of the unconscious from the theory of sexuality, so he wants to detach the experience of pleasure from a psychological theory of sexual desire, of sexual subjectivity.[1] The modification of the subject aimed at by the true discourse of the science of sexuality uses the conceptual structure of *desire* to excavate the real identity of the subject, and so to delimit the domain of psychological intervention. Desire has psychological *depth;* desire can be latent or manifest, apparent or hidden; desire can be repressed or sublimated; it calls for decipherment, for interpretation. True desire expresses what one really wants, who one really is, while false desire hides or masks identity, one's true subjectivity. No doubt this is a main part of the reason Foucault could not bear the word *desire* (see Deleuze 189).

Although we have no difficulty talking about and understanding the distinction between true and false desires, the idea of true and false pleasures (and Foucault understood this point even if he never put it in exactly this way) is conceptually misplaced. Pleasure is, as it were, exhausted by its surface; it can be intensified, increased, its qualities modified, but it does not have the psychological depth of desire. It is, so to speak, related to itself and not to something else that it expresses, either truly or falsely. There is no coherent conceptual space for the science of sexuality to attach itself to pleasure, and no primacy of the psychological subject in the experience of pleasure. Structures of desire lead to forms of sexual orientation, kinds of subjectivity; different pleasures do not imply orientation at all, require no theory of subjectivity or identity formation. The circumscription of true desire is a procedure of individualization; the production of pleasure is not.

In a famously enigmatic passage of *The Will to Know,* Foucault identifies bodies and pleasure, in contrast to sex-desire, as the point of support for the counterattack against the apparatus of sexuality (see *Volonté* 208). Whereas desire and the science of sexuality are internal to this apparatus, pleasure can function as a point or line of resistance to the structures and mechanisms of that very apparatus. Foucault is less enigmatic about this contrast in his interview "Le gai savoir," originally conducted in 1978:

> I advance this term [pleasure] because it appears to me to escape those medical and naturalistic connotations that this notion of desire bears within itself. That notion was used as a tool, a setting of intelligibility, a calibration in terms of normality: "Tell me what your desire is and I will tell you who you are, if you are normal or not, I will therefore be able to admit or disqualify your desire." One certainly finds this "hold" [*prise*] which goes from the notion of Christian concupiscence to the Freudian notion of desire, while passing through the notion of the sexual instinct in the 1840's. Desire is not an event, but a permanence of the subject, on which all this psychologico-medical armature is grafted. The term "pleasure," on the other hand, is free of use, almost devoid of meaning. There is no "pathology" of pleasure, no "abnormal" pleasure. It is an event "outside the

subject," or at the limit of the subject, in that something which is neither of the body nor of the soul, which is neither inside nor outside, in short, a notion not assigned and not assignable. (The French text is qtd. in Halperin 217 n. 181.)[2]

Desire allows a hold or grip on the subject that is central to the constitution of a science of sexuality, while pleasure escapes the discourse of pathology and abnormality, the discourse of *scientia sexualis;* its "location" at the limit of the self in fact disturbs, disrupts the primacy of the subject. This is one philosophical context in which we should place Foucault's extraordinary remarks delivered in 1979 at the meeting of Arcadie:

> Pleasure is something that passes from one individual to another; it is not a secretion of identity. Pleasure has no passport, no identity card. (The French text is qtd. in Eribon 271.)

We can easily invert Foucault's remarks and say that desire is a secretion of identity; it does possess an identity card. And as with other kinds of passports, it can be authentic or counterfeit, representing more or less faithfully who one is. Pleasure does not represent anything; there are no counterfeit pleasures.

Although other texts of Foucault could be cited to support this interpretation, these claims do directly raise the question of how one is to understand his remarks, both here and in *The Will to Know,* about that other pleasure, the "pleasure of analysis" (*Volonté* 94–96). For this specific pleasure seems to belie the conceptual division between desire and pleasure on which I have insisted. Indeed, Foucault's invocation of the pleasure of analysis is intended to complicate the strict distinction between *ars erotica* and *scientia sexualis,* leading us to ask whether, "at least in certain of its dimensions," *scientia sexualis* may not function as an *ars erotica* (95). Without denying the numerous relations between this art and this science, I want to note that Foucault's own remarks question the status of this "pleasure of analysis" in ways that mark it out as not being homogeneous with the pleasures that can function as points of resistance to the apparatus of sexuality. In addition to placing this pleasure within quotation marks, Foucault explicitly refers to this category as containing "ambiguous pleasures," a characterization used nowhere else. But even more importantly, his characterization of this pleasure employs verbs, all of which partake of the grammar of desire—in "The West and the Truth of Sex," *fouiller, traquer, interpréter;* in *The Will to Know,* verbs such as *exposer, découvrir, débusquer.* These are all activities whose object is typically *desire* and not pleasure, and this is the only instance in which Foucault attaches them to "pleasure," evidence enough of the ambiguous status of this pleasure. Moreover, in "The West and the Truth of Sex," speaking of the way in which the science of sex still belongs to the erotic art, Foucault himself refers not to the pleasure of analysis but to people who "spend so much money to buy the biweekly right to formulate laboriously *the truth of their desire,* and patiently to await the *benefit of interpretation*" (my emphasis), as if to say that the formulation of true desire and the benefit of interpretation fill in the content of the pleasure of analysis.[3]

At the end of his discussion in *The Will to Know,* Foucault raises a set of questions that already indicates the gap between this pleasure and the body-pleasure-intensification axis that I have previously discussed. After identifying the pleasure of analysis, he asks:

> Should one believe that our *scientia sexualis* is but a singularly subtle form of *ars erotica* and that, of this apparently lost tradition, it is the Western and quint-essential version? Or should one suppose that all these pleasures are but the by-products of a sexual science, a benefit that supports its innumerable efforts? (*Volonté* 96)

This latter question can only be coherently asked of the pleasures of analysis, and that fact alone shows the distinctiveness, the peculiarity, of this kind of pleasure. It is a pleasure that has neither the epistemological nor the political force of those other pleasures advanced by Foucault; in a word, it does not disrupt the sovereignty of the subject.

Foucault's interest in the dissolution of the psychological subject of *scientia sexualis* is not only compatible with but also, in my view, required by his final concern with ethical subjectivation. But rather than pursuing these latter concerns, I want to give a final example of the stakes involved in the dissolution of the psychological subject. Perhaps the clearest exem-plification of this dissolution remains Pierre Guyotat's *Éden, Éden, Éden,* to which Foucault devoted a very brief but brilliant and theoretically powerful text. Guyotat's book, without saving "the subject, the self, the soul," without protecting the "primacy of the subject, the unity of the individual," without representing sexuality as the "fundamental or primi-tive desire of the individual," is able to enact a rupture (Foucault, "Il y aura scandale, mais . . ." 75).[4] In this book the individual

> is but the precarious extension of sexuality, provisional, quickly effaced; the individual, in the end, is but a pallid form that arises for a few moments from

a great repetitive, persistent source. Individuals, the quickly retracted pseudo-pods of sexuality. . . . If we want to know what we know, we must give up what we suppose about our individuality, our self, our subject position. . . . In your text, it is perhaps the first time that the relations of the individual and of sexuality are plainly and decidedly reversed . . . : sexuality passes to the other side of the individual and ceases to be "subjected" [assujettie]. ("Il y aura scandale, mais . . ." 75)[5]

The inaccessibility of *Éden, Éden, Éden,* its unreadability, its new form of extremeness are marks of its exteriority and of its resistance to the apparatus of sexuality. Our inability to imagine what this text sounds like attests to the hold of that "anthropological slumber" that Foucault was ceaselessly combating ("Philosophie et psychologie" 448). We should not underestimate, as we so often do, the severe difficulty of dissolving the subject. If psychology, in all of its forms, has been an "absolutely inevitable and absolutely fatal impasse" of our thought since the nineteenth century, then its rupture will be experienced as a kind of death (448). So let us not forget, in this context, these shocking remarks of Foucault:

> I think that pleasure is a very difficult behavior. . . . I would like and I hope I'll die of an overdose of pleasure of any kind. Because I think it's really difficult, and I always have the feeling that I do not feel *the* pleasure, the complete total pleasure, and, for me, it's related to death. . . . I think that the kind of pleasure I would consider as *the* real pleasure would be so deep, so intense, so overwhelming that I couldn't survive it. I would die. ("Michel Foucault: An Interview by Stephen Riggins" 129)[6]

I hope we are in a position to take Foucault's remarks conceptually, and not psychologically, and to use them to ask ourselves a question he often asked himself, a question to which we still do not have a satisfactory answer: What is the pleasure of sex, what does it do to us?

Notes

1. In what follows, I restrict my discussion to the desire and pleasure of sexual experience.

2. Halperin's book remains the indispensable discussion of Foucault on desire and pleasure.

3. The corresponding sentence in *La volonté de savoir* does refer instead to the "pleasure of analysis" (see 95–96).

4. I am indebted to Daniel Defert for having first made me aware of this text.

5. The fact that Foucault here singles out a literary text merits further discussion.

6. This interview was conducted in English.

References

Davidson, Arnold I., ed. *Foucault and His Interlocutors*. Chicago: U of Chicago P, 1997.

———. "Structures and Strategies of Discourse: Remarks Towards a History of Foucault's Philosophy of Language." In Davidson, *Foucault and His Interlocutors* 1–17.

Deleuze, Gilles. "Desire and Pleasure." Trans. Daniel W. Smith. In Davidson, *Foucault and His Interlocutors* 183–92.

Eribon, Didier. *Michel Foucault et ses contemporains*. Paris: Fayard, 1994.

Foucault, Michel. *Dits et écrits: 1954–1988*. 4 vols. Ed. Daniel Defert and François Ewald, with the collaboration of Jacques Lagrange. Paris: Gallimard, 1994.

———. *Histoire de la sexualité*. Vol. 1: *La volonté de savoir*. Paris: Gallimard, 1976.

———. "Il y aura scandale, mais . . ." 1970. In *Dits et écrits* 2:74–75.

———. "Interview avec Michel Foucault." Interview with I. Lindung, March 1968. In *Dits et écrits* 1:651–62.

———. "Lacan, le 'libérateur' de la psychanalyse." Interview with J. Nobécourt, September 1981. In *Dits et écrits* 4:204–5.

———. "Le jeu de Michel Foucault." Interview with D. Colas, A. Grosrichard, G. Le Gaufey, J. Livi, G. Miller, J. Miller, J.-A. Miller, C. Millot, and G. Wajeman, July 1977. In *Dits et écrits* 3:298–329.

———. "Michel Foucault: An Interview by Stephen Riggins." June 1982. In *Ethics: Subjectivity and Truth*. Ed. Paul Rabinow. Trans. Robert Hurley and others. New York: New P, 1997. 121–33.

———. "Philosophie et psychologie." Interview with A. Badiou, March 1965. In *Dits et écrits* 1:448–64.

———. "Qu'est-ce qu'un auteur?" February 1969. In *Dits et écrits* 1:789–821.

———. "Sexualité et vérité." 1977. In *Dits et écrits* 3:136–37.

Halperin, David M. *Saint Foucault: Towards a Gay Hagiography*. New York: Oxford UP, 1995.

2

THE WEST AND THE
TRUTH OF SEX

Michel Foucault
Translated by Daniel W. Smith

. . . .

Toward the end of the nineteenth century, an Englishman who left no name wrote an immense book, of which only a dozen or so copies were printed; it was never put on sale and wound up in the hands of a few collectors or in rare bookstores. One of the most unknown of books, it was entitled *My Secret Life*. In it, the author gives a meticulous narration of a life that had, for the most part, been devoted to sexual pleasure. Night after night, day after day, he recounts his slightest experiences, without ostentation, without rhetoric, with the sole aim of saying what happened, how it happened, with what intensity and what quality of sensation.

With this sole aim? Perhaps. For he often speaks of this task of writing down the daily details of his pleasure as a pure duty. Since it is a heavy obligation, somewhat enigmatic, which he cannot refuse to subject himself to, *he must say everything*. Yet there is something else. For this obstinate Englishman, it is a matter of combining within this "wordplay" pleasure, true discourse on pleasure, and the pleasure given by stating this truth. It is a matter of making use of this journal—whether by rereading it out loud, or by writing it as he goes along—in the unfolding of new sexual experiences, in accordance with the rules of certain strange pleasures in which "reading and writing" would play a specific role.

Steven Marcus devoted several remarkable pages to this obscure contemporary of Queen Victoria (see *Other Victorians*). For my part, I would
not be overly tempted to see him as a shadowy character, relegated to the
"other side" in an age of excessive prudishness. Is his indeed a discrete
and sneering revenge against the prudery of the era? To me, he appears
to be situated rather at the point of convergence of three lines of evolution that are hardly secret in our society. The most recent is the one that
led the medicine and psychiatry of the era to a quasi-entomological interest in sexual practices, with all their variants and disparity: Krafft-Ebing
is not far off (see *Psychopathia sexualis*).[1] The second, older line is the one
that, since Rétif and Sade, had inclined erotic literature to seek its effects
not only in the vivacity or rarity of the scenes it was imagining, but also
in the relentless search for a certain truth of pleasure. An erotics of truth,
a relation between the true and the intense, is characteristic of this new
"libertinage" inaugurated at the end of the eighteenth century. The third
line is the oldest; it has traversed the entire Christian West since the
Middle Ages: it is the strict obligation of every person to seek out, in the
depths of his or her heart, through penitence and the examination of
conscience, the slightest traces of concupiscence, even if they are imperceptible. The quasi-clandestine nature of *My Secret Life* must not mislead
us, then;[2] the relation of true discourse to the pleasure of sex had been
one of the most constant concerns of Western societies. And that, for
several centuries.

.   .   .   .   .   .

What has not been said about this society—bourgeois, hypocritical, prudish, sparing with its pleasures, obstinately refusing either to want them
or to recognize them or name them? What has not been said about the
heavy heritage it received from Christianity—the sex-sin? And about the
way the nineteenth century used this heritage for economic ends—work
rather than pleasure, the reproduction of forces rather than the pure ex-
penditure of energies?

And what if these were not the essential points? What if there were
very different mechanisms at the center of the "politics of sex"? Not rejection and occultation, but incitation? What if the essential function of
power were not to say *no*, to forbid and to censure, but to link together
coercion, pleasure, and truth in an indefinite spiral?

We need think only of the zeal with which our societies have multiplied,
for several centuries now, all those institutions whose aim is to extort the

truth of sex, and thereby to produce a specific pleasure. Think of the enormous obligation toward avowal, and of all the ambiguous pleasures that both disrupt it and make it desirable: confession, education, relations between parents and children, doctors and patients, psychiatrists and hysterics, psychoanalysts and patients. It is sometimes said that the West has never been able to create a single new pleasure. Does the desire to excavate, to track down, to interpret, in short, the "pleasure of analysis," in the large sense of the term, count for nothing?

Rather than a society devoted to the repression of sex, I would see ours as devoted to its "expression." You will pardon me for using this devalued word. I would see the West as relentlessly devoted to extracting the truth of sex. The silences, blockages, and evasions must not be underestimated; but they could not have come into being and produced their formidable effects without the background of a will to know that traverses our entire relation to sex. A will to know at this point so imperious, and in which we are so enveloped, that we not only seek the truth of sex, but demand from it our own truth. We expect it to tell us who we are. From Gerson to Freud, an entire logic of sex was constructed, which has organized the science of the subject.

We readily imagine that we belong to a "Victorian" regime. It seems to me that our kingdom is rather the one imagined by Diderot in *Les bijoux indiscrets:* a certain mechanism, barely visible, makes sex speak in an almost unstoppable babble. We are in a society of sex that speaks.

· · · · · ·

Perhaps we must also interrogate a society on the way it organizes its relations of power, truth, and pleasure. It seems to me that two principal regimes can be distinguished. The first is that of *ars erotica.* Here, truth is extracted from pleasure itself, gathered as experience, analyzed according to its quality, followed along its reverberations in the body and the soul; and this quintessential knowledge, under the seal of a secret, is transmitted by magisterial initiation to those who have shown themselves worthy, and who will know how to use it in their own pleasure, in order to intensify it, to make it more acute and more complete.

Western civilization, at least for several centuries, has had little experience of erotic art; it has linked the relations of power, pleasure, and truth in a completely different mode: that of a *scientia sexualis.* A type of knowledge where what is analyzed is less pleasure than desire; where the function of the master is not to initiate, but to interrogate, listen, decipher; a long process whose aim is not the increase of pleasure but the modification of the subject (who is thereby pardoned or reconciled, cured or emancipated).

The relations between this art and this science are too numerous to make it a line of division between two types of society. Whether it is a question of the direction of conscience or of the psychoanalytic cure, the knowledge of sex carries with it the imperatives of a secret, a certain relation to the master, and an entire game of promises that still belong to the erotic art. Do you believe that, without these murky relations, people would spend so much money to buy the biweekly right to formulate laboriously the truth of their desire, and patiently to await the benefit of interpretation?

My project—*The History of Sexuality*—would be to trace the genealogy of this "science of sex." An undertaking, I am well aware, that is hardly novel; many people are at work on it today, showing how the refusals, the occultations, the fears, the systematic misunderstandings have for a long time kept at bay any possible knowledge of sex. But I would like to attempt this genealogy in positive terms, starting from the incitations, focal points, techniques, and procedures that have permitted the formation of this knowledge; I would like to follow, starting with the Christian problem of the flesh, all the mechanisms that have imposed a discourse of truth on sex, and organized around it a mixed regime of pleasure and power. Given the impossibility of following this genesis globally, I will try, in distinct studies, to pinpoint some of its most important strategies: with regard to children, with regard to women, with regard to perversions, and with regard to the regulation of births.

The question that has been traditionally asked is this: Why then has the West culpabilized sex for so long? And how, given the background of this refusal or fear, has one come to ask it, despite so much reticence, as the question of truth? Why and how, since the end of the nineteenth century, have we undertaken to dispel part of the great secret, and that with difficulty, to which Freud's courage still attests?

I would like to pose another question: Why has the West continually interrogated itself about the truth of sex, and required everyone to formulate it for him- or herself? Why has it obstinately wanted our relation with ourselves to pass through this truth? We should then be surprised that toward the end of the twentieth century we have been seized by a great and new culpability, that we have begun to experience a kind of historical remorse that has made us believe that for centuries we have been at fault with regard to sex.

It seems to me that what is systematically misunderstood in this new culpabilization, of which we are so fond, is precisely this great configuration of knowledge, which the West has ceaselessly organized around sex, through religious, medical, and social techniques.

I suppose I will be granted this point. But immediately someone will say: "All this fuss about sex, the constant concern with it, didn't it have a single objective, at least until the end of the nineteenth century, namely, to forbid the free use of sex?" Certainly, the role of interdictions has been important. But is sex first and above all forbidden? Or, rather, are the prohibitions mere traps within a complex and positive strategy?

We here touch on a more general problem that will have to be treated in counterpoint with this history of sexuality—the problem of power. In a spontaneous manner, when we speak of power, we conceive of it as a law, as an interdiction, as prohibition and repression; and we are indeed disarmed when we try to follow it in its mechanisms and its positive effects. A certain juridical model weighs heavily on the analyses of power, granting an absolute privilege to the form of the law. We would have to write a history of sexuality organized not around the idea of a repression-power, a censure-power, but around the idea of an incitation-power, a knowledge-power; we would have to try to disengage the regime of coercion, pleasure, and discourse that is not inhibiting but constitutive of this complex domain which is sexuality.

I would like this fragmentary history of the "science of sex" to function equally as the sketch for an analytic of power.

Notes

1. The second edition develops the study of "contrary sexual sensibility": *Psychopathia sexualis, mit besonderer Berücksichtigung der conträren Sexualempfindung. Eine klinisch-forensische Studie* (1887). See English edition of 1965.

2. Extracts appeared in French under the title *My Secret Life. Récit de la vie sexuelle d'un Anglais de l'époque victorienne* (1977).

References

Anonymous. *My Secret Life*. 11 vols. Amsterdam, 1890. Reprinted, New York: Grove P, 1964.

————. *My Secret Life. Récit de la vie sexuelle d'un Anglais de l'époque victorienne.* Trans. C. Charrnaux, N. Gobbi, N. Heinich, M. Lessana. Preface by Michel Foucault. Paris: Les Formes du secret, 1977.

Krafft-Ebing, Richard von. *Psychopathia Sexualis: A Medico-Forensic Study.* Trans. Harry E. Wedeck. New York: G. P. Putnam's Sons, 1965.

————. *Psychopathia sexualis, mit besonderer Berücksichtigung der conträren Sexualempfindung. Eine klinisch-forensische Studie.* Stuttgart: Ferdinand Enke, 1887.

Marcus, Steven. *The Other Victorians: A Study of Sexuality and Pornography in Mid-Nineteenth Century England.* New York: Basic, 1966.

3

THE DEATH OF LACAN

Michel Foucault
Translated by Daniel W. Smith

. . . .

These remarks stem from an interview Foucault conducted with Didier Eribon in September 1981 (shortly after Lacan's death) that was never finalized. Eribon reproduced them thirteen years later as rough notes from that interview, as we do here, respecting that this is not a final essay by Foucault.

Sartre and Lacan were exact contemporaries. They passed through the same intellectual, cultural, and political landscapes.

They both took part in this movement of the 1930s, when an antinationalistic and anticonservative reaction occurred in France, along with a return to an interrogation of German thought, which had been banned for fifteen years: Hegel, the old dragon concerned with all the representations of philosophy; the long-misunderstood novelty of Husserl, who had been around since 1900 but remained unknown. Freud as well, who until then was not well-known and was vilified. And the very recent novelty of Heidegger.

The rise of Nazism and its triumph, far from sidelining the interrogation of German thought, intensified it, because one wanted to oppose true thought to barbarism.

Throughout the 1930s Sartre, like Lacan, was with a whole series of intermediaries, Wahl, Kojève, Koyré. It turns out that Sartre and Lacan had been alternate contemporaries. They were not contemporaneous.

Whenever one of them took a step, it was by breaking with the other, but in order to take up again the same type of problems. For example, one could say that Sartre possibly had been the first to introduce Freudian themes into creative philosophical reflection. But he introduced them up to a certain point in order to reduce them, notably with his refusal of the unconscious. For the subject thought in phenomenological terms, but also in traditional Cartesian terms, the unconscious could not exist. And Sartre forged the concept of bad faith in order to substitute it for that of the unconscious.

Lacan's whole trajectory: To take up again the philosophical landscape he had in common with Sartre (Lacan had been Hegelian, and Hyppolite had participated in his seminar); he had been Heideggerian (Heidegger put in question the entire philosophy of the subject from Descartes to Husserl, which Sartre took up again, or it was thought he took it up again).

Armed with all this, Lacan's encounter with linguistics, which showed a play of significations on a material objectifiable in terms of knowledge that was no longer assimilable to the intentionalities of consciousness: something happened in the subject, through the subject . . . which allowed Lacan to ask the question of the subject again.

We here touch on a serious misunderstanding in the history of structuralism: it is not an objectivist philosophy. It is a matter of saying: The old theory of the subject can no longer be used. An interrogation of the subject, a step back from the conception of the subject.

The first pages of Sartre's *Flaubert* are unreadable because of five or ten initial pages on language that were seventy-five years late, ignorant of what linguistics had discovered.

Merleau-Ponty spoke of Saussure in 1948. The problem of linguistics: encountered when he was obliged to do child psychology at the Sorbonne. He then oriented himself along a new linguistic path; Heidegger.

Reflection on language that distances itself from a phenomenology of perception and from Sartre.

It turns out that the people who had been taken with the question of the subject, most of them, had been caught up in the movement of agitation, or "mobilization," of the 1960s, who were all Lacanians, and who found themselves converging with Sartre, while Lacan stayed on his couch.

Sartre died a contemporary of those who had learned a thought that had been formed by breaking with him. All these thoughts were thoughts that were preoccupied only with the problems of the subject and truth (history of the sciences). Two things Sartre did not speak about: He had an inherited conception of truth. He couldn't have cared less about it. For him: the structuralist movement was cold, apolitical. But the people who participated in May 1968 were Althusserians.

What is being said now: false in relation to what had been historically real.

CLOSING UP THE CORPSES

Diseases of Sexuality and the
Emergence of the Psychiatric Style of Reasoning

Arnold I. Davidson

. . . .

1.

In *The Birth of the Clinic* (1963), Michel Foucault charts the emergence and the effects of the conjunction of pathological anatomy and clinical medicine, and he emphasizes the significance of pathological anatomy as a foundation for the description and classification of diseases. At the beginning of the nineteenth century, assertions like Jean-Baptiste Bouillaud's in his *Philosophie médicale* were to determine the fate of medicine:

> If there is an axiom in medicine it is certainly the proposition that there is no disease without a seat. If one accepted the contrary opinion, one would also have to admit that there existed functions without organs, which is a palpable absurdity. The determination of the seat of disease or their localization is one of the finest conquests of modern medicine. (qtd. in Foucault, *Clinic* 140)

The history of this fine conquest is replete with surprises and ironies, the complete story of which still remains to be fully recounted. But we can summarize the hopeful, revolutionary enthusiasm of the pathological anatomists with these words from Marie-François-Xavier Bichat's *Anatomie générale:*

For twenty years, from morning to night, you have taken notes at patients'
bedsides on affections of the heart, the lungs, and the gastric viscera, and all is
confusion for you in the symptoms which, refusing to yield up their meaning,
offer you a succession of incoherent phenomena. Open up a few corpses: you
will dissipate at once the darkness that observation alone could not dissipate.
(qtd. in Foucault, *Clinic* 146)

And so Foucault concludes that "the great break in the history of Western
medicine dates precisely from the moment clinical experience became
the anatomo-clinical gaze" (146).

One of the great breaks in the history of Western psychiatry comes precisely during the time when the anatomo-clinical gaze is in steady decline.
The story of psychiatry's emergence, in the nineteenth century, as an autonomous medical discipline, and specifically its autonomy from neurology and cerebral pathology, is, in part, the history of this decline. Pathological anatomy could not serve psychiatry as either an explanatory theory
for so-called mental diseases or disorders, or as the foundation for the
classification and description of these diseases. But the gradual and virtually anonymous disappearance of pathological anatomy in psychiatry is
not merely the history of decline. For with this decline came the proliferation of whole new kinds of diseases and disease categories, a revitalization
and reworking of nosologies the consequences of which stamp us even
today. Foremost among these new disease categories was the class of functional diseases, of which sexual perversion and hysteria were the two
most prominent examples. Although the hope that these functional diseases would yield to pathological anatomy was held out long after there
was any evidence for this hope, in clinical practice, and later in theory as
well, these diseases were fully describable simply as functional deviations
of some kind; in the case of sexual perversion, for instance, one was faced
with a functional deviation or abnormality of the sexual instinct. Admitting pure functional deviations as diseases was to create entire new species
of diseased individuals, and to radically alter our conceptions of ourselves.

In this essay I focus on the diseases of sexual perversion and try to
show how the history of this disease category is intertwined with the fall
of pathological anatomy. The results of this history determine some of
our concepts of mental disease today, as shown, for example, by the third
edition of the diagnostic and statistical manual of the American Psychiatric Association. More important, the effects of this history have helped
determine how we now categorize ourselves, have contributed to our current epistemology of the self. We are all potential perverts. How has this
come to be?

2.

It is convenient to divide the history of sexual perversion into three stages, each stage depending upon a different understanding of what these diseases were thought to be diseases of. It is perhaps best to think of each stage as characterized by a different mode or form of explanation, the third stage constituting a decisive break with the first two, since it inaugurates an entirely new style of reasoning about perversion. In the first, most short-lived stage, sexual perversion was thought to be a disease of the reproductive or genital organs, a disease whose basis was some anatomical abnormality of these organs. The second stage, although in clinical practice recognizing perversions to be abnormalities of the sexual instinct, insisted that the psychophysiology of the sexual instinct (and so of its diseases as well) would eventually, with advances in knowledge, come to be understood in terms of the neurophysiology and neuroanatomy of the brain. These first two stages of explanation shared a commitment to the anatomo-pathological style of reasoning. The third stage took perversions to be pure functional deviations of the sexual instinct, not reducible to cerebral pathology. Perversions were to be viewed and treated at the level of psychology, not at the grander level of pathological anatomy. The psychiatric style of reasoning emerged clearly and definitively at this third stage.

Of course, this three-stage structural partition does not precisely coincide with historical chronology; the three forms of explanation were often mixed together, sometimes even in the same article. But they are capable of being distinguished and it will help our understanding to so distinguish them. More specifically, the second and third stages are not separated by some exactly datable dividing line. Indeed, these two stages overlap to such an extent that many of the psychiatrists who are most responsible for our current conception of the perversions were also strongly wedded to the dominance of brain pathology. So that although for analytical and historiographical reasons we must carefully separate these last two stages, as a matter of historical account no such neat division will be found.

In the years between 1870 and 1905 psychiatry was caught between two conceptual grids; in one of which it was aligned with neurology, in the other with psychology. Most psychiatric disease categories, including the perversions, were swept along in this battle over what kind of science psychiatry was to be. The fact that the majority of the great European psychiatrists at the end of the nineteenth century were trained as neurologists meant that they paid at least theoretical homage to their mother discipline. But it was not merely biographical considerations that prompted a constant appeal to the neural sciences. During this span of time, no one really knew what it would mean to conceive of diseases like perversion in purely functional terms. It would be like admitting functions without organs, which, as Bouillaud reminds us, was a palpable absurdity. So the hold of pathological anatomy remained to mask the fact that this palpable absurdity was already reality. In fact, the professions of these brain anatomists in almost no way affected the description and classification of the perversions. From very near the beginning of psychiatry's emergence as an academic discipline, functional diseases were a recognized part of clinical experience. Theories about the neuropathology of the brain had no clinical effects; they were part of an almost useless conceptual space. So although we can, and should, distinguish between perversions as functional deviations ultimately reducible to brain disease and perversions as pure functional diseases, if we look at the *descriptions* of those who advocate these second and third modes of explanation, they are practically identical. The real break, the new style of reasoning, is to be located at that point when the sexual instinct and its functional diseases were introduced together. Functional diseases were diseases of something—not an organ, but an instinct (see Foucault, "Confession").

3.

In one of the earliest articles on what we have come to call perversion, probably the earliest article on the subject in French, Dr. Michea takes up the case of Sergeant Bertrand, accused of having violated female cadavers. Although like all of the discussions prior to 1870, Michea is concerned primarily with the question of Bertrand's legal and moral responsibility for his actions, his article is distinguished by the fact that he does consider, in passing, the classification of what he names *les déviations maladives de l'appétit vénérien*. He classifies these deviations into four kinds, in order of their frequency: first, Greek love, the love of an individual for someone of his own sex; second, bestiality; third, the attraction for an inanimate object; and fourth, the attraction for human cadavers (339). Michea's paper is significant in that he argues that Bertrand suffers not from vampirism or destructive monomania but from some deviation of the venereal appetite, a form of erotic monomania. Arguments of this type were crucial in providing grounds for isolating diseases of sexuality as distinct morbid entities, and thus not reducing them to mere effects of other, prior disease processes. But for our purposes, the most interesting aspect of Michea's short paper is his discussion and explanation of "Greek love," to which he devotes, by far, the greatest space. (Indeed, Michea claims that there is only one previous case in judicial records of the attraction for human cadavers, the disease from which Bertrand is supposed to suffer.) After arguing that Greek love should be considered an unhealthy deviation of the venereal appetite, Michea wonders what might explain this strange disorder. His explanation relies on the work of Weber, a professor of anatomy and physiology, who had recently described, in great detail, the location and anatomy of the "masculine uterus." Michea points out that Weber's description of the masculine uterus has already been successfully used by Akermann to explain a hermaphrodite (Michea 339). On the basis of this successful application of Weber's anatomical discovery, Michea concludes:

> If these anatomical facts are verified, if, above all, one proceeded to discover that the masculine uterus can have sometimes a greater and sometimes a lesser development, one would perhaps be justified in establishing a relation of causality between these facts and the feminine tendencies that characterize the majority of individuals who engage in Greek love. (339)

Nothing could be more natural than to expect these feminine tendencies to have some anatomical basis; and nothing could constitute a more appropriate anatomical basis than a masculine uterus. The uterus, that almost always diseased female organ, was responsible for masculine deviations as well!

Although perhaps extraordinary in some of its details, Michea's form of explanation is not as uncommon as one might have expected. Writing in English in 1888, J. G. Kiernan puts great emphasis on the biological facts of bisexuality and hermaphroditism in the lowest orders of life. Combining these facts with the fact that the human embryo is not originally sexually differentiated, Kiernan proposes to explain sexual perversions according to a "principle of atavism" (Prince, "Sexual Perversions" 89–90):

> The original bisexuality of the ancestors of the race shown in the rudimentary female organs of the male could not fail to occasion functional if not organic reversions when mental or physical manifestations were interfered with by disease or congenital defect. (Kiernan 129)

Or as he puts it later:

> Males may be born with female external genitals and vice versa. The lowest
> animals are bisexual and the various types of hermaphroditism are more or less
> complete reversions to the ancestral type. (Kiernan 130)

Writing a year later in *Medical and Surgical Reporter*, G. Frank Lydston elaborates on the observations and hypothesis:

> It is puzzling to the healthy man and woman, to understand how the practices
> of the sexual pervert can afford gratification. If considered in the light of rever-
> sion of type, however, the subject is much less perplexing. That maldevelop-
> ment, or arrested development, of the sexual organs should be associated with
> sexual perversion is not at all surprising; and the more nearly the individual
> approximates the type of fetal development which exists prior to the com-
> mencement of sexual differentiation, the more marked is the aberrance of sexu-
> ality. (255)

Whether it be the increased development of the masculine uterus or the
failed development of sexual differentiation, the forty-two years between
Michea and Lydston persist in anatomo-pathological explanations of the
perversions. The explanatory ideal here is that of physical hermaphroditism. Since it was natural to suppose that all behavioral disorders had an
organic basis, and since the behavioral manifestations in question were
diseases of sexuality, it seemed inevitable that the sexual organs themselves must be the seat of the perversions. And it was no accident that
the vast majority of the clinically reported cases of perversion were cases
of "contrary sexual instinct" or homosexuality. Male organs led to male
behavior and female organs to female behavior. Investigate the anatomy
of the organs and behavioral science would be on a secure foundation.
How this explanatory ideal of physical hermaphroditism was to explain
the other perversions was never clear. But these other perversions were
sufficiently rare in comparison with contrary sexual instinct that they
could be theoretically neglected, at least at first, without much worry.
This straightforward style of pathological anatomy wished to trace the
behavioral abnormalities of perverts back to some gross physical deformity (or deficiency) of the reproductive organs, and in this way a clear
and epistemologically satisfying causal link would be established between
organs and functions. The anatomy of the body would continue to be
explanatorily supreme.

Medical doctors took great solace in this brute physicalism, insisting on the power of their science to explain even the most bizarre acts. Their attitude is clearly expressed by Lydston, whose article was originally delivered as a clinical lecture to the College of Physicians and Surgeons, Chicago, Illinois. Here is a synoptic passage:

> The subject has been until a recent date studied solely from the standpoint of the moralist, and from the indisposition of the scientific physician to study the subject, the unfortunate set of individuals who are characterized by perverted sexuality have been viewed in the light of their moral responsibility rather than *as the victims of a physical and incidentally of a mental defect.* It is certainly much less humiliating to us as atoms of the social fabric to be able to attribute the degradation of these poor unfortunates to a physical cause, than to a wilful viciousness over which they have, or ought to have, volitional control. Even to the moralist there should be much satisfaction in the thought that a large class of sexual perverts are physically abnormal rather than morally leprous . . . the sexual pervert is generally a physical aberration—a lusus naturae. (Lydston 253; my emphasis; see also Gley)

Most of the cases of contrary sexual instinct reported in the nineteenth-century medical literature explicitly record the anatomy of the reproductive organs of these unfortunate patients. And to the consternation of the pathological anatomists, the conclusion is virtually always the same— genital organs, normal; no physical malformations of the reproductive organs. Physical hermaphroditism could no more explain homosexuality than it could any of the other perversions. This grossest level of anatomy proved to be, in this arena, a useless explanatory space. Julien Chevalier had gotten the surprising conclusion correct when he wrote of "sexual inversion" in 1885: "It is characterized by the absence of anatomo-pathological lesions of the sexual organs" (155). But if pathological anatomy was to survive this startling claim, it had to retreat. And it quickly found its site of retreat in the brain.

4.

In the second edition of his acclaimed *Mental Pathology and Therapeutics,* Wilhelm Griesinger, holder of the first chair of psychiatry in Germany, and founder of the *Archiv für Psychiatrie und Nervenkrankheiten,* began with the following proclamation:

The first step towards a knowledge of the symptoms [of insanity] is their local-ity—to which organ do the indications of the disease belong? What organ must necessarily and invariably be diseased where there is madness? The answer to these questions is preliminary to all advancement in the study of mental disease.

Physiological and pathological facts show us that this organ can only be the brain; we therefore primarily, and in every case of mental disease, recognize a morbid action of that organ. (1)

Fewer than ten pages later, commenting on the state of knowledge in brain anatomy, Griesinger continues:

Cerebral pathology is, even in the present day, to a great extent in the same state which the pathology of the thoracic organs was in before the days of Laennec. Instead of proceeding in every case from the changes of structure of the organ, and being able to deduce in an exact manner the production of the symptoms from the changes in the tissue, it has very often to deal with symp-toms of which it can scarcely give an approximation to the seat, and of whose mode of origin it is completely ignorant. It must keep to the external phenom-ena, and establish the groups of diseases according to something common and characteristic in the symptoms altogether independently of their anatomical basis. (8)

Griesinger admits that although in many diseases of insanity anatomical changes in the brain "cannot be ocularly demonstrated by pathological anatomy, still, on physiological grounds it is universally admitted" (4). And he frankly acknowledges, at the beginning of his chapter on the forms of mental disease, that "a classification of mental diseases *according to their nature*—that is, according to the anatomical changes of the brain which lie at their foundation—is, at the present time, impossible" (206; my emphasis).

Writing about diseases of sexuality almost twenty years later, Paul Mo-reau, a prominent French chronicler of aberrations, claims:

Genital excitation, physical or psychical, is the result of a special physiological or pathological excitement, resulting from the localisation or augmentation of a real morbid process to a center of genital functions. But this center, where is it?—In the cortex, the cerebellum, the medulla?

On this point we confess our ignorance and with Esquirol we repeat: we know nothing about it. (146)

Yet again, over twenty-five years later, Kraepelin, in the seventh edition of his textbook for psychiatrists, insists:

The principle [*sic*] requisite in the knowledge of mental diseases is an accurate definition of the separate disease processes. In the solution of this problem one must have, on the one hand, knowledge of the physical changes in the cerebral cortex, and on the other of the mental symptoms associated with them. Until this is known we cannot hope to understand the relationship between mental symptoms of disease and the morbid physical processes underlying them, or indeed the causes of the entire disease process. . . . Judging from experience in internal medicine, the safest foundation for a classification of this kind is that offered by pathological anatomy. Unfortunately, however, mental diseases thus far present but very few lesions that have positive distinctive characteristics, and furthermore there is the extreme difficulty of correlating physical and mental morbid processes. (115–16)

I have reproduced these pronouncements, separated by forty-five years, because they present us with a significant problem: How are we to understand this obsession with brain anatomy coupled as it is with the constant admission of its theoretical and clinical uselessness? A naive hypothesis is that at the end of the nineteenth century, after the work of Broca and others, brain anatomy was just beginning to prove fruitful. Thus, this hypothesis continues, although brain pathology was perhaps not yet helpful in the classification and explanation of mental diseases, these physicians knew that with the slow progress of scientific knowledge it would soon become, both theoretically and clinically, of supreme importance. There was good evidence, so the claim concludes, on which to base an optimistic prediction about the explanatory power of the brain sciences. I have called this hypothesis "naive" because it takes at face value and as the whole story the statements of these neuropsychiatrists. I have no doubt that Griesinger and his descendants would have replied as this hypothesis suggests.[1] But their own avowed replies are not an accurate index of the historical circumstances. At this time in the history of psychiatry only certain kinds of statements about disease processes could count as either true or false; not every such statement was a possible candidate for the status of truth or falsehood (see Hacking, "Language"; Foucault, "Truth"). Specifically, explanations of disease states had to be referred to organs; any explanation not of this type was not so much false as not even in the domain of the true and false. An explanation that did not at least attempt to anatomically localize the disease was more a part of theology than of science (Kiernan 130; Griesinger 5–7). Since it was believed that there were distinct diseases of sexuality, and since these diseases could not be explained by defects of the reproductive organs, the only plausible organ that remained to provide an explanation was the brain. The dominance of brain pathology was as much a consequence of a complicated web of epistemic and conceptual conditions as it was of any empirical evidence. Indeed, for these early psychiatrists it does not seem as if anything could have counted as evidence against the proposition that sexual perversions are ultimately traceable to brain disease. Postmortem examinations that demonstrated no pathological lesions, and should have constituted such evidence, were always explained away; the necessary changes in brain structure were undoubtedly "so fine that with ordinary instruments they are not demonstrable postmortem" (Krafft-Ebing, *Textbook* 21). Whatever evidence was to be amassed had to be placed within the given framework of pathological anatomy. To affirm explicitly that sexual perversions or other mental diseases were functionally autonomous from the brain would have been to pass from basic truth to palpable absurdity, something beyond falsity.[2]

The epistemological stranglehold of pathological anatomy on psychiatry is perhaps best illustrated by Moriz Benedikt's *Anatomical Studies upon Brains of Criminals*. In this book Benedikt reproduces, in extraordinarily painstaking detail, the results of his investigations of the anatomical structure of the brains of twenty-two criminals. Believing that we think, feel, desire, and act according to the anatomical construction and physiological development of our brain, Benedikt hopes that his dissections of criminals' brains will furnish the "foundation stones of a Natural History of Crime" (v–vii). He considers the brains of various kinds of criminals from different races—some habitual thieves, murderers, a banknote counterfeiter, someone who killed the husband of his priest's concubine at the priest's instigation, and numerous others. Whatever interest there may be in the details of his presentations, his conclusion is remarkable:

THE BRAINS OF CRIMINALS EXHIBIT A DEVIATION FROM THE NORMAL TYPE, AND CRIMINALS ARE TO BE VIEWED AS AN ANTHROPOLOGICAL VARIETY OF THEIR SPECIES, AT LEAST AMONG THE CULTURED RACES. (157; original emphasis)

The idea that criminals are an anthropological variety of their species, because of their atypical brains, is an idea that we today find no more than amusing. But Benedikt found little amusement in his results. Concerned with criminal deviation, and starting from the framework of pathological anatomy, he found the "evidence" necessary for the logical conclusion. We should be concerned less with his evidence than with his style of explanation and his epistemic framework. Benedikt himself was sometimes aware of this framework:

It is self-evident that the observations here collected are the result of the a priori conviction that the constitutional ("eigentliche") criminal is a burdened ("belastetes") individual; that he has the same relation to crime as his next blood kin, the epileptic, and his cousin, the idiot, have to their encephalopathic condition. (158)

It is this a priori conviction that sets the stage for neuropsychiatry. The sexual pervert was no less burdened an individual than the criminal, epileptic, or idiot. I do not know how many anatomical investigations were performed upon the brains of perverts. But we should be more surprised if there were not such dissections than if there were. Given the explicit theoretical conception of perversion common at this time, Benedikt's kind of anatomical investigation would have been the ideal diagnostic and explanatory tool.

Yet I have claimed that pathological anatomy did not substantially influence the clinical description and classification of the perversions. Indeed, the only person to even attempt a classification of the perversions on an anatomical basis was Paul Magnan, a distinguished medical psychologist and a sometime collaborator with Charcot. In a presentation to the Société Médico-Psychologique in 1885, Magnan divided the perversions into four classes, hoping that his anatomical classification would help to reduce the confusion that surrounded these aberrations. Perversions were to be understood, according to him, as (1) spinal, (2) posterior spinal cerebral (nymphomania and satyriasis), (3) anterior spinal cerebral (contrary sexual instinct), and (4) anterior cerebral (erotomania). As ultimately unsatisfactory as it was, Magnan's classification was at least headed in the right direction, assuming, of course, that pathological anatomy was as useful as was always claimed. But even in Magnan's hands this classification was more nominal than real. His explanation for why the different perversions were classified as they were was less than sketchy, and his classifications had, at most, a minimal influence on his presentation of cases. Magnan was better known among his colleagues for his extended description of contrary sexual instinct (*inversion du sens génital*) and for his linking of this perversion with degeneracy (Charcot and Magnan); in this respect his views were quite common and his work followed a long line of predecessors, beginning with Westphal. In fact, Falret, commenting on Magnan's 1885 presentation, mentions nothing about his supposed anatomical classification, but rather insists (as did Magnan) on the importance of the hereditary character of the perversions. Although Magnan's classification was adopted by a few other French physicians, such as Sérieux, it was without much effect. His classification never really caught on, and no one offered any more sophisticated anatomical classifications in its place. Magnan's attempt was offered more out of theoretical necessity than as a result of any genuine evidence or insight. His was a last effort to keep pathological anatomy alive.

5.

The best way to understand the nineteenth-century obsession with perversion is to examine the notion of the sexual instinct, for, as I have said, the actual conception of perversion underlying clinical thought was that of a functional disease of this instinct. That is to say, the class of diseases that affected the sexual instinct was precisely the sexual perversions. Of course, the pathological anatomists did not want the notion of a sexual instinct to escape their grasp. Griesinger himself had said that "there is nothing inconsistent in seeking to discover in certain parts of the brain the seat of the sensual instincts" (41). And Krafft-Ebing, in *Psychopathia Sexualis* (1886), asserts that the sexual instinct is a function of the cerebral cortex, although he admits that no definite region of the cortex has yet been proven to be the exclusive seat of this instinct (17). He speculates that since there is a close relation between the olfactory sense and the sexual instinct, these two centers must be close together in the cerebral cortex. Indeed, he accepts Mackenzie's observations that masturbators are subject to nosebleeds, and that "there are affections of the nose which stubbornly resist all treatment until the concomitant (and causal) genital disease is removed" (Krafft-Ebing 21). But besides these rather vague remarks, Krafft-Ebing says nothing that would help one to determine the anatomical foundation of the sexual instinct, or to lead one to believe that it was actually possible to find distinct cerebral lesions associated with the diseases of this instinct.

The appropriate way to understand the sexual instinct is in functional terms, not in anatomical ones. Without such a functional understanding, there would have been no conceptual foundation for classifying certain phenomena as perversions or diseases of the instinct. And Krafft-Ebing himself, as I shall show, understood the sexual instinct in this functional way; his pathological anatomy here is just so much window dressing. One of the most explicit recognitions of the importance of this functional characterization of the sexual instinct, a characterization shared by all the significant clinical work on perversion, appears in Legrain's *Des anom-*

alies de l'instinct sexuel et en particulier des inversions du sens génital, published in 1896:

> The sexual instinct is a physiological phenomenon in every normal being endowed with life. It is a need of a general order and in consequence it is useless to look for its localisation, as one has done, in any particular part whatever of the organism. Its seat is everywhere and nowhere. . . . This instinct is therefore independent of the structure itself of the external genital organs, which are only instruments in the service of a function, as the stomach is an instrument in the service of the general function of nutrition. (36)

By acknowledging the subservience of the genital organs to the function of the sexual instinct, Legrain makes overt what by 1896 nobody should have doubted. And by claiming that the seat of the sexual instinct was everywhere and nowhere, he told us to look for its diseases everywhere and nowhere. This "everywhere and nowhere" sometimes had a more common name in psychiatric discussions—it went under the name of *personality.* A functional understanding of the instinct allowed one to isolate a set of disorders or diseases that were disturbances of the special functions of the instinct. Moreau (de Tours), in a book that influenced the first edition of Krafft-Ebing's *Psychopathia Sexualis,* argued that the clinical facts forced one to accept, as absolutely demonstrated, the psychic existence of a sixth sense, which he called the genital sense (2). Although the notion of a genital sense may appear ludicrous, Moreau's characterization was adopted by subsequent French clinicians, and his phrase *sens génital* was preserved, by Charcot among others, as a translation of our "sexual instinct." So Carl Westphal's *conträre Sexualempfindung* became *inversion du sens génital.* The genital sense is just the sexual instinct, masquerading in different words. Its characterization as a sixth sense was a useful analogy. Just as one could become blind or have acute vision or be able to discriminate only a part of the color spectrum, and just as one might go deaf or have abnormally sensitive hearing or be able to hear only certain pitches, so too this sixth sense might be diminished, augmented, or perverted. What Moreau hoped to demonstrate was that this genital sense had special functions, distinct from the functions served by other organs, and that just as with the other senses, this sixth sense could be psychically disturbed without the proper working of other mental functions, either affective or intellectual, being harmed (3).[3] A demonstration such as Moreau's was essential in isolating diseases of sexuality as distinct disease entities.

The *Oxford English Dictionary* reports that the first modern medical use in English of the concept of perversion occurred in 1842 in Dunglison's *Medical Lexicon:* "'Perversion,' one of the four modifications of function in disease; the three others being augmentation, diminution, and abolition" (*OED* 11:619). The notions of perversion and function are inextricably intertwined. Once one offers a functional characterization of the sexual instinct, perversions become a natural class of diseases; and without this characterization there is really no conceptual room for this kind of disease. Whatever words of pathological anatomy he and others offered, it is clear that Krafft-Ebing understood the sexual instinct in a functional way. In his *Textbook of Insanity,* Krafft-Ebing is unequivocal in his claim that life presents two instincts, those of self-preservation and sexuality; he insists that abnormal life presents no new instincts, although the instincts of self-preservation and sexuality "may be lessened, increased or manifested with perversion" (79). The sexual instinct was often compared with the instinct of self-preservation, which manifested itself in appetite. In a section entitled "Disturbances of the Instincts," Krafft-Ebing first discusses the anomalies of the appetites, which he divides into three different kinds. There are increases of the appetite (hyperorexia), lessening of the appetite (anorexia), and perversions of the appetite, such as a "true impulse to eat spiders, toads, worms, human blood, etc." (*Textbook* 77–81). Such a classification is exactly what one should expect from a functional understanding of the instinct. Anomalies of the sexual instinct are similarly classified as lessened or entirely wanting (anaesthesia), abnormally increased (hyperaesthesia), and perverse expression (paraesthesia); in addition there is a fourth class of anomalies of the sexual instinct, which consists in its manifestation outside of the period of anatomical and physiological processes in the reproductive organs (paradoxia) (81). In both his *Textbook of Insanity* and *Psychopathia Sexualis,* Krafft-Ebing further divides the perversions into sadism, masochism, fetishism, and contrary sexual instinct (*Textbook* 83–86; *Psychopathia* 34–36; I discuss masochism in "Sex").

In order to be able to determine precisely what phenomena are functional disturbances or diseases of the sexual instinct, one must also, of course, specify what the normal or natural function of this instinct consists in. Without knowing what the normal function of the instinct is, everything and nothing could count as a functional disturbance. There would be no principled criterion to include or exclude any behavior from the disease category of perversion. So one must first believe that there is a natural function of the sexual instinct and then believe that this function is quite determinate. One might have thought that questions as momentous as these would have received extensive discussion during the nineteenth-century heyday of perversion. But, remarkably enough, no such discussion appears. There is virtually *unargued unanimity* both on the fact that this instinct does have a natural function and on what that function is. Krafft-Ebing's view is representative here:

> During the time of the maturation of physiological processes in the reproductive glands, desires arise in the consciousness of the individual, which have for their purpose the perpetuation of the species (sexual instinct). . . . With opportunity for the natural satisfaction of the sexual instinct, every expression of it that does not correspond with the purpose of nature—i.e., propagation—must be regarded as perverse. (*Psychopathia* 16, 52–53; for other representative statements, see Krafft-Ebing, *Textbook* 81; Moll 172, 182; and Laupts)

Nineteenth-century psychiatry silently adopted this conception of the function of the sexual instinct, and it was often taken as so natural as to need no explicit statement. It is not at all obvious why sadism, masochism, fetishism, and homosexuality should be treated as species of the same disease, for they appear to have no essential features in common.[4] Yet if one takes the natural function of the sexual instinct to be propagation, it becomes possible to see why they were all classified together as perversions. They all manifest the same kind of perverse expression, the same basic kind of functional deviation. Thus this understanding of the instinct permits a *unified* treatment of perversion, allows one to place an apparently heterogeneous group of phenomena under the same natural disease kind.[5] Had anyone denied either that the sexual instinct has a natural function or that this function is procreation, diseases of perversion, as we understand them, would not have entered psychiatric nosology.

I have already indicated that most nineteenth-century clinical reports of perversion were cases of so-called contrary sexual instinct, and I have offered a hypothesis to explain why this may have been so. In the rest of my discussion of the medical literature on perversion I shall concentrate on these cases, other forms of perversion requiring a separate treatment (which I have provided elsewhere). We can conveniently place the origin of contrary sexual instinct, as a medicopsychological diagnostic category, in 1870, with the publication of Carl Westphal's "Die conträre Sexualempfindung" in *Archiv für Psychiatrie und Nervenkrankheiten*. Westphal's attachment to pathological anatomy did not prevent him from giving the first modern definition of homosexuality. He believed that contrary sexual instinct was a congenital perversion of the sexual instinct, and that in this perversion "a woman is physically a woman and psychologically a man and, on the other hand, a man is physically a man and psychologically a woman" (94). I have called this the first modern definition because it presents a purely psychological characterization of homosexuality, and, detached from Westphal's meager explanatory speculations, it provides us with the clinical conception of this perversion operative in almost all of the subsequent medical literature. Later issues of the *Archiv* contained similar reports of contrary sexual instinct, and some of Krafft-Ebing's most important early work appeared in this journal.

With the publication of Charcot and Magnan's paper in *Archives de Neurologie* in 1882, an epidemic of contrary sexual instinct, equal to that of Germany, was soon to plague France.[6] An Italian case appeared in 1878 (see Tamassia); and the first case in English, in 1881 (see Krueg). The latter case was reported by a German physician and some English-speaking psychiatrists did not consider it "a contribution to the study of this subject by English science" (Shaw and Ferris 198). In 1883 Shaw and Ferris, writing in the *Journal of Nervous and Mental Diseases,* summarize all of the German, French, Italian, and English cases, and conclude that there have been eighteen documented cases of contrary sexual instinct, to which they add one more, bringing the grand total to nineteen. Westphal's psychological characterization of homosexuality is, in effect, the psychiatric transformation of a previous, although nonmedical, understanding of this disorder. Karl Heinrich Ulrichs, a Hanoverian lawyer, had achieved some notoriety with his autobiographical description of contrary sexual instinct, published in the middle 1860s. Ulrichs gave the name "urnings" to those who suffered from these desires, and supposed that a woman's soul dwelled in a man's body (*anima muliebris in virili corpore inclusa*) (Shaw and Ferris 100). And of course, throughout the 1870s and 1880s, there were the obligatory anatomical claims that these desires were the result of "the brain of a woman in the body of a man and the brain of a man in the body of a woman" (Sérieux 37; Kiernan 130). These three ideas of same-sex sexual behavior represent three central places where the phenomenon was thought to reside—the soul, the brain, and the psyche or personality. And, although not always in this historical sequence, theology, pathological anatomy, and psychiatry each took its own opportunity to lay claim to a complete explanation of perverse desires.

The significance of a psychological description of homosexuality is amply illustrated by *Psychopathia Sexualis:*

> After the attainment of complete sexual development, among the most constant elements of self-consciousness in the individual are the knowledge of representing a definite sexual personality and the consciousness of desire, during

the period of physiological activity of the reproductive organs (production of semen and ova), to perform sexual acts corresponding with that sexual personality—acts which, consciously or unconsciously, have a procreative purpose. . . .

With the inception of anatomical and functional development of the generative organs, and the differentiation of form belonging to each sex, which goes hand in hand with it (in the boy as well as in the girl), rudiments of a mental feeling corresponding with the sex are developed. (186)

With this picture of the definite sexual personality in hand, Krafft-Ebing says of contrary sexual instinct:

It is purely a psychical anomaly, for the sexual instinct does in no wise correspond with the primary and secondary sexual characteristics. In spite of the fully differentiated sexual type, in spite of the normally developed and active sexual glands, man is drawn sexually to the man, because he has, consciously or otherwise, the instinct of the female toward him, or vice versa. (*Psychopathia* 35–36)

The normal sexual instinct expresses itself in a definite personality or character; functional disorders of the instinct will express themselves as psychical anomalies. Since the sexual instinct was thought to partake of both somatic and psychic features, any functional abnormality of the instinct could be expected to manifest itself psychically. In this way, these functional disorders and psychology were very closely connected. As Moll says, "To understand the homosexual urge we should consider the genital instinct not as a phenomenon apart from the other functions but rather as a psychic function" (171).

During this period of near-frenetic psychiatric classification, many attempts were made to provide detailed classifications of different degrees and kinds of homosexuality. Psychiatrists were not content with single categories, but rather subdivided the perversions into innumerable kinds so that, before long, the psychiatric world was populated by a plethora of strange beings (see Foucault, *History* 36–49). Krafft-Ebing believed that, "clinically and anthropologically," there were four degrees of development of homosexuality:

1. With the predominant homosexual feeling there are traces of heterosexual sensibility (psychosexual hermaphroditism).
2. Exclusive inclination to the same sex (homosexuality).
3. The whole psychic existence is altered to correspond with the abnormal sexual feeling (effemination and viraginity).

4. The form of the body approaches that which is in harmony with the abnormal
   sexual feeling. However, there are never actual transitions to hermaphrodites.
   (*Textbook* 85)[7]

It is important to note here that the degrees or kinds of homosexuality
are differentiated according to psychic features, namely, the degree of homosexual sensibility or feeling that is present. Only the rarest and most
severe form of homosexuality is accompanied by any somatic changes,
and even these changes are subordinate to the abnormal sexual feeling.

This psychological/functional understanding of contrary sexual instinct is not limited to the German medical literature of the time. In 1896
Legrain could warn us not to make a mistake about the true sex (*le sexe
vrai*) of a "uranist." Even though registered at birth as a man, if in his
contacts with men, he has the feelings that men normally have toward
women, then he is a woman (51). Psychological characteristics, expressions of the sexual instinct, are decisive for the categorization of the sexes:

> And this psychical differentiation is a fact of principal importance, for in my
> view in it alone rests the categorization of the sexes; as long as it is not a com-
> plete fact, the individual is really sexually neutral, whatever his genital struc-
> ture. (37–38)

This priority of the psychological provided some of the conditions necessary for statements such as Kraepelin's:

> It [contrary sexual instinct] is more prevalent in certain employments, such as
> among decorators, waiters, ladies' tailors; also among theatrical people. Moll
> claims that women comedians are regularly homosexual. (510)

It is clear from what Kraepelin says later that he does not believe that
these employments are causally responsible for this perversion of the sexual instinct. Rather, he must believe that once the psychic anomalies of
the perversion are manifest, one tends to choose employment that is
more appropriate to these psychical abnormalities (510–14). With remarks like these, the death of pathological anatomy is secured.

One of the most notable facts about this early psychiatric literature on
perversion is that no explanatory framework is proposed to account for
purely functional diseases. None of the writers I am familiar with ever
suggests that these so-called functional diseases are not true diseases, are
not part of the legitimate domain of medical science. Yet, at the same
time, there was no already clearly formulated concept of disease under

which they could readily fall. Clinical practice came first; explanatory theory lagged far behind. No doubt the circumstances are complicated by the fact that all of the early writers expressed an allegiance to pathological anatomy. But even after pathological anatomy became an obvious explanatory failure, psychiatry did not regroup and address itself to the question of whether these perversions were really diseases. One unequivocal path to take would have been to claim that precisely because no anatomical changes underlay the perversions, they could not be considered diseases, and physicians must leave their regulation to others more qualified. But clinical practice had already constituted the perversions as diseases, and by the time the hold of pathological anatomy was loosened, they were already a recognized part of psychiatric nosology. This precedence of clinical practice to theory is officially endorsed by the American Psychiatric Association, whose *Diagnostic and Statistical Manual* is meant to be theoretically neutral (6–8). But such theoretical neutrality is as unprincipled as it is expansive; indeed, its expansiveness is partially a function of its lack of principle. On a straightforward interpretation, it sanctions the view that whatever psychiatrists do in fact treat as diseases are diseases. So what could not become a disease? The American Psychiatric Association recognizes telephone scatologia, among others, as a psychosexual disorder. Moreover, phenomena do not exhibit their disease status to everyone's untutored vision. To count something as a disease is to make a theoretical classification. The hope of reading diseases straight off of nature, independent of theory, is as philosophically naive as it is historically suspect.

One of the first comprehensive attempts to provide an explanatory framework for functional diseases is Morton Prince's 1898 paper, "Habit Neuroses as True Functional Diseases."[8] Prince considers the whole class of diseases for which there are no anatomical changes different in kind from those that occur in health (sexual perversion being one subclass of functional disease). Not surprisingly, his explanations are of a thoroughly psychological nature, relying mainly on the laws of association. Simply put, his theory was that phenomena may become so strongly associated that their occurrence together is automatic, independent of volition. He thought that we may

> by a process of education be taught to respond to our environment or to internal stimuli in such a way as to generate painful sensations or undesirable motor effects. . . . The painful (disagreeable, undesirable) motor and sensory and other phenomena thus developed constitute so-called disease. ("Habit Neuroses" 589)

He refers to these diseases as habit neuroses, association neuroses, neuro-mimesis, or true functional diseases (590). Prince's framework bears a striking resemblance to Freud's attempt to "pass over into the field of psychology" to explain that other great functional disease, hysteria. Freud's explanations in "Some Points for a Comparative Study of Organic and Hysterical Motor Paralyses" (1893) also rely on the effects of associations in the genesis of mental disorders, and were published in French five years earlier than Prince's paper. Both papers help to culminate the gradual process by which psychiatry became independent of neurology and annexed itself instead to psychology. I have given these two examples (there are others as well) so as not to be accused of claiming that there were no theories of functional diseases. The important point is that theories of this kind were developed after the fact, after the recognition, in standard psychiatric manuals, of whole new disease categories. These new diseases appeared almost full-blown in clinical practice, and silently, anonymously, became part of psychiatric nomenclature. The effect of this quiet, undisturbed recognition was vastly to enlarge psychiatric therapy and intervention. Psychiatry was not to be concerned solely with the extreme forms, the limits, of the human condition, such as madness. Instead, the entire domain of the unnatural and abnormal was to become its province. And one need not have waited until Freud's *Three Essays on the Theory of Sexuality* (1905) to realize that this clinical arena was as common as it was "unnatural"; no one was to escape the psychiatric gaze.[9]

6.

In a groundbreaking essay on the traditional philosophical problem of other minds, Stanley Cavell concludes by saying:

> We don't know whether the mind is best represented by the phenomenon of pain, or by that of envy, or by working on a jigsaw puzzle, or by a ringing in the ears. A natural fact underlying the philosophical problem of privacy is that the individual will take *certain* among his experiences to represent his *own* mind—certain particular sins or shames or surprises of joy—and then take his mind (his self) to be unknown so far as *those* experiences are unknown. (265)

Nineteenth-century psychiatry took sexuality to be the way in which the mind is best represented. To know a person's sexuality is to know that person. Sexuality is the expression of the individual shape of the personality. And to know sexuality, to know the person, one must know its anomalies. Krafft-Ebing was quite clear about this point:

> These anomalies are very important elementary disturbances, since *upon the nature of sexual sensibility the mental individuality in greater part depends.* (*Textbook* 81; my emphasis)

Sexuality individualizes, turns one into a specific kind of human being— a sadist, masochist, homosexual, fetishist. This link between sexuality and individuality explains some of the passion with which psychiatry investigated the perversions. The more details one has about these anomalies, the better one is able to penetrate the covert individuality of the self. The second edition of Laupts's book on homosexuality announces the first thirteen volumes in a "Bibliothèque des Perversions Sexuelles." Here one can read about the perversions of one's choice, gathering as much information as possible about the most profound truths of the individual.

7.

The question I now wish to ask is: Were there any perverts before the later part of the nineteenth century? Strange as it may sound, the answer to this question is, *no.* Perversion and perverts were an invention of psychiatric reasoning and of the psychiatric theories I have surveyed. (I again restrict myself to the case of homosexuality, but a similar history could be recounted for the other perversions.) I do not wish to be misunderstood— intercourse between members of the same sex did not begin, I dare say, in the nineteenth century; but homosexuality, as a disease of the sexual instinct, did. One will not be able to understand the importance of these new diseases of sexuality if one conflates contrary sexual instinct with sodomy. Sodomy was a legal category, defined in terms of certain specifiable behavior; the sodomite was a judicial subject of the law. Homosexuality was a psychic disease of the instinct, of one's sensibility, not to be reduced to merely behavioral terms. Westphal's *conträre Sexualempfindung* is literally a contrary sexual sentiment or sensation, in which the notion of behavior plays, at most, a subsidiary role; the homosexual is a medical patient of psychiatry. Psychiatrists were forever concerned with carefully distinguishing sodomy from homosexuality; Laupts's book reports the views of D. Stefanowski, which are representative of attempts to differentiate the two. Stefanowski gives a point-by-point comparison of pederasty and "uranism," of which the following are some of the more interesting contrasts. In pederasty "the manner of feeling and acting in matters of love remains masculine, the inclination for women exists everywhere," and "the outward appearance always remains masculine; the tasks and habits remain manly"; on the other hand, in uranism "the manner of feeling and acting is completely feminine: it is accompanied by an envy and hatred towards women," and "the outward look sometimes becomes entirely effeminate; the tastes, habits, and pursuits become those of a woman." Moreover, "pederasty can sometimes be restrained and repressed by a vigorous effort of the will," while "uranist passion is completely outside of the domain of the will." Finally, "pederasty as a vice or profession should be repressed and forbidden by the law, male prostitution should be strictly prohibited"; but "uranism, as an innate moral deformity, can never be punished or prosecuted by the law, still its manifestations must necessarily be repressed, in the name of public morality, but one should judge its manifestations as an expression of a diseased state, as a sort of partial mental illness" (Laupts 200–1). These passages make clear how distinct homosexuality and sodomy were considered to be. Homosexuality was a disease, a "perversion" strictly speaking, whereas sodomy was a vice, a problem for morality and law, about which medicine had no special knowledge. The crucial distinction in this area of investigation was made by Krafft-Ebing:

> *Perversion* of the sexual instinct . . . is not to be confounded with *perversity* in the sexual act; since the latter may be induced by conditions other than psychopathological. The concrete perverse act, monstrous as it may be, is clinically not decisive. In order to differentiate between disease (perversion) and vice (perversity), one must investigate the whole personality of the individual and the original motive leading to the perverse act. Therein will be found the key to the diagnosis. (*Psychopathia* 53)

Every psychiatrist writing during this period acknowledged the difference between perversion and perversity, even if they also quickly admitted that it often proved difficult to distinguish the two. Only minutely detailed examination could help to determine that a given patient was a genuine pervert, and not merely evil or wicked. Before the later part of the nineteenth century, questions of sexual perversity were not cloaked in silence or secrecy, but were dealt with primarily in treatises of moral philosophy, moral theology, and jurisprudence, and not in medicine. A good example is the work of Immanuel Kant. Besides his three great critiques on epistemology, moral philosophy, and aesthetic judgment, Kant wrote on just about every imaginable topic that was philosophically interesting. His *Anthropology from a Pragmatic Point of View* (1798) contains a discussion of mental illness in which he distinguishes among hypochondria, mania, melancholia, delirium, and other forms of mental derangement (82–89). Not a word about sexual perversion appears anywhere in this book, however, even though there are chapters on the cognitive powers, the appetitive powers, temperament, character, and a section on the character of the sexes. But matters of sex did not escape Kant's pen, for if we turn to a book published a year earlier, *The Doctrine of Virtue,* which is Part II of *The Metaphysic of Morals,* we find Kant devoting an entire section to "carnal self-defilement" in his chapter on "Man's Duties to Himself as an Animal Being" (*Doctrine* 87–89). Moreover, he explicitly considers whether the sexual power may be used without regard for nature's purpose in the intercourse of the sexes (namely, procreation), and he uses the concept of "unnatural lust" here (89). So it is not as if Kant was silent on the topic of sexual deviations, as if he was subject to some pre-Victorian reticence. It is rather that the epistemic and conceptual conditions necessary to formulate the notion of *diseases of sexuality* did not yet obtain, and sexual unnaturalness could no more be seen unequivocally through the lens of medicine than could any other fundamentally moral problem. The reassignment in regulating the perversions, from law/morality to medicine, was not simply a new institutional division of labor; it was to signal a fundamental transformation, and the inauguration of whole new ways of conceptualizing ourselves.

Perversion was not a disease that lurked about in nature, waiting for a psychiatrist with especially acute powers of observation to discover it hiding almost everywhere. It was a disease created by a new (functional) understanding of disease, a conceptual shift, a shift in reasoning, that made it possible to interpret various types of activity in medicopsychiatric terms. There was no natural morbid entity to be discovered until clinical psychiatric practice invented one.[10] Perversion was not a disease candidate until it became possible to attribute diseases to the sexual instinct, and there were no possible diseases of the sexual instinct before the nineteenth century; when the notion of diseases of this instinct loses its last remaining grasp upon us, we will rid the world of all of its perverts.[11]

Of course, I do not for a moment deny that nineteenth-century psychiatry took itself to be discovering a real disease, and not inventing one. Many of the books I have discussed include entire chapters attempting to demonstrate the presence of these diseases throughout history. Moreau, for instance, after one such historical excursion, insists that we need no longer ascribe these frightful debaucheries to the anger of God or to the rebellion of Satan against God. We can now regard them from a scientific point of view, in conformity with "modern ideas" (67–68). This particular reinterpretation of history was part of the "retrospective medicine" that was so prominent during the nineteenth century, and which consisted in the reinterpretation of misunderstood past phenomena according to medical categories (see Littre). Charcot, to take a more famous instance, was another one of the practitioners of this revisionist medicine, and his *Les Démoniaques dans l'art,* written with Paul Richer, argues that artistic representations of demonic possession are in fact representations of hysteria (see esp. vi; and Goldstein). So we need not be at all surprised to find it repeatedly claimed that these sexual perversions can be seen everywhere in history. These claims, however, should not detain us; all we find before the nineteenth century are descriptions of sodomy, as an actual reading of these pre-nineteenth-century descriptions will confirm. Perversion is a thoroughly modern phenomenon.

8.

I want to discuss very briefly one last problem before drawing some conclusions. One of the concepts most often linked to sexual perversion is that of the degenerate. This concept derives from B. A. Morel and is understood by him to be an unhealthy deviation from the normal type of humanity; one of the essential characteristics of degeneracy is its hereditary transmissibility (*Traité* 4–5).[12] The theory of degeneracy was used as a pseudoexplanatory framework for practically every serious psychopathological state dealt with by nineteenth-century psychiatry. Degeneracy functioned as one of the central ties between what Foucault, in Volume One of *The History of Sexuality,* has called the anatomo-politics of the human body and the bio-politics of the population (139). Everyone from Westphal to Charcot considered sexual perversion to be one instance of this ever present degeneracy. Krafft-Ebing took the functional anomalies of the sexual instinct to be "functional signs of degeneration" (*Psychopathia* 32); Kraepelin, in his grand classificatory scheme of psychopathology, placed contrary sexual instinct under the general category of "constitutional psychopathic states (insanity of degeneracy)" (485). One advantage of regarding perversion as an inherited degenerate state was that, under this hypothesis, it was difficult to doubt that it was a true disease. Since the etiology of perversion was thought to be constitutional, independent of volition and cultivation, the distinction between perversity and perversion was in principle easily drawn. Yet with this clear advantage of allowing, even requiring, psychiatry to treat perversion as a disease came an unfortunate disadvantage "from a social and therapeutic point of view" (Prince, "Sexual" 85). It was natural to assume that it was impossible to modify or remove a congenital, inherited condition, and so the theory of degeneracy led to "therapeutic nihilism and social hopelessness" (85). As Kraepelin put it, "There can be no thought of treatment of an anomaly like this, which has developed with the development of the personality and has its origin deep within it" (qtd. in Schrenck-Notzing 145). How was psychiatric intervention to be justified in a case where, as a matter of theory, there could be little therapeutic efficacy? Since there was no hope in attempting to treat these patients, psychiatry might seem severely limited in how it could exercise its knowledge and power over the perversions. A. von Schrenck-Notzing was perhaps the first to argue in detail that extraneous influences and education were actually the most significant etiological factors in the genesis of the perversions. He treated thirty-two homosexual patients with hypnotic suggestion and found that 70 percent were greatly improved and 34 percent were cured (304). As he puts it in the preface to his book,

> The favorable results obtained in "congenital" urnings by psychical treatment in the hypnotic state placed before me the alternative either to assume that suggestion is capable of influencing congenital abnormalities of the mind or to prove that in the idea of homo-sexuality at present prevalent the hereditary factor is overestimated, to the disadvantage of educational influences. (v)

He chose, without hesitation, the latter alternative, emphasizing that individuals who actually suffered from contrary sexual instinct found the theory of heredity convenient, for they "find in it a very welcome excuse for their peculiarity" (146). Von Schrenck-Notzing said that the aim of his book was to demonstrate that "useful members of society can be made of such perverted individuals," and he hoped that his work would "open to workers in the domain of suggestive therapeutics a new and productive field of activity and humane striving!" (305). Morton Prince also recognized that the educational theory of the perversions offered "hope and possibilities," possibilities of successful therapeutic intervention that brought with them that social hopefulness that has always been so much a part of American psychiatry ("Sexual" 85). But Prince insisted as well that the theory that perversion was acquired or cultivated, owing to the effect of education, unconscious mimicry, external suggestion, example, and so forth, had its own unfortunate disadvantages. On this theory, weren't perversions really vices rather than diseases, perversity instead of true perversion ("Sexual" 95)? And if this was so, then there was still a difficulty in justifying psychiatric intervention. How could psychiatry legitimately interfere in purely moral problems; ought it not to be limited to real mental diseases, to the domain of medical science?[13] The matrix of psychiatric power/knowledge would be maximized if one could claim both that sexual perversion was not congenital and that it was a disease. If it was not congenital, then therapeutic intervention could be efficacious; if it was a disease, then therapeutic intervention would be required. This is exactly where Prince relied on his theory of habit neuroses and true functional diseases. He believed that in order to maintain that perversion, although acquired, was nevertheless a disease, one had to demonstrate that intensely cultivated habits could eventually become automatic, independent of volitional control. The pervert was then subject to "real imperative sensations and ideas":

> Analogy with what takes place in other fields of the nervous system would make it intelligible that sexual feelings and actions may by constant repetition (cultivation) become associated together and developed into the sort of quasi-independent neural activities, which may then become practically independent of the will—or, in other words, a psychosis. ("Sexual" 95)

Prince could then argue that, given this theory, it is up to "countereducation to replace the morbid processes by healthy ones" (96). Under countereducation one could include almost anything one pleased, and so psychiatry was on its way to an unlimited disciplinary regulation of the sexual life. This theory of perversion as an acquired disease induced one to leave completely the domain of pathological anatomy and embed oneself firmly in psychology. Morton Prince, after all, founded both the *Journal of Abnormal Psychology* (1906) and the American Psychopathological Association (1910). The sexual personality was created so much the better to control the body.

9.

It was Immanuel Kant who argued that we can never know the self as it is in itself, but only as it appears to us (*Critique* B68–B69). Kant thought that he could give a deduction that would exhibit the determinate and unchanging categories through which everything, including our own self, must appear to us. Even if we reject Kant's own deduction, we ought not to reject his basic idea. The categories and conceptualizations of the self determine not only how others view us, but also how each person conceives of him- or herself. And conceptions of ourselves greatly influence how we actually behave. Part of Foucault's "genealogy of the subject in Western civilization" must consist in an investigation of the origin of new categories of the self. These categories may come from the strangest and most diverse places. Ian Hacking has shown that the grand statistical surveys of the early nineteenth century provided many new classifications of the self (see "Biopower" and "Invention"). It will not be as surprising to be told that psychiatry is another fertile source for new conceptualizations of the self. The concept of perversion, once exclusively a part of specialized nineteenth-century discussions, became, in the twentieth century, a dominant way of organizing our thought about our own sexuality. People diagnosed as perverts came to think of themselves as diseased, as morbid, an experience that was not possible before the heyday of the pervert that I have described. Westphal believed that contrary sexual instinct was always accompanied by consciousness of the morbidity of the condition (see also Gley 83–84). Being classified as a pervert could alter everything from one's self-conception to one's behavior to one's social circumstances. And even those of us who are not full-fledged perverts have had to reconceive of ourselves; every little deviation of the sexual instinct may be a sign of our impending perversion. We are all possible perverts. It is perversion as a possible way of being, a possible category of the self, that is the legacy of nineteenth-century psychiatry. The notion of perversion has so penetrated our framework of categories that it is now as natural and unquestioned to think of oneself as a pervert as it was once odd and questionable.

Ian Hacking has argued that

> the organization of our concepts, and the philosophical difficulties that arise from them, sometimes have to do with their historical origins. When there is a radical transformation of ideas, whether by evolution or by an abrupt mutation, I think that whatever made the transformation possible leaves its mark upon subsequent reasoning. ("How" 17; see also Hacking, *Emergence* and "Leibniz")

The problem of perversion is a case in point. All of our subsequent reasoning about perversion is afflicted by the historical origins of the concept.

Moreover, we cannot think away the concept of perversion, even if we no longer claim to believe that there is any natural function of the sexual instinct. We are prisoners of the historical space of nineteenth-century psychiatry, "shaped by prehistory, and only archeology can display its shape" (Hacking, "Leibniz" 188). The archaeology of perversion is a crucial stage in understanding the genealogy of the twentieth-century self. Perhaps there will come a time when we can think to ourselves, "How do I love thee; let me count the ways," and no longer fear our possible perversion.

Notes

This essay, first written in 1982, although not published until 1990, has a long history that I will not recount here. In order to assess fully the implications of the arguments in this essay, the reader should place it in the context of two other of my papers, "Sex and the Emergence of Sexuality" and "How to Do the History of Psychoanalysis." I am grateful to Michael Lavin, John McNees, and Alan Stone for comments on an earlier version of this essay. I owe two special debts of gratitude. Conversations with Michel Foucault in 1976 were crucial in helping me conceptualize these issues. And discussions with Ian Hacking contributed to this paper in a multitude of different ways.

1. Another discussion of cerebral pathology that bears attention is Krafft-Ebing's *Textbook of Insanity;* see esp. 20–24.

2. The same set of problems surrounds Charcot's introduction of the ambiguous notion of "dynamic lesion" in reference to hysteria. See *Diseases* 12–14. I briefly discuss this notion in "Assault."

3. Moreau classifies as *"perversion génital absolue"* bestiality, the profanation of corpses, and rape. He also discusses erotomania, satyriasis, and nymphomania. Remarkably, he has no discussion of contrary sexual instinct.

4. In eighteenth-century medicine, masturbation was considered exclusively as a causal factor, omnipresent of course, in the genesis of disease processes. It was not considered a distinct and autonomous disease. See Tissot, *L'onanisme dissertation sur les maladies produites par la masturbation,* first published in Latin in 1758. In the nineteenth century, it came to be thought of as both a distinct morbid entity and a significant causal factor in the genesis of other diseases. For the later understanding, see Moreau (de Tours) 168.

5. It is instructive to compare this conception of perversion with Aquinas's treatment of unnatural vice. St. Thomas believed that there was a distinct kind of lustful vice, "contrary to the natural order of the venereal act as becoming to the human race: and this is called the unnatural vice." He considered onanism, bestial-

ity, sodomy, and the sin of not observing the right manner of copulation all to be unnatural vices. He thought them to be not only distinct from but also worse than incest, adultery, rape, and seduction. See *Summa Theologica,* Question 154, Articles 11 and 12. One must be careful, however, not to assimilate this moral conception of perversion to the nineteenth-century medical conception; see Davidson "Sex." I am indebted to John McNees for discussion on this point.

6. A case reported by Legrand du Saulle appears in *Annales médico-psychologiques* in 1876, Tome IV. But this case is not nearly as well documented as those of Charcot and Magnan.

7. By the fourth category Krafft-Ebing seems to have in mind those cases where "the secondary physical sexual characteristics approach that sex to which the individual, according to his instinct, belongs." He refers to these cases as pseudohermaphroditism (see *Psychopathia* 36).

8. Binet's "Le Fetichisme dans l'amour" must be mentioned as one of the earliest articulations of the associationist point of view. His associationism still left room for the notion of congenital morbid states, however, which he also invoked as part of his explanation of fetishism.

9. I have deliberately left aside Freud's views on the perversions. The best brief discussion of this topic is the entry on perversion in Laplanche and Pontalis 306–9. See also Davidson, "How."

10. Charcot was greatly disturbed by critics who claimed that hysteria was an artificial creation, not to be found in nature, but rather learned through imitation by "patients" who visited the Salpêtrière. He vigorously affirmed that the truth is *"que la grande attaque dont j'ai formulé les caractères, est bel et bien un type morbide naturel; ce n'est pas un création artificielle; elle appartienent à tous les ages, à tous les pays"* (*Leçons* 105).

11. Of course, the general doctrine of scientific realism has come under increasingly detailed attack. For some of the most important recent critiques, see Putnam, *Meaning, Reason,* and *Realism;* Cartwright; and Hacking, *Representing.*

12. Morel also uses the notion of a "functional lesion [*lésion functionnelle*]" (53). For some examples of the use of the theory of degeneracy, see Borel and Corbin.

13. See Krafft-Ebing's preface to the first edition (1886) of *Psychopathia Sexualis* (xiv).

References

American Psychiatric Association. *Diagnostic and Statistical Manual of Mental Disorders.* 3rd ed. Washington, DC: APA, 1980.

Benedikt, Moriz. *Anatomical Studies upon Brains of Criminals: A Contribution to Anthropology, Medicine, Jurisprudence, and Psychology.* 1878. Trans. Edward Payson Fowler. New York: Wm. Wood, 1881.

Binet, Alfred. "Le Fetichisme dans l'amour." *Revue philosophique* 24.1 (1887): 143–67; and 24.2 (1887): 252–74.

Borel, Jacques. *Du concept de dégénérescence à la notion d'alcoolisme dans la médicine contemporaine.* Montpellier: Caues et cie, 1968.

Cartwright, Nancy. *How the Laws of Physics Lie.* New York: Oxford UP, 1983.

Cavell, Stanley. "Knowing and Acknowledging." *Must We Mean What We Say? A Book of Essays.* New York: Scribner's, 1969. 238–66.

Charcot, J.-M. *Diseases of the Nervous System.* Vol. 3. London: New Sydenham Society, 1889.

———. *Leçons du Mardi à la Salpêtrière. Policlinique 1887–1888.* Tome 1. Paris: Aux Bureaux du Progrès Médical, 1892.

Charcot, J.-M., and P. Magnan. "Inversion du sens génital." *Archives de neurologie* 3.7 (1882): 53–60; and 4.12 (1882): 296–322.

Charcot, J.-M., and Paul Richer. *Les Démoniaques dans l'art.* Paris: Delahaye et Lecrosnier, 1897.

Chevalier, Julien. *De l'inversion de l'instinct sexuel au point de vue médico-légal.* Paris: O. Doin, 1885.

Corbin, Alan. *Les Filles de noce: Misère sexuelle et prostitution.* Paris: Aubier Montaigne, 1978.

Davidson, Arnold I. "Assault on Freud." *London Review of Books* (July 5–19, 1984): 9.

———. "How to Do the History of Psychoanalysis: A Reading of Freud's *Three Essays on the Theory of Sexuality.*" In *The Trial(s) of Psychoanalysis.* Ed. Françoise Meltzer. Chicago: U of Chicago P, 1988. 39–64.

———. "Sex and the Emergence of Sexuality." In *Forms of Desire: Sexual Orientation and the Social Constructionist Controversy.* Ed. Edward Stein. New York: Routledge, 1992. 89–132.

Foucault, Michel. *The Birth of the Clinic: An Archaeology of Medical Perception.* 1963. Trans. A. M. Sheridan Smith. New York: Pantheon, 1973.

———. "The Confession of the Flesh." *Power/Knowledge: Selected Interviews and Other Writings, 1972–1977.* Ed. Colin Gordon. New York: Pantheon, 1980. 194–228.

———. *The History of Sexuality, Volume 1: An Introduction.* 1976. Trans. Robert Hurley. New York: Pantheon, 1978.

———. "Truth and Power." *Power/Knowledge* 109–33.

Freud, Sigmund. "Some Points for a Comparative Study of Organic and Hysterical Motor Paralyses." 1893. *Standard* 1:157–72.

———. *The Standard Edition of the Complete Psychological Works of Sigmund Freud.* Ed. and trans. James Strachey. 24 vols. London: Hogarth, 1953–74.

Gley, E. "Les Aberrations de l'instinct sexuel." *Revue philosophique* (janvier 1884): 83–89.

Goldstein, Jan. "The Hysteria Diagnosis and the Politics of Anticlericalism in Late Nineteenth-Century France." *Journal of Modern History* 54.2 (1982): 209–39.

Griesinger, Wilhelm. *Mental Pathology and Therapeutics.* London: New Sydenham Society, 1867.

Hacking, Ian. "Biopower and the Avalanche of Printed Numbers." *Humanities in Society* 5.3–4 (1983): 279–95.

————. *The Emergence of Probability: A Philosophical Study of Early Ideas about Probability, Induction and Statistical Inference.* Cambridge: Cambridge UP, 1975.

————. "How Should We Do the History of Statistics?" *I & C* 8 (1981): 15–26.

————. "The Invention of Split Personalities." *Human Nature and Natural Knowledge, Boston Studies in the Philosophy of Science* 89 (1989): 63–85.

————. "Language, Truth and Reason." In *Rationality and Relativism.* Ed. Steven Lukes and Martin Hollis. Oxford: Blackwell, 1982. 48–66.

————. "Leibniz and Descartes: Proof and Eternal Truths." *Proceedings of the British Academy* LIX (1973). London: Oxford UP, 1975. 175–88.

————. "Making Up People." In *Reconstructing Individualism: Autonomy, Individuality, and the Self in Western Thought.* Ed. Thomas C. Heller et al. Stanford: Stanford UP, 1986. 222–36.

————. *Representing and Intervening.* Cambridge: Cambridge UP, 1983.

Kant, Immanuel. *Anthropology from a Pragmatic Point of View.* The Hague: Nijhoff, 1974.

————. *Critique of Pure Reason.* New York: St. Martin's, 1929.

————. *The Doctrine of Virtue.* Philadelphia: U of Pennsylvania P, 1964.

Kiernan, J. G. "Sexual Perversion and the Whitechapel Murders." *The Medical Standard* 4.5 (1888): 129–30; and 4.6 (1888): 170–72.

Kraepelin, Emil. *Clinical Psychiatry: A Textbook for Students and Physicians.* London: Macmillan, 1907.

Krafft-Ebing, Richard von. *Psychopathia Sexualis.* 1886. New York: Stein and Day, 1965.

————. *Textbook of Insanity.* Philadelphia: F. A. Davis, 1904.

Krueg, Julius. "Perverted Sexual Instincts." *Brain* 4 (1881): 368–76.

Laplanche, Jean, and Jean-Bertrand Pontalis. *The Language of Psychoanalysis.* Trans. Donald Nicholson-Smith. New York: Norton, 1973.

Laupts, Dr. (G. Saint Paul). *L'homosexualité et les types homosexuels: Nouvelle édition de perversion et perversités sexuelles.* Paris: Vigot, 1910.

Legrain, M. P. *Des anomalies de l'instinct sexuel et en particulier des inversions du sens génital.* Paris: Carré, 1896.

Littre, E. "Un fragment de médicine rétrospective." *Philosophie positive* 5 (1869): 103–20.

Lydston, G. Frank. "Sexual Perversion, Satyriasis and Nymphomania." *Medical and Surgical Reporter* 61.10 (1889): 253–58; and 61.11 (1889): 281–85.

Magnan, Paul. "Des anomalies, des aberrations et des perversions sexuelles." *Annales médico-psychologiques* (septième série, tome premier, 1885): 447–74.

Michea, Dr. "Des déviations maladives de l'appétit vénérien." *Union médicale* 17 (juillet 1849).

Moll, Albert. *Perversions of the Sex Instinct.* 1891. Newark: Julian, 1931.

Moreau (de Tours), Paul. *Des aberrations du sens génésique.* Paris: Asselin, 1880.

Morel, B. A. *Traité des dégénérescences physiques, intellectuelles et morales de l'espèce humaine*. Paris: J. B. Ballière, 1857.

Prince, Morton. "Habit Neuroses as True Functional Diseases." *Boston Medical and Surgical Journal* 139.24 (1898): 589–92.

———. "Sexual Perversion or Vice? A Pathological and Therapeutic Inquiry." *Journal of Nervous and Mental Diseases*, April 1898. Rpt. in Prince, *Psychotherapy and Multiple Personality: Selected Essays*. Ed. Nathan G. Hale, Jr. Cambridge: Harvard UP, 1975. 83–98.

Putnam, Hilary. *Meaning and the Moral Sciences*. London: Routledge and Kegan Paul, 1978.

———. *Realism and Reason*. Cambridge: Cambridge UP, 1983.

———. *Reason, Truth and History*. Cambridge: Cambridge UP, 1981.

Schrenck-Notzing, A. von. *Therapeutic Suggestion in Psychopathia Sexualis*. Philadelphia: F. A. Davis, 1895.

Sérieux, Paul. *Recherches cliniques sur les anomalies de l'instinct sexuel*. Paris: Lecrosnier et Babé, 1888.

Shaw, J. C., and G. N. Ferris. "Perverted Sexual Instinct." *Journal of Nervous and Mental Diseases* 10.2 (1883).

Tamassia, Arrigo. "Sull'inversione dell'istinto sensuale." *Revista sperimentale di freniatria* (1878): 97–117.

Tissot, S. A. *L'onanisme dissertation sur les maladies produites par la masturbation*. Paris: Bechet, 1823.

Westphal, Carl. "Die conträre Sexualempfindung." *Archiv für Psychiatrie und Nervenkrankheiten*. Band ii (1870): 73–108.

5

FREUD AND
HOMOSEXUALITY

Paul Robinson

. . . .

In this essay I'm going to address, in a somewhat abbreviated fashion, the question, "Has Freud been good or bad for homosexuals?" The question is worth asking because a number of recent scholarly writings have represented Freud as among the foremost inventors of modern homophobia— just as, a quarter of a century ago, Kate Millett represented him as the forefather of modern misogyny. I am thinking of books like Jonathan Ned Katz's *The Invention of Heterosexuality* (1995) and Daniel Boyarin's *Unheroic Conduct: The Rise of Heterosexuality and the Invention of the Jewish Man* (1997), in which Freud appears as a chief architect of the modern medical category of the homosexual (as well as that of the heterosexual). These categories—so the argument goes—created the tendentious notion that humanity is divided between those (presumably a small minority) devoted exclusively to sexual relations with their own sex and those (the vast majority) no less exclusively devoted to relations with the opposite sex.

I think this conception is fundamentally wrong. But it contains an element of truth, especially if we broaden our view to include not just Freud himself but the psychoanalytic tradition as a whole, notably its American variant in the middle years of the twentieth century.

I don't want to get into the broader argument about whether in fact "the homosexual" was invented—or merely codified—by turn-of-the-century sexologists (an argument that has pitted what are called "essentialists" against "social constructionists"). The kernel of truth that links Freud to what can legitimately be considered a homophobic discourse is his famous developmental conception of identity formation, according to which heterosexual object-choice is seen as the ideal, or at least the "normal," outcome of the child's psychic evolution. As Jonathan Ned Katz points out, Freud repeatedly, almost compulsively, refers to heterosexuality as the "normal" result, and he uses "normal" not just in a statistical sense but evaluatively, equating it with psychic maturity (72–80). By way of contrast, homosexuality in this scheme is always construed as regressive: Freud invariably speaks of it as an atavism, in which the child gets stuck—fixated—at some more primitive stage of psychic evolution, whether it be narcissistic, oral, or anal. Freud's language, in other words, is "normalizing," although one needs to point out that Freud's feelings about "normality," like his feelings about "civilization," were ambivalent: An important strain in his thought protested against the libidinal sacrifice that "normal" adult genitality entailed, and, as thinkers like Herbert Marcuse and Norman Brown argued years ago, one can read Freud as, at least in part, a critic of normalization and a prophet of a liberated, "polymorphously perverse" sexuality. In *Civilization and Its Discontents* (1930), for example, he gives a distinctly critical account of the sacrifices that so-called psychic maturity entails. "As regards the sexually mature individual," he writes, "the choice of an object is restricted to the opposite sex, and most extra-genital satisfactions are forbidden as perversions. The requirement, demonstrated in these prohibitions, that there shall be a single kind of sexual life for everyone, disregards the dissimilarities, whether innate or acquired, in the sexual constitution of human beings; it cuts off a fair number of them from sexual enjoyment, and so becomes the source of serious injustice" (104).

Although Freud's treatment of homosexuality was "normalizing," it was not "pathologizing." The distinction is important, because later on American psychoanalysts would argue, unambiguously, that homosexuality was a sickness. But Freud insisted that it was not a sickness. He did so most famously in his 1935 letter to the mother of an American homosexual ("Letter"). In fact, one can argue that Freud conceived of homosexuality as the opposite of sickness. As he said, more than once, the neuroses were, in his view, the "negative" of the perversions, by which he meant that homosexual urges become pathogenic only when repressed. The person who acted on his homosexual impulses was in theory immune to neurosis, whereas those impulses became dangerous precisely when they were driven into the unconscious. Perhaps the best known instance of the phenomenon is Freud's theory of paranoia, worked out in the essay on Schreber's memoirs, where paranoia is said to be caused by repressed homosexual desire.

Even more fundamentally, however, the notion that Freud participated in the radical conceptual separating of homosexuals from heterosexuals gets the story exactly backward. On the contrary, he opposed any notion that homosexuality can be so isolated, or that homosexuals constitute an essentially separate class of persons and that heterosexuals are thus safe from homosexual contamination. Freud expressly opposed the version of this idea advanced by a number of homophile theorists, such as Karl Heinrich Ulrichs and Magnus Hirschfeld, even though he supported the political goal that the conception was meant to advance—namely, the decriminalization of homosexuality—because, he contended, it ignored the evidence, turned up by psychoanalysis, that homosexuality is universally present in psychic development. As he says in *Three Essays on the Theory of Sexuality* (1905), "All human beings are capable of making a homosexual object-choice and have in fact made one in their unconscious" (145n). To use the language invented by Eve Kosofsky Sedgwick in *Epistemology of the Closet*, Freud's conception of homosexuality is unambiguously "universalizing," as opposed to the "minoritizing" ideas advanced not only by homosexuals like Ulrichs and Hirschfeld but by such influential straight thinkers of the period as Richard von Krafft-Ebing and Havelock Ellis (see, respectively, *Psychopathia; Studies*). In Freud's psychic universe, homosexuality is everywhere, insinuating itself into the psychic lives of the most impeccably "normal" and presentable individuals. Indeed, no one has done more to destabilize the notion of heterosexuality than Freud. In Freud's universe there simply are no heterosexuals, at least not psychologically. Similarly, he insists that manifest heterosexuality, far from being a fact of nature, is a precarious psychic achievement, and one that needs to be accounted for. As he writes, again in *Three Essays,* "The exclusive sexual interest felt by men for women is also a problem that needs elucidating and is not a self-evident fact based upon an attraction that is ultimately of a chemical nature" (146n). Nor did Freud exempt himself from this universalizing conception: He frequently diagnosed his relationship with Wilhelm Fliess as the manifestation of a passive homosexual attachment on his own part, most famously at the time of his fainting spell in Munich in 1912 when, speaking of his long connection with Fliess, he remarked in a letter to Ernest Jones, "There is some piece of unruly homosexual feeling at the root of the matter" (qtd. in Jones 317).

This universalizing conception is most spectacularly on display in the famous case histories. The only one who appears to be innocent of homosexual desire is the Rat Man, and here we almost feel that Freud missed the obvious homosexual implications of the Rat Man's rat fantasy. With the exception of Leonardo, all of the male protagonists of the essays and case histories (I'll come to the women in a moment) were manifest heterosexuals. Yet homosexual urges are found in each of their psychic lives, most emphatically, of course, in the examples of the Wolf Man and of Schreber, where the repression of their desire to be sodomized by the father, Freud argues, is the fundamental source of their illness. I would also suggest that Freud's attitude toward these men ranges from admiration (in the essay on Leonardo, with whom Freud profoundly identified) to at the very least dispassionate interest and sympathy, although one can argue that he is most enthusiastic about a homosexual like Leonardo who has sublimated his desires (and thereby become a culture bearer— rather like the Jews in *Moses and Monotheism* [1939]). He is made more nervous by passive anal sex (which, as Leo Bersani has complained, he illegitimately equates with castration, and thus with feminization; see *Homos* 108–12) than he is by fellatio, which, as he notes in the essay on Leonardo (1910), is "loathsome" in the eyes of "respectable society" but, he goes on to say, "may be traced to an origin of the most innocent kind," namely, the child's sucking at its mother's breast (*Leonardo* 86–87). I would point out that, from a historian's point of view, one of the most remarkable things about Freud's discussions of homosexuality is their astonishing rhetorical evenhandedness, which contrasts not only with the habitual prejudice of his society but also with the more judgmental tone of even such relatively enlightened figures as Krafft-Ebing and Havelock Ellis. As he says when introducing the sexual aberrations in the *Introductory Lectures* (1916–17), "What we have here is a field of phenomena like any other" ("Sexual Life" 307).

The story is very different, of course, when it comes to the two most famous lesbian case histories, Dora (Ida Bauer) and the anonymous woman of 1920. These cases, as Mary Jacobus has shown, are remarkably alike: Both involve prepossessing young women in their late teens who react to Freud with marked hostility and whom he treats with a corresponding contempt, which of course invites the suspicion that the real problem is Freud's, not his patients' (Jacobus 66). Put another way, I see in Freud's failure to extend to lesbians the same dispassion he lavishes on his male homosexuals a reflection of his larger problem with women. Indeed, I think it is difficult to separate lesbianism from femininity in

Freud's conceptual universe, since both are analyzed by him in terms of women's psychic problems with the penis and their disappointment in men. It's also interesting that while Freud insists that in men there is no necessary connection between homosexual object-choice and "character inversion" (that is, effeminacy), he makes just the opposite assertion about lesbians: In his view they are nearly always mannish. In other words, I don't think Freud's hostile treatment of lesbianism—which contrasts substantively and above all rhetorically with his treatment of male homosexuality—can be separated from his misogyny.

More important, finally, than any of the issues I've addressed so far—all of which might be said to belong to the "sticks and stones" category—is the question of therapy: whether homosexuality can be treated, or, more radically, cured. Although Freud often said that (manifest) homosexuality was probably grounded in some constitutional predisposition, the general thrust of his thinking was to insist that homosexuals are made rather than born, which seems to leave him open to the possibility that they might be "unmade," that is, turned into heterosexuals. But in fact Freud took just the opposite position. Although his pronouncements aren't absolutely categorical, he comes very close to saying that homosexuality is entirely beyond the range of not only analytic therapy but any therapy whatsoever. His statement in the 1920 case of the young woman is representative: "In general," he writes, "to undertake to convert a fully developed homosexual into a heterosexual does not offer much more prospect of success than the reverse" ("Psychogenesis" 151).

Freud's humane therapeutic pessimism must be contrasted with the profoundly homophobic and insanely utopian therapeutic optimism of his American acolytes, above all the evil trio of Edmund Bergler (a European transplant), Irving Bieber, and Charles Socarides—who, alas, is still among the quick and still issuing the same mad pronouncements. Not only do they call all homosexuals pathological—as well as manipulative liars—but they also insist that the homosexual's only hope rests in converting to heterosexuality. Bergler went so far as to claim that such "cures" could be effected "in 99.9 percent of all cases of homosexuality" (qtd. in Lewes 112). Here we are no longer dealing with "sticks and stones" but with a brutally oppressive therapeutic practice that did profound damage to a generation of American gay men in the middle decades of the twentieth century. If you want to take the measure of that damage in an individual life, I recommend the autobiography of Martin Duberman, entitled *Cures*, which documents the horrific treatment that Duberman received at the hands of three American Freudians in the

1950s and 1960s. In other words, American psychoanalysts exactly reversed Freud's ideas as well as his therapeutic practice. They transformed homosexuality into a disease, and a curable one at that, and they categorically separated it from "normal" heterosexuality by expressly rejecting Freud's universalizing notion of constitutional bisexuality. They even reversed Freud's prejudices on the subject, because in the mid-century American literature lesbianism is ignored, while male homosexuality, toward which Freud had a distinct softness, is thoroughly demonized. As the historian of this unhappy story, Kenneth Lewes, has said, in America the Freudian theory of homosexuality ceased to be a matter of the history of ideas and became instead a matter of the history of prejudice. And as Lewes further suggests, the transformation had much more to do with the Cold War and McCarthyism—and with the eagerness of foreign-born analysts to ingratiate themselves with their American hosts—than with anything that Freud ever wrote on the subject.

There is a sweet Freudian footnote to this lamentable history: Richard Socarides, son of the last and arguably the most vulgar of the American psychoanalytic homophobes, Charles Socarides, is not only a gay man himself but an activist in the cause who served as Bill Clinton's principal liaison to the gay community. I like to think of it as the return of the repressed.

References

Bergler, Edmund. *Homosexuality: Disease or Way of Life?* New York: Hill and Wang, 1956.

Bersani, Leo. *Homos*. Cambridge: Harvard UP, 1995.

Bieber, Irving, et al. *Homosexuality: A Psychoanalytic Study*. New York: Basic, 1962.

Boyarin, Daniel. *Unheroic Conduct: The Rise of Heterosexuality and the Invention of the Jewish Man*. Berkeley: U of California P, 1997.

Brown, Norman O. *Life against Death: The Psychoanalytical Meaning of History*. 1959. Middletown, CT: Wesleyan UP, 1985.

Duberman, Martin B. *Cures: A Gay Man's Odyssey*. New York: Dutton, 1991.

Ellis, Havelock. *Studies in the Psychology of Sex*. 7 vols. Vol. 4: *Sexual Selection in Man*. Philadelphia: F. A. Davis, 1911.

Freud, Sigmund. *Civilization and Its Discontents*. 1930 (1929). *Standard* 21:57–145.

———. *Leonardo da Vinci and a Memory of His Childhood*. 1910. *Standard* 11:63–137.

———. "A Letter from Freud." April 9, 1935. *American Journal of Psychiatry* 107 (1951): 786–87.

———. *Moses and Monotheism: Three Essays*. 1939. *Standard* 23:3–137.

———. "The Psychogenesis of a Case of Homosexuality in a Woman." 1920. *Standard* 18:145–72.

———. "The Sexual Life of Human Beings." *Introductory Lectures on Psycho-Analysis.* 1916–17. *Standard* 16:303–19.

———. *The Standard Edition of the Complete Psychological Works of Sigmund Freud.* Ed. and trans. James Strachey. 24 vols. London: Hogarth, 1953–74.

———. *Three Essays on the Theory of Sexuality.* 1905. *Standard* 7:123–245.

Hirschfeld, Magnus. *The Homosexuality of Men and Women.* 1914. Trans. Michael A. Lombardi-Nash. Introd. Vern L. Bullough. Buffalo: Prometheus, 1999.

Jacobus, Mary. "Russian Tactics: Freud's 'Case of Homosexuality in a Woman.'" *GLQ: A Journal of Lesbian and Gay Studies* 2.1–2 (1995): 65–79.

Jones, Ernest. *The Life and Work of Sigmund Freud.* 3 vols. Vol. 1. New York: Basic, 1953.

Katz, Jonathan Ned. *The Invention of Heterosexuality.* New York: Dutton, 1995.

Krafft-Ebing, Richard von. *Psychopathia Sexualis: A Medico-Forensic Study.* 1886. New York: Putnam's, 1965.

Lewes, Kenneth. *The Psychoanalytic Theory of Male Homosexuality.* New York: New American Library, 1988.

Marcuse, Herbert. *Eros and Civilization: A Philosophical Inquiry into Freud.* New York: Random House, 1955.

Millett, Kate. *Sexual Politics.* Garden City, NY: Doubleday, 1970.

Sedgwick, Eve Kosofsky. *Epistemology of the Closet.* Berkeley: U of California P, 1990.

Socarides, Charles W. *Homosexuality.* New York: Jason Aronson, 1978.

Ulrichs, Karl. *The Riddle of "Man-Manly" Love: The Pioneering Work on Male Homosexuality.* 2 vols. Trans. Michael A. Lombardi-Nash. Buffalo: Prometheus, 1994.

LACAN AND
THE *HOMMOSEXUELLE*

"A Love Letter"

Ellie Ragland

. . . .

1. Lacan and Sexual Difference

Freud could never figure out how the anatomical differences between males and females caused radical psychical distinctions between the sexes. Translating the little girl's "virile" sexuality into activity and aggressivity equal to that of the little boy, Freud was perplexed as to why girls suddenly become passive around the time of puberty. Baffled by the feminine, he conflated femininity with passivity and masochism, after trying for many years to decipher the riddle of feminine sexuality ("Some Psychical").

According to Jacques Lacan, however, neither gender identity nor libidinal object-choice can be explained by developmental accounts of the cause of feelings and thoughts. These accounts represent a biological sequence of stages correlating with mental development, as in Freud's early work on the sexual stages he called the "oral," "anal," and "genital." Freud hypothesized that the biological body is the cause of its own effects. Lacan, by contrast, found the kernel of his own theory at points of impasse in Freud's work. A person's sexual identity—or sexuation—resides, he argues, in *unconscious* subjective identifications assumed in the oedipal interpretation of the real, symbolic, and imaginary orders.

Lacan began reconceptualizing psychoanalysis where Freud left off in "Analysis Terminable and Interminable" (1937), arguing that even the best analysis founders on the rock of castration anxiety (on the side of the male) and penis envy (on the side of the female; see "Analysis" 250–53). In Lacan's terminology, male castration anxiety translates into the fear of being confronted with a tenuous basis for masculinity. The concept of female penis envy was Freud's attempt to describe the desire not to be wholly Other to the symbolic, invisible. Lacan's axiom that "there is no sexual relation" means quite simply that there is no signifier for gender—masculine or feminine—*in the unconscious.* The drama of sexual difference is played out around an image whose presence creates an absence—a negative *place*—in the signifying chain.

Parting company with psychoanalysis as practiced by the International Psychoanalytic Association—whether from the perspective of classical Freudianism, object-relations theories, or the myriad combination of these two extended into psychology and psychiatry—Lacan stated the obvious. Those who enter psychoanalysis tell but one story. Despite all their best efforts, discontent remains a constant within each subject's life, as well as in civilization (see Freud, *Civilization*). In the sphere of *jouissance*—which Lacan developed in 1975 as a knowledge system equal in force and impact to the linguistic field of representations—neither love nor sexual relations brings ongoing harmony or a lasting cure for unhappiness (see Lacan, *Television;* also Miller, "A Reading").

More specifically, Lacan did not retain Freud's idea of a preoedipal period. According to Lacan, nothing can be known of the real of primordial experience. One has access only to the alienated language that seeks to represent (or cover up) the real experience of *jouissance,* which is beyond the pleasure principle. For this and other reasons, Lacan's mapping of "self"-identification—one's sexuation—runs counter to Michel Foucault's idea of the subject as constructed by society. Diana Fuss, for example, argues persuasively in *Essentially Speaking: Feminism, Nature, and Difference* that subjects are invented constructs. Yet when it comes to saying from what they are invented or how, Fuss, like Foucault, makes history the agent, not parental desire or symptomatic *jouissance.*

In developing Freud's radical discovery—that sexuality is neither innate nor natural, but is constituted by an other and the Other, from the outside—Lacan argues that *persons are not masculine or feminine along lines of anatomy or gender.* Contrary to recent arguments about sex and gender, such as Judith Butler's, Lacan claims that insofar as there are only ever two anatomical sexes—excepting rare cases of hermaphroditism—there are only two psychical *positions* in sexual identification: the masculine and the feminine. A woman may be inscribed on the masculine side in sexuation and a man on the feminine side, but these effects derive from *asymmetrical* psychical differences that structure sexuation in the *oppositional relation* of both sexes to each other and to the mother. Additionally, the opposition is not binary, but involves the imaginary deciphering of difference itself.

One of Jacques-Alain Miller's statements about homosexuality in *Les divins détails* helps us grasp Lacan's suggestion that a subject is masculine or feminine at the level of desire, not at the level of anatomy:

> In the sexual order of things, nothing is automatic in psychoanalysis. Furthermore, the problem that is difficult to understand is why men love women. There is truly nothing natural in that. That is to say that homosexuality puts no one apart in this regard because, for analysis, in a certain fashion—that's Freud's thesis anyway—of course there is unconscious homosexuality. The object-choice of one's own sex is found on the same plane as the heterosexual object-choice. That is, the whole panorama, the countryside of the object-choice is made independent of whatever sex the object has. . . . Freedom of choice extends equally to masculine and feminine objects. It is afterwards that . . . the restriction [that] installs itself becomes, one can say, the condition of love. What I am saying is that men and women do not relate to their sexual love-object except by the bias of more or less precise conditions. That men love women is not an evident thing. It's a problem. (*Les divins details* 39; March 8, 1989)

Once one grasps that for Lacan the unconscious subject who desires is constituted as masculine or feminine in response to the oedipal experience of castration, one begins to understand his reinterpretation of Freud's oedipal *myth* away from the idea of masculine or feminine positions as gender specific or essential. Desiring positions arise, rather, within clinically differential traits. Pierre-Gilles Gueguen explains the implications of this reinterpretation for our understanding of sexuality: "It is a clinical position of Lacan['s] not to approach homosexuality as such, but rather as a *trait* included in a clinical structure, either neurosis, perversion, or psychosis. There is no doubt that credit has not been given to the modernity of this position, and notably that it avoids a moralizing treatment of the question" (41). The imaginary confusions that typically conflate sex with gender, opposing heterosexual to homosexual, disappear in Lacan's teaching. For one can be homosexual in any of the above-named structures of desire—or heterosexual. Suddenly, the issue of masculine and feminine takes on a thornier, more shadowy, but, for all that, truer face. No one is what or who he or she *appears* to be.

Consistent with this perspective, the Lacanian clinic transforms Freud's diagnostic categories into *structures* of desire. And insofar as desire always refers to a lack-in-being (excepting psychosis), Lacanian structures can never be reduced to Freud's positivistic categories according to which an analyst diagnoses developmental or cognitive deficiencies as disorders ("disorder" itself presupposing a category of normal or natural order). Nothing is natural in sex, Lacan taught. Yet at the base of the many fields that Freud's theories influenced—including psychology, pedagogical theories, and clinical therapies of all kinds—one finds the imaginary supposition of a whole, autonomous person who can be healthy, happy, realistic, successful, and adapted to reality if he (or she) develops his ego, or builds *self*-confidence. And this is opposed to the idea of the pathological person whose deficiency is supposed to lie in his or her *not being whole.*

By contrast, in Lacan's teaching, the logic of *not whole* or *not all* typifies health. Indeed, one aim of analysis is to enable analysands to accept their lack(s) so they can live more constructively in the larger sphere of the social. Lacan *begins* by disagreeing with the "and they lived happily ever after" supposed ending to analysis. No, "they lived unhappily ever after," he says, as they deny lack (that is, castration) and wait to be made whole by goods, events, better partners, or better sex. Lacan's axiom—"There is no sexual relation"—does not mean, of course, that there are neither sexual couplings nor good orgasms nor good relationships. It means that the *structure* of the human subject is such that there is no natural or mature developmental model that can lead to genital harmony between the sexes, as many post-Freudian analysts would like to believe. In Lacanian terms, the unspoken paradigm on which many analysts base their theory of adult sexual happiness is the romanticized ideal of a good mother symbiosis between the infant and parent.

Without these clarifications, the idea of distinguishing between the masculine and the feminine sounds regressive, seeming to go backward to Jung and before. Jung, as we know, in trying to break with Freud's anatomical reductions of the masculine and the feminine to simple biology, hypothesized that every woman had a dark shadow of the man within her—the *animus*—and every man, a shadow of the woman—the *anima*—in him. Lacan was critical of all such reductions of sexual difference to binary oppositions, arguing that these theories end up in an impasse similar to Hegel's resolution of the thesis and antithesis in the merger of a false synthesis. Jung, for example, proposed an ideal type, a mythical figure of the androgyne who contains an equal portion of masculine and feminine attributes.

2. Sexuation, Sexuality, and the Drives

Lacan's theory of sexuation takes on its larger meaning relative to his rethinking *how* the drive is constituted. This is the innovation in his thought: The drive, which is neither natural nor instinctual, links sexuality to the Other, so bringing its function into the field of representations. And Lacan further distinguishes between "sexuality," taken as an erotics submitted to the law of the signifier, insofar as words are *pulsional*—that is, interconnected with the partial drives (oral, anal, invocatory, and scopic)—and "sexuality" understood as the response to the real that arises from the polarity of active and passive. In the first case, sexuality would be inscribed in the real via the drives. In the latter, sexuality overlaps with sexuation in symbolic and imaginary interpretations of the real.

Conflating the sexual with the real—the order of trauma and primordial repressions—Lacan added a category to knowledge that skews the opposition of mind and body characteristic of theories of sexuality throughout the centuries. We desire at the unsayable level of the real of the flesh, Lacan argues. But the *cause* of such desire does not emanate from hormonal chemistry, or even from the actual objects desired (his theory is neither biological nor phenomenological). Rather, individuals desire things or sex acts because *lack* and *loss* are structural components of being.

In *Donc,* a course Miller gave in the Department of Psychoanalysis at the University of Paris VIII (Saint-Denis), he describes the real as a category of essence—that is, of *jouissance*—that the signifier enters to decomplete: $S(\emptyset)$. In the same course, Miller also argues that Lacan's joining of mind to body via the *structure* of desire goes a long way toward explaining another major question that Freud never entirely answered: What *are* the drives? By trying to connect mind directly to the biological body, Freud ended up, in "Instincts and Their Vicissitudes" (1915), in the impasse of having to argue that the drives are a mythology. In Lacan's teaching, however, the drives are closer to a montage of images, language effects, and affect that gives rise to desire (*Four Fundamental* 161–73). Such associational meanings of the imaginary, symbolic, and real are introjects of the *bric-à-brac* material of the world, which Miller later called "divine details."

In his 1988–89 course of the same title, Miller suggests that this *bric-à-brac* quickly gets conflated with a partner, sex act, and fetish object. Evoking evanescent memories, the drives refer to meanings taken from the repressed unconscious Other that is radically absent from conscious scrutiny (Miller, "Analytic"). In this sense, Lacan's theory is not a correspondence theory, but a disappearance-of-the-referent theory (Miller, "Language"). The referent, here, is the object *a*—the cause of desire—which is created by loss of the first corporal "partial objects": the voice, the gaze, the phoneme, the breast, the feces, the urinary flow, the (imaginary) phallus, and the nothing ("Subversion" 315).

Freud called the drives a mythology, but he did not view the quest for libidinal "objects" as mythical. And Lacan gave the name the object *a* to what Freud called his myth of the drives. But Lacan's object *a* is no myth. The quest for objects becomes, rather, the quest for libidinal pleasure, for a *jouissance* of the real. Moreover, *jouissance* is sought not actually in one's partner, but in the particular details present in the partner, details that first made of *jouissance* a constellation of meaning. Yet one chases after *jouissance* within the field of the partial drives where the drives bear on the real of flesh. Because these drives do not remain attached to the body, but also have an effect on memory—that is, they become attached to images and language—they enter language as pieces of *jouissance,* placing an extralinguistic component in language itself. Consequently, sexuality is inseparable from language and thought.

Although Lacan's sexuation graphs in *Seminar 20: Encore* clearly depict the connection between fantasy and desire, he never figured out how to link *jouissance* to love. He says in "A Love Letter": "What it is all about is the fact that love is impossible, and that the sexual relation founders in non-sense" (158). To help explain this, Miller argues in *Donc* that the partial drives' linkage to genital sexual pleasure stems from each subject's unconscious hope that sex acts will reconnect her (or him) to first encounters with the real. These encounters have already constituted a repressed ur-lining as primordial, symbolic, maternal gifts (the breast, the voice, the gaze, fecal care) that lay down the basis for love in *jouissance.*

Grasping Miller's theory opens up a new perspective on the meaning of sex acts themselves—homosexual or heterosexual—that may break up the simplistic reduction of sexual desire to heterosexual or homosexual object-choice. Moreover, Lacan's point regarding the teleology of sex is crucial to any serious rethinking of homosexuality and heterosexuality: Sex, in and of itself, is not the point in love relations. If sexual bliss were the only goal, then sex would not remain the problem, linked as it is to fantasy, desire, love, pleasure, and *jouissance*. That each of these elements works by its own logic, and moreover in three registers of meaning—the real, symbolic, and imaginary—considerably complicates the effort to reduce the *finesse* of human sexual *non*relations to some idealized correspondence of gender with gender, whether heterosexual or homosexual. For the one truth that remains in sexual relations is that sex itself just misses the mark of bringing the hoped-for rapport that is *supposed* to unite one person with another. How can two be one? asks Lacan. Sex requires repeating, which entails encountering the impasse of *jouissance* in desire that Lacan calls the real (in this way, redefining Freud's theory of repetition in the death drive in *Beyond the Pleasure Principle* [1920]).

Insofar as a person's sexual desire is only secondarily the masculine or feminine outcome of that subject's response to the phallus and castration—the phallus signifying what one seeks at the level of desire in compensation for what one *lacks-in-being*—any individual's object-choice has a built-in instability. One's partner is mistaken for the source of what comes from one's own unconscious Other. It is in this sense that Lacan says the sexual partner of each person is the Other. In "A Love Letter" he suggests that partners cannot be linked around the object *a* because the Other that supports the *a* is self-enclosed, with no referent beyond itself (154). Miller's placing of the extimate object within the symbolic helps him formalize a connection between love and *jouissance*. This is a departure from Lacan's theory of the link between love and sex in *Encore,* as we shall see in Miller's discussion of André Gide.

3. Homosexuality and *L'hommosexuelle*

The Lacanian desiring positions are not coordinated with anatomy or gender, then, but indicate a posture of *desire* taken toward a set of real traits that hold out the promise of wholeness. Not only is Lacan's account of sexuality nonrelational, but it offers a logic of the drives at precisely the point where ethical systems have tended to produce moralities that deny the sexual real in the name of some supposed sexual norm.

Lacan taught that moralities belong to the obscenity and ferocity of superego pronouncements, which enunciate totalizing laws concerning how one should act as a sexual being. He insists that although Freud departed from ethical moralities of old in his discovery of a pleasure principle at the heart of human action, he never figured out why repeated and continued pleasure is impossible. Consequently, Freud ended up opposing Thanatos to Eros in *Beyond the Pleasure Principle,* so begging the question of how the repetition of pleasure could turn into displeasure. Lacan reads Freud's constant return to the presence of a death drive at the heart of being as a structural idea that there is an impossibility in the idea of a sexual harmony between man and woman.

Within this framework, one can see why Lacan's account of homosexuality diverges significantly from Freud's frequent conflation of homosexuality with pathological narcissism. "I am going to allow myself a break by reading you something I wrote for you a while back . . . simply from where it might be possible to speak of love," Lacan says in "A Love Letter" (154). He wonders how scientific discourse has failed to remark that speaking (about love) is itself a *jouissance,* for it brings one to the pleasure principle, which Lacan designates in his mathemes as the relation between the object *a* and the S(Ø) on the feminine side of the sexuation graph, where he locates the soul in the relation of the object *a* to the void in the Other.

At this point in "A Love Letter," Lacan develops his theory of the *hommosexuelle,* portraying him as an obsessional man who seeks the soul of the other in love. Playing on the combination of *man (homme)* and *homosexuel,* Lacan argues provocatively that the *hommosexuelle*—a man who loves Woman as an ideal—defines himself by the division between this ideal love and the possible choice of keeping his ideal sexually pure. Although the *hommosexuelle* may therefore confuse his quest with sexual pleasure, his goal is not orgasm, but refinding a lost Other that left behind mere traces of its form in the sublime objects that occasion *jouissance.* Indeed, the soul itself derives from whatever is *hommosexuelle,* Lacan says, defining the soul as "love's effect." But what does this mean? "The soul could only be spoken as whatever enables a being—the speaking being to call him by its name—to bear what is intolerable in its world, which presumes this soul to be alien to that world, that is to say, fantasmatic" (155). Moreover, "there is no sex in the affair. Sex does not count" (155). The soul exists in the "divine details" of the shedding, dropped skin layers of lost objects. According to Lacan, the lover who seeks his soul in the other seeks the Good, or God.

The Lacanian soul is not a theological one. The soul is Woman, the dark-sided face of God. By this, Lacan denotes a point "outsidesex"—an *horsexe*—where love and the soul connect (155). Lacan's theory resonates on several levels, while suggesting that Freud's theory about narcissistic love causing homosexuality is not entirely wrong. The difference between Freud and Lacan here is that Lacan does not mistake narcissism for pathology. Indeed, narcissism for Lacan is the basis for all love. He also argues that love is false insofar as it is narcissistically imaginary. Its deeper truth lies in the real. Love of the same—the other you, your soul, the distant interior—bears on knowledge, in Lacan's teaching, not on sex. One loves one's own Other. One loves oneself in the Other. The *hommo-sexuelle* loves what, in the Other, is like himself, and he does so for the purpose of repudiating castration, in order to claim that the Woman (as ideal) does exist.

Lacan characterizes heterosexual man and heterosexual woman as well as the *hommosexuelle*. The heterosexual man does not manifest a pure love for Woman as does the *hommosexuelle*, for the heterosexual man takes Woman as woman only insofar as she is differentiated from soul, is "defamed" (*diffâmée*). He cannot take her in desire except as the object *a* of his particular perversion (157). Insofar as the rapport between the sexes is impossible, Lacan points to the obvious (which Freud missed): Man can reach his partner only via the mediation of perverse traits (of the version whore versus virgin) in the fantasy (151).

In his 1988–89 course *Sur André Gide,* Miller develops Lacan's unstated assumption in "A Love Letter" that desire and love are split. The object one desires is often not the same as the person one loves. While the *hommosexuelle* loves Woman—her *agalma,* the essence of the feminine—he sometimes loves a woman as well. Lacan points out the fetishizing of some object between that woman and the *hommosexuelle,* as, for example, Gide's letters to his wife Madeleine, whom he loved but did not desire. The homosexual woman often loves Woman, as doubled, and desires man only as a point of anchorage—a name—in the symbolic, not sexually. While the split in his desire and love for the same person tortures the heterosexual man, the heterosexual woman desires a man *because* of her love for his *savoir (faire)*. What the heterosexual woman tends to love in a man is not so much his sexuality, Lacan argues, as the way he faces the knowledge he "souls for"—his cause (158).

4. *L'hommosexuelle* and the Object *a*

In Lacanian psychoanalysis, the object *a* is taken as a *positive* cause of desire precisely because its loss leaves behind a definite set of *jouissance* effects whose traits are concrete and countable (Frau K.'s adorable white body; Dora's father's cigar smoke; the wolf in the window). This point is crucial for coming to terms with the idea that desire—not anatomy—

determines destiny.[1] The difference between psychoanalysis and psychology concerns the object *a*, Lacan claims, around which the impossibilities in sexual (would-be) relations waltz. In "A Love Letter," he defines the object *a* as that which, concerning the sexual relation, cannot be stated or written:

> Up till now, in relation to knowledge nothing has ever been conceived of which did not share in the fantasy of inscribing a sexual tie—and we cannot even say that the subjects of the ancient theory of knowledge were not conscious of the fact.
>
> For example, simply take the terms active and passive which dominate everything which has ever been thought up on the relationship of form to matter, a relationship which is so fundamental and which Plato, and then Aristotle, refer to at every step they take regarding the nature of things. It is visibly, palpably the case that these propositions are only upheld by a fantasy of trying to make up for what there is no way of stating[;] that is, the sexual relation.
>
> The strange thing is that something, albeit something ambiguous, has none the less come out of this crude polarity, which makes matter passive and form the agency which brings to life, namely, that this bringing to life, this animation, is nothing other than the *a* whose agency animates what?—it animates nothing, it takes the other for its soul. ("A Love Letter" 153)

Far from setting up categories of normative sexuality, as Freud often did, in which man is supposed to love women naturally, Lacan locates the love of Woman on the feminine side of sexuation and the *act* of making love on the masculine side of lack. Thus, his concern in "A Love Letter" is the *a*-moral that he calls a subversion of knowledge, a perverse kind of knowledge—a know-how with *jouissance*. Freud confused the phallus with the penis and argued that male homosexuals fetishize the penis, unconsciously attributing a penis to the mother. What Freud failed to understand, Lacan argues, was that the penis qua imaginary phallus (-φ) is a negativized image of a lost object. Loss is, in turn, marked by a unary trait that returns from the real to create an actual hole, a concrete void place in the signifying chain. There, traits of the *a* (a, a_1, a_2, a_3 . . .) create a dialectical discontinuity around the presence or absence of a given piece of the *a* (Lacan's *bouts* [ends] of the real)—the *agalmata* one seeks in the symbolic.

In a probing article "Fetish Envy," Marjorie Garber cites Lacan's remark in "Guiding Remarks for a Congress on Feminine Sexuality" (1958) to the effect that the imaginary motive for most male perversions is the desire to preserve the phallus, and that the absence of fetishism in women leads one to suspect a different fate for female perversions. "'Having' the phallus, having the fetish, becomes therefore a matter of one's position in the symbolic register and in the economy of desire. 'Men' have the phallus; 'men' have the fetish. What is at stake . . . is the ownership of desire," Garber argues (120).

But Lacan does not equate the phallus with the fetish. The fetish is, rather, the metonym for an organ, such as the image of a high-heeled shoe, a piece of blue velvet, a razor strap. In this sense, men do not have the phallus any more than women. Each person owns only his or her particular unconscious desire, which is quite precisely that part of one's knowledge one does not want to know. As such, unconscious desire plays its role veiled, like the phallus. What Lacan emphasizes from Freud's theory is that individuals do not want to know the incestuous knowledge that makes up the fundamental fantasy that Freud found in infantile sexuality, in which love and sex are first linked through their reference to the father.[2]

Trying to explain what energy motivates humans to act in certain ways, Freud first divided "drive" into two parts: The self-preservative drives he called ego drives and the pleasure-seeking drives he named sexual drives. He later sought to explain the relation of Eros to Thanatos in terms of two myths—the oedipal myth and that of the drives. Lacan gives these myths a different twist, allowing one to equate the oedipal myth with Freud's ego-preservative drives. Insofar as sexuation is a response to the oedipal experience, one can say that it takes on the force of an ego drive—one defends it as if it were an ideology. Lacan's theory of partial drives, which arise out of the partial object-causes-of-desire, describes more precisely the drives Freud called sexual in *The Ego and the Id* (1923). Although the cause assigned to these two drives since Freud has been biological—the ego drives one to seek food, and so on, for purposes of physical survival, and the sex drives ensure the survival of the species—Lacan connects sexuation to sexuality such that there is no opposition between ego and sexual drives (or id), as Freud claimed.

Insofar as our first fantasies of reunion are laid down in relation to the object of our first love, these fantasies surround partial objects, not a whole person. Later lovers confront us with the dilemma of the other qua partner who—in sexual relations—is metonymically related to these partial objects. But since no one, homosexual or heterosexual, solves the problem of the sexual drives at the level of sexuation—by identification as masculine or feminine in fundamental fantasy—sexual relations are replete with impasses, rather than with harmonious complementarity.

Yet from the beginning of recorded history, cultural practices have advanced the idea that man can be made whole by his love of the feminine. Lacan points to the medieval system of courtly love, which appeared as an anomaly in history, elevating The Woman to a symbolic order signifier, and so placing love and sexuality at the center of social concerns. Courtly love

> appeared at the point when hommosexual *âmusement* had fallen into supreme decadence. . . . It must have become noticeable that on the side of the woman, there was something [that] really would no longer do. The invention of courtly love is in no sense the fruit of what history usually symbolises as the thesis-antithesis-synthesis. . . . Courtly love blazed in history like a meteor. . . . After the blazing of courtly love, it was assigned once more to its original futility by something [that] sprang from an entirely different quarter. It took nothing less than scientific discourse, that is, something owing nothing to the suppositions of the ancient soul. ("A Love Letter" 156–57)

Lacan implies that history rectifies the very real impasses that manifest from the sexual nonrapport when the social is threatened by its own practices, to the point that producing children and rearing them is jeopardized. When Woman is taken as a cultural signifier, she, paradoxically, becomes a phallic signifier (Φ). This makes structural sense in terms of Lacan's proposal that Woman can also be represented by a man, just as one of the names of the Father is Woman. But this poses another problem at the level where Woman represents a limit in knowledge, at a point where the real is itself a boundary. Woman, thus, stands as a cipher for the silence of the drives within language. This is logical insofar as the real is organized in the following way: The primordial mother is one with the drives in fundamental fantasy, bringing about a conflation of the feminine with a supposed consistency in reality that gives rise to the *myth* of the essential feminine. The fantasy of *La Femme* responds to the structural reality of lack, the flaw in being.

Heterosexual men tend to confuse Woman with a particular woman, while the *hommosexuelle* is faithful to Woman in figures or guises that hold out a hope of "redemption" from lack through a *jouissance* of Oneness. In turn, such *jouissance* is sought through sublimation of the drives in sexual acts that re-create scenes, fetishistically reminiscent of the castration trauma itself. On his sexuation graph, Lacan placed the object *a*—a semblance of what any lover wants to incorporate of the beloved—on the side of the feminine, the right-hand side of the graph. Freud's passive partner has become Lacan's beloved. The feminine (one) is courted, is the one who inspires desire. The object *a* on the feminine side of the sexuation tables is inseparable from the masculine side. Veering back toward the lover ($), it offers whatever the lover thinks will fulfill his (or her) fantasy of love or sex.

Although the love illusion mistakes the lure object—be it a person, an organ, a sex act, a fetish, or a fantasy ritual—for the point of satisfaction, love really aims the drives at something beyond the object, something intangible that will eradicate the *angst* that produces doubt. Yet, in the place of the object *a* in the Borromean knot where imaginary, real, and symbolic orders intersect—

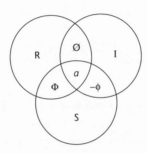

—there is no whole object. There is only the density of an affective *jouissance* made up of traits left over from the primordial effects of loss and trauma. Lacan first named this *place* the object *a* of condensed *jouissance* in *Le séminaire, livre VIII: Le transfert, 1960–1961*. Here he presents Socrates from Plato's *Symposium* as Alcibiades' beloved, the one who inspires desire in Alcibiades. Later, in "La troisième jouissance," a discourse he delivered in Rome in 1974, he makes it clear that the particular conditions of love are embodied in the object *a* sought in fantasy ($ ◊ *a*), as already constituted in the three distinct orders. Consequently, the *jouissance*-object that inspires desire is far from a simple object of the world. It contains properties from all three orders, as well as from the *sinthome* (or order of the knot) that links the three orders in reference to the Father's Name signifier. Socrates is the soul that Alcibiades wants to incorporate as his Ideal. But Socrates sees beyond the immediacy of Alcibiades' imaginary demand for *jouissance*, a demand for substitute—or imaginary—love. What he wants from Socrates is what Socrates does not have to give anyone—his emptiness ($), his *agalma*.

The object is a lure in the imaginary, where cultural stereotypes mime the desirable object of the always already constituted sociohistorical moment. And Socrates was desirable. He was an object whose positive traits in the symbolic were redolent of the social ideal of a real teacher. Socrates saw through his pupils' imaginary games in love and sex. But Socrates too was blinded. He told Alcibiades a lie, claiming that Alcibiades desired Agathon, the beautiful new, erotically appealing pupil. Yet it was Socrates that Alcibiades loved; Socrates he wanted to touch. Alcibiades' *hommosexuelle* love of the feminine *agalma* unveils the lie in the lure-objects that mask the emptiness beyond a beautiful form. Socrates possessed this *agalma*, Lacan argues, this *substance* that Lacan locates somewhere between the real and the imaginary.

5. *L'hommosexuelle* and the Woman Who Does Not Exist

Insofar as the hole in knowledge (Ø) appears at the intersection of the imaginary and real orders—R Ø I, showing the limits of *semblance* or appearance in the join between the images of things and the real of the drives—the void has always posed a problem for the symbolic order (see Lacan, "La troisième"). It has had many names throughout history—God, the supernatural, intuition, the feminine, and so on. In keeping with his antiprogressivist theory of history, Lacan assigns a structurally primary and identical cause to the secondary content of any such doctrine, or myth, in whatever historical era: Woman (qua mother) is unconsciously conflated with The Woman (*La Femme*), who is taken as a guarantee that nothing is lacking. Yet Lacan argues that the belief that Woman can guarantee continuity in being is based on a lie. To make his point, he struck a bar through T̶h̶e̶ Woman. There is no essential T̶h̶e̶ in Woman.

Consequently, Lacan proposes that there is no such thing as bisexuality. Rather, humans are *nullisexuel*—troubled by the void (*nulle*) that he aligns with the order of the real that inserts the impasses and holes that perforate the seemingly smooth narratives of the symbolic and (pseudo)-consistencies of the imaginary. When he writes *hommosexuelle* as a combination of *homme* and a feminine component in the *sexuelle,* it is in keeping with his larger theory of male sexuality as perverse in toto. The *père-version,* the father version, means that every man's cause is his phallic *jouissance,* inseparable from the base narcissism of his being. Marie-Hélène Brousse writes the symbols for male sexuality as the fetish object (the *a*) and the phallic signifier (the Φ). She represents the symbols for female sexuality as $ and Ø ("Symbols"). One can deduce from this that the major difference between the masculine and feminine in sexuation— whether heterosexual or homosexual—is linked to sexuality by one constant in each register. The Φ—the phallus—is always present in masculine sexuation and the $—which symbolizes the lack of the phallus—is always present in feminine sexuation.

Thus, the one constant in the sexuality of males and females, and in the sexuation of both, is the phallus. Freud argued that there was only one libido, the masculine one, which Lacan translates into the phallus, the male symbol of sexuality *as each sex symbolizes it.* "The phallus is the privileged signifier of that mark where the share of the logos is wedded to the advent of desire" ("signification"). The male takes sexual pleasure in reference to the Φ—the phallic signifier that resonates in all four orders—while the female may love a male in order to cover over lack and compensate for loss. This difference offers another example of the asymmetry in masculine and feminine sexuality.

In "God and the *Jouissance* of T̶h̶e̶ Woman," the chapter preceding "A Love Letter" in *Encore,* Lacan anticipates his theory of the *hommosexuelle* as developed in "A Love Letter":

> Let us first take things from the side where every x is a function of Φx, that is to say from the side where man arranges himself. One places oneself there, finally, by choice—open to women to place themselves there if that it please them. Everyone knows that there are phallic women, and that the phallic function does not prohibit men from being homosexual. But it also gives them a way to situate themselves as men, and to approach the woman. For the man . . . at least of castration, that is to say who has something which says no to the phallic function, there is no chance that he will have *jouissance* of the woman's body, in other words make love with her. . . . That does not prevent him from desiring woman in all kinds of ways, even when this condition [of desire] is not realized. Not only does he desire her, but he does for her all kinds of things that are astoundingly similar to love. Contrary to what Freud advanced, it is the man—I mean the one who finds himself male without knowing what to do about it . . .—who approaches woman, who can believe that he approaches her. . . . Only, what he approaches, is the cause of his desire, that I have designated by the object *a.* That is the act of love. To make love, as the name indicates it, is poetry. But there is a world between poetry and the act. The act of love is the polymorphous perversion of the male. (143; trans. mod.)

Love is the name Lacan gives to the belief that one can take another as one's very soul, while *desire* takes its proper name on the slope of perversion. Two years after he delivered the seminar *Encore,* Lacan made a major departure from Freud in *Television.* He concludes there that no one attains one's partner sexually *except* via perverse elements in fantasy, which designate those remnants of the object *a* left over after language has alienated the body from the immediacy of the drives. In other words, perversion is on the side of the object *a,* on the side of the feminine. This gives a meaning to perversion very different from Lacan's earlier claim that perversion is always on the side of the male, on the perimeter of the phallus.

Although contemporary gender studies tends to divide sexual desire into three possibilities—man and woman, man and man, woman and woman—such divisions do not take into account that fantasy already divides all sexual partners from each other, linking every subject to the solitude of his or her position in the Other. In giving the name *sexuation* to the propensity to identify as masculine or feminine, regardless of gender, Lacan puts his finger on the truth hidden within fantasy—a truth neurotics hide from others at all costs—that sheds new light on the reality of sexuality. For example, no Lacanian analyst would be surprised to find, in a heterosexual couple, the presence of a hysteric whose *jouissance* depends on lesbian fantasies or "dreams"—the absence of the phallic organ—as Lacan calls them. That politically right- and left-wing women have lesbian fantasies, as Andrea Dworkin insists, does not mean, as Dworkin concludes, that all women are lesbians. It suggests instead that since the mother qua primordial object of satisfaction is dispersed into pieces of *jouissance* dreams, and is thereby lost as a total object, the real of the drives will always bear on the relation of the phallus to the real of Woman's body. According to Lacan, both the *hommosexuelle* and the hysteric put the existence of the idea of a soul into *cause* as an *effect* of love within sexual fantasies ("A Love Letter" 155–56).

Questioning the connection between desire and love in fantasy, Lacan proposes that desire is the desire for an organ, whereas love is the desire for a name. Miller has given another meaning to love by showing the intersection for both sexes between the mother's primordial gifts and the drives. But rather than locate the preoedipal mother at this site, as Freud does, he places the drives there, giving a new meaning to the injunctions against Eros. Put another way, fantasies try to assess how body parts coalesce with some cause of love that one might call the soul.

In *Donc,* Miller answers a question Lacan left dangling when he separated desire from love. Arguing that desire is linked to *jouissance* by love, he defines love as the "demand for nothing," that is, "nothing much" but the demand for a repetition of the particular details of *jouissance* already constitutive of the drives where every person was first fed, bathed, touched, seen, heard. In this sense, every subject was first passive—feminine or beloved—not virile, as Freud hypothesized. What one seeks in sex is a return to this more in *jouissance* than orgasm. What one seeks in love is a real repetition of the symbolic. This is a notion quite different from IPA Freudianism, in which the object is mistaken for a parental figure for whom love-objects, including the analyst, are thought to substitute.

Freud's view of male homosexuality as a narcissistic oedipal problem is, we might say, the opposite of Lacan's idea that male homosexuality attests to an extreme love of the feminine. Indeed, one might summarize Lacan's concept of feminine sexuation as an unconscious subjective position in which one identifies *as* the phallus—that is, the object—that will fill the Other's lack. Whether one encounters the female hysteric who has made a subject position out of serving others—be it Florence Nightingale or Madonna—or the *hommosexuelle* who makes himself an object to serve the Other's *jouissance,* Lacan discovered that being-for-another can be a subjective identity position. For this reason, he does not make the Freudian assumption that the feminine is a masochistic position. Rather, he sees it as an epistemological position, a recognition of castration or the *not all*—not being all, not knowing all, not having it all—which overlaps with an awareness of the lack-in-being.

Another way in which Lacan's theory of homosexuality differs from Freud's theory—in which a man cannot *unconsciously* accept that his mother lacks the penis—lies in the *hommosexuelle*'s identification as radically Other to the symbolic, rather than as the moralistic convener of its conventions and laws. Having placed himself under the sign of the love of Woman, he has this in common with women: He too is on an endless quest for love. Even if he does not find his ideal love in a sexual partner, the *hommosexuelle* may well find this love in a woman, according to Miller. But like André Gide, he may not find it *all*—everything he wants—in the same place. In "Jeunesse de Gide," Lacan proposes that Gide wrote to give himself a name, to elevate himself above his fellowman. And he addresses his words to a woman, his cousin Madeleine, who incarnates The Woman who exists for him as an unsullied ideal. But where is Gide's desire? Miller asks in posing a psychoanalytic structural question—not a question about Gide's *jouissance,* which lay primarily with Arab boys. Gide's desire, Miller claims, resides with the dead phallus insofar as his denial of castration is the equivalent of a denial of the lack-in-being. Gide nonetheless recuperates his desire in writing to The Woman. And, Miller adds, Madeleine knew this. She knew that her burning his letters could touch his lack-in-being.

In *Sur André Gide,* Miller emphasizes that Lacan had little to say about Gide's homosexuality. His interest was, rather, in the split between the object of love and the object of desire. Arguing that Gide made a distinction between his love of an essential Woman—embodied in cousin Made-leine, whom he married—and the boys he desired, Miller traces this split to the way Gide's mother, a cold, pious, religious woman, introduced him to love. Love was an obligation and sex was a sin. Transferring the dutiful love he had given his mother to his cousin, Gide dedicated reams of love letters to her. But the love was platonic, desexualized. Miller's point is that although the *hommosexuelle* may love the sexual partner he desires—or will find attractive traits in a woman he idealizes—his unconscious fantasy rejects the possibility that certain women lack anything.

Gide repudiated the idea that anything was lacking in Woman, Miller argues, a repudiation consistent with Lacan's maintaining that the struc-ture of perversion is one response to the oedipal drama. The only way for the *hommosexuelle* to keep Woman pure, free of "sin"—that is, virginal—is not to have sexual congress with substitute versions of her. Since desir-ing a woman turns her into Eve, a seductress and betrayer, the *hommosex-uelle* avoids confronting this side of Woman.

In *Sur André Gide,* Miller also links love to desire in relation to his own theory of the two mothers. In Gide's case, his "two" mothers were his own mother, who served as mother of the law, and his aunt, who took on the function of the "mother," opening the door of sexual desire to him. Miller writes such a logic—a mother who is against desire—as a negative function of desire (-ϕ). This experience of maternal desire ($\phi°$), in Gide's case, was strong enough to leave the signification of the phallus outside the law of castration. In this context, Miller describes castration as "an articulation between the positive and negative incidence of desire" ("Sur le Gide" 30–31). He refers to a comment Lacan made on perversion in "On a Question Preliminary to Any Possible Treatment of Psychosis" as the basis for his linking the structuration of desire to the real of mater-nal love: "The whole problem of the perversions consists in conceiving how the child, in his relation to the mother, a relation constituted in analysis not by his vital dependence on her, but by his dependence on her love, that is to say, by the desire for her desire, identifies himself with the imaginary object of this desire in so far as the mother herself symbol-izes it in the phallus" ("On a Question" 197–98). Gide's subsequent con-flict between love and what his mother's desire had constituted as his possible *jouissance* is to be found in an unexpected place, Miller claims, namely, in his rapport with *la lettre.* Gide's mother's ambition for her son was ferocious. Ambition, the duty to love her, the suppression of the fa-ther's name—these ingredients can be found not in the mask over the truth of Gide's life, but in the mask itself. "One is the dupe of the mask," Miller says, "if one looks behind it. . . . The truth of the screen is not behind, it is above, which is the opposite of any psychology or depth-psychoanalysis" ("Sur le Gide" 16).

Miller's statement could also be read as meaning that heterosexual men are—as one can observe at the surface—split around the issue of love and desire for women. One might suggest that the very concept of sin, or any other sexual prescription based on a moral law, is a signifier by which men have marked the trauma of discovering the mother's sexual difference from themselves. This is a narcissistic trauma of some magnitude, Lacan argues, a narcissistic wound to the male infant's developing mirror-image of a body and to his sense of being One with his mother in the drives. Why, for example, should a man in a gay bar recoil in horror upon discovering that the woman he is touching is actually a "real woman"? Why, too, should Fergus love Dil any less in *The Crying Game* upon discovering that s/he has a penis and, therefore, is not a "real woman"? Sartre called the response of disgust "nausea." Freud called it anxiety—castration anxiety. Lacan called it the inverse face of desire. Miller speaks of the particular conditions of love.

If the *hommosexuelle* is marked by his love of Woman, in Lacan's doctrine the male heterosexual displays the masculine conflict surrounding that fact that no one attains his or her partner sexually except via perverse elements in fantasy or through perverse acts. As Miller explained in his 1981–82 course at the University of Paris VIII (*First Course*), fantasy unveils the remnant of *jouissance* left over after linguistic taboos have alienated one's body from the immediacy of satisfaction in the drives. Male heterosexuality quickly becomes patriarchal in response to the conflict aroused by castration, which splits his desire into the desire for a pure Woman and desire for the woman who is not pure. History provides ample evidence of the moralisms that try to regulate the real in the feminine, thereby relegating *jouissance* to silence. Thus one could say that cultural systems elaborate sexual orientation in such a way that the normative heterosexual man confuses his own master signifiers with objective reality. Lacan equated the Name-of-the-Father with sublimating the *jouissance* of meaning, a strictly ideological process. But rather than resolving anything, such ideological "solutions" unveil the impasse in heterosexual relations that Lacan calls "the sexual *non-rapport*" (see *Seminar* 20:79).

According to Lacan, human culture is itself a product of the fact that there is no natural rapport between the sexes, no device to draw men and women together in harmony (Ragland, "How the Fact"). Society maintains itself as a supposedly coherent group of interlinked beings—a social body—because most people believe sex and love can make them whole. Homosexuality bears shock value for the normative male or his counterpart—the normative (that is, castrated) female—only insofar as the master discourse has the structure of *repression*. Relying on the belief in some natural agency that will yield an ideal rapport—the right person, the right technique—the heterosexual lie allows heterosexually identified men and women to dissimulate the most obvious truth: Their *relations* simply do not work.

The fear that homophobia tries to screen out is not a matter of unenlightened response or simple prejudice. Rather, the *hommosexuelle* confronts those in the heterosexual masquerade with an unbearable truth: There is no Oneness to be found *between* the sexes. Heterosexuality might even be thought of as an ideology reflecting the structural refusal to accept the mirror stage as only a mythical symbiosis. But the structure of the masquerade is not to be taken lightly. At stake is a belief in the natural goodness of the infant-mother dyad. In "La mère et l'enfant," Brousse argues that idealized images of this dyad underlie various historical conceptions of romantic love. Such images also underlie theological concepts, political concepts, and those of the IPA, as well. The heterosexual masquerade is, by definition, an attempt to keep at bay the real, which perforates with discontinuities and disturbances such myths of wholeness and harmony, thereby generating anxiety. By confronting heterosexuals with the sexual *non-rapport*, which problematizes normative fantasies, the *hommosexuelle* faces a colossal enemy. By his very existence, he tears at the underpinnings of culture, based as it is on a sexual lie.

Notes

1. This sense of the object *a* differs from Žižek's interpretation of this object as a negative kernel, always absent. See Žižek, *Tarrying with the Negative*.

2. See also Lacan's treatment of this fantasy in *Le séminaire, livre IV: La relation d'objet*, and Miller's discussion in his course *Du symptôme au fantasme et retour* (1982–83).

References

Brousse, Marie-Hélène. "La mère et l'enfant." Ph.D. diss., University of Paris VIII, Saint-Denis, 1990.

———. "The Symbols of Masculine and Feminine Sexuation." Paper presented at the VIIIth Rencontre of the Freudian Field: La sortie de la cure. Paris, July 1994.

Butler, Judith. *Bodies That Matter: On the Discursive Limits of "Sex."* New York: Routledge, 1993.

The Crying Game. Dir. Neil Jordan. 1992.

Dworkin, Andrea. *Right-Wing Women: The Politics of Domesticated Females.* New
York: Putnam, 1983.

Freud, Sigmund. "Analysis Terminable and Interminable." 1937. *Standard* 23:
209–53.

———. *Beyond the Pleasure Principle.* 1920. *Standard* 18:1–64.

———. "'A Child Is Being Beaten': A Contribution to the Study of the Origin of
Sexual Perversions." 1919. *Standard* 17:175–204.

———. *Civilization and Its Discontents.* 1930 (1929). *Standard* 21:59–148.

———. *The Ego and the Id.* 1923. *Standard* 19:1–66.

———. "Instincts and Their Vicissitudes." 1915. *Standard* 14:109–40.

———. "On Narcissism: An Introduction." 1914. *Standard* 14:67–107.

———. "Some Psychical Consequences of the Anatomical Distinction between the
Sexes." 1925. *Standard* 19:241–58.

———. *The Standard Edition of the Complete Psychological Works of Sigmund Freud.* Ed.
and trans. James Strachey. 24 vols. London: Hogarth, 1953–74.

Fuss, Diana. *Essentially Speaking: Feminism, Nature, and Difference.* New York: Routledge, 1989.

Garber, Marjorie. *Vested Interests: Cross-Dressing and Cultural Anxiety.* New York:
Routledge, 1991.

Gueguen, Pierre-Gilles. "Un trait de perversion: remarques sur un cas de Lacan."
Quarto 43 (1991): 40–42.

Lacan, Jacques. *Écrits: A Selection.* Trans. Alan Sheridan. New York: Norton, 1977.

———. *Feminine Sexuality: Jacques Lacan and the école freudienne.* Ed. Juliet Mitchell
and Jacqueline Rose. Trans. Rose. New York: Norton, 1982. 149–61.

———. *The Four Fundamental Concepts of Psycho-Analysis.* Ed. Jacques-Alain Miller.
Trans. Alan Sheridan. New York: Norton, 1977.

———. "God and the *Jouissance* of the Woman." 1973. *Feminine Sexuality* 138–48.

———. "Guiding Remarks for a Congress on Feminine Sexuality." 1958. *Feminine
Sexuality* 86–98.

———. "Jeunesse de Gide ou la lettre et le désir." 1958. *Écrits.* Paris: Seuil, 1966.
739–64.

———. "A Love Letter." 1973. *Feminine Sexuality* 149–61.

———. "On a Question Preliminary to any Possible Treatment of Psychosis." 1959.
Écrits: A Selection 179–225.

———. *Le séminaire, livre IV: La relation d'objet, 1956–1957.* Ed. Jacques-Alain Miller.
Paris: Seuil, 1994.

———. *Le séminaire, livre VIII: Le transfert, 1960–1961.* Ed. Jacques-Alain Miller.
Paris: Seuil, 1991.

———. *Le séminaire, livre XX: Encore, 1972–1973.* Ed. Jacques-Alain Miller. Paris:
Seuil, 1975.

————. *The Seminar of Jacques Lacan, Book 20: Encore: On Feminine Sexuality, The Limits of Love and Knowledge, 1972–1973*. Ed. Jacques-Alain Miller. Trans. Bruce Fink. New York: Norton, 1998.

————. "The Signification of the Phallus." 1958. *Écrits: A Selection* 281–91.

————. "The Subversion of the Subject and the Dialectic of Desire in the Freudian Unconscious." 1960. *Écrits: A Selection* 292–325.

————. *Television: A Challenge to the Psychoanalytic Establishment*. Ed. Joan Copjec. Trans. Denis Hollier, Rosalind Krauss, Annette Michelson, and Jeffrey Mehlman. New York: Norton, 1990.

————. "La troisième jouissance." 1974. *Lettres de l'école freudienne* 16 (1975): 178–203.

Miller, Jacques-Alain. "The Analytic Experience: Ways and Means." In Ragland-Sullivan and Bracher 83–99.

————. *Les divins détails*. Course of 1989–90, Department of Psychoanalysis, University of Paris VIII, Saint-Denis. Unpublished.

————. *Donc*. Course of 1993–94, Department of Psychoanalysis, University of Paris VIII, Saint-Denis. Unpublished.

————. *Du symptôme au fantasme et retour*. Course of 1982–83, Department of Psychoanalysis, University of Paris VIII, Saint-Denis. Unpublished.

————. *First Course*. Course of 1981–82, Department of Psychoanalysis, University of Paris VIII, Saint-Denis. Unpublished.

————. "Language: Much Ado about What?" In Ragland-Sullivan and Bracher 21–35.

————. "A Reading of Some Details in *Television* in Dialogue with the Audience." *Newsletter of the Freudian Field* 4 (1990): 4–30.

————. *Sur André Gide*. Course of 1988–89, Department of Psychoanalysis, University of Paris VIII, Saint-Denis. Unpublished.

————. "Sur le Gide de Lacan." *Revue de psychanalyse, la cause freudienne* 25 (1993): 7–38.

Ragland, Ellie. "How the Fact That 'There Is No Sexual Rapport' Gives Rise to Culture." In *The Subject of Lacan: A Lacanian Reader for Psychologists*. Ed. Kareen Malone and Stephen Friedlander. Albany: SUNY P, 2000. 251–63.

Ragland-Sullivan, Ellie, and Mark Bracher, eds. *Lacan and the Subject of Language*. New York: Routledge, 1991.

Žižek, Slavoj. *Tarrying with the Negative: Kant, Hegel, and the Critique of Ideology*. Durham: Duke UP, 1993.

7

HOMOSEXUALITY AND THE
PROBLEM OF OTHERNESS

Tim Dean

. . . .

If it were possible to admit that any relevant forms of otherness operate in homosexuality, then the main feature of heterosexual self-understanding would be lost. MICHAEL WARNER, "HOMO-NARCISSISM; OR, HETEROSEXUALITY" 202–3.

In an article composed on the cusp of queer theory's emergence, Michael Warner initiated a critique of psychoanalytic thinking whose implications have not been fully grasped. Rather than launching an attack on "heterosexual self-understanding," Warner's account can be understood more precisely as a critique of heterosexist epistemology—a critique, that is, of the assumption that heterosexuality represents the principal axis of one's relation to the other. This assumption permeates not only psychoanalytic thinking but also certain feminist critiques of psychoanalysis, where it takes the form of an insistence that otherness and difference be understood primarily in terms of sexual difference. Perhaps Warner's critique has been passed over in silence because it implicitly challenges the primacy of sexual difference that for several decades feminism has struggled to foreground as an explanatory category. I want to argue not that sexual difference is unimportant, but that it should be relegated to secondary status in any psychoanalytic account of otherness that takes the unconscious—and, indeed, homosexuality—seriously as a concept.

Of course, homosexuality is not a psychoanalytic concept but a sexological one. Though Freud rarely stops talking about homosexuality, he never actually theorizes it as a distinctly psychoanalytic idea. Homosexuality features in Freud's psychoanalytic theories of the unconscious, narcissism, infantile sexuality, and the Oedipus complex without ever fully commanding his speculative attention as an idea in its own right. The absence of a coherent Freudian conceptualization of homosexuality suggests that this ostensibly self-evident term *homosexuality* unifies and homogenizes what is actually a heterogeneous field of phenomena. We misrecognize the refractory nature of desire when we take homosexuality to be a coherent and epistemologically unproblematic category. If, in other words, the gender of object-choice is understood to override all other possible discriminations in erotic life, then the idea of homosexuality must represent an imaginary construct, an idea that makes sense only in terms of the synthetic illusions of consciousness. Homosexuality makes sense only from the perspective of the ego. This suggestion helps illuminate—albeit from a different angle—why Freud describes homosexuality in terms of narcissism. "Homosexual object-choice originally lies closer to narcissism than does the heterosexual kind," he declares in his *Introductory Lectures on Psychoanalysis* (426).

Narcissism represents Freud's most notorious explanation of homosexuality, though certainly not his only one.[1] This explanation achieved notoriety because versions of it have been used to pathologize same-sex desire in both the psychoanalytic clinic and twentieth-century American culture more generally (for example, Gus Van Sant's recent remake of *Psycho* treats this psychoanalytic narrative as so familiar as to be readily available for camp mockery). When Freud accounts for homosexuality in terms of narcissism, he confines his discussion to male homosexuality. Since I remain skeptical that the gender of object-choice should be regarded as the most salient factor in any theory of sexual relations, I question the plausibility of discussing men's and women's homosexualities as if they could be comprehended within the terms of a single conceptual model. A better understanding of same-sex desire might result from discussing lesbian sexuality quite independently of gay men's desire: If lesbianism has anything to do with female narcissism, it may do so differently from narcissism in men. My point is not simply that we should resist conceiving lesbian and gay sexualities as analogous, but more fundamentally that understanding them both in terms of "same-sex desire"—as if the sameness of gender were the principal determinant in homosexuality—misconstrues what is most crucially at issue in lesbian and gay sexualities. Thinking about homosexuality primarily within the framework of gender risks returning our account to the sexological models of desire from which psychoanalysis tried to break a century ago.

The Freudian break from earlier models of desire, while decisive, remains incomplete—and nowhere more so than on the question of homosexuality. Explaining male homosexuality as a form of narcissism, Freud conceives it in terms of the sameness not of gender but of the self: Homosexuality appears to Freud as self-love rather than love of another, and this explains why homosexuality can be so readily pathologized. As a form of narcissism, homosexuality can seem intolerant of difference—especially sexual difference—and thus may look like an ethical as well as a psychological problem. In this paper I consider male homosexuality in relation to psychoanalytic and philosophical theories of otherness (principally those of Lacan, Laplanche, and Levinas) with the aim of formulating a new ethics of narcissism. I am interested particularly in forms of narcissism that, though they entail a commitment to sameness, do not exclude otherness. By elaborating a distinction between otherness and difference, this paper extends Warner's critique of the heterosexist ethics of difference while challenging his account of psychoanalytic theories of otherness.

1. If You've Met a Gay Man, You've Met His Mother[2]

The classic psychoanalytic topos for explaining male homosexuality in terms of narcissism is Freud's 1910 essay on Leonardo da Vinci, in which he introduces the concept of narcissism to account for the artist's "manifest, if ideal [sublimated], homosexuality"—a characterization raising a number of problems that the essay fails to resolve. Attempting to explain the genesis of Leonardo's "type" of homosexuality, Freud traces the libidinal fate of a boy who is overly attached to his mother:

> The child's love for his mother cannot continue to develop consciously any further; it succumbs to repression. The boy represses his love for his mother: he puts himself in her place, identifies himself with her, and takes his own person as a model in whose likeness he chooses the new objects of his love. In this way he has become a homosexual. What he has in fact done is to slip back to auto-erotism: for the boys whom he now loves as he grows up are after all only substitutive figures and revivals of himself in childhood—boys whom he loves in the way in which his mother loved *him* when he was a child. He finds the objects of his love along the path of *narcissism,* as we say; for Narcissus, according to the Greek legend, was a youth who preferred his own reflection

to everything else and who was changed into the lovely flower of that name. (100; original emphases)

This passage gives us Freud at his most inventive, revealing a thinker who is neither wholly the mouthpiece of his culture's biases nor yet the radical innovator we prefer to emphasize. In this case the figure of Narcissus, while still attached to his original Greek myth, is also becoming part of an equally bizarre narrative of Freud's own construction—as if Freud felt compelled to rival Ovid's imaginative genius by creating a story of implausibly elaborate metamorphosis: the transformation of a boy into his mother. Since this is only the second time that Freud has used the term *narcissism* in print, an air of self-consciousness hovers about his coinage. And in his reference to "the lovely flower of that name" at the end of this passage, we may hear also a tone of feyness that hints at how the objects of Freud's investigation—homosexuality and the less than normatively masculine practice of artistry—contaminate his own ostensibly scientific discourse.

By associating homosexuality with narcissism at this point in his theory—that is, well before his paper "On Narcissism: An Introduction" (1914)—Freud permits the ominous implications of each idea to affect our understanding of the other. We know that narcissism must be pathogenic because of Narcissus's fate, and so, by virtue of the intuitive association between self-love and love of the same, homosexuality takes over this connotation of impending doom. Mediating between homosexuality and narcissism is the notion of autoerotism, a term that may function here as a placeholder for an account of the self as a libidinal object that Freud remained unable to formulate fully until "On Narcissism," several years later. The alignment of autoerotism, homosexuality, and narcissism in this passage also reinforces the sentiment that same-sex object-choice represents a psychological regression or a sign of arrested development: "What he has in fact done is to slip back to auto-erotism." Once Freud has properly differentiated the concept of narcissism from that of autoerotism, however, the idea of homosexuality as a developmental failure becomes harder to sustain.

Indeed, the psychical transformations this boy undergoes suggest not developmental arrest but rather developmental acceleration or excess: "The boy represses his love for his mother: he puts himself in her place, identifies himself with her, and takes his own person as a model in whose likeness he chooses the new objects of his love." In this complex narrative, which could be read as an ingenious strategy for dealing with loss, the boy conforms to the mandate that he relinquish his attachment to Mother by becoming her. We might call this the Norman Bates solution to oedipal crisis. Rather than seeking substitutes of his mother as love-objects, the boy seeks substitutes of himself; and by desiring versions of his boyish self from the position of maternal love, this boy seems para-doxically to ensure that his homosexuality is underwritten by an unshake-able heterosexuality, albeit of an incestuous sort. Like Norman Bates, this boy exhibits a potentially pathological splitting of his ego, since by as-suming the wrong gender, he identifies with difference rather than with sameness; he thus can be considered non-self-identical from the begin-ning. In this version of male narcissism, there seems to be too much dif-ference rather than not enough. Homosexuality results here not from sameness but from difference, and the conceptual priority of desire as invariably hetero is thereby maintained.

Freud complicates this heterosexual priority in "On Narcissism" by dis-tinguishing between narcissistic and anaclitic (or attachment) object-choices. In this distinction, which inaugurates the properly Freudian the-ory of narcissism, gender fades into irrelevance as a determinant of erotic desire. Anaclisis determines object-choice based on parental care, since, according to Freud, a person makes an anaclitic object-choice when he or she loves the woman who feeds him, the man who protects him, or the succession of substitutes who take their place ("On Narcissism" 90). By contrast, narcissistic object-choice entails a person loving (a) what he himself is, (b) what he himself was, (c) what he himself would like to be, or (d) someone who was once part of himself (90). The anaclitic-narcissistic distinction is supposed to correlate with the hetero-homo dis-tinction, but there is abundant evidence that this correlation cannot be sustained. The boy who makes an anaclitic object-choice based on pater-nal care and protection is as liable to turn out gay as is the boy who makes a narcissistic object-choice and loves himself from his adoring father's perspective. Indeed, the enormous appeal of Daddy-Boy relationships and fantasies within gay male subculture could be explained by recourse to either narcissistic or anaclitic modes of object-choice.

Further, it is clear that if loving "someone who was once part of him-self" counts as a narcissistic object-choice, then a mother's love for her child conforms to this model—an idea that Freud himself confirms: "Pa-rental love, which is so moving and at bottom so childish, is nothing but the parents' narcissism born again, which, transformed into object-love, unmistakably reveals its former nature" ("On Narcissism" 91). In this case it would be not homosexuality but the bastion of heterosexuality, the nu-clear family, that is the haven of narcissism. Yet the narcissism revealed by parental care also leads the child who is the object of this attention beyond him- or herself and toward the other. While Freud does not develop his point about parental narcissism in this direction, Jean Laplanche's revisionist psychoanalytic theory sees in the ministrations of parental care a primal seduction that installs the other at the heart of the child's subjectivity, thereby compromising infantile narcissism from the beginning. In Laplanche's account (to which I shall return), parental narcissism encourages a form of attention that disrupts infantile narcissism by establishing the primacy of the other in the child's subjective economy.

This paradox may be illuminated by pursuing Freud's distinctions in "On Narcissism." The difference between anaclitic and narcissistic object-choices seems to be based on a fundamental difference between self and other, since narcissistic desire fastens upon a self-substitute, whereas anaclitic desire searches out surrogates of those original others who cared for the infant self. Yet the example of the boy in Freud's Leonardo case makes plain why this self-other distinction—and the narcissistic-anaclitic distinction that depends on it—is untenable. The boy in the Leonardo case is said to make a narcissistic object-choice because he loves "what he himself is" or "he himself was." However, according to Freud, his object-choices are determined by the boy's passionate love for his mother, and thus the anaclitic logic of parental care motivates this boy's desire as much as the narcissistic logic of self-love. Freud's prototypical homosexual contravenes the model of narcissism that he is supposed to illustrate because he loves self-substitutes *from another's point of view*. It is thus not he but the other who determines the direction of this ostensibly narcissistic boy's desire.

Freud attempts to resolve this contradiction by asserting not what Laplanche will call the primacy of the other, but, on the contrary, the primacy of narcissism: "We say that a human being has originally two sexual objects—himself and the woman who nurses him—and in doing so we are postulating a primary narcissism in everyone" ("On Narcissism" 88). In thus universalizing narcissism, Freud could have said—according to his own logic in the essay on Leonardo—that psychoanalysis posits a primary *homosexuality* in everyone. Indeed, just one year later, in a famous footnote appended to the third edition of his *Three Essays on the Theory of Sexuality*, he comes close to saying exactly that:

> By studying sexual excitations other than those that are manifestly displayed, [psychoanalytic research] has found that all human beings are capable of making a homosexual object-choice and have in fact made one in their unconscious. Indeed, libidinal attachments to persons of the same sex play no less a

part as factors in normal mental life, and a greater part as a motive force for illness, than do similar attachments to the opposite sex. On the contrary, psychoanalysis considers that a choice of an object independently of its sex—freedom to range equally over male and female objects—as it is found in children, in primitive states of society and early periods of history, is the original basis from which, as a result of restriction in one direction or the other, both the normal and the inverted types develop. (145–46n.)

It is striking that in this passage Freud posits a primary bisexuality—a subjective "freedom to range equally over male and female objects"—as his explanatory touchstone, even though by 1915 he has at his disposal the concept of primary narcissism. Somehow the self-other problematic that defines narcissism has been transposed into a gender problematic and a question of constitutional bisexuality. Another way of putting this would be to say that, in the footnote to *Three Essays*, the problem of otherness is being understood in terms of difference—specifically, sexual difference.

By contrast, Lacan sees in Freud's theory of narcissism the possibility of a relation to otherness before any relation to difference.[3] Without this conceptual prospect, it remains impossible to differentiate primary narcissism from primary homosexuality, because love of oneself appears indistinguishable from love of the same. During the 1950s Lacan dedicated his seminar to rethinking the Freudian theory of narcissism in order to show why love of oneself should *not* be considered love of the same. In these early seminars Lacan lays great stress on the fact that Narcissus loves not so much himself as an *image* of himself. Hence Lacan's conceptualizing narcissism in terms of what he calls the imaginary register of experience. Narcissus falls in love with a mirage, a visual phenomenon that appears to be out there in the world but in fact has no objective existence. It is to this dimension of illusoriness that Lacan is referring when he describes the alienation of the ego in a specular image. In narcissism Lacan discerns a subjective relation to otherness prior to any relation to difference as a consequence of the ego's identification with an image outside itself, a reflection. We might call this the otherness of the visual: a dimension of alterity specific to the imaginary register.

2. *Je est un autre*[4]

Discussing the relation between ideal-ego and ego-ideal, Lacan points to the paradox of primary narcissism in amorous relations, claiming that "it's one's own ego that one loves in love, one's own ego made real on the imaginary level" (*Seminar* 1:142). Significantly, the example Lacan uses to illustrate this proposition is a heterosexual one—Werther's falling in love with Lotte, in Goethe's *The Sorrows of Young Werther:*

> Remember the first time Werther sees Lotte, as she is cuddling a child. It's an entirely satisfying image for the *Anlehnungstypus* on the anaclitic plane. It is the way the object coincides with Goethe's hero's fundamental image that triggers off his fatal attachment. (142)

According to Lacan's reading of Goethe, the image of Lotte cuddling the child gels with Werther's ideal image of his infantile self being cuddled by his mother. Werther makes an anaclitic object-choice, desiring Lotte on the model of parental care, but desiring too the idealized, lovable image of himself. In other words, his object-choice is also narcissistic because he loves his own ego in the objectified form in which he encounters it in this image of Lotte caressing the child. This is what Lacan means by saying that, when in love, one loves "one's own ego made real on the imaginary level."[5]

Lacan may be drawn to a literary illustration in this instance because the notion of one's own ego made real on the imaginary level remains ineluctably fictive. It should go without saying that it is not humanly possible to realize the mirage of the ego in objective form. Hence Lacan's suggestion concerning the irrationality involved in love: "When you're in love, you are mad" (*Seminar* 1:142). Lacan considers narcissism pathogenic as a consequence not of homosexuality but, more generally, of the ego's delusional attachment to a mirage. Although there is a relation to otherness in narcissism, it is invariably a pathological relation, characterized by rivalry, aggression, and fierce intolerance of difference (see "Aggressivity"). From a Lacanian perspective, primary narcissism presents us with the problem of how to get outside the closed circuit of the ego: How might we love or desire beyond the imaginary register? Can we love or respect others only if we're able to identify ourselves in them?

The psychoanalytic postulate of primary narcissism raises broadly ethical and political questions. These questions are particularly pressing in the case of homosexuality because same-sex love tends to be understood as love of the same, and hence as a refusal or exclusion of otherness. While the imaginary is founded upon a relation to the other, I am arguing that that relation cannot form the basis for an ethical disposition toward alterity. Even after the clinical depathologization and social acceptance of homosexuality have been fully achieved, we will be left with the ethical issue of otherness in homosexuality. Thus far queer theory has focused on sexual politics to the neglect of sexual ethics, perhaps out of a sense that ethics entails norms; and, following an often reductive interpretation of Foucault, queer theory sets itself against all norms. However, Foucault stressed, particularly in his late works, that ethics should be differentiated from the normalizing implications of moral codes, because ethics concerns a more expansive and creative sense of obligation toward the other than what can be codified in rules, morals, or etiquette (see *History* and "On the Genealogy").

If ethics can be distinguished from the moralisms that remain so inhospitable to those who fall outside the pale of "the normal," then ethics should also be differentiated in turn from the sexual politics familiar to queer theory. Whereas politics involves strategically negotiating the ideological field on behalf of individual or group interests, the strand of ethics that concerns me entails subordinating all self-interest to the well-being of the other. By prioritizing the other's well-being, I am referring not simply to the claims of collective welfare over individual advantage, but, more radically, to thinking of the other independently of any well-being from which one might benefit oneself (for example, the communitarian benefits accruing from a good society). It may be especially challenging for socially disempowered groups to envision such an ethical practice, because the disenfranchised usually feel a strong imperative to better their own lot. Yet Foucault insisted that such groups—the lesbian and gay movement is implied—should struggle to meet the challenge of ethics beyond that of politics: "Most of us no longer believe that ethics is founded in religion, nor do we want a legal system to intervene in our moral, personal, private life. Recent liberation movements suffer from the fact that they cannot find any principle on which to base the elaboration of a new ethics" ("On the Genealogy" 255–56).

Having in mind the ethical philosophy of Emmanuel Levinas as well as Foucault's late works, I am interested in how an ethics that prioritizes the other over any politics or morality of altruism might be articulated with psychoanalysis, since both Lacan and Laplanche also privilege alterity in their different accounts of subjectivity. What I find particularly useful in these psychoanalytic accounts is their conceiving "the other" as something more than another person or the representative of a social differential. I would like to develop an ethics of sexuality that does not reduce otherness to either personhood or difference—hence the ostensibly paradoxical enterprise of formulating a sexual ethics that is *not* centered on sexual difference. While for feminist philosophers such as Luce Irigaray psychoanalysis remains ethically impoverished owing to its comparative neglect of sexual difference, I consider psychoanalysis ethically constrained by its heterosexist propensity for translating otherness into the terms of sexual difference (see Irigaray). Psychoanalysis offers the inestimable conceptual and ethical benefits of an account of alterity that distinguishes otherness from both personhood and difference. However, it dissipates that advantage every time subjective relations to alterity are framed in heterosexual terms. This is a complex argument that I would like to lay out as clearly as possible.

Philosophy generally conceives our relation to the other in terms of two broad problematics: How we know the other, and how we should behave toward him or her. The first question—How do I know the other?—is epistemological; the second—How should I behave toward him or her?—is ethical. It would appear that how we answer the second question depends on how we resolve the first. Indeed, as Elaine Scarry argues in a very interesting essay on the problem of otherness, "our injuring of others . . . results from our failure to know them" (44). Scarry points out that the two-sided problematic of knowing the other and behaving ethically toward him or her is mediated by the question of how we imagine others—a question that entails aesthetics, as well as psychology and ethics. She argues compellingly that "the human capacity to injure other people is very great precisely because our capacity to imagine other people is very small" (45). However, an exception to this rule, which Scarry barely acknowledges, lies in our virtually limitless capacity to imagine other people *enjoying*. This imaginative capacity readily produces the conviction that others are enjoying themselves at our expense, and it is this conviction that sparks the desire to injure others. For example, gay men are often pictured as having access to forms of *jouissance*—more sex, more disposable income, freedom from the ties of family and tradition, et cetera—that responsible, law-abiding citizens are denied. From this perspective it is not the failure to imagine others, but, on the contrary, the avid willingness to do so that leads to violence against them.

Rather than assuming that ethical behavior toward the other depends on our knowledge of him or her, we may question this link between epistemology and ethics, asking whether an ethical relation to the other might not be quite independent of knowing him or her. Indeed, ethics may stem from our accepting the impossibility of epistemologically comprehending alterity. To put this claim at its most basic: We should not need to understand or be able to imagine others in order to grant them the same measure of respect that we accord to those whom we know and those with whom we already sympathize. Ethical treatment depends not on familiarity and likeness, but comes into its own when we confront the other's strangeness. Only in these terms may we hope to achieve an ethical disposition—not just toward other persons but also toward different species and the nonsentient world. This conception of the ethical relation pertains to more than an ecological awareness of the environment: It also bears implications for those who consider homosexuals a different species. In short, it's exactly when one fails to recognize anything of oneself in the other—including a species commonality—that ethical behavior becomes paramount.

The epistemological project of knowing others goes by the name, in philosophy, of "the problem of other minds." Psychoanalysis substantially reorients this philosophical problematic by pointing to the otherness of one's own mind. Since the alterity of one's own mind differs from the alterity of the other as another person, the psychoanalytic concept of the unconscious, by indicating a further dimension of otherness, makes the philosophical question of other minds more intimate and pressing. We might say that psychoanalysis reveals the otherness within sameness, and so explodes the myth that sameness involves only self-sameness. To take just one example: The boy in Freud's Leonardo case, by installing his mother in and as his own mind, has become other to himself. A major consequence of the psychoanalytic reframing of this philosophical problem is that our epistemological and ethical relations to other persons can be seen as predicated upon a newfound relation to ourselves—a relationship, that is, with our own otherness.

Although he did not pursue the issue in psychoanalytic terms, Foucault explored this problematic in his discussions of Greek ethics, specifically, in his account of the care of the self as an "aesthetics of existence." Within his genealogy of techniques of the self, Foucault distinguishes ancient ethical practices of *epimeleia heautou* (care of the self) from later techniques of normalization, arguing that the care of the self situates the subject in a different relation to power. He contends that Christianity displaced this Greek ethical practice by denouncing care of the self as a form of self-love—or what today we would disparage as excessive narcissism ("Ethics" 284). Yet Foucault shows why an aesthetics of existence should not be collapsed into self-love, since care of the self entails working on a relation to one's own otherness. In this respect, care of the self is homologous with psychoanalysis, rather than contrary to it, as Foucault implies ("On the Genealogy" 271). Both aesthetic and clinical practices assume the self's nontransparency to itself, and therefore both remain antithetical to self-indulgence.

Taking care of one's own otherness is, for Foucault and Lacan alike, the necessary precondition of any ethical relation to other persons: "Care for others should not be put before the care of oneself," Foucault insists. "The care of the self is ethically prior in that the relationship with oneself is ontologically prior" ("Ethics" 287). Although Foucault did not couch this problematic in terms of a relationship with *one's own otherness*—perhaps because the vocabulary of otherness was for him too closely associated with French psychoanalysis and existentialism—it was in fact the self's difference from itself that concerned him. Psychoanalysis calls this self-alienation the unconscious. Hence psychoanalysis can contribute to ethical discourse because, at least in its continental variants, it concerns nothing but subjective relations to alterity.[6]

The ethics of psychoanalysis involves not only ideas pertaining to clinical practice, but also a distinctive account of human relationality in general. From the point of view of French psychoanalysis, the Anglo-American tendency to conceive of human relations intersubjectively tends to restrict ethics to the interpersonal and thus to the imaginary realm. My discussion of narcissism above suggests how ethically inadequate it is to conceive of relationality imaginarily, as a question of mutual recognition.[7] What French psychoanalysis offers is a theory of alterity in which the other remains irreducible to another person. This psychoanalytic approach keeps open ethical possibilities by refusing to domesticate—we might even say *normalize*—the Other's inhuman strangeness. It is not the recognizable other but the unrecognizable Other—that which defies our imaginary coordinates and our capacity for what Scarry terms "generous imaginings"—that most urgently calls for an ethical attitude.

3. The Missing Piece Meets the Big O[8]

It has become commonplace in contemporary criticism to observe that the subject is constituted through its relation to an other. Often the claim is made that the subject constitutes him- or herself through some act of violence upon the other—by repressing or excluding the other, as if from an ethical perspective subjectivity were inherently troubling.[9] This line of argument tends to identify "the other" that is excluded or repressed with various social positions—with disequilibriums of gender, race, and class. Often "the other" becomes simply a shorthand way of talking about women, ethnic and racial minorities, sexual minorities, and poor people. From a psychoanalytic perspective, the central problem with this mode of reasoning lies in its tendency to overlook the alterity specific to language itself, as if the alienating effects of symbolic existence could be elided with various forms of social disenfranchisement. Whereas much contemporary theory insists on the imperative to specify otherness with respect to gender, race, and class (supplemented by sexuality, ethnicity, and other variables), Lacan suggests instead that we specify otherness in terms of three different registers: imaginary, symbolic, and real.

Lacan is interested in something more than the alterity specific to the imaginary register that I discussed earlier, because he realizes that subjectivity exceeds the confines of the ego. Since psychoanalysis concerns itself with the unconscious more than with the ego, Lacan's emphasis falls on the alterity specific to the symbolic register, alterity with a capital *A—le grand Autre*, or what Lacanians call "the big Other." In Lacanian discourse, the distinction between lowercase *o* and capital *O*—between the *other* and the *Other*—involves the difference between imaginary and symbolic forms of otherness. It thus entails a distinction between ego and subject, according to which Lacan conceives subjectivity as an effect of the unconscious rather than of consciousness.[10] These distinctions clarify the means for getting beyond an imaginary ethics of the ego—that is, for finding modes of relationality other than those of intersubjective recognition, empathic identification, or repudiation. The distinction between imaginary and symbolic forms of otherness differentiates a psychoanalytic ethic from the therapeutic ethic of mutual recognition and its political correlate, the democratic ethic of liberal tolerance.

Lacan insists on the alterity of language in order to emphasize a degree of subjective alienation that no amount of therapeutic empathy or intersubjective validation can overcome. In the alterity of language, he sees another dimension of the human subject's strangeness to itself.[11] This kind of strangeness defies recognition. By taking the strangeness of the unconscious as foundational rather than contingent, Lacan proposes that our relation to other persons—others with a lowercase *o*—depends on our relation to language and what is beyond it—the big Other, the Other with a capital *O*. Intersubjective relations depend on the self's essentially impersonal relationship to symbolic mediation. Far from this impersonal, abstract Other signaling a failure on the part of psychoanalysis to particularize alterity in terms of its sociohistorical variables (as many critics complain), I would argue that the ethical relation to other persons depends on our upholding the distinction between particular and general forms of alterity.[12]

When one conceives of alterity in symbolic rather than imaginary terms, it immediately becomes evident that homosexual relations are no more guilty of excluding otherness than are the heterosexual kind; all sexual relations are symbolically mediated. Thus Lacan's answer to the problem of how we might love or desire beyond the imaginary register lies in acknowledging that the big Other—the alterity of symbolic existence—affects us from the beginning. The distinctness of Lacan's conception of the big Other—its designating something more than language as such—has to do with a form of alienation that precludes subjective identification. Whereas the alterity of imaginary relations confers upon the subject an alienated identity that we call ego or self, symbolic alterity impedes the formation of any identity, even an alienated one. Our identities, including sexual identity, invariably conflict with our unconscious. Hence the forms of otherness entailed by imaginary and symbolic registers of experience are neither compatible nor sequential (human subjects do not progress *from* the imaginary *to* the symbolic), but heterogeneous.

A distinct advantage issues from this ineluctable making-strange of symbolic alienation. Since nobody's place in the symbolic order is fully guaranteed—there is no social position awaiting merely one's identification with it—his or her subjective destiny cannot be programmed in advance. Neither heterosexuality nor homosexuality is subjectively predetermined, whether biologically *or socially.* No regime of socio-symbolic construction can produce heterosexual subjects without fail, since the fit between human forms and symbolic systems remains imperfect. Lacan's theory of the symbolic order thus refutes determinist views of human subjectivity and sexuality. It is to this underdetermination of the subject that Lacan is referring when he announces that the big Other is incomplete, lacking, or missing. If the subject lacks something, it is only because the big Other is already missing a piece. In the symbolic order, as distinct from the imaginary, the picture is always incomplete. Subjectively speaking, this incompleteness can be a source of frustration, since our identifications are not fully secure and the possibility of self-mastery therefore remains forever out of reach. Yet this incompleteness and the consequent elusiveness of self-mastery also present an opportunity for creativity—or what Foucault calls an aesthetics of existence. "From the idea that the self is not given to us," Foucault suggests, "I think that there is only one practical consequence: we have to create ourselves as a work of art" ("On the Genealogy" 262).

4. Sexual Secrets

The form of agency called *creativity,* which is distinct from what Foucault meant by the term *resistance,* may be illuminated by turning to Jean Laplanche's theory of alterity. I am interested here in Laplanche's account of the primacy of the other because it has inspired recent speculations concerning the ethical possibilities that may inhere in homosexual narcissism—or in what Leo Bersani terms *homo-ness*. Bersani's transvaluation of the sameness in homosexuality from an ethical weakness to an ethical strength bears some investigation.

For Laplanche as for Lacan, narcissism is unavoidably compromised by the subject's relation to otherness.[13] Focusing on what he calls the primacy of the other in the genesis of subjectivity, Laplanche at once differentiates two axes of alterity—that of the other person and that of the unconscious—and insists on their interdependence. He takes this distinction between two kinds of otherness from Freud's discriminating between the masculine noun, *der Andere,* to refer to another person, and the gender-neutral noun, *das Andere,* to refer to the "other thing" of the unconscious (Laplanche, *Essays* 255–56). The other person ensures the alienness of the subject's unconscious because he or she unwittingly introduced it in the first place. In this sense, one's own unconscious can be understood as a foreign body that has been installed by another's alienation from him- or herself. For Laplanche this intersubjective emergence of an otherness that remains irreducible to the alterity of another person testifies to the constitutive failure of mutual recognition. Paradoxically, it is somebody else's unrecognizability to him- or herself that constitutes one's "own" unconscious.

Laplanche explains this paradox by recourse to the theory of the *enigmatic signifier,* a term he borrows from Lacan.[14] Parental care transmits to the child who is its object messages that the child is unable to comprehend; these messages are enigmatic to the child because they are enigmatic to the person who transmits them. According to Laplanche, the circumstances of infantile care—touching, caressing, rocking, kissing, bathing, diapering, and so on—call forth in the adult caretaker unconscious fantasies that inadvertently are communicated to the child and necessarily remain enigmatic. This transmission and its consequences determine what Laplanche calls *seduction theory:* The child is seduced into intersubjectivity by meanings it cannot fathom, and these incomprehensible communications form the child's own unconscious. The otherness of the unconscious precipitates from those baffling residues of asymmetrical exchanges.

Laplanche's account situates epistemological concerns at the heart of human relations by making the other's secret the motive force of intersubjectivity. From this perspective, the philosophical problematic of other minds sublimates the more basic problem of the other's secret—the idea that the other has something to which I am denied access; hence our fantasies of penetrating or incorporating the other in order to learn his or her secret. The enigmatic signifier makes intersubjective relations antagonistic, characterized by paranoid fascination and the struggle for possession. Such fantasies play out especially keenly in sexual relations, because sex is the primary form the secret assumes in our culture. For historical reasons laid out by Foucault, sexuality has become the site of the enigma and hence, apparently, of the truth of our being.

According to Laplanche, one's subjective itinerary is determined by how he or she responds to the enigmatic message of the other's unconscious. The type of agency I'm calling creativity consists in multiplying the potential forms this response might take. Both the care of the self and the experience of psychoanalysis involve enlarging the horizon of possibilities for responding to otherness. One aim of psychoanalysis—at least from a continental perspective—is to grasp that the solution to the mystery of one's being is lacking not only in him- or herself, but also in the Other. In the end there may be no mystery to penetrate. This is also the trajectory Foucault was pursuing in his multivolume *History of Sexuality:* Care of the self does not entail locating the truth of the self. In this view, the other may be seen not as a threatening source of alien enigmas, but rather as that with which one can have less antagonistic kinds of relationship. The other would remain other without having to be either reassuringly identical to oneself or markedly different. When the distinction between identity and difference dissolves, the other does not disappear along with it but simply assumes a less ominous aspect.

This, in fact, is what Bersani proposes in his idea of homo-ness, or what he speaks of elsewhere as "inaccurate self-replication." Bersani sees in homosexuality the potential for a different relation to sameness—a relation that we might describe as a nonimaginary kind of narcissism. This way of apprehending otherness would enable forms of relationality liberated from the tyranny of the enigmatic signifier. While the theory of the enigmatic signifier centers intersubjectivity on epistemological questions, Bersani counters by pointing to the ontological register of relatedness, in which a nonimaginary narcissism would consist in finding and losing oneself in the ongoing communication of forms. In this account of human relations, the communication of meaning (accompanied by its blockages and enigmas) gives way to a communication of being that renders secrets, especially sexual secrets, obsolete.[15]

This brief characterization begins to suggest how differently Bersani views homosexuality than do most contemporary critics. Impatient with queer theorists' tendency to romanticize the subversive power that they see in nonnormative sexual practices, Bersani emphasizes how gay modes of relating can be just as exploitative as normative heterosexual ones. Nevertheless, he finds in the attraction to sameness that characterizes homosexuality as an idea (if not always in practice) a mode of relating that challenges the distinction between sameness and difference upon which relational hierarchies are founded.[16] In other words, Bersani's locating in homosexuality a model of sociality depends on his distinguishing homosexuality as an ontological category from gayness as a psychological identity. As he and Ulysse Dutoit conclude their study of Derek Jarman's film *Caravaggio:*

> These slippages of identity from one body to another, this interchangeability of being, help us to re-define homosexuality: no longer (merely) a particular sexual orientation, it can be seen as the sexuality most appropriate to a perceived solidarity of being in the universe. Identities are never individual; homosexual desire is a reaching out toward an *other sameness*. Homosexuality *expresses* a homoness that vastly exceeds it but that it none the less has the privilege, and the responsibility, of making visible. (79–80; original emphases)

5. There Is No Other Sex[17]

Bersani's work elaborates some ways of thinking about otherness outside the binary polarization of identity and difference. And, as I have suggested, continental psychoanalytic theory offers distinctions between registers of alterity that support this effort to differentiate otherness from difference. Yet when it comes to sexual ethics, there remains within psychoanalysis a countervailing impulse to conceptualize alterity in terms of sexual difference. Despite its innovations, psychoanalysis has not yet dissociated itself fully from the epistemic horizon in which the other's enigma is apprehended in primarily sexual terms. This limitation may represent one more instance of what Laplanche calls the *fourvoiement*, or going-astray, of psychoanalytic thinking, since, according to him, the development of Freudian theory tends to mimic a subjective trajectory in which the radical otherness of the unconscious and its relation to sexuality is recentered and normalized through the agency of the ego (*Essays* 52–83). While Laplanche maintains that there is something inevitable about this normalizing process, I want to suggest that the collapsing of alterity into difference results in part from a residual heterosexism in French psychoanalysis.

This problem is most evident in Lacan's elaboration in *Encore* of the notion of "the Other sex," where Other bears a capital *O* and there is an implicit ethical imperative to engage otherness by engaging "the Other sex." Lacan is surprisingly candid about this conflation, insisting that "the Other, in my terminology, can thus only be the Other sex" (*Seminar* 20:39). Yet to conceive of symbolic otherness in terms of difference, especially sexual difference, is an imaginary and, ultimately, a heterosexist gesture. When we make sexual difference the paradigm for alterity in the field of sexual ethics, we fail to escape the imaginary lures of the ego that the question of ethics was invoked to circumvent.

Another way of indicating this heterosexist slippage in psychoanalysis would be to question the gendering of each side of Lacan's sexuation graphs in *Encore* (*Seminar* 20:78). Although his axiom that "there is no sexual relation" counters the heterosexist assumption of complementarity between the sexes, Lacan's explanations of this axiom nevertheless are invariably couched in terms of male and female failures to relate to each other, rather than in terms of relationality's failure as such, regardless of gender. The impediments to relationality that stem from symbolic mediation—that is, from the big Other's intervening in all subjective relations—have nothing to do with gender, and therefore Lacan occludes his original insight by formulating relational failure in terms of man's nonrelation to Woman.[18]

This problem becomes even clearer when we consider the third register of alterity that Lacan specifies. Here we are dealing with neither the imaginary other (lowercase *o*) nor the symbolic Other (capital *O*), but with the *objet petit a* (where *a* stands for *autre*). This form of otherness entails an ethics of the real. What I take to be most original about Lacan's theory of the object *a* as the "cause of desire" is that it explains desire's origins in the effects of language on my own body, thereby implying a different conception of autoerotism. Since in this account desire originates in a making other to myself of my own corporeal *jouissance*, there is no way that desire can be, in the first instance, heterosexual. All desire entails the presence of the symbolic Other, but since this Other has no gender—there is no "Other sex"—desire involves a relation to otherness independent of sexual difference. This important point evaporates (or is perhaps repressed) when Lacan positions the object *a* on the woman's side of his sexuation graphs. This positioning negates his own theory of the object.[19]

Permit me to get at this question of the relation between otherness and sexual difference from one further angle. Following Freud, Lacan maintains that there is no signifier for sexual difference in the unconscious. If so, then in the unconscious heterosexuality does not exist. At the level of the unconscious—where Lacan locates both the subject and desire—we are concerned not with primary narcissism but with something that may appear to be primary homosexuality (see *Revue de psychanalyse*). To Freud's list of the distinctive characteristics of primary process thinking—that it knows no negation, no contradiction, nothing of time—we are obliged to add that the unconscious knows nothing of heterosexuality. Since there is alterity without sexual difference in the unconscious, our translating otherness into sexual terms begins a process of betraying the unconscious—and hence betraying the psychoanalytic ethic. Consequently the psychoanalytic problematic of the unconscious bears further investigation by queer theory.[20]

The bizarre fact of there being no signifier for sexual difference in the unconscious means that sexual difference cannot *determine* erotic desire. It is not that sexual difference has no bearing on sexual desire, but that the latter is not determined fully by the former. Since we live in a social world where there is more than one sex, however, we are obliged to respond to this difference. Perhaps more creative responses to sexual difference may come not from insisting on discovering in it the key to our alterity, but rather from keeping the margin between otherness and difference open. One's ethical relation to the other inevitably narrows when sexual difference is interpreted as its primary axis. By contrast, in the ontology—if not the psychology—of homosexuality lies an ethic that, as Foucault intuited, is more open to the inventions of otherness than psychoanalysis itself sometimes is. When read outside the normalizing lenses of both orthodox psychoanalysis and gay identity, homosexuality points toward a nonimaginary narcissism that may benefit gays and straights alike, even as it challenges erotic identities as we know them.

Notes

Earlier versions of this paper were presented at SUNY-Buffalo, University of California at Berkeley, and University of Illinois at Urbana-Champaign. I would like to thank my audiences on those occasions, particularly Joan Copjec, Leo Bersani, and Peter Garrett, for inviting me to present this material. Special thanks are owed also to Nancy Blake and Lisa King, formal respondents to my presentation at University of Illinois, and to Jason Friedman, Christopher Lane, and Ramón Soto-Crespo for help with subsequent drafts.

1. Freud remarks in his study of Leonardo da Vinci that "what is for practical reasons called homosexuality may arise from a whole variety of psychosexual inhibitory processes; the particular process we have singled out is perhaps only one among many, and is perhaps related to only one type of 'homosexuality'" (*Leonardo* 101).

2. Modern gay proverb.

3. My thanks to Ramón Soto-Crespo for this formulation.

4. "I is an other." Poet Arthur Rimbaud, in a letter to Paul Demeny, May 15, 1871 (Rimbaud 275); Rimbaud's formulation is quoted by Lacan (*Seminar* 2:7).

5. By way of qualification I should like to emphasize two points. First, in this sentence Lacan is using the word *real* in the ordinary sense, not the sense he develops later in his work, where *real* designates the third register, along with *imaginary* and *symbolic*. Second, although Lacan's account of love shifts later in his work too, even twenty years afterward he can be found insisting that "analysis demonstrates that love, in its essence, is narcissistic" (*Seminar* 20:6).

6. Hence, of course, Lacan's devoting a year-long seminar to ethics. The issue of Foucault's account of psychoanalysis and his relation to it is too complex to take up properly here. My point is simply that the place of psychoanalysis in his genealogy of techniques of the self is not fully accounted for by what Foucault himself said on the matter.

7. My argument here is directed against the liberalist assumptions of contemporary psychoanalytic thinkers such as Jessica Benjamin, who has developed a feminist psychoanalytic ethic of intersubjectivity based on mutual recognition (see *Bonds* and *Like Subjects*). For Benjamin, one's ethical relation to the other depends on recognizing him or her as a "like subject," whereas I am arguing that the ethical relation depends on precisely the failure of that recognition—and on a corresponding acknowledgment of the other's irreducible alterity.

8. This phrase forms the title of a popular children's storybook by Shel Silverstein. I am grateful to Andrew Moss for presenting me with this document of Americana after he heard an earlier version of the present paper. If Shel Silverstein had not existed to write this book, it would have been necessary for Slavoj Žižek to invent him.

9. Such claims are exemplified in, though not restricted to, Judith Butler's recent work, particularly her would-be psychoanalytic argument about subjection in *The Psychic Life of Power*.

10. Here I am condensing a set of distinctions that I lay out more fully in "Two Kinds of Other and Their Consequences," where I argue that collapsing the Other into the other fuels social antagonisms because the symbolic Other introduces a subjective alienation or privation that, when it becomes confused with social others and their different styles of life, breeds hatred toward sexual and ethnic minorities.

11. This theme also has been pursued by Kristeva, in her aptly titled *Strangers to Ourselves*.

12. Here I am arguing also against critics such as Scarry, who, though lodging no particular complaint against psychoanalysis, nevertheless formulates in its starkest terms the kind of position I wish to discredit. Scarry argues for "the importance of creating laws that eliminate the structural position of the Other" (55), when, from a psychoanalytic perspective, such an aim is not only impossible to achieve but also dangerously counterproductive.

13. Laplanche's insistence on the primacy of the other leads him to emphasize anaclitic over narcissistic modes of object-choice. He first develops the concept of anaclisis—from the German *Anlehnung,* or "leaning-on"—in his important distinction between drive and instinct: The drive leans on, or props itself on, instinctual activities such as feeding, from which it subsequently detaches itself (see *Life and Death* 8–24). Laplanche's theory of the drive and his prioritizing of the other thus go hand in hand. From this it follows that drive theory, which often is thought to be part of a "one-body psychology," should be understood as inseparable from, rather than mutually exclusive with, an emphasis on intersubjectivity.

14. In his "Agency of the Letter in the Unconscious" (1957), Lacan writes: "Between the enigmatic signifier of the sexual trauma and the term that is substituted for it in an actual signifying chain there passes the spark that fixes in a symptom the signification inaccessible to the conscious subject in which that symptom may be resolved—a symptom being a metaphor in which flesh or function is taken as a signifying element" (166).

15. From the self-shattered ego of *The Freudian Body* to the critique of narcissism in chapter 2 of *The Culture of Redemption,* through the concept of homo-ness in *Homos* to the idea of inaccurate self-replication in his writing on art with Ulysse Dutoit (see *Arts* and *Caravaggio's Secrets*), Bersani has been considering the concept of narcissism for well over a decade. While it is therefore impossible to do justice to his reformulations of this psychoanalytic idea here, in a discussion of Bersani's work elsewhere I unpack the paradox of a nonimaginary narcissism (see "What's the Point").

16. In a fascinating study of urban transformations, Samuel R. Delany suggests how certain gay sexual practices challenge relational hierarchies in ways that point toward more democratic forms of sociality. Discussing recent changes in New York City's Times Square area, Delany distinguishes between two forms of social interaction: contact, which he associates with interclass connections, and networking, which he defines in terms of connections within a comparatively homogeneous social grouping. One of Delany's principal examples of "contact" is the gay cruising and casual sexual encounters that flourished in the old Times Square. His account of this phenomenon avoids the easy nostalgia that it might seem to invite because Delany compellingly shows how the corporate makeover of Times Square facilitates networking-style interactions while narrowing possibilities for contact-style interactions—to the detriment of cosmopolitan life as a whole. Delany's remains the most illuminating analysis of gay public sexual culture—and, more broadly, urban democracy—that I've read.

17. An axiom derived from the present argument.

18. This blind spot appears particularly dramatically in Dany Nobus's comprehensive account of the status of sexuality in Lacanian theory. Having elaborated Lacan's formula that "there is no sexual relation" in exclusively heterosexual terms, Nobus paradoxically selects as his example to illustrate this axiom the relationship between Alcibiades and Socrates in Plato's *Symposium.* That is, he uses an ideal—we might say sublimated—homosexual relationship to illustrate a principle put forth in purely heterosexual terms. As if dimly aware of this inconsistency, Nobus subsequently asserts that the formula "there is no sexual relation" still holds for a male-male relationship because "biological males" can occupy the woman's side of the sexuation graph (120). But this compounds the problem rather than resolving it, since such formulations maintain a heterosexist principle of desire as flowing only between masculine and feminine positions, at the same time as the declaration—regularly repeated to me by Lacanians—that in gay relationships an anatomical man can occupy the woman's side of the graph veers disconcertingly close to the prepsychoanalytic idea of homosexuality as betraying "a female soul in a man's body," or vice versa. Often it seems that homosexuality represents the unconscious—the unthought—of Lacanian psychoanalysis.

19. In a brilliant and heterodox reading of Lacan's sexuation formulae, Molly Anne Rothenberg and Joseph Valente argue that subjectivity as such is impossible if restricted to either side of the sexuation graph. Their argument confirms my sense that the two sides of the graph cannot legitimately be gendered, but instead should be understood as diagramming differential modalities that inform every subject. Perhaps Lacan's sexuation formulae can be grasped as a mathematical rewriting of Freud's hypothesis about constitutional bisexuality—a hypothesis that, I have suggested, itself rewrites primary narcissism in gendered terms.

20. I pursue some implications of this idea in *Beyond Sexuality.*

References

Benjamin, Jessica. *The Bonds of Love: Psychoanalysis, Feminism, and the Problem of Domination.* New York: Pantheon, 1988.

———. *Like Subjects, Love Objects: Essays on Recognition and Sexual Difference.* New Haven: Yale UP, 1995.

Bersani, Leo. "Erotic Assumptions: Narcissism and Sublimation in Freud." *The Culture of Redemption.* Cambridge: Harvard UP, 1990. 29–46.

———. *The Freudian Body: Psychoanalysis and Art.* New York: Columbia UP, 1986.

———. *Homos.* Cambridge: Harvard UP, 1995.

Bersani, Leo, and Ulysse Dutoit. *Arts of Impoverishment: Beckett, Rothko, Resnais.* Cambridge: Harvard UP, 1993.

———. *Caravaggio.* London: BFI, 1999.

———. *Caravaggio's Secrets*. Cambridge: MIT P, 1998.

Butler, Judith. *The Psychic Life of Power: Theories in Subjection*. Stanford: Stanford UP, 1997.

Dean, Tim. *Beyond Sexuality*. Chicago: U of Chicago P, 2000.

———. "Two Kinds of Other and Their Consequences." *Critical Inquiry* 23 (1997): 910–20.

———. "What's the Point of Psychoanalytic Criticism?" *Oxford Literary Review* 20 (1998): 143–62.

Delany, Samuel R. ". . . Three, Two, One, Contact: Times Square Red, 1998." In *Giving Ground: The Politics of Propinquity*. Ed. Joan Copjec and Michael Sorkin. London: Verso, 1999. 19–85.

Foucault, Michel. *The Essential Works of Michel Foucault, 1954–1984*. Vol. 1: *Ethics: Subjectivity and Truth*. Ed. Paul Rabinow. Trans. Robert Hurley. New York: New P, 1997.

———. "The Ethics of the Concern of the Self as a Practice of Freedom." *Essential Works* 1:281–301.

———. *The History of Sexuality. Volume 3: The Care of the Self*. Trans. Robert Hurley. New York: Random House, 1986.

———. "On the Genealogy of Ethics: An Overview of Work in Progress." *Essential Works* 1:253–80.

Freud, Sigmund. *Introductory Lectures on Psychoanalysis*. Part 3. 1916–17. *Standard* 16:243–463.

———. *Leonardo da Vinci and a Memory of His Childhood*. 1910. *Standard* 11:57–137.

———. "On Narcissism: An Introduction." 1914. *Standard* 14:67–102.

———. *The Standard Edition of the Complete Psychological Works of Sigmund Freud*. 24 vols. Ed. James Strachey. London: Hogarth, 1953–74.

———. *Three Essays on the Theory of Sexuality*. 1905. *Standard* 7:123–243.

Irigaray, Luce. *An Ethics of Sexual Difference*. Trans. Carolyn Burke and Gillian C. Gill. Ithaca: Cornell UP, 1993.

Kristeva, Julia. *Strangers to Ourselves*. Trans. Leon S. Roudiez. New York: Columbia UP, 1991.

Lacan, Jacques. "The Agency of the Letter in the Unconscious or Reason Since Freud." *Écrits* 146–78.

———. "Aggressivity in Psychoanalysis." *Écrits* 8–29.

———. *Écrits: A Selection*. Trans. Alan Sheridan. New York: Norton, 1977.

———. *The Seminar of Jacques Lacan, Book 1: Freud's Papers on Technique, 1953–1954*. Ed. Jacques-Alain Miller. Trans. John Forrester. Cambridge: Cambridge UP, 1988.

———. *The Seminar of Jacques Lacan, Book 2: The Ego in Freud's Theory and in the Technique of Psychoanalysis, 1954–1955*. Ed. Jacques-Alain Miller. Trans. Sylvana Tomaselli. Cambridge: Cambridge UP, 1988.

———. *The Seminar of Jacques Lacan, Book 7: The Ethics of Psychoanalysis, 1959–1960*. Ed. Jacques-Alain Miller. Trans. Dennis Porter. New York: Norton, 1992.

————. *The Seminar of Jacques Lacan, Book 20: Encore: On Feminine Sexuality, The Limits of Love and Knowledge, 1972–1973.* Ed. Jacques-Alain Miller. Trans. Bruce Fink. New York: Norton, 1998.

Laplanche, Jean. *Essays on Otherness.* Ed. John Fletcher. London: Routledge, 1999.

————. *Life and Death in Psychoanalysis.* Trans. Jeffrey Mehlman. Baltimore: Johns Hopkins UP, 1976.

Levinas, Emmanuel. *Entre Nous: On Thinking-of-the-Other.* Trans. Michael B. Smith and Barbara Harshav. New York: Columbia UP, 1998.

Nobus, Dany. "Theorising the Comedy of Sexes: Lacan on Sexuality." In *The Klein-Lacan Dialogues.* Ed. Bernard Burgoyne and Mary Sullivan. New York: Other P, 1999. 105–24.

Revue de psychanalyse 37 (October 1997). Spec. issue: "L'inconscient homosexuel."

Rimbaud, Arthur. *Poems.* Trans Paul Schmidt. New York: Knopf, 1994.

Rothenberg, Molly Anne, and Joseph Valente. "Against an Ethics of *Jouissance.*" *Paper Tigers: A Guide to the Crisis of Agency in Cultural Theory Today.* Cambridge: Cambridge UP, forthcoming.

Scarry, Elaine. "The Difficulty of Imagining Other Persons." In *The Handbook of Interethnic Coexistence.* Ed. Eugene Weiner. New York: Continuum, 1998. 40–62.

Silverstein, Shel. *The Missing Piece Meets the Big O.* New York: HarperCollins, 1981.

Warner, Michael. "Homo-Narcissism; or, Heterosexuality." In *Engendering Men: The Question of Male Feminist Criticism.* Ed. Joseph A. Boone and Michael Cadden. New York: Routledge, 1990. 190–206.

GAY
SEXUALITY
2

8

FREUD ON GROUP PSYCHOLOGY

Shattering the Dream of a Common Culture

Christopher Lane

. . . .

Sexual desires do not unite men but divide them. FREUD, *TOTEM AND TABOO* 144

Recent psychoanalytic work on culture and aesthetics routinely has noted Freud's inadequate theorization of sublimation and group relations. Although the reasons given for this inadequacy vary, the consensus seems clear: Freud's account of group identification is marred by his inability to resolve the sexual—especially the homosexual—status of group bonds. The superficial response to this difficulty is to conclude that Freud was oddly intransigent in linking sublimation to inhibited homosexuality. In responding thus, critics deduce that Freud either came to an honorable defense of homosexuals, granting them "a special aptitude for cultural sublimation," as he put it in 1908, or that he perpetuated a classical and Victorian stereotype that could tolerate homosexuality only in nonsexual forms ("'Civilized'" 190). Although both deductions rely heavily on biographical assumptions, the latter argument, at its most extreme, implies that any conceptual incoherence damages psychoanalysis as a whole, making it irrelevant for and even inimical to queer theory (for elaboration, see Dean 124–25).

This essay aims to engage with Freud's difficulty on a deeper level, showing how his conception of sublimation and group identification stems from a specific argument about male homosexuality and attachment in *Group Psychology and the Analysis of the Ego* (1921). "In groups [*der Masse*]," Freud maintains, referring largely to crowds and mass psychology,[1] "there can evidently be no question of [directly] sexual aims. . . . We are concerned here with love instincts which have been diverted from their original aims, though they do not operate with less energy on that account" (103). According to Freud, group psychology could be explained by examining the influence of such diverted "love instincts" on individual consciousness. Sociability, in other words, might be viewed as an effect of various psychic displacements of homosexual desire. Modifying Gustave Le Bon's notion of the "racial unconscious" in *Psychologie des foules* (1895) and William McDougall's thoughts on crowd mentality in *The Group Mind* (1920), Freud also used his thesis on group psychology to sharpen his overall claims about metapsychology. *Group Psychology* anticipates his thoughts on the superego and intrapsychic violence in *The Ego and the Id* (1923).

By examining the role that Freud assigned to "love instincts" in groups and crowds, this essay addresses his problems in distinguishing the social orientation of the group from its "presocial" homosexual origins. Beyond merely elaborating this difficulty, however, I want to show why this argument still has heuristic value—why Freud's near-tautological claims in *Group Psychology* signal the emergence of a very interesting argument about sociality and the "emotional tie [*Gefühlsbindung*]" (103; *Massenpsychologie* 113). In Freud's text this tie is imbued with "sensuous" regard but also rendered inseparable from "feelings of aversion and hostility . . . , contempt, . . . [and] an almost insuperable repugnance" for neighbors, rivals, and strangers (101). Whether critics acknowledge this or not, a similar argument often recurs in contemporary debates about the community, the crowd, and the nation, as homosexuality for these entities tends to be socially foundational yet psychically inadmissible.

We have perhaps grown used to the critical argument that the expulsion of homosexuality is a precondition for the definition and coherence of many cultures (see *Group* 100). In *Homos,* however, Leo Bersani usefully extends this claim, arguing that contemporary tolerance for some homosexuals rests on an implicit demand that they be devoid of sexuality (4–5, 34). He finds this demand so ubiquitous—and conventional modes of reform so limited, owing to widespread hostility to desire—that he pushes conceptually for a "force" ("homoness") capable of generating "a massive redefining of relationality" (76). In *Group Psychology,* by contrast,

Freud stopped short of this wholesale undertaking, though his theory, as François Roustang explains, "aimed at dismantling some of the structures essential to the functioning of Western civilization" (17). (Roustang is referring to Freud's arguments against the Church and the army, which Freud expressed candidly: "Cruelty and intolerance towards those who do not belong to it are natural to every religion" [*Group* 98].) In a partial illustration of the reason these arguments persist, Bersani begins *Homos* by engaging with "Don't ask, don't tell, don't pursue," the U.S. compromise policy for coping with gays and lesbians in the military.

Clearly, *Group Psychology* is not as radical or extensive in its critique as *Homos*. Yet in describing—and sometimes solidifying—the perceptual emptying of desire from identification that Bersani turns into an all-out critique of sociality, *Group Psychology* remains provocative. Freud suggests that admiration for homosexuals and their achievements can persist alongside a powerful aversion to gay sex, an argument Bersani puts more stringently in "Is the Rectum a Grave?" (1987; see 198; and *Group* 91, 103). Against various forms of conventional wisdom, Freud also shows us that resistance to homosexual desire is neither incidental nor superficial, but structural. "In this way," he says, commenting generically on identification, "a wedge [is] driven in between a man's affectionate and sensuous feelings, one still firmly fixed in his erotic life to-day" (141). He deepens our understanding of homophobia, in other words, binding it not only to emotional attachments—our relation to leaders, beliefs, other countries, and so on—but also to our very notion of what it means to be human (see 102–3). To this extent, his account proleptically makes clear why, after several decades of feminism, poststructuralism, and civil rights movements, heterosexuality is still invoked today as men's and women's natural sexuality.

Group Psychology partly demonstrates this by insisting, as Mikkel Borch-Jacobsen puts it, that "homosexuality condense . . . within itself the most contradictory predicates" (*Freudian* 84). One of several outcomes of this argument, as we'll see, is that Freud designates homosexual sex as presocial, as a force capable of unbinding the myth that heterosexuality *is* natural and our only nonpathological expression of desire. This is just one illustration of the way *Group Psychology* anticipates Bersani's interest in "homoness" and queer theory's emphasis on same-sex structures and normative regulations of desire: "There is no doubt," writes Freud, "that the tie which unites each individual with Christ is also the cause of the tie which unites them with one another. The like holds good of an army" (*Group* 94). The reason homosexuality alone has this power in Freud's

1921 book is worth investigating, for it indicates how Freud intervened in existing social theory and established that a "malaise" besets modern society, the principal thesis of *Civilization and Its Discontents* (1929, revised 1930).

1. History and Psychobiography

As the introduction to this collection of essays stresses, Freud did not promulgate a single theory of homosexuality. Although in *An Autobiographical Study* (1924; 1925), he insists that "psycho-analysis enables us to point to some trace or other of a homosexual object-choice in everyone" (38), an argument building on the famous footnotes to *Three Essays on the Theory of Sexuality* (1905), he later declares that "[a] man's heterosexuality will not put up with any homosexuality, and *vice versa*" ("Analysis" 244). This last observation highlights the internal antagonism between ego and desire that affects every subject, regardless of sexual preference (the "ego," confirms Lacan, "is frustration in its essence" ["Function" 42]). Because Freud engages with drives rather than instincts, his account of sexuality preempts conventional biological arguments about desire and pleasure. By "free[ing] desire from heterosexuality," he raises a set of questions about the relationship—and nonrelationship—between sexuality and society (Dean 129).

My reading of the conceptual impasses of *Group Psychology* has significant precedents in the work of Jean Laplanche, Bersani, and Borch-Jacobsen. Following Laplanche, Bersani has argued that the category of the "nonsexual" beleaguered Freud's account of sublimation insofar as sublimation must be related—but not reducible—to sexuality. "In this form of sublimation," Bersani observes in *The Freudian Body* (1986), "we would have *a nonreferential version of sexualized thought*" (45; original emphasis). Freud stressed this psychic difference between sexual and nonsexual forms of satisfaction, arguing that whereas genital drives carry a stronger cathexis and thus a more intense "economic" discharge than sublimated drives, the latter are more amenable to creative use, though they consequently inhibit the subject's experience of sexual pleasure. In *Group Psychology*, Freud took this theory beyond aesthetics and implicated it in groups and crowds, maintaining that

> it is precisely those sexual impulsions that are inhibited in their aims which achieve such lasting ties between people. But this can easily be understood from

the fact that they are not capable of complete satisfaction, while sexual impulsions which are uninhibited in their aims suffer an extraordinary reduction through the discharge of energy every time the sexual aim is attained. (115)

In *The Culture of Redemption* (1990), Bersani observes that Freud failed to explain why the subject would substitute creative production for sexual release. Instead of amplifying this distinction between the "sexual" and the "nonsexual," Freud seems to displace it in "On Narcissism" (1914) and *The Ego and the Id* by associating sublimation respectively with narcissism and the formation of the ego-ideal (see also Gay 199–201). Describing this "upward" movement of psychic drives may have desexualized the concept of narcissism, but it did not resolve Freud's problems with the "nonsexual"; instead, his argument about the ego's self-transformation became increasingly tautological.

Borch-Jacobsen offers a related analysis of this problem in *The Freudian Subject* (1982), but he arrives at different conclusions. He argues that Freud's account of the subject's "subjectification" enabled psychoanalysis to repress its own conceptual origins. Instead of suggesting that Freud alighted on a profound hermeneutic dilemma affecting psychoanalysis *and* society, or that his dilemma might indicate that he was asking the right questions, Borch-Jacobsen argues that Freud became disingenuous at this moment. Having founded psychoanalysis on filial rivalry, Freud apparently naturalized this origin as an arche-history of modern civilization. He did so, Borch-Jacobsen contends, by inventing the myth of the primal horde, which solved at a stroke the enigma of the subject's prehistory, turning psychoanalysis into the primary reader of this and other myths (Oedipus and Narcissus). In this way, Freud apparently could separate psychoanalysis from related disciplines, such as psychology and anthropology, while distinguishing himself from potential rivals, such as Jean-Martin Charcot, Josef Breuer, Alfred Adler, Wilhelm Fliess, Carl Jung, Sándor Ferenczi, Otto Rank, and Karl Abraham, to say nothing of Le Bon and McDougall.

Championed by poststructuralists and anti-Freudians hoping to limit Freud's argument to a textual and biographical difficulty, Borch-Jacobsen's claim that Freud's theory of ontogenesis mimes the historical origins of psychoanalysis is theoretically misleading in substituting Freud (and subsequently Lacan) for the Primal Father.[2] Like François Roustang in *Dire Mastery* (1976), Borch-Jacobsen limits the full resonance of his arguments by tying the most prescient "discoveries" of psychoanalysis to disputes between its earliest practitioners, thereby construing the entire field of psychoanalytic knowledge as a replication of jealous conflicts among professional rivals. "That Freud describes his disciples as a savage horde can be related to what he says in *Totem and Taboo*," claims Roustang. "The sons kill each other in order to take the place of the father. We propose the following hypothesis: When creating his own myth, Freud simply looked around him" (16).

Although this interpretive move is popular today even among critics spurning psychobiography and the intentional fallacy, it is neither rigorous nor convincing to turn disputes over the inheritance, definition, and appropriation of psychoanalysis into explanations for aporias in the psychoanalytic theory of the subject. To see the obvious flaws of this argument, one need only imagine the response to suggestions that Marxism is best comprehended by revisiting the biographical details of its founder.[3] Much more interesting (if contentious) is Roustang's subsequent claim about *Group Psychology*, to which I alluded earlier: "It is as if Freud, who radically criticized the foundations of two societies typical to our culture [the Church and the army], was unable to find another model on which to base a society composed of supporters of a practice, a technique, and a theory aimed at dismantling some of the structures essential to the functioning of Western civilization" (17).

Strongly indebted to Roustang's argument and approach, Borch-Jacobsen's characterization of subjective and social relations compounds this palpable difficulty in Freud's work. Arguing that Freud could theorize group identification only by displacing intrapsychic conflict into social antagonism, Borch-Jacobsen claims that Freud defined the social in subjective terms, and thus falsely conflated both elements. Because Borch-Jacobsen ultimately connects everything to biographical details, he ends up suggesting that sexual difficulty in this model is best viewed as a sign of professional antagonism (see 19, 47, 59–61, 71, 74, 76–78). According to Borch-Jacobsen, Freud's psychoanalysis of the "social" is indistinguishable from psychology or anthropology, which ruins Freud's attempt in *Group Psychology* to represent psychoanalysis as a separate discipline responsive to the unconscious.

Owing, it seems, to sexual jealousy and disappointment over his disciple challenging his professional authority, Freud stressed the influence of sexual drives over Jung's psychology of the ego.[4] But the intellectual value of Freud's theory is irreducible to the circumstances that helped spawn it. One could as easily claim that Freud's theory of the unconscious proved conceptually incompatible with Adler's individual psychology or Jung's desexualized understanding of the libido and stress on symbols, archetypes, and even alchemy. After all, Jung was prepared to say:

I see the real value of the concept of libido not in its sexual definition, but in its energic view. . . . We were deceiving ourselves when we believed that we could make the *libido sexualis* the vehicle of an energic conception of psychic life. . . . Consequently the critics are right when they object that the libido theory purports to explain things which do not properly belong to its sphere. (119)

Freud's rejoinder is worth restating for its stress on psychosocial difficulty: "The truth is that these people [Adler and Jung] have picked out a few cultural overtones from the symphony of life and have once more failed to hear the mighty and powerful melody of the [drives]" ("On the History" 62).

By contrast, Borch-Jacobsen ends up arguing—as Jung came close to doing—that Freud's theory of group and mass cohesion was "much more rivalrous than sexual" (77). The implication of his reading is that if Freud had not been dogged by jealousy and unanalyzed homosexual desire for his friends and rivals, he would have theorized the social quite differently. Had he also not argued with Fliess and Jung, we infer, psychoanalysis might have become a theory of alchemy and selfhood!

Borch-Jacobsen's psychologistic approach is in one sense surprising, because his analysis of Freud's conceptual problems with male homosexuality is often remarkably astute, helping us see why Freud reproduced some of this theoretical insufficiency in "On Narcissism" and *The Ego and the Id*. As Laplanche, Bersani, and Borch-Jacobsen argue meticulously, Freud wanted a concept of group identification that would be influenced, but not distorted, by sexual interest. These critics demonstrate why male homosexuality seemed to alleviate Freud's dilemma, describing a useful "passage" between the subject and the group. Same-sex desire could anchor identification for the group and simultaneously deter the male subject from sexual interest in another male. To sustain homosexuality's paradoxical role, Freud proposed a sharp, if theoretically untenable, distinction between sexual and "socialized" libido. However, the distinction collapsed because "socialized libido" is psychically oxymoronic, and homosexual desire supports a libidinal charge that resonates long after fulfilling its function as a social "fixative." As Borch-Jacobsen puts it, "*Without* a common libidinal bond, no identification would be established, either among Oedipal 'brothers' or among members of the group. This has been a constant theme of our reading" (*Freudian* 204; original emphasis).

Borch-Jacobsen is right to note Freud's inconsistent account of the group's "sexual" origins. Yet his explanation for this inconsistency not only mischaracterizes Freud (and thus psychoanalysis), but also radically curtails the effects of Freud's theorizing *sociality.* Since this difficulty informs contemporary accounts of enmity, territorial rivalry, and the "sexual" composition of the group, Freud's argument has implications far beyond concerns internal to psychoanalysis, as Borch-Jacobsen shows when revisiting some of this material in *The Emotional Tie: Psychoanalysis, Mimesis, and Affect* (1992; see esp. 1–35).

The sexual cannot completely define the social, Freud helps us see, because it isn't equivalent or reducible to this entity. Freud couldn't accept the suggestion of equivalence because it would oversexualize competition among brothers of the horde and so "ruin" their identification with the Father. We recall the sentence from *Totem and Taboo* (1913), cited as my epigraph: "Sexual desires do not unite men but divide them" (144). As Borch-Jacobsen attests, Freud was keen to solve this impasse and restricted his definition of group motivation to "love instincts" (*Group* 91). Emphasizing the nonsexual mechanism of identification, he tried to uphold a shaky distinction between object relations that are sexual and object bonds that are not. This distinction hinges on the psychic difference between the *geliebte* and the *ungeliebte:* In the model of identification that *Group Psychology* advances, the ego discovers "a common quality shared with some other person who is not an object of the sexual instinct" (108). Thus the ego apparently takes as its model not the beloved (*geliebte*), but a person (or object) that isn't loved (*ungeliebte*). Accordingly, the "emotional tie" accompanying identification is inseparable from "a readiness for hatred, an aggressiveness, the source of which is unknown" (*Group* 102; see also Nancy 1–42).

The Freudian Subject quickly obscures this problem by deemphasizing the sexual properties of the group and crowd; Borch-Jacobsen redefines the problem in terms of *homosociality,* never the clearest concept at the best of times (*Freudian* 78). *Homosociality* is an oxymoron for psychoanalysis because the social is "homo" in the sense neither of unity nor of single sexuality, nor, ultimately, of one gender. If the phenomenon of homosexuality is always split, nonidentical, exceeding sameness, as Freud and others have argued, the social field cannot reproduce and maintain a consistency of which homosexuality itself is incapable. When critics suggest, by contrast, that this consistency is imaginary, and that social relations expose the repeated failure of this fantasy, they are probably more indebted to parts of *Group Psychology* than they realize. In repeating this argument about the homosocial, however, queer theory ultimately eclipses the dilemma Freud encountered in 1921, turning his interpretive difficulty into homosexual panic (his own, apparently, as well as his culture's), and so rendering Freud's profound inquiry into this subject in the 1910s and 1920s almost inherently normalizing. Like Eve Kosofsky Sedgwick—whose own work follows a trajectory closer to Jung's in moving from homosocial desire to homosexual panic, and then to shame and self-psychology—Borch-Jacobsen ultimately reduces Freud's intricate model of partial drives and fantasy to an argument shaped and modified by persons.

These simplifications help account for the inadequacy of the "either/or" model that Borch-Jacobsen finally proposes: The social must be exclusively "homosexual" in origin or it must be determined wholly by social rivalry. These options won't get us far enough. By representing identification as an act of mimesis (imaginary affiliation to the same sex) and homosexual sex as nothing more than a genital act, Borch-Jacobsen ignores the symbolic and real dimensions of identification, as well as the sexual composition of phobia and hatred that violently governs identification and desire. In Freud, the mnemonic form is always attached to a drive; and consequently any account that relies solely on a mimetic—that is, imaginary—model of identification will misrepresent his theory.

In distinguishing among psychoanalysis, social constructivism, and popular psychology, I am suggesting that Freud proposed, but never finally endorsed, a relation between the sexual and the social; this is what makes *Group Psychology* by turns frustrating and sophisticated. Although Borch-Jacobsen suggests that homosexuality represented for Freud an "instant translation of the egoistic into the erotic, of sociality into sexuality" (*Freudian* 75), Freud never simply "translated" the sexual into the social, or vice versa; he came closer to interpreting what would be at stake in their transposition, if the "translation" could successfully occur. Freud also questioned the imaginary and sexual supports on which identification relies, though he was alternately imprecise and overly schematic about the elements of which they consist.

2. Object Relations

Despite this gap between the aims and the necessary limitations of his argument, Freud put the category of homosexuality to work "because it opens the way to object orientation in general" (*Freudian* 81). Borch-Jacobsen derives this point from a developmental tendency in Freud's 1905 account of sexuality, in which homosexuality precedes narcissism as a recognition of genital similarity in a same-sex object. "Without that first narcissistic wound or break," writes Borch-Jacobsen, "no relation to the other as such could come about, nor—consequently—any social relations at all. On this account, homosexuality is an archisociality, or the primary 'social instinct'" (81). Yet Borch-Jacobsen correctly infers from Freud's account that "homosexuality can also become social in the strict or narrow sense of the term, when it is combined with the ego instincts. This is where it would seem to be distinguished from hetero-sexuality" (81).

This second proposition requires amplification: It stems from Freud's claim that the subject's identification with the group thwarts its homo-sexual drives, transforming them into "love instincts," whereas hetero-sexual drives define the conventional path of sexual development. As Freud put it schematically in his 1911 account of Senatspräsident Schreb-er's *Memoirs*, "the line of development" places homosexuality as a "half-way phase between auto-erotism and object-love" (61). Homosexuality precedes heterosexuality. But "after the stage of heterosexual object-choice has been reached," Freud continues,

> the homosexual tendencies are not, as might be supposed, done away with or brought to a stop; they are merely deflected from their sexual aim and applied to fresh uses. They now combine with portions of the ego-instincts and, as "attached" [*Angelehnte*] components, help to constitute the social instincts, thus contributing an erotic factor to friendship and comradeship, to *esprit de corps* and to the love of mankind in general. (61)

Freud's argument implies paradoxically that although homosexual de-sire founds the social and sexual body, the group's erotic composition is in fact *neither* social *nor* homosexual, but something else entirely. The paradox stems partly from Freud's early tendency—clearly visible here—to conceive of sexuality developmentally, establishing a chronology to which the subject seems to adhere in order to attain sexual maturity. In his later work, as we'll see, a more nuanced and ethically salutary model emerges that makes "an almost insuperable repugnance" integral to both social relations and subjectivity, without reducing the first entity to the second (*Group* 101). The observations in *Civilization and Its Discontents* that man is a wolf to man (*"Homo homini lupus"*) and that the "primary mutual hostility of human beings" is ineradicable from society surface alongside passages describing an internal "war" among different psychic registers. Crucial distinctions among these arguments (including Freud's remarks on the superego) finally break apart any possibility of internal symmetry (111–12). In *The Ego and the Id,* too, Freud insists that the super-ego is not a simple representative of external forces, such as law and culture (26, 54). Far from offering an "instant translation of the egoistic into the erotic, of sociality into sexuality," then, Freud in fact brings together two registers that, for important reasons, *cannot* be homologous (*Freudian* 75).

Freud's basic constituent of the social is less homosexuality as such than a modified form of *narcissism,* with all its attendant anxiety about the neighbor's *jouissance* (*Group* 102–3; Lacan, "Function" 42). He emphasizes the "social" properties of narcissism by arguing that narcissism represents a break between the subject's primary object and the object with which it identifies. As Borch-Jacobsen repeatedly notes, homosexuality never works for Freud as a conceptual path to the social body because the social requires an alterity that is shaped less by "desire" for the father than by the antagonism dividing and driving every subject, regardless of gender. When Lacan speaks of the superego as the "neurosis of self-punishment" governing the "'emancipated' man of modern society," he likewise insists that "this pitiful victim, this escaped, irresponsible outlaw, . . . is condemning modern man to the most formidable social hell" ("Aggressivity" 28–29).

Where Borch-Jacobsen is most astute, and Freud most troubled and incoherent, concerns the difference between identification and desire. Borch-Jacobsen shows effectively how Freud's reading of group identification first relies on—and then, for theoretical consistency, pronounces as incidental—the "sexual." If the homosexual drives central to Freud's account of group identification are "merely deflected," why are they invested with social possibility ("Psychoanalytic Notes" 61)? Throughout *Group Psychology,* Freud tries to distinguish between the "asocial" tendency of the heterosexual couple and the unifying "herd instinct" among social "brothers." But he doesn't simply reproduce the classical Hellenic model, in which, ideally, an older man's erotic and affectionate attachment to a younger man seems inseparable from his devotion to the polity. Freud adds to Plato's accounts of creativity, eros, philia, and social responsibility a distinction between sublimation and repression that accounts for the subject's converting "homosexual object-choice" into "*esprit de corps* and . . . the love of mankind in general" ("Psychoanalytic Notes" 61).[5] Defining his category of the "nonsexual," this second distinction is perhaps most important in Freud's argument. While sharpening the arguments about eros and self-division that appear in Plato's *Symposium,* Freud gives us a theory of phobia and hatred that complicates the Hellenic model, rendering disgust integral to any psychoanalytic theory of desire (see Bersani's and Dollimore's essays in this collection).

When addressing Freud's suggestion that homosexuality hinges on a distinction between sublimation and repression, Borch-Jacobsen comments usefully:

> The fact remains (and this is what makes the whole argument so strange) that something seems to predestine homosexuality in particular—and homosexuality alone—to social sublimation. Why? Because homosexuality is a little less sexual than heterosexuality, because it is *already* somewhat desexualized? Because, by opening up the relation to the other in general, it is already opening up the properly social relation to the other? Or is it because sublimation, conversely, would *always* bear upon homosexuality? (*Freudian* 82)

In Freud's model, I stress (and Borch-Jacobsen has already shown this), homosexuality in fact *doesn't* open "the relation to the other in general"; this relation is precipitated by a "cut" between the infant and its primary object—a cut that shapes all subsequent forms of alterity and alienation.

3. The Feminine Attitude

Hostility to the father is unavoidable for any boy who has the slightest claim to masculinity. FREUD AND BULLITT, *THOMAS WOODROW WILSON* 44

Although Borch-Jacobsen argues convincingly that Freud's argument in *Group Psychology* makes any rigorous distinction between "object-choice" and "object-bond" impossible to sustain, he leaves unexamined two related issues stemming from this difficulty, to which I must now turn: the psychic effects of the boy's identification and the significance attached to his "feminine attitude" toward the father.

Since Freud made the boy's identifications coeval with subject formation—and extrapolated from the boy's path a related, but asymmetrical, development for the girl—he designated the father as the boy's "ideal" before any question of oedipal rivalry or sexual difference could arise (*Group* 105). Although Lacan explained that the subject carries an imago of both parents, or significant substitutes, Freud was adamant that the subject's nonsexual imago is of its own sex only, and that this imago guides all subsequent development, later evolving into the boy's ego-ideal. The argument is bewildering because Freud not only seems to overlook the boy's primary attachment to the mother, but also gives the boy a proleptic knowledge of sexual difference before the Oedipus complex. He assumes, in effect, that the boy is *always already gendered.*[6] Although it permeates *Group Psychology,* this assumption is incommensurate with the very tenets of psychoanalysis, which hold that the subject's possible identifications are not fixed in "nature."[7] Psychoanalysis also refutes the notion of equivalent trajectories for the girl and boy, instead presupposing a gender-specific account that can't be inverted to "accommodate" an equivalent narrative for girls and women.

The second issue that Borch-Jacobsen barely mentions is the boy's "feminine attitude" toward his father. For reasons we'll see below, Freud, in chapter 7 of *Group Psychology,* represents the "negative" Oedipus complex as a fait accompli, as contributing only to male homosexuality; it doesn't sexualize father-son identification in any way. In fact, Freud stresses that the boy's preoedipal idealization of his father "has nothing to do with a passive or feminine attitude towards his father (and towards males in general); it is on the contrary typically masculine. It fits in very well with the Oedipus complex, for which it helps to prepare the way" (105). If this compatibility between "feminine attitude" and paternal regard were missing—or the paternal imago *governing* identification were less influential—the boy would adopt the psychic position of a girl.

One way Freud tried to *prevent* the "feminine attitude" from corrupting his account of masculine identification was by transforming the "feminine attitude" into male homosexuality *tout court,* arguing in *Leonardo da Vinci and a Memory of His Childhood* (1910) that "the boy represses his love for his mother: he puts himself in her place, identifies himself with her, and takes his own person as a model in whose likeness he chooses the new objects of his love. In this way he has become a homosexual" (100).

Neo-Freudians for many years were content to accept this summary as *the* psychoanalytic model of male homosexuality, prevailing over even Freud's extensive revisions to his argument.[8] Elsewhere in his oeuvre, however, Freud was more successful at curbing any predominance of the "feminine attitude." In "Dostoevsky and Parricide" (1928), for example, he considers the influence of the "feminine attitude" on the boy's disposition to bisexuality, arguing that

> under the threat to the boy's masculinity by castration, his inclination becomes strengthened to diverge in the direction of femininity, to put himself instead in his mother's place and take over her role as object of his father's love. But the fear of castration makes *this* solution impossible as well. The boy understands that he must also submit to castration if he wants to be loved by his

father as a woman. Thus both impulses, hatred of the father and being in love
with the father, undergo repression. (183–84; original emphasis)

By resolving all nonsexual desire for the father, the threat of castration
performs a crucial conceptual *and* psychic function in Freud's account of
masculine identification. I raise one caveat, however, to which Freud himself alluded: Repression does *not* in fact erase the "feminine attitude"; the
superego reproduces it in an altered form. As Freud explains in "Dostoevsky and Parricide," the ego learns to respond to the strictures of the superego "in a feminine way" (185)—that is, by submission and apology. The
ego's submission to the superego is thus not only an indication of femininity, but also implicit punishment for it. As the paternal influence is
incorporated by the ego, "every punishment is ultimately castration and,
as such, a fulfillment of the old passive attitude towards the father" (185).
Freud's previous explanation of the difference between repression and
inhibition is thus repeated (in "Dostoevsky and Parricide") in his claim
that the source of desire is finally the agent that represses it. This argument is frustratingly circular. Whatever desire for identification that the
father causes apparently must explain why the father is undesirable as
an object.

4. The Faltering Polity

The notion of impossibility disappears for the individual in a group. FREUD, *GROUP PSY-
CHOLOGY* 77

Although *Group Psychology* represents homosexuality tautologically, the
impasse it reaches concerning group and individual identification indicates where the sexual is untranslatable as the social, and vice versa. Homosexuality in Freud's account is neither "homo" nor simply "sexual";
and the interstitial realm ostensibly replacing both categories is a "sensuous" regard never wholly devoid of violence or phobic constraints. As
Freud put it bluntly in his and William Bullitt's "psychological study" of
Woodrow Wilson, written between 1928–32 and revised in 1938, "If man
had been nothing but aggressive activity and woman nothing but passivity, the human race would have ceased to exist long before the dawn of
history, since the men would have murdered one another to the last
man" (47). Phobia and hatred, Freud argues, are central to the psychic
development of the masculine subject and the social body, creating a de-

mand for the boy to be *like* his father, but not to like him too much. This precarious balance between homosexuality and homophobia produces a social body replete with eroticism on condition that homosexual desire be irreducible to a single object, and that the one who "misreads" this desire—the homosexual—be pathologized.

I am suggesting that Freud's limited engagement of the concept he defines—the boy's "feminine attitude"—points up its ongoing psychic and conceptual relevance. The "feminine attitude" later compelled Freud to theorize some "homo" influences on social relations that would distinguish the social body from the "regressive" status of *the* homosexual. This inquiry also forced him to disband the idea that sexuality is normative and developmental. By contrast, the developmental model of sexuality that returned after Freud's death in 1939 assumes that narcissism has no influence on heterosexuality, and that homosexuality, regressive but self-contained, has no alterity, since the "homo" here is designed to *protect* the "hetero" from its "anterior" sexual forms (see Warner; Dean in this volume).

But what remains of the social bond when the cohesive effect of homosexual desire is taken away, and when the unconscious is considered intrinsic to all theories of group identification? It seems to me ethical, rather than frivolous or dishonest, that Freud struggled with this question when defining "the nature of these ties which exist in groups," to the extent that the social body still partly relies on affective, fraternal relations. In his "Postscript," Freud writes: "There is scarcely any sense in asking whether the libido which keeps groups together is of a homosexual or of a heterosexual nature, for it is not differentiated according to the sexes" (141). This pansexual solution never appealed to him, however, in part because it entails an instant loss of the unconscious and its related difficulties. Indeed, Freud ultimately could *not* accept categorical distinctions between hetero- and homosexuality, and thus would not follow sexology in homosexualizing perversion. It is to his credit that he insisted that the social ultimately is neither homo nor hetero. Yet partly for this reason—for instance, in wishing to avoid a nebulous universality indifferent to homosexual desire—Freud would not give up positing the idea that some form of "homosexuality" influences group identity. Thus, he restates one paragraph later: "It seems certain that homosexual love is far more compatible with group ties, *even when* it takes the shape of uninhibited sexual impulses—a remarkable fact, the explanation of which might carry us far" (141; my emphasis).

This is indeed a remarkable *assertion,* and its acceptance might carry

us far! Since homosexual "love" is not the same as libido, these statements are not contradictory. Yet for conceptual reasons, Freud could not
accept the full implications of his proposition that the "libido" of the
group and crowd is "not differentiated according to the sexes." In its alternating use of the terms *libido, love object,* and *sensuous object-tie, Group
Psychology* precedes both Lacanian psychoanalysis and queer theory, insofar as Freud could maintain a binary opposition between neither the subject and the group, nor identification and desire. Freud's difficulty in fact
paved the way for Lacan's later stress on the irrelevance of object-choice
for psychic desire. As Lacan never tired of stressing, the question for psychoanalysis was not *what* is one's desire, but *where* it can be found: "This
is what Freud tells us," Lacan insists. "Let us look at what he says—*As far
as the object in the drive is concerned, let it be clear that it is, strictly speaking,
of no importance. It is a matter of total indifference*" (*Four* 168; original emphasis). Lacan also dramatically modifies Freud's account of enmity,
making clear that conventional interpretations of hostility as thwarted
homosexuality miss Freud's deeper assessment of this violence: "The aggressivity experienced by the subject at this point has nothing to do with
the animal aggressivity of frustrated desire. This assumption, which seems
to satisfy most people, actually masks another that is less agreeable for
each and every one of us: the aggressivity of the slave whose response to
the frustration of his labour is a desire for death" ("Function" 42).

The "sublimation" of homosexuality therefore seemed to resolve
Freud's problem, maintaining the illusion of a common culture around
the force of sexual disturbance. Yet as Freud would later admit, "We cannot for long enjoy the illusion that we have solved the riddle of the group
with this formula" (*Group* 117). Finally unable to divest the group of sexual conflict or eliminate its brothers' sexual interest in each other, Freud
insisted that they sacrifice an element of sexual pleasure for the purpose
of group definition. This is the predominant lesson critics take from
Freud's book, though as we've seen it is arguably the least compelling one.

Owing to homosexuality's haunting relation to group ties, Freud's inability to distinguish the social from the sexual was surely a productive
failure. Since it reveals the complexity of the subject's sexual difficulty
relative to its "community," *Group Psychology* demonstrates why humanity endlessly falls short of democracy. The book's uncomfortable lesson is
that no redemptive appeal to the "community" can afford to ignore the
"furious hatred" that manifests in groups and crowds (*Group* 78). Indeed,
although the fantasy that society consists of harmonious brethren is one
we inherit from religious, social, and political mythology, all of these entities, as Freud observes, exhibit "cruelt[ies] and intolerance[s]" of their

own (*Group* 98). His stress on the psychic violence governing norms helps us question an unrealistic, and paradoxically intolerant, appeal to "humanity"—the type of appeal that seems horrifically to sanction the murder of young men such as Matthew Shepard.

In a similarly bleak, if resolute, conclusion to his chapter on Freud's 1908 essay "Character and Anal Erotism," Bersani raises the following caution: "The potentially murderous atonements of order can repeat—literally, historically—the fantasmatic devastations they punish" (*Culture* 46). Eighty years after the publication of *Group Psychology and the Analysis of the Ego*, the fantasy that we have experienced the "caring '90s" now seems overwhelmed by the horror of recurring genocide and ethnic cleansing. For that reason, let us recall that *Group Psychology* voiced a similar warning against further "atonements of order" and the repetition of their "fantasmatic devastations." In the aftermath of the First World War, Freud voiced a haunting thesis that tried to explain why subjects, communities, and nations fight over respective interests. The thesis may have failed, but the rationale behind it remains striking. The petty tyranny of groups still heeds the death drive in inviting us to slide from esprit de corps to the abject devastation of the corpse.[9]

Notes

I thank audiences at the University of Sussex, the University of London, and SUNY-Buffalo for invaluable feedback on earlier versions of this essay. I am also grateful to Joan Copjec, Tim Dean, and Jason Friedman for additional comments and assistance.

1. Although in many instances Freud's *Massenpsychologie* would be better translated as "Mass" or "Crowd Psychology," I have decided to avoid confusion by adopting throughout this essay the *Standard Edition*'s translation, "Group Psychology." One reason for this is that I reproduce from *Civilization and Its Discontents* part of Freud's discussion of the neighbor, a noun that seems closer to our conception of the group than to our more impersonal conception of crowds. Second, although we refer in English to "group identification" and "group ties," it makes little sense to talk about "crowd identification" or "mass ties." The reader should bear in mind, though, that in many passages here, Freud explicitly addresses mass psychology, and thus the social as a psychic entity. Whenever relevant, I have tried to indicate this by writing "groups and crowds."

2. The critique that follows coincides largely with Melville's.

3. It is curious that those making this critique of psychoanalysis rarely extend it into more general accounts of the production and transmission of critical knowl-

edge. The historically fraught lineage of Marxism, for example, with its crises over the "inheritance" of Leninism, Trotskyism, and Stalinism, suggests that all knowledge and every discipline are beset by struggles over "correct" interpretation. That psychoanalysis theorizes the tension between the "legacy" and the "inheritance" of knowledge implies that the discipline Freud founded relies on the transmission of an indeterminate factor: the unconscious. As Felman, among others, has noted, the unconscious disturbs authoritative control over knowledge, while the mythical function of parricide undermines the logic of mastery by rewriting psychoanalysis as a fundamentally "ungovernable" discipline.

4. For readings attentive to the homoerotic dimensions of Freud's rivalry with Fliess, see Garner; Boyarin.

5. See *Group Psychology* 91 and Plato's *Symposium,* esp. 202E, 206C, 211C. I elaborate on Freud's differences with Plato in *Burdens,* esp. xvi–xvii, 168–69, 173.

6. In making a similar argument about the trajectory of masculine identity for the boy, Fletcher argues that "what is lacking in both these fantasies and the Freud-Fenichel analysis is either an erotic or theoretical recognition respectively of the place of the father. . . . What we might divine in the form taken by desire, an imaginary mother-child relation (whether son or daughter), is an active *refusal* to identify with and take up the place of the father" (112; original emphasis). For additional discussion of the boy's "feminine attitude," see Silverman 356–73.

7. Had Freud taken the girl as representative for this model, identification with the mother would have been indistinguishable from the girl's desire for her, and the girl's putative ideal would have been hopelessly confused with her primary object (see *Ego* 32). Freud, in fact, could not conceptualize the girl's establishing a maternal ideal *before* her attachment to the mother as an object.

8. These revisions appear in Freud's famous footnotes to *Three Essays on the Theory of Sexuality,* "Some Neurotic Mechanisms in Jealousy, Paranoia and Homosexuality" (1921), and "A Seventeenth-Century Demonological Neurosis" (1923). For psychoanalytic accounts that modify Freud's original account of male homosexuality, see Ferenczi; Greenson; de Oliveira; and Lagache.

9. I am referring in part to the notorious murders of Matthew Shepard and, somewhat earlier, of Allen Schindler by Terry Helvey and accomplice, Charles E. Vins, in Sasebo, Japan, on October 27, 1992. Schindler, an openly gay sailor, was so brutally assaulted by Helvey that his mother could identify him only by the tattoos on his arms. According to a report in *The Advocate,* "The Navy doctor testified that Helvey's blows had the effect of a crash in a low-speed plane or a high-speed car" (Schoofs 37). The U.S. Navy took over six weeks to concede that Schindler's murder was even related to homophobia.

References

Anderson, Perry. *In the Tracks of Historical Materialism.* London: Verso, 1983.
Bersani, Leo. *The Culture of Redemption.* Cambridge: Harvard UP, 1990.

———. *The Freudian Body: Psychoanalysis and Art*. New York: Columbia UP, 1986.

———. *Homos*. Cambridge: Harvard UP, 1995.

———. "Is the Rectum a Grave?" 1987. In *AIDS: Cultural Analysis/Cultural Activism*. Ed. Douglas Crimp. Cambridge: MIT P, 1988, 1993. 197–223.

Borch-Jacobsen, Mikkel. *The Emotional Tie: Psychoanalysis, Mimesis, and Affect*. 1991. Trans. Douglas Brick and others. Stanford: Stanford UP, 1992.

———. *The Freudian Subject*. 1982. Trans. Catherine Porter. Stanford: Stanford UP, 1988.

———. *Lacan: The Absolute Master*. Trans. Douglas Brick. Stanford: Stanford UP, 1990.

Boyarin, Daniel. "Freud's Baby, Fliess's Maybe: Homophobia, Anti-Semitism, and the Invention of Oedipus." *GLQ: A Journal of Lesbian and Gay Studies* 2.1–2 (1995): 115–47.

Dean, Tim. "On the Eve of a Queer Future." *Raritan* 15.1 (1995): 116–34.

de Oliveira, Prado. "La libération des hommes, ou la création de la pathogénèse." *Cahiers confrontation* 6 (1981): 187–95.

Felman, Shoshana. "To Open the Question." In *Literature and Psychoanalysis: The Question of Reading: Otherwise*. Ed. Felman. Baltimore: Johns Hopkins UP, 1982. 5–10.

Ferenczi, Sándor. "On the Part Played by Homosexuality in the Pathogenesis of Paranoia." 1912. *Sex in Psycho-Analysis: Contributions to Psycho-Analysis*. Boston: Gorham, 1916. 154–84.

Fletcher, John. "Freud and His Uses: Psychoanalysis and Gay Theory." In *Coming on Strong: Gay Politics and Culture*. Ed. Simon Shepherd and Mick Wallis. London: Unwin Hyman, 1989. 90–118.

Freud, Sigmund. "Analysis Terminable and Interminable." 1937. *Standard* 23: 209–53.

———. *An Autobiographical Study*. 1924, 1925. *Standard* 20:1–74.

———. *Beyond the Pleasure Principle*. 1920. *Standard* 18:1–64.

———. *Civilization and Its Discontents*. 1930 (1929). *Standard* 21:57–145.

———. "'Civilized' Sexual Morality and Modern Nervous Illness." 1908. *Standard* 9:181–204.

———. "Dostoevsky and Parricide." 1928. *Standard* 21:173–94.

———. *The Ego and the Id*. 1923. *Standard* 19:1–66.

———. *Group Psychology and the Analysis of the Ego*. 1921. *Standard* 18:65–144.

———. "On the History of the Psychoanalytic Movement." 1914. *Standard* 14: 1–66.

———. *Leonardo da Vinci and a Memory of His Childhood*. 1910. *Standard* 11:59–138.

———. *Massenpsychologie und Ich-Analyse*. 1921. *Gesammelte Werke*. Unter Mitwirkung von Marie Bonaparte. 18 vols. Frankfurt am Main: Fischer Verlag, 1940–68. 13:71–161.

———. "On Narcissism: An Introduction." 1914. *Standard* 14:67–104.

———. "Psychoanalytic Notes on an Autobiographical Account of a Case of Paranoia (Dementia Paranoides)." 1911. *Standard* 12:1–82.

———. "A Seventeenth-Century Demonological Neurosis." 1923 (1922). *Standard* 19:67–108.

———. "Some Neurotic Mechanisms in Jealousy, Paranoia and Homosexuality." 1922 (1921). *Standard* 18:221–34.

———. *The Standard Edition of the Complete Psychological Works of Sigmund Freud.* Ed. and trans. James Strachey. 24 vols. London: Hogarth, 1953–74.

———. *Three Essays on the Theory of Sexuality.* 1905. *Standard* 7:123–243.

———. *Totem and Taboo.* 1913 (1912–13). *Standard* 13:1–161.

Freud, Sigmund, with William C. Bullitt. *Thomas Woodrow Wilson, Twenty-Eighth President of the United States: A Psychological Study.* 1928–32, revised 1938. Boston: Houghton Mifflin, 1967.

Garner, Shirley Nelson. "Freud and Fliess: Homophobia and Seduction." In *Seduction and Theory: Readings of Gender, Representation, and Rhetoric.* Ed. Dianne Hunter. Urbana: U of Illinois P, 1989. 86–109.

Gay, Volney. *Freud on Sublimation: Reconsiderations.* Albany: SUNY P, 1992.

Greenson, Ralph R. "Dis-Identifying from the Mother—Its Special Importance for the Boy." *International Journal of Psychoanalysis* 49 (1968): 370–74.

Jung, C. G. *The Theory of Psychoanalysis.* 1913. *Freud and Psychoanalysis.* Trans. R. F. C. Hull. Bollingen Series XX. Princeton: Princeton UP, 1961, 1985. 83–226.

Lacan, Jacques. "Aggressivity in Psychoanalysis." 1948. *Écrits* 8–29.

———. *Écrits: A Selection.* Trans. Alan Sheridan. New York: Norton, 1977.

———. *The Four Fundamental Concepts of Psycho-Analysis.* 1973. Ed. Jacques-Alain Miller. Trans. Alan Sheridan. New York: Norton, 1978.

———. "The Function and Field of Speech and Language in Psychoanalysis." 1953. *Écrits* 30–113.

Lagache, Daniel. "Contribution à l'étude des idées d'infidelité homosexuelle dans la jalousie." *Revue française de psychanalyse* 10 (1938): 709–19.

Lane, Christopher. *The Burdens of Intimacy: Psychoanalysis and Victorian Masculinity.* Chicago: U of Chicago P, 1999.

Laplanche, Jean. "To Situate Sublimation." Trans. Richard Miller. *October* 28 (1984): 7–26.

Le Bon, Gustave. *Psychologie des foules.* 1895. Paris: F. Alcan, 1913.

McDougall, William. *The Group Mind: A Sketch of the Principles of Collective Psychology, with Some Attempt to Apply Them to the Interpretation of National Life and Character.* New York: G. P. Putnam's, 1920.

Melville, Stephen. "On Mood, Time, and *The Freudian Subject.*" *Oxford Literary Review* 12.1–2 (1990): 215–25.

Nancy, Jean-Luc. *The Inoperative Community.* 1986. Ed. Peter Connor. Trans. Connor, Lisa Garbus, Michael Holland, and Simona Sawhney. Minneapolis: U of Minnesota P, 1991.

Plato. *Lysis, Symposium, Gorgias.* Trans. W. R. M. Lamb. Cambridge: Harvard UP/ Loeb Classical Library, 1925, 1991.

Roustang, François. *Dire Mastery: Discipleship from Freud to Lacan.* 1976. Trans. Ned Lukacher. Baltimore: Johns Hopkins UP, 1982.

Sedgwick, Eve Kosofsky. *Between Men: English Literature and Male Homosocial Desire.* New York: Columbia UP, 1985.

Schoofs, Mark. "Life after Death." *The Advocate* 633 (July 13, 1993): 32–38.

Silverman, Kaja. *Male Subjectivity at the Margins.* New York: Routledge, 1992.

Warner, Michael. "Homo-Narcissism; or, Heterosexuality." In *Engendering Men: The Question of Male Feminist Criticism.* Ed. Joseph A. Boone and Michael Cadden. New York: Routledge, 1990. 190–206.

9

LOVING CIVILIZATION'S
DISCONTENTS

Reich and *Jouissance*

Jason B. Jones

. . . .

Somewhere my political-psychological theory has an enormous loophole where all the facts
I try to gather slip through my fingers. The more I attempt to cling to the idea of human
decency, the more man behaves in an indecent, unintelligent, stupid fashion. WILHELM
REICH, *BEYOND PSYCHOLOGY* 249

During his lifetime, Wilhelm Reich's work brought him extraordinary ha-
rassment, even persecution. Excluded from both the International Psychoanalytic Association (IPA) and the Communist Party, he was hounded
from four countries and then, after finally settling in the United States,
arrested on contempt of court charges. Within months of his arrest, the
U.S. Food and Drug Administration burned all of his books and equip-
ment in a grotesque power ploy. Despite this hostility from his contemporaries, however, Reich's work still resonates today. For example, his *Mass
Psychology of Fascism* (*Die Massenpsychologie des Faschismus* [1933]) is
widely influential in political and cultural theory, and his *Character Analysis* (1933) continues to be a standard text in psychoanalytic training in-
stitutes. Perhaps counterintuitively, Reich's work persists because it tells
us what we want to hear: Deep down, Reich says, we are fundamentally
good, and although society has corrupted us, the corruption can be reversed, restoring us to our biologically ordained sexual happiness.

My wager is that Reich's self-diagnosis, reproduced in my epigraph, is correct: His theory *does* have an "enormous loophole," because he refuses to account for *jouissance* and other internal obstacles to the subject's well-being.[1] His emphatic claim that humans are essentially "decent" cannot incorporate the psychoanalytic argument that they are constitutively split, with desires running counter to their own good that are irreducible to social interpellation. By tracing and interpreting Reich's representation of homosexuality in *Mass Psychology,* his major political work, I hope to sketch the consequences of this exclusion: The *jouissance* that Reich excludes from his theory returns apocalyptically in his rhetoric. Because Reich's theory hangs on the assumption of human decency, he eventually constructs an eschatological perspective to explain the genocide and other geopolitical atrocities of the 1940s and 1950s.

1. Reichian Self-Diagnosis

Although the goal of this essay is to not rehearse Reich's rise and fall, I would like to sketch some pertinent facts.[2] In the 1920s Freud and those close to him considered Reich to be among the most brilliant analysts of the younger generation.[3] In 1922 Reich founded the Seminar on Psychoanalytic Therapy in Freud's Vienna institute, which he also directed from 1924–30. He quickly emerged as a leader of the politically radical analysts, and Otto Fenichel and Erich Fromm each saw Reich as the first theorist to yoke Freud and Marx in a systematic critique of society's sex-economic conditions. At least since 1926, though, when Reich gave Freud a copy of *Die Funktion des Orgasmus*[4]—a book dedicated to Freud—problems began to emerge. Freud treated Reich with increasing coldness, and Reich, in turn, began to attack Freud's cultural arguments, especially those advanced in *Civilization and Its Discontents* (1929, revised 1930). Thus, when Reich published *Character Analysis* and *Mass Psychology* in 1933, his imminent expulsion from the IPA was not especially surprising. As Reich acknowledged in 1934, the split had been long coming:

> The gap between two irreconcilable tendencies, which I discovered some eight years ago and which has in the meantime become unbridgeable, does indeed exist, and . . . my exclusion means simply that one of these tendencies is responsible for the field of psychoanalysis. You will already have guessed that I am referring here to the gap between the representatives of the death instinct theory and the theoreticians of the libido theory. (*Beyond* 3)

However, the theory of the death instinct was not his only source of trouble. The communists deemed his work on fascism reactionary, and therefore excluded him from the Communist Party. His first wife, Annie, left him, taking their children with her. And when the Nazis took power in Germany, Reich had to flee first to Denmark, then Sweden, and finally to Norway, where he worked for five years before moving permanently to the United States.[5]

Despite the turmoil Reich experienced during these years, his two major publications, *Character Analysis* and *Mass Psychology,* remain influential (see Jacoby 79; Cohen 24, 26). Reich's theory of fascism depends entirely on his model of the psyche—he opens *Mass Psychology* with an explanation of his tripartite model of the mind and insists repeatedly that "'fascism' is only the organized political expression of the structure of the average man's character" (xiii). For this reason, I must first lay out his models of the psyche and of repression to make clear how he derives the structure of fascism from psychic organization.

The commonplace today that fascism is a social-sexual phenomenon stems largely from Reich's original insistence in the 1930s. According to *Mass Psychology,* socioeconomic conditions shape the psyche, which responds in turn with a desire for fascism. Reich bases this argument on the essentially good *nature* of humanity, and in doing so he redescribes the psyche. Whereas for Freud mental life must be either conscious or unconscious, Reich divides psychic life among three dimensions: the surface layer ("personality"), the middle layer ("the repressed"), and the innermost layer ("the deep biologic core"):

> On the surface layer of his personality the average man is reserved, polite, compassionate, responsible, conscientious. There would be no social tragedy of the human animal if this surface layer of the personality were in direct contact with the deep natural core. This, unfortunately, is not the case. The surface layer of social cooperation is not in contact with the deep biologic core of one's selfhood; it is borne by a *second,* an intermediate character layer, which consists exclusively of cruel, sadistic, lascivious, rapacious, and envious impulses. It represents the Freudian "unconscious" or "what is repressed"; to put it in the language of sex-economy, it represents the sum total of all so-called "secondary drives." . . . [T]he Freudian unconscious, that which is antisocial in man, [is] a secondary result of the repression of primary biologic urges. If one penetrates through this destructive second layer, deeper into the biologic substratum of the human animal, one always discovers the third, deepest layer, which we call the *biologic core.* In this core, under favorable social conditions, man is an essentially honest, industrious, cooperative, loving, and, if motivated, rationally hating animal. (xi; original emphases)

One consequence of Reich's argument is that it renders psychic conflict an effect of external conditions. The "biologic core" is a utopian vision of humankind as self-harmonious; repression, a sign of psychic conflict, comes from outside (I elaborate later on this point). From the start of his argument, then, Reich claims that it is possible to conceive of a subject without internal difficulty. He is trying to evacuate *jouissance* and the death drive from the psyche; the goal of analysis apparently is to reach the biologic core. And in order to reach this core, analysis must "penetrate through the destructive second layer." As we'll see, this conceptual move has apocalyptic implications. For Reich, unlike for Freud, there is a cure for subjectivity. The third layer seems to have been added simply to retain a faith in human goodness. It signals a break from Freud, whose perspective on humanity was somewhat more jaundiced—or reasonable, depending on one's perspective. For example, in *Civilization and Its Discontents*, a key text illustrating Reich's break with Freud, the latter famously announces, *"Homo homini lupus"*: Man is a wolf to man (111; see Rycroft 19–20 and Robinson 31–36).

Reich views the three layers of the psyche as sedimentary: Society represses the biologic core, so producing the middle layer; and the third layer is required to make humans tolerate each other.[6] But this definition of the biologic core is puzzling: Reich claims that "under favorable social conditions" man is good. While insisting on a tripartite structure, Reich never explains how the biologic core remains unaffected by the millennia of repression it has endured. If the core were truly biological, for example, it would surely be subject to evolutionary pressures, creating a more perfect fit between life and its environment. Perhaps more difficult to understand is the reason the second layer intervenes. If the inner and outer layers are both good and essentially conflict-free, why does repression take place? Unlike Freud, Reich does not claim that society is impossible without repression—in fact, he repeatedly pointed to Bronislaw Malinowski's analysis of the Trobriand islanders as a society with a self-regulated sex-economy ("Imposition" 104–61). This raises a new question: How could "unfavorable social conditions" arise if man is *by nature* "honest, industrious, [and] cooperative" (see Mitchell 137–93)? Reich's argument is tautological here; without repression, humanity lives in Eden, yet repression is possible only under dystopic conditions. Finally, as sexuality apparently is not complicated in the biologic core, complete satisfaction of the "primary biologic urges" seems possible. Reich attaches such importance to this idea that, in *Character Analysis*, he tells us that when an "individual is capable of reacting biologically," he or she has a "genital character," whose "genital libido . . . [is] gratified directly" (364,

167). Indeed, the "term 'genital character' is justified by the fact that only genital primacy and orgastic potency . . . guarantee an orderly libidinal economy" (165).[7]

More relevant for us here, Reich declares that the third layer is—almost by definition—heterosexual, because he insists on opposing "natural" heterosexuality to "secondary" homosexuality. The way to reach reactionary adolescents, he claims, is "to pit the natural genital demands against the secondary (homosexual) and mystical drives" (*Mass* 163–64). Reich even attributes to heterosexual intercourse an ability to satisfy homosexual desires: "An existing homosexual tendency . . . will have little significance if at the same time heterosexuality is satisfied" (*Character* 168). In short, repression makes people perverse, antisocial, and homosexual. I shall argue that Reich's faith in the heterosexuality of the biologic core is a consequence of his attempt to exclude *jouissance* from his theory of the subject. Because the biological core of humanity is harmonious, industrious, and cooperative, Reich must first explain the self-imposed "problems" of perversion and fascism, and he does so by making them tautological, eclipsing political factors.

2. Repression and Fascism

As Reich makes repression entirely an external phenomenon, it supports the interest of those in power. Thus Foucault was correct in calling his model of sexuality a "repressive hypothesis" (131, 3–7; see Lane, *Burdens* 1–43, and "Experience"). As Reich declares:

> If one studies the history of sexual suppression and the etiology of sexual repression, one finds that it cannot be traced back to the beginnings of cultural development; suppression and repression, in other words, are not the presuppositions of cultural development. It was not until relatively late, with the establishment of an authoritarian patriarchy and the beginning of the divisions of the classes, that the suppression of sexuality begins to make its appearance. (*Mass* 29)

Thus, culture demands that repression "serve the purposes of the ruling powers . . . precisely" (54). We are meant to hear a rebuke of Freud here: In an interview in the 1950s, Reich claims that "*Civilization and Its Discontents* was written specifically in response to one of my lectures in Freud's home. I was the one who was '*unbehaglich in der Kultur*' ['dis-eased in civilization']" (Higgins and Raphael, *Reich Speaks* 44).[8]

Because of his tautological approach, however, Reich could never make clear how repression obtains. Despite claiming that "the psychic structures of the supporting strata of a society are so constructed that they fit the economic framework and serve the purposes of the ruling powers as precisely as the parts of a precision machine," he nonetheless admits that this "fit . . . will long remain an unsolved riddle" (*Mass* 54). Society's power structures reproduce themselves faultlessly in each individual's psyche. Since Reich insists that sexuality is benign, he cannot make it the grounds for resistance. Although Reich writes at length about "orgastic potency" and "genital character," sexuality in his model turns out to be politically useless, defeated at every turn by society's precise repressions. Freud, however, recognized that sexuality does not simply drive the subject toward its good. In "On the Universal Tendency to Debasement in the Sphere of Love" (1912), Freud asks us to "reckon with the possibility that something in the nature of the sexual instinct itself is unfavourable to the realization of complete satisfaction" (188–89). Freud indicates here that the subject is stymied by intractable internal elements, and that this resistance is irreducible to social causes. Already in 1912, he is voicing arguments about the death drive.[9] While believing that psychic conflict comes partly from outside, Freud reserves a significant remainder for internal factors.

Despite his inability to determine its origin or the means of its efficacy, Reich was certain that repression creates a fear of sexuality. Because he identifies sexuality primarily with the life-force, he considers sexuality conducive to the subject's submission to authoritarianism:

> The moral inhibition of the child's natural sexuality . . . makes the child afraid, shy, fearful of authority, obedient, "good," and "docile" in the authoritarian sense of the words. It has a crippling effect on man's rebellious forces because every vital life-impulse is now burdened with severe fear; and since sex is a forbidden subject, thought in general and man's critical faculty also become inhibited. (*Mass* 30)

The subject therefore recoils not only from those in authority, but also from the lifting of repression: The subject fears the force of "dammed up sexual excitation" (xxix). Although this latter fear is fascinating and resembles Freud's perspective on the repugnance intrinsic to sexuality, Reich insists that this anxiety stems from external causes.[10] Although Reich writes passionately about the "inhibition" and "repression" facing the subject's sexuality, he leaves himself considerable leeway. He claims, too, that apparently healthy displays of sexuality are evidence for his model:

> The authoritarian familial tie presupposes the inhibition of sensuous sexuality. Without exception, all children brought up in a patriarchal society are subject to this sensuous inhibition. No sexual activity, no matter how showy and "free" it appears to be, can delude the expert as to this deeply rooted inhibition. In fact, it is precisely this *inhibition* of the capacity for orgastic experience that lies at the bases of many pathological manifestations that occur later in sexual life, such as indiscriminate choice of partners, sexual restlessness, proclivity to pathological extravagances, etc. (136; original emphasis)

Central to Reich's argument is the idea of "sensuous sexuality," which he associates with humanity's "primary urges." Sensuous sexuality, however, can mean only heterosexuality since, as we've seen, the biologic core is naturally heterosexual, and "perversions" are effects of repression. Although heterosexuality as such is not inherently revolutionary, Reich believes that heterosexual intercourse between persons with "genital characters" is. The "revolutionary negates perverse and pathological pleasure," he writes, "because it is not *his* pleasure, is not the sexuality of the *future*, but *the pleasure born of the contradiction between morality and instinct;* it is the pleasure of a dictatorial society, *debased, sordid, pathological pleasure*" (141; original emphases). If the ideal of orgastically potent heterosexual intercourse is revolutionary, sexuality in the current regime is not. In fact, in the authoritarian state (and Reich is nebulous about what this is, referring generally to Western civilization), authentic heterosexuality may not even exist. Reich claims that the repression of childhood sexuality produces passivity and homosexuality. In other words, as a result of repression,

> a youth's sexual drive develops in a passive homosexual direction. In terms of the drive's energy, passive homosexuality is the most effective counterpart of natural masculine sexuality, for it replaces activity and aggression by passivity and masochistic attitudes, that is to say, by precisely those attitudes that determine the mass basis of patriarchal authoritarian mysticism in the human structure. (163)

This bizarre claim clashes with Reich's model of the psyche: Although the biologic core was supposed to be harmonious and cooperative, Reich characterizes "natural masculine sexuality" as "aggressive," while also falsely linking homosexuality with masochism and passivity.[11] Within the conceptual economy of Reich's model, the repression of children's sexuality apparently forces their drives into "passive homosexuality," making sexuality under fascism passive, masochistic, and homosexual. As we saw earlier, Reich considers "perverse" sexuality to be "the pleasure of a dictatorial society." That is, Reich is arguing that elites repress "natural" sexuality in order to bind the masses libidinally to a system that oppresses them.

We are thus in a position to unravel Reich's tautological claims about fascism. Mankind, he has told us, is essentially good and loving, but repression produces a society of sex-fearing individuals who display passive, masochistic, homosexual behavior. And this psychical model apparently is the key to understanding politics: "The various political and ideological groupings of human society correspond to the various layers of the structure of the human character" (xii). So fascism, at least here, is the political counterpart to the psyche's second layer: "'Fascism' is only the organized political expression of the structure of the average man's character. . . *'fascism' is the basic emotional attitude of the suppressed man of our authoritarian machine civilization and its mechanistic-mystical conception of life"* (xii; original emphasis).

According to this passage, we are all potentially fascist. Yet Reich's assertion is possible only because his model is conceptually impoverished: It cannot clarify differences among actually existing political systems, and so fails to explain how some nations remain democratic, others fascist, and so on. Second, because Reich's argument is an effect of his topography of the mind and theory of repression, it begs the question how fascism comes into being: In order for fascism to gain power, either primary repression must exist (which Reich explicitly denies), or humanity's innermost core must not be completely wholesome. He disavows this, too.

3. Homo-Fascism

Reich insists that homosexuality subtends fascism. The mechanistic-mystical ideology of fascist society apparently "draws its power from the suppression of genital sexuality, which, on a secondary level, entails a regression along the line of passive and masochistic homosexuality" (163). The fascist state is thus viewed as a community of masochistic homosexuals governed by sadistic ones. Reich does not claim merely that the masses develop a passive homosexual structure, causing them to crave authoritarianism. He goes much further, asserting that the authoritarian elites are themselves homosexual:

The sexual structure of the fascists, who affirm the most severe form of patriarchy and actually reactivate the sexual life of the Platonic era in their familial
mode of living—i.e., "purity" in ideology, disintegration and pathology in actual practice—must bear a resemblance to the sexual conditions of the Platonic
era. Rosenberg and Blüher recognize the state solely as a male state organized
on a homosexual basis. (93)

Reich is entirely categorical about this, claiming erroneously that the
"male supremacy of the Platonic era [was] entirely homosexual," and,
later, that the "same principle governs the fascist ideology of the male
strata of leaders" (91, 91 n. 8). Moreover, Reich comes very close to making fascism an effect of homosexual enjoyment, a clearly ridiculous claim:
"The shifting of power and of wealth from the democratic gens to the
authoritarian family of the chief was mainly implemented with the help
of the suppression of the sexual strivings of the people" (90). We have
just seen that suppressing the sexual striving of the people "produces"
homosexuality—and that is apparently caused by homosexuals. Not only
does Reich thus claim that homosexuals cause sexual misery, but he also
asserts outrageously that they cause *economic* oppression as well. Genitally satisfied heterosexuals, Reich quixotically insists, once lived in a system called "work-democracy," which he claims actually existed and was
founded on "love, work, and knowledge, and is developed organically"
(xxxi). The patriarchal, authoritarian system, Reich avers, was created to
hoard dowry money within individual families. So, by repressing the
"natural" heterosexuality of "the people," homosexuals (who in this account are also those in power) transfer to themselves enormous amounts
of psychic energy and wealth. In addition to noting the complete absence
of historical evidence for this set of claims, we note at least two fatal
errors in Reich's logic: He cannot explain why members of the "natural
work-democracy" (90), comprised of genitally satisfied heterosexual persons, would either start to hoard money or manifest perverse desires. This
difficulty about cause is rooted fundamentally in Reich's hydraulic model
of the psyche. By refusing to recognize the subject's *jouissance*, Reich
forces himself continually to contort history and logic in order to account
for the fact that humans can't get along.

Reich claimed that he could cure fascism and, implicitly, homosexuality. By teaching people to overcome their fear of sexuality, he believed
that he could free up their orgastic potential and help them resist the
state. For adults, this meant a combination of physical massage and an
attempt to reconcile the ego and the sexual instinct. Successful character

analysis would entail making the analysand lose "the childhood fear of masturbation[,] and as a result thereof genitality demands gratification, then intellectual insight and sexual gratification are wont to prevail" (181). We see here how sexual gratification apparently culminates in and sustains psychic harmony in general. If lifting repression gives patients access to the deep biologic core, abating repression on a mass scale apparently facilitates the reunion of man and nature: "Originally and naturally, sexual pleasure was the good, the beautiful, the happy, that which united man with nature in general" (148). Reich insists that *"the abolition of this 'morality' . . . is the precondition of the abolition of immorality, which it seeks to eliminate in vain"* (183; original emphasis). Reich does not ask us here to rethink immorality; he offers his sex-economic work as a more effective means of *abolishing* immorality. All homosexuality and all fascism, he implies, obtain from repression on society's behalf. If analysis could undo the effects of repression, society apparently would rid itself of both fascism *and* homosexuality.

Reich's homophobic and potentially genocidal account of fascism permits us to qualify one of the critiques that Andrew Hewitt levels at psychoanalysis in *Political Inversions: Homosexuality, Fascism, and the Modernist Imaginary* (1996). Hewitt coins the term *homo-fascism* to undermine the alarming commonplace of positing homosexuals *as* fascist. In such theories, as he justly points out, homosexuals—clearly the victims of fascism—are converted into its cause. In Hewitt's valuable study, homo-fascism therefore does not refer to individuals who are homosexual and fascist; he reserves the term for those who locate the source of fascism in homosexuality and who identify both as problems needing eradication. This can take many forms, ranging from a contributor's claiming in *Salmagundi* in 1982–83 that "the [Sturmabteilung] . . . was among other things, a cult of decadent homosexual toughs" (qtd. in Hewitt 4), to the subtle victim-blaming involved in the pop-psychological position that "the fascist fears homosexuality because he somehow 'is'—or fears he will become, or reveal himself to have always already been—homosexual" (11). Perhaps most alarming is the fact that the disturbing prevalence of this idea warrants its own label.[12]

Hewitt also attributes homo-fascism to post-Freudian psychoanalysis. He claims quite startlingly that in the "postwar theoretical discussion of homosexuality and fascism, psychoanalysis has permitted a return to ideological distortions [that is, homo-fascism] that Klaus Mann already discredited in the earliest years of Nazism" (6). In particular, Hewitt faults the "reworking of Freud at the hands of Wilhelm Reich and the members of the Frankfurt School" for sustaining this perspective on homosexuality (9). Because Reich and the Frankfurt School tried to meld Freud and Marx, naming only Freud in this formula could suggest that these theorists' encounter with Freud somehow tainted otherwise theoretically pure Marxists. As I've shown, however, at least Reich explicitly broke from Freud in order to advance his theory of fascism. And Hewitt repeatedly acknowledges the role of the Left and of popular opinion in shaping homo-fascism, claiming, for instance, that "far from being an abstraction in leftist ideology, the conflation of homosexuality and fascism seems to have marked an opportunistic capitulation of theory in the face of popular sentiment" (9). While he therefore does not exclusively blame psychoanalysis—nor indeed blame all of it—his pronouncements such as "psychoanalysis has permitted a return to ideological distortions," cited above, have considerable rhetorical impact, and probably should be more inflected with qualifiers such as "American," "'psychoanalysis,'" and "Freudo-Marxist." Moreover, Hewitt is not the only critic to charge psychoanalysis with reactionary tendencies, especially in its theorization of fascism.

Klaus Theweleit's two-volume *Male Fantasies—Volume 1: Women, Floods, Bodies, History* (1977; trans. 1987) and *Volume 2: Male Bodies: Psychoanalyzing the White Terror* (1978; trans. 1989)—sets a new standard for theoretical descriptions of the fascist imaginary. His work draws on a rich collection of material from diaries and novels written by or about the Freikorps—private, authoritarian armies flourishing in Germany after World War I. What is especially interesting in this context is Theweleit's engagement with Reich, which partially determines his approach to homosexuality. Theweleit's general perspective on Reich is that he ruined his own thought by sticking to Freudian terminology: "Wilhelm Reich's psychoanalytic terminology was basically outmoded or, more specifically, always off-target because of its internal inconsistence. The inconsistency stems from the fact that, in many respects, Reich had ventured for [sic] from Freud in his conception of human psychic processes" (*Male* 1:223). For example, Theweleit inaccurately claims that "Reich attacked only the 'death drive,' while appropriating the Freudian 'ego' concept in its entirety for his character analysis" (223). Theweleit admires Reich—at least initially—for his attempt to avoid what he calls the biologism of Freud's death drive. Yet he, too, ultimately faults Reich for focusing too narrowly on external causes: "The force of human desiring-production, in whatever form—whether as a force for life or for destruction—always necessarily represents a force that produces not only the organization of industrial production, but every other form of social existence" (*Male* 2:417). According to Theweleit (following Deleuze and Guattari), Reich fails in the "insertion of desire into the economic infrastructure itself" (*Anti-Oedipus* 118). Although I agree with Theweleit—as well as with Deleuze and Guattari—about Reich's overemphasis of external factors, I think they each fundamentally ignore the question of *jouissance,* leaving unexamined what we do with desires that work against the subject's well-being (see Žižek, *Ticklish* 250–51).

In *Male Fantasies, Volume 1,* Theweleit dismisses the value of the term *homosexuality* in discussions of fascism. He asserts that the concept's psychoanalytic use "sets in motion a series of prejudices, false ideas, and personal-defense mechanisms, to reach the strained-but-safe conclusion that homosexuals are always first and foremost the *others"* (1:55; original emphasis). In volume 2 he continues this critique of received notions of homosexuality by noting that it "is not a problem for doctors; it is a political problem that touches every one of us. Any theoretical attempt to divorce homosexuality either from masculinity or from the fate of sexuality in general has to be seen as contributing to the maintenance of a *status quo* in which *specific* forms of homosexual practice are denounced and pathologized" (2:336; original emphases).[13] Yet while Theweleit is rightly skeptical of certain moments in Freudian thought that specify developmental models of homosexuality, he downplays his own similarity to Freud. For example, Freud argues in *Three Essays on the Theory of Sexuality* (1905) that "psycho-analytic research is most decidedly opposed to any attempt at separating off homosexuals from the rest of mankind as a group of a special character" (145n). In other words, far from treating homosexuals as "others," Freudian psychoanalysis makes the far more radical claim that it may be impossible to distinguish homosexuality from heterosexuality in psychic terms. Freud often gives us an important, anti-heterosexist vocabulary of fantasy and desire (see Lane, *Burdens* 1–43, 224–45; Dean, "Psychoanalysis," "Eve," and *Beyond*). To avoid the homo-fascist fallacy, then, we must first eschew the temptation to identify homosexuality as a psychically discrete entity that can be extracted from "normal" masculinity, femininity, or heterosexuality without profoundly coercive implications (see Freud, *Three* 145n).

4. A Politics of *Jouissance*

When asked what led to his split with Freud, Reich invoked the death drive, characterizing it as apolitical. Reich recalls, "The great question was: '*Where does that misery come from?'* And here the trouble began. While

Freud developed his death-instinct theory which said 'the misery comes from inside,' I went out, out where the people were" (Higgins and Raphael, *Reich Speaks* 42; original emphasis). As Jacqueline Rose points out, Reich's insistence that misery comes from "out where the people [are]" means that the people have *only* an "outside, since whatever they are and suffer is a direct effect of a purely external causality and constraint" (90). Reich's failure to accept Freud's theory of the death drive, as well as the psychical role of aggression and negativity, leads in Rose's view to a misguided reading of psychoanalysis as "apolitical," and a dangerous presumption that the political field must strive toward wholeness. If we reproduce the Lacanian axiom that "what is foreclosed in the symbolic returns in the real" (*Seminar* 3:13), we'll see in Reich's theory the consequences of assuming the subject as primally harmonious and self-identical: Factors (such as *jouissance*) splitting the subject are simply projected onto another, which is identified as the source of all difficulty and the problem that must be eliminated.

That Reich excluded *jouissance* from the content of his theory, so forcing it to return in other forms, is not simply an a priori objection to his work. In his 1952 interview with Kurt Eissler, Reich gave midcentury events an eschatological gloss:

> In order to get to the core where the natural, the normal, the healthy is, you have to get through the middle layer. And in that middle layer there is terror. There is severe terror. Not only that, there is murder there. All that Freud tried to subsume under the death instinct is in that middle layer. He thought it was biological. It wasn't. It's an artifact of culture. It is a structural malignancy of the human animal. Therefore before you can get through to what Freud called Eros or what I call orgonotic streaming or plasmatic excitation, you have to go through hell. . . . All these wars, all the chaos now—do you know what that is to my mind? *Humanity is trying to get at its core, at its living, healthy core. But before it can be reached, humanity has to pass through this phase of murder, killing, and destruction.* (Higgins and Raphael, *Reich Speaks* 109; original emphasis)

It is interesting to note an obvious contradiction here in Reich's inaccurate account of Freud's death drive: On the one hand, Reich claims that the death drive is an "artifact of culture"; on the other hand, he argues that it is a "structural malignancy of the human animal." By *structural*, however, Reich seems to mean "the result of a structure imposed by repression," rather than "immanent," "necessary," or any other possible meaning. And it is precisely his failure to consider the death drive as a structural condition of the psyche that gives him conceptual trouble. Further, Reich's argument is eschatologically disturbing: Humanity in his view is purging itself to get back to the beatific inner core; thus, the Holocaust is merely a sign that humanity is returning to its healthy, natural core, while suffering some inevitable birth pangs along the way. Ironically, given Reich's hostility toward religion and his claim that it functions as a key institution of repression, it isn't difficult to see that this emphasis is still popular among American fundamentalist groups keen on eradicating homosexuality while re-creating Eden (Lane, "Beyond" 116–17). Reich and his fundamentalist inheritors project their disavowed *jouissance* onto homosexuals, who thus become the obstacle that must be eliminated so that others might reach paradise.

This remark is not simply an offhand comment in an interview; Reich first elaborated this perspective in a journal entry of December 7, 1945:

> Society will have to pass through a phase of chaotic events, including mass murder and killing, before it arrives at a social order based on the human animal's biological core. . . . The discovery of the biological core of the human animal offers us hope, but it also reveals the necessity of passing through this inferno of the middle layer in order to arrive at the core. Exactly the way it happens in therapy. (*American Odyssey* 315–16)

Considering that there are no recorded instances of murder in a Reichian therapy session, we are left wondering why the social application of his theory mandates genocide. I have tried to suggest that this eschatological perspective represents but one consequence of Reich's account of homosexuality and his related refusal to consider the role of *jouissance* in the psyche. In the remainder of the essay, I want to underscore this point by indicating the importance of the death drive in theories of fascism.

I selected the quotation from Reich's journal as an epigraph for this essay because, while indicating a rare moment of self-doubt, it uncannily reproduces the drama of *jouissance*. The citation ends: "The more I attempt to cling to the idea of human decency, the more man behaves in an indecent, unintelligent, stupid fashion" (*Beyond* 249). Our first impulse might be to read this as extreme megalomania: It is as if Reich laments, "It is not *I* who am indecent, unintelligent, and stupid, but those around me. Look at how well I behave!" (see Žižek, *For They Know Not* 70–72). However, this journal entry echoes another crucial moment in *Civilization and Its Discontents,* a passage that proved central to Lacan's theory of *jouissance:* Reflecting on the commandment to "Love thy neighbor as thyself," Freud remarks that "anyone who follows such a precept in present-day civilization only puts himself at a disadvantage vis-à-vis the person who disregards it" (143). Both Reich and Freud seemed to believe that behaving "decently" toward others is the same as making oneself vulnerable to them. And Freud already made clear the consequences of disadvantage relative to one's neighbor:

> Men are not gentle creatures who want to be loved, and who at the most can defend themselves if they are attacked; they are, on the contrary, creatures among whose instinctual endowments is to be reckoned a powerful share of aggressiveness. As a result, their neighbour is for them not only a potential helper or sexual object, but also someone who tempts them to satisfy their aggressiveness on him, to exploit his capacity for work without compensation, to use him sexually without his consent, to seize his possessions, to humiliate him, to cause him pain, to torture and to kill him. *Homo homini lupus*. (*Civilization* 111)

Freud emphasizes the aggressivity that civilization must overcome in order to produce a social bond. Especially interesting in this passage is Freud's focus on the *temptation* the neighbor poses, rather than simply his imminent threat. That is, the unquestionably over-the-top list of temptations one faces with one's neighbor points up Freud's dual interest in aggressivity: First, the subject is stymied by drives that undermine its well-being; second (and related), Freud ethically refuses to locate the source of violence outside the subject. Lacan, in his seminar on *The Ethics of Psychoanalysis*, glosses Freud's recoil thus:

> Every time that Freud stops short in horror at the consequences of the commandment to love one's neighbor, we see evoked the presence of that fundamental evil which dwells within this neighbor. But if that is the case, then it also dwells within me. And what is more of a neighbor to me than this heart within which is that of my *jouissance* and which I daren't go near? For as soon as I go near it, as *Civilization and Its Discontents* makes clear, there rises up the unfathomable aggressivity from which I flee, that I turn against me, and which in the very place of the vanished Law adds its weight to that which prevents me from crossing a certain frontier at the limit of the Thing. (7:186)

In Lacan's reading of Freud, "the neighbor" is already within us; it is the death drive, the *jouissance* around which our subjectivity is elaborated.[14] In this way, Lacan indicates the full measure of Reich's break with Freud. In Reich's theory of the subject, as we've seen, the core of being is self-harmonious, a viable foundation for harmonious social relations. However, Freud and Lacan ask us to consider the possibility that this core might well be "the evil I desire, and that my neighbor desires also" (*Seminar* 7:187). This is what Reich's apocalyptic fantasies exploit but never adequately explain—or even consciously acknowledge.

Lacan's theory of *jouissance* is not simply a cautionary tale about the limits of human happiness. It also constitutes the paradoxical ground for psychoanalysis's political claims.[15] It is thus particularly tragic that ostensibly radical analysts such as Reich disputed Freud's theory so vehemently and misunderstood it so extensively. Reich's project, as we saw, was to attain the biologic core, to reunite humanity with nature; that is, to produce a harmonious subjectivity. As a consequence of that project, Reich began to read history in eschatological terms. But this may be an inescapable dilemma. As Slavoj Žižek explains, "All 'culture' is in a way a reaction-formation, an attempt to *cultivate* this imbalance, this traumatic kernel, this radical antagonism. . . . It is not only that the aim is no longer to abolish this drive antagonism, but the aspiration to abolish it is precisely the source of totalitarian temptation: the greatest mass murders and holocausts have always been perpetrated in the name of man as harmonious being" (*Sublime* 5).

Reich's journal entry illustrates this paradox, for he found that the more he tried to believe in the fundamental decency of humanity, the worse he tended to perceive its actions. The fantasy of harmonious subjectivity exacerbates the malign impact of *jouissance*. When Reich asks, *"Why shouldn't we have happiness on earth? Why shouldn't pleasure be the substance of life?"* (*Mass* 141; original emphasis), he summons into being his later, apocalyptic perspective. If humans are "naturally" harmonious, yet harmony and pleasure cannot coexist, then some external force must be preventing them from coming into being. Some other group has the "secret" of happiness, we infer, and is preventing us from achieving pleasure. The results are predictable. As Tim Dean puts it, *"He whom I suppose to know how to enjoy, I hate"* ("Psychoanalysis" 112; original emphasis).

Sadly, at the end of his life, Reich did in fact believe that a specific other was stealing our pleasure: UFOs. He became increasingly convinced that representatives from another planet were mining our atmosphere of useful orgone energy and were seeding it with destructive orgones (DOR).[16] And as Paul Robinson notes, orgone energy "was . . . embarrassingly concrete. It was blue in color and could be observed in such natural phenomena as the bluish glimmer of 'red' corpuscles or the blue coloration of sexually excited frogs" (64). In addition to Reich's politically reprehensible tolerance for genocide, one might view the plasmatic excitations, bions, orgone energy, and especially DOR symptomatically, as a return of the real. In fact, Reich himself began to make this connection toward the end of his life. In "Re-emergence of the Death Instinct as 'DOR' Energy," despite maintaining "strong opposition to [the] death instinct theory, he saw certain connections between Freud's ideas and what he conceptualized as DOR" (Sharaf 402). However, his death in federal prison one year after the essay's publication precluded any possibility of conceptual rapprochement. Reich continued to call the death drive a "structural malignancy of the human animal," and though he meant the phrase as criticism, I should like to reclaim it as one of psychoanalysis's crucial contributions to antiheterosexist and antifascist thought. For *jouissance*'s "malignant" opposition to the good paradoxically opens up a space for psychic freedom. Without this loophole, we are (as Reich felt himself to be) at the mercy of social forces that shape and manipulate us; with it, however, we are pathologically free.

Notes

This essay has benefited from generous, patient, and multiple readings by Robin Pickering-Iazzi, Aimee Pozorski, and especially Christopher Lane. Additionally, I would like to thank Robert A. Paul and a lively audience in the Emory Psychoanalytic Studies Program Brown Bag series for helping me further sharpen my claims. Finally, I thank Tim Dean and Christopher Lane for kindly allowing me to consult work still in manuscript.

1. I'll be developing the idea of *jouissance* in more detail; for now it may suffice to cite Miller's concise definition: *Jouissance* is the "secret satisfaction which . . . is at the heart of the symptom and attaches the subject to [its] symptom" (Morel 8). Further, as Miller points out, there is no relationship between the death drive and *jouissance,* for they are in essence the same thing: "The death drive is at bottom the Freudian figure that Lacan deciphers through *jouissance. Jouissance* doesn't work for the good of the individual" (Morel 9).

2. It is difficult to recommend biographies of Reich, as they inevitably get caught up in the fiercely partisan debates over his theoretical affiliations and mental health. To take just one example, in her introduction to *Beyond Psychology,* Higgins cites only "two bitter disappointments in Freud," both of which occurred in 1926: his cool reception of Reich's *The Function of the Orgasm* [published in English in 1980 as *Genitality in the Theory and Therapy of Neurosis*] and a technical dispute over the handling of material in analysis (xii). She omits any mention of Freud's nearly simultaneous refusal to analyze Reich (for details, see Rycroft 5–6), a blow

that Reich took personally. The most generous and evenhanded assessments of Reich's life are Jacoby 76–97; Cohen; and Rycroft 1–12; a somewhat more skeptical view is available in Mitchell. The two full-length biographies of Reich (Boadella, *Wilhelm Reich;* Sharaf) are both works of advocacy, written by supporters, but they are nonetheless useful. My account of Reich in this paragraph draws principally on Jacoby and Rycroft.

3. It must be noted that, against Cohen's claim that "Reich was once Sigmund Freud's star pupil" (24), Reich's value was always held to lie in his therapeutic results, not in his theoretical power (Jacoby 72–73, 90; Fleiss 104). One of Reich's theoretical limitations was his incapacity to distinguish between fact and metaphor; as Mitchell argues, "Reich concretized all concepts, [and] took phantasy for fact or made it into a neurotic irrelevance" (170). For elaborations on this idea, see Mitchell 170–72, 174, 215; Robinson 15–16.

4. Reich's oeuvre is a bibliographer's nightmare. Despite appearances to the contrary, *Die Funktion des Orgasmus* is *not* the same text as *The Function of the Orgasm.* Reich often rewrote entire sections of books between editions, or, as in this case, simply gave an old title to a new book. There are no pristine editions of his work.

5. Given the real and imaginary persecution that, after 1933, plagued Reich throughout his career, my claim that his work tells us what we long to hear might seem outrageous. However, there is evidence that Reich was not particularly tolerant of criticism, and that he may have manufactured some of his own enemies. As Rycroft notes, even "Reich's greatest admirers admit that he was a difficult and autocratic man" (8). Robinson goes further, arguing that as Reich's "self-esteem exceeded all limits of sanity, not to speak of modesty, he developed a sense of persecution which was nothing short of paranoiac. He identified with every great martyr from Socrates to Marx, and with none so intimately as Jesus Christ. He hypostatized all critics of his theories as 'the Emotional Plague,' proving himself more than Freud's equal in the art of *ad hominem* argument" (71–72). Also, some of his persecution has to be placed in the various contexts of the institutional histories of psychoanalysis and communism, the European political situation of the 1930s, and American Red-hunting in the late 1940s and 1950s. For quite disparate discussions of how Reich's thought has served as an unacknowledged source for much contemporary political thought, see Mitchell 197–201; Sharaf 4, 481.

6. As Mitchell puts it, "Reich's thesis really amounts to saying that man has animal instincts (his 'unconscious') which are outgoing ('toward the world') but which then hit the conflicting social pressures moving against them. In the ensuing conflict man builds himself like an armour-plated monster, suppressing his instincts and using the hostile attitudes of the world as the main component of his armour-plating" (186). Mitchell usefully demonstrates how Reich confuses the concepts of "the unconscious" and "instincts," with deleterious theoretical consequences. For a characteristic example of the hydraulic principles driving Reich's model, see the opening paragraphs of Boadella, "Genital."

7. "Orgastic potency" is the "capacity for surrender to the flow of biological energy without any inhibitions, the capacity for complete discharge of all dammed-up sexual excitation through involuntary pleasurable contractions of the body" (qtd. in Boadella, *Wilhelm Reich* 16).

8. One can grasp that Reich's insisting that culture does not presuppose repression directly repudiates Freud's claim in *Civilization and Its Discontents* that "it is impossible to overlook the extent to which civilization is built up upon a renunciation of instinct, how much it presupposes precisely the non-satisfaction (by suppression, repression, or some other means?) of powerful instincts" (97).

9. Laplanche and Boothby have each argued convincingly that Freud's arguments about the death drive are implicit in his posthumous *Project for a Scientific Psychology* (1950 [1895]). It is possible to dismiss Reich's curious insistence that Freud's early theory is radically incompatible with the death drive. For example, he claimed to have asked Freud "many times, 'Where are we going? This libido theory is dying.' (The death-instinct theory came up about 1924 or 1925.) And he said many times, 'Don't worry.' . . . Freud definitely knew that he was betrayed in his sexual theory" (Higgins and Raphael, *Reich Speaks* 25).

10. *Inhibitions, Symptoms, and Anxiety* (1926) helped drive Reich from Freud, for in that text Freud modifies earlier pronouncements on anxiety that Reich found congenial (Higgins and Raphael, *Reich Speaks* 241–50).

11. For a speculative argument that masochism may be the basis of sexuality as such, and that homosexuality may, in the heterosexual imaginary, constitute a privileged example of masochism, see Bersani, *Freudian*; "Rectum"; and *Homos*.

12. Hewitt is properly unflinching on this score, marshaling an impressive array of evidence signaling the frequency of this structure, from the earliest antifascist propaganda on the Left (the KPD, or German Communist Party claimed in 1932 that "the Hitler racket is based on homosexual tendencies and hypocrisy" [qtd. in Hewitt 20]) to the various theories of fascism advanced by the Frankfurt School, to a variety of plays, novels, and avant-garde art pieces produced in France and Germany over the last fifty years. Hewitt identifies convincingly a sort of representational transubstantiation: If homosexuality is traditionally "the love that dare not speak its name" and fascism—especially after the Holocaust—is identified as "unrepresentable," then the two unspeakable things are apparently exchangeable and can represent each other.

13. Indeed, while Theweleit here identifies homosexuality as a problem, Freud in 1915 wrote that the problem is sexuality itself: "Psycho-analysis considers that a choice of object independently of its sex . . . is the original basis from which, as a result of restriction in one direction or the other, both the normal and inverted types develop. Thus from the point of view of psycho-analysis the exclusive sexual interest felt by men for women is also a problem that needs elucidating and is not a self-evident fact" (*Three* 145–46n).

14. This is what Lacan refers to when he speaks of "extimacy [*extimité*]": It is something at the heart of the subject that is nevertheless strictly inassimilable to it. For an elaboration of this idea, see Miller.

15. For attempts to theorize the political dimensions of the death drive, see Rose; Dean, "Transsexual," "Psychoanalysis," and "Eve"; Lane, "Beyond"; and the entirety of Žižek's oeuvre.

16. Even Reichians cannot follow this step. Sharaf downplays the issue (413, 461), while Boadella concedes that Reich may have finally started to break with reality (*Wilhelm Reich* 299–305).

References

Bersani, Leo. *The Freudian Body: Psychoanalysis and Art*. New York: Columbia UP, 1986.

———. *Homos*. Cambridge: Harvard UP, 1995.

———. "Is the Rectum a Grave?" 1987. In *AIDS: Cultural Analysis/Cultural Activism*. Ed. Douglas Crimp. Cambridge: MIT P, 1988, 1993. 197–223.

Boadella, David. "Genital Contact and Sexual Hangups." *Energy and Character* 10.1 (1979): 23–29.

———. *Wilhelm Reich: The Evolution of His Work*. 1973. Chicago: Henry Regnery, 1974.

Boothby, Richard. *Death and Desire: Psychoanalytic Theory in Lacan's Return to Freud*. New York: Routledge, 1991.

Cohen, Hal. "A Secret History of the Sexual Revolution: The Repression of Wilhelm Reich." *Lingua Franca* 9.2 (March 1999): 24–33.

Dean, Tim. *Beyond Sexuality*. Chicago: U of Chicago P, 2000.

———. "On the Eve of a Queer Future." *Raritan* 15.1 (1995): 116–34.

———. "The Psychoanalysis of AIDS." *October* 63 (1993): 83–116.

———. "Transsexual Identification, Gender Performance Theory, and the Politics of the Real." *Literature and Psychology* 39.4 (1993): 1–27.

Deleuze, Gilles, and Félix Guattari. *Anti-Oedipus: Capitalism and Schizophrenia*. 1972. Trans. Robert Hurley, Mark Seem, and Helen R. Lane. Minneapolis: U of Minnesota P, 1983.

Fleiss, Robert. "Characterology." In *The Psycho-Analytic Reader: An Anthology of Essential Papers with Critical Introductions*. Ed. Robert Fleiss. New York: International Universities P, 1948. 104–5.

Foucault, Michel. *The History of Sexuality. Volume 1: An Introduction*. 1976. Trans. Robert Hurley. New York: Vintage, 1990.

Freud, Sigmund. *Civilization and Its Discontents*. 1930 (1929). *Standard* 21:57–145.

———. "On the Universal Tendency to Debasement in the Sphere of Love." 1912. *Standard* 11:177–90.

———. *The Standard Edition of the Complete Psychological Works of Sigmund Freud*. Ed. and trans. James Strachey. 24 vols. London: Hogarth, 1953–74.

———. *Three Essays on the Theory of Sexuality*. 1905. *Standard* 7:123–243.

Hewitt, Andrew. *Political Inversions: Homosexuality, Fascism, and the Modernist Imaginary*. Stanford: Stanford UP, 1996.

Higgins, Mary Boyd. "Introduction: Reich's Development, 1922–1934." In Reich, *Beyond* vii–xxiii.

Higgins, Mary Boyd, and Chester M. Raphael. *Reich Speaks of Freud: Wilhelm Reich Discusses His Work and His Relationship with Sigmund Freud.* Trans. Therese Pol. New York: Farrar, Straus and Giroux, 1967.

Jacoby, Russell. *The Repression of Psychoanalysis: Otto Fenichel and the Political Freudians.* Chicago: U of Chicago P, 1983.

Lacan, Jacques. *The Seminar of Jacques Lacan, Book 3: The Psychoses, 1955–1956.* Ed. Jacques-Alain Miller. Trans. Russell Grigg. New York: Norton, 1993.

———. *The Seminar of Jacques Lacan, Book 7: The Ethics of Psychoanalysis, 1959–1960.* Ed. Jacques-Alain Miller. Trans. Dennis Porter. New York: Norton, 1992.

Lane, Christopher. "Beyond the Social Principle: Psychoanalysis and Radical Democracy." *JPCS: Journal for the Psychoanalysis of Culture and Society* 1.1 (1996): 105–21.

———. *The Burdens of Intimacy: Psychoanalysis and Victorian Masculinity.* Chicago: U of Chicago P, 1999.

———. "The Experience of the Outside: Foucault and Psychoanalysis." In *Lacan in America.* Ed. Jean-Michel Rabaté. New York: Other P, 2000. 309–47.

Laplanche, Jean. *Life and Death in Psychoanalysis.* 1970. Trans. Jeffrey Mehlman. Baltimore: Johns Hopkins UP, 1976.

Miller, Jacques-Alain. "Extimité." In *Lacanian Theory of Discourse: Subject, Structure, and Society.* Ed. Mark Bracher, Marshall W. Alcorn Jr., Ronald J. Corthell, and Françoise Massardier-Kenney. New York: New York UP, 1994. 74–87.

Mitchell, Juliet. *Psychoanalysis and Feminism: Freud, Reich, Laing, and Women.* New York: Vintage, 1975.

Morel, Jean-Paul. "Interview with Jacques-Alain Miller." *Le Matin* (26 septembre 1986). Trans. Dennis Porter. *Newsletter of the Freudian Field* 1.1 (1987): 5–10.

Reich, Wilhelm. *American Odyssey: Letters and Journals 1940–1947.* Ed. Mary Boyd Higgins. Trans. Derek and Inge Jordan, and Philip Schmitz. New York: Farrar, Straus and Giroux, 1999.

———. *Beyond Psychology: Letters and Journals 1934–1939.* Ed. Mary Boyd Higgins. Trans. Derek and Inge Jordan, and Philip Schmitz. New York: Farrar, Straus and Giroux, 1994.

———. *Character Analysis.* 1933. 3rd ed. Trans. Theodore P. Wolfe. New York: Orgone Institute P, 1949.

———. "The Imposition of Sexual Morality." 1932. *Sex-Pol: Essays 1929–1934.* Ed. Lee Baxandall. Trans. Anna Bostock, Tom DuBose, and Baxandall. New York: Random House, 1966. 89–249.

———. *The Mass Psychology of Fascism.* 1933. 3rd ed. Ed. Mary Higgins and Chester M. Raphael. Trans. Vincent R. Carfagno. New York: Farrar, Straus and Giroux, 1970.

Robinson, Paul A. *The Freudian Left: Wilhelm Reich, Géza Róheim, Herbert Marcuse.* New York: Harper and Row, 1969.

Rose, Jacqueline. *Why War? Psychoanalysis, Politics, and the Return to Melanie Klein.*
    Oxford: Blackwell, 1993.

Rycroft, Charles. *Wilhelm Reich.* 1969. New York: Viking, 1972.

Sharaf, Myron. *Fury on Earth: A Biography of Wilhelm Reich.* New York: St. Martin's,
    1983.

Theweleit, Klaus. *Male Fantasies: Volume 1: Women, Floods, Bodies, History.* 1977.
    Trans. Steven Conway, Erica Carter, and Chris Turner. Minneapolis: U of Min-
    nesota P, 1987.

———. *Male Fantasies: Volume 2: Male Bodies: Psychoanalyzing the White Terror.* 1978.
    Trans. Erica Carter, Chris Turner, and Steven Conway. Minneapolis: U of Min-
    nesota P, 1989.

Žižek, Slavoj. *For They Know Not What They Do: Enjoyment as a Political Factor.* New
    York: Verso, 1991.

———. *The Sublime Object of Ideology.* New York: Verso, 1989.

———. *Tarrying with the Negative: Kant, Hegel, and the Critique of Ideology.* Durham:
    Duke UP, 1993.

———. *The Ticklish Subject: The Absent Centre of Political Ontology.* New York:
    Verso, 1999.

10

HETEROSEXUALITY TERMINABLE OR INTERMINABLE?

Kleinian Fantasies of Reparation and Mourning

Ramón E. Soto-Crespo

. . . .

You are afraid that I shall not be able to distinguish between psychoanalytic treatment and buggery. HANNA SEGAL, *PSYCHOANALYSIS, LITERATURE AND WAR* 98

In his 1937 essay "Analysis Terminable and Interminable," Sigmund Freud provides us with a peculiar passage on the heterosexual-homosexual relationship:

> It is well known that at all periods there have been, as there still are, people who can take as their sexual objects members of their own sex as well as of the opposite one, without the one trend interfering with the other. We call such people bisexuals, and we accept their existence without feeling much surprise about it. We have come to learn, however, that every human being is bisexual in this sense and that his libido is distributed, either in a manifest or a latent fashion, over objects of both sexes. But we are struck by the following point. Whereas in the first class of people the two trends have got on together without clashing, in the second and more numerous class they are in a state of irreconcilable conflict. A man's heterosexuality will not put up with any homosexuality, and *vice versa*. If the former is the stronger it succeeds in keeping the latter

latent and forcing it away from satisfaction in reality. On the other hand, there is no greater danger for a man's heterosexual function than its being disturbed by his latent homosexuality. (243–44)

Significantly, this passage positing homosexuality and heterosexuality as latent drives of each other—and in a state of irreconcilable conflict—comes in the middle of Freud's discussion of masochism and the activity of the death drive.

Thirteen years later, on the same topic of psychoanalytical termination, Melanie Klein (1882–1960) explains the death drive in terms of mourning. For Klein the work of mourning is key because it deals with not only the process of "establishing within the ego the person who is mourned," but also the resurgence of the depressive position ("On the Criteria" 44). This position, according to Klein, works by "re-establishing the first loved objects, which in early infancy were felt to be endangered or destroyed by destructive impulses" (44). Whereas Freud's examples concerning termination verge on homosexuality, in Klein the examples concern a heterosexual depressive castration anxiety and the relationship between "potency and heterosexuality" (45). Klein informs us about male heterosexual impotence: "This fear [castration] is mixed with depressive anxiety in so far as it gives rise to the feeling that he cannot fertilize a woman, at bottom that he cannot fertilize the loved mother and is therefore unable to make reparation for the harm done to her by his sadistic impulses" (45). Klein adds the dimension of mourning to Freud's description of heterosexuality and its phantasies. But she also points to a certain negativity that is key in understanding a different structure of sexuality, phantasy, and sexual difference. The two essays from which I have quoted bring to mind a series of questions about sexual identity and gay men's ambivalent relationship to psychoanalysis. How does a homo deal with his latent heterosexuality? And who *is* the homo when he has heterosexual phantasies? More important, are these heterosexual phantasies better described as phantasies of mourning? To pursue these questions we must confront the difficult relationship between homosexuality and psychoanalysis.

Psychoanalysis and gay and lesbian studies (as well as more recent queer theory) have been at odds since the 1970s in their assessment of the subject's development. Psychoanalytic theories have located homosexuality as a phase in a developmental process that allegedly ends in heterosexual normativity. Gay, lesbian, and queer theorists have combated the location of homosexuality as a phase by demystifying the supposed normativity of heterosexuality, arguing that it is merely one outcome among many others. Theorists have also pointed out that what drives the heterosexual matrix is the fear of an identifiable sexual otherness in a phase that supposedly "everybody goes through." It seems, therefore, that the debate has been fueled by questioning not the terminability or interminability of psychoanalysis, but that of homosexuality. This type of institutional questioning has encouraged the establishment of "reactionary" programs for reversing homosexuality into heterosexuality—so-called "reparative therapy." What has been obscured in this debate, of course, is any exploration of *heterosexuality's* status as terminable or interminable.

Misled at the outset, this debate has been derailed by framing its terms as sexual choice versus natural determinism, thereby replicating the discursive constraints of free will and determinism that characterized philosophical debates of previous centuries. In order to address the issue differently, this essay attempts to view sexualities as neither fluid nor determined, since fluidity is just as much a conceptual constraint as determinism. I want to avoid essentializing heterosexuality, while at the same time refusing to buy into an aporetic understanding of sexuality as ambiguous or fluid. This last conception of sexuality as fluid stems from thinking of it in terms of loci of identification. Fluidity is contingent upon alternate points of sedimentation. I consider it urgent to problematize the post-structuralist logic of fluidity, in order to posit a more conceptually acute and productive paradigm. We need an account of sexuality as something more than a mobile space of experiences where phantasies play only a part.

I shall contend that sexuality is constituted through phantasies of reparation in a process of mourning for lost objects. I find useful the Kleinians' distinction between phantasy and fantasy. *Phantasy* in this distinction refers to an unconscious process that begins at birth and affects psychic reality from then on. *Fantasy,* by contrast, refers to the conscious processes of daydreaming, imagination, creative writing, or visual narratives such as film.[1] Although in preserving the difference between unconscious and conscious systems in such a clear-cut manner the Kleinians may be accused of establishing illusory demarcations, their use of *phantasy,* in fact, refers as well to adult clinical fantasies "modeled on" or "given shape" by past phantasies. This is to say not that unconscious phantasies give rise to conscious fantasies, but that action, thinking, and fantasizing are rooted in the oscillating inner world of unconscious phantasies. Since I find this distinction of great theoretical importance, I would like to retain the implications of this distinctively Kleinian concept in the present essay.

In Kleinian theory, sexuality derives from a mental space of unconscious phantasies. Because they are neither fluid nor static, they form
a cohesive and overlapping variety of phantasmatic structures such as
sexuality. This essay discusses the role of these phantasies from the perspective of the Kleinian school, which has contributed extensively to our
understanding of mourning and its function in sexuality. Specifically, I
shall argue that phantasies of mourning create sexual drives that are later
understood in terms of constitutive elements of identities. In a sense,
phantasies *create* sexualities. Jean Laplanche and Jean-Bertrand Pontalis's
understanding of the formation of sexuality through phantasy is congru-
ent with Klein's account of phantasy's function. As Laplanche and Pontalis argue, "The 'origin' of auto-erotism would therefore be the moment
when sexuality, disengaged from any natural object, moves into the field
of fantasy and by that very fact becomes sexuality" (25). Thus this essay
revolves around two important points, worth emphasizing from the start:
First, sexuality is formed *through* phantasy, and, second, phantasy is circumscribed by loss. These points bring to light the role of unconscious
phantasy in the formation of the subject of sexuality and, hence, the
importance of mourning in the formation of fantasy, and later, sexuality.
By rethinking sexuality and mourning, we may reach a different understanding of heterosexuality's terminable or interminable status as a sexual phantasy.

1. Melanie Klein and Homosexuality

Discussion of Melanie Klein's account of homosexuality has been limited.
Criticism on this topic mostly follows a purely demystifying approach. For
example, in *Wild Desires and Mistaken Identities: Lesbianism and Psychoanalysis* (1993), Noreen O'Connor and Joanna Ryan devote a chapter to Klein
in which they attempt to expose her essentialism—her theory's reliance
on biological or anatomical foundations. Basically, they argue that Klein
theorized sexuality as "intrinsic to gender differences" (75). This is due,
they insist, to Klein's blindness—specifically, her claims to present "the
'objective' truth of human development without sufficiently addressing
the issue of her own inevitable historical, cultural and psychic biases"
(74). According to O'Connor and Ryan, Klein lacks self-consciousness. Of
course, this objection could be leveled at any psychoanalytic theorist
from earlier in the century, and O'Connor and Ryan proceed to argue
that in Klein, "as in Freud, homosexuality is designated as a negative

choice and results from a failure adequately to negotiate oedipal conflicts" (76).

From this aspect of Klein's theory, O'Connor and Ryan infer that a homosexual relationship in Klein would amount to a "part-object relationship" (80). Although this is a valid point, we should take into consideration the definition of *part-object* in Klein's theoretical paradigm. This term may strike us as implying a shortcoming or as belittling the relationship in question, and it may be so from a particular point of view; but in another sense the term provides the possibility of a different understanding of sexuality. According to Klein, the child's first object is a part-object (that is, the breast, the mouth, and so on) and this corresponds to both the paranoid-schizoid position and an inner world of phantasy. By contrast, it is in the depressive position that the child will encounter not solely reality (reality-testing) but the "whole" object as well.[2] This signifies a healthy relationship with the subject's reality. It is the position where, as it were, the subject repairs its phantasy-driven inner life by reevaluating the object based on external reality. This is the part that offers integration and cure. O'Connor and Ryan tackle here the implications of Klein's *terms* rather than the meaning and function of her theoretical *concepts*.

Another important point of contention in O'Connor and Ryan's summation is that "in assuming the existence of an 'inner world' Klein ignores all twentieth-century advances in hermeneutic theory which systematically criticise divisions between thought and language, and spatial metaphors of 'inside' and 'outside' arising from that dualistic split" (82). Klein's failure in this regard, they argue, is "in line with many essentialist, universalist, foundational theories" (83). O'Connor and Ryan's critique of inherent gender bias in Klein—and of her lack of self-reflexivity concerning essentializing foundations—is necessary and valuable. However, I would like to move beyond this critique to focus more systematically on how Klein's theoretical model deploys homosexuality. Does it serve as a simplified object that secures a specific normativity, or does it reveal— beyond Klein's intentions—a more complex and dislocating possibility in the logic of her metanarrative? And if so, how does the category *homosexuality* reveal rather than conceal the underside of its own logic? These are crucial questions that Kleinian psychoanalytic theory has yet to pursue.

These questions also could be posed to the larger psychoanalytic movement. In psychoanalytic theory, one generally finds the contention that the genital phase is the apex of sexual maturity. This assumption invariably is explained in relation to perversion as "derived from the constituent elements of infantile sexuality" (Gillespie 38). Since homosexuality has been for decades included under the rubric of perversion, it has often been understood as a "psychic formation" (38). Homosexuality has been seen as attached to the Oedipus complex, that is, as a libidinization of castration anxiety. In the face of this pervasive and prejudicial psychoanalytic understanding of homosexuality, Klein's account of the Oedipus complex offers a reading of sexuality that could be considered queerer, less orthodox, and even anti-oedipal (in the Freudian sense).

This means not that Klein is beyond criticism, but that there are certain insights that O'Connor and Ryan overlook in their rush to critique the essentialist basis of Kleinian psychoanalysis. Although Klein does not devote any particular treatise to homosexuality, the issue recurs in clinical examples throughout her work. In Klein, homosexuality offers itself not only as a phase or an anomaly, but also as a form of negativity and, hence, in Kleinian language, as an affirmative and contentious conceptual underside. This revealing possibility will become more intelligible as we explore the key Kleinian concept of phantasy and her controversial ideas about a world of mental objects.

2. The Otherness of Objects

Reading *The Psycho-Analysis of Children,* one can almost feel she describes too many phantasies, too many defenses. HANNA SEGAL, *MELANIE KLEIN* 89

Phantasies, moreover, may be used as defences against other phantasies. HANNA SEGAL, *INTRODUCTION TO THE WORK OF MELANIE KLEIN* 5

Ever since Freud located the Oedipus complex at the heart of childhood sexual phantasies, infantile sexuality has been a contested field in sexual politics. The most hotly debated point has been the foundational presuppositions of the Oedipus complex; that is to say, its key role in establishing sexual difference (its heterosexual bias) and the consequences of its developmental logic (heterosexual normativity and homosexual deviancy).

The duration and emergence of the superego in childhood development was a major point of controversy in these wars of the nursery (see Geissmann and Geissmann's *History*). For Klein, the superego has its prototype before the oedipal phase. This contrasts sharply with Freud's insistence that the superego emerges to reconcile phantasy (desire) and reality (impossibility) *after* the oedipal conflict. Following her father, Anna Freud determined that the superego emerges as a compromise formation during the oedipal phase, in a compromise between reality and the inner world of phantasy. These disputes between the Anna Freudians and the Kleinians are known as "The Controversial Discussions"—intense debates about the formation of the superego that led inevitably to fundamental disagreement concerning the relationship between phantasy and external reality (see King and Steiner). These discussions about the nature and function of phantasy consolidated further the strong Kleinian position on the psychosomatic foundation of sexual difference as an instinctual phantasy, as I will explain later in the essay. And this strong assertion from the Kleinian school with regard to phantasy undergirds its distinctive mode of clinical practice. Since these analysts believe the child has innate knowledge of sexual difference, the Kleinians do not hesitate to address sexuality and intercourse very explicitly in the clinical setting. In a sense, the sexual enlightenment of children, which Klein tirelessly advocated in her writings, does not amount to new knowledge for the child, because he or she already possesses such knowledge in the form of an innate unconscious phantasy.[3] According to Klein, the child has always already been sexually enlightened with respect to sexual difference. But what the child lacks in understanding is the cultural meaning and value judgment of that knowledge. There are two major points that need to be understood with respect to Kleinian psychoanalysis: First, infants have sexual fantasies (there is no myth of innocence), and, second, infants are full of sadistic aggression (there is no myth of original goodness). These presuppositions have been debated extensively elsewhere, but are assumed by Klein and her most important followers—Joan Riviere, Susan Isaacs, and Hanna Segal.

In her seminal essay "The Nature and Function of Phantasy," Isaacs clarifies this school's account of sexuality by following the Kleinian logic of psychoanalytic phantasy. The partly psychic and partly somatic composites of phantasy mark the distinction between unconscious phantasy (the inner world of mental objects) and conscious fantasy (or imagination). The images of phantasy—or imagos—draw their power, she argues, "from their repressed unconscious somatic associates in the unconscious world of desire and emotions, which form the link with the id; and which do mean in unconscious phantasy that the objects to which they refer are believed to be inside the body, to be incorporated" (106). Isaacs illustrates the connection of somatic bodily impulses and phantasies in the formula "It is all right if it comes out of my anus as flatus and faeces, but it mustn't come out of my mouth as words" (106). Klein's concept of the internal object is best defined as a "phantasy of the object inside the body" (Perlow 39). This definition illuminates Isaacs's understanding of the body in the composite structure known as *phantasy*. It is not only that the body feels physically what the ego desires—or that unconscious phantasies tend to trigger the derailment of conscious bodily functions (that is, in sex acts, desire, speech acts, and so on)—but that all conscious processes are based on unconscious phantasies. Isaacs declares: "I wish to state here my opinion that the primary content of all mental processes are unconscious phantasies. Such phantasies are the basis of all unconscious and conscious thought processes" (King and Steiner 271–72).

For Klein the infant is born phantasizing. Phantasies guide his or her relations to a world of part-objects—a world in which the infant is vaguely aware of external reality and lacks precise knowledge of the boundaries between inner and outer objects. This paradoxical standpoint emerges because these external and internal objects are initially assessed through projection, introjection, and splitting. Klein considers objects partial because when the infant encounters something in external reality, this encounter triggers in the infant the formation of a world of imagos, or internal phantasied objects. The infant supplements the part-object with phantasy and therefore makes of it his or her psychic "reality." This world of unconscious phantasy is indeed a "complex structure in which drives and phantasies have added to, and distorted, the realistic basis. As such it is composed of conscious and unconscious components" (Perlow 12). Since imagos are mental constructs almost independent of the realistic images of objects, Klein made this breach of perception between the real-life parents and the virtually autonomous entities of the imagos the basis of her psychoanalytical approach. According to Klein, the child's behavior reflects "his or her phantasied behaviour with these imagos" (Perlow 35), rather than his or her relation with the real parents. The infant creates his or her own reality based on phantasmatic mental structures that for the most part to do not refer to an external reality, but to an unconscious phantasy world of imagos. In her "Symposium on Child Analysis" (1927), Riviere summarizes this breach inherent in the formation of objects: "The objects of unconscious phantasies are imagos formed to some extent after the pattern of real people, but not to a material extent on real experience" (84). In order to understand Klein, therefore, there are two major points to consider: First, the phantasmatic nature of the infant's mental objects; and second, the infant's relationship with these phantasmatic imagos as the basis of his or her relationship with external objects.

These distinctions lead us to appreciate the centrality in Kleinian thought of introjected objects, particularly the superego. According to Klein, the inner world of imagos is far from innocent and peaceful; instead, it is the site of the most ferocious and voracious "self"-inflicted punishments. Judith Butler characterizes this inner world of psychic reality as the tormented site of an endlessly lacerating and "self-annihilating soliloquy" (181). Indeed, the infant's sadomasochistic world of phantasies resembles a torture chamber—a place of endless torments that take the form of cannibalistic persecution, envy, and pain. This conception of the child's inner world is tied to Klein's assertion that the superego is formed from introjected objects—an assertion anticipating Freud's last account of the superego.[4] In "A Contribution to the Theory of Intellectual Inhibition" (1931), Klein explains:

> In those cases in which the significance of reality and real objects as reflections of the dreaded internal world and imagos has retained its preponderance, the stimuli from the external world may be felt to be nearly as alarming as the phantasied domination of the internalized objects, which have taken possession of all initiative and to which the ego feels compulsively bound to surrender the execution of all activities and intellectual operations, together of course with the responsibility for them. (245)

This possessive, or negative, nature of the imagos becomes central to Klein's clinical cases. The case of Rita is an illuminating example: "I would now go further in my interpretation," Klein insists. "To the phantasied attacks on [Rita's] body by her parents as external figures corresponded fear of inner attacks by the internalized persecuting parent-figures who formed the cruel part of her superego" ("Oedipus Complex" 403). The Kleinian superego, we learn here, is founded on a deep breach between reality and phantasy.

The formation of the superego marks an asymmetrical relation to external reality. But this asymmetry provides the foundation for the sadism crucial to homo- and heterosexualities in the oedipal formation. In an earlier essay, Klein argues that "the parents are the source of the superego, in that their commands, prohibitions, and so on become absorbed by the child itself. But this superego is not identical with the parents; it is partly formed upon the child's own sadistic phantasies" ("Criminal Tendencies" 179). Thus, as she explains one year later (1928), the superego that fills the breach between external and internal realities is formed through the child's own sadistic phantasies and becomes something that "bites, devours and cuts" ("Early Stages" 187). By 1930, in sharp contrast to Freud, Klein was arguing that the superego becomes something that aims to "possess himself of the contents of the mother's body and to destroy her by means of every weapon which sadism can command" ("Symbol Formation" 219).

The concept of phantasy in Kleinian thought introduces us to a detailed account of the composite aspect of the superego. According to Klein, the child's sadistic phantasies fuse the mother's breast and the father's penis into a single entity. We could say that the phallic breast and the vaginalized penis are phantasies of sexual difference that embody both signifiers. Klein illustrates this phantasy in the following way:

> The father's penis, which from the sucking oral point of view is equated with the breast, and so becomes an object of desire, is thus incorporated and in the boy's phantasy very rapidly transforms itself, in consequence of his sadistic attacks against it, into a terrifying internal aggressor and becomes equated with dangerous, murderous animals or weapons. ("Intellectual Inhibition" 241–42)

The mother's breast becomes the repository of the phantasy of sexual difference. Klein explains that the mother's body also becomes a repository of the phallus, because inside her body she conceals the father's penis. Nevertheless, there is an otherness underlying the Kleinian logic of sexual difference as it is structured through phantasy. This is the otherness of objects signaling phantasy that is asymmetrical to the purportedly innate knowledge of sexual difference. The otherness of objects in phantasy guides sexuality toward not a normative heterosexuality, but rather a world of monstrous phantasies, meshed bizarre libidinal crossings, and chimerical aberrations. Indeed, the inner world of the child amounts to "a cave full of dangerous monsters" ("Manic Depressive States" 272)—or, in the words of Robert M. Young, a world of "craziness and nastiness" (69).

These descriptions of the inner world, which recur over and again in Klein's oeuvre, prompted Lacan to refer to the inner world as a "witch's cauldron . . . at the bottom of which stir, in a global imaginary world . . ., the container of the mother's body, all the primordial phantasies present from the beginning and tending to structure themselves in a drama which seems prefigured" (qtd. in Burgoyne and Sullivan 189). Lacan shows his keen eye in making this classification, for Klein does indeed picture the inner world like a "witch's cauldron," in which bodies, wishes, and desires are participating in a great "S/M" orgy of endless hallucinations, drives, and pleasures. In this inner world of confusion between the sexes, sexual difference is constantly obliterated, demarcated, and exorcised. In a sense, the inner world is not the space where sexual difference prevails in its normative characteristics, but is, on the contrary, the space where it becomes known outside its normative artifice. In the inner world, sexual difference fails. This is so because endlessly conflicting and conflating chimerical phantasies rule the inner world.

Therefore, for Klein the object initially does not exist in itself but is rather a compound and chimerical part-object of an unconscious phantasy. The object could be described as a coordinate structural phantasy that persists in the mind as a result of the processes of projection-introjection. And unconscious phantasy dislocates the idea of innate sexual difference as determining sexuality, because phantasies undermine sexual difference by constantly combining them in chimerical forms of desire. The subject is haunted by compound sexual monsters. Since sexuality for Klein is all about phantasy and to some extent drive (or strong passions), heterosexuality does not exist as such, but seems to be reduced to the phantasy formation of an instinctual drive that searches for fulfillment in aberrant chimeras. These phantasy formations are referred to by Klein as *positions* and are key to ascertaining an unmanageable and structural asymmetry in her theory of sexuality through phantasies of mourning.

3. Phantasies of Mourning

In normal mourning the lost object is retained in the mind in an alive way while the mourner is also aware of its real absence. But if the loss leads to the feeling of a concrete presence of a corpse inside one's body then the mourning processes cannot proceed. You cannot bring a real corpse to life, any more than you can change faeces back into milk. HANNA SEGAL, *PSYCHOANALYSIS, LITERATURE AND WAR* 35

"Mourning and Its Relation to Manic-Depressive States" (1940), one of Klein's most famous essays, expands the ideas Freud developed in "Mourning and Melancholia" (1917). Her essay holds both biographical significance—Klein wrote it after the death of her eldest son—and conceptual significance for its analysis of the inner world and the mechanisms of reparation (see Grosskurth 212–31). There are two major contributions to psychoanalytic theory in this piece: the idea of the depressive position and the concept of reparation. The first one, the depressive position, entails the advent of guilt after aggression has been enacted against the "good" object. The second one, reparation, involves an attempt to repair the damage done by sadistic aggression. The work of mourning re-evokes this depressive position, and, according to Klein, this position recurs through life. Apropos this recurrence, Klein claims that "the course of libidinal development is thus at every step stimulated and reinforced by the drive for reparation, and ultimately by the sense of guilt" ("Oedipus Complex" 410). Primordially the child mourns a fundamental, internal loss. The desire to make reparation originates at the moment when the child realizes that she or he is dependent on the object and that his or her sadistic omnipotence was a phantasy. According to Klein, this reparative position is tied to phantasy, because the child's priority is to repair the inner world by restoring the external world.[5] Thus, in "Criminal Tendencies in Normal Children," Klein argues:

> The impression I get of the way in which even the quite small child fights his unsocial tendencies is rather touching. . . . One moment after we have seen the most sadistic impulses, we meet with performances showing the greatest capacity for love and the wish to make all possible sacrifices to be loved. . . . It is impressive to see in analysis how these destructive tendencies can be used for sublimation . . . how the phantasies can be liberated for most artistic and constructive work. (176)

Reparation takes place through phantasy. But these are phantasies of mourning for the "good" object that the child fears has been killed by phantasies of aggression. The infant appropriates the "whole" object, the predominately good object, not the ideal or perfect object.

Contemporary theorists such as Leo Bersani have criticized this idea of a "whole" object. According to Bersani, an impossibility lies at the heart of this phantasy of reparation. He categorizes these phantasies as "regressive attempts to make up for failed experience" (22). In his view, Klein's inner world is "a complex nonverbal syntax of fantasmatic introjections and projections" (19). Bersani acutely perceives one of the central problems in Klein's idea of phantasies of reparation, arguing that "from the perspective of Klein's later theory of sublimation, the ego's 'new' object relations are, by definition, new relations to old fantasy objects . . . as the ego develops, its relations become more spectral or fantasmatic" (20). Phantasies of reparation represent for Bersani a spiraling of self-referentiality: "What is restored therefore never existed; the 'perfect' object is nothing more than a function of the attacked object" (21).

Indeed, for Klein there is an endless reversion to ever more primitive phantasies. One of Klein's complications is the prevailing dual narrative of phantasy. The theoretical complication occurs not so much in the impossibility of reparation (as Bersani suggests) as in the need for phantasy in the process of mourning. In Klein's system, phantasy is key to reparation, as it is through mourning that the subject can phantasize the distinction between reality and phantasy. And in Kleinian terms, this means being able to avoid concretizing phantasies, that is to say, ensuring that a mental object not be phantasized as an internal organ. As Segal states, "If the dead person is felt as a concrete dead body, or as faeces, inside oneself, then normal mourning is not possible" (*Dream* 37). Klein's formulation of "going through mourning" ("Mourning and Its Relation" 369) refers to a de-idealization of the object of loss, since that loss fails the subject because it refers to the imago of a loss that was the result of an idealization in the first place.

The inner world is a complex conundrum of phantasies that we associate with forms. Nevertheless, this does not imply an inborn heterosexuality; instead, heterosexuality (the oedipal) involves a phantasy of loss that as such should be mourned. In a sense, it is a mourning of the infant phantasy of genital difference. Sexual difference, therefore, is central to the loss that we endlessly mourn through phantasy. On this issue, Jacqueline Rose explains Klein's paradoxical position relative to heterosexuality and phantasy: "Hence the well-known paradox that, in Klein's account, homosexuality arises out of the anxieties of heterosexual phantasy; that if heterosexuality is somewhere pre-established for the subject, it is so only as part of an unmanageable set of phantasies which are in fact incapable, in the theory, of ensuring heterosexuality itself" (167).

This curtailing unmanageability is illustrated well by the case of "Mr B," Klein's major case dealing with male homosexuality. Klein addressed the issue of homosexuality in other cases, such as that of "Mr A" (discussed in *The Psycho-Analysis of Children*), but it is in the case of Mr B (1932) that she referred to the subject as—in the language of identity—a "true homosexual" (*Psycho-Analysis* 265). Hanna Segal provides a useful summary of the case:

> He hated and feared women's bodies because of their "sticking-out parts"—breasts and buttocks. In the analysis it appeared that his unconscious phantasy was that women's breasts and buttocks were so full of sadistic penises and excrement that they were bursting. He also had a frightening phantasy of breasts as harpies. . . . Split off from these bad part-objects, he had a phantasy of an idealized penis, first represented by his pacifier and the bottle, then by the penis of an elder brother with whom he practiced fellatio. (*Melanie Klein* 114)

Klein considers Mr B's phantasies as typical of delusions of omnipotence, which she explains in the following way:

> By means of the magical attributes of excrements and thoughts, poisonous faeces and flatus are introduced into the bodies of his objects in order to dominate or destroy them. In this connection the child's faeces are the instruments of his secret attacks upon the inside of his objects and are regarded by him as evildoing objects or animals who are acting in the interest of his ego. These phantasies of grandeur and omnipotence play a great part in delusions of persecution . . . and in delusions of being poisoned. (*Psycho-Analysis* 261)

According to Klein, these illusory faeces are seen as "coming from his parents and entering his anus" (262n); in the case of Mr B, "his belief in the omnipotence of his excrements was stronger than is usual in boys" (269). The complication emerges when Mr B's "true homosexuality," based on a stronger than usual "omnipotence of excrements," is shown to conceal an unconscious heterosexual position:

> Although Mr B's homosexual position had been established so early on and so strongly, and although he consciously rejected a heterosexual one, he had always unconsciously kept the heterosexual aims in view towards which, as a small boy, he had striven so ardently in his imagination, and as an adult never quite relinquished. To his unconscious his various homosexual activities represented so many bypaths leading to this unconsciously desired goal. (271)

Klein here suggests that the "omnipotence of excrements" signals *not* homosexuality but an unconscious heterosexuality. She identifies in the "deeper layers of the unconscious" the traces of an unconscious heterosexuality in the "real homosexual" subject—in the form of "magnanimous" faeces. Nevertheless, this discovery is occluded by positioning it under the cloak of an oedipal phantasy:

> The homosexual act is designed to realize his early childhood desire of having an opportunity of seeing in what respect his father's penis differs from his own and to find out how it behaves in copulating with his mother. He wants to become more adept and potent in sexual intercourse with his mother. (263)

But what takes place is something different: Klein's logic of sexual difference has shown its underside, and she immediately makes use of the oedipal phantasy as theoretical framework. In doing so, she equates the heterosexual unconscious with the father's penis and the omnipotence of excrements with the omnipotence of the phallus. In this underside of phantasy, in which sexual difference takes the form of chimeras, homosexuality and heterosexuality lose their fixity and take on the attributes of positions. Klein argues: "The child's desire to castrate his father so as to get his penis and be potent in sexual intercourse with his mother urges him towards a homosexual position" (263).

Klein's chimerical, combinative understanding of phantasy leads her to theorize both homosexuality and heterosexuality as positions:

> In addition to this, he wants to put "good" penises and "good" semen inside himself so as to make the interior of his body whole and well. And this wish is heightened in the genital stage by his belief that if his inside is unimpaired he will be able to give his mother "good" semen and children as well—a situation which goes to increase his potency in the heterosexual position. If, on the other hand, his sadistic trends predominate, his desire to get possession of his father's penis and semen by means of the homosexual act will also in part have a heterosexual aim. (263)

In this understanding of sexuality as other than identity, Klein posits homosexuality and heterosexuality as positions. Although she tries to prioritize heterosexuality and normativity, her attempt is doomed to fail. Klein's concepts undermine convention. And it is this unmanageability and unruliness of concepts that provide an innovative understanding of sexuality. As formations of unconscious phantasies, these positions are neither overcome as phases, nor do they disappear in a fluid pansexual plethora of perverse pleasures. Instead they are phantoms that recur to be mourned and, as such, they do not signal a sexual truth but a possibility of creative growth.

In her *Introduction to the Work of Melanie Klein*, Segal reveals the importance of Klein's concept of positionality as innovative in psychoanalysis. This concept radically alters the orthodox psychoanalytic dependency on a stage-based or phase-based developmental understanding of sexuality:

> Melanie Klein chose the term "position" to emphasize the fact that the phenomenon she was describing was not simply a passing "stage" or a "phase," such as, for example, the oral phase; her term implies a specific configuration of object relations, anxieties and defences which persist throughout life. The depressive position never fully supersedes the paranoid-schizoid position; the integration achieved is never complete and defences against the depressive conflict bring about regression to paranoid-schizoid phenomena, so that the individual at all times may oscillate between the two. (xiii)

This understanding of homosexuality and heterosexuality as positions pushes the theory of sexuality beyond psychoanalytical conventions of a ruling genital imaginary, and even beyond the cultural capital of sexual "fluidity." Klein conceives a sexuality that oscillates around phantasies of mourning; she renders homosexuality and heterosexuality as positions structured by the phantasies of the inner world. They are not identities but sexual chimeras—formations of phantasy that endlessly mourn the ever-recurring phantasy-objects of sexual otherness.

4. Mourning Heterosexuality

Phantasies evolve. HANNA SEGAL, *DREAM, PHANTASY AND ART* 26

In a key essay on the topic of termination, Hanna Segal concedes that "in fact, fluctuations remain throughout life" (*Psychoanalysis* 109). This conclusion applies to not only subjectivity, but also sexuality and its phantasies. Reparative phantasies are bound up with ambivalence toward an internal object (generally the entities that come to form the superego). Sexual identity derives from a logic that is very similar to that of a necrophilic phantasy, in which the subject confronts his or her inner world of objects in the problem of "how to share a life between the two of us. . . . It is either you or I" (Segal, *Work* 170). This illustrates a condition in which what is not mourned becomes a corpse.

Segal refers to this confrontation with the otherness of objects when describing a heterosexual subject horrified at his own homosexuality. In this case the patient's failure to work through mourning led to the phantasy of a concretized corpse as ideal sexual object:

> He then started extolling the virtues of a corpse as a sexual object. He described with relish the feeling of power and security that he could enjoy in making love to a corpse: it is there when wanted; you put it away when finished with it; it makes no demands; it is never frustrating, never unfaithful, never reproachful; persecution and guilt, he said, could be quite done away with. (*Work* 166)

This idealization of the corpse derived from an inability to mourn the otherness of objects that short-circuits the phantasy of sexual difference: "He idealized it so intensely in order to deny his overwhelming fear of disintegrating, stinking, putrid corpses, their bits and pieces forever attacking him[,] claiming his very life. . . . The old woman's vagina was 'empty and stinking'" (168). The phantasy of mourning revisited in the depressive position allows for a symbolization that emphasizes the development of an understanding of the interminability of mental objects and of sexuality. This is a very different account of sexuality, one that bases its health in the fluctuating nature of sexual positions and in the cyclical revisiting of mourning. At every fluctuation we revisit our position anew by traversing a phantasy of mourning the otherness of our inner world.

In this model, sexuality is far from a straight line that passes through developmental phases; it is constituted instead through endless fluctuations among positions. At the same time, sexuality is not fluid because it is bound to a specific set of phantasies or mental structures that become ever-recurring positions of failed subjectivity. In short, sexuality involves structural fluctuations of phantasies about reparations that fail. Neither subjects nor objects are integrated fully or perfectly, but instead oscillate around phantasies. These phantasies are structured around losses that recur and therefore are not completely fluid or polymorphous. According to Klein, these phantasies of reparation allow a sexual position to perform by permitting sexual difference to fail. In this failure, sexuality is tied not to genitalia but to phantasies of objects constantly mourned, objects that fluctuate interminably between phantasies of faeces and corpses.

Heterosexuality, therefore, is *terminable* as a sexual practice, but *interminable* as an unconscious phantasy in the homosexual subject. This makes heterosexuality not the hidden truth of homosexuality; instead, the recurrence of heterosexual phantasies means that gay identity revisits its phantasies of losses. Through the recurring mourning of those phantasies, sexuality unravels its otherness. It becomes, for Klein, a recurrent mourning for the phantasmatic burdens of its interminable otherness.

Notes

1. See Isaacs: "The English translators of Freud adopted a special spelling of the word 'phantasy,' with the *ph*, in order to differentiate the psycho-analytical significance of the term, *i.e.* predominantly or entirely unconscious phantasies, from the popular word 'fantasy,' meaning conscious day-dreams, fictions and so on. The psycho-analytical term 'phantasy' essentially connotes unconscious mental content, which may or may not become conscious. This meaning of the word

has assumed a growing significance, particularly in consequence of the work of Melanie Klein on the early stages of development" (81). See also Hinshelwood, *Dictionary* 32–46, 68–83; and *Clinical* 25–31.

2. A note on basic Kleinian terminology is in order here. In Kleinian psychoanalysis two major fluctuating positions structure the infant human psyche: the paranoid-schizoid position and the depressive position. The paranoid-schizoid position is the earliest state of mind, in which persecutory anxiety is met by processes that threaten to fragment the mind. These splitting processes "typically lead to projection of parts of the self or ego . . . into objects, with a depleting effect on the self" (Hinshelwood 156). The paranoid-schizoid position is countered by the depressive position, characterized by "a particularly poignant sadness." In an effort to "maximize the loving aspect of the ambivalent relationship with the damaged 'whole object,'" the subject in the depressive position attempts to "integrate his or her fragmented perceptions of mother, bringing together the separately good and bad versions (imagos) that he or she has previously experienced. When such part-objects are brought together as a whole they threaten to form a contaminated, damaged or dead whole object" (Hinshelwood 138).

3. Klein discusses in depth the issue of the enlightenment of children in the following essays: "The Development of a Child" (1921), "Inhibitions and Difficulties at Puberty" (1922), "Early Analysis" (1923), "A Contribution to the Psychogenesis of Tics" (1925), "The Psychological Principles of Early Analysis"(1926), and "Criminal Tendencies in Normal Children" (1927).

4. Following one of Freud's theories of the formation of the superego, Klein interprets the superego as formed through a combination of factors; but it still retains its amorphous or impersonalist trait. For Freud, the superego was formed in various ways: through introjection in *Group Psychology and the Analysis of the Ego* (1921); drives versus reality in *Civilization and Its Discontents* (1930); later development in *New Introductory Lectures on Psycho-Analysis* (1933); and internal object in *An Outline of Psychoanalysis* (1940). It is the Freud of *An Outline* that is most akin to Klein's depictions of the inner world.

5. For a contemporary social theory based on Klein's theory of reparation vis-à-vis the Frankfurt School, see Alford 170–98.

References

Alford, C. Fred. *Melanie Klein and Critical Social Theory: An Account of Politics, Art, and Reason Based on Her Psychoanalytic Theory.* New Haven: Yale UP, 1989.

Bersani, Leo. "Death and Literary Authority: Marcel Proust and Melanie Klein." *The Culture of Redemption.* Cambridge: Harvard UP, 1990. 7–28. In Phillips and Stonebridge 223–44.

Burgoyne, Bernard, and Mary Sullivan, eds. *The Klein-Lacan Dialogues.* New York: Other P, 1999.

Butler, Judith. "Moral Sadism and Doubting One's Own Love: Kleinian Reflections on Melancholia." In Phillips and Stonebridge 179–89.

Freud, Sigmund. "Analysis Terminable and Interminable." 1937. *Standard* 23: 209–53.

———. *Civilization and Its Discontents.* 1930 (1929). *Standard* 21:59–148.

———. *Group Psychology and the Analysis of the Ego.* 1921. *Standard* 18:67–144.

———. "Mourning and Melancholia." 1917. *Standard* 14:237–48.

———. *New Introductory Lectures on Psycho-Analysis.* 1933. *Standard* 22:3–184.

———. *An Outline of Psychoanalysis.* 1940. *Standard* 23:139–208.

———. *The Standard Edition of the Complete Psychological Works of Sigmund Freud.* Ed. James Strachey. 24 vols. London: Hogarth, 1953–74.

Geissmann, Pierre, and Claudine Geissmann. *A History of Child Psychoanalysis.* London: Routledge, 1998.

Gillespie, William H. "The Structure and Aetiology of Sexual Perversion." In *Perversions: Psychodynamics and Therapy.* Ed. Sandor Lorand. New York: Random House, 1956. 28–41.

Grosskurth, Phyllis. *Melanie Klein: Her World and Her Work.* Cambridge: Harvard UP, 1987.

Hinshelwood, R. D. *Clinical Klein: From Theory to Practice.* New York: Basic, 1994.

———. *A Dictionary of Kleinian Thought.* 2nd. ed. Northvale, NJ: Jason Aronson, 1991.

Isaacs, Susan. "The Nature and Function of Phantasy." In *Developments in Psycho-Analysis.* Ed. Joan Riviere. London: Hogarth, 1952. 67–122. A different version appears in King and Steiner 264–414.

King, Pearl, and Riccardo Steiner, eds. *The Freud-Klein Controversies in the British Psycho-Analytical Society, 1941–45.* London: Routledge, 1991.

Klein, Melanie. "A Contribution to the Psychogenesis of Manic-Depressive States." 1935. *Love, Guilt and Reparation* 262–89.

———. "A Contribution to the Psychogenesis of Tics." 1925. *Love, Guilt and Reparation* 106–27.

———. "A Contribution to the Theory of Intellectual Inhibition." 1931. *Love, Guilt and Reparation* 236–47.

———. "Criminal Tendencies in Normal Children." 1927. *Love, Guilt and Reparation* 170–85.

———. "The Development of a Child." 1921. *Love, Guilt and Reparation* 1–53.

———. "Early Analysis." 1923. *Love, Guilt and Reparation* 77–105.

———. "Early Stages of the Oedipus Conflict." 1928. *Love, Guilt and Reparation* 186–98.

———. *Envy and Gratitude and Other Works, 1946–1963.* London: Hogarth, 1975.

———. "The Importance of Symbol Formation in the Development of the Ego." 1930. *Love, Guilt and Reparation* 219–32.

———. "Inhibitions and Difficulties at Puberty." 1922. *Love, Guilt and Reparation* 54–58.

————. *Love, Guilt and Reparation and Other Works 1921–1945*. London: Virago, 1988.

————. "Mourning and Its Relation to Manic-Depressive States." 1940. *Love, Guilt and Reparation* 344–69.

————. "The Oedipus Complex in the Light of Early Anxieties." 1945. *Love, Guilt and Reparation* 370–419.

————. "On the Criteria for the Termination of a Psycho-Analysis." 1950. *Envy and Gratitude* 43–47.

————. *The Psycho-Analysis of Children*. Trans. Alix Strachey. London: Hogarth, 1932.

————. "The Psychological Principles of Early Analysis." 1926. *Love, Guilt and Reparation* 128–38.

Laplanche, Jean, and Jean-Bertrand Pontalis. "Fantasy and the Origins of Sexuality." 1964. In *Formations of Fantasy*. Ed. Victor Burgin, James Donald, and Cora Kaplan. London: Methuen, 1986. 5–34.

O'Connor, Noreen, and Joanna Ryan. *Wild Desires and Mistaken Identities: Lesbianism and Psychoanalysis*. New York: Columbia UP, 1993.

Perlow, Meir. *Understanding Mental Objects*. London: Routledge, 1995.

Phillips, John, and Lyndsey Stonebridge, eds. *Reading Melanie Klein*. London: Routledge, 1998.

Riviere, Joan. "Symposium on Child Analysis." *The Inner World and Joan Riviere. Collected Papers: 1920–1958*. Ed. Athol Hughes. London: Karnac, 1991. 80–88.

Rose, Jacqueline. *Why War? Psychoanalysis, Politics, and the Return to Melanie Klein*. Oxford: Blackwell, 1993.

Segal, Hanna. *Dream, Phantasy and Art*. London: Routledge, 1991.

————. *Introduction to the Work of Melanie Klein*. New York: Basic, 1964.

————. *Melanie Klein*. New York: Viking, 1979.

————. *Psychoanalysis, Literature and War: Papers 1972–1995*. Ed. John Steiner. London: Routledge, 1997.

————. *The Work of Hanna Segal: A Kleinian Approach to Clinical Practice*. New York: Jason Aronson, 1981.

Young, Robert M. "Phantasy and Psychotic Anxieties." In Burgoyne and Sullivan 65–81.

THE EROTICISM OF DESOLATION

Catherine Millot
Translated by James Swenson

. . . .

Everything that is not consumed rots. ROGER CAILLOIS, *L'HOMME ET LE SACRÉ*

1.

Mishima shared with Gide the bitter certainty of being "barred" (*forclos*). Both of them, unique objects of a feminine solicitude completely and narrowly enclosed upon them, experienced a childhood of constant illnesses, riven by a precocious eroticism that was both solitary and associated with the most unseemly representations. The immobilization of their bodies by an almost constant surveillance was avenged by the aberrations of their imaginations, which remained unmoderated by contact with other children. Like André Gide as a child, Yukio Mishima lacked the self-image that is formed through the image of another in whom one recognizes oneself. These children had no peers, no others like them. Despite being the objects of an overwhelming attachment, they seemed to be missing the love that compares and thereby places one in the human community. Unique, each was without equal, lacking a rival. The love they did get had given them no outline, as if it were addressed to something in them without form or name.

This lack of an image is perhaps the source of what is too easily called homosexual narcissism. This subject seeks in himself not so much the lost image of the mother's beloved child as something that never gave this love a human face. Desire to have and desire to be, longing for possession and longing for an inaccessible confraternity, will remain forever indissociable for him.

The solitary child watches the others play through a window. He knows that it will always be like this. A spell separates him from ordinary humanity. He has been denied the fundamental right of sharing the common fate, the pleasures and the pains of everyone else. He alone, for example, can never eat "blue-skinned fish" (*Confessions* 26), nor, later, marry the young woman he loves: an inexplicable impossibility. The risk of death hangs over him; every form of life is suspected as a source of fatal contamination from which he must be sheltered. But what can be done when one secretes his own poison?

Kimitake Hiraoka, the future Mishima, was raised in a darkened room, much like the heir to the imperial throne. On the fiftieth day after his birth, his grandmother took him from his mother. This child, her son's firstborn, was sacrificed like the first fruits of the harvest. The old woman, who suffered from horrible neuralgia, closed him in with her far away from noise and light. Often at night the child heard her scream with pain. Such suffering was like a chasm into which he had been thrown in hope of an unlikely reparation.

Illness is often the only available cry of distress for the child who knows the abandonment of being the other's thing. Kimitake fell victim to violent allergies; at least once a month he showed all the signs of poisoning and was thought to be at the point of death. The diagnosis of autointoxication gave the grandmother an alibi to clutch him even tighter, a justification for his seclusion. His rebellion, as is often the case, served only to subjugate him further. Everyone marveled at the way he never complained about the grandmother's regime and submitted so gracefully to his exclusion from the family life that his younger brother and sister led with his parents. His stoicism was cause for astonishment. His unruffled face evoked the masks of the Noh theater. Nothing shook him; nothing seemed even to move him. One day, hoping to toughen him, his father held him up at arm's length in the wind created by a train passing at top speed, but the child did not bat an eyelash.

Beyond the physical harm done by this sort of sequestration, one's being an object of barter—treated like a commodity that is fought or bargained over—does not leave much room for desire to develop unless you eroticize the very condition imposed upon you. Extreme dispossession of the self, variously transposed, thus became the recurrent theme of the young Mishima's mental theater. Any evocation of a fate to which someone had been subjected without choice—a difficult task or a dangerous mission (like cleaning sewers or going off to war)—aroused in him a voluptuous sorrow. Representations of heroic or sacrificial death took his sensual excitement to its peak.

The rending unity of abjection and glory, eroticism and desolation, was abruptly realized by a scene that Mishima's 1949 autobiographical novel, *Confessions of a Mask,* describes as originary. When he was four, Kimitake's encounter with a young cesspool cleaner—a "night-soil man" in Japanese—fixed the child's desire in a vision as definitive as a vocation. The beauty of the red-cheeked face, of the agile body in the soiled cotton clothes, gracefully balancing on his shoulder two buckets full of excrement, would later detach itself from the depths of memory with the luminous precision, the almost surreal clarity characteristic of the "fixed images" Freud speaks about with respect to screen memories. "This image," Mishima writes in *Confessions,* "is the earliest of those that have kept tormenting and frightening me all my life" (8). It was a programmatic image that fixed and announced a destiny, like a "menu" that he would spend his whole life figuring out until everything had been consumed. The night-soil man, with his clinging pants and strange job, instantly became the object of the child's irremediable fascination: Thenceforth, he wanted to "be him," to become like him a collector of excrement, and like him to wear the tight cotton pants that outline his thighs. This sudden desire cuts through him like a sharp pain, like "a yearning for a piercing sorrow" (9). The night-soil man, in his intimacy with obscure dangers, seemed to the child to be carrying out a heroic duty closely related to martyrdom. His shining grace was the sort conferred by the sovereign detachment of one who has consented to self-sacrifice. In Japan, where excrement is the symbol for earth, his fearsome mission doomed him to "the malevolent love of the Earth Mother" (8).

The chasm of the Earth Mother, like a gaping jaw above which all life is suspended, calls upon certain beings to assume the burden of its insatiable avarice. Some even long to throw themselves into it. But are not all men, being mortal, doomed to end up there? Are we not, in Mishima's words, "fodder to garnish a gizzard"?

A little-known detail of Japanese society, intimately tied to its religious foundations, may explain why the night-soil man had a tragic aura in the child's eyes. Surrounded by a silence comprising shame and denial, a caste of untouchables, the *"burakumin,"* still exists in Japan today, according to Jean-François Sabouret. Descendants of ancient pariahs dedicated to impure tasks (those that brought them into contact with blood and death, rottenness and excrement), the *burakumin* are still excluded from marriage and jobs, despite the legal abrogation, over a century ago, of the caste system. Employers and families often enlist private detectives to investigate the ancestry of a job candidate or prospective spouse. "Won't you find out if he's not a bit different?" the detective is asked. The word *burakumin* is not pronounced, a sign of its taboo character. Admitting a descendant of one of these pariahs into one's family or business is thought to bring pollution and malediction upon it.

The *burakumin* are split into two groups with distinct social status: the *eta*—the impure, the "defilement abundant"—and the *hinin,* the "nonhuman." The former worked at jobs that brought them into contact with blood, death, and human waste. They were butchers, tanners or cobblers, grave diggers, cemetery keepers, garbage collectors, and night-soil men. They were allowed to live only on the periphery of cities and villages, on the mountainside or near the riverbed: These ghettos still exist today. The center of the city was forbidden to them, as was marrying outside of their group or taking jobs other than those reserved for them. One was born an *eta,* but the *hinin,* the nonhuman, had been provisionally cut off from the human community by some criminal act or impure activity. Actors and other performers, magicians, and prostitutes were part of this group. The *hinin* are supposed to have invented the Kabuki theater.

Japanese sociologist Masao Yamaguchi has pointed out the topological relation that exists in Japanese society between the emperor and the *burakumin.* If this society is compared to what is called an open set in mathematics, a set that excludes its own limits, then they constitute its exterior poles, the "top" and "bottom" limits. Simultaneously foreign to the community and founding it by their very exclusion, the emperor and the *burakumin* are equally sacred, the one by an excess of purity and the other by an excess of impurity. The two meet in what constitutes a sphere of danger for the rest of society. They have identical functions as scapegoats, assuring the unity of the group through self-sacrifice.

The ambivalence inherent in the notion of the sacred, which originally designated "a person or thing that cannot be touched without being defiled or defiling what touches it" (qtd. in Caillois 46), is well known. Roger Caillois notes that profane existence is limited by two exclusions: that of the pure on account of its proximity with the gods, and that of the impure, whose proximity to animality reminds man of his condition as a living thing—the blood of menstruation and childbirth, the cadaver. "It is worth remarking that the same prohibitions that protect against defilement also isolate holiness and protect against contact with it. The sovereign-god of the mikado type, like the menstruating woman, must not touch the ground or be exposed to the light of the sun" (Caillois 53). The sacred is bipolar. It is made of two abysses that may form only one, pollution inverting itself into benediction, the impure becoming the path of purification. If the law that founds the human order is sacred, so is its transgression, and the pomp of princes is only the luminous face of filth. At Golgotha, the thief and the son of God are side by side. Christ's crown of thorns, set on a black-and-red background, served as an emblem on the flag of the Suiheisha, the movement to defend *burakumin* rights, founded in 1922. It was kept by the BKD, which succeeded it and which is still fighting discrimination today.

The pure and the impure—their ties to blood, death, and sacrifice— are at the heart of Mishima's work. His fateful encounter with the young, red-cheeked night-soil man bears witness to Mishima's relation to the theme of the pariah. Nowhere in his work are the *burakumin* discussed, but for all Japanese the figure of the night-soil man cannot be dissociated from these untouchables. The horror they inspire explains the gesture of the woman, whether mother or governess, who violently pulls the child back when the young man passes.

And how can we not think of the other *burakumin*, the *hinin* or nonhu- mans, when considering Tenkatsu, the famous female magician whom the child of *Confessions of a Mask* admires at the theater? Her violent makeup, her arms weighed down with glittering jewels, and her brightly colored clothing fascinate him. He is taken with the "melancholy har- mony" that the "brazen luster [of] shoddy merchandise" emits. Once again, he immediately wants to "become Tenkatsu," even as he feels the difference between this desire and the desire to "become a night-soil man." A "tragic quality" is lacking in this new desire: "In wishing to be- come Tenkatsu I did not have to taste that bitter mixture of longing and shame" (*Confessions* 17).

Shortly thereafter, he enters his mother's room, takes her most sump- tuous kimono, wraps an obi around and around his waist, powders his face, and runs into his grandmother's room screaming, "I'm Tenkatsu!" He is brutally recalled to reality when he sees his mother completely pale, her eyes lowered: "I understood. Tears blurred my eyes" (19). But what did he understand? Which was the greater shame for his mother, that her son was dressed as a woman or that he had taken the role of a *hinin*?

Recent studies have suggested that Mishima might have had *burakumin* in his ancestry.

In the option of "becoming Tenkatsu," the shame seems to remain someone else's. The little boy did not give up the pleasures of transvestism, which merely became clandestine. His impersonation of Cleopatra, whom he had seen at the movies, took up where Tenkatsu left off, but this time with the complicity of his brother and sister, who helped dress him up. Transvestism, for Mishima, seems to require the regard of another, whereas "becoming a night-soil man" remains confined to the secret recesses of his conscience. "Becoming Tenkatsu" could be avowed; it allowed him to escape the bitter vocation of sacrifice entailed by "becoming a night-soil man." "Being Tenkatsu" meant having the powers of the lower realm, controlling the magic of counterfeit, being delivered from the "tragic fate" of the former desire.

Throughout Mishima's childhood a pariah identity developed around his feeling of being "barred," to which his slow discovery of homosexuality gave meaning only retroactively. The silent conviction of being different, excluded from the common destiny, haunted his youth, always holding him back on the threshold of engagements, war, marriage, a profession. This constitutes a leitmotif of *Confessions of a Mask*. His becoming a writer took account of this feeling of tragic exclusion and represented a path of return, a way of finding a separate place—but still *a* place—among men; that is, his becoming a writer provided a way of "being Tenkatsu" and exercising the very real powers of illusion, all the while deferring his accomplishment of a fatal destiny. Being a novelist, a man of the theater, an actor, as Mishima was, meant playing with the resources of fiction and the games of illusion so as to create "a thing which is not a thing," a work, a fetish, the costume jewelry that onstage shines brighter than the real thing. That Mishima situated himself as a writer on the side of "being Tenkatsu" is confirmed by the many feminine heroines who have the burden of representing him in books such as *Thirst for Love* (1950), *After the Banquet* (1960), and *A School for the Flesh* (1964). And the fetishistic value that words have for him is explicitly formulated in *Sun and Steel* (1968).

The bipolarity of his desire—the double wish to "become a night-soil man" and to "become Tenkatsu"—is at the foundation of the splitting of the ego from which Mishima never ceased to suffer. His personality offered such contrary aspects that he often seemed to others to wear masks, and occasionally even he no longer knew which was his true face. According to Freud, the unity of the ego is the price that must be paid to avoid renouncing incompatible desires, and above all to evade the reality of the mother's "castration" and the threat it bears. In this respect, the divergent desires to "become Tenkatsu" and to "become a night-soil man" represent two "solutions," each of which gives the lie to maternal castration and that reinforce each other even though they are contradictory, resting as they do on the two aspects of "being" and "having."

"To be a night-soil man" apparently means immolating oneself in "the malevolent love of the Earth Mother," in the chasm of her murderous voracity, making oneself equal in death to the absent phallus—or at least erecting oneself as its substitute, the stiffened muscles in the taut clothing, the whole body become a fetish. "To be Tenkatsu," the illusionist, means on the contrary exhibiting the insignia of power, even and especially if they are factitious, since fraudulence is an essential index of their symbolic value. Costume jewelry is exemplary of the fetish when worn by a woman: The affirmation of her phallicism is denied in the same breath, the avowal of her castration by the same movement that misrecognizes it—and hence is realized the unity of two contrary propositions. Tenkatsu is the idol in its splendor as a simulacrum.

In the first case, the object chosen by the fascinated child *is* the phallus, conditional on the possession of an organ; in the second, it is the *objet a* in the explicit mode of counterfeit. Both "solutions" rescue one from the impossible mission of having and being the phallus at the same time—of having it "for real" as a man and of being it for the mother (or, in this case, for the grandmother). Both "solutions" also rescue one from the tyranny of having really to be this sacrificial object dedicated to the Other's lack, of being in the reality of one's own body the appendage, the living prosthesis of the Other's infirm body. In both cases, the solution resides in the liberating delegation that consists in being it and having it *in the object,* in a doubled object, fetish on one side and idol on the other. The movement of identification—wanting to "be like"—in fact comes down to affirming a nonidentity; this identification supposes a separation from the thing that one was for the other, a way of casting off the burden of having to be it. Mishima notes this relief: "It seemed to be that my grief at being eternally excluded was always being transformed in my dreaming into grief for those persons and their ways of life" (*Confessions* 10).

There exists a disparity between the two solutions, however. "Becoming Tenkatsu" is the least ruinous. It represents a ludic manner, not entirely lacking in derision, of settling the question of the woman's "castration" by upholding both exigencies: that she has the phallus, which liberates, and that she does not, which leaves reality its rights. Although the object of a ludic identification, Tenkatsu is never an object of erotic desire for the narrator of *Confessions of a Mask*. The burden of desire, as well as the "tragic quality" connected with it, belongs entirely to the figure of the night-soil man and his successive avatars (railway ticket collectors, knights killed in war, assassinated princes, and Christian martyrs). Here the tragic excludes the ludic: Fetishistic value is intimately associated with the fact of being "fated for death" (20), and desire is thus indissociable from "bitter sorrow." Here too the phallus is both affirmed and denied at once, although in a different mode than with Tenkatsu. On the one hand, the presence of the masculine organ under the clothing is indispensable to the object's erotic value. On the other hand, virility cannot be dissociated from death: It exalts in its own destruction, as if supreme castration brought it to an incandescent state.

It is in the homosexual option (as opposed to the transvestite option) that we can observe the particular seesaw movement between desire and identification generally attributed to the narcissistic component of a same-sex object-choice. In this case, to love is to want to "be like." From his first encounter with the night-soil man, Mishima's experience of desire for the other and his longing to be like him are affirmed as fundamentally indissociable. And when, later, the narrator of *Confessions* gets a crush on Omi, a young classmate, he experiences an incessant oscillation between erotic excitement and jealous envy vis-à-vis the plenitude of being that Omi incarnates in his eyes. This oscillation enables an ever-increasing self-deception about the truth of his inclinations, and he convinces himself that he wants only to resemble his ideal, whereas in reality he wants to take sensual pleasure in him.

This seesaw movement is nevertheless irreducible to a mirror relation, that is, to the erotic and aggressive tensions that flow from such a relation and that make desire for one's self-image tantamount to a theft either of one's desire or of one's image. This seesaw refers rather to a coupling of two heterogeneous terms. One of Freud's well-known formulations, later revised, is that homosexual love for younger men rests on an unconscious identification with the mother, whose chosen object the homosexual had previously been (see Freud, *Leonardo*). But here Mishima falls in love with the night-soil man and later with Omi to replace his grandmother—she who was his "true-love sweetheart, aged sixty" (37) when he was nine years old. And when he longs to "be like" Omi and the night-soil man, it is not so much a matter of identifying with the ideal image of the child beloved by the old woman as it is of longing to be swallowed by the abyss of her *jouissance*—and thereby to fulfill the destiny that dooms him to an obscure sacrifice (and by which he identifies with the missing phallus). In other words, the seesaw movement oscillates not between the self and a mirroring other, but between the two poles of the maternal Other and the phallus. This doubling is less like that of the subject and his mirror image than it is like the two infinite series of reflections obtained by placing an object between facing mirrors. The oscillation from one position to the other is sometimes so fast that, as Phyllis Greenacre has remarked, the look never stops passing from one reflection to the other (see *Trauma*).

The narrator of *Confessions of a Mask* at one point tries to superimpose the two and make himself both subject and object of desire: "I would enact the double role of both Omi and myself" (87–88). In order to become Omi's "stand-in" and transform his pleasure at Omi's sight into the pleasure that Omi himself would feel, he begins to seek upon his frail body the timid reflection of the other's sumptuous virility. One day at the seashore, he suddenly catches sight of his own underarms and discovers that Omi's exuberant pilosity, the object of his jealousy, has begun to grace his own barely pubescent body with a glorious shadow. A "mysterious sexual desire" (88) overtakes him at once and, taking the dark thickets of his underarms as his object (in the image of those he had fetishized), he masturbates in the open air for the first time, alone beneath the blue sky: "My body was shaken with a strange grief. I was on fire with a loneliness as fiery as the sun" (89). The solitude of his own, mysterious exclusion is reawakened by a feeling of emptiness before the plenitude of the sea and joined, in this moment of solitary pleasure, with the solitude that has attracted him in Omi, "a loneliness born of the fact that life had enslaved him" (87). Eroticism once again transforms desolation into triumph.

These cascading rifts—becoming Tenkatsu/becoming a night-soil man, desiring Omi/becoming Omi—constitute so many zigzagging ramparts against the "tragic fate" of actually being sacrificed. They defuse and distance the lethal desire of the Other by derealizing it in fantasy. Doubtless this is also the function of anonymity in perverse fantasy (for example, the passive voice of the fantasy "A child is being beaten"), which allows the subject not to appear in the fantasy but to slide under either of its terms.

The protective function of this rift is demonstrated *a contrario* by the fact that the urge to overcome it—essentially in the purified form of the split between words and the body explored by *Sun and Steel*—pushed Mishima to fulfill his "tragic fate" in the form of an ultimate sacrifice to a lost cause, that of the emperor's "divinity." But perhaps he had also reached the limits of the two "solutions," homosexuality and writing, that had sustained him for so long. Of his writing he declared, in the catalog for an exhibition dedicated to him shortly before his death, "What I have written departs from me, never nourishing my void, and becomes nothing but a relentless whip lashing me on" (Scott-Stokes 115).

2.

At the entry to adulthood, the narrator of *Confessions* encounters a new fact that cannot be integrated into the "solutions" elaborated up to this point, an "unknown" that ruins his calculations. Love for Sonoko comes crashing down on him, confronting him with the violence of a grief that shakes the very foundations of his existence and revives his old feeling of being permanently excluded from common life. The suffering that he had managed to eroticize by making it the other's, a suffering experienced by the pariah yet shrouded in the halo of a martyr's glory, returns to him—this time purified of all sensuality because confronting the impossibility that a woman's love represents for him. While the "piercing sorrow" inspired by his sight of the night-soil man was associated with a desire mixed with shame, in this case a mysterious feeling of guilt prevails, one so difficult to delimit that Mishima describes it with the expression "remorse as prelude to sin."

The tragic character of his encounter with Sonoko is different from that in the fantasmatic scenarios that destine the hero to death. It resides, on the contrary, in the fact that, in a sense, this encounter never took place. The pain of this enigmatic nonevent is compared to "that of a person who waits one bright midday for the roar of the noon-gun and, when the time for the gun's sounding has passed in silence, tries to discover the waiting emptiness somewhere in the blue sky. His is . . . the horrible doubt that it may never come after all. He is the only man in the world who knows that the noon-gun did not sound promptly at noon" (206).

The narrator never stops examining what he, inexplicably, had been lacking. Was it this same weakness that led him to get himself declared unfit for service even as he believed, in his fantasy, that he wanted to die at war, "among strangers, untroubled, beneath a cloudless sky"? In his half-conscious evasion, he had missed the call and nothing could ever redeem this cowardice: "I realized vividly that my future life would never attain heights of glory sufficient to justify my having escaped death in the army" (138). Mishima did not hide the fact that, in this respect, his story in *Confessions* was faithful to reality. His subsequent bodybuilding appears derisory and pathetic in this light, as do his paramilitary training and his creation of a private militia.

In his failed marriage, as in the episode of military service, he lacked access to ordinary virility, the kind that dissociates the penis from any fetishistic value and that does not covet death as a *jouissance*. He was missing the "solution"; he didn't know how to use it. The narrator of *Confessions* writes: "My grief resembled that of a fainthearted student who has failed an examination: I made a mistake! I made a mistake! Simply because I didn't solve that X, everything was wrong" (206–7). But how can one risk one's life when he believes himself immortal? How can one love a woman when he doesn't desire her? It appears that he has reached here the very root of his sense of exclusion: "You're not human. You're a being who is incapable of social intercourse. You're nothing but a creature, nonhuman and strangely pathetic" (230).

Despite his "unendurable" grief (168), and desolated as he was by this unfulfilled love, he lived the separation from Sonoko as a "delight." This pleasure dissimulated what was irreparable, affirming his victory over loss: "I had an odd ability to enjoy everything in this way. Because of this perverse talent my cowardice was often mistaken, even in my own eyes, for courage" (171). Mishima's eroticism shows that *jouissance* is the royal road to denying castration. Such a victory may be shrewd, but it does not evade culpability. If Mishima's exclusion stems from the immemorial constraint suffered by his unwilling body—experienced in his childhood as a "compulsion" to be different (81) and resulting in a mysterious malaise at the thought of growing up—it is nonetheless accompanied by a feeling of guilt, for there is no subject position that, in the last resort, is not the result of a decision, however unfathomable its origin.

Beyond the evasion of his military obligations, the narrator's culpability in *Confessions of a Mask* is based on a more fundamental desertion. He has broken with ordinary obligations and failed to acquit himself of what the community of men requires of its members, and he is the only one to know it; hence his feeling of imposture and his sensation of having a sword of Damocles suspended above him. He sees the cracked and chapped hands of Sonoko's brother, on leave from the front, as witnesses for the prosecution. And as he resolves to escape from loving Sonoko, he feels even more deeply the "guilty conscience of a fugitive from justice" (156).

This feeling of being cut off from common existence intensifies the day he walks with Sonoko in the streets of a just-bombarded Tokyo: "As we went along the passageway we did not receive even so much as a reproachful glance. We were ignored. Our existence was obliterated by the fact that we had not shared in their misery; for them, we were noth-ing more than shadows" (160). Nevertheless, on that day, observing a distress that seems connected to the deepest bonds of love, he momen-tarily glimpses the possibility of rejoining the human community. A wave of confidence lifts him up and seems to dissipate on the spot his "doubts concerning the fundamental requirement of manhood." This "sudden in-sight into truth" arises, bizarrely, in response to the idea that the men and women whose misfortune he views have just been confronted with one of those exceptional situations in which it is "permissible to kill one person in order that another might live," in which it is "none other than the child who murdered his own mother when she was trying to save it." Evoking a mother who dies by giving life, whose sacrifice makes her child her murderer, the narrator is suddenly overtaken by a "hot feeling of con-fidence" (161). An obscure link seems to unite the acceptance of the gift of love—even in its mortal extremities—with the possibility of assuming the demands of ordinary life.

In Mishima's work the feeling of being "barred" from humanity merges with that of being barred from love. It is not feeling but receiving love that is impossible, and when Sonoko begins to love him the narrator takes flight for good. The mechanism of this impossibility lies precisely in the idea that momentarily seemed to remove it—that the child is po-tentially his mother's murderer. The Other of love must be protected from the danger the subject himself threatens. His certainty of threatening this Other with destruction is thus the source of his unconscious despair and his sense of worthlessness. In this respect, his homosexuality serves as much to protect the mother by identifying with her as to protect himself from her grasp. But this identification is unstable, and the subject finds himself thrown back to the other pole—his identification with the de-structive phallus—whenever a lover takes the position of maternal other.

Love for young men also runs up against the impossible. If his love for Sonoko was free of any sensuality, unfortunately disincarnate, his love for young men, on the contrary, will have to be free of any intellectuality. Like Omi, a boy is desirable only if he is, in some way, deprived of lan-guage—as if his body thereby becomes purer, more carnal, and acquires through this privation the "tragic" dimension essential to erotic value. Desire's condition that the intellect play no part engages love in a logical aporia, since the reciprocity required by love demands of the narrator a "revolt against reason" that contradicts his nature (65). Thus the scission of flesh and spirit goes so far as to necessitate that they be held at an implacable distance from each other, forbidding any relation and render-ing the metaphor of love impossible.

This scission is so implacable that it makes coexistence of the two terms impossible. The narrator of *Confessions* cannot accept the common banalization of amorous life that consists, as Freud put it, in loving where there is no desire and desiring where there is no love ("On the Universal" 183). If his desire is directed at boys, he cannot love Sonoko: If one statement is true the other must be false. Like two contradictory propositions, homosexual desire and love for Sonoko cannot both be true. This requirement for wholeness, this refusal of the normal division of subjectivity and its compromises (and here we see incontrovertibly that the splitting characteristic of perversion is in no way reducible to this division), leads the narrator of *Confessions* to a desperate attempt to escape the double truth of his love and his desire by denying one of the terms of the contradiction. Thus he is led to question the authenticity of each term, one after the other. At one moment he kids himself that he is like everyone else "in every respect" (106). Occluding his homosexual desires, he rushes headlong into an obsession with normality. At other times he attempts to free himself from his love's implacable certainty by imagining himself as an unscrupulous seducer. His love for Sonoko confronts him with a painful presentiment of its impossibility and hence with guilt ("remorse as prelude to sin").

Thus he struggles to believe that he is lying to himself by making himself believe that he loves her, for if it is false that he loves her, then his pain is fictitious: QED. Once again, he can believe that he has escaped the ineluctability of loss and failure. But it is characteristic of a lie to turn around on itself: If lying to himself is his truth, "then my feeling of wanting to regard Sonoko's attraction for me as sheer counterfeit might be nothing but a mask to hide my true desire of believing myself genuinely in love with her. So maybe I am becoming the sort of person who is incapable of acting contrary to his true nature, and maybe I do really love her . . ." (153).

A vertiginous turning movement is thus set in motion between homosexual desire and love for Sonoko. As on a Möbius strip, where one traverses front to back without crossing any border, the narrator of *Confessions* never stops seeing his truth transformed into a lie and his lie becoming true, sliding as on a toboggan from one side of himself to the other:

> My powers of self-analysis were constructed in a way that defied definition, like one of those hoops made by giving a single twist to a strip of paper and then pasting the ends together. What appeared to be the inside was the outside, and what appeared to be the outside was the inside. Although in later years my self-

analysis traversed the rim of the hoop more slowly, when I was twenty it was doing nothing but spinning blindfolded through the orbit of my emotions, and lashed on by the excitement attending the war's final disastrous stages, the speed of the revolutions had become enough to make me all but completely lose my sense of balance.

Thenceforth, overcome by the sense of imposture, he feels himself becoming "the sort of person who can't believe in anything except the counterfeit" (153).

His imminent enlistment in the army and departure for the front, signifying an almost certain death, delivers him from the exhausting rift between his desire and his love. Death turns out to be the only possible solution to his doubleness and the only thing capable of checking the incessant movement from one pole of his shredded subjectivity to the other: "The blind devotion I felt for Sonoko and my ever-present unnatural desires of the flesh had now been fused within me into a single homogeneous mass and had pinned me immobile to each succeeding instant of time as a human being without any self-contradictions" (182).

Only the perspective of martyrdom allows him a hope of escape from this torment whose terms, beyond the cultural differences, Dostoyevsky had already set forth in the passage from *Brothers Karamazov* inscribed as an epigraph to *Confessions of a Mask:*

> Within beauty both shores meet and all contradictions exist side by side. . . . Truly there are mysteries without end! Too many riddles weigh man down on earth. . . . I cannot bear the thought that a man of noble heart and lofty mind sets out with the ideal of the Madonna and ends with the ideal of Sodom. What's still more awful is that the man with the ideal of Sodom in his soul does not renounce the ideal of the Madonna, and in the bottom of his heart he may still be on fire, sincerely on fire, with longing for the beautiful ideal, just as in the days of his youthful innocence. . . . The dreadful thing is that beauty is not only terrifying but also mysterious. God and the devil are fighting there, and their battlefield is the heart of man.

3.

Mishima himself chose the solution of suicide. One of his last books, *Sun and Steel* (1968), written "on the verge of non-communication" (46), strives to circumscribe the untranslatable and to reveal the terms of the dialectic that led him to this point. The longing to seal the rift at the foundation of his subjectivity seems to have set him on a path whose only logical endpoint is suicide. "In me there was a cleavage, pure and simple, between spirit and flesh," concludes the narrator of *Confessions* (241). Twenty years later, *Sun and Steel* takes up where the earlier book left off, and in the form of an autobiographical essay retraces the development through the years of the split opposing the "body" (curiously assimilated to "reality") and "words."

His frail and cloistered childhood allowed language and its magic their fullest sway. For this child, words came first and the flesh, awakened only later, was "sadly wasted" by them. According to him, language is as fearful a thing for the living being as "white ants." Normally, "first comes the pillar of wood, then the white ants that feed on it. But for me, the white ants were there from the start, and the pillar of plain wood emerged tardily, already half eaten away" (8). He declared a war to the death between the realm of words and the empire of reality, whose heart is the body. Reality was endangered by the "corrosive function" of words, for the concrete—that which is particular, singular—is threatened with destruction by the abstract, universalizing nature of language (8). Eventually even words themselves came under attack from their own corrosive power, capable of autointoxication like Mishima was as a child. On the other hand, reality was capable of turning words away from the purity of their function. Thus it was necessary—and Mishima's labors were dedicated to this mission—to avoid as much as possible entering into contact with reality by means of words, so as to maintain their purity; and, inversely, to "maintain a constant watch on the corrosive action lest it suddenly come up against some object that it might corrode" (10).

Like the sentry on the ramparts, the writer watches, from the height of the fortress of words and by means of words, both to protect them and to protect the world from them by preventing all contact between the two. Novelistic writing fulfills this function, substituting for reality a world of words, a fictional universe. A relation to reality was allowed "only in fields where words had no part whatsoever" (10), such as bodies (so long as they be totally foreign to the intellect) or carnal beauty (provided that it be taciturn, its muteness serving to guarantee its purity).

This kind of cleavage cannot be reduced to the opposition, tirelessly described by Melanie Klein, between pure and impure (good and bad; see for instance "A Contribution" 262, 285). It is not so much a question of separating the wheat from the chaff as of constituting two poles of purity and perfection, two absolutes, by a separation that excludes their mixture and prevents them from harming each other. Impurity stems from contact. It is born merely from the action of relating the two terms, which introduces the relative and consequently leads to the downfall of the absolute. One can recognize here the thematics elaborated by Kashiwagi, the clubfoot in Mishima's novel *The Temple of the Golden Pavilion* (1959), for whom the beautiful feet of a woman must never come into contact with his own deformed feet. It is not that the latter are unworthy of the former and might defile them, but rather concerns the fetishistic value that each in its own way contains: Both clubfeet and beautiful feet, equally but not together, can be the object of a worshipful adoration.

This is indeed what the body and words became for Mishima: equally objects of worship, fetishes, inasmuch as they are kept at an infinite distance from each other. The fetish is essentially private, because the "absolute" separates. There is a despair of purity at these two poles, a desolation born of a mutual exile. Mishima's position is related to the Cathar heresy. "Was it not to purity that I had sworn allegiance?" he wrote in *Confessions* (132). This purity finds its final expression in the refusal of the Incarnation, which is perhaps the true sin against the Spirit, the only one that is irredeemable, because in the end it is only a choice between despairs. But despair itself might be the true purity if—as Mizoguchi in *The Temple of the Golden Pavilion* suggests—hope turns out to be the impurity par excellence: "I wondered what it was that made mother so particularly ugly. Then I understood. What made her so ugly was—hope. Incurable hope, like an obstinate case of scabies, which lodges, damp and reddish, in the infected skin, producing a constant itching, and refusing to yield to any outer force" (223).

In the case of those youths whose bodies attain incandescence only at the price of being exiled from part of their humanity, namely speech, exile envelops them in a shroud of sadness, surrounding them with the halo of "that fierce melancholy proper to the flesh," as if they were sacrificed to the expansion of their own vital force. But exile also encloses the writer in the prison house of language, between the walls of unreality that language builds, always distancing from himself the feeling of life, to the point that sometimes he no longer knows if he is dead or alive, or if he really exists. Nevertheless, these two absolutes, body and language, continue to exchange their attributes chiasmatically yet, strangely, without attenuating their cleavage—in fact, widening the abyss that separates them in the very effort to bridge it.

Thus the writer appropriates the literary ideal of imitating physical beauty, in order to tear its prerogative from the body, seeking a beauty exempt from any corrosion:

> This was an obvious self-contradiction, since it represented an attempt to de-prive words of their essential function (corrosion) and to strip reality of its es-sential characteristics (taciturnity and beauty). Yet, in another sense, it was an exceedingly clever and artful method of ensuring that words and the reality they should have dealt with never came face to face. In this way my mind, without realizing what it was doing, straddled these two contradictory elements and, godlike, set about trying to manipulate them. It was thus that I started writing novels. And this increased still further my thirst for reality and the flesh. (*Sun and Steel* 12)

In order to escape this dualism, Mishima set out in search of a "language of the flesh." Having situated himself entirely on the side of words, he then undertook the transformation of his body in order to make it con-form to his physical ideal. He began to haunt weight rooms, learned to box, then—dissuaded by his friends from boxing because of the beatings he kept taking—turned toward the martial arts. "Becoming like Omi" predominated, under the sign of the sun discovered in Greece and the steel of weightlifting. He could not fail to encounter upon this path what he called the "intellectualization" of the flesh: The body became a con-cept, a "metaphor for ideas," and thereby "achieve[d] a closer intimacy with ideas than the spirit" (16).

What he then discovered was a new chiasmus between the attributes of language and those of the body. The physical exercise that raised his body to the pure, ideal form also rendered it abstract. As it approaches classical perfection, the body acquires a universal character, the particu-larity of individual differences being considered a mark of "degenera-tion." Rejoining the "general pattern," the universality of the species, en-tails reaching a concept free from the "corrosion" associated with words' destructive power over reality. Furthermore, "a burgeoning of this type of triumph of the non-specific" brings with it another victory, that of "knowing that one was the same as others" (30), that one has at last managed to take one's place in the ranks of the human community and to recognize one's likeness with others, in the mortality that binds men together. The vulnerability of beauty, the ephemeral glory of the flesh, leads to a confrontation with the idea of death that alone makes it pos-sible to escape the ridicule that lies in wait for a beautiful physique, giving it the halo of tragedy without which beauty cannot exist. Universality and existence are thus reconciled in the body. The sentiment of existence, always described by Mishima as precarious, at last found a solid founda-tion in the crucible of physical effort, in which he thought he had attained "a sense of power as transparent as light," the only true antithesis of words, and which became "the focus of [his] whole thinking" (33).

While he stripped his body of its particularity and thereby succeeded in raising it to the universal, Mishima's artistic practice in turn subjected words to an inversion of their usual function by using them for artistic ends. In effect the writer turns the universality of words around on themselves, using them against the grain in order to "universalize [his] own individuality. . . . Seeming at first glance to strive after universality, in fact [the verbal arts] concern themselves with subtle ways of betraying the fundamental function of words, which is to be universally applicable" (30). Every work of literature is thus "no more than a beautiful perversion of words," and it is this perversion that is called style. Did not this double possibility of inversion promise a solution to the split between flesh and spirit? The project of unifying art and life according to "the old Japanese ideal of a combination of the literary and martial arts" (49) took hold of Mishima, in whose eyes style became entirely comparable to muscles, erecting itself as a rampart against the excesses of a sensibility and an imagination in which he thenceforth located the powers of corruption.

Nevertheless, the trench separating words and the body, opposing love and desire, the demands of literature and those of sex, was not thereby filled up. On the contrary, the man's energy had thenceforth to be divided between the two poles of muscle and sentence, watching over the tension of each in turn, dividing the day between them. Mishima submitted to alternations in the direction of his effort, to its incessant inversions from one pole to the other, just like an alternating current. He seemed to experience "an ever-wider split in the personality, yet in practice [there was] created at each moment a living balance that was constantly being destroyed and brought back to life again. The embracing of a dual polarity within the self and the acceptance of contradiction and collision—such was my own blend of 'art and action'" (49).

This new chiasmus emphasized the irremediable incompleteness of each of its terms, however, as well as their mutual alienation. Each of these paths found its truth only in the other, thereby being not complementary but rather doubly deprived. The artificial flowers of art, which "possess a weird eternal life," and the perishable flowers of action each turn out to be the other's ideal. But "to be utterly familiar with the essence of these two things—of which one must be false if the other is true . . . is secretly to destroy the ultimate dreams of one concerning the other" (50).

The *jouissance* of the instant and that of eternity respond to contrary wishes. Death alone can resolve their discordance, for only death gives reality to the oxymoron of an eternal instant. Only the hero's beautiful death conjoins art and action, intellectual vision and objective beauty. Death is the dream of an existence that would not be diminished by the consciousness of being, that would not be fissured by subjective division. At times of imminent danger there are instants when one is projected into such a world without future and one experiences, like Mishima after a parachute jump, "an absolute rest for the spirit, a beatification of the flesh" (61).

This existence, achieved during violent physical exercise, seems to have required strange conditions, far from what one might have thought of as the simplicity of the body. Indeed, it required the reunion of what Mishima calls "concepts"—almost "fetishes," he adds—associated with the body through the agency of words: "The army, physical training, summer, clouds, sunset, the green of summer grasses, the white training suit, sweat, muscle, and just the faintest whiff of death . . ." (61). If all the pieces of this strange puzzle are brought together, then at last arises the feeling of existing, the "joy of being one with the world" (61–62). From "a being that created words," the writer has become "one that was created by words" (63), his body sufficiently sculpted to incarnate what it was literary art's purpose to create: "The basis of my happiness, obviously, lay in my having transformed myself, albeit for only a moment, into a phantom formed by the shadows cast by far-off, moldering words from the past" (63–64).

Yet does this secure anything but "the momentary shadow of existence" (63)? As soon as the moment of euphoria is past, duality is reborn. The split now divides consciousness and being. How can one be certain of existence without consciousness? From the moment of its appearance, is not consciousness irremediably separate from being? And does not sight place the one who sees at an unbridgeable distance from the thing seen? Were consciousness able to turn around on itself, the antinomy between seeing and existing would not be resolved. If we compare the self to an apple (setting aside the hypothesis of introspective psychology that wants the apple to be transparent), we must admit that its dark heart will remain hidden from sight and thus the perfection of its being will remain uncertain: "There is only one method of solving this contradiction. It is for a knife to be plunged deep into the apple so that it is split open and the core is exposed to the light. . . . Yet then the existence of the cut apple falls into fragments; the core of the apple sacrifices existence for the sake of seeing" (65). In *Sun and Steel,* at the end of his quest, Mishima concludes that the only way to resolve the knot of his contradictions is to cut it. Like the blind core of the apple, his consciousness "was driven to desire certain proof of its existence so fiercely that it was bound, sooner or later, to destroy that existence" (66). Death alone can fill "the logical gap between seeing and existing" (67) to which his subjective cleavage has been reduced by this point.

Like the apple, both the ego and the body are endowed with a surface and a depth that divide them between interiority and exteriority. Only once, during a privileged experience, did Mishima believe he had succeeded in abolishing this antinomy that ordinarily frames our mental universe. On board a supersonic fighter jet, at the moment the sound barrier was broken, speed suddenly became indistinguishable from immobility:

> If this stillness was the ultimate end of action—of movement—then the sky about me, the clouds far below, the sea gleaming between the clouds, even the setting sun, might well be events, things, within myself. At this distance from the earth, intellectual adventure and physical adventure could join hands without the slightest difficulty. This was the point that I had always been striving towards. (102)

The plane seemed to float like a silver phallus in an azure uterus, while "the inner world and the outer world had become completely interchangeable" (102). The Möbius strip, which had formerly illustrated his psychological alternations, here becomes the symbol of their reconciliation, in the form of a circle of clouds encircling the earth like the mythical snake of eternity "that resolves all polarities" (103).

Mishima pursued this final dissolution of all oppositions to the extreme point of that ultimate eroticization of death that was his suicide. He stabbed himself in the stomach as a young disciple beheaded him in the ritual of seppuku, reserved for samurai warriors. This act—by its extravagance, its mixture of horror and beauty—will continue to trouble "the dreams of timid ruminators who have never been tempted by the abyss," as Caillois puts it. So theatrical a death was necessarily the object of many interpretations, and the most contradictory significations were woven together and came unraveled in it.

Kanshi: By this "suicide of remonstration" Mishima addressed himself to the emperor, whose "human declaration" had ruined, he thought, the meaning of the suicide squads' sacrifice. In an ultimate *père-version,* the seppuku is offered to restore the emperor's divinity, proving that the "pervert" is indeed, as Lacan put it, the defender of the faith. Cutting one's guts open, traditionally, is a way of displaying one's "visible sincerity," the final token of his refusal to give ground relative to his desire, and the law that sustains it.

Choosing one's own time and manner is also a way of stealing some of death's authority, removing oneself in extremis from the laws of an inflexible nature ("we are fodder to garnish a gizzard"), from its voracious *jouissance*. An ultimate self-affirmation by which one destroys oneself in order to exist, this eminently contradictory gesture is also a way of making oneself equal to the impossible object that is the mother's phallus. Does not Mishima's self-sacrifice repeat the one that was made of his young life for the sake of his valetudinarian grandmother? Is not all this spilled blood—following the example in his novel *The Sailor Who Fell from Grace with the Sea* (1965)—an ultimate transfusion intended to give back to a dying universe the desire that threatens to withdraw from it forever? Is not opening one's guts (the site par excellence of intimacy and mystery) and seeking in one's own entrails the blindside of all vision, an attempt, acting as one's own midwife, to extirpate from the mother, open like a rose, the hateful object that is none other than oneself, finally brought forth in an unnameable exhibition?

Like a trail of fire and blood across the rottenness of the world, seppuku adorned itself forever that day in the luster of a strange, Rilkean sadism: "What is so ghastly about exposed intestines? . . . Why does there have to be something inhuman about regarding human beings like roses and refusing to make any distinction between the inside of their bodies and the outside? If only human beings could reverse their spirits and their bodies, could gracefully turn them inside out like rose petals and expose them to the spring breeze and to the sun . . ." (*Temple* 78).

References

Caillois, Roger. *L'homme et le sacré*. Paris: Gallimard, Folio, 1988.
Freud, Sigmund. "'A Child Is Being Beaten': A Contribution to the Study of the Origin of Sexual Perversions." 1919. *Standard* 17:175–204.
———. *Leonardo da Vinci and a Memory of His Childhood*. 1910. *Standard* 11:63–137.
———. *The Standard Edition of the Complete Psychological Works of Sigmund Freud*. Ed. and trans. James Strachey. 24 vols. London: Hogarth, 1953–74.
———. "On the Universal Tendency to Debasement in the Sphere of Love (Contributions to the Psychology of Love II)." 1912. *Standard* 11:179–90.

Greenacre, Phyllis. *Trauma, Growth, and Personality.* 1952. New York: International Universities P, 1969.

Klein, Melanie. "A Contribution to the Psychogenesis of Manic-Depressive States." 1935. *Love, Guilt and Reparation and Other Works 1921–1945.* London: Virago, 1988. 262–89.

Mishima, Yukio. *Confessions of a Mask.* 1949. Trans. Meredith Weatherby. New York: New Directions, 1958.

———. *Sun and Steel.* 1968. Trans. John Bester. Tokyo: Kodansha International, 1980.

———. *The Temple of the Golden Pavilion.* 1959. Trans. Ivan Morris. New York: Berkeley Medallion, 1971.

Sabouret, Jean-François. *L'autre Japon: les Burakumin.* Paris: Editions de la Découverte, 1983.

Scott-Stokes, Henry. *The Life and Death of Yukio Mishima.* New York: Ballantine, 1974.

Yamaguchi, Masao. "La royauté japonaise." *Esprit* 2 (1972): 315–43.

3

LESBIAN

SEXUALITY

12

"THE COMMUNITY OF DOLPHINS" V. "THE SAFE SEA OF WOMEN"

Lesbian Sexuality and Psychosis

Judith Roof

. . . .

Preamble

The lesbian loves the law; the law is what she hates, envies, evades, wields. And the law loves the lesbian, stalking her through culture, representations, politics, binding itself to her as the condition of her existence. The lesbian dresses herself in the law, in her fascination with definition. Without the law, the lesbian cannot exist; but she also cannot exist within the law.

The Law is the intersection of the lesbian and the psychotic, the Möbius strip of the inside and outside, the locus of their inversion, one to the other, their conflation and misidentification. The lesbian's love of the law is the psychotic's foreclosure of it. Reflecting supreme presence and supreme absence, the lesbian and psychotic meet in the place that is all law and no law, outlaw and prelaw, utopian community of women under one law and chaos of undifferentiated mothers/daughters in antecedent ignorance of the law.

1. Definitions

A. Lesbian sexuality is defined via the law of sexual difference as sexual activity, real or imaginary, between two women.
B. Lesbian sexual behavior is not limited to those who identify as lesbians.
C. All lesbians who identify as such do not necessarily become lesbians in the same way.

2. The Law of the Case

The Name-of-the-Father, the *post facto* agent of separation, is a metaphor whose necessary limit not only installs and perpetuates desire, but also maintains difference. The Name-of-the-Father prefigures and sustains social law, the literal limits imposed in the name of order whose real function is to hide pervasive chaos.

3. The Party of the First Part

Attracted to and repulsed by the imaginary outlaw, discussions of feminism and the feminine locate the lesbian in the place of the psychotic (see Irigaray's various analyses in *This Sex Which Is Not One*). Although some psychotics claim to be lesbians in their psychosis, most lesbians are not psychotic.[1] What is it about the cultural understanding of the lesbian that makes lesbianism a possible identity for psychotics? What enables culture to conflate the two so easily, and what does their relation tell us about the system of sexuality, gender, and representation as it currently operates?

In her essay on maternity and the ascendance of the Virgin, "Stabat Mater" (1976–77), Julia Kristeva hypothesizes that relations among women reproduce "forgotten body relationships with their mothers" (257). Located in the body, these relations are nostalgic and bereft of the symbolic order, of the Law: "Complicity in the unspoken, connivance of the inexpressible, or a wink, a tone of voice, a gesture, a tinge, a scent. We are in it, set free of our identification papers and names, on an ocean of preciseness, a computerization of the unnameable" (257). Kristeva's juxtaposition of two economies of signification characterizes the relation between communities of women and patriarchal culture as both emancipation and loss. One of Kristeva's economies is the signifying body, which exists in undefined space outside the aegis of the symbolic; the other describes the empty systems of legalistic individuation evoked by "identification papers," "preciseness," "names," "a computerization." For her, the symbolic order is an empty form among women who, without it, lose not only individuality and differentiation, but also their ability to communicate as individuals. Kristeva writes, "No communication between individuals but connections between atoms, molecules, wisps of words, droplets of sentences. The community of women is a community of dolphins" (257).

Posed against the symbolic, against the individuation that constitutes the "other" woman, as well as against the text on the other side of the split column in Kristeva's essay, the community of women is the underside of her symbolization of the unique, in this case the Virgin Mary. But there is pathology in the reproduction of "forgotten body relationships"—something alluring, irretrievable, and deadly in the watery pleasure of aquatic mammals whose "atomic connection" we do not yet understand. Kristeva's evocation of the dolphin, a benign image, evokes the danger of the womb's watery deep seduction. More a fear than a briny frolic, the specter of "molecular" relations among women stands at the furthest verge of memory, recalled, even enjoyed safely from the symbolic shore just this side of consciousness.

Kristeva's "community of dolphins" is neither overtly lesbian nor recalled for its own sake. Its represented position in the left column of her essay, contrasted with the text in the right column, makes the dolphins part of an extended argument about the symbolic function of the Virgin Mary relative to maternity. Replaying in her columns the logic of patriarchy, Kristeva depicts the woman oscillating between two extremes: "Within this strange feminine see-saw that makes 'me' swing from the unnameable community of women over to the war of individual singularities, it is unsettling to say 'I'" (258–59). Yet this "I" is the real danger in women's relations; it is the one real impossibility in the logic opposing even momentarily the "feminine" imaginary to the "masculine" symbolic. The "I" is also the one combination Kristeva avoids in her evocation of the community of women who are linked to one another via maternity and who finally can find meaning only in motherhood. The woman who is singular and stays in the community of dolphins not only is condemned as "masculine," but inaugurates psychosis. She introduces the nonsense of singularity into the logic of body memory—the inseparability of fragments—that maternal relations endow.

Choosing to be an "I" instead of a mother means repudiating "the other sex (the masculine)" (261). Kristeva connects the "I"—woman, the unmentionable lesbian—to psychosis:

Feminine psychosis today is sustained and absorbed through passion for politics, science, art. . . . The variant that accompanies motherhood might be analyzed perhaps more readily than the others from the standpoint of the rejection
of the other sex that it comprises. To allow what? Surely not some understanding or other on the part of "sexual partners" within the pre-established harmony of primal androgyny. Rather, to lead to an acknowledgment of what is
irreducible, of the irreconcilable interest of both sexes in asserting their differences, in the quest of each one—and of women, after all—for an appropriate
fulfillment. (261–62)

"Fulfillment" comes from an acknowledgment of "differences," from not
"repudiating" the "other" sex. Fulfillment is "appropriate" if it reifies this
difference, which Kristeva depicts as denied in the community of dolphins. Even though Kristeva's right-column inclusion of psychosis clearly
includes all women, the relation between psychosis and sexual difference—here a specific variant accompanying motherhood—suggests that
the "fulfillment" arising from the recognition of differences is always described in heterosexual terms. In this maternal context, the repudiation
of the other sex becomes a rejection of the third "person" or "party"—
that is, the "child, the nonperson, God," otherness, the Law (261). The
left-column community of dolphins becomes psychotic through its foreclosure of otherness, but even more so through its failure to reproduce.
No child means that no differences mingle and complete one another.
Feminine psychosis means staying in the water too long while a woman
says "I" and means it.

This discourse on the community of women is a small part of Kristeva's
discussion in "Stabat Mater." Yet it reveals how visions of a mass of
women detached from men get tied to psychosis through an argument
about the repudiation or unseemly appropriation of the masculine. This
link ultimately is owing to an unnamed and imaginary vision of the lesbian. Kristeva's notion of feminine psychosis takes the form of "count-
ercathexes in strong values, in strong equivalents of power" (261), which
depends on the imaginary outlaw, the one who lives beyond the Name-
of-the-Father, outside the quest for sexual difference in that arena seen as
but never named "lesbian." The psychotic becomes one who substitutes,
who compensates with "strong equivalents of power," the mistaken "I,"
the masculinized faux phallus making love to women—the travesty of
the artificial in the place of the third term, the limit, the paternal law
regulating sexual relations. What is odd about this is how the community
of women that Kristeva poses on the left side, across from the maternal
right, loses its place as a preoedipal utopia and becomes the monstrous
challenger to the symbolic order itself.

4. The Party of the Second Part

Psychoanalysis, itself a law, perpetually haunts discussions of lesbian sexuality, even (perhaps especially) those conducted by lesbians. In her 1975 cultural sketch of lesbians in western culture, *Lesbian Images,* Jane Rule links psychoanalysis to what she calls the irrational and "random" patriarchal condemnation of lesbian sexuality. She introduces her collection of essays on twelve lesbian writers with two chapters, "Myth and Morality, Sources of Law and Prejudice" and "From Sin to Sickness," which treat in a broadly historical way the intersections of law, sexuality, and culture. Rule, whose work reflects fairly widespread ideas of '70s (and even '80s) American nonacademic lesbian-feminism, argues that law—consisting of tradition combined with the random selection of attitudes supporting male privilege—perpetuates irrational ideas about lesbian women, which in turn authorizes their legal and social mistreatment. Connecting the Name-of-the-Father to psychoanalysis itself, Rule situates the lesbian again as the outlaw. But unlike Kristeva's community of women, Rule's lesbian outlaw is not out-of-the-law; she is against the law, an outcast by virtue of the conspiratorial misunderstandings of the "medical community" and its confusion of "morality" with medicine. Rule's lesbian would rather be legal.

Although Rule contrasts the legal conventions of dominant culture with a continuing underground lesbian tradition, she believes in and relies on an idea of law as the limit whose responsible figuration would end lesbian oppression. Rule's analysis implies that a just law—a law empty of patriarchal prejudices, one recognizing the equality of genders—would permit more of the truth of lesbian existence. What is most important here is not that gender be eliminated or that homosexualities become the rule, but that the conspiracy of Law, masculinity, and privilege be untangled to allow a more egalitarian participation—a shift from the Name-of-the-Father to simply the name of the law. Rule's lesbian is a creature of a "correct" law.

According to Rule, the law most skewed and stubbornly ingrained is psychoanalysis, which governs how other laws control lesbian lives. After briefly and critically analyzing every psychologist and psychoanalyst from Freud to Charlotte Wolff, Rule concludes:

> For anyone who would genuinely like to understand the nature of lesbian experience, the field of psychology should probably be off limits since just this brief, incomplete survey exposes the state of conflict and confusion which exists among the "experts." But the myth that psychology has the answers about

human experience is now deeply embedded in our culture and people do turn
there to increase their understanding or relieve their suffering. (45)

Psychoanalysis and psychology represent the arch-law that invisibly perpetuates the "myths" about "human experience" that support the misguided laws of the fathers. Rule's belief in its errant virility suggests simultaneously her acute understanding of the relationship between culture
and psyche and her grudging insight that the lesbian is somehow a psychoanalytic (rather than a juridical) subject.[2]

What is intriguing and symptomatic about Rule's collection of essays
is its subtle but insistent fix on the law. Rule maintains as the substance
of her argument that the law is prejudiced, reflecting only the selfish
needs of patriarchy, represented often as the needs of individual men. In
this sense, the law is neither absolute nor universal, but compromised
and therefore not really law at all. Literalized, the symbolic order seems
to fail. In this sense, the lesbian is lawless, out of the law, but not an
outlaw, as there really is no law and apparently only lesbians know this.

However, Rule's dismissal of the law ultimately refers to an even
greater sense of law elsewhere—an ideal Law, a deferred symbolic order
beyond the bounds of the patriarchy by which Law is already disqualified.
Although Rule's appeal is to a higher justice, the effect of her rejecting
law for a Law beyond patriarchy means that she reiterates superficially
the rule of nondifferentiation, of a place beyond the limits of the father
where women can exist as women among themselves. Yet even as Rule's
version of the Law beyond the law seems to refer to a woman's space, it
reinscribes the Law as powerful and as elsewhere.

5. Jus Tertii[3]

The psychoanalysis Kristeva overwrites and Rule underwrites enters the
scenario as the Law of the father, whose despairing ignorance of lesbian
sexuality—premised on its very acceptance of the cultural biases of gender, rather than gender's truth—causes half the trouble. The liability of
psychoanalysis is precisely its status as law and specifically as the law that,
correctly formulated, could explain lesbian sexuality, even and especially
to those who hate psychoanalysis. The truth of psychoanalysis does not
make it a third term; rather, lesbians and culture in general position psychoanalysis as the literal law of the limit—a third term—by which lesbianism is perpetually misunderstood (castrated). Culturally linked to phal-

locentrism and patriarchy, psychoanalysis is cast as the Law that defines and oppresses lesbians.

It is not surprising, then, that Jacques Lacan comments that the female homosexual "will not accept" that the "incestuous object"—in this case, the father—"only assumes its sex at the price of castration" ("Guiding Remarks" 97).[4] The lesbian's continued belief in the identity of penis and phallus, phallus and father, Desire and Law—in short, her belief in the father's noncastration—apparently sustains her "courtly" "pride" in "being the love which gives what it does not have, so it is precisely in this that the homosexual woman excels in relation to what is lacking in her" (96). What is "lacking" is not the phallus, however, but lack itself, the lack of a signifier of lack, "the envy of desire" (97). Lacan suggests that "the naturalness with which such women [female homosexuals] appeal to their quality of being men" reveals "the path leading from feminine sexuality to desire itself" (97). Characterizing feminine sexuality "as the effort of a *jouissance* wrapped in its own contiguity (for which all circumcision might represent the symbolic rupture)," he locates lesbian desire as a version of feminine desire recognizing the virtue of lack "to be *realised in the envy* of desire, which castration releases in the male by giving him its signifier in the phallus" (97; original emphasis).

By believing in an imagined potency of the father (and the law) and his lack of lack in a reified arena of sexual difference, the lesbian becomes subject and outlaw, courtly lover and adulterer, thief of women and the one who can fulfill them. This "fulfillment" is depicted as a contiguity, "lips speaking together," a pan-erogeneity that iterates a figure of wholeness rather than lack or desire.[5] This is not to say that there is no lesbian desire; rather, that such desire in Lacanian terms is premised not on lack but on desire itself, on the desire for a desire representing the conditions of lack—the law of castration and separation—by which desire is possible. This desire for desire is a yearning for the Law by which lack and desire are created and sustained.

As evidence of this dynamic of desire, Lacan cites Ernest Jones as having "detected here the link between the fantasy of the man as invisible witness and the care which the subject shows for the enjoyment of her partner" (97). Introducing an element of lesbian exhibitionism via Jones, Lacan simultaneously interjects a voyeurism that, not even hinted at in the work of Kristeva, suggests a patriarchal investment in the lesbian. Imagined as one who wishes to be watched, she becomes the guarantor of the Law's power. Quoting Jones, Lacan refers not literally to man, but to man as a referent of the Law: It is the Law as the Moile, the executor of God's covenant, that one imagines watching. This watching, whose scenario is the represented imaginary of the woman, is the fantasy of being the object who is also a subject. It introduces a duplicity that evokes a metonymy from the "watching" law to castration and limit. Being watched from the place of lack—from the place of desire—causes a desire for desire. This doubling of desire reproduces desire infinitely in a reciprocity that threatens never to end. Hence such lesbian sex lore as "orgasm is not important," "women have multiple orgasms," "my whole body is an erogenous zone," and "I don't know where I end and she begins."

Lacan, in his parting questions of "Guiding Remarks for a Congress on Feminine Sexuality" (1958), observes and anticipates the error of such formulations as Kristeva's social "allegory" of lesbian sexuality as "a sort of entropy tending towards communal degradation," suggesting instead that the "eros of feminine homosexuality" might convey "the opposite of social entropy" (98). By multiplying desire, the lesbian produces; she expands instead of contracting into entropy or stasis. Opposed to simple patriarchal ideologies of reproduction and narrative, Lacan's insight that the lesbian generates desire and energy implies that the lesbian is a disruption that must be actively quelled by an insecure patriarchy.

While the structure of lesbian sexuality has everything to do with this otherness, the structure of psychosis has everything to do with its absence. Psychotics are transsexual, as Ellie Ragland-Sullivan observes, for they confuse "1 and 2—symbiosis and castration—they are fused with the mother and so not subject to the father's Name, which she contains; both woman and man; or neither" (*Jacques Lacan* 277). The Law means an absence of identity—the lack of a position within the symbolic. This results in what Ragland-Sullivan and Mark Bracher call "delusional reformulations of the universe" that "bring agony and despair, often suicide, rather than the supposedly joyful pleasure to be found on *mille plateaux* in an imaginary poetic weave of being to language and sexuality" ("Introduction" 7). The "joyful pleasure" denied the psychotic is another vestige of a cultural nostalgia or fantasies of premirror stage unity. Like preoedipal bliss, "joyful pleasure's" substitution for agony in representations of psychosis comes from the vantage point of the symbolic, whose superimposition initiates the distortions of subjectivity and culture that prefer to see the law itself as the pain. Such distortions displace psychotic angst into the realm of never-never land.

The uncanny link between law and lesbian suggests that the lesbian has somehow everything to do with the law, while the psychotic is the lesbian inverse. Each position on one or other side of the law reflects its other, seeming to coalesce within some mirrored terrain, some watery zone, some "safe sea of women" or "community of dolphins." But these positions enter this liquidity from opposite directions: the lesbian from the side of the law and Kristeva's women from that of the preoedipal. Their marine alliance stimulates their conflation, but their difference is all the difference in the world.

6. Conditions

The series of representational gambits by which lesbianism is linked to or collapsed into images of psychosis reflects a nineteenth-century rather than a contemporary (or even Freudian) understanding of lesbian etiology. Only in the most hackneyed pop-psychological terms do images of lesbian sexuality have anything to do with psychoanalytical understandings of it. In fact, the obverse of both Freudian and Lacanian theories, cultural myths and representations of the psychic structure of lesbian desire render the lesbian lover of Law a destroyer of Law. This confusion exists generally throughout Western culture, championed alike by right-wing ideologues and radical lesbians. There are, however, political and ideological stakes in this rendering of the lesbian: It bolsters the family, displaces and contains patriarchal pathologies, and neutralizes the fear of the "feminine." For example, in her analysis Rule represents two kinds of appeal to law—law as unjust and oppressive versus the Law as ultimately fair and true. The relation between them reverses the analogy of the psychotic's foreclosure of the Law, where an imaginary "law" takes the place of the missing third-term Law by which the subject would know its limits and understand castration and separation. The difference between the two is that whereas the lesbian's "laws" are both too symbolic and literal, the psychotic's imaginary suture of otherness is not symbolic enough. Even so, their respective performances of excess around the issue of law enable their representational confusion in a system where the law itself is a sometimes unstable metaphor. Here, then, is one proximate cause of the confusion between lesbian sexuality and psychosis: The contiguity of feminine sexuality and its revelation in lesbian desire are mistaken. The imagery of their communal degradation begins to resemble the psychotic's lack of limits. This similarity is not an accident but the result of a failure or inability to distinguish among outlaws.

Like Kristeva, Rule locates the lesbian outside the law, the male law that in Rule's formulation cannot comprehend the nonpatriarchal.

Whereas Kristeva's dolphins have neither law nor regulation of difference, Rule's lesbians know their difference and have an overdeveloped sense of the power of both the law and the symbolic. The "safe sea of women" is a highly legislated place. The contradiction between Rule's analysis and her assumptions—between an apparent rejection of the symbolic and its veneration—seems a kind of schizophrenia, but the confusion stems from her ardent belief in the Law's power. It is no accident, for example, that in the 1993 Gay and Lesbian March on Washington, the dominant plea was for inclusion into the family—the desire to become "in-laws."[6]

Rule begins a tradition of lesbian antipsychoanalytic critiques, which continues through the '70s and '80s in the name of an alternative psychology premised on a rejection of literal patriarchy. In this tradition, lesbian critics don't reject psychoanalysis; they want to change its terms—its laws—to the more "authentic" terrain of a "women-centered" world. Lesbian accounts of lesbian psychology, which replaces psychoanalysis, tend to ground themselves in the idea of a community: the "safe sea" of women Kristeva rejects.[7] Revisiting the imaginary realm of what is either a healthy celebratory company of women or the borders of psychosis, lesbian psychologies tend to resituate the "law" of human development in a place where mother *is* father; they shift the gender of the law, not its idea. Evocations of matriarchy and woman-centeredness, whether existing to combat patriarchal systems or simply to provide an alternative (and more palatable) premise for understanding lesbian identity, reiterate Rule's curiously schizophrenic relation to the Law. The substitution of mother for father phallicizes the mother, turning her into the Law. The community of women from which she derives both insulates and isolates lesbians; as a world—a community—it reenters the fray, pitting itself against a very powerful and certainly not vanquished world of men.

The underside of this schizophrenia is not psychosis or a lack of limit, but a very real belief in the limit. Lesbian faith in the law has everything to do with a lesbian understanding of castration, of the lesbian's limits in the symbolic. This juridical respect is a lesbian constant, though it is difficult to generalize about lesbian psychology: Lesbian sexual behaviors have many explanations, and several different versions of sexuality and identity may occupy the cultural position named "lesbian." This respect may even make the position of lesbian useful to psychotics. Lesbian feminism as one example of lesbian sexuality suggests not only the successful introjection of otherness, but also a tendency to overestimate the power of men. This in turn suggests a reluctance to believe in male castration, generating confusion between the penis and the phallus. Hence the need constantly to debunk the phallus, positing an alternative, all-female world where castration—in a staunch return to the gender logic of patriarchy—is irrelevant. The paradoxical recognition of an "irrelevant" castration makes it possible to posit an imaginary female world whose existence and communal relations are impossible without a sense of castration—without Law.

The representational similarity of psychosis and lesbian sexuality demonstrates a way of dispensing with their respective tortuous relations to the Law, relations that disturb through excess or absence of the paternal metaphor. The illusory absence of law conveyed by such images as the "community of dolphins" or the "safe sea of women" or "in the imaginary poetic weave of being to language and sexuality" gets linked to the superficial commonality of their structures of the law's displacement. Seeing both lesbian sexuality and psychosis as "outside" purges lesbianism of its interlopers. Envisioning psychosis and lesbian sexuality as joyful, and in that joy pathological, situates them both as exemplary warnings of the dangers of seeking pleasure where freedom and anguish collide, and where the body meets god. This conception ultimately consolidates and normalizes the Name-of-the-Father as metaphor, as neither literal nor lacking, playing against the disorder of these outsiders whose very confusion reveals the similarity of their function.

In this roundabout way, lesbian sexuality and the psychotic's evocations of lesbian sexuality are linked through the confusion of sexual engagement without a "real" penis (the literal lesbian scene) with a foreclosure of the Name-of-the-Father (the structure of psychosis). Lesbian sexuality exists in the cultural imaginary along a spectrum of positions that, in seeming to eschew the Name-of-the-Father along with the literal penis, are relegated to a frontier of sameness associated with the preoedipal, adolescence, narcissism, and misdirected utopian community. In their apparent lack of law or structure, these realms of sameness are represented as perverse, pathological, sterile, and lost.

As an effect of this confusion, the model of pathology (through which lesbian sexuality remains appended to psychoanalysis) survived the American Psychiatric Association's judicious 1973 depathologization. Lesbian sexuality is not simply a literal disease with its contagion, disablement, and pathos, but a continuing madness, a lack of reason, control, and acquiescence to social norms (in this instance, patriarchy). While this pathologized lesbian and her inherent contagion underwrites a fearful imaginary in most media representations of lesbians, she also evokes a more dangerous and substantial challenge to the logic of the system itself. As teachers, lesbians might proselytize; as athletes, they might recruit; as military personnel, they create disorder; and as feminists, they threaten patriarchal order. Lesbians are the germs of a sickness infecting the family, the condensed site of the law of limits, deities, and patriarchy. If lesbians can exist and even reproduce without men, then the ultimate "truth" of the patriarchal system is apparently confronted. If in order to function, the Name-of-the-Father must be universal, and if this metaphorical "law" is confused with literal patriarchy, which is itself confused with men— then lesbians appear, at least superficially, to have circumvented the gendered orders by which cultural sense and history are made. Thus lesbians are an aberration, a sickness, not unto themselves but unto the system by which they are defined as aberrant in the first place. They are the out-of-laws.

The pathology linked to the lesbian is actually a displacement of the feared pathology of patriarchal culture. For this reason, culture must figure the lesbian in the realm of nonsense, of linguistic and narrative impossibility, insofar as language and narrative both depend on systems of complementary opposites sustained by law. This lesbian region of no logic is a zone without law, the place of the "psychotic criminal" who knows no bounds. The very challenge to order contained in representations of lesbians is restrained by depictions that, in their evocations of nonsense or pathology, disenfranchise the out-of-the-law as the outlaw. That is why lesbians are often figured as murderers, and vice versa. The murderous lesbian characters in Paul Verhoeven's *Basic Instinct* (1992), as well as the association of lesbians with vampires in such films as Tony Scott's *The Hunger* (1983) and Harry Kümel's *Daughters of Darkness* (1971), highlight fears that lesbians threaten the death of patriarchy.

The representational existence of the outlaw lesbian is, of course, necessary for maintaining the system of binary, heterosexual logic, including Jane Rule's. The out-of-order guarantees order. The lesbian, more than the male homosexual, is the point of failure certifying that the rest of the system—the complementary opposites, heterosexuality—continues to work. The system thereby rids itself of sameness, which is represented by the lesbian's incomprehensible, undifferentiated feminine ground. This representation of the lesbian as sameness—this policing function—conceals the operations of a coexistent but different logic of difference. And this logic is based not on the binaries of sexual (or even racial or age) differences, but on a logic of separation premised on castration—the Law lesbians in their guise as fake men appear to deny.

This is not to say that lesbians don't exist under the law of castration; they may in fact know rather more than others do about their relation to castration. Instead, it is to say that within the representational logic already in place, they seem to have ignored gender and its principles of limitation. They are the women who ignore their "castration," who behave as "men," who suggest that the tongue is mightier than the sword. The price they pay for their disdain is their representational relegation to a kind of preoedipal, precastrated space. They represent a mass of fragmented and indistinguishable beings that, lacking the single signifier of desire and combination, exist in a pure *jouissance* tantamount to stasis, the error to which Lacan points. This postoedipal, preoedipal lesbian—denying reproduction, and hence signification—carries with her a mythical etiology that casts her as the result of everything from retarded emotional development to the deleterious effects of ignoring the laws of sexual difference. The image of the out-of-time lesbian evokes a nostalgia both envied and castigated.

It is important, finally, that lesbian sexuality be confused with psychosis. Ideologically, lesbian sexuality must be mad; its overvaluation of the Law makes a parody of it; its excessive respect implies the law's usurpation. The image of lesbian as psychotic imprisons lesbians for their own good, contains them safely away from the culture they confound, and protects them for their own survival.

7. Remedies

Claiming that lesbians love the law is likely to be misunderstood either as a capitulation to patriarchy or as a recapitulation of a confusion between the metaphorical and the literal: as either treason or blindness. Certainly, all those who identify themselves as lesbians or who participate in lesbian desire do not share in the same overvaluation, especially if we understand humans as intrinsically bisexual or comprehend that psychotics may accept the label of lesbian to locate themselves culturally. No matter the origins of images of contiguity, they are an important part of lesbian erotica in works from Virginia Woolf to Monique Wittig. They are also part of an aesthetic deemed feminine, even if that definition, itself reiterating the traits of psychosis, relies for its meaning on heterology.

The Law is, however, the premise of most theories of lesbian praxis, founding Judy Chicago's and Judy Grahn's evocations of goddess and matriarchy, Elaine Marks's politics of excess, Judith Butler's claims for performativity, and Wittig's supposition of the materiality of language.[8] All these play with the law as Law, shifting it, exposing it, and even destabilizing it, but always with reference to the Law outside that Law that can see, understand, and appreciate Law's transmogrifications. The law is always a matter of otherness: No matter what its identity or label, the third term will function as the Law, as the agent of separation and castration, as the symbolic through which these discussions can be held at all. Every attempt to circumvent the law—even by those that substitute formlessness, lawlessness, silence, and excess—evokes another law, a better, truer Law, that of the castrator elsewhere in the locus of desire.

This lesbian play of law is not, however, recuperative or recuperated. It is one site of the change in Law as the Other itself shifts through culture. While the Law will not disappear, the nature of cultural investments in Law and gender can and do change. If the Name-of-the-Father is a historical construct, then it can, and perhaps is, changing to a different metaphor as patriarchy itself dissolves through the effects of technology, overpopulation, and widespread changes in familial paradigms. The lesbian just might be the harbinger of a different order threatening the Name-of-the-Father with a new name, boiled up from that not-so-safe sea.

Notes

1. Three (of four) case studies of psychotics presented at Sainte-Anne Hospital in Paris during June 1989 contained some episode of lesbian identification. Lacan's 1932 study of psychosis, *De la psychose paranoïaque dans ses rapports avec la personnalité,* followed Freud in linking paranoia to homosexuality in cases specifically involving women.

2. In *Odd Girls and Twilight Lovers,* Faderman systematically attributes lesbian oppression to the "freudians," whom she sees as the archenemy.

3. This is a legal term, translated as "the rights of the third party."

4. The "incestuous object" might refer to the mother—the mother as an object is only an effect of the homosexual girl's disbelief in the father's castration. Lacan's rereading of Jones's analysis replaces the latter's structures of identification with the father with a position vis-à-vis lack that situates the lesbian squarely within the realm of the symbolic instead of the imaginary (and potentially psychotic).

5. Irigaray in "When Our Lips Speak Together," Wittig in *The Lesbian Body,* and Brossard all present this image as both an erotic and a critical one.

6. The phrase comes from Robyn Wiegman, who suggested for this essay the example of the rhetoric surrounding the 1993 Gay and Lesbian March on Washington.

7. See the diverse essays on lesbian counseling, development, and problems in *Lesbian Psychologies: Explorations and Challenges.* See also Garner, "Feminism, Psychoanalysis, and the Heterosexual Imperative" 164–81.

8. See for example Grahn, *The Common Woman;* Marks, "Lesbian Intertextuality"; Butler, *Gender Trouble;* and Wittig, "The Straight Mind."

References

Basic Instinct. Dir. Paul Verhoeven. 1992.

Boston Lesbian Psychologies Collective, ed. *Lesbian Psychologies: Explorations and Challenges.* Urbana: U of Illinois P, 1987.

Brossard, Nicole. *Picture Theory.* Trans. Barbara Godard. New York: Roof, 1990.

Butler, Judith. *Gender Trouble: Feminism and the Subversion of Identity.* New York: Routledge, 1990.

Daughters of Darkness. Dir. Harry Kümel. 1971.

Faderman, Lillian. *Odd Girls and Twilight Lovers: A History of Lesbian Life in Twentieth-Century America.* New York: Columbia UP, 1991.

Garner, Shirley Nelson. "Feminism, Psychoanalysis, and the Heterosexual Imperative." In *Feminism and Psychoanalysis.* Ed. Richard Feldstein and Judith Roof. Ithaca: Cornell UP, 1989. 164–81.

Grahn, Judy. *The Common Woman.* Oakland: Women's, n.d.

The Hunger. Dir. Tony Scott. 1983.

Irigaray, Luce. "When Our Lips Speak Together." *This Sex Which Is Not One.* 1977. Trans. Catherine Porter with Carolyn Burke. Ithaca: Cornell UP, 1985. 205–18.

Kristeva, Julia. "Stabat Mater." 1976–77. *Tales of Love.* Trans. Leon Roudiez. New York: Columbia UP, 1987. 234–63.

Lacan, Jacques. *De la psychose paranoïaque dans ses rapports avec la personnalité, suivi de premiers écrits sur la paranoïa.* 1932. Paris: Seuil, 1975.

———. "Guiding Remarks for a Congress on Feminine Sexuality." 1958. *Feminine Sexuality: Jacques Lacan and the école freudienne.* Ed. Juliet Mitchell and Jacqueline Rose. Trans. Rose. New York: Norton, 1982. 86–98.

Marks, Elaine. "Lesbian Intertextuality." In *Homosexualities and French Literature: Cultural Contexts/Critical Texts.* Ed. George Stambolian and Elaine Marks. Ithaca: Cornell UP, 1979. 353–77.

Ragland-Sullivan, Ellie. *Jacques Lacan and the Philosophy of Psychoanalysis.* Urbana: U of Illinois P, 1986.

Ragland-Sullivan, Ellie, and Mark Bracher. "Introduction." *Lacan and the Subject of Language.* Ed. Ragland-Sullivan and Bracher. New York: Routledge, 1991. 1–17.

Rule, Jane. *Lesbian Images.* 1975. Trumansburg, NY: Crossing, 1982.

Wittig, Monique. *The Lesbian Body.* Trans. David LeVay. Boston: Beacon, 1986.

———. "The Straight Mind." *Feminist Issues* 1.1 (1980): 47–54.

13

UNREQUITED LOVE

Lesbian Transference and Revenge in Psychoanalysis

H. N. Lukes

. . . .

1.

What does a lesbian want? Freud's quandary about "what woman wants" would seem to flower into a double conundrum when it concerns lesbians. Yet based on his one clinical experience with an "actual" homosexual woman, Freud seems to have had no problem answering the question at all: Lesbians want revenge. In his case history "The Psychogenesis of a Case of Homosexuality in a Woman" (1920), Freud determines that the patient feels a kind of unrequited love for her father and, in revenge for his rejection, takes a female lover in order to vex and anger him. Freud concludes that her attitudes toward analysis, ranging from indifference to mockery, signal a transference of this revenge onto her analyst as a stand-in for the father. Queer sympathists cannot help but find this plainly heterosexualizing account of female homosexual desire unsatisfying, if not offensive, and they have acted accordingly. In fact, to read the last ten years of lesbian-focused queer theory, one might conclude that lesbians are not women who want to fuck other women, but women who want to fuck with psychoanalysis.[1]

Apparently there is no love lost between lesbians and psychoanalysis.

In this essay, however, I argue that we do witness a kind of love between Freud and his analysand, as well as in the contemporary queer hostilities toward psychoanalysis that such cases have engendered. As Jacques Lacan states clearly, the effect of transference *is* love, even if it is vengeful. By this, he means that transference is not simply a repetition of primal structure, but a discrete reaction to the clinical scene. Transference at first enables—before blocking—the emergence of the unconscious, just as love addresses, and thereby arrests, the flow of desire. In thus reorienting our understanding of transference to love, Lacan helps us see that a homosexual woman's failure to find a productive transference in analysis bears more similarity to her unrequited love for her lover than either relation does to what Freud extrapolates as her relationship to her father.

Comparing these two love relations in Freud's case history—the patient's relationship to Freud and to her lover—helps us rethink the political and critical impasse arising between psychoanalytic and queer discourses. However, trying to determine either the ontological status of the lesbian or psychoanalysis's epistemological limitations relative to that status leads to nothing but a conceptual dead end. In discussing the lesbian, I shall redirect our attention instead to the field of ethics. According to Lacan, psychoanalysis shows us how the very parameters of ontology and epistemology are contingent on the subject's foundation, figured in this theory as a primal ethical decision that stems from a confrontation with trauma. If we accept Lacan's thesis, elaborated below, that both the subject as such and the practice of psychoanalysis are situated in the realm of ethics, rather than in that of ontology or epistemology, we might view the lack of understanding between psychoanalysis and lesbian subjects as a unique ethical encounter. The relational difficulties besetting the lesbian subject and analyst arguably signify less a particular failure between Freud and one female homosexual than an ethical question about the relative position and status of each.[2] Revenge, I shall argue, is the ethical dilemma that lesbianism poses to fundamental notions of subject formation and symbolic structure.

It may seem misleading to read this missed relationship between psychoanalysis and the lesbian subject as one concerning love. In a Lacanian paradigm, however, love is exactly the statement of this paradox, since it makes up for the lack of sexual relationship. When Lacan says, "There is no such thing as a sexual relationship," he means, primarily, that there is no necessary or natural relation between the sexes. On this plane, queer theory and Lacanian psychoanalysis share the same basic premise. However, Lacan also means that sexuality and desire as such are always addressed to a lack that can never be filled, and therefore that no sexual relationship—whether heterosexual or homosexual—can culminate in anything but more desire. Love compensates for this failure of satisfaction by forging reciprocity between self and other in the imaginary realm, and thus carries on as "a passion that involves ignorance of desire" (*Seminar* 20:4). On this imaginary level, homosexual and heterosexual loves are equivalent. Love is the narcissistic projection of one's ego onto the other, and is therefore by definition mutual, regardless of what we take to be the subject's "sexuality."

It would seem, then, that there is no such thing as unrequited love in the Lacanian idiom. I shall argue, however, that the one form of unrequited love legible in psychoanalytic terms is the relationship between the analyst and the lesbian.[3] The lesbian signifies the analysand who refuses transference, yet nonetheless wants to continue investigating through gender the traumas of desire. When the lesbian confirms through her same-sex object-choice that there is no such thing as a sexual relationship between men and women, arguably she acknowledges this truth from a perspective quite different from Lacan's. What comes out in the impossibility of the transference between the analyst and the lesbian is a perspective Lacan calls *anamorphic*—that is, an oblique glimpse of the other looking at this same fact of nonrelationality.

Lesbian love is not the same love of which Lacan speaks—his notion of love concerns the subject who would force reciprocity between the sexes. Whereas one may view homosexual desire as a sort of cop-out in the battle of the sexes, a Lacanian perspective helps us see heterosexuality, ironically, as a stronger renunciation of the trauma around sexuation than we find in homosexuality. I will argue that the figure of the lesbian in analysis—mythically rendered through Freud's female homosexual analysand—sublimates the question of gender as such. This action has two objects and two modes of conduct: When addressed to the sublime lover, the lesbian performs a kind of chivalric courtly love. When addressed to the analyst, however, who enables the articulation of this sublime position, she enacts revenge.[4]

I want to pursue this argument by exploring Lacan's thesis about the ethics of psychoanalysis. This discussion will help me explain how transference functions as a clinical process. I will then consider Lacan's theory of sexual differentiation, which inspires what I call *hysterical sublimation*. Through this notion of sublimation, I'll conclude by demonstrating that Freud's failure in "Psychogenesis" crystallizes the limits of analytical practice in a way that political and epistemological critiques of psychoanalysis have hitherto neglected.[5]

2.

Why is it important to understand the lesbian in terms of ethics? Perhaps a better question would be whether it is even possible to isolate homosexuality from the ethical field, since, as Michel Foucault points out, its status as a category of character has arisen out of the problem of *what to do* with such people. To this day, concerns about whether homosexuality is behavioral or identitarian, genetic or social, personal and/or political hinge on whether we condemn, celebrate, tolerate, or try to cure whatever we define as "homosexuality." In this context, it may be more fruitful to turn our questions from what a lesbian is or how we know her, to *why* it is important to attribute content to lesbians in the first place.

Lacan formalizes this ethical problem underlying homosexuality, and warns that we miss its significance when deferring to psychological conceptions of the subject. By rewriting Melanie Klein's understanding of the "bad object" in his *Ethics of Psychoanalysis,* Lacan argues that an ethical choice inaugurates subjectivity. In the grips of a mythical primal trauma, the infant enters the compromise forged by the pleasure and reality principles. The process of reality testing is essentially a set of ethical decisions by which the infant determines which objects are good and which bad. In representing its inside as good and its outside as bad, the ego creates a contradiction whereby the mother—held to be the original, missing good object—is refigured as bad. Through this paradox arising from primal judgment, Lacan challenges what he sees as the foundational concept of ethics deriving from presumptions of a "sovereign good." According to psychoanalysis, the instigating desire for an object pushes the subject to represent it as "good" even though the object is always encountered with ambivalence. In this respect, Lacan shifts our understanding of ethics from codes of conduct aimed at achieving "the good" (the conventional definition of ethics) to the field that underwrites the possibility of judgment as such.

Attributing content to the *unconscious* results in what Lacan calls "a new type of alienation," the invention of "a *homo psychologicus*" ("Intervention" 64). And the notion of an intelligible lesbian identity is but one manifestation of this *homo psychologicus,* stemming in part from a distortion of the psychoanalytic imperative to "know thyself." In psychoanalytic terms, this psychological characterology creates alienation because self-identity always entails misrecognition, and because the subject cannot fully assess the inherently divisive functions of desire. While for the past century most representations of lesbian identity have fallen under the rubric of psychology, Lacanian psychoanalysis offers us a unique model of subjectivity in place of the *homo psychologicus,* where we can view lesbianism as an ethical position.

Instead of the psychological subject, Lacan represents the subject of unconscious desire. He translates Freud's *"Wo es war, soll Ich werden"* as *"Whatever it is, I must go there,* because somewhere the unconscious reveals itself" (*Four* 33). This underscores the predominance of ethics over ontology, because "whatever" indicates that the unconscious's status as "there" is more important than the nature of its content. The subject imagines she will encounter the Other there, but in fact she discovers only the Other's lack. In searching for what the Other lacks and presumably wants, the Other's desire becomes hers.

Lacan not only defines the status of the unconscious as ethical, but also represents psychoanalysis itself as ethical, since Freud's *wo es war* is viewed as an imperative for the subject. The content of analysis's ethical code therefore consists in this question: "Have you acted in conformity with the desire that is in you?" (*Seminar* 7:314). That is, have you gone to where the unconscious reveals itself?

Putting aside for now the significance of lesbian desire in this process, we might perceive how this ethical imperative passes through the medium of transference, as Lacan explains in his "Intervention on Transference" (1951):

> What is involved is a scansion of structures in which truth is transmuted for the subject, affecting not only her comprehension of things, but her very position as subject of which her "objects" are a function. This means that the conception of the case-history is *identical* to the progress of the subject, that is, to the reality of the treatment. (64; original emphasis)

Analysis, Lacan tells us, does not entail plunging into psychological depth to recover psychic material from elsewhere; rather, the subject *happens* in analysis.

Lacan frames the analytic scene as a place where the asymmetrical desires of two subjects cross. The desire of the analyst implies both a problem and a lure for the understanding of the analysand's desire. As a discipline that strives to know the subject while accounting for the ways in which epistemologies ineluctably alter the objects they represent, psychoanalysis defines the ethical realm as marking the limits of knowledge. Psychoanalysis in theory aims not only to articulate that limit, but also to go into it, positing an arena in which the subject may emerge. As an instrument for knowing desire that is itself permeated with the desires of two subjects, the process of analysis yields the subject as necessarily a contaminated product.

The creature that emerges ephemerally in analysis holds a distinctly twentieth-century subjectivity that, following Lacan's cue, I will call *homo psychoanalyticus*. As a character who grew up, so to speak, within the institution of psychoanalysis, the lesbian emerges as the quintessential *homo psychoanalyticus*, a subject who redefines the limits of psychoanalytic practice and identitarian thinking. As we'll see in the next section, the lesbian also is the analysand who can exploit and protest the psychic structures that psychoanalysis must posit in order to represent itself as a theory of subjectivity. By shifting queer discussions of the lesbian from the current theoretical tendency to dismiss or revise psychoanalysis toward the subject of revenge, raised by Freud's own lesbian analysand, we might consider the lesbian as a subject who logically and historically emerges from psychoanalysis, yet threatens to wreak havoc on it as a theory.

The lesbian as *homo psychoanalyticus* is born of Freud's misuse and neglect, as portrayed in the cases of Dora and the female homosexual, respectively. By this, I don't mean that actual lesbians reacted politically to the way he treated these patients. Instead, through his ethical decisions before lesbian desire, Freud rendered female homosexuality inscrutable and inadvertently represented it as a kind of ethical Other to psychoanalysis. In order to understand this transformation—or creation, if you will—we must investigate further how transference operates in analysis.

3.

Since Lacan rewrites ethics as the condition through which judgment becomes intelligible, he gives transference paradigmatic importance. Whereas other psychoanalysts commonly view transference as an affective element of resistance requiring "liquidation," Lacan widens the frame of transference in order to see it as the necessary condition of analytic engagement. Analysis hinges on the probability that the analyst will appear as a love object—that the nature of his desire is not a dangerous by-product of analysis, but rather an object of the analytic scene. Lacan claims that transference signifies a primary function of the analysand's ethical encounter with the Other in the avatar of the analyst: "This means that the transference is not, of its nature, the shadow of something that was once alive" (*Four* 254). He adds that the love that emerges in analysis works in conjunction with the traumatic nature of the process for the analysand: "The subject, in so far as he is subjected to the desire of the analyst, desires to betray him for this subjection, by making the analyst love him, by offering of himself that essential duplicity that is love" (254).

The distinction between love and hostility is not especially significant on a structural level; these emotions are simply flip sides of an imaginary relation of the patient's ego to the analyst's. Either instance refers to an identification that the analysand would make with the analyst in order to avoid the more troubling vicissitudes of desire—hence Lacan's calling love duplicitous. A relation that is always reciprocal though never symmetrical, love ostensibly veils the impossibility of intersubjective relations. Even as it misses its object as surely as does desire, love fixes the position of an imaginary object of affection rather than presuming a lack (as desire does). While love therefore entails misrecognition, it manages to arrest the movement of desire.

So how does transference go wrong? Freud's encounters with female homosexuality seem to chart the inherent risks of the analytic process, and Lacan is the first to condemn Freud as heterosexist. If the role of the analyst is not only to point out the subject's unconscious desire, but also to hold her radically accountable to that desire, then the analyst must maintain a neutrality amounting to a kind of amoralism. This stems from the analyst's refusal to collude with the defensive structures of either the analysand's ego or his own. Herein lies the difference between the ethics of psychoanalysis and the moralism of patriarchal culture. In his "Intervention on Transference," Lacan criticizes Freud's treatment of Dora less for its misinterpretation than for the bad decision it reveals. Lacan argues that in his identification with Herr K. and his urge to see heterosexuality as natural, Freud allowed his countertransferential desires to supersede his responsibility to the desire of his analysand. This supersession resulted in his failure to recognize Dora's homosexual desire for Frau K.

In *Séminaire IV*, Lacan takes Freud to task for similar issues regarding the lesbian analysand. When Freud's analysand begins to fabricate dreams about sleeping with men, he recognizes that she wants to deceive the analyst. Lacan accuses Freud of taking this deception personally and so allowing his transferential feelings to supersede the structural suggestions of her transference. He adds that, as in Dora's case, Freud identifies with a straight male in her narrative, in this instance the lesbian's father, while finding her attractive. Again, Freud could not allow himself to think outside a heterosexual matrix. In this case—perhaps wanting to avoid repeating his mistakes with Dora—Freud calls off the analysis and suggests that she find a female analyst.

Yet Lacan doesn't go far enough in criticizing Freud's failure to realize his role as analyst. Beyond the veil of heterosexist morality resides a specific form of female homosexual desire that does more to account for Freud's flustered reaction than does any suggestion of his socially conservative leanings. Lacan, however, misses the form and consequence of this unique lesbian structure when focusing on purifying the desire of the analyst. He poses this desire as an "experienced desire" that strives "to obtain absolute difference" and results in an analyst's ethical imperative to recognize his or her own desire as a subject and extract it from the progress of the analysis (*Four* 276). The radical renunciation inherent in the analyst's desire teaches the analysand about the truth of her (or his) castration, which may lead to the only true love Lacan acknowledges:

> Love, which, it seems to some, I have down-graded, can be posited only in that beyond, where, at first, it renounces its object. This also enables us to understand that any shelter in which may be established a viable, temperate relation of one sex to the other necessitates the intervention—this is what psychoanalysis teaches us—of that medium known as the paternal metaphor. (276)

This leap to reconcile the sexes and accept the paternal metaphor should give us pause. Is this what the lesbian subject realizes? Although Lacan posits this love as "outside the limits of the law"—as a type of transcendence through acceptance—the lesbian subject swerves from this limit precisely when defying the paternal function. As heroizing as this claim may seem, however, the structural justification for this unique lesbian subject is embedded in Lacanian logic itself.

4.

The Lacanian notion of subjective structure involves a number of overlapping schema describing different aspects of psychic function and formation. The most important of these structures is contained in the three orders: the symbolic, imaginary, and real. For Lacan, the real does not describe reality as we perceive it, but something similar to Kant's world of "things as such," from which we are cut off by symbolization, the famous castration by the signifier. The ethical negotiation of reality-testing mediates the traumatic cancellation of the real in the symbolic by creating an imaginary reality dictated by the ego.

The subject's experience of these orders is inseparable from its relationship to sexual difference, which Lacan theorizes in *Seminar 20: Encore* when defining male and female structures: Men are completely castrated under the sign of the phallus and attribute the *objet a* to the Other as woman. Women, by contrast, are castrated by the phallic function as well, though not entirely. They attribute the phallus to masculine structure and seek the "signifier of the lack in the Other" positioned on the female side of structure. However, since for Lacan "there is no such thing as a sexual relation," these structures are neither naturally nor diacritically related on the level of symbolic understanding. Instead, they establish different and asymmetrical relations to a third term, the phallus as signifier, which neither sex owns. Hence biological men can be psychically women, and vice versa.[6]

Homosexuality might seem to reverse this structure, whereby the subject solves the gender dilemma with her certainty that she is a woman who desires other women. This assurance may in fact be deemed an imaginary compensation for the perpetual unknowability of gender in the form of an egoistic lie. Nonetheless, Lacan notes in his essay on transference that a "homosexual tendency" is a "constant" in hysterics and, correspondingly, that Dora's interest in Frau K. is aimed at "a mystery, the mystery of her femininity, by which I mean her bodily femininity" ("Intervention" 69, 67). So in this sense, the literalism around gender identification and desire in female homosexuality appears as a further intensification of the hysterical questioning of gender.

By assigning the question "What gender am I?" to the female structure, Lacan establishes a sort of productive redundancy. Whereas the average hysteric aggressively questions her gender, the lesbian seems to answer the question of her feminine status while introducing her female object-choice as another aspect of certainty. Rather than denying the desire of hysteria, the lesbian apparently sublates the paradox of holding a gendered position that is burdened exclusively with questioning the fact of gender differentiation. In a conventional Lacanian description of structure, lesbians are psychic women who select imaginary—which is to say, biological and socially normative—women. The lesbian of whom I speak describes an ethical position beyond this psychic structure. To this extent, lesbianism interrogates ethically the very terms of sexual structure by asking, "Why gender?"

5.

These elements of ethics, transference, and structure converge in Freud's "Psychogenesis of a Case of Homosexuality in a Woman" (1920). The case is on two levels a story of unrequited love: The younger woman's love for the older woman is not returned, and the young woman rejects Freud when she refuses the transferential medium of analysis. Let us first examine how the analysand's unrequited love for the woman illuminates the ethical status of the lesbian. The father's concern for his daughter seems as much about the gender of her would-be lover as it is about this woman's reputation as a "*cocotte*" (123). The lover bears a distinguished family name, but has fallen short of money and has been taken in by a wealthier female friend with whom she apparently has sex. She also entertains the attentions of a number of men. The young analysand worships this woman, whose pedestal is supported precisely by the dichotomy of her usual promiscuity and her exceptional refusal to accommodate Freud's patient. The young woman takes this refusal as proof of the noble nature of their love, which Freud reads as her "making a virtue of necessity" (129).

There is another way to read this virtue. Although Freud renounces the idea that the young woman is a gender invert, he notes her chivalric attitude toward the "Lady" (to whom he continually refers in quotes and a capital letter) as evidence of the "humility and sublime over-estimation of the sexual object so characteristic of the male lover" (131). The very language Freud uses to describe her resonates with the Lacanian explication of courtly love in *Seminar 7*. She is chivalric in almost identical ways, except that the Lady here is a Viennese coquette. In these parallels, we may conclude that, like the courtly knight, the young lesbian is performing a type of sublimation.

Lacan disputes Freud's idea that in sublimation the drive replaces its object. Instead, he depicts sublimation as reconstellating desire around the same object, such that it is elevated "to the dignity of the Thing" (*Seminar* 7:112), the presumed object of primal loss that survives symbolization in the form of the *objet a*. Lacan teases out a sense of the sublime in the act of the sublimation. Far from rescuing the object from the trials of desire, this sublimation puts the subject in a position to suffer all the more intensely the signifier's cancellation of the Thing. Lacan does, however, concur with Freud's idea that the sublimated object must also be culturally glorified. We may suppose that the promiscuous, bisexual coquette holds an iconic role in the early twentieth century akin to the medieval Lady's. This is apparent when Freud compares this lesbian love "relation" with that of a male "youth for a celebrated actress" and the masculine fantasy of "rescuing" a fallen woman ("Psychogenesis" 137, 138).

More important than these historical specificities is the analysand's own status as female and the way in which this sublimation reveals a fundamental trauma concerning the symbolic order's differentiation from the imaginary. I suggest that the lesbian in Freud's case history demonstrates a type of hysterical sublimation. The masculine sublimation epitomized by courtly love works in the register of objects, since the male obsessional neurotic pursues the *objet a*, situated between the symbolic and the real (*Seminar 20*).[7] Feminine structure, however, revolves around not an object, but gender as a fundamental point of indeterminacy. As the sublimation of a question rather than of an object, clinical lesbian structure might appear as a more difficult but truthful ethic of giving a traumatic impasse the significance of a fundamental lack.

Freud's lesbian elevates her lover to the status of the Thing precisely by sublimating the very fact of gender itself, the mystery of the feminine body pursued more conventionally by Dora. Both the lover's bisexuality and ambivalence toward the younger woman promote a hysterical questioning of the nature of gender, just as the courtly Lady's chastity furthers her elusive appeal as an avatar of the *objet a*. This model of hysterical sublimation is an alternative to both the Freudian notion of the drive's substituted object and the Lacanian notion of the object's rearrangement relative to fantasy. Instead, the subject of this hysterical sublimation takes from masculinist tradition an already sublime object of the "Lady" and appropriates it for herself. In doing so, she grants herself a sublime image. The lesbian sublimates her own subject position and calls herself into being.

This model of sublimation allows us to reinterpret this lesbian's resistance in analysis. If we view the analysand's self-enforced trials—including her suicide attempt—as a sublimated reconstitution of knightly duty, we might also consider her alleged "revenge" in analysis as an elevation of symbolic engagement. Her calculated deception of Freud and flagrant performances before her father prop these characters up as dragons before her chivalric task. Indeed, Lacan recognizes this defiance as "showing the father how one is, oneself, an abstract, heroic, unique phallus, devoted to the service of a lady" (*Four* 39). He claims that her suicide attempt after her father confronts her is a sincere response to his contempt for her lame approximation of the phallus. I read her suicide attempt, by contrast, not as an admission of defeat, but as a further provocation of paternal authority. As Lacan makes clear in the same passage regarding Dora, hysteria aims at sustaining the desire of the father as Other. If we follow his logic of transference, it hardly matters whether that effort takes the form of support or defiance.

In his reading of this lesbian case, Lacan makes an oversight similar to the one of which he accuses Freud: He fails to read transference as an address to the Other. On an imaginary level, the young woman does exactly what Lacan claims her father does to her: She demonstrates her disdain for the inadequacy of the paternal phallus. Her boredom with psychoanalysis concerns the fact that she cannot suspend her disbelief in the process, since she knows the denouement: that the Other lacks. If her suicide attempt is a way to get her father to take her homosexual mission seriously, the act parallels how she plays with her symptoms, dreams, and the analytic situation itself. In what seems open hostility, an anamorphic relation between the lesbian and psychoanalysis appears in their mutual address to truth, the inexpressible signifier of the Other's lack. The lesbian's joint provocations of Freud and her father demonstrate her will not to be a unique phallus, but to advance an ethics of "going there," her movement toward the impossible signifier.

The unrequited nature of Freud's countertransference becomes apparent here. Freud prefaces his conclusion that she is taking revenge on paternal figures by discussing how transference in general fails through doubt. According to him, the analysand's persistent skepticism is a transferential shield for her neurosis. This idea of doubt resonates with Lacan's argument that the Freudian unconscious represents the subject of doubt, yet in Freud's account only the analyst may doubt on the level of transference. In provoking Freud to continue with his heterosexist interpretations through her false dreams, the lesbian analysand demonstrates clearly that she recognizes the existence and form of Freud's countertransference. That this doubt is available to the analyst, but apparently signifies only resistance in the analysand, reveals an asymmetry at the heart of psychoanalytic ethics and transference.

If transference is the imaginary lie that nonetheless presents a sincere urge to love the analyst, then knowing deception approximates the doubling inherent in the liar's paradox. I am referring to the inaccessible truth of the statement "I am lying," which Lacan has no problem dissolving, since he recognizes that the "I" who speaks—that is, the unconscious subject—is not the same as the "I" in the sentence, the ego. The analyst must maintain exactly this awareness in his desire for "absolute difference," a desire that the lesbian arguably manifests in her retaliation by trying to isolate Freud's desire in the analytic situation. Freud cannot recover from the way she has flipped the analysis and so he terminates the analysis.

The liminality of the lesbian in psychoanalysis's clinical and theoretical terrain implies that revenge signifies an anamorphic and mutually defining hostility between psychoanalysis and lesbianism. Since lesbians and analysts recognize that there is no such thing as a sexual relationship, the paternal metaphor cannot provide the ground for either transference or a love beyond the limits of the law. However, this mutual refusal of transferential love is not a fruitless impasse, as transference itself is best viewed as a productive failure. Instead, the mutual ambivalence between lesbians and analysts yields the lesbian as a belated breed of analysand who uniquely addresses the signifier of the lack in psychoanalysis. Perhaps we might even propose a revision of Freud's ethical commandment "*Wo es war, soll Ich werden*" that includes the analyst more thoroughly in the frame of psychoanalytic inquiry: Where the lesbian was, so the analyst must come to be. By this "where" I mean the couch itself, the lack freshly rendered by the lesbian who has left the scene of analysis.

Lesbian analysands may be theorized, then, less as the oversight of psychoanalysis than as its limit. If lesbian analysands sublimate their relation to the always-absent signifier, they may not have or be this signifier, but they do bear its subjective trace as *jouissance*. Revenge, the Freudian lesbian's "keenest desire," should—at least tentatively—find a place in psychoanalysis as a desire intimately other to analysis that is impervious to psychogenetic explication and the liberal accommodation that seeks to dissolve this fundamental hostility ("Psychogenesis" 160). In confronting this model of transference, psychoanalysis may make a place for the lesbian's revenge. However, psychoanalysis must also be willing to take a necessary step closer to its own abnegation, permitting a traumatic ethical encounter that includes the desire of psychoanalysis itself.

Notes

I thank George Edmondson, Sonnet Retman, Ken Reinhard, and Roshni Sharma for their generosity in reading and commenting on earlier versions of this essay.

1. I refer here to a loose collection of critics arguing on behalf of a redemptive lesbian politics. Toward this end, many of their works display an interesting will to perversion, which in psychoanalytic theory signals a disavowal of castration. These theorists include Grosz; de Lauretis; Adams; and, most recently, McCallum, whose interest in fetishizing fetishism formalizes this wider urge to escape from the psychoanalytic description of subjectivization. While most of her work addresses the logical problems of psychoanalysis, Butler's analysis of the lesbian phal-

lus in *Bodies That Matter* displays a similar theoretical trajectory in its attempt to imagine a nonpsychotic space beyond the symbolic. Most of these theories—Adams's excepted—often fail to indicate that deconstructing a structure does not automatically make it available for political action and subjective change.

2. In *Homos*, Bersani provides a useful model for the kind of reading I am attempting here. He does so by articulating a homosexual value of "sameness" that resists how epistemologies of difference neutralize *jouissance* and help naturalize oppressive social regimes.

3. For an explication of the unique relation that gay men have to the ethics of psychoanalysis, see my article "Is the Rectum *das Ding*? Lacan, Bersani, and the Ethics of Psychoanalysis."

4. In the cases where I use "she" for the analysand and "he" for the analyst, I am taking Freud's case history of the homosexual woman as an urtext, in this way reading the analytical situation as a kind of mythos addressed to what the analysand in this case imagined to be a fundamental gender drama.

5. Lesser and Schoenberg's volume marks the limit of such political deconstructive accounts of Freud's lesbian case history. The essays by Fuss, Wineapple, and de Lauretis (who begins her inquiry with a question almost identical to mine, "What does the homosexual woman want?" [38]) do much to unpack the epistemological limitations of Freud's study. Without offering an ethical framework for these concerns, however, the political insistence implicit in their critiques can only repeat the hysterical declaration of a lack in psychoanalysis as Other. I suggest not that this questioning stop, but that we envision a way to enjoy it as a lesbian theoretical symptom. Whereas these essays offer a purer readerly critique, the volume's other essays—particularly those by analysts—tend to call for a redemptive revision of psychoanalysis along the lines of inclusivity. It seems to me that these gestures conform to imaginary adjustments that may have an ineluctable effect of normalizing and heteroizing the homosexual analysand. Calling for a psychoanalysis that can accommodate lesbians is akin to the violence Freud and Lacan see in the Levitican commandment to love thy neighbor. Such inclusion enacts repressions that will heighten an aggressive return elsewhere. Lesbian analysands offer histories tainted with oppression and clinical misrecognition, while marking a theoretical impasse around the very idea of psychogenesis as a form of epistemology. Assuaging the harms of these traumas by clinically clearing space for a lesbian imaginary is in fact downright antipsychoanalytic. Instead, we might view the mythical and historical trauma of the analyst's encounter with the lesbian as an occasion to push clinical practice into a new, more rigorous, and frankly frightening exploration of the ethical world that Lacan introduced.

6. For this reason, it is also possible to have a male lesbian.

7. See the diagrams at the beginning of chapters 7 and 8 in *Seminar 20*. My reading aims to mediate the relationship between the S($\text{\textbar}$A) and *objet a* in these two charts, which represent sexuation and the triad of the symbolic, imaginary, and real, respectively.

References

Adams, Parveen. "Of Female Bondage." In *Between Feminism and Psychoanalysis*. Ed. Teresa Brennan. New York: Routledge, 1989. 247–65.

Bersani, Leo. *Homos*. Cambridge: Harvard UP, 1995.

Butler, Judith. *Bodies That Matter: On the Discursive Limits of "Sex."* New York: Routledge, 1993.

de Lauretis, Teresa. *The Practice of Love: Lesbian Sexuality and Perverse Desire*. Bloomington: Indiana UP, 1994.

Freud, Sigmund. "The Psychogenesis of a Case of Homosexuality in a Woman." 1920. *The Standard Edition of the Complete Psychological Works of Sigmund Freud*. Ed. and trans. James Strachey. 24 vols. London: Hogarth, 1953–74. 18:145–72.

Grosz, Elizabeth. *Space, Time, and Perversion: Essays on the Politics of Bodies*. New York: Routledge, 1995.

Lacan, Jacques. *The Four Fundamental Concepts of Psycho-Analysis (The Seminar of Jacques Lacan, Book 11)*. 1973. Ed. Jacques-Alain Miller. Trans. Alan Sheridan. New York: Norton, 1981.

———. "Intervention on Transference." 1951. *Feminine Sexuality: Jacques Lacan and the école freudienne*. Ed. Juliet Mitchell and Jacqueline Rose. Trans. Rose. New York: Norton, 1982. 62–73.

———. *Le séminaire, livre IV: La relation d'objet, 1956–1957*. Ed. Jacques-Alain Miller. Paris: Seuil, 1994.

———. *The Seminar of Jacques Lacan, Book 7: The Ethics of Psychoanalysis, 1959–1960*. Ed. Jacques-Alain Miller. Trans. Dennis Porter. New York: Norton, 1992.

———. *The Seminar of Jacques Lacan, Book 20: Encore: On Feminine Sexuality, the Limits of Love and Knowledge, 1972–1973*. Ed. Jacques-Alain Miller. Trans. Bruce Fink. New York: Norton, 1998.

Lesser, Ronnie C., and Erica Schoenberg, eds. *That Obscure Subject of Desire: Freud's Female Homosexual Revisited*. New York: Routledge, 1999.

Lukes, H. N. "Is the Rectum *das Ding*? Lacan, Bersani, and the Ethics of Psychoanalysis." *Oxford Literary Review* 20.1–2 (1998): 103–42.

McCallum, E. L. *Object Lessons: How to Do Things with Fetishism*. Albany: SUNY P, 1999.

14

HOMOSEXUALITY AND PSYCHOSIS IN THE CLINIC

Symptom or Structure?

Daniel L. Buccino

. . . .

Traveling across the deserts of the southwestern United States, a truck stops to pick up a young hitchhiker with long hair and drab clothes. It is not clear whether this hitchhiker is male or female, and after a while of riding in silence, the passenger asks the driver, "Well, aren't you going to ask me?" "Ask you what?" counters the trucker. "If I'm a boy or a girl," replies the hitchhiker. To which the trucker responds: "Don't matter. I'm gonna screw you anyway!"

1. To Begin: The Moment of the Look

For decades now, the American psychoanalytic establishment has endeavored to move in two opposing directions away from Freud's theories of homosexuality. Although these attempts arise from basic misconstruals of Freud's positions, the analytic community's machinations about homosexuality are nevertheless instructive. In seeking to update analytic wisdom about homosexuality, several contemporary American analysts merely underline the profound complexity of Freud's original claims. Freud's work engages not only sexual orientation and the essential differences, if any, between homosexuality and heterosexuality, but also the more profound question of gender identity and what it means to be a man or woman. In returning to Freud through the slippages of mainstream analytic revisionism, we confront the work of Jacques Lacan. And by reviewing some influential literature on homosexuality produced by the American clinical psychoanalytic community (and academic theorists of psychoanalysis), we find ourselves on Freud's primary bedrock of bisexuality. From there, I will argue, in part through a clinical vignette, that the seemingly vexing questions of homosexuality versus heterosexuality are in fact screens for more difficult Lacanian questions about phallic knowledge and the clinical structure of psychosis.

2. Homosexuality and American Psychoanalysis

American psychoanalysis has adopted two contrary stances about homosexuality. Stereotypically, the analytic establishment has been understood to hold a fundamentally pathologizing view of both male and female homosexuality. Charles Socarides is perhaps the strongest proponent of this position, which sees homosexuality as prima facie evidence of ego weakness, profound preoedipal pathology, and lack of impulse control— and which therefore requires radical restructuring of the ego and sexual-partner reorientation in psychoanalytic treatment. According to Socarides, although the homosexual requires corrective treatment, most homosexuals are unanalyzable because of their denials of the trauma inflicted by their homosexual drives. In this position, there is no such thing as "ego-syntonic (unconflicted) homosexuality": Homosexuality is seen as entirely defensive and pathologically conflicted. Perhaps Socarides found this extreme a necessary correction to Freud's ambiguous perspectives on sexuality. But owing to positions such as Socarides's, the American analytic community has suffered from bad public relations.

The analytic community has also tried to develop another, more progressive line of revisionism, following too from Freud's ambiguous positions. This position, advanced by Richard Isay, is lent quasi-scientific substantiation by the work of Richard Friedman ("Toward a Further Understanding"; *Male Homosexuality*) and Robert Stoller (*Observing*). In this view, homosexuality is not inherently pathological, and the goal of analytic treatment need not be to alter partner preference. In fact, Isay, the first "out" gay analyst in the American Psychoanalytic Association, even contends, contra Socarides, that a patient's apparent discomfort with his homosexuality should not be taken at face value. Isay sees homosexuality as "immutable from birth" (21), though early experiences can affect its expression. Isay focuses not on etiology or pathogenesis, but on approaches to facilitating satisfying homosexual expression and sustaining relationships; he also argues that treatment should focus on challenging homophobia, which is often internalized even by gay men. Although Isay's articulation of the self-denigrating repercussions of internalized homophobia is useful, the polarized positions of Isay and Socarides effectively cancel each other in the dialectics of debate within the American psychoanalytic community.

Kenneth Lewes has characterized the American psychoanalytic community's basic positions on homosexuality as revealing at bottom a "brittle and exaggerated solicitude for conventional sexual values" (139). Despite some resistance from analysts, Lewes sees American psychoanalytic theories of homosexuality not only as homophobic, but also as "gynecophobic"; "homosexuals were seen as deeply flawed and defective, because they shared certain psychic characteristics with women" (237). In American psychoanalysis, it seems, one can be neither content nor discontented with one's homosexuality.

Friedman gamely elaborates Isay's view that homosexual preference must be biological, and therefore immune from (psycho-) pathologizing. Unfortunately, however, Friedman's attempts to bring Freud into twentieth-century neurology and developmental psychology prove no more illuminating than was Freud himself. Friedman concludes that there must be a "critical period" in which a homosexual's neurological structure accretes in the brain, during which a central sexual fantasy is adopted and a core gender identity developed. This perspective resembles the suggestive but still unproven arguments that there are critical periods for the acquisition of speech and language ability (Rymer) and that there is a gene for mental illness, which we allegedly get daily closer to pinpointing. The possibility of a biological basis for homosexuality might help diminish its current stigma and status as a pathology within professional and lay communities, but finding such a basis would do little to illuminate the psychic conflicts involved in *any* sexual preference.

That much of this is biological may turn out someday to be true, as the work of Dean Hamer and Peter Copeland (*The Science of Desire*) and Simon LeVay (*The Sexual Brain*) increasingly contend. Hamer and Copeland have found evidence of a specific, transmissible "gay gene," and LeVay has speculated on the role of different hypothalamic structures in gay men than in straight men. But although the work of LeVay and Hamer and Copeland is scientifically rigorous and intriguing, and their larger arguments both sober and progressive, they admit that even less is

certain regarding female homosexuality. And beyond even this, the finding of these biological substrates by themselves ultimately will be uninter-
esting to any psychoanalyst concerned with the way the body and the
biological take on symbolic and imaginary meanings. We must remind
ourselves that the Freudian subject is always internally conflicted about
its psychosexual development and identity, regardless of object-choice.[1]

In his classic reading of Freud on sexuality and the drives, Jean Laplanche makes clear that internal sexual conflict is a critical aspect of sexuality. Primary masochism, Laplanche argues, "is intimately connected with
the notion of fantasy as an alien internal entity and with the drive as an
internal attack, so that the paradox of masochism, far from deserving to
be circumscribed as a specific 'perversion,' should be generalized, linked
as it is to the *essentially traumatic nature of human sexuality*" (105; original
emphasis). Not only is a stable sexual identity difficult to secure for the
subject, but concerns about symptomatic expressions—beliefs in a core
self, identity, or personality—are only the beginnings of the properly psychoanalytic domain and must not remain exclusive foci in treatment.

In a letter to Karl Abraham at a time when American psychiatry increasingly opposed him, Freud wrote that "personality . . . is a loosely defined
term from surface psychology that does nothing in particular to increase
understanding of the real processes, that is to say, *meta-psychologically*, it
says nothing. But it is easy to believe that one is saying something meaningful in using it" (qtd. in Leys 24; original emphasis). It is easy to see
how American psychoanalysis has been persuaded by a set of American
psychiatric concerns with symptomatic description and classification,
losing track of deeper "meta-psychological" conflicts in subjectivity, identity, and sexuality. For Freud, these conflicts emerge from within the subject as much as from the subject's conflict with the external world.

One of the most interesting and influential American researchers on
human sexuality is Stoller. He has been a shrewd and nonjudgmental
observer of the multiple possibilities of human sexual experience, and he
allows that most sexual solutions are indeed classically Freudian compromise formations. In elaborating the logical premises of Stoller's arguments, however, we are stymied again in categorizing homosexuality as
distinct from heterosexuality. For the sake of argument, let us assume,
following Stoller, that there are four components of the gender identity/
sexual orientation scale. One starts with the foundation of "anatomy,"
which all too often is thought to be a simple bodily matter. From anatomical attributes, Stoller assumes that "core gender identity" follows developmentally. Logically, what follows next in the Stollerian scheme is

Figure 1   PERMUTATIONS OF SEXUALITY

(GENITAL) ANATOMY	♀ ♂ ♂	♂ ♀ ♂	♀ ♂ ♂
(CHROMOSOMAL/ HORMONAL) BIOLOGY	♀ ♀ ♂	♀ ♀ ♂	♀ ♂ ♂
CORE GENDER IDENTITY	♀ ♀ ♀	♂ ♂ ♀	♂ ♂ ♂
GENDER ROLE IDENTITY (PERFORMANCE)	♀ ♀ ♀	♂ ♀ ♀	♂ ♂ ♂
PARTNER ORIENTATION/ OBJECT CHOICE	♀ ♀ ♀	♀ ♂ ♂	♀ ♂ ♂
"LOVE INTEREST"/ OBJECT IN FANTASY	♀ ♀ ♂...	♂ ♂ ♀...	♂ ♀ ♂...

"gender role performance"; and, finally, "sexual orientation," partner preference, or object-choice. As figure 1 indicates, the assumption of secure identity in each realm is problematic enough. What happens, then, if there are inconsistent identities? If one is seen as male in one domain and identifies as female in another? Even in the apparently simplest realm of anatomy, science has shown us that there is much more involved than meets the eye. The question of hermaphroditism complicates the truth of anatomy on one level, and quite recent Olympic spectacles about whether female athletes are indeed female have complicated it on another.

By expanding the realm of science to include chromosomal and hormonal identities, recent laboratory tests have pushed the quest to certify the anatomical distinction between the sexes to new levels of precision and new crises of confusion (Burr; Kolata). For example, it no longer seems adequate for Olympic physicians simply to inspect athletes' genitalia before permitting them to compete. Sophisticated new chromosomal and hormonal tests have found athletes who look female and, like women, have two X chromosomes, yet have "masculinized" muscle mass due to hormonal imbalances. Females with any male genes or masculinization, however, have been declared ineligible for competition as women. So even the definition of anatomy is open to different medical, genital, hormonal, and chromosomal interpretations, showing how difficult it is to establish the ultimate truth of gender identity on a biological, anatomical, or genetic basis alone.

In attempting to incorporate late-twentieth-century scientific advancements, American psychoanalysis betrays Freud (by attending to a surface psychology and a nearly subatomic, chromosomal neural biology), while unwittingly revalorizing him; as such, advanced science ultimately reveals the fundamental psychic complexity of sexuality and identity. In the contradictions between its more gay-affirmative moments and its most egregiously homophobic, American psychoanalysis leads us back to Freud's sophisticated claims about constitutional bisexuality. I submit that Freud never really abandoned this position, advanced initially and perhaps most succinctly in his *Three Essays on the Theory of Sexuality* (1905).

Later attempts by Freudian revisionists to privilege one oedipal solution over another, or to pathologize homosexuality, turn out to be conflicted, ambivalent oscillations and enactments of a fundamental bisexual core. The more that contemporary American psychoanalysis tries to stake out a position on sexual identity opposed to Freud, the more progressive Freud's own positions are revealed to be. Since it has been so difficult for American psychoanalysis to distinguish normal from pathological development in the field of gender identity and sexual orientation, we can view most theorists as not departing from Freud, but implicitly returning to him.

Contemporary efforts to illuminate the essential characteristics of what it means to be straight or gay, or even male or female, frequently collapse into assumptions about passivity and activity; ironically, such efforts reveal a profoundly Freudian nucleus of bisexuality and polymorphous perversity. Contemporary American analysis struggles in its attempts to account for nontraditional oedipal resolutions and to explain the concepts of phallic women and castrated men. To forgo the concept of bisexuality and explain most variants of sexuality via the mere presence or absence of a penis is to lose the specific utility of Freudian psychoanalysis, while falling into fundamentally essentialist understandings of sexual difference.

Freud certainly was not an essentialist, and as we will see in our exploration of Lacanian theory, the phallus certainly is not simply a piece of flesh; indeed, gender identity and sexual orientation are established in complicated topological relationships in at least three registers, each concerning the phallus.

Through the following case study of a lesbian patient, I shall discuss how bisexuality and psychosis may be raised in the transference of a treatment relationship, and then move to a Lacanian conclusion about the relation between bisexuality and stable sexual identity. Ultimately, I shall claim that the case hinges on an understanding of the distinction between neurosis and psychosis, and not between male and female, or gay and straight desires.

3. Case History: Ms. D.

For four years I treated a middle-aged lesbian. Ms. D. is proud to profess her status as a "butch dyke," indeed enacting a conventionally masculinized "gender role performance." She spent much of her first two years in treatment grieving the loss of a long-term lover, Ms. E., and berating this woman for dumping her in favor of an openly bisexual woman, Ms. F., a "piece of trash" who would occasionally turn male "tricks."

Ms. D. was most perturbed by her former partner's renunciation of her lesbian "purity" in favor of "anyone who'd been with guys!" Ms. D. had great difficulty understanding how her long-term companion could make such a shift. It called into question their time together, ultimately provoking a question about whether Ms. D. herself had bisexual traits, perhaps a component of initial interest in Ms. E.

Ms. D. spent many sessions "teaching" me about how "pure" homosexuality and lesbianism should be and what was "correct" behavior for each; Ms. E.'s betrayal was clearly impolitic. Ms. D. was certain that she herself had no bisexual inclinations, but that Ms. E.'s contact with Ms. F., who had "been with guys," somehow had "contaminated" Ms. D. Ms. D.'s denunciation of bisexuality and her denial of any sexual variance beyond the most essentially lesbian seemed a bit vociferous, a little too concerned that a lesbian be attracted "only" to other lesbians without any bisexual history.

Indeed, it became clear that the question of her own homosexuality and what it meant to be a "Lesbian" (stressing, as in Ms. D.'s mind, the apparent universality of the capital L) gave her a certain amount of grief and anxiety. What was most striking was less the effect of this grief and anxiety, than the tenacity with which Ms. D. clung to her certainty regarding what a lesbian could be, how a homosexual must act, and the effects of a lover's variant practices on her own self-definition as "homo or het," "butch or femme," and even "male or female." Ms. D. was also quite strident in her belief that "real" lesbians maintained a butch stance and that "lipstick lesbians" were of a somewhat lower order. These issues and Ms. D.'s certainty of their relevance finally became diagnostically suggestive.

In a Lacanian view, Ms. D.'s conviction (not to mention her increased anxieties, linguistic disorganization, and diminished self-care) generated such acute turmoil in her life that she began to manifest psychotic traits. The Lacanian diagnosis of psychosis hinges on precisely the *certainty* that the patient ascribes to her knowledge of sexual difference. When the paternal metaphor is foreclosed entirely from consciousness, the psychotic cannot recognize lack-in-being and thus is able only to "teach" others, in the transference specifically, about the certainty of her often-delusional worlds.

By comparison, the neurotic possesses a question, rather than a conviction, about sexual difference. And the hysteric's question, too, often entails asking what it means to be male or female, specifically, what it takes to be a woman. In both cases, the structural diagnosis indicates a certain position for the analyst to adopt in the transference, which allows him or her to avoid being too distracted by the movements of the patient's symptoms and self-assurances. In this case, the traditional place as "subject supposed to know" was not open to me in the transference, because it was she, Ms. D., who knew the truth of her condition. Therefore, I was left to occupy the position of "substitute Name-of-the-Father" as a place of limits and containment. This would aid the patient in grafting a neurotic structure onto her psychotic core, or otherwise transforming her psychotic certainty into a neurotic question that might be amenable to therapeutic interventions. In trying to assume the position of "substitute Name-of-the-Father," I tried to offer some structure in the treatment relationship that would allow Ms. D. to experience and tolerate moments of uncertainty regarding her phallic knowledge; I hoped that this uncertainty might help her continue to see the value in treatment.

Ms. D.'s loss of Ms. E. to the putatively bisexual Ms. F. was a crisis that hastened many serious symptoms and revealed her psychotic structure. But it would not be long before the patient experienced another crisis of confrontation, which occasioned both a psychotic explosion and the beginnings of a retreat from her prior convictions.

While out one evening in her usual haunts, Ms. D. was propositioned by a very attractive woman, Ms. G. In her rigid epistemology, Ms. D. knew this woman *had* to be lesbian because, in her mind, no one but lesbians—no one different from her—frequented the same establishments as her. Ms. D. quickly became infatuated with Ms. G., since it had been a very long time since anyone as attractive as Ms. G. had expressed such amorous interest in her. After several evenings of flirtation and "dirty dancing," Ms. D. was ready to take Ms. G. home with her. At this point, the manager of the establishment where they were courting, an acquaintance of Ms. D.'s, informed her that Ms. G. was in fact a male-to-female transsexual, a rather notorious flirt, and a not-infrequent bisexual prostitute. In shock, dismay, and humiliation, Ms. D. fled the bar and Ms. G.; Ms. D. soon began showing such an array of floridly psychotic and classically psychiatric symptoms that she required hospitalization.

After her discharge and stabilization, Ms. D. continued treatment, during which it became apparent that her psychotic explosion was not only a recapitulation of the loss of her true love, Ms. E., but also that Ms. D.'s encounter with Ms. G., together with subsequent disappointments, hastened a confrontation with her own *un*certainty regarding her homosexuality and what it means to be a lesbian. This second psychotic crisis, occurring after two years of treatment, unexpectedly allowed the patient to recall aspects of her own history that she had "forgotten" in establishing the certainty of her sexual identity. It was through an acutely psychiatric psychotic crisis that Ms. D. was able to begin to readjust her psychoanalytically psychotic certainties into more "normal" neurotic questions.

In treatment following her discharge from hospital, Ms. D. revisited her grim childhood, born as she was into a loveless marriage between a cruel, indifferent mother and an abusive, alcoholic father. Ms. D. was shuttled between numerous foster homes, where she was apparently sexually abused and began to exhibit a wide array of behavioral disturbances. In her teens, Ms. D. found solace in the arms of a slightly older woman, but felt the need to renounce as socially unacceptable her burgeoning homosexuality, despite her continued exhibition of other "socially unacceptable" academic and vocational behavior. In a last-ditch effort to reconcile with her own mother, Ms. D. married in her early twenties and bore a child.

Her husband had resembled her father (abusive, alcoholic) and their marriage was short-lived. Most notably, Ms. D. soon gave her son up for adoption; she began to establish fully her lesbian identity and vigorously renounced all her prior involvement with men: her abusive father, foster fathers, and husband, as well as the product of this last involvement in the person of her young son. The development of Ms. D.'s own definitions of lesbianism apparently required her to leave behind all reminders of her past and to generalize her experiences to all other lesbians. Additionally, Ms. D. had never quite had a female presence in her life that could function structurally as a representative of the Name-of-the-Father. By reviving some of the painful compromises in her past history, Ms. D. was able to shift gradually in her treatment from her psychotic certainty regarding the meaning of being lesbian to a more neurotic, "hysterical" uncertainty regarding what it means to be a woman.

From this vignette, understood implicitly in Lacanian terms, we now turn to explicitly Lacanian formulations, following the impasse in American psychoanalysis that points to Freud's original insights regarding primary bisexuality. This will allow us to shift clinical focus from symptomatic preoccupations with homo- or heterosexuality onto more useful structural observations regarding neurosis, psychosis, and perversion.

4. Lacanian Analysis and Structural Diagnosis

Marie-Hélène Brousse gives us perspective on a Lacanian understanding of both homosexuality and psychosis. In "Feminism with Lacan," she makes two introductory points that help contextualize the present discussion. The first is to emphasize that "psychoanalysis is a *clinical* approach to sexuality in human beings as subjects of the unconscious" (119; my emphasis).

Brousse also distinguishes a Lacanian psychoanalytic understanding of sexuality from the impasses of a more Anglo-American position. As I suggested above, American psychoanalysis inadvertently revealed the Freudian truth of bisexuality when it ran aground on faulty distinctions among anatomy, development, fantasy, identification, and behavior. American psychoanalysis has trouble holding apart the differences among biology (in an attempt to obtain pseudoscientific legitimation), conscious and unconscious mentation, and behavior. Rather than pursuing any one avenue as essentially constitutive of subjectivity or sexuality (as American psychoanalysis is wont to do), Brousse reminds us that "to give a specificity to the psychoanalytical approach to sexuality, we have to keep in mind this distinction between organism, body, and subject, a distinction which can be related to the three dimensions Lacan invented: Real, Imaginary, and Symbolic" (118). This can be illustrated with the simplest of Lacanian topologies, as shown in figure 2. This mapping corresponds to the specific problems we saw in the clinical case, as illustrated in figure 3.

The three dimensions of real, symbolic, and imaginary overlap in places, and contain specific questions for our particular patient. But what is most liberating in this Lacanian approach is the possibility—indeed the necessity—of considering all three dimensions simultaneously without giving priority to any, a necessity that is foreign to American literalness and singularity. Brousse concludes: "There is no such thing as the corre-

Figure 2

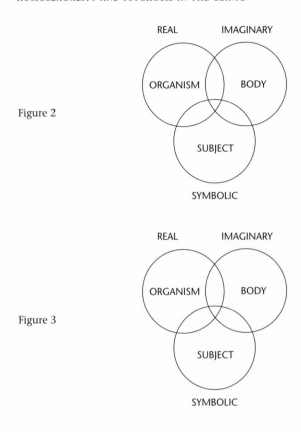

Figure 3

spondence or mutual covering of these three concepts: in consequence, subjective sex is not the psychical transcription of the biological sex, nor of the body image" (118). On the one hand, Brousse's contribution points to the precision of a properly Lacanian psychoanalytic approach in the midst of the confusion of Anglo-American and theoretical-applied psychoanalysis. On the other hand, Brousse treats the question of sexuality as a clinical question, one that concerns the unconscious and therefore cannot be answered by general, theoretical laws of the body or the mind.

Confronted with questions about her own gender identity and sexual orientation in her encounter with the beautiful transsexual, Ms. D. witnessed her own "certainties" regarding her identity and identifications simultaneously challenged and reinforced. In glossing Lacan, who canonized Joan Riviere's 1929 article, "Womanliness as a Masquerade," Brousse points up the difficulties in Ms. D.'s encounter: "Femininity manifests itself in a masquerade, but behind the phallic mask, we do not find any truth about femininity. Femininity is nothing but the mask itself, or the mask itself is the truth of femininity as a phallic emblem. This posits femininity as one of the figures of fetishism. . . . By placing herself as semblant of the object, she produces a fiction of femininity and reveals the truth of femininity as a masculine fantasy" (124). Although in Ms. D.'s case the question of which or whose masculine fantasy was operating remains open, we do see not only that questions of femininity and womanhood were problematized for her, but, more important, that any sense of sexual identity based on rigid gender identifications is prone to collapse as well. I want to stress the clinical and conceptual repercussions of this argument.

In an ambiguous near-conclusion to her article, Brousse points to Lacan's famous aphorism "Woman only encounters Man in psychosis" (125). Brousse glosses this aphorism: "Let us assert that this particular encounter with Man as universal (and not a man, any man) is a way to affirm, in return, Woman as *La femme*, without the bar on the *La*" (125). Invocation and interpretation of Lacan here becomes tricky, as Lacan himself said in *Television:* "It follows that woman—since we cannot speak of more than one—a woman only encounters Man [*L'homme*] in psychosis" (40).

As is often the case in Lacan, what appears to be a relatively straightforward statement is actually profoundly elusive. Small differences between, for instance, what is capitalized or not—which become even harder to differentiate aurally, thereby further opening the unconscious by way of puns—can have major and quite divergent implications. In the passage above we see Lacan referring, it appears, to an encounter between a specific woman (with a small *w*) and the structure of phallic knowledge as imaginarized in the Universalized Man (with a capital *M*).

Lacan specifies carefully that only a woman encounters "Man" in psychosis. As noted, Lacan seems to want to formalize the logic of an encounter between a specific woman and the generalized man of the supposedly universal Phallus and Knowledge. Rather than recognizing the reality of castration that all specific and rigidly designated men and women traverse in confrontation with the Phallus, the psychotic woman is unable to recognize either the phallus or castration and thereby enacts a reciprocal fantasy of the Universal Woman (with a capital *W*). Additionally, in the case of Ms. D., we see a specific refusal of and foreclosure in the Name-of-the-Father in literal terms of abuse, abandonment, and foster care, and in Lacanian terms in the three registers.

But the somewhat ambiguous capitalizations in Brousse's citation seem to indicate that the woman's encounter with Man affirms for her a psychotic certainty of *La femme* to counterbalance *L'homme* and to obtain security—if only in the truth of psychosis—of her own essential gender identity. We might say that such capitalizations exist only in psychosis. It follows logically that if a woman can assume an encounter with Man, then she must be equivalent to Woman—a logical error, but one that assures the certainty of psychosis regarding the universality and essential quality of Man and Woman. There are of course many other symptoms of psychosis, but this dimension of certainty is most characteristic, enabling the clinical, structural diagnosis of psychosis. It is worth reemphasizing that the structural diagnosis of psychosis can be made clinically only when the foreclosure of the Name-of-the-Father engenders a specific certainty in the transference regarding sexual difference, sexual identity, and the "subject supposed to know." This does not mean that every vigorously argued conviction is an example of psychotic certainty—only the absolute certainty about sexual difference that emerges in the transference established by treatment, the "clinic" of psychosis as it were.

Although it may seem an unlikely place to look for further elucidation of the enigmas of gender identity and sexual orientation, Lacan's third seminar, *The Psychoses* (1955–56), provides insight into the function of certainty and phallic knowledge in the clinical structure of psychosis.

5. A Psychotic Certainty?

Surely, certainty is the rarest of things for the normal subject. If he questions himself about this matter, he will be aware that certainty emerges in strict correlation to an action he undertakes. . . . But, contrary to the normal subject for whom reality is always in the right place, he is certain of something, which is that what is at issue—ranging from hallucination to interpretation—regards him.

Reality isn't at issue for him, certainty is. Even when he expresses himself along the lines of saying that what he experiences is not of the order of reality, this does not affect his certainty that it concerns him. The certainty is radical. The very nature of what he is certain of can quite easily remain completely ambiguous, covering the entire range from malevolence to benevolence. But it means something unshakable for him. (*Seminar* 3:74–75)

The psychotic shows himself in his or her *certainty* as different from the "normal" subject, for whom *reality* stays in place. Although reality is elusive and ultimately specific to each subject, the psychotic is certain something concerns him, even if this is whether s/he is a man or woman, or straight or gay. In his third seminar, which we could subtitle "The Book of the Real" (as *Seminar 1* could be "The Book of the Imaginary" and *Seminar 2*, "The Book of the Symbolic"), Lacan makes clear his views regarding the certainty of psychosis and the specific clinical dimension of psychoanalysis. It is in the transference—in the clinic of psychoanalytic practice—that we find one of the few approaches to the structure of speech and language that constitutes sexuality. This is outside the "reality" of essentialized, embodied differences thought to obtain, within precincts of American psychoanalysis at any rate, between male and female:

> The distinction I introduced at the beginning of our course between certainty and reality is what counts. It introduces us to differences which, to our mind, as analysts, are not superstructural but structural. It's a fact that this can be the case for us alone, because contrary to all other clinicians we know that speech is always there, whether articulated or not, present in an articulated state, already historicized, already caught in the network of symbolic couples and oppositions. (*Seminar* 3:111)

For Lacan, subjectivity and sexuality are questions of language, rather than of the body, and therefore reaching a certain conclusion about one's body, mind, or sexuality without considering the structuring function of language can only lead one astray. In an effort to find the biogenetic essence of homosexuality, scientific discourse and American psychoanalysis inadvertently end up in the impasse of bisexual potentiality. They then endeavor to impose another sort of certainty on the patient concerning distinctions between homo- and heterosexuality, consequently making it more difficult to determine the patient's symbolic position in language. "Psychoanalysis," Lacan observes in *Seminar 3*, "should be the science of language inhabited by the subject. From the Freudian point of view man is the subject captured and tortured by language" (243).

Just as the subject's relation to the signifier characterizes psychosis, so too is it the central function within sexuality and for psychoanalysis more generally. Although the psychotic often symptomatically plays with his language as if it were music, this is because s/he is so certain about other things that s/he is able to do so. "Psychotics love their delusion like they love themselves" (*Seminar* 3:157). The psychotic loves her symptom(s), her delusional certainty, like herself because her delirium *is* herself.[2] What characterizes psychosis is not any single symptom (paranoia, transsexuality, thought disorder, delusions, hallucinations, and so on), but the certainty behind the symptoms to which the subject clings, in order to avoid alienation in "the little other" that comes with full entry into the symbolic; this entails negotiating sexual difference and castration. The mechanism of the foreclosure of the paternal function in psychosis may cause some problems, but it prevents others—namely, the mechanisms of neurosis that hinge on the alienating entry into the symbolic via castration.

The psychotic trades one form of alienation (in castration) for another (difficulty communicating in reality), but is not fazed by this discrepancy. The psychotic embodies the old adage "Ignorance is bliss," or rather, "Certainty is bliss" (though the psychotic is not without suffering), and has made an accommodation to nontruth regarding the "idea of the father" and the paternal function, the psychical incorporation of which makes possible a capacity for neurotic questioning. "It seems to me," argues Lacan,

> that in this work [*Moses and Monotheism*] we find confirmation yet again of what I'm here trying to make you feel, namely that analysis is absolutely inseparable from a fundamental question about the way truth enters into the life of man. The dimension of truth is mysterious, inexplicable, nothing decisively enables the necessity of it to be grasped, since man accommodates himself to non-truth perfectly well. (*Seminar* 3:214)

Here it seems that, for Lacan, the certainty of psychosis corresponds to an accommodation to nontruth regarding the father, whereas neurosis can be equated with accession to the truth vis-à-vis the *idea* of the father, the paternal function, and castration. Indeed, the homosexual, like the heterosexual, maintains questions and establishes accommodations to the idea of the father while maintaining maternal and paternal identifications. But truth is alienating, though it liberates entry into the symbolic. Nontruth is certainty and security, though it forecloses full entry into the symbolic.

This discussion of the *idea* of the father more baldly invokes the core questions of hysterical and obsessional neurosis. I stress, however, that it is the absence of a question (in the transference), the lack of a struggle in identifying with a particular position, that can lead to psychosis:

> We have indicated in passing that what characterizes the hysterical position is a question that refers precisely to the two signifying poles of male and female. The hysteric addresses it with all his being—how can one be either male or female?—which implies that the hysteric nevertheless has reference to it. The question is this—what is it that the entire structure of the hysteric, with his fundamental identification with the individual of the sex opposite to his own by which his own sex is questioned, is introduced into, suspended from, and preserved in? The hysterical manner of questioning, *either . . . or . . .* , contrasts with the obsessional's response, negation, *neither . . . nor . . .* , neither male nor

female. This negation comes about against a background of mortal experience and of hiding his being from the question, which is a way of remaining suspended from it. The obsessional is precisely neither one nor the other—one may also say that he is both at once. (*Seminar* 3:249)

Whereas the hysteric and the obsessional struggle with the logical possibilities of the conjunction either/neither, the psychotic ultimately is secure in the logical choice entailed by a truly disjunctive either/neither, in which the assumption of one position forecloses the assumption of the other. To put this another way, as the psychotic is able to be so certain about male and female, then for him or her any question attached to the terms *straight* and *gay* is truly inconsequential, though they may provide an additional level of certainty.

Lacan's observations above return us, with Freud (and, ironically, with the American analysts such as Isay and Friedman), to the question of bisexuality. Although individuals can adopt alternative positions to bisexuality and shifting identifications in the different registers of real, symbolic, and imaginary, their primary, structurally diagnostic questions have not necessarily been answered. Such shifting identifications are strategies to avoid the troubling questions of constitutional bisexuality and give rise to either neurotic or psychotic structural organizations for the subject of psychoanalysis:

> The Freudian discovery teaches us that all natural harmony in man is profoundly disconcerted. It is not just that bisexuality plays an essential role. This bisexuality is not surprising from the biological point of view, given that the means of access to regularization and normalization in man are more complex than and different from what we observe in mammals and in vertebrates in general. Symbolization, in other words the Law, plays an essential role here . . .
> . . . [I]f we are a man, for example, [we can] completely satisfy our opposite tendencies by occupying a feminine position in a symbolic relation, while perfectly well remaining a man equipped with one's virility on both the imaginary and the real planes. This function which, with greater or lesser intensity, is a role of femininity, may thus find the means to satisfy itself in this essential receptivity that is one of the fundamental existing roles. This is not metaphorical—we do indeed receive something in receiving speech. Participating in speech relations may have several senses at once, and one of the meanings involved might be just that of obtaining satisfaction in the feminine position, as such essential to our being. (*Seminar* 3:83–84)

Because one can take different positions in the symbolic, imaginary, and real registers, the nucleus of bisexuality remains unchallenged (see figure

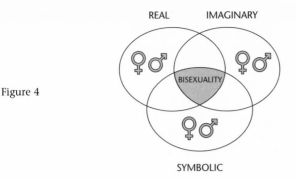

Figure 4

4). It is in relation to the Other in the transference, however, that one finds the subject's relation to speech and language. From there one can determine the structural resolutions of questions regarding the certainty of sexuality; this certainty arises relative to the law of the paternal function.

In his summary of *Seminar 3*, which appears in *Écrits* as "On a Question Preliminary to Any Possible Treatment of Psychosis" (1957–58),[3] Lacan reemphasizes the place of the phallus, the paternal function, and the castration complex in establishing the coordinates of symbolic, imaginary, and real for each subject and his or her sexuality (198). Considering the certainty of psychosis, Lacan reminds us that "uncertainty about one's sex is precisely a common feature in hysteria" (191). This definition of hysteria creates an antinomy pointing to psychosis, about which Lacan avers: "What is involved here, in fact is an effect of the signifier, in so far as its degree of certainty (second degree: signification of signification) assumes a weight proportional to the enigmatic void that first presents itself in the place of the signification itself" (185). For the hysteric, there is too much (imaginary) uncertainty, whereas for the psychotic, the void and the place of signification itself entail an uncertainty in the symbolic, which is covered over by certainty in the real. This certainty involves steadfast maintenance of and belief in the psychotic symptom—whether thought-disordered speech, hallucinations, or unwavering conviction regarding one's sexuality.

6. Lacan, Millot, and the Transsexual's Certainty

The work of Lacanian analyst Catherine Millot is especially instructive on these points. In *Horsexe: Essay on Transsexuality* (1983; trans. 1990), she reminds us that symptoms—whether neurotic, psychotic, or perverse—

are not the same as structures; nor are fantasies the same as diagnostic structures of neurosis, psychosis, or perversion. Every neurotic (structurally) has perverse fantasies, and such "perverse" practices as sodomy, obsessionality, and sadomasochism can be found in those with psychotic structures. Further, Ms. D. in our clinical case report isn't asking what it means to be a woman, as is the hysteric. In her highlighting of lack, "less" is imaginarized as "more," and she is interested in both playing at and creating woman in her own certain terms, in her own image. So the question of sexual orientation here becomes coextensive with that of gender identity. Certain of his or her own identity, the psychotic subject plays at being—in order to capture the essence of—man or woman, a game that would not admit the ambiguities of constitutional bisexuality or the uncertainty of, say, hysteria (neurosis). This is a consideration that arguments about sexuality as performative tend to downplay or ignore entirely (see Butler, "Imitation," *Gender,* and even *Bodies;* Sedgwick, *Epistemology;* and Sedgwick and Parker).

Although Millot's text focuses on transsexuality, her argument engages the question of certainty and therefore makes clear our discussion of sexual orientation and gender identity, as well as our clinical example:

> In the final analysis, sexual difference, which owes much to symbolic dualisms, belongs to the register of the *real.* It constitutes an insuperable barrier, an irreducible wall against which one can bang one's head indefinitely. . . . Transsexuals who claim to possess a female soul imprisoned in a man's body are perhaps the only ones who can boast a monolithic sexual identity, one that admits of neither doubts nor questions. (15)

Although not necessarily including homosexuality, the transsexual's certainty is Millot's interest. Millot posits that sexual difference is *real,* an irreducible wall and an all-constraining limit. Since sexual difference is perhaps *the* fundamental question of the real, imaginary or symbolic solutions can be only inadequate or symptomatic. However, any approach to the real always provokes anxiety, and therefore the nature of sexual difference is never exactly clear. For this reason, any solution to this enigma in the real establishes a structural position. As we've seen, the neurotic, particularly the hysteric, is always waiting and always questioning in order to avoid the pain of castration. The psychotic, finally, has neither a sense of urgency nor a particular question; in her certainty about sexual difference, gender identity, and partner orientation, the psychotic has no questions. Charles Shepherdson's excellent essay on Millot elaborates some of these Lacanian points in ways useful for cultural studies, though they are a bit far from the clinical realm, especially in identifying which aspects of transsexualism may be psychotic. It is also significant that the medical establishment has recently been much less willing than Millot and Shepherdson presumably are to accommodate the transsexual's demand for "sex reassignment surgery" (see McHugh). Although prompted by economics and normalizing ethics, the medical community's resistance to sex reassignment surgery has had the effect of asking the transsexual who s/he is and of suggesting that the "problem" is as much in the mind and in the unconscious as it is in the body.

Apropos of our clinical example, Millot discusses "the case of [male-to-female] transsexuals who become 'lesbians' a few years after their metamorphosis, and who, abandoning the quest for love relations with men who might confirm their femininity, instead seek this recognition in women" (16). This field of "recognition" is what made our patient's barroom encounter so complicated. In apparently seeking recognition through Ms. D., the transsexual was not only looking to confirm her own femininity but was also able to offer our patient a chance to resituate relative to sexual difference. This opportunity is often perceived as a crisis, as it was for Ms. D., because it problematizes established solutions to the central questions in the real. In Ms. D.'s encounter, the transsexual was originally male, now seeking to confirm her feminine identity, and she collided with our patient, essentially female, but seeking both to confirm her butch role and to maintain an essentialized category of Woman. This sort of encounter is psychically unpredictable, as it was for Ms. D.; as Freud wrote, however, there are always at least four participants in *any* sexual encounter.[4] At such moments, "political" responses to gender and sexuality are of limited value; they cannot predict how people will feel compelled to act, or establish what they will say or think. As a response to this confusion, we must again differentiate the orders of real, symbolic, and imaginary in which we respond to each other, and in clinical work establish the structural positions (neurotic, psychotic, or perverse) occupied by each subject as a function of the unconscious. Millot reminds us again:

> A structural definition of psychosis relegates the symptomatic aspect to a secondary status. In other words, the absence of psychotic symptoms does not necessarily exclude the presence of a psychotic structure; and the presence of a given symptom does not in itself give any indication of structure. Indecision as to one's sex, or as to one's homosexuality, for example, may be thought of

as imaginary formations, and in this sense they correspond to effects derived from diverse structural positions. No symptom can itself be assigned to a particular structure. . . . Lacan argued the existence in psychosis of a clear tendency towards transsexuality. (26)

What points to psychosis, for Lacan, is the certainty of one's belief in the truth, in the real: the decisiveness of one's solutions to sexual difference. And who but the transsexual can be more certain that he *really* is either male or female? "Indecision as to one's sex, or . . . homosexuality" can arise in multiple structural positions, precisely because there is a preoccupation with imaginary formations, whereas certainty in the real can point to psychosis. Homosexuality itself is not psychotic; but *certainty* regarding one's sexual orientation reveals psychosis. This certainty is most clearly seen in the transsexual, but it is also present in the homosexual and, of course, the heterosexual. Certainty about the naturalness and primacy of heterosexuality also implies a sort of cultural psychosis that may be most evident in homophobia. Indeed, from a Freudian perspective, heterosexuality is as symptomatic of a compromise formation as is homosexuality. Heterosexuality and homosexuality are equally conflicted psychical options; the structural diagnosis of neurosis or psychosis emerges only in relation to the certainty with which the positions are held.

The paradigmatic transsexual whom Millot describes is the clearest clinical example of the ways subjects' structural certainties drive sexual performances and thereby structure sexual identity. Despite what his body has yielded him, the transsexual knows he is in fact a woman, precisely because sexuality is all in the mind. But what casts the transsexual as psychotic is that he knows too much, too securely, and cannot allow any (neurotic) ambiguity into his sexual orientation. What should be interesting to the psychoanalyst is not what the transsexual does, and with whom, but rather the strenuousness with which he clings to his knowledge of what he is. And whether "in fact" he is male or female, or seen by others as male or female, it is the degree of certainty with which he maintains his identity, not his behavior, that indicates a psychotic structure. Punning on "the Name-of-the-Father" (*le nom du père*), Lacan says in *Seminar 21* "les non-dupes errent": Concerning sexuality, the more one presumes to know, the less one is able to acknowledge the truth of castration and admit ambiguity and bipotentiality.

7. A Moment to Conclude

As we have seen, recent American efforts to advance Freudian theory have only confirmed Freud's original insights, though such efforts threaten to return us to a quasi-scientific, pre-Freudian morass quite useless to psychoanalysts. It is only through speech and language that a subject can ascribe meaning to, or derive it from, his body. Lacan's insights, elaborated by Brousse and Millot, show that unconscious sexuality and identity can be staged differently in the three registers of the symbolic, imaginary, and real simultaneously. Further, specific symptoms or sexual performances are of only marginal interest to the analysts who seek to make a structural diagnosis of neurosis, psychosis, or perversion. Because subjects with a different clinical structure can exhibit identical behaviors, treatment interventions depend on making an accurate *structural* diagnosis.

It is only in the transference, in the clinical setting, where the subject's relation to phallic knowledge is both forged and clarified, that such structural diagnosis can be made. Until then, the subject's discourse on the essences of homo- versus heterosexuality can be heard only as the masterful teachings of a psychotic who may evince some information on the structure of psychosis, but who is in no position to comment meaningfully on sexual difference, sexual identity, or sexual orientation.

One's certainties about being male or female, straight or gay, or even a coherent "self" are all imaginary identities, ruses of the ego. This structuring of subjectivity and sexuality as eternally divided, prone to deceptions and misidentifications, is not equivalent to the clinical structures of neurosis, psychosis, and perversion that we have discussed; nor is it equivalent to the structuring of the symbolic, imaginary, and real. The Lacanian attention to multiple structures helps us avoid confusing the clinic with the classroom, and enables us to maintain a respectfully rigorous attention to the particularities and potentialities of each subject and his or her sexuality.

So we end where we began, with the image of the (ungendered) trucker traversing the desolate American sexual landscape, comfortable enough with the fundamental conflicts and polymorphously perverse possibilities of identity and sexuality not to require essential definitions of what it means to be straight or gay, or how to act as a result. The trucker's tale underscores our theoretical explorations in pointing to the bisexual bedrock of sexuality, and our conclusion that any solution within the unconscious, whether male/female or homo/hetero, entails conflict, compromise, and the capacity to withstand the uncertainty entailed by castration.

The more certain one is of the truth of one's identity and its universality, the more clearly psychotic one proves oneself. And though there are many important psychosexual and sociopolitical questions regarding what it means to be man or woman, straight or gay, answering them definitively can only impede further discussion and foster polarization all around.

Notes

1. Describing the rise of American psychiatric hegemony, Ruth Leys underscores that "Freud conceptualizes the self as the site of an insistent, psychosexual conflict in a way that makes the failure of stable sexual identity normal and inevitable" (26).

2. The personal pronoun here is obviously meant to echo the preceding analysis. Alternating in this sentence between *him* and *her* would also be syntactically clumsy.

3. I think Lacan means "possible" because psychosis is as much a potentially immutable, structural, diagnostic position as it is a pathology amenable to treatment.

4. Freud remarked to Wilhelm Fliess in 1899: "I am accustoming myself to regarding every sexual act as an event between four individuals" (*Ego* 33n. 1).

References

Brousse, Marie-Hélène. "Feminism with Lacan." *Newsletter of the Freudian Field* 5.1–2 (1991): 113–28.

Burr, Chandler. "Homosexuality and Biology." *Atlantic Monthly* (March 1993): 47–65.

Butler, Judith. *Bodies That Matter: On the Discursive Limits of "Sex."* New York: Routledge, 1993.

———. *Gender Trouble: Feminism and the Subversion of Identity.* New York: Routledge, 1990.

———. "Imitation and Gender Insubordination." In *Inside/Out: Lesbian Theories, Gay Theories.* Ed. Diana Fuss. New York: Routledge, 1991. 13–31.

Freud, Sigmund. *The Ego and the Id.* 1923. *Standard* 19:1–66.

———. *The Standard Edition of the Complete Psychological Works of Sigmund Freud.* Ed. and trans. James Strachey. 24 vols. London: Hogarth, 1953–74.

———. *Three Essays on the Theory of Sexuality.* 1905. *Standard* 7:125–245.

Friedman, Richard. Book review of Socarides, *Homosexuality*. *Journal of the American Psychoanalytic Association* 31 (1983): 316–23.

———. *Male Homosexuality: A Contemporary Psychoanalytic Perspective*. New Haven: Yale UP, 1988.

———. Reporter on panel: "Toward a Further Understanding of Homosexual Men." *Journal of the American Psychoanalytic Association* 34 (1986): 193–206.

Hamer, Dean, and Peter Copeland. *The Science of Desire: The Search for the Gay Gene and the Biology of Behavior*. New York: Simon & Schuster, 1994.

Isay, Richard A. *Being Homosexual: Gay Men and Their Development*. New York: Farrar, Straus and Giroux, 1989.

Kolata, Gina. "Who Is Female? Science Can't Say." *New York Times* (News of the Week in Review; February 16, 1992): 1.

Lacan, Jacques. "On a Question Preliminary to any Possible Treatment of Psychosis." *Écrits: A Selection*. Trans. Alan Sheridan. New York: Norton, 1977. 179–225.

———. *The Seminar of Jacques Lacan, Book 3: The Psychoses, 1955–1956*. Ed. Jacques-Alain Miller. Trans. Russell Grigg. New York: Norton, 1993.

———. *Television: A Challenge to the Psychoanalytic Establishment*. 1974. Ed. Joan Copjec. Trans. Denis Hollier, Rosalind Krauss, Annette Michelson, and Jeffrey Mehlman. New York: Norton, 1990.

Laplanche, Jean. *Life and Death in Psychoanalysis*. 1970. Trans. Jeffrey Mehlman. Baltimore: Johns Hopkins UP, 1976.

LeVay, Simon. *The Sexual Brain*. Cambridge: MIT P, 1993.

Lewes, Kenneth. *The Psychoanalytic Theory of Male Homosexuality*. New York: Simon & Schuster, 1988.

Leys, Ruth. "Types of One: Adolf Meyer's Life-Chart and the Representations of Individuality." *Representations* 34 (1991): 1–28.

McHugh, Paul. "Psychiatric Misadventures." *American Scholar* 61 (1992): 497–510.

Millot, Catherine. *Horsexe: Essay on Transsexuality*. 1983. Trans. K. Hylton. New York: Autonomedia, 1990.

Payne, Edmund. Reporter on panel: "The Psychoanalytic Treatment of Male Homosexuality." *Journal of the American Psychoanalytic Association* 25 (1977): 183–99.

Rymer, Russ. *Genie: An Abused Child's Flight from Silence*. New York: HarperCollins, 1993.

Sedgwick, Eve Kosofsky. *Epistemology of the Closet*. Berkeley: U of California P, 1990.

Sedgwick, Eve Kosofsky, and Andrew Parker, eds. *Performance and Performativity*. New York: Routledge, 1995.

Shepherdson, Charles. "The *Role* of Gender and the *Imperative* of Sex." In *Supposing the Subject*. Ed. Joan Copjec. New York: Verso, 1994. 158–84.

Socarides, Charles. *Homosexuality*. New York: Jason Aronson, 1978.

Stoller, Robert J. *Observing the Erotic Imagination*. New Haven: Yale UP, 1985.

———. *Perversion: The Erotic Form of Hatred*. New York: Pantheon, 1975.

Wolfson, Abby. Reporter on Panel: "Toward a Further Understanding of Homosexual Women." *Journal of the American Psychoanalytic Association* 35 (1987): 165–73.

15

LUST FOR INNOCENCE

Lynda Hart

. . . .

Very strange, this economy regulating the father-daughter relations! And it is odd that, in the whole adventure of female sexuality as described by Freud, the father makes his appearance only at the end and in such a dim, secondary, even "passive" role. With no desires, no instincts, no dealings, of any kind, in regard to his daughter. Neutral and benevolent. But why? LUCE IRIGARAY, *SPECULUM OF THE OTHER WOMAN* 62

In the November 1995 issue of *Harper's,* Katie Roiphe bemoans the proliferation of contemporary novels about incest. "Incest," she writes, "has become our latest literary vogue" (65). She attributes the abundance of these narratives to the "mirage of the zeitgeist," an alchemical production of the marriage of academia and politics, "a mainstream fascination with victims of all kinds," made particularly compelling by a "pop-feminist sensibility" (68). With the exception of a few writers she considers genuinely talented, Roiphe finds the plots of these novels not only prosaic, trendy, and banal, but also disturbing in their crude "pornographic precision" (70). This, apparently, is simply a way "to spice up sex scenes," unlike the minimalist, engaging innuendo of a truly "classic" novel like F. Scott Fitzgerald's *Tender Is the Night* (71n).

While Roiphe's article "Making the Incest Scene" announces her scorn for what she considers narratives that cater to the prurience of the "masses," her title also refers to the problem of making incest visible in her punning, perhaps unconscious, homophone—"scene/seen." In the unconscious, where the signifier is literal, the "joke" of this homology does not translate—does not "reproduce"—two into one. Roiphe objects particularly to a plot device she finds consistent in all the novels she previews, a style of delivery that is insistently revelatory, as if the narrators of these fictions were saying, *"I am the first person ever to have written about this"* (71). Reading her essay, one gets the impression that Roiphe's first preference would be for these novels never to have been written. Or, if these women *must* speak, then they could at least have the good grace and literary skill to present their narratives in a voice that would seem to say, *"Well here we go again with this same sad, banal, boring story."* Of course, Roiphe is partly right: Incest is banal, common, ordinary, everyday. Indeed, it is part of the structure of civilization as some of us know it for men to have the prerogative to violate the incest taboo while maintaining its violence as a transgressive fantasy that hysterical women—and their "predatory" therapists—engage and encourage.

Despite the near-canonical status, at least in women's studies, of Toni Morrison's *The Bluest Eye,* Maya Angelou's *I Know Why the Caged Bird Sings,* and Alice Walker's *The Color Purple,* Roiphe is also right to notice that the tone of *revelation* is a marked feature of contemporary incest narratives. She mentions Morrison, Walker, and Angelou, only to dismiss them as "heirs" of southern (white) "gothic imaginations" (68). The scene that can or cannot be imagined by women of color constitutes a particularly vexed site of inquiry, given the widespread supposition among theorists that psychoanalytic discourse lacks the socioeconomic perspective and historical specificity to address racial and class differences.

Among the few academic theorists who have taken on this problem, Hortense Spillers has made a particularly compelling claim that psychoanalysis might be a productive place to work through a racial unconscious. Having no "evidence that what are . . . the major topics of the field are not in fact stringently operative in the African-American community" (87), Spillers's article by no means tries to use psychoanalytic models to understand an African American "Oedipus." Instead, it rethinks what, if anything, an oedipal scenario might lend to an investigation of the psychic structures of a community "historically fraught with laws that at one time overdetermined the legal status of the child as property" (87). The seemingly "special status" accorded the three novels mentioned above, all written by women of color, as somehow outside of, before, or exceptional to the vogue of these times, suggests that they occupy

that special place in our racist fantasies, where the breaking of the incest taboo *can* be articulated without having much impact on "civilization as we know it."[1] We apparently can even allow these novels some
literary merit; they are kept within the confines of a minority discourse
where white critics tolerate strange, inexplicable, and extraordinary dis-
ruptions without too much anxiety about their "truth-value" or effects
on the dominant culture. Indeed, their "exceptional" status may be regarded as a kind of elision, reinforcing Spillers's compelling observation
about Freudian psychoanalysis:

> Freud could not "see" his own connection to the "race"/culture orbit, or could
> not theorize it, because the place of their elision marked the vantage point from
> which he spoke. Because it constituted his enabling postulate, it went "without
> saying." Perhaps we could argue that the "race" matrix was the fundamental
> *interdiction* within the enabling discourse of founding psychoanalytic theory
> and practice itself. (89)

When white women—especially white heterosexual women[2]—add
their voices to such narratives by women of color and white lesbians, we
seem to return to the "scene" of the original crime, where Freud's upper-
class white female patients were trying to make the incest seen. We know
what "scene" resulted from that historical conjuncture. Rather than re-
hearsing that history, in this essay I want to focus on the differences between incest scenes that are represented as conscious, eroticized fantasies
of women and the more usual narratives that are about forgetting/re-
membering and the traumatic aftermath of sexual abuse.

In "Women and Madness: the Critical Phallacy," Shoshana Felman
cites Phyllis Chesler: "The *sine qua non* of 'feminine' identity in patriarchal society is the violation of the incest taboo, i.e., the initial and continued 'preference' for Daddy, followed by the approved falling in love and/
or marrying of powerful father figures" (7). Men *uphold* the incest taboo;
women violate it. It is "our" lust for "their" innocence, therefore, that
maintains and supports heteropatriarchy. We are, if you will, doing it *for*
daddy. But the women in Pat Califia's collection *Doing It for Daddy* are not
really doing it *for* Daddy—they are doing it with him. One gay character
says, "I didn't know lesbians had 'daddies.'" Well, that's what you think.
Our daddies are Daddy's girls, not daddies' incarnations. Robin Sweeney
writes:

> Sometimes I'm Daddy's girl. I feel like a drag queen when I wear lingerie,
> until the moment I stop trying to figure out who I am and just be the girl I get
> to be so rarely. Daddy wants me, and it doesn't matter who I think I am.

Other times, Daddy is something meaner and I get back to some basic fear-and-thrill connection, and hope that this person who can hold my life in her hands will try to hurt me too much, and push me too hard, and stop just before I really can't take it. Right now, I'm just focusing on the fear part, vaguely aware that the thrill part is there, waiting. Is this the time that Daddy will want to hurt me more than I can handle? And what will I do if she doesn't try to hurt me, at all? (92)

Interestingly, the sex scenes in Califia's collection are mostly about whipping. As Elizabeth Freeman observes in her smart review of *Between the Body and the Flesh: Performing Sado-Masochism,* my book is curiously silent about the practice of whipping. I want to try to address that absence here. The closest I came to it is in my first chapter, "Knights in Shining Armor," which discusses Anna Freud's case study of a teenage girl (most likely herself) who was troubled by beating fantasies. At the end of this chapter, I tentatively suggested that Anna Freud's case study points to what I called a "bottom ground." In the second phase of Freud's theory, "'A Child Is Being Beaten'" (1919), the girl imagines that she is no longer the witness to the boy being beaten by his father, but is instead the child who is herself being beaten. "My father is beating me"—this is the phase that Freud insists must remain unconscious, but he doesn't explain why. Freud says simply that there is no testimony, no *evidence,* to support it, yet it must be inferred as the middle of two phases. It is curious indeed that this phase must remain unconscious, for of course it is an incest fantasy, the beating substituting for the girl's desire to be sexual with her father. Freud writes: "This second phase is the most important and the most momentous of all. But we may say of it in a certain sense that it has never had a real existence. It is never remembered, it has never succeeded in becoming conscious. It is a construction of analysis, but it is no less a necessity on that account" ("'A Child'" 185).

As Chesler candidly puts it, the woman's *obligation,* under heteronormativity, is to desire the father. On the other hand, it is Freud's psychoanalytic experience that this testimony is unavailable. Indeed, when women did report that their fathers and father figures were sexually accosting them, the biggest challenge to Freud's career and the most stunning and tenacious theoretical breakthrough came forward in tandem. These women, in short, were fantasizing about having sex with their fathers, a fantasy so forbidden, so taboo, that they could only imagine it as a form of sexual abuse. Hence, the birth of the Oedipus complex. Following psychoanalytic orthodoxy, the incest taboo is what founds and maintains "civilization as we know it." The ultimate violation of that taboo is not doing it *for* daddy; on the contrary, that is the requisite role of women as the keepers of civilization. Doing it *with* Daddy, on the other hand, renders conscious the obligatory unconscious middle phase. Such narratives are perhaps "striking off on another path that will no doubt intersect with the previous one, will in some way take up where it had left off, but in a zigzag fashion that defies all resumption of a linear discourse and all forms of rigor as measured in terms of the law of [the] excluded middle. Here the unconscious is speaking" (Irigaray, *Speculum* 17).

As Daddy fantasies become increasingly prominent in lesbian pro-sex writing, we witness the manifestation of a fantasy that was, at all costs, to remain tacit and inarticulate. As more and more women articulate incest fantasies, what is at stake is no less than a representational upheaval of civilization as we have known it—a way out of the paradox. These daddies' girls do it with daddies' *girls,* who are ejected from the economy of the market where the goods are marked. The middleman disappears, and the lust for innocence is revealed as the chimera it already was.

These pro-sex "daddy/incest" fantasies have twin sisters, doubles, in a much more widely circulated, indeed somewhat "popular" genre, that has amassed hundreds of titles in contemporary women's and some men's fiction, poetry, testimonials, plays, autobiographies, and films. One might even say that "incest" has gone mainstream, or that it is certainly making the scene.

It is neither my intent nor my interest in this essay to reenter the fray of arguments about whether incest really happens or if it is women's ubiquitous fantasy. It does happen, frequently and routinely. And it is a pervasive fantasy. Turning this issue into a question of "truth versus fiction/fantasy" leaves us at an impasse, encouraging us to forget that we live on a moment-by-moment basis within the fantasies of heterosexual white men, to which we are bound to refer as reality. Let us not forget that

> it is neither simply true, nor indeed false, to claim that the little girl fantasizes being seduced by her father, since it is equally valid to assume that the father *seduces his daughter* but that, because (in most cases, though not in all) he refuses to recognize and live out his desire, *he lays down a law that prohibits him from doing so.* . . . [This] law . . . reduces to the state of "fantasy" the little girl's seduced and rejected desire—a desire still faltering, barely articulate, silent perhaps. . . . *In place of the desire for the sexuate body of the father*—a desire labeled a "seduction fantasy" that must be verbalized and submitted to interpretation— we find a law proposed and imposed, that is, a discourse that institutionalizes and is already institutionalized. In some measure as a defense. (Irigaray, *Speculum* 38; original emphases)

Despite Irigaray's brilliant elucidation of this law of the father, the force of this institution remains powerful. For the "daughters" are presumed to be seduced. And even the daddies tremble a bit before the altar of the seduction fantasy. Nonetheless, a few have dared to tread upon this boundary. Candor being our crime, here is one of our accomplices, a psychoanalytic Daddy, Jean Laplanche, who takes this risk (perhaps of being relegated to the "feminine" position, the risk of hysteria):

> My first topic is the *seduction/seduction fantasy* controversy, in which I accord seduction priority over the fantasy. I do not mind if I am therefore seen as a softy or—as the case may be—a terrible crank. We all surely know what unitary visions lead to. . . . The whole question turns here on the term "reality," on the kind of reality at issue, and whether or not psychoanalysis has contributed anything new in this field, whether it has affirmed the existence of a *third domain of reality*. (167, 169; original emphases)

Laplanche then distinguishes this third domain of reality from what is "psychological" and "material." This third domain of reality—"*neither* the pure materiality of the gesture (assuming that this could in any case be grasped) *nor* the pure psychology of the protagonist(s)"—is the "reality of the message and the irreducibility of the fact of communication. What psychoanalysis adds is a fact of its experience, namely that this message is frequently compromised, that it both fails and succeeds at one and the same time" (169). Thus Laplanche persists in saying "seduction" rather than "seduction fantasy." For readers who doubt me, I offer his words to accompany and bolster my own assertion—that incest occurs frequently and routinely and that it is an international women's fantasy. In representation and in reality, the last decades of the twentieth-century have manifested an explosion of interest in incest narratives.

As Janice Haaken points out, "We are currently witnessing a revival of the early dissociation construct linked to a trauma model, with childhood sexual abuse again the central etiological factor" (133). This model, she explains further, "permits the recognition of psychic injury while closing off possibilities for the expression of prohibited desire" (135). Haaken's point about the trauma/dissociation model partly explains why incest narratives are so often couched in language that is at once hidden, disguised, and *revelatory*. But the revelation is often signified in a form that resonates with Gothic undertones, or extrapsychic phenomena. This excerpt from Rebecca Brown's story "The Princess and the Pea" is exemplary:

Then I see something stirring in the bed. The sheets are pulled away and she's uncovered. She gasps, she tries to pull her body in, she puts her fist against her mouth to keep from crying out. There is the pressure of something on the bed. My heart is beating, terrified. I try to shout, to stop the thing except I can't. There is the pressing in the bed, I hear the muffled cries, the pleas, then there's a hand, a mouth, against the mouth, there is the sob, the gasp for breath, the creak of something moving in the bed. She tries to go inside herself, she tries to fold up far inside where nothing else can get. She tries to fly above herself, above the awful bed. Then I see in the dark above the bed, as far away as she can get, a shape. It's like a vapor, a hologram. It is a shape, inside of her where nothing else can get. It stays above the awful bed and sees the hiding self. I know that I can't stop it, I cannot undo what's done. But in my mind I cry to her, I tell her that I see. (72–73)

In this scenario, the lesbian lover witnesses the manifestation of the incest scene that her partner is unable to witness for herself. The woman who has had the experience can recall it only through its current symptoms. Her lover, however, sees for her, and in some sense occupies her space—or desires to take her place—but she cannot do so, and the relationship is severed through and because of this witnessing. The story ends thus: "This happened once upon a time, a long, long time ago, before we had learned what happened to us." The incest scene functions in the present tense of their relationship rather like the "open secret" of homosexuality. They both know, but they cannot know together, nor can either of them articulate its memory in speech. It is, again, the speaking body of the "hysteric" that somatizes the past in the present. In such narratives, the women can remember, but they cannot re-member or change what has been done.

Brown's narratives in *What Keeps Me Here* are some of the best examples of the traumatic model that Cathy Caruth theorizes in the terminology of the "crying wound":

While . . . the suffering [one] recognizes through the voice [one] hears represents the experience of an individual traumatized by his own past—the repetition of his own trauma as it shapes his life—the wound that speaks is not precisely [his] own but the wound, the trauma, of another. It is possible, of course, to understand that other voice . . . to represent the other within the self that retains the memory of the "unwitting" traumatic events of one's past. (8)

In contrast to these "*unclaimed* experiences," the lesbian sex narratives in Califia's "soft S/M"—Daddy stories permitting sexual encounters beyond the S/M "scene"—represent women who speak with each other quite graphically about incest memories and ways to act them out in the present with each other. In Laura Federico's "Ask Me," one character says to the other: "'You're giving yourself another chance' . . . and pulls me into her arms. It's so warm and solid there. . . . I hadn't realized how rigid I'd been, bracing myself. . . . 'I don't know what's happened to you, honey, but I know you're brave right now, I know you're looking for a way to handle it. This is no rerun of your past. You've chosen this. And you can change your mind anytime'" (193). In Califia's "It Takes a Good Boy to Make a Good Daddy," Doyle puts Kip through a series of "tests" to see if she can play the part of Daddy's boy. First Kip serves Doyle an elegant dinner wearing only a jockstrap and boots, reciting poetry while Doyle works her way through four courses. Then Doyle whips and paddles her for her services. But Kip is thrown when Doyle then wants to fuck her. She wasn't expecting the intimacy of sex. When Kip resists this next move, Doyle offers her a choice, anal or vaginal penetration. Of course, Kip has the option to refuse either, but Doyle's top trick—to "threaten" Kip with anal sex—helps her choose vaginal penetration. Then Doyle adds another twist to the scene: She asks Kip to spend the night with her, which brings on a rush of emotion that sends Kip running for the door. Doyle blocks her exit. Kip wants to be *made* to exercise her desire, and Doyle knows how to "force" her—by setting limits within a certain range of options, and rewarding Kip each time she makes a bolder surrender. Still Kip refuses to call Doyle "Daddy," though in her fantasy formations she is screaming the word silently. Finally Doyle asks Kip to fuck her, and refers to herself as Daddy. Instead of the incest scene blocking the way to these women's desire and severing the relationship, as it does in most mainstream lesbian narratives, these quasi-S/M scenarios use incest to facilitate a sexual relationship, maintain it, and thus keep it erotic.

Three years after writing "Making the Incest Scene," Katie Roiphe is back in the January 1998 issue of *Vogue,* making a startling revelation of her own. This time her essay is entitled "The End of Innocence" and is a narrative of her own affair at the age of sixteen with a thirty-six-year-old man. On the second page, Roiphe's photograph of herself at sixteen, wearing an orange bikini with a flower in her hair, is reprinted with the caption "Girl Interrupted: The Author at the Time of the Affair." Roiphe describes her affair as both "eros and theater," and curiously represents its strangest feature as "secrecy." "I couldn't tell anyone without endangering his position in the community, and so I slipped away at night without saying where I was going, and lied to almost all my friends, my sisters, and my parents. The deception made me feel important." In this piece Roiphe says: "There is definitely something wrong with a man who yearns for what Vladimir Nabokov called a 'childish something,' but what about me?" (46).

Roiphe looks retroactively at this relationship as a "rite of passage rather than some form of abuse," though she allows:

> There may have been a darker side of this relationship that's been softened and erased by time. There may be ways in which it haunts me that I am not even aware of. In the diaries I kept during those months, every account of the Older Man is obliterated with black paint, every kiss, every night by the fire, every phone call. The black paint reveals a level of shame and horror that I don't remember feeling. And it is true that after more than ten years, the smell of brandy [his drink] makes me feel sick. (46)

Does Roiphe's criticism of the *sameness* of the revelation scenes (hers now included) point, as she initially argued, to a thematic appropriation of a subject that now has great marketing appeal, a form of prurience for the masses? If so, what has seduced her into participating in it? Could it be that this sameness indicates a formula for revelation that is circumscribed, and therefore repeated, by writers who are unable to articulate the experience beyond the boundaries of permissible visibility? Mainstream publishers and audiences seem to recognize two modes of expression for incest. The first and certainly most popular is the aforementioned "open secret"—the story that can never be told except as something that has been forgotten and manifests itself in inexplicable, but still more or less "readable," symptoms. Then there is the story of the young girl's complicity, Roiphe's second story, the rite of passage rather than a story of abuse. But these stories, like all narratives, speak much more than such formulaic summations of them imply. Can they tell us what cannot enter into the symbolic order of representation and interpretation and therefore, in their omissions, silences, and obliqueness, evoke how the incest taboo is being transformed from an unspeakable, impossible act into a prescriptively representable prohibition? Has what was once foreclosed now passed through negation—the first sign of the lifting of repression— and entered into representation, albeit in forms that are limited to what the dominant culture has assimilated as its founding taboo? Freud's etymological analysis of taboo highlights its grammatical doubling—that which embodies, at once, the sacred and the profane (sacred, we might add, precisely because it is profane). What is "alien" and is general and "familiar." *The incest taboo is precisely revelatory and banal.*

Representations that address the experience of incest seem to reflect and constitute subjectivities that, in deviating from the "norm," are later fully accommodated by it. As Haaken reminds us, "Both the incest taboo and its violation signify the girl's entry into a symbolic order that privileges the claims of men" (129). In her discussion of fantasy as the mediator between the symbolic and the "real," Haaken highlights this paradox of becoming a "woman" in a patriarchal culture. Whether the "incest" is real or fantastical, the girl must still participate in the oedipal struggle, and either way she is *obliged* to desire Daddy. "But in cases of overt incest," Haaken writes,

> the father acts out *his* Oedipal desires, robbing the daughter of her own process of self-discovery, including the imaginative exploration of both the dangers and the pleasurable possibilities posed by her own desires. Her discovery of her own capacity for pleasure has to take into account the father's prior invasion and knowledge of her. What is true on a symbolic level for *all* women, expressed and managed through fantasy, becomes dangerously immediate for incest survivors: the power of the father is more than a threat; it is an act that closes off the possibilities of using fantasy creatively, as a realm of more open meanings and as an impetus for new avenues of development and self-assertion. (130; second emphasis mine)

What is at stake in incest narratives is surely the "reality" of the message—that is, its revelatory credibility. But to phrase the issue in this way is to misunderstand the concept of revelation. Indeed, while the message of incest narratives is enigmatic, as all communications are, let us not fall into the error of thinking that only some messages are delusional. For if we consider some communications as delusional, we must allow that others are illusory; the opposite of delusion is illusion, not "truth." Laplanche reminds us that in *The Future of an Illusion* (1927) Freud includes delusion in the context of illusions as "the part that is demonstrably inconsistent with reality" (186). Yet if illusion is itself a fantasy that cannot be read according to its truth-value, it is itself inconsistent with reality. What purportedly distinguishes between illusion and delusion in fact unites them. "The inadequacy of [Freud's] theory of delusion is plain," writes Laplanche. "An illusion could become a delusion according to the state of our knowledge at a given moment" (186). There is thus no "reason" to believe that incest narratives are more mediated than are other narratives, for always the communications of others constitute what we define as our historical "truths." The issue is neither credibility nor truth-value, but desire—what we desire to believe, what we wish, what gives us pleasure.

Can incest narratives give us pleasure? Whose pleasure and "innocence" is at risk in these revelations?

The end of innocence perhaps comes earlier for the incest survivor, but the *lust* for innocence is surely amplified, magnified, until it resembles the *aim* of her sexual desire. Must this mean that the incest survivor is forever foreclosed from sexual enactments that are presumably opened through the creative imaginings of other women? The literature on incest survivors suggests that two "types" or "symptomatologies" often appear, and, as we might expect, they represent extremes: the woman who is sexually cautious (formerly called "frigid") and the woman who is sexually active (formally called "promiscuous"). One can't say yes; the other can't say no. As I discuss at length in *Between the Body and the Flesh,* mainstream feminism has participated in a prescriptive discourse on women's sexuality that advocates the elimination of what some feminists call "internalized misogyny," that is, violence against women. The "cure" proposed for a woman's sadistic and masochist fantasies has been abstinence and therapeutic rehabilitation—what S/M feminists call "vanilla sex."

While I am not arguing *against* such a process—to each her other—I am criticizing the proscriptive rhetoric that denies the value of other ways of making the incest scene. As the therapeutic language has shifted from "victim" to "survivor," and the latter term has come to represent a heroic stance, there is also, as Haaken shrewdly observes, "a potential in this feminist stance . . . for a repressive idealization of feminine innocence and purity; repressive because it denies women the capacity for hostile and vengeful impulses, even moral agency and human complexity" (139). Haaken also points out that many feminist critiques of male violence leave out the "problem of men's impoverished capacities to read and interpret complex and conflictual emotional cues" (140). As we know, the establishment of the woman's "innocence" within legal discourse is usually the determining factor for the male perpetrator's guilt. Again, the paradox of innocence for women is that it certifies her claim to victimization and denies her moral agency and human complexity. Feminist debates about these questions are often locked into this both/and impasse. Whether one argues for or against women's innocence, they are still victimized by the rhetoric alone. One way or another, then, women must make the incest scene seen.

Consider Jane Gallop's account of Irigaray reading Freud in "The Father's Seduction." Having gone through a heterosexual phase in my youth, I can, up to a point, follow Gallop's logic without much difficulty. And this, for me, is the sticking point. I am focusing on the last section of Gallop's essay where she asks why women must comply in the vicious circle whereby the only way to seduce the father "is to please him, and to please him one must submit to his law which proscribes any sexual relation" (71). Only a fool would wait for an answer, Gallop says, but the answer, which she asks us to wait for as she proceeds in her close reading, "is not to set up another homosexual economy, [though] . . . that may be necessary as one step to some hetero-sexuality" (73–74). Women, Gallop argues, must take this step, "must demand 'the same,' 'the homo' and then not settle for it, not fall into the trap of thinking a female 'homo' is necessarily any closer to a representation of otherness, an opening for the other" (74). She then critiques Irigaray for the moment in her text when she reproduces the "precision" that she has avoided all along, so as not to reproduce the reign of the One, the unity of the Phallus. This moment of precision in Irigaray's text occurs when she writes: "That is not to say that the father *should* make love with his daughter—from time to time it is better to state things precisely—but that it would be good to call into question this mantle of the law with which he drapes his desire, and his sex (organ)" (qtd. 77; original emphasis). Irigaray "will not lay down a law about how to lift the law," Gallop argues, for if she did "it would, like all laws, mask and support a desire" (77).

Although Gallop admits to having been seduced and then shut out by Luce's "tighten[ing] up," she is—like Irigaray—careful not to arrive at too precise a conclusion, to lay down yet another law. At the end of her essay, she suggests that Irigaray may be more threatened by "making love," which is "entangled with the question of women's complicity; [and] may be the bribe which has persuaded her to agree to her own exclusion" (79). Irigaray does state her desire boldly: "What I want and what I'm waiting to see is what men will do and say if their sexuality releases its hold on the empire of phallocratism" (*This Sex* 136). Unlike her, however, Gallop ends by suggesting not that "we" wait, but that we choose at this moment "to be momentarily blind to father-love; it may be politically effective to defend—tightly, unlucidly—against its inducements, in order for a 'relation between the sexes,' in order to rediscover some feminine desire for a masculine body that does not respect the Father's law" (79). So, while Gallop critiques Irigaray for waiting and being seduced by the father of psychoanalysis, Gallop herself participates with Irigaray in maintaining the Freudian teleology of sexual development, whereby autoeroticism leads to narcissism, and then to homoeroticism, before culminating apparently in heterosexuality. Following Irigaray's own (problematically antigay) critique of "hommo-sexuality" and Eve Sedgwick's more nuanced and developed theory of the homosocial, any feminist theorist worth her paltry salary knows by now that we are operating within a

discourse in which there is no relation *between* the sexes—or as Lacan
puts it, "the sexual relation is impossible."

Heterosexuality is the big joke of psychoanalysis, and the joke is on
"Woman," who does not exist. Of course, masculinity is also a fiction, as
Gallop, Irigaray, and the rest clearly recognize. Nonetheless, we are *still*
doing it for Daddy. We wouldn't be speaking at conferences and publishing if we were not, and that's the game we all play. Not that there is
not a chain that leads back to male authority—the woman who has the
authority to make a place for the "other" woman has usually been given
that authority by a man. So why don't we just come clean, and, like Irigaray's "marine lover," make candor our crime? If we are all doing it *for*
Daddy, why don't we just openly do it *with* him? Gallop argues that "if
the father were to desire his daughter he could no longer exchange her,
no longer possess her in the economy by which true, masterful possession
is the right to exchange. If you cannot give something up for something
of like value, if you consider it nonsubstitutable, then you do not possess it any more than it possesses you" (76). If the father's (overt) desire
for the daughter would remove him from the homosocial commerce in
which women are exchanged between men, what would the daughter's
overt desire for the father imply? Could she not remove *herself* from that
market by exchanging her place in that economy for something of *like
value,* something that she considers nonsubstitutable, something she no
more possesses than it possesses her? Something like another woman
who has also made the same self-exchange?

Califia's story represents this possibility when Kip "want[s] to say the
forbidden word. Giving in to the desire to say it out loud would make
her orgasm more intense. But she [can]not. She [winds] up screaming
silently, jamming her face into the pillow as if she were actually making
a noise that had to be hidden" (235). Doyle takes Kip further than anyone
else had, but she still can't make her say the "forbidden word," *Daddy.*
However, Doyle has another trick. Topping Kip from below, Doyle demands that Kip fuck her now. Poised above her, her hands planted on
either side of Doyle's head and her hips settled between Doyle's legs, Kip
looked "really different from this perspective . . . awfully much like a
girl." "'You'd better call me Daddy now,' Doyle said, putting her arms and
legs around Kip and taking her full weight" (237).

What is restored in this representation that boldly fantasizes a father-
daughter "incest scene" *between two women?* First, the "law of the excluded middle" is blatantly *included* in this scene. Second, the "father"
in this scenario speaks "her" desire to have sexual intercourse with the
"daughter," thus violating "his" *own* prohibition against incest. Third,

rather than being jilted by her father in the name of the law, the "daughter" in this fantasy submits to "his" seduction. If this is a sadomasochistic scenario, it differs radically from psychoanalytic orthodoxy, in which women are arrested in the stage of primary or erogenous masochism. As Irigaray reminds us, "Freud states that this 'primary' or 'erogenous' masochism will be reserved to woman and that both her 'constitution' and 'social rules' will forbid her any *sadistic way to work out these masochistic death drives*" (*Speculum* 54; my emphasis). In Califia's story, what is perhaps most radical is the permission given to a woman to perform the "sadistic" role. Doyle not only takes Daddy's place, she also demands that *her desire* be realized in Kip's submission to her own unarticulated fantasy. She demands, quite simply, that Kip act out the scene of father-daughter incest. This is no simple repetition of the excluded (unconscious) middle phase of "'A Child Is Being Beaten.'" Granted, it partly conjures that scene, but it does not reproduce it. The message that Doyle sends Kip is *not* the enigmatic message of the psychoanalytic father's seduction—a message that is *not* spoken, or, rather, that is conveyed *only* by its repression. This is not to say that the message is now "clear," rather than enigmatic. Although Doyle's message retains the enigmatic nature of *all* messages, there is a *breach* in the already permeable envelope of the unconscious. Laplanche explains:

> With the *message,* there is the idea that an existing, pre-existing sense is offered to the subject, of which, however, he is not the master and of which he can become the master only by submitting to it. With the concept of *enigma,* a break in determinism appears: to the extent that the originator of the enigmatic message is unaware of most of what he means, and to the extent that the child possesses only inadequate and imperfect ways to configure or theorize about what is communicated to him, there can be no linear causality between the parental unconscious and discourse on the one hand and what the child does with these on the other. (160; original emphases)

Even within the primary incestuous scene, Laplanche's emphasis on the enigmatic nature of the message and his correlative concept of *translation* opens up the possibility for a break, a reshaping, which he likens to "a metabolism that breaks down food into its constituent parts and reassembles them into a completely different entity" (160). It is, at once, far too simple and much too complicated to say that representations such as those in *Doing It for Daddy* are therapeutic, as we scarcely know what constitutes "therapy." What I meant to achieve in this essay was simply an observation of representations that elude *both* models of popular incest narratives—the traumatic narrative and the "Lolita" scenario. We

should hesitate before the possibility that something is entering representation that translates our unspoken desires into a different, if not *completely* different entity.

Postscript

When I began this essay, I had no idea that the lust I would be writing
about was more than in part my own. I conceived the title flippantly,
then caught a glimpse of the remnants of a defensive desire that I wore
like a lifelike prosthesis. I never lusted after women who could not discern
its inauthenticity. My desire was not to want what was, but only what
could have been or might be. Like the child, or the "primitive," who does
not "rack his brains about the enigma of life and death . . . beside the
body of his slain enemy," I did not know that I was going to die (Freud,
"Thoughts" 293). I had not really imagined my own death. I was still
nostalgic. Nostalgic for a time before, an infinite regression to the "real"
moment of oblivion, I mourned for my innocence.

Now like Demeter from the depths of hell, I have been reprieved. And
like Irigaray's "Marine Lover,"

> I am coming back from far, far away. And my crime, at present, is my
> candor. . . .
> You had fashioned me into a mirror but I have dipped that mirror into the
> waters of oblivion—that you call life. And farther away than the place where
> you are beginning to be, I have turned back. I have washed off your masks and
> make up, scrubbed away your multicolored projections and designs, stripped
> off your veils and wraps that hid the shame of your nudity. I have even had
> to scrape my woman's flesh clean of the insignia and marks you had etched
> upon it.
> That was the most painful hour. For you had so deeply implanted these
> things into me that almost nothing was left to recall me to the innocence of
> my life. All that was left—barely—was a breath, a hint of air and blood that
> said: I want to live. . . . If you care nothing for living, then death will be for
> you a surer place of eternal peace. (*Marine Lover* 4)

So it is time to breathe and come clean. And in this mourning,
"mourning the loss of something I never had," to paraphrase Bone, Dorothy Allison's bastard, death and sex, our inevitable Siamese twins, came
together for me in a new way. When death was no longer sexy, sex became sexier. Imagine my surprise. No longer doing it anyway, just doing it.

Notes

1. Notable examples of more recent incest narratives by women of color garnering some literary attention include Sapphire's *Push* and Alleyne's *Crazy.* Sapphire's novel is mentioned repeatedly in Roiphe's article as a particularly "bad" example of the genre. But what seems to bother Roiphe most about *Push* is the amount of advance money that this "unknown" author received from publishers competing for the rights to the novel. A detailed exploration of racial differences in the reception of incest narratives is beyond the scope of this essay, which focuses simply on the difference between those incest scenes that are acted out consciously and the more usual narratives that are about forgetting/remembering and the traumatic aftermath of sexual abuse. From my survey of incest narratives, however, I can say that they are dominated by white, and mostly heterosexual, women. In the longer project that this essay initiates, I mean to pursue the issue of racial and other cultural differences.

2. Karen Finley's recent performance *Shut Up and Love Me* (unpublished) contains a lengthy monologue in which Stella, a young woman whose father is paying for her therapy, gets fed up with the therapeutic process and goes to her father demanding that he fuck her. She tries various methods of seduction, all of which fail. Her father's refusal to meet her demands and the audacity of her request make this piece viciously funny—in Finley's inimitable style. What I find interesting about this performance is that it does seem to reproduce the fantasy of the father's seduction in its most orthodox psychoanalytic form. That is, the father "seduces" the daughter, but then it becomes *her* fantasy structure that is problematic and the talking cure is designed to manage this "problem." The father in this monologue participates in the incest economy by paying for his daughter's therapy *and* by refusing her advances. In this economy, as Irigaray writes, "The girl's only way to redeem her personal value, and value in general, would be to seduce the father, and persuade him to express, if not admit, some interest in her" (*Speculum* 87). This is precisely the scenario that Finley performs. That Stella's "seduction" *fails* makes this piece a testimony to the status quo, rather than an intervention. Nonetheless, it advances on the trauma models, in which women are shown as simply tragic victims of their remembered or forgotten incest experiences. Although Stella cannot effect an intervention, at least she voices the *problem* dramatically and succinctly.

References

Alleyne, Vanessa. *Crazy: A Black Woman's Story of Incest.* Toronto: Sister Vision, 1997.

Angelou, Maya. *I Know Why the Caged Bird Sings.* New York: Random House, 1970.

Brown, Rebecca. "The Princess and the Pea." *What Keeps Me Here: A Book of Stories.* New York: HarperCollins, 1996. 63–73.

Califia, Pat, ed. *Doing It for Daddy: Short and Sexy Fiction about a Very Forbidden Fantasy.* Los Angeles: Alyson, 1994.

———. "It Takes a Good Boy to Make a Good Daddy." In Califia 215–37.

Caruth, Cathy. *Unclaimed Experience: Trauma, Narrative, and History.* Baltimore: Johns Hopkins UP, 1996.

Federico, Laura. "Ask Me." In Califia 171–202.

Felman, Shoshana. "Women and Madness: The Critical Phallacy." *diacritics* 5.4 (1975): 2–10.

Fitzgerald, F. Scott. *Tender Is the Night.* 1934. Harmondsworth: Penguin, 1986.

Freeman, Elizabeth. "(This Review Will Have Been) Impossible to Write: Lesbian S/M Theory as Academic Practice." *GLQ: A Journal of Lesbian and Gay Studies* 5.1 (1999): 63–72.

Freud, Sigmund. "'A Child Is Being Beaten': A Contribution to the Study of the Origin of Sexual Perversions." 1919. *Standard* 17:175–204.

———. *The Standard Edition of the Complete Psychological Works of Sigmund Freud.* Ed. and trans. James Strachey. 24 vols. London: Hogarth, 1953–74.

———. "Thoughts for the Times on War and Death." 1915. *Standard* 14:273–302.

Gallop, Jane. "The Father's Seduction." *The Daughter's Seduction: Feminism and Psychoanalysis.* Ithaca: Cornell UP, 1982. 56–79.

Haaken, Janice. "Sexual Abuse, Recovered Memory, and Therapeutic Practice: A Feminist-Psychoanalytic Perspective." *Social Text* 40 (1994): 115–45.

Hart, Lynda. *Between the Body and the Flesh: Performing Sado-Masochism.* New York: Columbia UP, 1998.

Irigaray, Luce. *Marine Lover of Friedrich Nietzsche.* 1980. Trans. Gillian C. Gill. New York: Columbia UP, 1991.

———. *Speculum of the Other Woman.* 1974. Trans. Gillian C. Gill. Ithaca: Cornell UP, 1985.

———. *This Sex Which Is Not One.* 1977. Trans. Catherine Porter with Carolyn Burke. Ithaca: Cornell UP, 1985.

Laplanche, Jean. *Essays on Otherness.* Ed. John Fletcher. New York: Routledge, 1999.

Morrison, Toni. *The Bluest Eye.* 1970. New York: Knopf, 1993.

Roiphe, Katie. "The End of Innocence." *Vogue* (January 1998): 38–46.

———. "Making the Incest Scene." *Harper's Magazine* (November 1995): 65, 68–71.

Sapphire. *Push.* London: Secker and Warburg, 1996.

Spillers, Hortense J. "'All the Things You Could Be by Now, If Sigmund Freud's Wife Was Your Mother': Psychoanalysis and Race." *boundary 2* 23.3 (1996): 75–141.

Sweeney, Robin. "Daddy." In Califia 89–100.

Walker, Alice. *The Color Purple.* 1982. New York: Harcourt Brace Jovanovich, 1992.

CLINICAL

PERSPECTIVES

4

16

CAN PSYCHOANALYSIS UNDERSTAND HOMOPHOBIA?

Resistance in the Clinic

Joanna Ryan

. . . .

In the last decade, homosexuality has been the cause of considerable debate in the psychoanalytic world, and the forms that this debate has taken tell us much about the operation and nature of power in the psychoanalytic field. We are now witnessing many changes concerning psychoanalytic representations of homosexuality. What these changes mean and why they have occurred can best be addressed historically; as we have learned from other fields, ignoring or trivializing history creates a problematic present. Rather than trying to offer a full history here, I want to situate current debates in their appropriate historical context, especially regarding the interplay between forms of challenge and what is so challenged. These processes of change shed light on the mechanisms of power and resistance governing this discursive field.

As an aspect of human sexuality, homosexuality has always been central to psychoanalysis. Freud began his *Three Essays on the Theory of Sexuality* (1905) by postulating the issues he believed homosexuality posed for his general theory of sexuality. Although much has since changed in psychoanalytic thought, much also has *not* occurred that psychoanalysis initially made possible. Since Freud, the increasing restrictiveness and conservatism of psychoanalytic perspectives on homosexuality—especially following the Second World War—is an important historical phenomenon that critics have only recently begun to document. These effects are notable not only for their intrinsic importance and damaging consequences, but also for helping us understand sources of influence within psychoanalysis. In *The Psychoanalytic Theory of Male Homosexuality*, Kenneth Lewes describes from a predominantly American angle the consequences of this history for male homosexuality. And Noreen O'Connor and I, in *Wild Desires and Mistaken Identities*, provide a partly historical perspective on psychoanalytic theories about lesbianism.

At the risk of summarizing a vast amount of important detail, we can underscore a major theme of both these works: the passage from Freud's inclusion of homosexuality as part of everyone's sexuality to its being viewed as a pathology and consigned to the category of perversion. This transformation involved writers from many diverse schools, and it occurred over a substantial period with varying degrees of vilification and denigration. In this, we do not idealize Freud. As both Lewes and O'Connor and I describe, much is contradictory, ambiguous, and normative in Freud's writings, and the assertion of heterosexuality's primacy accompanies his radical deconstruction of its presumed naturalism. There is some danger that this history will be forgotten or rewritten as attitudes toward homosexuality become more inclusive. For example, in her most recent book, *The Many Faces of Eros: A Psychoanalytic Exploration*, Joyce McDougall appears to have substantially altered her ideas about homosexuality, from a theoretical position in earlier works that included homosexuality among the perversions to this book's more inclusive and apparently accepting stance. However, in *The Many Faces of Eros*, McDougall scarcely refers to her previous, extremely influential theories. It is as if she never published them and need say nothing about them. Nor does she explain why she modified her ideas.

In *Wild Desires*, O'Connor and I describe the paucity of dissenting voices and theories—as well as the lack of debate about predominant theories of homosexuality—in psychoanalysis. It is no exaggeration to call this, until recently, a hegemonic state of affairs. Although since the late sixties many outside psychoanalysis have critiqued its attitudes to and theories about homosexuality, these works have had little impact on mainstream psychoanalytic thought. We see a parallel here with contemporaneous feminist critiques leveled at psychoanalytic theories of woman. In both cases, the more orthodox and conservative aspects of psychoanalysis were attacked and viewed as representative of the whole, with the result that psychoanalysis was dismissed as having little value for feminism and no value for gay liberation. However, in the case of feminism, feminist voices from within the profession defended psychoanalysis's more radical and creative potential, leading eventually to a flowering of diverse work on psychoanalysis and feminism. This did not occur with the gay and lesbian critiques. No gay and lesbian voices emerged from within the profession, and there were few sympathetic ones to argue that homosexuality's nonsymptomatic status and an understanding of the diversity of sexuality were to be found in Freud's work, though not in the most prevalent forms of psychoanalysis then circulating. For reasons we discuss in *Wild Desires,* feminist writings often ignored lesbianism.

One consequence of these external critiques—and the profession's failure to respond creatively to them—was that gay men and lesbians often kept away from therapy and psychoanalysis, fearing that their sexuality would be judged. This represents a serious deprivation of therapeutic help. It also meant that most analysts and therapists had few, if any, gay and lesbian patients; their theories were based on the few, often very disturbed, individuals who found their way into therapy and on those who wished to change their sexual orientation. The result—a startling degree of analytic ignorance about the diversity and vicissitudes of homosexualities—remains with us today. In her description of the state of many psychoanalytic organizations, Rachel Cunningham attributes this ignorance to a form of splitting, whereby homosexuality is not considered a form of relating but tends instead to "remain raw and unprocessed . . . not a repressed entity or complex, but a disavowed one, projected or split off into the external world . . . where it can only be seen as threatening, pernicious" (50).

Only recently have voices within the profession challenged prevailing arguments and practices, also altering the balance of power. This is due largely to the presence of openly gay and lesbian therapists and analysts, a relatively new phenomenon established at considerable professional risk to the individuals involved. As with feminism, this presence is likely to create new considerations and new ways of theorizing: How far will the mainstream allow itself to be affected?

In what follows I draw on my own experience of trying to bring about change in this area. I also discuss recent writings about power, dominance, inclusion, and exclusion in this field. These texts include *Disorienting Sexuality: Psychoanalytic Reappraisals of Sexual Identities* (1995), a collection of essays mainly by American gay and lesbian psychoanalysts and psychotherapists. Eloquent and dignified, this book documents many of

the experiences of being at the cutting edge of psychoanalytic homophobia; as dispatches from the front line, the essays constitute essential historical material. *Disorienting Sexuality* also includes many papers addressing what may be involved clinically, theoretically, and institutionally in
reshaping psychoanalysis so that it can incorporate more adequately the
diversity of human sexuality. This ambitious project also asks us to consider what is arguably fundamental to this enterprise: A different approach to homosexuality involves not just dropping prejudicial attitudes
and discriminatory practices (welcome as that would be), but also, as
O'Connor and I argue in *Wild Desires,* reconsidering many taken-for-
granted aspects of psychoanalytic theory. This is likely to cause considerable opposition and resistance.

My second source is Elisabeth Young-Bruehl's mammoth study *The
Anatomy of Prejudices* (1996), a kind of psychoanalytic sociology of racism,
anti-Semitism, sexism, and homophobia. This book provides the most
extensive understanding I have yet found in the psychoanalytic field of
the little-studied subject of homophobia. Psychoanalysis arguably clarifies the fears and anxieties that homosexuality arouses, as well as the consequent prejudice and intolerance, but there is extraordinarily little psychoanalytic writing on this subject—a seldom-cited 1964 paper by Ralph
Greenson is a neglected exception. The paucity of psychoanalytic concern about homophobic phenomena is striking, especially compared with
the volumes of psychoanalytic writing on the supposed etiologies and
pathologies of male and female homosexuals, and on attempted therapeutic "cures." These volumes demonstrate the field's prevailing concerns
and as such undoubtedly illustrate the operation of power. In the concluding chapter of *Disorienting Sexuality,* Mark Blechner also asks why psychoanalysts have devoted so much effort to "explaining" homosexuality
and so little to explaining why so many people hate or fear homosexuals.
Psychoanalysis, he claims, is in fact better suited to respond to the latter
than the former issue; I would add that psychoanalysis is unique in this
respect. As many since Foucault have pointed out, what is not spoken or
represented in discourse may be as significant as what is said, indicating
the presuppositions, values, and normative demands of that discourse.

Among other things, Young-Bruehl emphasizes the plurality of forms
that prejudices can take, their complexities, and their context-specific na-
tures. She devises a typology of prejudices that draws on the psychoanalytic categories of hysteria, obsessional neurosis, and narcissism, providing much that can help us understand specifically psychoanalytic forms
of homophobia.

My third source includes some aspects of Judith Butler's writings. In

The Psychic Life of Power (1997), Butler extends Foucauldian notions of power in a psychoanalytic direction, in relation to the constitution of subjects. She refers to the unavoidable paradoxes inherent in gay and lesbian "identities," in ways that shed light on the implicitly homophobic aspects of psychoanalysis itself. She also addresses the psychic forms that power can take. This is directly relevant to what is tellingly but inadequately known as "internalized homophobia"; Butler pushes theories of this phenomenon beyond arguments about the internalization of victim or oppressed status.

The first and third sources above draw explicitly on Foucauldian theories of power, Young-Bruehl's approach representing a more traditional left/feminist position with perceptive analyses of the dynamics of oppositional groups. I have found Foucault's emphasis on the "how"—rather than the "who"—of power especially useful in describing the various "micro-operations" that for so long have sustained the dominance of orthodox psychoanalytic theories about homosexuality. Foucault's emphasis asks us to look at specific practices, technologies, strategies, and mechanisms involved in the maintenance of a virtually hegemonic state of affairs concerning homosexuality. We can identify—by no means exhaustively—some of the effects of these practices. For example:

- The psychoanalytic categories operating in a range of writings depicting homosexuality as a perversion and/or as a form of immaturity; the assumption that homosexuality inevitably has a psychopathological status, with a corresponding lack of conceptions of "healthy" homosexualities.
- The credibility given to the notion that psychotherapy can change a patient's orientation from homosexual to heterosexual. This assumption entails not only flagrantly abandoning an analytic stance, but also an abuse of transference.
- The theoretical conflation of gender identity issues with those of object-choice and sexual orientation; homosexuality was thereby designated a gender identity disorder.
- An ignorance or denial of important clinical issues, especially countertransference phenomena involving gay and lesbian patients. Accompanying this is a failure to work on, theorize, or teach in this area.
- Overgeneralization and reification of gay and lesbian issues, often collapsed into problems facing *the* homosexual.
- An absence of alternative or dissenting views, including little reporting of case material with homosexual outcomes to therapy, or material in which a patient's homosexuality was not seen symptomatically.
- The prohibition on lesbians and gay men entering psychoanalytic—and sometimes—psychotherapeutic training. Homosexuality also disqualifying a candidate's admission into training programs.

• The separation of psychoanalytic theory and practice from considerations of the social world, homophobia, the evolution of lesbian and gay identities, and what these mean for therapeutic work and theory.

Much could be said about these practices, which I list here to summarize the mechanisms that have helped exclude homosexuals from the field of psychoanalysis. I will elaborate on some of these practices.

How did such a state of affairs occur in the psychoanalytic field, and why has the psychoanalytic mainstream been so resistant to what for many are necessary and desirable changes? Once when I was giving a clinical paper to one of the more orthodox organizations, a distinguished psychoanalyst said about my description of some psychoanalytic positions, "This is not the psychoanalysis that I know." This remark, which perhaps captures the feelings of many therapists and analysts when confronted with such critiques, was undoubtedly sincere, but it was also a comfortably insulated denial, expressing satisfaction with the status quo. Only by a certain ignorance or denial could psychoanalysts and therapists take up a liberal position without conflict or personal risk. Many liberal practitioners were shocked when the United Kingdom's Association of Psychoanalytic Psychotherapists invited Charles Socarides to give a prestigious lecture in 1995. The ensuing protest, an attempt to get the profession to disown homophobic positions, had a vital educational function, as well as garnering considerable professional support (see Ryan, "Homophobia"). However, the number of therapists and analysts who for professional reasons felt afraid to associate themselves with the protest, although they agreed with it, is a concern. Here we see a particularly crude but intimidating form of patronage and power at work.

Most overt homophobic psychoanalytic work is an aberration of basic psychoanalytic tenets, values, and ideas. Why has such work had such credibility, and why has it not been disowned? And when will we see some acknowledgment of the far-reaching damage that has been wrought, both for patients who were inappropriately subjected to such treatments and for the culture-wide influence of psychoanalysis in supporting the pathologization of homosexuality? Whether or not they agree with this history, constructive acknowledgment of it by its current inheritors would facilitate more valuable thought on this subject, and perhaps bring the rich and creative thinking now taking place in queer and feminist theory more into alignment with contemporary psychoanalytic practice.

In the meantime, it is possible to understand key theoretical moves within psychoanalysis that pathologized homosexuality, and to see these relative to what we know about homophobia. We can identify the following:

- The abandonment in many quarters of Freud's position on bisexuality (however qualified or contradictory this was in Freud's work). Sandor Rado was a leading proponent of this abandonment (see Lewes 101–2), which continued in the form of widespread psychoanalytic endorsement of heterosexuality as biologically ordained, natural, fitting, mature, the essence of human sexuality and relationships, the instantiation of difference and complementarity between men and women.
- The unexamined shift from Freud's differentiation of homosexuality as inversion from perversion to the categorization of homosexuality as perversion par excellence. We see this transition in the work of Helene Deutsch, in the move from her sensitive clinical descriptions of lesbian eroticism in 1933 ("Homosexuality") to her later, more censorious account of lesbianism as a perversion in 1944 (*Psychology*). Subsequent publications even describe Freud as having categorized homosexuality as a perversion (see Socarides, *Overt*). This extraordinary rewriting of history seems to have gone largely unnoticed.
- The gendered split between identification and desire, inaugurated by Freud and basic to most versions of the Oedipus complex. O'Connor and I elaborate on this in *Wild Desires*, and other authors have commented on it (see Fuss). This split has led to the common and largely uncontested designation of homosexuality as a gender identity disorder in many mainstream psychoanalytic writings.

It is useful to consider these theoretical issues relative to the mechanisms identified earlier, as well as to aspects of homophobia operating within psychoanalysis.

Overgeneralization and reification (as in *the* homosexual) are hallmarks of all prejudices, but Young-Bruehl argues that homophobia is a prejudice of categorization, in a way that other prejudices are not, or are less centrally. She notes how the category itself functions as an accusation (as in "Faggot!" "Poof!" "Queer!" and so on); naming someone as homosexual can be an act of aggression and denigration. Categorization, she argues, is fundamental because the word *homosexual* cannot comprise a group unless it is made to refer to one, as in sexology's well-documented history, or when individuals decide to organize around it. Psychiatry, she argues, was historically the keeper of definitions of homosexuality—the "official pathologizer" of the homosexual—and there is much overlap here between psychiatry and sections of psychoanalysis. Psychiatry indeed—and psychoanalysis, too—became a prime target of attack in much gay liberation literature of the 1960s and 1970s, with its insistence that homosexuality is neither a sickness, disorder, nor disease, but is instead a normal variant of human sexuality.

Unlike with many—though not all—other categories or groups, it is less clear with homosexuality who should or should not be included in the term—hence all the debates about bisexuality and what constitutes homosexuality. One aspect of homophobia, Young-Bruehl argues, is the assertion of control over the category of homosexuality, so that self-identification means nothing. Rather, those she describes as homophobes "try to seize the power of definition" not only in the form of aggressive accusations about membership of such a category, but also, more widely, in typologies of various kinds (143). This corresponds with what Foucault calls the introduction of the homosexual as a subspecies, near the end of the nineteenth century, in sexology and related disciplines (*History* 43). In psychoanalysis, from Freud's "Psychogenesis of a Case of Homosexuality in a Woman" (1920) on, many case histories involve naming and labeling patients as "female homosexuals" without regard to their self-perception, or the trajectories of these individuals' developing sexualities. Categorization has also spawned subcategories, such as "true," "primary," and "secondary" homosexuality.

In elaborating her notion of homophobia as a prejudice of categorization, Young-Bruehl claims that prejudice is often aimed at the lifestyles and acts that "characterize" the people in question. Certainly this seems to fit the attitudes of two major institutions in which homophobia is currently challenged—the Church and the military. In these cases a prevalent form of homophobia is to tolerate the person but not her or his sexual acts—as in celibacy for openly gay and lesbian priests; loving the sinner but hating the sin; don't ask, don't tell in the U.S. military; and so on. And psychoanalysis has also exhibited a form of this brand of homophobia, in the tacit acceptance of some closeted analysts and therapists, but not of open ones; in the injunction to be "discreet" (see Ellis 513); and in analytic misunderstandings about the importance of being able to be "out" as lesbian or gay in psychoanalytic organizations. *Disorienting Sexuality* describes many of these misunderstandings, in which out therapists have been accused of "flaunting" their sexuality, and fears have been expressed about their imagined inappropriate disclosure to patients, as if openly gay or lesbian therapists were more likely to do this than any other therapist. The contributors record many instances of other kinds of inappropriate disclosure, for example, the breaking—by presumptively heterosexual therapists—of confidentiality about a lesbian or gay therapist's sexuality, often in situations of training or supervision, and even to patients. Also described are unsought assertions of a therapist's or analyst's heterosexuality in response to the presentation in clinical situations concerning homosexual material or information. Such breaking of the usual boundaries, by an unwarranted resort to these categories, represents a level of unacknowledged and irrational anxiety about homosexuality that should concern us all. Again, the assignment to a category seems to bear—or to speak to—a weight of unprocessed anxiety.

Young-Bruehl argues that for those most affected by homophobic anxieties, the category is all that stands between homosexuals and themselves. In this way, the category seems to block the universality of these acts by attributing them only to one class of persons, although anyone may engage in or fantasize about these acts. She maintains that this anxious emphasis on categorization and difference represents a repressed but shared desire, and calls this an hysterical form of prejudice.

In this prejudice's most extreme forms, homosexuality is viewed as unnatural and contagious, and homosexuals are seen as an inferior species that must be excluded, underpinning the vital differences that must be preserved against apparently dangerous encroachments. That psychoanalysts overturned Freud's formulation by categorizing homosexuality as a perversion signifies the kind of distinction they have found necessary to draw between homosexuality and heterosexuality. This redefinition of homosexuality is not only widespread today in many psychoanalytic writings, but also relevant to discrimination in blocking a person's admission to training. Some training programs specify that perversion is a disqualifying criterion, without explicitly saying whether homosexuality is included in this heading.

Before I elaborate further on hysterical aspects of homophobia, we should acknowledge other forms that it can take. Young-Bruehl designates as obsessional the kinds of prejudice evident in the writings of psychoanalysts who most denigrated and vilified homosexuals—Edmund Bergler, Irving Bieber, Frank Samuel Caprio, and Socarides—especially at the height of antihomosexual psychoanalytic writing in the late 1950s and early 1960s. What she calls obsessional is the preoccupation with how homosexuals were allegedly undermining American values and nuclear families, and the danger they supposedly constituted to children. Although such explicit antihomosexual attacks by psychoanalysts are less common today, obsessional anxieties are nonetheless evident among some psychoanalysts and therapists. Hanna Segal's remarks, in her 1990 interview with Jacqueline Rose, about children who are brought up by lesbians are examples of this, based entirely on speculation rather than on clinical material. In my account of the Socarides affair in England, I describe the kinds of anxieties expressed by analysts and therapists who in many ways were concerned not to discriminate in matters of training—these were anxieties especially about lesbians having babies and the well-being of their children (see Ryan, "Homophobia"). The irrational content of these anxieties was apparent from the fact that the mother, not the child, was the patient in these instances, and from the speakers' complete ignorance about and uninterest in the extensive psychological research available about children brought up in lesbian (and gay) families (see, for example, Tasker and Golombok). This exhibits one of the features of obsessional anxiety—that fears cannot be assuaged by contrary and well-established evidence.

Although I am loath to draw parallels among different forms of prejudice, I have found some of Stuart Hall's writings on racism useful in highlighting certain comparable dynamics in homophobic prejudices. He observes thus about the intertwining of envy and desire: "The play of identity and difference which constructs racism is powered not only by the positioning of blacks as the inferior species, but also and at the same time by an inexpressible envy and desire; and this is something the recognition of which displaces many of our hitherto stable categories, since it implies a process of identification and otherness which is more complex than hitherto imagined" (444–45). The idea that some highly repressed homosexual desires and longings are involved in homophobic prejudices has perhaps become a well-worn cliché, a way of knowing that blocks fuller understanding of what is involved in all kinds of homophobia. Part of the difficulty here may be that knowing and acknowledging are themselves threatening to the very repression that apparently is so necessary. Young-Bruehl's work helps us take this understanding more seriously, and it is interesting that Adam Phillips, in his commentary on Butler's work, also analyzes what he calls "the culturally pervasive hostility . . . toward homosexuality [that] is based on envy" (Phillips 154). Psychoanalysis is uniquely placed to understand the complexity of these feared wishes and identifications, and their accompanying envy.

Within psychoanalysis, the historical exclusion of lesbians and gay men from psychoanalytic training—whether covert or overt, past or in some quarters still present—is arguably an example of hysterical prejudice. The lesbian or gay man is apparently always the patient, never the analyst—them, but never us. The idea of a lesbian psychoanalyst or gay psychotherapist—or even of a gay man or lesbian speaking from the position of the analyst or therapist—has been seen as oxymoronic and impossible, or else as anxiety provoking. In this respect we can say that lesbians or gay men generally have been barred from taking up positions as analyst-subjects; they have not been able to enter psychoanalytic discourse as analysts or therapists.

I would now like to turn to the contribution Butler's work makes to understanding the interplay of forms of stigmatization and challenge, as well as the discursive basis of homophobia. Butler aims to describe how power forms the subject. In doing so, she takes us away from Young-Bruehl's methodology, which is closer to the framework of the repressive hypothesis. Butler's analysis surpasses the idea that we internalize prevailing norms. Instead, she insists that norms, practices, and values are the very conditions of the subject's existence. Internalizing norms creates the psyche's interiority, she argues; it *"fabricates the distinction between interior and exterior life"* (19; original emphasis). Thus, instead of a distinct "we" or "I" that can accept or refuse these terms, the "we" or "I" depends on these terms for its existence. Butler views the desire for social existence as one exploited by regulatory power. Subjection is thus our "fundamental dependency on a discourse we never chose, but that, paradoxically, initiates and sustains our agency" (2). In this respect, the power that appears as external assumes a psychic form that constitutes a subject's identity: "Power is both external to the subject and the very venue of the subject" (15).

Butler applies her analysis to the formation of the heterosexual subject, which, she argues, depends on a form of prohibition she calls "foreclosure" rather than "repression." Foreclosure is a rigorous barring of desire, constituting the subject through a certain kind of loss: "The foreclosure of homosexuality appears to be foundational to a certain heterosexual version of the subject. The formula 'I have never loved' someone of similar gender and 'I have never lost' any such person predicates the 'I' on the 'never-never' of that love and loss" (23).

Butler then asks what happens when the foreclosure of love becomes the condition of possibility for social existence. This is an apposite way of describing the dilemmas that gays and lesbians have often faced; it also pinpoints what happens for those constituted as heterosexual when they find themselves barred from recognizing any homosexual desires. She describes the ensuing sociality as melancholic, for loss cannot be grieved and it cannot be recognized as loss; what is lost was never entitled to exist. From a psychoanalytic perspective, it is not difficult to see the pathological consequences of unrecognized foreclosure—unconscious hostility, panic, and denial. Owing to the taboo on homosexuality, Butler views social sanctions as operating by foreclosure, rather than by repression. And she claims that persisting in alterity—through categories, terms, names, and so on, that indicate a primary violence—is the only way we can persist as subjects—"a subject emerges against itself in order, paradoxically, to be for itself" (28).

It seems to me that many struggles against discrimination, homophobia, and so on are attempts at changing the terms of social existence in order to inaugurate different kinds of subjects—the lesbian or gay man as an out psychoanalyst, parent, priest, or even as a general. Some of these struggles have been attempts at reversing and resignifying prejudicial categories. For example, the much maligned slogan "We're here, we're queer, get used to it!" and the term *queer theory* are assertive resignifications, opposing norms by reversing the terms of discourse that constitute certain subjects as acceptable and others not. This is a very different tactic from trying to function within existing terms, which leads only to silence, the closet, and passing as heterosexual. Within the psychoanalytic world, the conditions for social existence used to be—and often still are—the apparent heterosexuality of the analyst; the psychotherapeutic equivalent of stating "We're here, we're queer" has challenged these conditions, while shattering their related silences. This has not happened without risk to the practitioners involved (risks still operating in terms of selective patronage), however, and it has required an exposure through identity, which for those working within a psychoanalytic framework is complex, but not insuperable.

Concerning resignification, Butler asks how it is possible to occupy the place of discursive injury, as in adopting injurious terms. "Called by an injurious name," she writes, "I come into social being"; and owing to the narcissism attached to any term that confers social existence, "I am led to embrace the terms that injure me because they constitute me socially" (104). This points up the inherent paradox of identity politics. According to Butler, adopting injurious terms makes resistance and opposition possible, for it "recast[s] the power that constitutes me as the power I oppose" (104). Any mobilization against subjection must use subjection as a resource; and because psychoanalysis elaborates on the intricacies of unconscious power—its "traumatic and productive iterability"—it is especially useful in this regard. Butler contrasts this approach with the idea of unacknowledged external power, which in many psychoanalytic texts claims a universality—regardless of culture or context—that ignores the unconscious. In such a picture, the exteriority of the law and of the social regulation of desire is presumed. Butler turns this assumption on its head, arguing (with Foucault and Lacan) that there is no desire without the law that forms and sustains what it prohibits.

What are the implications of taking seriously Butler's claim that heterosexuality is based on a radical foreclosure of homosexual desire? I suggest that it gives us a necessary context for understanding homophobia in its psychic forms. Butler is producing not a psychology, but an account of discourses with which we are often overfamiliar. So for her what matters is that individuals find themselves unable to avow and mourn the loss of homosexual attachments, and that foreclosure is ritualized and repeated by our social and cultural discourses.

Clearly, the precise intertwining of gender and sexuality within subjects is infinitely varied. When applied to psychoanalysis, Butler's analysis is also complex. She uses psychoanalytic insights about mourning, loss, and identification to understand what she calls the "melancholia of gender" and the consequent lack of possibility for acknowledging properly homosexual love and desire. Butler's analysis is also complex because psychoanalysis is precisely the discourse that deconstructs naturalized and assumed distinctions between heterosexuality and homosexuality. As Freud famously said, in a passage quoted over and again: "Psycho-analytic research is most decidedly opposed to any attempt at separating off homosexuals from the rest of mankind as a group of a special character . . ." (*Three* 145n).

Unfortunately, as I have outlined here, this separation happened extensively in the subsequent history of psychoanalysis. Contradictions writ large in Freud's work have thus been suppressed and ignored. Butler's analysis and our argument in *Wild Desires* point up the moves that enabled this outcome, which has barred homosexual subjects from the field of psychoanalysis, as well as discussion of related issues of immense clinical importance. These include psychoanalytic perspectives on homophobia that might have been usefully generated; the full theorization of countertransference issues; and a better understanding of aspects of gay and lesbian experiences.

According to Young-Bruehl, one of homophobia's functions is to shore up core gender identities. By contrast, Butler makes clear how masculinity and femininity are traces of an ungrieved and ungrievable loss—symptoms of a pervasive disavowal. The status of "masculinity" and "femininity" as concepts in psychoanalytic theory crucially underpins psychoanalytic notions of homosexuality as a gender identity disorder, while upholding heterosexuality as the standard for sexual desire. That homosexuality as a variant of human sexuality has been transformed into a key issue of gender identity illustrates where psychoanalysis betrays itself. Freud led the way for this transformation when making the distinction between identification and desire pivotal to most versions of the Oedipus complex, while rendering as normative and universal the obligatory gendering of desire as heterosexual. In this way, forms of homophobia became institutionalized as received theory and consequently invisible.

References

Bergler, Edmund. *Homosexuality: Disease or Way of Life?* New York: Hill and Wang, 1956.

Bieber, Irving, et al. *Homosexuality: A Psychoanalytic Study.* New York: Basic, 1962.

Blechner, Mark J. "The Shaping of Psychoanalytic Theory and Practice by Cultural and Personal Biases about Sexuality." In Domenici and Lesser 265–88.

Butler, Judith. *The Psychic Life of Power: Theories in Subjection.* Stanford: Stanford UP, 1997.

Caprio, Frank Samuel. *Female Homosexuality: A Psychodynamic Study of Lesbianism.* 1954. New York: Citadel, 1960.

Cunningham, Rachel. "When Is a Pervert Not a Pervert?" *British Journal of Psychotherapy* 8.1 (1991): 48–70.

Deutsch, Helene. "Homosexuality in Women." *International Journal of Psycho-Analysis* 14.1 (1933): 34–56.

———. *The Psychology of Women: A Psychoanalytic Interpretation.* New York: Grune and Stratton, 1944.

Domenici, Thomas, and Ronnie C. Lesser, eds. *Disorienting Sexuality: Psychoanalytic Reappraisals of Sexual Identities.* New York: Routledge, 1995.

Ellis, Mary Lynne. "Lesbians, Gay Men and Psychoanalytic Training." *Free Associations* 32 (1994): 501–17.

Foucault, Michel. *The History of Sexuality, Volume 1: An Introduction.* 1976. Trans. Robert Hurley. New York: Pantheon, 1978.

Freud, Sigmund. *The Standard Edition of the Complete Psychological Works of Sigmund Freud.* Ed. and trans. James Strachey. 24 vols. London: Hogarth, 1953–74.

———. *Three Essays on the Theory of Sexuality.* 1905. *Standard* 7:123–245.

———. "The Psychogenesis of a Case of Homosexuality in a Woman." 1920. *Standard* 18:145–72.

Fuss, Diana. *Identification Papers.* New York: Routledge, 1995.

Greenson, Ralph R. "On Homosexuality and Gender Identity." *International Journal of Psycho-Analysis* 45 (1964): 217–19.

Hall, Stuart. "New Ethnicities." *Stuart Hall: Critical Dialogues in Cultural Studies.* Ed. David Morley and Kuan-Hsing Chen. New York: Routledge, 1996. 441–49.

Lewes, Kenneth. *The Psychoanalytic Theory of Male Homosexuality.* New York: New American Library, 1988.

McDougall, Joyce. *The Many Faces of Eros: A Psychoanalytic Exploration.* New York: Norton, 1995.

O'Connor, Noreen, and Joanna Ryan. *Wild Desires and Mistaken Identities: Lesbianism and Psychoanalysis.* New York: Columbia UP, 1993.

Phillips, Adam. "Keeping It Moving: Commentary on Judith Butler's 'Melancholy Gender/Refused Identification.'" Rept. in Butler 151–59.

Rose, Jacqueline. "Hanna Segal Interview." *Women: A Cultural Review* 1.2 (1990): 198–214.

Ryan, Joanna. "Homophobia and Hegemony: A Case of Psychoanalysis." In *Who's Afraid of Feminism? Seeing through the Backlash.* Ed. Ann Oakley and Juliet Mitchell. London: Hamish Hamilton, 1997. 129–43.

Socarides, Charles W. *The Overt Homosexual.* New York: Grune and Stratton, 1968.

Tasker, Fiona L., and Susan Golombok. *Growing Up in a Lesbian Family: Effects on Child Development.* New York: Guilford, 1997.

Young-Bruehl, Elisabeth. *The Anatomy of Prejudices.* Cambridge: Harvard UP, 1996.

17

SPEAKING OF THE SURFACE

The Texts of Kaposi's Sarcoma

Suzanne Yang

· ·

This essay addresses a question at the heart of any discourse said to be clinical: how to intervene in suffering in the face of the unknown. It also offers a perspective on the future anterior, the way the present will have been mistaken relative to knowledge that is yet to come.[1]

It is impossible to empathize without sensing a danger—one's own vulnerability to the disease called AIDS. We are accustomed to speaking of the patient's perspective and the lived experience of this disease, reading traces of subjectivity in cultural representations and individual testimony.[2] But we are unable to perceive clearly what barriers—affective, bodily, or scientific—block empathy and comprehension, impeding understanding in the same way that life cannot but misunderstand death.[3] In what follows, I will focus on Kaposi's sarcoma (KS) in order to examine the subject of medical discourse about AIDS-related changes to the body and one's sense of self. Through close study of the scientific language of diagnosis and treatment in this particular disease manifestation, I shall advance questions for further research in the psychodynamics of the medical treatment of AIDS.

1. Cutaneous Manifestations

If AIDS is really the sickness of the other, how can we get infected? What provides the bridge and how can it be broken? RONALD FRANKENBERG, "THE OTHER WHO IS ALSO THE SAME" 83

Over 90 percent of persons with AIDS develop opportunistic skin conditions during the course of the illness (see Zalla et al.; Duvic; Muggia and Lonberg). These are rarely the immediate cause of death in AIDS. As the most prevalent group of symptoms, however, they seem to exemplify, to characterize, the disease. AIDS—acquired immunodeficiency syndrome— is a disease of boundaries, of the relation between self and environment, and of vulnerability both specific and diffuse to the challenges posed from within and outside the body. These challenges reveal the persistent struggle and overcoming that the immune system ordinarily accomplishes in silence.

The skin doubles as a biological site of the disease and as a site of cultural and clinical meaning. The skin is thus a focus of voyeuristic judgments, of stigma that arises from the wealth of significance at the surface, the availability of the surface to multiple investments. A dermatological tautology would insist that the skin is an important site of manifestation *because* it is the organ system of the body most accessible to vision. Thus by way of the skin, *the body shows,* and the skin becomes the place of its expression, exemplary of outwardness. When we consider the skin, there is an ambivalence that reflects our suspicion that there is much more than meets the eye.

According to Didier Anzieu, "The skin is both permeable and impermeable, superficial and profound, truthful and misleading . . ." (17). By literalizing the body image as a function of the skin (the imago that Lacan theorized in his essay on "The Mirror Stage"), Anzieu shows how subjectivity depends on superficial phenomena. The surface marks a threshold between inner and outer, and is supposed to make known the internal contents and events. In his concept of a "skin ego," Anzieu merges the biological reality, imaginary anatomy, and symbolic appropriations of the skin into an elastic construct that the subject deploys in its experience of the world. The skin ego is a psychical effect, he argues, a self-perception in which the integument—imaginary, real, and symbolic—serves many functions. It is a container of depth, a marker of the threshold with the world, and a site of exchange with others. In this last function, the skin ego is scarred by openings, insignias of passage, orifices through which it makes itself known as the insufficient container and threshold on which the subject depends. Porosity—the penetrability of the body surface—installs our knowledge of a body's depth (Deleuze 286).

Only through such ruptures does a body become capable of speaking. It is through the mouth, for instance, that a baby makes its insufficiency and needs known. In this way, speech represents the disruption and restitution of the subject's coherence. Implicit in Anzieu's model is the idea that the skin ego is self-referential, that it encourages a correspondence, albeit inexact, between the psychical effect and physical presence of the body. He sketches the emergence of different pathologies from defects in this correspondence, suggesting that it is possible, and desirable, to achieve a coherent relation between the two. And mouths may achieve this, the speaking subject momentarily anchoring his or her name in relation to the body. Yet the superimposition of a skin ego on the surface of the body tears at its integrity, leaving holes that words inadequately fill, opening new holes as they cover.

The outward and interrupted surface of the skin maintains the body's social aspect, exposed to public capture, imaging, and diverse symbolizations. It is a short step from acknowledgment of one's appearance to the extraordinary investments the skin is made to carry. The skin is often a factor in one's acceptance or disapproval, real or imagined, by others; it is a means of self-consciousness and a mode of communication.[4] Patients and clinicians often consider dermatological problems related to AIDS as social signs; they are visible indicators of a disease that remains severely stigmatizing and that is still associated with socially marginalized groups.[5] A destruction of the surface, an invasion into the body's integrity, visually represents the perceived danger that epidemics pose to the larger social order.[6] Among these eruptions, KS seems especially undeniable as a sign of AIDS.

Many of the cutaneous manifestations of AIDS are opportunistic varieties of skin conditions present in milder form in the absence of HIV. Clinicians have emphasized the importance of accurate diagnosis both in treating the particular manifestation and in determining whether it is indeed an indication of underlying HIV infection (Berger et al. 1739; Krown et al., "Medical Management" 235). Of these skin manifestations of AIDS, KS was the focus of special attention in the medical literature because of its prevalence and specificity as a marker for AIDS. Previously a rare disease, KS, along with *Pneumocystis carinii* pneumonia, quickly became known to the public as one of the characteristic manifestations of AIDS. In the early days of the epidemic, KS, a relatively slow-developing neoplasm, was often the presenting symptom, the first indication, of AIDS.[7] Among ambiguous "flulike symptoms" and "weight loss," the prominent purplish lesions of KS seemed to be a reliable diagnostic marker of AIDS. Although far short of being a pathognomic sign—KS is not present in every case of AIDS—non-AIDS-related KS is so rare and demographically restricted that the presence of these lesions could with some certainty be attributed to the AIDS process.

Yet in the absence of knowledge about etiology, the importance of KS in diagnosing AIDS and in defining AIDS as a specific disease entity was disproportionate to its significance to mortality in AIDS. As Kaplan, Wofsy, and Volberding have shown, KS among persons with AIDS is rarely a direct cause of death.[8] Thus criteria for treatment must be established more in terms of subjective effects—discomfort or pain, and the patient's perception of changes in appearance and social presentation—than of physiological survival (see Fox et al.; Epstein and Silverman; Groopman; Boudreaux et al.).[9] KS is a matter of life or death only with respect to the larger picture it captures. Descriptions of KS and the criteria physicians must consider in determining treatment consistently emphasize the impact of the disease on the patient's appearance and self-image: *cosmetic effect, disfigurement, aesthetic considerations* are prominent categories in discussions of treatment (LaCamera et al.; Ficarra et al.; Kaplan et al.; Boudreaux et al.). These criteria include a locus of subjectivity, a place for the patient's informed decision, a determination of the necessity of palliation based on his or her own experience (see Smith et al.). Yet this subjectivity, constituted relative to its representation, remains inaccessible to direct experience, finding itself the effect and cause of elaborate signs and symbols, of which medical science is but one of many.

2. The Time of the Lesion

As the testimony of those afflicted with AIDS makes clear, medical discourse cannot avoid "contaminating" experience. In this respect, it is pointless to invoke subjects experiencing AIDS who could be identified without the terms and parameters of scientific medicine.[10] In our time, the time of AIDS, medicine has become postbacteriological. Even as scientists question the validity of our current concepts of infectious disease, they are not free to forget the legacy that a century of certainty and apparent progress has bestowed. The medical field is organized by a particular orthodoxy in which microbes and antisera serve as the central models of disease causation and cure. The experiences of AIDS and of Kaposi's sarcoma cannot be separated from the subjectivity of the patient as portrayed in medical discourse, the subject seen from the perspective of the scientific observer. The clinical language of diagnosis and treatment positions the subject.[11]

The individual subject of experience becomes a function of the various discourses purporting to serve it. AIDS may be described as an experience of dispossession—loss of one's health, immunity, employment, insurance, housing, family, and other forms of security. Bodily conditions, unpredictable and uncanny, dictate the directions of movement, delivering the person over to the care of medical personnel. Future hopes are directed at the possibility of vaccines and antisera to reverse the damage; and scientists concentrate on trying to disclose the cause, the etiological agent whose mechanism remains obscured. Others have placed their hopes in epidemiological effects, in the potential deceleration of the spread of HIV, which eventually could lead to its extinction.[12] In the meantime, medical scientific paradigms have focused on the prevention and treatment of opportunistic infections in those already infected.

It is difficult to prevent KS, or to tackle it aggressively, as it has not been known to be fully eradicated once the process has begun (Ficarra et al.; Safai et al. "Interferon"). KS is a "multifocal neoplasm": It cannot be said to spread from any particular point of origin; destruction of an early appearing tumor therefore does not prevent the emergence of new lesions at distant sites (Cotran et al. 511–12). There are thought to be systemic "cofactors" required for the activation of KS.[13] Clinical efforts either have concentrated on the local treatment of individual lesions or have concentrated on the prognostic value of the lesions; the former, as discussed above, relies on the patient's determination of the subjective impact of the disease.

The effort to read the lesions prognostically extends the diagnostic value already conferred on KS. KS has been read as an index of AIDS. Up until the early 1980s, Kaposi's sarcoma had been understood in the medical literature as a neoplasm limited to white males of Mediterranean descent over the age of sixty and young black Africans in areas known to have a high endemic incidence (Cotran et al. 511). The gradual accumulation of isolated cases of Kaposi's sarcoma in young white males erupted into a quantitatively significant phenomenon in the first half of 1981, as clinicians in urban medical centers compared their observations.[14] Correlation of KS with unusual vulnerability to opportunistic infections, including *Pneumocystis carinii* pneumonia, allowed for the early constitution of AIDS as an identifiable disease entity (see Shilts; Fee and Fox; Grmek). In current diagnostic manuals and textbooks, KS in a patient under the age of sixty, even in the absence of HIV, is considered an unambiguous demonstration of the AIDS process.[15] Thus, as a diagnostic tool, the lesion of KS serves as positive indication of the larger disease entity, the syndrome, the complex of phenomena gathered under the acronym AIDS.

But *syndrome* (from the Greek root meaning "combination") names only a pattern—one presumed to refer to a central cause that is not yet disclosed. From the earliest understandings in antiquity of a relation among symptoms to the efflorescence of the specificity concept in early-nineteenth-century French medicine, the making of specific disease entities served to organize the physicians' observations and assessments for the purpose of intervention. However, only in modern times has the notion of specificity been linked to scientific efforts to rationally assess the efficacy of therapeutic measures. The emergence of such an aim, natural as it seems to us now, was not simple. As Foucault has rigorously shown in *The Birth of the Clinic* (1963), a methodology for the precise description of distinct pathological states dates back to the late eighteenth century in the large hospitals of Paris. The presence of large numbers of patients suffering from many of the same diseases helped physicians to correlate observed clinical symptoms with anatomical lesions garnered through postmortem inspection. Historians have supposed that physicians in these opening decades of scientific medicine neglected therapeutics in favor of ever-finer diagnostic schemata of modest consequence. More recently, historians have suggested that the apparent therapeutic nihilism of early-nineteenth-century medicine reflects only present-day standards applied to a time before the startling advances of the late nineteenth and early twentieth centuries.[16] Compared to the development of the antitoxin for diphtheria—and the Wassermann test, 606 Salvarsan, and penicillin in the diagnosis and treatment of syphilis (Quétel; Crissey and Parish)—mid-nineteenth-century efforts to establish diagnostic categories and more effective ways to administer the same old remedies that had been around for centuries, such as mercury in the case of syphilis, seemed hopelessly simplistic. *How could they not know what we know now?* This is the retrospective version of the question we now ask ourselves about AIDS: *What prevents us from knowing what we will surely know—it is only a matter of time—in the near future?* This question is misguided, not only in its assumption that mastery is inevitable, but also in its certainty that current methods and current definitions of knowledge are adequate to the problems they address.

We have reason to believe that these problems will be resolved in time, and tremendous research efforts are devoted to finding an answer. But the questions remain: What are we to do in the meantime, and how is what we do in the meantime going to generate this desired answer? Before antibiotics and the advances of bacteriology, pathological anatomists sought to ameliorate medical uncertainty through the precise correlation of symptoms with lesion complexes found within the body. Knowledge of these complexes was to enable physicians to diagnose specific diseases and to improve the administration of various therapeutic measures. Of crucial importance in this enterprise was the pathognomic sign, a characteristic marker of the disease, often an internal lesion, which was necessarily present in all instances of the specific disease (see Foucault; Matthews). The pathognomic sign offsets the sliding of elements, the melee of physical signs of disease, and confers on them their meaning under a disease nomenclature, or diagnosis (Žižek 87). The pathognomic sign fastens a certain point of reference in the field of floating bodily significations, a master signifier (S_1) relative to which all other indicators attain meaning.

Early on, within the confusing array of manifestations of AIDS, KS was assumed to provide this point of reference. As particular symptoms and signs may be said to connote AIDS (sudden weight loss, flulike symptoms, leukoplakia), the presence of KS, in medical terms, apparently designated the disease entity. KS is presumed to be a clinical marker of the larger disease process, just as HIV is presumed to indicate its cause. But both these signs are far from meeting criteria for pathognomic certitude: KS is a sufficient but not necessary manifestation of AIDS (many patients with AIDS do not develop KS). Like HIV, KS has been observed to correlate with the overall process named AIDS, but its relationship to the cause of the disease has not been demonstrated mechanistically. For a time, this was the nearest approach to diagnostic certainty, a clinical impression amid unreliable signs. The problem remains that if this is certainty, then we seem to be on shaky ground—a sentiment corroborated by everyone's sense of what we don't yet know about AIDS treatment.

At such a moment, in this situation of ignorance, we are inclined to amplify what certainty we do possess into a yet greater one obtained through better methods of reading. Medical scientists, taking KS as a reasonable index of the presence of the AIDS process, looked toward the prognostic value of the lesions, attempting to turn a designation of the disease into a prediction of its future. The clinical course of AIDS-related KS was seen to vary widely, the lesions sometimes slow to develop, indolent, at other times rapid and fulminant, penetrating deeper into the body to affect visceral organs. Nevertheless, physicians observed that neither the initial site of appearance of KS nor the extent of "tumor load" or progression correlated with the prognosis of the skin disease (see Safai et al., "Natural History"). In the mid-1980s, the most reliable indicator of the progression of KS in AIDS was a period of observing and assessing the tempo of lesion development (Kaplan et al.). In 1986, however, investigators began to speculate that immune-system status might be a valuable parameter in the staging classification of KS in AIDS (Vadhan-Raj et al.). The extent of KS previously had been measured in morphological terms, based on lesion size, shape, and location. But reports in 1987 and 1988 noted a correlation between overall level of cellular immunosuppression, the degree of development of KS, and survival time in patients with AIDS (Groopman; Ficarra et al.). A new staging classification for KS was developed that included CD4 counts as one of the factors in severity of the disease. Given the possibility that cytomegalovirus was a necessary cofactor in the KS process, and owing to observed links between immune status and this skin disorder, interferon was explored as a possible treatment for KS (Safai et al., "Interferon").[17] Researchers found that the interferon treatment of KS was most effective in patients whose immune function was relatively intact, and that immune status was both the strongest predictor of therapeutic success and the strongest indicator of good prognosis—slow tempo of progression—in KS.

In the mid-1990s, the arrows of influence were again reversed, with physicians reading immune-system status as a prognostic indicator for KS, and KS as a prognostic indicator for the overall process of AIDS. Studies showed that AIDS patients for whom the only initial presenting manifestation was KS fared better in the long run than did patients presenting with infections or KS with infections (Ficarra et al.; Niedt et al.; Tappero et al.). Microscopic studies of biopsies led to the conclusion that KS prognosis could be discerned from histological evidence.[18] Through acts of interpretation, KS was first construed diagnostically as a marker, something like a pathognomic sign. KS also was understood prognostically, in time, as (1) an indicator of its own progression, (2) a correlate of the progression of immune system debilitation, (3) an indicator of the overall progression of AIDS in the patient, (4) a histological predictor of its own development, its pace, *and* that of the general disease process. This last perspective leads to a shift from the lesion being seen as an indicator of itself, to its being viewed as an index of a larger process to which it contributes.

The unreliability of KS lesions for prognosis accentuates the already

unstable status of KS as a pathognomic sign, however, extending and illuminating the illegibility of the sarcoma relative to the larger disease that
it is said to represent. Something else must be supposed at the heart of
AIDS. The failure of the lesion to mark prognosis exposes the limitations
of conceptions of AIDS as a disease entity (Krim 3). Like other illnesses,
AIDS as it is experienced afflicts the subject in ways not registered by the
framework of science. From the perspective of science, the visibility of
the lesion affords the prospect of certitude in diagnosis and treatment. KS
compensates for a lack of certainty, presenting as its image or latent
meaning precisely the flaw that is symptomatic of its nondesignation.

However, the use of a bodily phenomenon as a definite sign of disease
raises a question about a subjective relation to the body and its transformations. For whom is the sign significant? Is the subject of KS to be defined by clinical medicine, laboratory science, the patient—or in the ver-
nacular? The modes of interaction among these definitions may be
affected by the structures in which they are introduced and contested.
How can the labeling of disease offer anything but simple alienation?
And how, if it is possible, may the indicator be appropriated in favor of
the patient's empowerment?

3. "Microbes" in Place of the Object *a*

There are not only "social" relations . . . for everywhere microbes intervene and act. . . .
Microbes are everywhere third parties in all relations. BRUNO LATOUR, *THE PASTEUR-
IZATION OF FRANCE*

The correlation of positive sign and underlying process of disease seems
apt but insufficient. Just as cultural representations have sought a signifier
for AIDS (as Tim Dean has argued), so has medicine pursued knowledge
and diagnostic procedures that surpass the superficial complex of symptoms, the "syndrome" of AIDS. AIDS, for the time being, refers to an entity
whose ultimate cause, presumed to be singular, remains obscured.

Ever since the Pasteurian revolution, the cause sought by medical
science has been the microbe, of one species or another. It is as if the
parasite, or foreign body, were a positive rendition that establishes the
specificity of disease entities (Latour; Salomon-Bayet; Léonard; Dagognet,
Méthodes and *Pasteur*). It is plausible to trace a simplified trajectory, from
observation of associated symptoms and their grouping into presumed
"first-order" disease entities, to a "second-order" correlation of symptom

complexes with lesion complexes; in this second order, the pathognomic sign fulfills the nosologist's wish. This trajectory extends to what, in the time of AIDS, we might call "third-order" disease. Here, a specific entity comprises a complex of different opportunistic infections and disorders, each component itself a specific disease, configured characteristically with the others in the complex known as AIDS. In each of these conceptions of disease specificity, a set of elements (symptoms, lesions, and infections) is organized about a central anchor, a definitive point. Up until the last decades of the nineteenth century, this point was the object of medical theory, a speculation whose place was marked by the pathognomic sign that bore spurious relationship to the cause of disease. As Georges Canguilhem has shown, bacteriology ended such speculations by providing a microscopic visibility at the center, a causative agent, the microbe to which all effects could be traced.

Before AIDS the microbe's role seemed indisputable. Ten years ago activists and scientists, albeit in antagonistic relation, remained equally optimistic that conventional understandings of infectious disease and methods of investigating the disease mechanism would lead, in time, to vaccines and antidotes. In the early 1990s conferences witnessed confusion as all parties acknowledged that there might be a fundamental flaw in conceptions of the disease. If it is true that "causation is a theoretical relationship and can only be established relative to a specific theoretical framework" (Carter 56), then the "cause" of AIDS may be much more elusive than we previously thought. On further reflection we recall that in the early days being gay was seen as a "cause" of AIDS; then, that having sex with IV-drug users was a cause of AIDS; government silence later was acknowledged as a cause of AIDS; and so on. Perhaps causation relates to different ideologies circling about a void, a central absence whose effects feed our wish to know. As with the object a, there is in AIDS a little piece of the real that overturns our aim, that defies definition and almost cannot receive a name. The desire of the scientist may be constituted in terms of what he or she believes is lacking, and conventionally one seeks microbes in this place; but nothing ever really takes the place of the object a.[19] There, where knowledge is lacking, there will be discourses, and a progress assessed through the livability of the void.

It is tempting to assert that the scientist, the activist, the patient, the epidemiologist, all wonder after the same thing. More likely, a lack becomes differentiated, as it is constituted by distinct epistemologies in which characteristic desires are furrowed. A discourse proper to the subject of AIDS, if there were such a discourse, might entail the (re)appropriation of the work of science, biology, and bacteriology to the point of questioning, to that point where "the subject is subject of a question," as Žižek observes. Yet "it is not the subject which is asking the question; the subject is the void of the impossibility of answering the question of the Other" (Žižek 178). Who articulates the question of the Other, explicitly or implicitly, to receive answers from it? The vocabulary of positive and experimental science has become one of the privileged discourses of the Other in relation to which other discourses, including psychoanalysis, situate themselves.[20] The scientist, standing in for the Other, occupies the position pursued as the ideal of rational discourse.

The epistemologies devised to contend with ignorance and impossible questions overlap with one another, at times in conflict, to offer greater knowledge as livable responses to this Other. In the face of uncertainty and the inadequacy of current strategies, different groups constitute what is lacking and what is sought in order to complement their values and particular aims (Treichler, "AIDS, Homophobia").[21] The object a in discourses, plied toward specific desires, produces a multiplicity of solutions and future directions for resolving the problem provisionally unified by calling it AIDS. To the extent that AIDS is everybody's problem and refers to a definite phenomenon, however, the various ways of addressing the problem and negotiating a relation to it do not operate independently. Nor are they equal in efficacy and persuasiveness.[22] Within the network of relations established to contend with AIDS, the scientific fields—and more narrowly, the work in laboratories—have been privileged as the spearhead of hopes for a cure.[23] Yet scientific methods, especially the reductionist ones that prevail in laboratory research,[24] have evolved from a tradition in which the patient's subjectivity—or the observer's subjectivity, for that matter—is systematically eclipsed for the sake of uniformity and statistical coherence. These procedures and their technologies have generated a medical environment in which patients are implicitly asked to have faith in scientific solutions.

Many authors, notably in the nursing literature, try to reintroduce the subject into the technologies of treatment through a shift from curing to "caring."[25] The division of medical labor implicit in this separation of the components of treatment—between the technologically sophisticated or experimental and the affective—misses the point of reference created by this divide, the subject strewn between imaginary and symbolic registrations of the self. The person with AIDS is both a subject facing premature death and the subject of complicated technologies of treatment. In addition to conceptualizing the emotional experience of AIDS within the frame of the patient's life story beyond the hospital and the clinic, the task of caring for the subject requires that experience be resituated within parameters established by medical discourse. What is called for, in the context of urgent need and the AIDS pandemic, is a reading of the subjective consequences of these institutional and epistemological patterns.[26]

In the operations of medicine, in the regimented procedures, something is co-opted, a quiet remainder unexpressed by science. Perhaps it speaks anyway, unnamed, an improper and impossible discourse beneath the reasonableness of clinical trials. One person with AIDS writes emphatically, "I cannot see myself as contending with a biological virus. I do not think I am ever going to lose any war in this way. . . . I am not a battle-field. I am not a landscape, but rather the presence that matters in this landscape that my body has become in this illness" (qtd. in Daniel 548).[27] Nevertheless, many patients wage their struggle against the disease through the vocabulary of medical science, as a way of appropriating the disease.[28] *Their* disease, one's own disease. Not simply the disease as it afflicts everyone, or even those afflicted with currently active infections, but the disease as a singularity expressed through the language of universality. Oneself seen by science—a subject afflicted by something whose parameters have largely been defined by medical classifications.[29] Medical language implicitly promotes this belonging, this ownership of the disease, imposing it on the patient without articulating the impact or the meaning of this relation to the patient.[30]

4. An Obverse of the Psychosomatic Phenomenon

Unlike conversion (at least as theorists have defined it), the psychosomatic phenomenon (PSP) involves the lesioning of tissue, something occurring in the real that encounters the symbolic order not by submitting to it but by sticking to its edges, asserting a continuity between imaginary and symbolic domains.[31] And, astonishingly, psychosomatic phenomena often manifest themselves in lesions affecting the body's "edges"—the organs that present contactable surfaces: mucous membranes, the skin, the asthmatic lung (Valas 110).[32] Given the absence of any mediating symbolization, the unleashing of the drives submits the body directly to their forces. Indeed, patients describe the actions of symptoms in the passive voice, conflating the fantasm and its bodily expression, dispossessing the subject of both agency and symbolization (Valas 97). A holophrastic unit, the psychosomatic lesion is not yet a symptom (see A. Stevens 60).[33]

It is borne of a tissue that, having lent itself to the *jouissance* of the Other, recenters itself in the lesion, a form of stabilization through which a radically illegible internal condition awaits its significance (Guir 12–13; Castanet 57–58). Like the hysterical symptom, the psychosomatic phenomenon takes advantage of a somatic effect, a basal level of physiological activity or a preexisting disturbance, transforming it into a kind of signifier, the way random noise becomes troped, elaborated, and amplified through investment (A. Stevens 52).

The psychosomatic phenomenon, however, does not quite signify. It is as if the hysterical symptom, already short-circuited on its way to the Other (as Monique David-Ménard explains), had taken a further detour, a purity of address not yet composable or decomposable into units of sense. The holophrastic expression, congealing the syntactic relation between signifiers, suspends the function of signification as such (A. Stevens 65). This consolidation of the interval and its materialization in the somatic phenomenon preempts the signifying break that was to have been introduced by the paternal metaphor (A. Stevens 65). The task of treating the psychosomatic phenomenon involves a kind of clipping of the holophrase into semantic units, an opening of the signifying relation (35).[34] Within the constrained circuit addressed to the Other and expressed in the lesion, the psychosomatic phenomenon is a type of appeal for signification that has been occluded in its passage, diverted from its mediation. This is a problematic situation for the clinician who would introduce an intermediate signifier in an interval that does not yet exist; the transference involved in the structure of the psychosomatic phenomenon bypasses the other person in the room. The illness addresses medicine itself (Guir), seeking a response from a discourse that is supposed to exclude the subject, and from technologies whose logic lies beyond the subject. Presumably, the patient presenting him- or herself for analytic treatment of psychosomatic disturbances somehow knows that there is more to the story.

Whereas the psychosomatic phenomenon is a subjective appropriation of somatic effects that hides meaning by submerging it within a concrete lesional expression in the real, there may be diseases whose course within the real precedes the subject's appropriation of them. To refer to a path in the real suggests the possible independence of the disease progression—its "natural history"—from human efforts to master it. Social constructionist interpretations of the epidemic have tended to take "the biological" for granted in order to analyze the discourses circulating about this point of certainty. This stabilization of "the biological" as a category is itself an ideology empowering radical social constructionist views, and consequently tends to grant the subject an unrealizable and misleading sense of liberation from the strictures imposed by the affliction. From a psychoanalytic perspective, the subject is easily distracted by an imaginary construct that can conceal its own falsehood. Such an imaginary construct fortifies itself against the incursion of the unexpected, discounting the vicissitudes of the disease's circulation within an epistemologically inaccessible domain. If we take the radical inaccessibility of this truth seriously, we must acknowledge the difficulty of eluding its absence. We must also consider the effect of that absence on the action we find it possible to pursue while waiting for clearer answers.

AIDS represents the activation of something real in the body, as well as the insistent impact of this real on the subject and its desire. It calls for the refashioning of the subject's libidinal investments relative to visible alterations of a body made vulnerable to lesioning. In the real, the body to some extent takes over the representation of the subject's *jouissance,* calling on the subjective moment to redirect its conception of the bodily ego. The disruptiveness of AIDS introduces new and painful circumstances into the life of the subject, a need for "adaptations," or more appropriately a "response," defined with respect to the patient's expectations of what it means to function well in daily life. The disease demands the patient's response, and treatments are assessed in terms of how effectively patients "respond" to medical modes of addressing the disease.[35]

5. What Remains to Be Said

As yet insufficient in its solutions, medicine addresses the speaking subject through the premise of the body. As Danièle Silvestre has argued, it is this subject—sheltered but also made vulnerable by the body—that a psychoanalytic perspective on disease makes legible ("Sur le statut"; see also Leguil and Silvestre). To state this is far from declaring a manifesto. Patients and clinicians already live and intimately know the subjectivity that psychoanalysis—as theory and practice—seeks to articulate more fully in its truth. For persons with AIDS, the inevitability of death is much too near, soon, and yet incalculable, determined by odds unknown. Psychoanalysis is the name that inserts itself at the place of this silence, as a way of giving voice to what remains quiet in the scientific aspect of AIDS treatment. To the physician-patient dyad, psychoanalysis adds the beckoning of a subject who no longer believes in personal agency—a subject not at peace with the anonymous and deathly place he finds secured in the symbolic, living under the weight of a disease that had been anybody's problem and is now irrevocably his own (Levine; L. Stevens and Muskin; Blechner).

These are actualities, subjective realities, included in the daily experience of AIDS. When the hope of medical curing is so blatantly suspended—suspended because it is not yet possible, but also is impossible to forget—the remedy invoked shifts from *curing* to *caring*,[36] a substituted vowel that leaves the intended accent unchanged. If there is a moment for this empathy, the active gift of caring for the patient's needs, there also is a place for its neutral counterpoint to emerge. This stance asks after the patient's singularity and would permit the person with AIDS to confront the final destiny that creates and destroys all meaning.[37] At the edge where death is in question, suspended between the hope of its deferral and the fantasy of its effacement, psychoanalysis, as theory or as practice, offers an intervention. It asserts that there is more knowledge than we believe, and yet that knowledge is not enough to treat the real.

My argument can be only brief here, knowing that there *is* a future of AIDS research—not because we desire it, but because what we desire requires it of us. If there can be hope, it is a hope that someday soon we will have the freedom to devote our attention to something other than AIDS. We continue to hope for a time when AIDS as we know it will no longer exist, and when the imperative to know it will have disappeared, passing into obscurity and freeing us to desire knowledge of other things. In the meantime, we keep going on with the persistent reformulation of this surface and its subject—depending, again, on what we think it is.

Notes

1. The paper is published here with few changes or updates, capturing a snapshot of the topic from the vantage of 1994, when the essay was completed. The treatment of AIDS and AIDS-related Kaposi's sarcoma has changed dramatically since then, in ways too numerous to recount here. Because the field is changing rapidly, persons with AIDS are advised to consult their physicians regarding the most current treatments for AIDS and Kaposi's sarcoma.

2. More frequently, we speak of *persons with AIDS* (PWAS). I have chosen here to call this person a "patient" to underscore the constitution of the subject as a subject of scientific medical discourse. In the very inability of medical science to en-

compass *persons*—persons with or without AIDS—we are reminded of a forgetting on which medicine is founded. If the unconscious is structured *like a language*, it may be that in medicine the subject, a person, is structured *like a patient*.

3. See Crimp's comments in Caruth and Keenan: "Because it seems that empathy only gets constructed in relation to sameness, it can't get constructed in relation to difference" (547). Also: "There might be some kind of psychic prohibition about identifying with the dead, because then it's really about confronting your own mortality" (555).

4. Montagu has discussed the erotics of the body surface. Gupta and Voorhees note that 40 percent of dermatologic disorders are accompanied by psychological morbidity, and that the psychological component "should be addressed and treated regardless of whether or not it is the cause or effect of the skin disorder" (92). They also caution that for this reason, physicians must remain aware of transference reactions in the treatment process.

5. Hall comments: "Psychological reactions in persons with HIV appear to be the consequence of adjustment before diagnosis and adaptations to changing physical status, such as the appearance of symptoms, and personal, social, and economic changes. Several clients of this author have framed their negative emotional reactions to the dermatological problems that are so common among HIV patients as social problems because they fear exposure of their HIV status to anyone looking at them" (191). See also Kaplan et al., who state, "One cannot underestimate the effect that visible cutaneous skin lesions have on a disease that is already extremely socially stigmatizing" (1370).

6. See accounts in Delaporte and Rosenberg. Frankenberg comments: "Epidemics are *social* sicknesses in which the whole social relationship between nature and culture is put in question for many individuals at the same time. . . . Epidemics are for these reasons accompanied by an attempt simultaneously to maintain and to redefine the boundaries of same and other and thereby to maintain and to replace modes of ritual and symbolic control. Sexually transmitted diseases that become epidemic, especially those with an expected fatal outcome within a relatively fixed period, represent for society as a whole and especially for its powerful the ultimate in loss of control over nature and the individual. They demand social explanation and redressive action over and above clinical cure and prevention" (80).

7. The use of the terms *neoplasm* and *cancer* has generated considerable debate about the character of KS. According to one textbook, "Neoplasia literally means 'new growth,' and the new growth is a 'neoplasm.' The term 'tumor' was originally applied to the swelling caused by inflammation. Neoplasms also may induce swellings, but by long precedent, the non-neoplastic usage of 'tumor' has passed into limbo; thus, the term is now equated with neoplasm. Oncology (Greek 'oncos' = tumor) is the study of tumors or neoplasms. *Cancer is the common term for all malignant tumors.* Although the ancient origins of this term are somewhat uncertain, it probably derives from the Latin for crab, 'cancer'—presumably because a cancer

'adheres to any part that it seizes upon in an obstinate manner like the crab'"
(Cotran et al. 241–42). Although it is clear that KS is a neoplasm, it remains unclear
whether it is a cancer, whether it is malignant—in the sense that cancers invade
and metastasize from one location to another. The multiple lesions of KS often
appear simultaneously and do not appear to originate one from the other. Unlike
most cancers, KS is rarely invasive of surrounding tissue, although it spreads. See
Isselbacher et al. 1604.

8. Krown ("Neoplasia") writes that "in some patients, particularly those with
respiratory symptoms from lung involvement, Kaposi's sarcoma may be directly
life-threatening and systemic cytoreductive treatment is clearly warranted. In the
absence of life-threatening organ involvement, however, many patients require
palliation of symptoms, particularly pain and edema. For others, the primary indication for treatment may be cosmetic or emotional. In the latter group, Kaposi's
sarcoma lesions on exposed areas may interfere with the ability to work and to
function effectively in society, and for many patients it is the sole visible sign to
themselves and the world of their diagnosis. However, as no treatment currently
is proved to affect the underlying cause of the tumor or to alter the natural history
of the underlying immunodeficiency, treatment for Kaposi's sarcoma may not be
indicated in patients with asymptomatic, indolent disease" (685).

9. Northfelt speculates that "morbidity and mortality attributable to AIDS-KS
may be increasing" due to increasing efficacy of treatment of infectious opportunistic manifestations, which are more treatable than KS (571).

10. Scott argues that "when the evidence offered is the evidence of 'experience,'
the claim for referentiality is further buttressed—what could be truer, after all,
than a subject's own account of what he or she has lived through? It is precisely
this kind of appeal to experience as uncontestable evidence and as an originary
point of explanation—as a foundation upon which analysis is based—that weak-
ens the critical thrust of histories of difference. By remaining within the epistemological frame of orthodox history, these studies lose the possibility of examining
those assumptions and practices that excluded considerations of difference in the
first place. They take as self-evident the identities of those whose experience is
being documented and thus naturalize their difference. They locate resistance outside its discursive construction, and reify agency as an inherent attribute of individuals, thus decontextualizing it. When experience is taken as the origin of
knowledge, the vision of the individual subject (the person who had the experience or the historian who recounts it) becomes the bedrock of evidence upon
which explanation is built. Questions about the constructed nature of experience,
about how subjects are constituted as different in the first place, about how one's
vision is structured—about language (or discourse) and history—are left aside. The
evidence of experience then becomes evidence for the fact of difference, rather
than a way of exploring how difference is established, how it operates, how and
in what ways it constitutes subjects who see and act in the world" (24–25).

11. It is important to remember that the experience of AIDS belongs not only

to the patient with AIDS, but to a subject of stigmatization and cultural discourses of AIDS, of which medicine is one among many.

12. In population-based studies, it is plausible to endorse a logic of mass effects whereby a *deceleration* of the spread of AIDS could eventually lead to its extinction. Within this logic, it makes sense for people to practice safe sex in order to lower the rate of HIV transmission, rather than simply to reduce their individual chances of acquiring AIDS. While this approach has its merits, it tends to view those already infected as reservoirs of disease.

13. The concept of "cofactors" has been extremely controversial in cultural discourses, because it implies that HIV is not indiscriminate but requires some other factor to trigger full-blown AIDS. In the early 1990s, this "other factor" was sometimes envisioned as specific to particular populations (for example, those who use illicit drugs, or homosexual men). Although it is crucial to understand the divergent manifestations of AIDS in different populations, the notion of "cofactors" sometimes contained overtones of blame or exceptional stigmatization above and beyond AIDS itself, hearkening back to the early days of AIDS when it was named GRIDS, for Gay-Related Immunodeficiency Syndrome.

14. Gottlieb relates the combination of serendipitous institutional structures, individual insights, and conversations that contributed to the reporting of what would later be described as AIDS-related KS at New York University.

15. See Berkow et al.; and Isselbacher et al. 1567. Many other diseases, including opportunistic infections, are diagnostic of AIDS even in the absence of HIV. Of these, the only other noninfectious manifestation besides KS is primary non-Hodgkin's lymphoma, which received less attention in popular accounts, perhaps because it was less easily recognizable in social interactions.

16. Coleman discusses the problem of determining how efficacy was to be measured in early clinical trials.

17. Interferon is a chemotherapeutic agent that enhances the body's own immune response to viruses and neoplasms.

18. Histological examination of biopsies involves fixing and staining a specimen with dyes and inspecting thin slices of it under a microscope, usually a light microscope. Although in the nineteenth century histology simply indicated a technique of inspecting tissues, it now entails the microscopic identification of specimens by structural features and the inference of function and pathology from the structure, and is considered the only definitive mode of diagnosis of neoplasms.

19. The object *a* operates as a kind of unidentified Freudian object from inner space—a shadow or recall cast upon the subject by the presence of another. By definition, it can attain positivity only by proxy.

20. Lacan (1966) argues that the subject of psychoanalysis *is* the subject of science, produced by the same division. Psychoanalysis is there to pick up the remainder of medical science; concretely, psychoanalysis was born as a result of the failure of neurological science to treat hysteria. In this and other ways, the emer-

gence and development of psychoanalysis has been co-extensive with the unfolding of modern science. In order to treat the malaise in civilization, the discourse of psychoanalysis is faced with the task of taking account of the science by
which some of this malaise is affected. Perhaps this explains Freud's initial efforts
to situate psychoanalysis within the scientific fields (1895), only to find later that
he could simply renew this effort tentatively, through speculation and metaphor
(see Freud, *Project*). The status of psychoanalysis as a science would remain antici-
patory, as yet to be realized. If psychoanalysis were a science, how would the parameters by which a science is defined be altered? A discussion of Lacan's elaboration of this problematic is beyond the scope of this essay.

21. Treichler writes: "If AIDS's dual life as both a material and linguistic entity
is important, the emphasis on *dual* is critical. Symbolic and social reconceptualiza-
tions of AIDS are necessary but not sufficient to address the massive social questions
AIDS raises. . . . But AIDS is to be a fundamental force of twentieth-century life, and
no barrier in the world can make us 'safe' from its complex material realities. . . .
Ultimately, we cannot distinguish self from not-self: for 'plague is life,' and each
of us has the plague within us; 'no one, no one on earth is free from it' (Ca-
mus). . . . We need to use what science gives us in ways that are selective, self-
conscious, and pragmatic ('as though' they were true). We need to understand that
AIDS is and will remain a provisional and deeply problematic signifier. Above all, we
need to resist, at all costs, the luxury of listening to thousands of language tapes playing in our heads, laden with prior discourse, that tell us with compelling certainty
and dizzying contradiction what AIDS 'really' means" ("AIDS, Homophobia" 69, 70).

22. Treichler elaborates a list of crucial questions: "What are the range of existing discourses in which HIV is mentioned? How is it articulated to the preexisting issues and codes in those discourses? How do discourses empower people
and people empower discourses? To what extent does a 'dominant' discourse on
HIV continue to be identifiable, under what circumstances and under whose aus-
pices did it emerge, and what kind of resources have been required to sustain its
authority? How are authoritative definitions constructed and deployed? Conversely, how are they challenged, evaded, disrupted, or redefined? How does discourse, in other words, work to articulate, codify, maintain, or challenge various
forms of authority, power, and control over material resources? And what difference does it make?" ("AIDS, HIV" 89). Patton comments: "Typically in medicine,
health educators and clinicians are viewed as the conduits for this knowledge
transferal, receiving scientific knowledge at one step removed and then paring it
down to pass on to the 'audience' or 'client.' Evaluation of whether knowledge
has been correctly conveyed proceeds by objectively testing the recipient and by
obtaining measures of the educator's ability to remain neutral, consistent, and
credible in the eyes of the recipient. This system of information conveyance is
thought to work best when the intermediaries add as little as possible, while at the
same time convincing the audience that they 'know what they are talking about.'
The clinician/health educator engages in a performance of scientific legitimation;

the success of that performance depends on the extent of her/his theatrical competence" (70). Rather than being a model involving the translation of discourses from one domain to another, a negotiation model would acknowledge that, in crossing from one community to another, a change must happen. The discourse undergoes a somewhat violent transformation that may render it more relevant to those who are able to hear it.

23. Treichler comments: "Scientific discourse is a form of shorthand in which facts, once admitted, need no longer retain the history of their fabrication. . . . The scientific culture that constructed the virus is now what most effectively disguises its existence as a cultural construction. Thus reified, HIV exhibits a number of predictable characteristics: It is referred to by a universally agreed upon signifier; conventional representations for it have been developed in journals, the media, three-dimensional glass models, and elsewhere; and its reality continues to be verified through ongoing laboratory and clinical operations . . ." ("AIDS, HIV" 86, 88).

24. Gagnon writes: "If the medical profession's gaze rarely rises above the level of the symptom in normal times, in HIV/AIDS times, it often focuses on the level of the cell, the molecule, or the gene" ("Epidemics" 35).

25. Carson and Green. See also Fox, Aiken, and Messikomer: "AIDS is unique among diseases in present-day societies because it is simultaneously acute, chronic, progressive, infectious, and fatal—and also affects young people. At our present stage of medical knowledge, there is no cure for the total collapse of the body's immune defenses that the AIDS virus causes. Despite recent improvements in pharmacologic therapies, for the great majority of symptoms that plague people with AIDS—ranging from the irritating to the excruciating—there are simply no substitutes for the hands-on, face-to-face forms of physical and interpersonal care that constitute the very core of nursing, and in which nurses, above all other health professionals, excel" (229).

26. Discussion of particular institutional differences in the literature is beyond the scope of this essay. Interestingly, the important work in different areas of AIDS research clusters about particular institutions with interests in differing aspects of the disease.

27. Daniel comments: "To determine who is living with AIDS today is a problem that cannot be solved in the laboratory. No blood test can determine who is living with AIDS. It can detect antibodies or viruses in the bloodstream, but not the established antibody of solidarity and its varieties—and of its contraries—in the stream of life today. HIV is following its biological course. Another complex of virulences (entering into the game of the usual metaphors of the AIDS age, we could simply call them ideological viruses) has spread through the social structure of AIDS, developing it into a three-dimensional photograph of contemporary civilization. Thus, it is no metaphor to assert that, on the planetary scale, humankind is seropositive. It is a historical and political axiom that merits an extensive explanation" (547).

28. See Ragsdale, Kotarba, and Morrow. The authors describe several "management styles" they have found among their patients: the "loner," the "activist" who

perceives the disease as largely a social and political phenomenon, the "victim," the "time-keeper" who measures his day according to a schedule of routine events, the "mystic," and the "medic." Of these, the latter style is the response most pertinent to the present discussion of the subject constituted by medical discourse: "The medic manages life by depending overwhelmingly on medical meanings for interpreting AIDS and related events. Medics typically refer to AIDS as *their* condition and *their* disease. They are frequently preoccupied with gathering as much information as possible on advances in surgical and medical treatments, physicians' reputations, sources of medications and so forth. Over time medics become virtual experts on HIV disease, so that they can converse intelligently with staff on the staff's linguistic terms. They read everything they can get their hands on and attend numerous seminars and lectures" (263). For the "medic," empowerment takes place when, as a subject, he is able to appropriate and speak the scientific language that would otherwise objectify his perspective.

29. Viney and Bousfield write: "In this narrative, the events which are interrelated are largely unspecified. AIDS becomes an 'it' to be coped with. 'It' becomes an influence or power in its own right. 'It' is viewed in this story as a force. Sometimes this is a physical force capable of achieving change to the physical being of the narrator. AIDS, as a physical force, is also capable of invoking other physical forces with this effect, such as medical treatments. Yet it can be a psychological force, with the greatest power of AIDS as being able to act on the feelings and thoughts of the story-tellers, in ways beyond their control. AIDS can also be an economic force, through its undermining of people's ability to make an appropriate living and increasing their financial dependence on others" (763).

30. Haraway notes: "The hierarchical body of old has given way to a network-body of truly amazing complexity and specificity. The immune system is everywhere and nowhere. Its specificities are indefinite if not infinite, and they arise randomly—yet these extraordinary variations are the critical means of maintaining individual bodily coherence" (385).

31. Castanet defines the distinction in terms of functional, readily reversible somatization and lesional expression. Nonreversible, or lesional, expression is a product of a subjective structure in which there is "no transition between imaginary and symbolic" (see A. Stevens esp. 55–59). As a mode of expression, the PSP short-circuits the signifier as such and engraves the message in the material of the body tissue. This leads to the supposition that reversibility requires a fictional space in which meaning can be constituted as a function of the signifier.

32. An interesting exception to the surface-directed character of psychosomatic expression is psychogenic hypertension; see Lacan, Lévy, and Danon-Boileau. If lesions of the surface express the subject's sense through localization, the pathology of high blood pressure resides in the diffusion of sense throughout the circulatory system, almost invisibly and without location.

33. See A. Stevens; and Lacan, *Seminar 1:* "There are phrases which cannot be broken down, and which have to be related to a situation taken in its entirety—

these are holophrases. . . . In what situation is the holophrase spoken? . . . a state of inter-gaze where each expects the other to decide on something which has to be done by the two, which is between the two, but which neither of them wishes to enter into. And, by the same token, you see clearly that the holophrase is not an intermediary step between a primitive assumption of the situation as a whole, which would be the register of animal action, and symbolisation. It is not some vague sort of original gluing together of the situation into a verbal mode. On the contrary, what is involved is something in which what pertains to the register of the symbolic composition is defined at the limit, at the periphery" (225–26).

34. Strictly speaking, foreclosure *of the paternal metaphor* is irreversible—it is impossible to reintroduce what never was. In the treatment of psychosomatic phenomena, we must posit a (re)introduction of the *signifying interval,* or what may be referred to as an alteration in the foreclosure *of the subject* whether as a subject of language or a subject of *jouissance.* There we could consider the *time* of foreclosure of this subject, a contraction and expansion that varies in temporal duration and sequence.

35. "Response," in medical terms, is rarely conceptualized linguistically or with reference to a subject of signification. The units of sense are defined by various systems of symbolization organized around different measurements of the desired "response." This raises the question of how the implicit addressee is constituted as a subject. See Krown et al., "Kaposi's Sarcoma."

36. Carson and Green write: "In a health care system focused on cure, the ultimate death of the PWA is a constant reminder that 'we don't have all the answers.'" And they continue: "When curing is not possible and physical ministrations prove inadequate, care providers must shift their priority to caring. Such a shift requires a transformation of thinking for many, because the tools are no longer pharmacological preparations and miracles of medical technology but rather the use of self to communicate acceptance of the sufferer, provision of emotional support through the dying process, education about the disease and its course, exploration of ways to improve quality if not duration of life, and existential support as the sufferer struggles to find meaning and purpose in his or her life" (210). See also Fox, Aiken, and Messikomer. And Ragsdale, Kotarba, and Morrow, who comment: "Quality of life should be viewed more as an accomplishment than as a variable. By accomplishment, we mean that quality of life results from the interaction among all members of the team during all phases of the health care encounter. Yet, the overall effectiveness of this process can only be assessed by the patient. . . . *Quality of life should be viewed as the relative effectiveness of a patient's chosen or ascribed management style in solving the practical problems associated with being 'seriously sick'"* (260).

37. Blechner articulates this very clearly: "While AIDS patients often need extraordinary care-giving, there is a good case to be made for the psychoanalyst maintaining his therapeutically-neutral position, while other care-givers meet the other needs of the patient. This situation allows the patient to bring his most

painful and destructive fantasies and emotions to the analysis. The analytic sessions can then function as a kind of crucible for these unmentionables, which allow the patient to carry on productively outside the sessions. If the patient actually needs the analyst for care-giving outside the sessions, this crucial function of the psychoanalyst is compromised" (72–73).

References

Anzieu, Didier. *The Skin Ego. A Psychoanalytic Approach to the Self.* Trans. Chris Turner. New Haven: Yale UP, 1989.

Berger, T. G., M. L. Obuch, and R. H. Goldschmidt. "Dermatologic Manifestations of HIV Infection." *American Family Physician* 41 (1990): 1729–42.

Berkow, Robert, et al., eds. *The Merck Manual of Diagnosis and Therapy.* 16th ed. Rahway, NJ: Merck Research Laboratories, 1992.

Blechner, Mark J. "Psychoanalysis and HIV Disease." *Contemporary Psychoanalysis* 29 (1993): 61–80.

Bosk, Charles L., and Joel E. Frader. "AIDS and Its Impact on Medical Work: The Culture and Politics of the Shop Floor." *The Milbank Quarterly* 68 (1990): 257–79.

Boudreaux, Alison A., et al. "Intralesional Vinblastine for Cutaneous Kaposi's Sarcoma Associated with Acquired Immunodeficiency Syndrome." *Journal of the American Academy of Dermatology* 8 (1993): 61–65.

Canguilhem, Georges. "Bacteriology and the End of Nineteenth-Century Medical Theory." *Ideology and Rationality in the History of the Life Sciences.* Trans. Arthur Goldhammer. Cambridge: MIT P, 1990. 51–77.

Carson, Verna Benner, and Harry Green. "Spiritual Well-Being: A Predictor of Hardiness in Patients with Acquired Immunodeficiency Syndrome." *Journal of Professional Nursing* 8 (1992): 209–20.

Carter, K. Codell. "The Koch-Pasteur Dispute on Establishing the Cause of Anthrax." *Bulletin of the History of Medicine* 62 (1988): 42–57.

Caruth, Cathy, and Thomas Keenan. "'The AIDS Crisis Is Not Over': A Conversation with Gregg Bordowitz, Douglas Crimp, and Laura Pinsky." *American Imago* 48 (1991): 539–56.

Castanet, Didier. "Corps, symptôme et jouissance dans la problématique psychosomatique." In GREPS 51–58.

Coleman, William. "Experimental Physiology and Statistical Inference: The Therapeutic Trial in Nineteenth-Century Germany." In *The Probabilistic Revolution.* Vol. 2: *Ideas in the Sciences.* Ed. Lorenz Krüger, Gerd Gigerenzer, and Mary S. Morgan. Cambridge: MIT P, 1987. 201–26.

Cotran, Ramzi S., Vinay Kumar, Stanley L. Robbins, and Frederick J. Schoen. *Robbins Pathologic Basis of Disease.* 5th ed. Philadelphia: W. B. Saunders, 1994.

Crissey, John Thorne, and Lawrence Charles Parish. *The Dermatology and Syphilology of the Nineteenth Century.* New York: Praeger, 1981.

Dagognet, François. *Méthodes et doctrine dans l'oeuvre de Pasteur.* Paris: Presses Universitaires de France, 1967.

——. *Pasteur sans la légende.* Le Plessis-Robinson: Synthelabo, 1994.

Daniel, Herbert. "We Are All People Living with AIDS: Myths and Realities of AIDS in Brazil." *International Journal of Health Services* 21.3 (1991): 539–51.

David-Ménard, Monique. *Hysteria from Freud to Lacan: Body and Language in Psychoanalysis.* 1983. Trans. Catherine Porter. Ithaca: Cornell UP, 1989.

Dean, Tim. "The Psychoanalysis of AIDS." *October* 63 (1993): 83–116.

Delaporte, François. *Disease and Civilization: The Cholera in Paris, 1832.* Trans. Arthur Goldhammer. Cambridge: MIT P, 1986.

Deleuze, Gilles. "The Schizophrenic and Language: Surface and Depth in Lewis Carroll and Antonin Artaud." In *Textual Strategies: Perspectives in Post-Structuralist Criticism.* Ed. Josué V. Harari. Ithaca: Cornell UP, 1979. 277–95.

Duvic, Madeleine. "HIV and Skin Disease: The Molecular Biology of the Human Immunodeficiency Virus." *American Journal of Medical Science* 304 (1992): 180–87.

Epstein, J. B., and S. Silverman Jr. "Head and Neck Malignancies Associated with HIV Infection." *Oral Surgery, Oral Medicine, and Oral Pathology* 73 (1992): 193–200.

Fee, Elizabeth, and Daniel M. Fox. *AIDS: The Burdens of History.* Berkeley: U of California P, 1988.

Ficarra, G., A. M. Berson, S. Silverman Jr., J. M. Quivey et al. "Kaposi's Sarcoma of the Oral Cavity: A Study of 134 Patients with a Review of the Pathogenesis, Epidemiology, Clinical Aspects, and Treatment." *Oral Surgery, Oral Medicine, and Oral Pathology* 66 (1988): 543–50.

Foucault, Michel. *The Birth of the Clinic: An Archaeology of Medical Perception.* 1963. Trans. A. M. Sheridan Smith. New York: Pantheon, 1973.

Fox, Renée C., Linda H. Aiken, and Carla M. Messikomer. "The Culture of Caring: AIDS and the Nursing Profession." *The Milbank Quarterly* 68 (1990): 226–55.

Frankenberg, Ronald. "The Other Who Is also the Same: The Relevance of Epidemics in Space and Time for Prevention of HIV Infection." *International Journal of Health Services* 22 (1992): 73–88.

Freud, Sigmund. *Beyond the Pleasure Principle.* 1920. *Standard* 18:1–64.

——. *Project for a Scientific Psychology.* 1950 (1895). *Standard* 1:283–397.

——. *The Standard Edition of the Complete Psychological Works of Sigmund Freud.* Ed. and trans. James Strachey. 24 vols. London: Hogarth, 1953–74.

Gagnon, John H. "Epidemics and Researchers: AIDS and the Practice of Social Studies." In Herdt and Lindenbaum 27–40.

Gottlieb, Geoffrey J. "Kaposi's Sarcoma in AIDS: The Early Experience at New York University." In *Kaposi's Sarcoma: A Text and Atlas.* Ed. Geoffrey J. Gottlieb and A. Bernard Ackerman. Philadelphia: Lea and Febiger, 1988. 173–77.

GREPS, ed. *Existe-il un sujet psychosomatique? Analytica* Paris: Navarin, 1989.

Grmek, Mirko. *History of AIDS: Emergence and Origin of a Modern Pandemic.* Trans. Russell C. Maulitz and Jacalyn Duffin. Princeton: Princeton UP, 1990.

Groopman, Jerome E. "Biology and Therapy of Epidemic Kaposi's Sarcoma." *Cancer* 59 (1987): 633–37.

Guir, Jean. "Modalités de l'acte analytique dans la cure de sujets souffrant de phé-
nomènes psychosomatiques." In GREPS 11–20.

Gupta, Madhulika A., and John J. Voorhees. "Psychosomatic Dermatology: Is It
Relevant?" *Archives of Dermatology* 126 (1990): 90–93.

Hall, Beverly A. "Overcoming Stigmatization: Social and Personal Implications of
the Human Immunodeficiency Virus Diagnosis." *Archives of Psychiatric Nursing*
6 (1992): 189–94.

Haraway, Donna. "The Biopolitics of Postmodern Bodies: Determinations of Self
in Immune System Discourse." *Knowledge, Power, and Practice: The Anthropology
of Medicine and Everyday Life*. Ed. Shirley Lindenbaum and Margaret Lock. Berkeley: U of California P, 1993. 364–410.

Herdt, Gilbert, and Shirley Lindenbaum, eds. *The Time of AIDS: Social Analysis, Theory, and Method*. Newbury Park, CA: Sage, 1992.

Isselbacher, Kurt J., et al. *Harrisons' Principles of Internal Medicine*. 13th ed. New
York: McGraw-Hill, 1994.

Kaplan, L. D., C. B. Wofsy, and P. A. Volberding. "Treatment of Patients with Acquired Immunodeficiency Syndrome and Associated Manifestations." *JAMA* 257
(1987): 1367–74.

Krim, Mathilde. "AIDS: The Challenge to Science and Medicine." *AIDS: The Emerging
Ethical Dilemmas, Hastings Center Report* special supplement, 15.4 (August
1985): 2–7.

Krown, Susan E. "Neoplasia in AIDS." *Bulletin of the New York Academy of Medicine*
63.7 (1987): 679–91.

Krown, Susan E., et al. "Kaposi's Sarcoma and the Acquired Immune Deficiency
Syndrome: Treatment with Recombinant Interferon Alpha and Analysis of
Prognostic Factors." *Cancer* 57 (1986): 1662–65.

Krown, Susan E., Patricia L. Myskowski, and Josephine Paredes. "Medical Management of AIDS Patients: Kaposi's Sarcoma." *Medical Clinics of North America* 76
(1992): 235–52.

LaCamera, D. J., H. Masur, and D. K. Henderson. "Symposium on Infections in
the Compromised Host: The Acquired Immunodeficiency Syndrome." *Nursing
Clinics of North America* 20 (1985): 241–56.

Lacan, Jacques. "La science et la vérité." *Écrits*. Paris: Seuil, 1966. 855–77.

———. "Science and Truth." Trans. Bruce Fink. *Newsletter of the Freudian Field* 3
(1989): 4–29.

———. *The Seminar of Jacques Lacan, Book 1: Freud's Papers on Technique, 1953–1954*.
Ed. Jacques-Alain Miller. Trans. John Forrester. Cambridge: Cambridge UP,
1988.

Lacan, Jacques, R. Lévy, and H. Danon-Boileau. "Considérations psychosomatiques
sur l'hypertension artérielle." *Ornicar?* 43 (1987): 5–16.

Latour, Bruno. *The Pasteurization of France*. Trans. Alan Sheridan and John Law.
Cambridge: Harvard UP, 1988.

Leguil, François, and Danièle Silvestre. "Psychanalystes confronté au SIDA." *Ornicar?* 45 (1988): 5–13.

Leibowitch, Jacques. *A Strange Virus of Unknown Origin*. New York: Ballantine, 1985.

Léonard, J. "Comment peut-on être pasteurien?" In Salomon-Bayet 143–79.

Levine, Robert J. "AIDS and the Physician-Patient Relationship." In *AIDS and Ethics*. Ed. Frederic G. Reamer. New York: Columbia UP, 1991. 188–214.

Matthews, J. Rosser. *Quantification and the Quest for Medical Certainty*. Princeton: Princeton UP, 1995.

Montagu, Ashley. *Touching: The Human Significance of the Skin*. New York: Harper and Row, 1971.

Muggia, Franco M., and Matthew Lonberg. "Kaposi's Sarcoma and AIDS." *Medical Clinics of North America* 70 (1986): 139–54.

Niedt, G. William, et al. "Histologic Predictors of Survival in Acquired Immunodeficiency Syndrome-Associated Kaposi's Sarcoma." *Human Pathology* 23 (1992): 1419–26.

Northfelt, Donald N. "Treatment of Kaposi's Sarcoma: Current Guidelines and Future Perspectives." *Drugs* 48 (1994): 569–82.

Patton, Cindy. "What 'Science' Knows about AIDS: Formations of AIDS Knowledges." *Inventing AIDS*. New York: Routledge, 1990. 51–75.

Quétel, Claude. *History of Syphilis*. Trans. Judith Braddock and Brian Pike. Baltimore: Johns Hopkins UP, 1990.

Ragsdale, Diane, Joseph A. Kotarba, and James R. Morrow Jr. "Quality of Life of Hospitalized Persons with AIDS." *IMAGE: Journal of Nursing Scholarship* 24 (1992): 259–65.

Rosenberg, Charles. *The Cholera Years: The United States in 1832, 1849, 1866*. Chicago: U of Chicago P, 1962.

Safai, Bijan, et al. "Interferon in the Treatment of AIDS-Associated Kaposi's Sarcoma: The American Experience." *Journal of Investigative Dermatology* 95 (1990): 166S–69S.

———. "The Natural History of Kaposi's Sarcoma in the Acquired Immunodeficiency Syndrome." *Annals of Internal Medicine* 103 (1985): 744–50.

Salomon-Bayet, Claire, ed. *Pasteur et la révolution pastorienne*. Paris: Payot, 1986.

Scott, Joan W. "'Experience.'" In *Feminists Theorize the Political*. Ed. Judith Butler and Joan W. Scott. New York: Routledge, 1992. 22–40.

Shilts, Randy. *And the Band Played On: Politics, People, and the AIDS Epidemic*. New York: St. Martin's, 1987.

Silvestre, Danièle. "Sur le statut du corps dans la psychanalyse." *Ornicar?* 41 (1987): 67–70.

Smith, Kathleen J., et al. "Iontophoresis of Vinblastine into Normal Skin for Treatment of Kaposi's Sarcoma in Human Immunodeficiency Virus-Positive Patients." *Archives of Dermatology* 128 (1992): 1365–70.

Stevens, Alexandre. "L'holophrase entre le psychose et le psychosomatique." *Ornicar?* 42 (1987): 45–79.

Stevens, L., and P. Muskin. "Techniques for Reversing the Failure of Empathy towards AIDS Patients." *Journal of the American Academy of Psychoanalysis* 15 (1987): 539–51.

Tappero, Jordan W., Marcus A. Conant, Steven F. Wolfe, and Timothy G. Berger. "Kaposi's Sarcoma: Epidemiology, Pathogenesis, Histology, Clinical Spectrum, Staging Criteria, and Therapy." *Journal of the American Academy of Dermatology* 28 (1993): 371–95.

Treichler, Paula A. "AIDS, Homophobia, and Biomedical Discourse: An Epidemic of Signification." *October* 43 (1987): 31–70.

———. "AIDS, HIV, and the Cultural Construction of Reality." In Herdt and Lindenbaum 65–98.

Vadhan-Raj, Saroj, et al. "Immunological Variables as Predictors of Prognosis in Patients with Kaposi's Sarcoma and AIDS." *Cancer Research* 46 (1986): 417–25.

Valas, Patrick. "Horizons de la psychosomatique." In *Le phénomène psychosomatique et la psychanalyse.* Ed. GREPS. Paris: Navarin, 1986. 87–112.

Viney, Linda L., and Lynne Bousfield. "Narrative Analysis: A Method of Psychosocial Research for AIDS-Affected People." *Social Science and Medicine* 32 (1991): 757–65.

Zalla, Mark J., W. P. Daniel Su, and Anthony F. Fransway. "Dermatologic Manifestations of Human Immunodeficiency Virus Infection." *Mayo Clinic Proceedings* 67 (1992): 1089–1105.

Žižek, Slavoj. *The Sublime Object of Ideology.* New York: Verso, 1989.

5

QUEER

RELATIONS

18

GENITAL CHASTITY

Leo Bersani

. . . .

Nothing, it would seem, is more difficult than to conceive, to elaborate, and to put into practice "new ways of being together." Foucault used this expression to define what he thought of as our most urgent ethical project, one in which gays, according to him, were destined to play a privileged role. Indeed, in an interview published in 1981 in the French magazine *Gai Pied,* he went so far as to argue—against what we might call psychoanalytic common sense—that what disturbs people about homosexuality is not "the sexual act itself," but rather "the homosexual mode of life," which Foucault associated with "the formation of new alliances and the tying together of unforeseen lines of force." Such alliances, such lines of force would somehow escape "the two ready made formulas"— both perfectly consistent with the normalizing coercions of the dominant culture—"of the pure sexual encounter and the lovers' fusion of identities." But we should remember that the "new ways of being together"— which, apparently, neither genital nor psychic intimacy would help us to imagine—are, for the most part, as yet "unforeseen." Foucault seems to have thought of cultural subversion and renewal as inherent in homosexuality, but, to a large extent, it is also something not yet realized. Homosexuality "is not a form of desire but something desirable. Therefore," he went on, "we have to work at becoming homosexuals." In so doing, we might, curiously and impressively, help to bring heterosexuals closer to what Foucault also called "a manner of being that is still improbable." "Homosexuality is a historic occasion to reopen affective and relational virtualities not so much through the intrinsic qualities of the homosexual but because the 'slant wise' position of the latter, as it were, the diagonal lines he can lay out in the social fabric allow these virtualities to come to light" ("Friendship" 136–38).

I want to suggest that in order to imagine "a mode of life" that would, as Foucault put it, "yield a culture and an ethics" (138), we might momentarily bracket some of the work that has been done in recent years and respond as if we had just heard Foucault's challenge for the first time. Let's start again, which means taking a foundational approach to the question of relationality. I will hypothesize a genealogy of the relational, more specifically, a certain threshold of entry into the relational. I am of course not referring to a historically locatable moment, one at which each human subject—and not only human subjects—might have the option of *not* moving, of *not* connecting. Such beginnings are both inexistent— there was never any moment when we were not already in relation—and structurally necessary: It is perhaps only by positing them that we can make existent relations intelligible. Or, more exactly, it is only through the figuration of such beginnings that we can see the being of relations, a being that at once grounds and is obscured by the complicated contingency of all relations. This is the enabling assumption of much of Beckett's fiction—of *Company,* for example, in which a life that is nearly over remembers itself *essentially* by remembering (which is to say, by inventing) its relational origins. The Beckettian narrator goes back to a place where he never was as the only way to account for his being anywhere, for it was from "there" that he was summoned into relations, called up from the immobility of perfect self-adequation to be displaced within a language that, before meaning anything, operates as a directional motor, an agent of spatial dispersion.

Because the representation of the birth of relations requires a figure of nonrelationality, the danger inherent in any such representation is the erasure of figurality itself. Nothing is more haunting in the work of artists otherwise so different from one another as Turner and Rothko than their reduction of the canvas to the wholly undifferentiated origins of the canvas's work. In the nearly unpunctuated whiteness of Turner's late paintings, in the blankets of dark sameness on the panels of the Rothko Chapel in Houston, we come as close as we can to suffering the truly rare privilege of seeing nothing—as if the lines of movement in space that art represents could, as it were, be ontologically illuminated only as they almost disappear within a representation of their emergence from nothing. If art is the principal site/sight (both place and view) of being as emergence into connectedness, then the metaphysical dimensions of the aesthetic—which may also be its aesthetically distinguishing dimension—is an erosion of aesthetic form. Origination is designated by figures of its perhaps not taking place; the coming-to-be of relationality, which is our birth into being, can only be retroactively enacted, and it is enacted largely as a rubbing out of formal relations. Perhaps traditional associations of art with form-giving or form-revealing activities are at least partly a denial of such formal disappearance in art. If art celebrates an originating extensibility of all objects and creatures into space—and therefore our connectedness to the universe—it does so by also inscribing within connectedness the possibility of its not happening. Relationality is itself related to its own absence. Emphatically present forms designate nonaesthetic functions and registers of being. Brutally authoritative interventions in space—presences secure in their legitimation—violate the ecological ethic for which art trains us.

The notion of an immobility before relations is a heuristic device designed to help us see the invisible rhythms of appearance and disappearance in all being. There is a further question: Why extend at all? Why do objects and living beings even begin to move? Again, there is no beginning of movement; nonetheless, relational movement requires an account of a foundational motor—in the case of human subjects, a fundamental motivation for all movement. "Requires" in the sense that all particular motivations of all particular movements share a founding structure of desire, by which I mean a structure that accounts for the *will to be* in all things. Somewhat unexpectedly, psychoanalysis, which has presented itself as the most finely elaborated theory of desire in the history of human thought, will not be of much help here. It has elaborated extremely tendentious accounts of desire, accounts that make of the world we live in a place inherently alien to any subject's desire. Psychoanalysis has conceptualized desire as the mistaken reaction to a loss; it has been unable to think of desire as the confirmation of a community of being.

"At the very beginning, it seems," Freud writes in the 1915 essay "Instincts and Their Vicissitudes," "the external world, objects and what is hated are identical." Not only at the very beginning: "As an expression of the unpleasure evoked by objects," he goes on, hate "always remains in an intimate relation with the self-preservative instincts" (139).

Given the (perceived) fundamental hostility of the world to the self, the very possibility of object relations depends on a certain mode of appropriation of the object. That appropriating mode is identification, which plays a major role in the psychoanalytic theory of self-constitution. The different internal agencies described in *The Ego and the Id* are sediments of object relationships, the result of the subject's having composed its multiple identificatory acts into a psychically individuating design. The identificatory appropriation of the other is especially striking in the Freudian account of love, where, as Freud writes in *Group Psychology and the Analysis of the Ego,* the object often "serves as a substitute for some unattained ego ideal of our own. We love it on account of the perfections we have striven to reach for our own ego, and which we should now like to procure in this roundabout way as a means of satisfying our narcissism" (112–13). "Roundabout" indeed: In this account the external world would have to be invented if it didn't already exist in order for the subject to suppress it. We need it in order to love ourselves, to have the illusorily objectified self-confirmation of a mirror. Freud famously—or infamously—associated narcissistic love with women and, as he writes in the essay "On Narcissism," "people whose libidinal development has suffered some disturbance, such as perverts or homosexuals" (89). But those of us who belong to one—or more—of those unfortunate categories can perhaps take some solace from the fact that Freud saw object love in the most privileged, the most happily developed group—heterosexual men—as also motivated to some degree by a nostalgia for the narcissism they have presumably given up. With this view of the straight man yearning to be the self-contained, self-sufficient woman he loves, the turning away from the other inherent in the Freudian account of sexual love is nearly universalized, although it is a turning away identical to an intense concentration on the other. Because what the man must appropriate as his is the woman's exclusion of him, he can narcissistically suppress her only by an intense, mimetic attention to her self-absorption, her utterly private pleasure in her own image.

I have used the word *appropriate* several times. The relational mechanisms studied most thoroughly by psychoanalysis—identification, projection, introjection—could perhaps only have been theorized in a civilization that has privileged an appropriative relation of the self to the world, one that assumes a secure and fundamentally antagonistic distinction between subject and object. While psychoanalysis has certainly demystified the subject's disinterested pursuit of truth, it has had great difficulty positioning the subject in a nonantagonistic, nonappropriative relation to the world. Indeed, in dramatically desublimating the entire epistemological project in which knowledge is the key to power, to mastery of the real, Freud did not free us from that project; rather, he transformed it into a psychic fate. Psychoanalysis has psychoanalyzed the subject's need to master otherness, and in so doing, it has exposed that need as the inescapable consequence of the equally inescapable dysfunctionality in the human subject's efforts to negotiate the world's difference.

In the Lacanian Imaginary, difference is denied before there is even an ego to oppose itself to difference. The jubilation with which the infant, in the mirror stage, anticipates a unifying ego in the specular mirage of itself as a unified physical form becomes, in the reenactments of Imaginary relationality, the subject's paranoid suspicion that the other is deliberately withholding the subject's being. In his seminar on *Freud's Papers on Technique*, Lacan emphasizes both the distinction and the correlation between physical and psychological maturation. The subject's imaginary mastery over its own body in the mirror stage is also, Lacan writes, an anticipation of psychological mastery, one that "will leave its mark [*donner son style*] on every subsequent exercise of effective motor mastery" (*Seminar* 1:79). But much more than an effect on physical mastery is involved: Lacan goes on to say that the anticipated mastery of the mirror stage is "the original adventure through which man, for the first time, has the experience of seeing himself, of reflecting on himself and conceiving himself as other than he is—an essential dimension of the human, which entirely structures his fantasy life" (79). By giving such enormous importance (and in spite of the possibility, indeed the necessity, of other relational registers to which I'll return in a moment) to this originating self-(mis)recognition, Lacan suggests that the subject's relation to the world will always bear traces of (Lacan actually speaks of our entire fantasmatic life being structured by) an original self-identification taking place before there is a self, or more exactly a conscious ego, to be identified.

Psychoanalytic accounts of a dysfunctional relation between perception and self-constitution can't help but legitimize—in the sense of demonstrating their necessity—projects of mastery, since psychoanalysis grounds all such projects in a biologically determined history of self-apprehension. Indeed, it endows power, or the impulse to master, with a certain pathos, since mastery turns out always to bear the mark of that "original adventure" in which we celebrated our capacity for mastery (our bodily coordination and unity) by locating it where it was not. That pathetically misconceived celebration is bound to become a ferocious antagonism toward a world that prevents me from joining my own being. The repetition of an original anticipation of psychological mastery necessarily takes the form of a sense of loss, of theft. A happy expectation is, retroactively, transformed into a hateful resentment.

Interestingly, Laplanche's recently elaborated theory of the enigmatic signifier provides yet another psychoanalytic version of relationality as initiated by misapprehension, by a failure to relate. Laplanche's concept of the enigmatic signifier (see *Seduction*) refers to an original and unavoidable seduction of the child by the mother, a seduction inherent in the very nurturing of the child. The seduction is not intentional; simply by her care, the parent implants in the child the "unconscious and sexual significations" (*Seduction* 188) with which the adult world is infiltrated, and that are received in the form of an enigmatic signifier—that is, a message by which the child is seduced but that he or she cannot read, an enigmatic message that is perhaps inevitably interpreted as a secret. The result of this original seduction would be a tendency to structure all relations on the basis of an eroticizing mystification. If we feel not only, as Freud proposed, that others threaten the stability the ego must defend for its very survival, but also, more dangerously, that we can be seduced by such threats—in Laplanchean terms, "shattered" into an ego-shattering sexuality—then it is reasonable to confront others with paranoid mistrust. The enigmatic signifier becomes a knowledge they are at once willfully withholding from me and using in order to invade my being. But this invasive secret can, in the final analysis, only be *about me:* The enigmatic signifier seduces me because it "knows" me, because it contains that which in me can be seduced, the very formula of a desire of which I myself am ignorant. It is Proust who, with his usual psychoanalytic profundity, both anticipates Laplanche's notion and explicitly draws from it the conclusion I have just proposed. "As there is no knowledge, one might almost say that there is no jealousy, save of oneself" (*Captive* 392–93). The withheld secret Marcel anxiously pursues in others is the fantasy formula of his own desires—in short, the formula of that which sexualizes him.

Intersubjectivity in the psychoanalytic accounts I have just briefly outlined is a drama of property relations. The world dispossesses me of myself; it threatens or steals the being that is properly mine, that is my property. The Proustian—the Laplanchean, the Freudian—the Lacanian imaginary subject must master the world in order to repossess its self. The projective, introjective, and identificatory techniques first studied by Freud are strategies designed to suppress the otherness in which my sameness is hidden from my consciousness. To paraphrase an author who made of this war between subject and object a gloriously lurid psychic drama (I refer to Melanie Klein), I must impose my good objects on the world in order to prevent the world from destroying me with my bad objects.

These are the most persuasive voices in psychoanalysis, far more persuasive than those comparatively cheerful theorists of object relations who postulate an adaptive fit between subject and object by simply dismissing the powerful speculative arguments, from Freud to Lacan, for an irreducibly intractable hostility between subject and object as well as between the individual and civilization. Significantly, when the thinkers I've been discussing imagine an alternative to the misapprehensions and the antagonisms that make of human relationality a striking case of dysfunctional evolution, they tend to do so at the expense of consciousness. In my previous work, I have, following Laplanche, given great emphasis to that antinormative strain of thought in the *Three Essays on the Theory of Sexuality* in which Freud speaks of sexual pleasure as "a by-product . . . of a large number of processes that occur in the organism, as soon as they reach a certain degree of intensity, and most especially of any relatively powerful emotion, even though it is of a distressing nature" (233). On the basis of passages such as this one, Laplanche has formulated a theory of sexual excitement as an effect of *ébranlement*—perturbation or shattering—on the organism, an effect that momentarily undoes psychic organization. I have pushed this to the point of arguing, especially in *The Freudian Body*, that sexuality—at least in the mode in which it is constituted—could be thought of as a tautology for masochism (see *Freudian* 37–39). In other words, I have been proposing that we think of the sexual—more specifically, of *jouissance* in sexuality—as a defeat of power, a giving up, on the part of an otherwise hyperbolically self-affirming and phallocentrically constituted ego, of its projects of mastery. Thus the subject enters into a Bataille-like "communication" with otherness, one in which the individuating boundaries that separate subjects, and that subjects for the most part fiercely defend, are erased.

Bypassing Laplanche, in whom it would apparently have displeased them to find any of this, the French *École lacanienne* has recently shown great interest in what it judges to be the closeness of certain aspects of American gay and lesbian studies to Lacan's reflections on *jouissance* in the 1970s. The meeting point between these improbable intellectual allies would be *"la question du non-rapport sexuel,"* as it was recently defined in the review *L'unebévue*—that is, the sexual as an *absence of relations, a failure to connect.* Jean Allouch evokes Foucault describing *"le délire amoureux"* as a "*perte de soi*," an experience in which the individual "no longer knows who he is," lives his pleasure as a "perpetual self-forgetting." Allouch goes on to quote, with approval, my own gloss in "Is the Rectum a Grave?" on Freud's association of sexual excitement with a loss of psychic organization and coherence—a gloss in which I say that Freud's definition "removes the sexual from the intersubjective" (217). Allouch praises the Lacanian resonance of this comment and concludes with a definition of fucking as "a defeat of the subjective as such" ("Pour introduire" 58–59).

Much of this now seems to me a rather facile, even irresponsible celebration of "self-defeat." Masochism is not a viable alternative to mastery, either practically or theoretically. The defeat of the self belongs to the same relational system, the same relational imagination, as the self's exercise of power; it is merely the transgressive version of that exercise. Masochism consents to, indeed embraces, that theft of being that mastery would remedy by obliterating otherness through a fantasmatic invasion of difference. Perhaps the crucial move here—I'm tempted to say the crucial mistake here—is an interpretation of desire as lack. The world perceived as inherently hostile to the self (Freud), the world as withholding the "secret" of the subject's sexual being (Laplanche on the enigmatic signifier), the world as containing the subject's future completion as a coordinated form (Lacan's relationally initiating mirror stage): In all these cases the subject is either in danger of being stolen or has already suffered a loss of self. Fantasmatic—and, if possible, real—mastery places the subject in the world on the subject's own terms; no longer an agent of loss, the world is now the coerced repairer of loss. Desire is polarized between lack and possession; the *activity* of desire is what moves the subject from the one to the other. Relationality is grounded in antagonism and misapprehension, which means that to meet the world is always to see the world as a place where I am not, or, if I am there, it is as alienated and/or unrecognizable being.

Finally, misapprehension remains a fundamental relational mode even in what is probably the most interesting attempt, within psychoanalytic history, to conceptualize a productive relation of the subject to the world. I refer to Lacan's theory of desire, a theory that depends, in its most psychoanalytically original move, on a depsychologizing of desire and an emphasis on what might be called desire's ontological dignity. Desire is grounded in loss—not the loss of any particular object, but rather of being itself. The sacrifice of being is the price we pay when we enter language, when we become creatures who have meaning. Wholly inexpressible, resistant to any kind of symbolization, being retroactively comes to signify lost presence and fullness. Desire is the doomed but limitlessly rich attempt to recover that fullness through objects that are ontologically incommensurable with it. There is no foundational object of desire, only what Tim Dean has called "the perpetual illusion of a secret located beyond language, and it is this enigma that elicits desire" (*Beyond* 250). In her most recent work, Kaja Silverman appeals to this Lacanian theory in order to put forth a brilliant argument about what she calls our "passion for symbolization" (*World* 62)—the way in which we allow other creatures and things to incarnate the originary nonobject of desire. The very lack of that originary object propels us toward the world and toward the future; lack and loss are the bases for our passionate interest in things, for desire's multiple relations with the world's appearances. Thus lack, in this account, is, intriguingly, the precondition for metonymic excess— for all our productively mistaken desires for real objects and real people. Logically, there is no limit to this productivity, since the objects we pursue, while they trace the design of our individual desiring histories, are meant to recover that which preexists all object-choices, to "repair" not the anecdotal, anatomical castration of oedipal anxieties, but, much more impressively, the ontological castration through which we presumably entered the human community of signification. No object could ever be an adequate substitute for an object-less being that never was. The ultimate foundation of desire's productivity in this account is the pursuit of, and nostalgia for, nothingness.

· · · · · ·

Is lack necessary to desire? Perhaps the founding text of desire as lack in the Western tradition is Plato's *Symposium*. It will therefore be all the more astonishing to see this extraordinary Platonic dialogue dismiss what appears to be its most unambiguously formulated argument. At a formal drinking party held in honor of the tragedian Agathon's first dramatic triumph, the guests agree to give speeches in praise of love. Socrates, the last to speak, is preceded by Agathon, who, complaining that those who preceded *him* had "congratulated human beings on the good things that come to them from the god" of love rather than praising him "first for what he is" (477), had eloquently enumerated Eros' qualities. Eros is beautiful, young, delicate, brave, temperate, just, and wise. Immediately after the enthusiastic applause with which the handsome tragedian's praise of love is received, Socrates, claiming—to the disbelief of the others—that he can only be tongue-tied "after a speech delivered with such beauty and variety," proceeds to demolish what Agathon has said—and, implicitly, to criticize the speeches given by all the others—for praising Eros, attributing to him "the grandest and most beautiful qualities," rather than telling the truth about him. The truth, as Socrates swiftly demonstrates in a characteristically coercive exchange with the docile Agathon, is that we desire only that which we lack: ". . . anyone . . . who has a desire desires what is not at hand and not present, what he does not have, and what he is not, and that of which he is in need; for such are the objects of desire and love." Thus, if love is the desire of "that of which it is the love," and if, as the others have agreed, love pursues, or makes men pursue, the beautiful and the good, then love itself must be without those qualities. Love can't *be* beautiful and good if it *desires* beautiful and good things—a conclusion Agathon finds so irresistible that he readily admits not knowing what he was talking about in his speech (481–84).

Desire is, then, a lack of being. The apparent importance of this position in the *Symposium* is underlined by the fact that it is the only philosophical claim made directly by Socrates; the rest of his contribution to this exercise in intellectual sociability is mediated through his memory of the lessons in love once given to him by the wise woman Diotima. Furthermore, dissatisfied with Agathon merely acknowledging that it "wouldn't be likely" for someone to "actually have what he desires and loves" at the very time of desiring and loving something, Socrates insists that they agree on the necessity of the inherence of lack in desire: "I can't tell you, Agathon, how strongly it strikes me that this is necessary" (482). Finally, in order to forestall one possible criticism of his argument, Socrates himself brings up the potential counterexamples of strong men who wish to be strong, tall men who wish to be tall—only to point out that what they mean is that they want to possess these things in time to come. Unable to desire things they already have, they are expressing their desire for the future health, the future tallness they now lack.

And yet even in the couple of pages in which the argument for desire as lack or need is so forcefully made, Socrates' coercive move is preceded by a logical confusion that makes us glimpse the possibility of love, or desire, as including within itself its object. Socrates begins his correction of Agathon by asking him if he agrees—and of course he will—that love must be a love of something rather than of nothing. He explains his question by saying that it's as if he were asking whether a father is the father *of* something or not—or whether a mother or a brother are mother and brother *of* something. But are these familial relations really analogous to the relation of desire to that which it lacks? If lack is intrinsic to desire, the object of desire must be absent from the activity of desiring. "Father," on the other hand, specifies a relation; not only is a father the father *of* something (as desire is the desire *of* something), but the word itself includes, and therefore largely defines, the other relational term. The analogy Socrates proposes in order to elucidate his notion of desire as lack actually raises the possibility of a desire the other term of which would be an extension, another version, of that which constitutes the very activity of desiring. "Father" is not a relation of need to an object it might seek to possess; it rather evokes what we might call inaccurate replications, or a modified sameness, of itself. That which is external to it is included in that which identifies, or individuates it. Thus by its very enunciation "father" moves toward "child," and this logical model of relationality not initiated by lacks or gaps of being might start us moving toward relationality acknowledged as an ontological necessity antecedent to lack. Presence is always relational; desire would be the affective recognition of something like our debt to all those forms of being that relationally define and activate our being. Desire mobilizes correspondences of being.

Much more decisively than the short passage I've been discussing, the entire text of the *Symposium* refutes the ostensibly privileged idea of love or desire as lack. If, on the one hand, we are tempted to give Socrates an authority none of the other figures in the dialogue enjoys, it is, on the other hand, difficult to locate authority in Plato's *Symposium*. To begin with, can we even be sure that this is an authoritative account of what took place, of what was said, at that celebrated banquet? The time of the narrative is several years after the event, which has, it seems, acquired a certain notoriety among Athenians interested in hearing about Socrates. The dialogue begins with a singularly convoluted account of how Apollodorus, who will report on the events in question, learned about them himself. To an unnamed acquaintance who asks him about that dinner long ago, Apollodorus responds that another friend—Glaucon—had just a few days before come to him with the same request. Knowing that Apollodorus has made it his job "to know exactly what [Socrates] says and does each day," Glaucon, who had heard a garbled version of the banquet from a man who had himself learned about it from Phoenix, mistakenly thought that Apollodorus—who in fact has been Socrates' companion only for the past three years—had himself been at the dinner. Apollodorus rather gruffly sets Glaucon straight and tells him that he himself learned about it from "the very same man who told Phoenix, a fellow called Aristodemus," who went to the party with Socrates. So Apollodorus, who had checked "part of" Aristodemus' story with Socrates ("who

agreed with his account"), told it to Glaucon and is now about to tell it
again to the "rich businessman" (458–59) whose question originally led
not to Apollodorus giving straightaway the account of things he had gotten from the banquet guest Aristodemus, but rather to that curious detour
that goes from Glaucon to the man with the garbled version to Phoenix,
who may or may not have made things garbled, back to Aristodemus.
The latter, however, according to Apollodorus, "couldn't remember exactly what everyone said," and, Apollodorus adds, "I myself don't remember everything he told me. But I'll tell you," he says to his friend, adding
two more qualifications, "I'll tell you what he remembered best, and what
I consider the most important points" (463).

So we may have a highly selective *and* approximate account of the
speeches given during the banquet. Remember also that the *Symposium*'s
most celebrated and presumably authoritative speech is actually Socrates'
report of what Diotima told him in a series of meetings that Socrates
himself may not remember with total accuracy but that he will report
on, he tells his fellow guests, "as best I can on my own" (484). Indirect
transmission, distance from the event, scattered sources, the perhaps
doubtful credibility of the sources: All this implicitly encourages us not
to lean too heavily on any one argument and perhaps even to reconsider
what we might mean by philosophical seriousness. This is not to put into
question Plato's intellectual commitment to the theory of Forms outlined
by Diotima, the progression from love of beautiful bodies to the love of
absolute Beauty. I do mean to suggest, however, that in the *Symposium*
that theory is less important than the textual relationality in which it has
its place, and, as a consequence, meaning itself is reconceived as a certain
kind of movement. Unable to be absolutely certain that we are getting it
right, that the report is entirely accurate, we are freer to attend to what
might be called the text's disseminated authority. We note, for example,
that instead of a single most authoritative voice, we have voices—and
indeed structures—that echo one another. Here are some of them: Apollodorus repeats to the businessman the account of the banquet he has
already given to Glaucon. The speeches about love are framed by the
arrivals of two uninvited guests: Aristodemus at the beginning, Alcibiades
at the end. After the speeches on love, Alcibiades begins what is at least
planned as a second series of encomia, this time with each man present
praising the guest to his right (or perhaps choosing the topic of the
speech to be given by that guest). Socrates begins his speech about love
by reporting that he "had told [Diotima] almost the same things Agathon
told [him] . . . : that love is a great god and that he belongs to beautiful

things." Diotima "used the very same arguments against [Socrates] that [he] used against Agathon; she showed how . . . love is neither beautiful nor good" (484). None of these repetitions is exact, and the difference in the final case is especially significant. Socrates' correction of Agathon goes no further than proving that need is inherent in desire, and that Eros, lacking good and beautiful things, can be neither good nor beautiful. With Diotima, Socrates, unlike Agathon with him, had drawn an apparently logical conclusion from this: "Is love ugly, then, and bad?" Shocked, Diotima admonishes him to "watch [his] tongue" and proceeds to instruct him—in a manner not unlike Socrates' instructional style with his partners in dialogue—that love is *between* wisdom and ignorance, *between* beauty and ugliness (484–85). Love, like all great spirits, according to Diotima, shuttles between opposites, between ignorance and wisdom, between what is mortal and what is immortal. This betweenness is a conceptual echo of our textual betweenness, of the reader's movement between the inaccurately replicative voices, structures, and ideas that constitute the *Symposium*'s text.

Ideationally, the replicative structure I find most interesting is constituted by Aristophanes' and Diotima's speeches. It may seem odd to refer to these speeches as echoes of one another. The differences between the two (including the difference between the whimsical turn of Aristophanes' fable and the pedagogical and philosophical solemnity of Diotima's speech) are obvious, but also somewhat misleading. Let's first of all note that Diotima significantly modifies Socrates' view that the lover of beautiful and good things desires to possess those things. The lover wants not beauty, she teaches, but rather "reproduction and birth in beauty" (490). Far from expressing an emptiness, Eros, according to Diotima, is the sign of a fullness, an inner plenitude that seeks to reproduce itself in the world. She speaks of someone "pregnant" with "wisdom and the rest of virtue" (491). In philosophical discourse with the beautiful soul that acts as a catalyst, or midwife, of this self-reproduction, the lover submits his own ideas to a dialogue in which he not only "educates" the other, as Diotima says, but also "corresponds" with the dialogic modulations of his own philosophical being. An important consequence, even goal of this exchange is to transform the loved one into a lover. This transformation is a recurrent motif in the *Symposium* (another replicative structure). In the first speech in praise of love, Phaedrus explains that the gods honored Achilles over Alcestis (who sacrificed her own life so that her husband Admetus might live) because Achilles, originally Patrocles' beloved, had made himself Patrocles' lover by his willingness to die in order to avenge Patrocles' death. With an important modification, Alcibiades, according to his own account, underwent the same transformation—now more complexly viewed—in his relation with Socrates. Alcibiades starts out by interpreting his seductive activity entirely as an acquisitive project—in terms of desire as lack. He assumed, he tells the banquet guests, that what Socrates wanted was him—to possess him—so he thought that if he "let [Socrates] have his way with" him, he, Alcibiades, would in turn make Socrates teach him "everything he knew" (499). In this exchange of possessions, the philosopher gets the body he wants and the young man gets the philosopher's wisdom. Socrates fails to take up the offer because, as Alcibiades obscurely recognizes, he's interested in a different kind of activity in the young men he apparently pursues. If, as Alcibiades somewhat humorously complains, Socrates "has deceived us all: he presents himself as your lover, and, before you know it, you're in love with him yourself" (503), it is because, in a sense, Socrates has nothing to offer, nothing to fill the gap of a lover's desire. Just as his young lovers' beauty is what excites Socrates to give birth to the ideas teeming in his own philosophically pregnant being, so he expects those he loves to respond to his spiritual beauty by giving birth to the virtue and the wisdom in themselves. In short, the goal of a relation of love with Socrates is the loving subject's communication with himself through the other—not the suppression of the other through such psychoanalytic strategies as projection and identification, but rather the bringing to term the other's pregnancy of soul. Self-delivery fertilizes the philosophical perspective, in dialogue, of otherness.

Aristophanes' fable has, of course, already given us the *Symposium*'s most unambiguous version of Eros as pursuit of the same. According to that fable, there were originally three kinds of human beings: male, female, and a combination of the two. Each spherically shaped person had four arms, four legs, two faces, two sets of sexual organs. As punishment for these powerful and ambitious humans' attempt to vanquish the gods, Zeus had the luminous idea of cutting each person in two, "the way . . . people cut eggs with hairs" (474). The result of this is that every human being is longing for his or her lost other half. "Love," Aristophanes tells his fellow guests, "is born into every human being; it calls back the halves of our original nature together; it tries to make one out of two and heal the wound of human nature" (474). Those who were originally all male pursue other men; those who were split from a woman are, as Aristophanes specifies, "oriented more towards women, and lesbians come from this class" (475), while the original androgynes are now heterosexuals (who, if the prelapsarian race were divided equally among the three types, would, curiously enough, make up only one-third of present humanity . . .).

Is this love for our lost half motivated by lack? This would certainly seem to be the case: A lover longs for what he or she no longer has, the missing half of his or her being. Love, Aristophanes concludes, is an attempt at repossession; it "is the name for our pursuit of wholeness, for our desire to be complete" (476). But what does it mean to lack oneself? If love in Aristophanes' fable is a desire motivated by lack or need, what the lover lacks is identical to what he is. *It is more of what he is.* This is a lack based not on difference (as in the view of Eros desiring that which is different from it, the beautiful and the good which it is not), but rather on the *extensibility of sameness.* Aristophanes' speech makes a mythic narrative, a story, out of what I am proposing as an ontological reality: All being moves toward, corresponds with itself outside of itself. This self-desiring movement defeats specular narcissism, for it erases the individuating boundaries within which an ego might frame and contemplate itself. The self loved in what I have called elsewhere an impersonal narcissism can't be specularized because it can't be personalized; the self out there is "mine" without belonging to me. Aristophanes also makes clear that once sameness is divided from itself, desire for the same can no longer be a relation between exactly identical terms. The "ideal," he says is to "recover (our) original nature." But where is that exactly identical other half? It is of course nowhere to be found, in addition to which the splitting in two is itself a phylogenetic memory. So, as Aristophanes concedes, "the nearest approach to [the ideal] is best in present circumstances. . . . Love does the best that can be done for the time being" (476).

We love, in other words, inaccurate replications of ourselves. The philosophical lesson of the fable is that we relate to difference by recognizing and longing for sameness. All love is, in a sense, homoerotic. Even in the love between a man and a woman, each partner rejoices in finding himself, or herself, in the other. This is not the envy of narcissistic enclosure that Freud thought he detected in male heterosexual desire; it is rather an expression of the security humans can feel when they embrace difference as the supplemental benefit of a universal replication and solidarity of being. Each subject reoccurs differently everywhere.

Finally, if, as I said earlier, art is the site of being as emergence into connectedness, the *Symposium* both thematizes that emergence in speeches about love and pedagogically performs (as befits the educative mission of Socrates) its own textual emergence as inaccurately self-replicating ideas and structures. At the beginning of our philosophical and literary tradition, Plato's dialogue makes an invaluable contribution to our own discussions of why human subjects intervene in the world, of what moves us to connect. The *Symposium* offers an account of connectedness according to which relations are initiated because they are already there. Its various registers of replication—of reoccurrence of the same— disclose, bring to being what is in truth our already established at-homeness in the world.

References

Allouch, Jean. "Pour introduire le sexe du maître." *L'unebévue* 11 (1998): 17–63.
Bersani, Leo. *The Freudian Body: Psychoanalysis and Art.* New York: Columbia UP, 1986.
———. "Is the Rectum a Grave?" 1987. In *AIDS*: Cultural Analysis/Cultural Activism. Ed. Douglas Crimp. Cambridge: MIT P, 1988, 1993. 197–223.
Dean, Tim. *Beyond Sexuality.* Chicago: U of Chicago P, 2000.
Foucault, Michel. "Friendship as a Way of Life." In *Ethics: Subjectivity and Truth.* Ed. Paul Rabinow. New York: New P, 1997. 135–40.
Freud, Sigmund. *The Ego and the Id.* 1923. *Standard* 19:1–66.
———. *Group Psychology and the Analysis of the Ego.* 1921. *Standard* 18:65–144.
———. "Instincts and Their Vicissitudes." 1915. *Standard* 14:115–40.
———. "On Narcissism: An Introduction." 1914. *Standard* 14:69–102.
———. *The Standard Edition of the Complete Psychological Works of Sigmund Freud.* Ed. and trans. James Strachey. 24 vols. London: Hogarth, 1953–74.
———. *Three Essays on the Theory of Sexuality.* 1905. *Standard* 7:123–245.
Lacan, Jacques. *The Seminar of Jacques Lacan, Book 1: Freud's Papers on Technique, 1953–1954.* Ed. Jacques-Alain Miller. Trans. John Forrester. New York: Norton, 1991.
Laplanche, Jean. *Seduction, Translation, Drives.* Ed. John Fletcher and Martin Stanton. London: ICA, 1992.
Plato, *The Symposium.* Trans. Alexander Nehamas and Paul Woodruff. *Complete Works.* Ed. John M. Cooper. Indianapolis: Hackett, 1997. 457–505.
Proust, Marcel. *The Captive.* Vol. 3, *Remembrance of Things Past.* Trans. C. K. Scott Moncrieff and Terence Kilmartin. New York: Random House, 1981.
Silverman, Kaja. *World Spectators.* Stanford: Stanford UP, 2000.

19

SEXUAL DISGUST

Jonathan Dollimore

. . . .

Why is it that we read so much about desire but very little about how it is haunted—even created—by its opposite, disgust? Might this suggest one of the more significant repressions of academic writing about sexuality?

Disgust is the strong word, *aversion* the weaker. And then there is the sometimes evasive alternative to both of these: *indifference*. If I use the strong word, it's because disgust is often in fact what is being felt, even though what is admitted is usually something else; sometimes aversion, but more usually a claimed indifference—"not my scene." The relationship between desire and disgust is especially significant in the arena of sexuality where complex responses are at once registered, concealed, and indeed repressed in that misleadingly simple designation, *sexual preference*.

Some would say that even to talk about sexual disgust is to be gripped by a residual puritanism. But if anyone remains in the grip of such a thing, it's those who would pretend that sexual or bodily disgust is only for Victorians and prudes. In fact, some of the most uninterestingly neurotic people one can meet are those who want everyone to know that they are really at ease with their own sexuality. And, as the politically correct counterpart of this personal bill of health, such people usually also insist that they are equally at ease with everyone else's sexuality.

Disgust, in both its subjective experience and social expression, is dense with cultural significance. It is a dynamic component of the most exalted philosophies and the most murderous political ideologies. It can work to protect cultural boundaries, but sometimes in ways that indicate their vulnerability to disruption, and the psychological and social cost paid for securing them. It can be a reaction that consolidates individual identity, or a disavowal of what threatens it; it can be a symptom of repressed or ambivalent desire for something with the potential to liberate or threaten the self, or to liberate *and* threaten it almost indistinguishably. This and more.

Disgust is typically experienced at the boundary of a culture, and of the individual identities of those who belong to it, and its focus is often what is excluded by that boundary, especially what is just the other side of it. Social cohesion requires that the securing of the boundaries of the larger culture, and the individual identities within it, should coincide, whereas in practice of course they often do not. From one angle, this emphasis on coincidence seems conclusive; from another, we see only the mismatch; from yet another, what matters is the seemingly unbridgeable gulf between those differently positioned in relation to the boundaries: What to one person is the most ecstatically beautiful experience in the world is, to another, so repulsive it deserves reprobation, punishment, mutilation, and death—and never more so than where sexuality is concerned. If disgust reveals a great deal about ourselves and our culture, it also suggests how little we really know about either—especially when we remember that sexual disgust (unlike most other kinds) may also be the ultimate temptation to sexual transgression. There is something mysterious about this and I want to hold it in mind throughout, not least because it focuses something important for the perspective I'm trying to take: Disgust—the experience and the concept—resists the X-ray vision of the analyst, and the reductive perspective of what I've elsewhere called wishful theory ("Bisexuality").

1. The Way People Go at It

In his frank and controversial 1920 autobiography, *Si le grain ne meurt* (*If It Die*), André Gide recalls witnessing a sexual encounter that took place in Algiers in 1897. Gide's friend Daniel fucks an Arab youth called Mohammed. Gide recalls that Daniel "looked gigantic leaning over this little body which he hid from view—he might have been a huge vampire feeding upon a corpse. I could have screamed in horror." Although undoubtedly exploitative, this sexual act was not rape: Gide confesses that he was horrified, equally, by "Daniel's way of going at it and by the willing cooperation of Mohammed." Gide does not judge; on the contrary he uses the occasion to reflect on not just the diversity of human sexual practice, but the irrational revulsion we experience—and the difficulty we have in understanding—how other people "go at it." Nothing, he adds, "is so disconcerting." If we were able to see the way our neighbors make love, it would seem as "strange, ridiculous and, let us admit it, as revolting" as the sexual coupling of animals and insects. And, crucially, "no doubt this is why misunderstandings in this matter are so great and intolerance so ferocious" (286–87). Undoubtedly, this thoughtful containment of personal revulsion was a crucial strand in Gide's rationalist defense of his own and others' sexual nonconformity, a defense whose historical importance needs to be remembered. Gide's response to Daniel and Mohammed is especially commendable in that Gide's own preference was for what today we might call "vanilla" sex; in his own words here, he "can only conceive pleasure face to face, reciprocal and gentle and . . . find satisfaction in the most furtive contact" (287). Vanilla or not, as Bersani shows in *Homos,* Gide's sexuality, or at least his representation of it in *The Immoralist,* intimates a kind of intimacy devoid of intimacy, a kind of eroticism with the potential to challenge nothing less than the Western conception of desire as "a drama of personal anguish and unfulfilled demands" (*Homos* 125, 128).

How interesting, then, to find Gide, in one of his journal entries, displacing his own disgust into exactly the intolerance he here avoids, and doing so at around the same time as he wrote up his recollection of the earlier traumatic episode.[1] It is a brisk early instance of a certain kind of identity politics—that self-exoneration inseparable from a distancing of others. Gide classifies homosexuals into three groups: the pederast, the sodomite, and the invert. In the process he declares that only inverts— men who like to be anally fucked—deserve the reproach of "moral and intellectual deformation" that is commonly addressed to all homosexuals. He adds: "Most often the differences among [homosexuals] is such that they experience a profound disgust for one another, a disgust . . . that in no way yields to that which . . . (heterosexuals) fiercely show toward all three" (*Journals* 2:246–47). Despite their alleged disgust for one another, homosexuals (collectively?) resist the homophobic disgust of straight culture. This ambivalent solidarity—one that incorporates, reproduces, and displaces what it also resists—persists today, albeit in different terms, and not only within gay identities.

Since Gide we have benefited from the sexual liberation to which he in no small part contributed. And liberation has greatly changed not just the objects of disgust, but the ways in which its expression is interpreted. For example, one conservative attitude has always regarded manifest disgust as a proper response to any sexual deviation. In our more liberal climate, that attitude survives but on a much-reduced scale. In fact, today we are more likely to turn the tables and pathologize not the deviant practice, but any extreme attitude of disgust toward it. Like *Hamlet*'s lady, the disgusted are thought to protest too much. Again, this change derives especially from the liberation movements of the postwar period that tended to demystify and/or pathologize disgust. To demystify disgust entailed seeing it as symptomatic of a repressive sexual ideology; to pathologize it, as symptomatic of a "screwed-up" individual. And in practice, of course, the latter usually, and conveniently, presupposed the former. One of the more successful examples of what I mean was the way that the gay liberation movement was able, with considerable success, to argue that the disgusted homophobe, and not the homosexual, was neurotic; and the reason homophobes were so disturbed was because they were concealing their own repressed and possibly unconscious homosexuality behind cultural bigotry. Additionally—and this is a nicely ironic instance of how disgust doesn't so much disappear as find new objects—the disgusted become vaguely disgusting.

This very example tells us that the influential origins of this reversal, whereby the experience rather than the object of disgust is pathologized, are in Freud. Yet my mention of Shakespeare's *Hamlet* might suggest the psychological insight that enables this reversal is much older (Freud would have agreed).

2. Closeted Disgust

Yet it seems to me that liberation, far from eradicating the kind of sexual disgust felt by Gide, may have intensified it; certainly it has helped produce new ways of concealing or repressing it, or of encouraging people to displace and project their experience of it into politically acceptable forms of bigotry. Disgust is still publicly expressed relative to anal sex, for example, and, probably most freely today, pedophilia. The virulence of such expressions of disgust is partly a consequence of the suppression of others. Misogynistic and racist disgust have been freely expressed for centuries.[2] Today, in certain important public contexts at least, the overt expression of such disgust has diminished. But it has not gone away.

It remains the case that the sexuality of some straight men is organized around not just a barely concealed contempt for, but also a fundamental disgust with, women. Crudely, they fuck them despite—or because of—not much liking them.[3] Ostensibly that has changed. Yet I would guess that for some men it hasn't changed very much, while for others, though much has changed, anxious aversions remain. Another instance: One of the most embarrassing aspects of gay history has been the overt misogyny of some gay men. Commendably, today gay men can be among our most vigilant critics of misogyny. But does this does necessarily mean that they themselves are free of anxieties about the female body? Might not this political vigilance in some cases also be symptomatic of the continuing shadowy presence of such anxieties, rather than their complete absence? One of the many deceptions of contemporary sexual politics is that the adoption of a progressive political attitude apparently can guarantee the presence of a "together"—that is, untroubled—psyche. One suspects that some people have adopted the first only by way of laying claim to the second. Does it work? Amusingly, Camille Paglia suggests not, at least not for those U.S. men who tried to make themselves more attractive by adopting the persona of "new man," only to find that the very feminists who demanded this are attracted to new men even less than to old men. Paglia is given to the odd overstatement, but the disjunction between desire and politics she identifies here is familiar enough.

The body has become a fashionable topic: Athletes work out; cultural theorists "work on" the body and with a tenacious abstraction that to me suggests anxiety if not aversion.[4] Here's an exchange between an older and a younger academic, overheard at a cocktail party (you'll guess which is which):

"So what do you work on?"
"The Body."
"The body—how interesting; [longish pause in which both sip drinks]. In what sense exactly?"
"I see the body as an effect of repressive discursive constructions and in particular the site of the inscription of power."
"Right. So this is a body in prison, as it were?"
"Well, yes and no: I also theorize the body as the site of subversion and subjugated knowledges."
"Interesting."

Explicit attention to the question of aversion puts back into the picture what the abstractions of postmodern "body theory" usually evade, namely the body. I'm not foregrounding disgust and aversion as the key terms in a new theory of desire. In one respect, the last thing I want is yet another theory of desire. I'm much more interested in using disgust to interrogate the limits of the theories we have. Bored by "body studies," I yearn for a body that is material in the sense that it is recalcitrant, impeding theory rather than surrendering to it. Not with the intention of repudiating theory—I still want it—but getting it to be more "worked out," more truthful. If William Miller's recent book *Anatomy of Disgust* is more enlightening about the body than any body theory could ever be, it's partly because his commonsense approach confronts the empirical realities of disgust that theoretical abstraction avoids. Similarly with Mary Douglas's pioneering work in *Purity and Danger*. Douglas shows how relatively small changes in the object or its location can precipitate us from one attitude into its opposite, from desire to loathing: Hence the famous formulation that dirt is [nothing more than] matter out of place.[5] The same food that was enticing on the plate becomes repulsive in the dustbin. And this spatial difference has a temporal counterpart: The food that is desirable on the plate *now* may be perceived as disgusting in exactly that same place several hours later.

3. Vile Bodies

Aversion to the body is hardly surprising since, for many human beings, nothing has greater potential to disgust. And if writers as diverse as Augustine and Freud are right in thinking that we are repulsed by the realization of having being born between feces and urine, it's even more pertinent that the very same bodily orifices that disgust because of their excretions—vomit, urine, and shit to name but three—also excite sexually. Which is, perhaps, why disgust in its "purest" form can be experienced *only* in relation to the human body—the very same body that, for those in love, can also be the most beautiful, the *least* disgusting, thing in the world. But if the truth were told, for most of our lives we are not in love, and the mundane fact remains: Where the bodies of most others are concerned, we experience not spontaneous attraction but a wish to keep them at a certain distance. And even then, is attraction ever completely spontaneous, completely free of the sense of how different it is from the norm?

I've already mentioned three types of the disgusted: the racist, the misogynist, and the homophobe. Now in each case we can, if we like, pathologize the disgust—that is, regard it only or mainly as a problem of individuals not like us. But expressions of disgust can sometimes be politically respectable even—dare I say, especially—for people like us. Not so long ago a feminist writer spent some time demolishing the myth that older men make better lovers. In the process she spoke of the supposed ailments of the aging male body with contempt and distaste. It was another woman who pointed out that had a man spoken of a woman in such terms, it would have been construed as virulent misogyny. Another example: Lesbian and gay people sometimes parody, and sometimes earnestly reciprocate, homophobia by expressing contempt for straight sex,[6] and both gays and straights have been known to express aversion to bisexuality; so much so that a new word has recently entered the arena of sexual politics: *biphobia*.

In current debates, bisexuals are sometimes categorized as pathologically greedy (they fuck everyone in sight). Some bisexuals turn the tables by celebrating this sexual openness as a measure of how pathology-free they are: At least they aren't afflicted with the constitutive aversions of the rigidly straight or rigidly gay. But, as we've already seen, it isn't that simple. I once heard of a (self-identified) bisexual male who had been interrogated by a psychiatrist intent on finding out whether he was really straight or gay. This bisexual confessed to finding some men's bodies repulsive in a way that he rarely found women's bodies repulsive. Relieved, the psychiatrist concluded that this proved his "patient" to be more straight than gay, and only in need of a little aversion therapy. Unfortunately, he didn't wait to hear that this bisexual also found his aversion to some men matched by an intensity of desire for others that he never quite felt for women.

Of course, this man does not *have* to be classified sexually. The utopian potential of refusing sexual classification is only now being imagined with the advent of queer erotics. At the moment many gays, as well as straights, share the psychiatrist's desire to pin down our bisexual on one side or the other; they too find the apparent sexual indeterminacy of the bisexual troubling to their own identity. So, if we can't resist the temptation to classify him, then I'd bet he was more gay than straight. So yes: I'm suggesting that to experience an aversion to some men matched by an intensity of desire for others may make him more gay than straight. And that has the interesting consequence that strong aversion to some people of the *opposite* sex may be a constituent part of heterosexuality, rather than—or as well as—homosexuality, while feelings of aversion to some members of the *same* sex may actually be prima facie evidence of homoerotic inclination. One thing is for sure: Sexual aversion isn't just a hostile dynamic between groups characterized by *different* sexual orientations—straight, gay, or bisexual. As the example of Gide just made clear, there's a long tradition of people of the same—the very same—sexual orientation being disgusted with each other. Proust of course made the same point, and there is a particularly challenging section in Bersani's *Homos* where he suggests that Proust deserves our attention for suggesting that "the aversion of inverts to the society of inverts may be the necessary basis for a new community of inversion" (131).

But to return to the question of orientation: What about feelings of aversion toward the *whole* of the opposite sex—surely that would be conclusive evidence of homosexuality? Presumably so; yet how many people really experience sexual desire in terms of such a blanket, almost a priori form of aversion and exclusion, any more than we feel a strong desire for *all* members of the same sex if we're gay, or the opposite sex if we're straight? And if, say, a gay man *does* experience total aversion to the opposite sex, isn't he being overdetermined by an identity formation that is historically very recent, and not unconnected to the "straight" person's total aversion to the idea of any kind of erotic contact with people of the same sex? The point of these questions is to suggest that the experience of aversion is all the while telling us more than we want to hear or know.

4. "Disgust Always Bears the Imprint of Desire"

One idea that became popular with sexual liberation was that disgust is always a masking symptom of repressed or unconscious desire: "Disgust always bears the imprint of desire."[7] It derived directly, if vaguely, from the Freudian idea that disgust was a reaction formation to a desire that was threatening the coherence of the civilized ego. Attractive as this idea may be, it is just wrong to believe that disgust is always an expression of a repressed desire whose return threatens mayhem. That it *may* be, however, is an indispensable insight that also contributes to an almost inevitable misuse and discrediting of psychoanalysis. If, for instance, we approach the subject from an anthropological perspective, a very different picture emerges: Aversion is not necessarily about a repressed desire for its object, but about protecting boundaries and maintaining the inner coherence of an existing formation of desire. This makes a real difference: In a strong Freudian model, the desire "inside" the disgust is a force for instability; identity is constantly being threatened or destabilized by its own repressed desires. In the anthropological account, though, aversion concerns less the surfacing of repressed desire than the policing and containing of a socially acceptable desire. Boundaries and identities are not being threatened but, on the contrary, secured.

Another problem with the repression model is that it can't quite explain why we sometimes construe things as disgusting just because we *consciously* desire them, and for diverse reasons. Perhaps because we're infatuated with someone we deem unworthy of us; perhaps because we *know* we desire what threatens our survival, even our very life. Then there is the related scenario in which the desire comes first and transmutes into disgust—what Miller calls "the disgust of surfeit" (120). If, for an instance of this, I glance back a couple of millennia, it is to indicate both the cultural continuity and relativity of what I'm describing. Plutarch (c. 46–c. 126) describes how in ancient Greece the love that a man felt for a boy would disappear abruptly when body hair appeared; a single hair, he says, would cancel the obsessive love just like that, turning desire to aversion.[8] (Another nice irony here: In Greece they were disgusted by men loving boys who were too old, while today most people are disgusted by men loving them too young. I like the way Paglia phrases this: "Greek pederasty honored the erotic magnetism of male adolescents in a way that today brings the police to the door" [*Sexual* 115].)

Consider another, more recent instance. In James Baldwin's *Giovanni's Room,* the narrator, David, describes how he comes to be disgusted by the body of his female partner:

> I trace it to something as fleeting as the tip of her breast lightly touching my forearm as she leaned over me to serve my supper. I felt my flesh recoil. Her underclothes, drying in the bathroom, which I had often thought of as smelling even rather improbably sweet and as being washed much too often, now began to seen unaesthetic and unclean. . . . I sometimes watched her naked body move and wished it were harder and firmer, I was fantastically intimidated by her breasts, and when I entered her I began to feel that I would never get out alive. All that once delighted me seemed to have turned sour in my stomach. (118–19)[9]

Anyone who has read this novel would probably agree that it is somewhat evasive to describe David as bisexual. But if we're to describe him as homosexual, that raises the prospect that his is a homosexuality somehow inseparable from a disgust with, and flight from, the female body. We could of course avoid such uncomfortable issues by simply dismissing David as a misogynist. But that too would be an evasion since, as Marjorie

Garber points out when citing this passage in *Vice Versa*, the body of a loved one becoming the focus for such disgust is a familiar if unwelcome recognition for many people—straights, gays, and bisexuals alike (129). In this novel, disgust surely finds expression in terms of a misogyny to which it is nevertheless irreducible. To engage in such a reduction is convenient but incorrect. Likewise with the charges of homophobia and racism: To see aversion only in these terms helps us avoid confronting the uncomfortable complexities of desire itself, and a crucial but partial truth becomes an evasion. To think harder about aversion might get us back to that complexity and force us to confront the evasion.

Note, for example, how in this passage from Baldwin, the disgust emerges neither from some new aspect of the other (as in the instance from Plutarch), nor from some hitherto unseen or ignored aspect of them, but from the *very same* details that hitherto were erotic—the "fleeting" contact of the breast on the forearm, the smell of the underclothes. What once was desirable has become disgusting. David feels this to be the physical manifestation of something much greater—the process "of love turning to hatred"; not indifference, note, but hatred. And this change is, he says, "far more terrible than anything I have ever read about it, more terrible than anything I will ever be able to say" (118).

Here disgust is, among other things, the compelling expression of the terrifying mutability of desire. So why has the simplistic interpretation of disgust as always being the symptom of repressed desire gained such currency—doubly erroneous here since repression is usually regarded as a constant rather than mutable factor in desire? (This is not to suggest that the mutability of desire never involves repression.) One obvious reason is that it is an interpretation empowering those who invoke it. The person experiencing the disgust as symptom is already psychically disqualified and "known" from a superior position: We diagnose his or her inner "truth" to be one of conflict, repression, insecurity, bad faith, inauthenticity; he or she is, in short, "fucked up." Disgust as a concept can be violently powerful. That is one reason for being suspicious of this simplistic idea. Another is that it works with a crude version of the Freudian theory of repression. A third is that it is in danger of becoming an uncritical orthodoxy in theory, or rather wishful theory.

The way that aversion and exclusion are "positive" components *of* desire is nicely treated in the German gay film *Taxi zum Klo*, literally "Taxi to the Toilet." In that film a gay teacher, on his way home, cruises some toilets. As I recall—and I fear I may be wishfully idealizing the scene— he's sitting in a cubicle waiting for action. Being a conscientious teacher, he's filling in time marking student essays. Suddenly there's interest from the next cubicle. Through the glory hole the teacher posts a note: "What are you into?" The message comes back: "Everything. Anything." Now who, I find myself wondering, could have been on the other side? Doubtless a postmodernist. Or maybe it was only the kind of person I mentioned earlier, at ease with their own sexuality and everyone else's. Whoever, our teacher does the only decent thing: He gathers together his scripts and leaves. He at least knows that discrimination is the essence of culture.

5. Freud: Overriding Disgust

I mentioned earlier that liberation discourse tends to demystify and pathologize disgust both at once, seeing it as symptomatic of a repressive sexual ideology and of the "screwed-up" individuals produced within that ideology. We might expect Freud to be the crucial precursor in the second respect (disgust as symptomatic of individual neurosis), but actually he's also a significant precursor in the first (symptomatic of repressive ideology). Since most of what follows will be critical, I want to say now that I believe there are ways in which Freud was quite right, and on both counts.

In brief, his theory is this: Disgust, along with morality and shame, are civilization's defensive strategies against unbridled instinct. Disgust keeps instinct in check; it is part of the process of repression that keeps illicit desire unconscious. For Freud, of course, there is an unending conflict between the demands of instinct and those of civilization. The evolution—not to say the very survival—of civilization depends on the repression and sublimation of sexual desire. Anal eroticism becomes a striking paradigm of all this; according to Freud, once upon a time, when we went around on all fours, we were all into anal sex. But as we got up on two legs, the evolution of civilization required the repression of anality. It becomes, says Freud, with a nice choice of word, "unserviceable" for civilization. Hence the disgust with which it is now regarded.

But there is an inherent, momentous instability in this process: "The sexual instinct in its strength enjoys overriding . . . disgust"; part of its very nature is to struggle against disgust and shame, which in turn— and presumably with less enjoyment—are struggling to keep the instinct within the bounds of the normal (*Three Essays* 152, 159, 162). A major challenge to civilization's defensive strategies comes from the sexual perversions; they especially transgress the cultural boundaries between desire and disgust. Actually, it might be more accurate to speak here not of transgressing boundaries but of shifting them: Perverse desire pushes back the boundaries, claiming ground from disgust. Rupert Haselden describes his feelings on visiting for the first time in the late 1970s the gay New York club The Mineshaft, legendary for its sexual extremism:

> I had never seen anything like it: fist fucking, racks, and the stench of piss and poppers and everything else and the heat and the men and the light was all red and I remember thinking standing there, adrenaline thundering round me and thinking, "This is evil, this is wrong." I remember being very frightened; it seemed so extreme. But later I was thinking about it a lot, and wanking when thinking about it, and the next thing I knew I was back there and within weeks it felt like home.[10]

Desire more or less permanently escapes aversion. Or does it? Often the boundaries close back in.[11] Whatever the case, for Freud there is, in the individual, a continuing struggle between desire and disgust that replicates the larger struggle between instinct and civilization. In a sense, the human subject is the walking casualty of that struggle.[12] And when we recognize that this struggle between desire and disgust can be intensified rather than resolved by sublimation, "casualty" does indeed seem the appropriate word.[13] Our psyche is the battleground for the opposition between these terms, even while our libido is energized by their violent, dialectical intimacy with each other. In other words, at one moment desire finds, in what was once disgusting, a pleasure whose intensity it could never have known without that history of disgust; at another moment desire gives way to a revulsion the more intense because its history is grounded in the very desire it displaces.

So far this theory begs questions, but it's reasonably consistent. It soon ceases to be so, as one would expect of something so central to what Freud wryly calls "the human privilege of becoming neurotic" ("Question" 211). Like other Freudian concepts, disgust becomes inconsistent as he elaborates it and extends its explanatory power to new instances. The most striking inconsistency is apparent in those places where Freud briskly announces that disgust is "purely conventional"—that is, something easily dismissed as a local, ignorant, and irrational prejudice (*Three* 151). In *Three Essays* he is even prepared to regard the most obdurate form of sexual disgust, namely the revulsion felt at the thought of anal intercourse, as also purely conventional. Indeed, Freud insists on this, even to the point of being concerned that he might be construed as a propagandist for the practice:

> I hope . . . I shall not be accused of partisanship when I assert that people who try to account for this disgust by saying that the organ in question serves the function of excretion and comes in contact with excrement . . . are not much more to the point than hysterical girls who account for their disgust at the male genital by saying that it serves to void urine. (152)

How does this square with his other argument, alluded to above, that anal eroticism has become "unserviceable" for civilization yet remains the site of the eternal struggle between instinct and civilization? On the one hand, disgust—here, specifically anal disgust—expresses a repression that is itself the necessary condition for the evolution of civilization; on the other, disgust is no more rational than hysterical girls who don't like the idea of sucking cock (and it is fellatio that Freud has in mind). Is the man who, for the same reason, also finds disgusting the thought of performing fellatio on another man, equally, irrationally, hysterical? I'd like to think so, if only because the implication would be that a bit of brisk rationalist therapy would have all the straight boys going down on each other all the time. A sexual revolution is just a lifted T-shirt away.

But never mind the boys; what about those hysterical girls? This is such a revealing moment in Freud; psychoanalysis bravely demystifies an inveterate cultural prejudice, but does so only by invoking another. These girls recall Dora, Freud's most famous hysteric. She, too, experiences disgust at the penis and is reprimanded by Freud for doing so. Rereading the extensive secondary literature on this case history, I was struck by how rarely this crucial issue of disgust was addressed directly. At one point, Herr K., a friend of her parents, tries to seduce Dora; he clasps her to him and kisses her. Freud writes: "This was surely just the situation to call up a distinct feeling of sexual excitement in a girl of fourteen who had never before been approached. But Dora had at that moment a violent feeling of disgust"—and broke free. Freud is unequivocal: For her to feel disgust rather than pleasure in this encounter was, he continues, "entirely and completely hysterical. I should without question consider a person hysterical in whom an occasion for sexual excitement elicited feelings that were preponderantly or exclusively unpleasurable" ("Fragment" 28).

Dora is suffering from what Freud calls "reversal of affect" (28). What this refers to here is a situation in which, because of repression, desire is transformed into disgust. I remarked earlier that to interpret disgust as a symptom of desire is fraught with danger, not because it is simply wrong, but precisely because it is sometimes right. The same is true with reversal of affect. It happens. That has led some people to construe others as saying the opposite of what they mean, and desiring the opposite of what they say or think they desire; of telling them, in effect, that their "no" really means "yes."[14] To his credit, Freud says that reversal of affect is "one of the most important and at the same time one of the most difficult problems in the psychology of neuroses," and admits that he hasn't yet cracked it (28).

Freud further interprets Dora's disgust as involving displacement. She remarked in analysis that she could still feel on the upper part of her body the pressure of Herr K.'s embrace. Freud concludes that during the embrace she *in fact* felt the pressure of his erect penis. But because this perception was disgusting to her, she repressed it and replaced it with this more respectable sensation. There occurs a displacement from the lower part of the body to the upper—from the disgusting to the respectable—a displacement that, he adds, psychoanalysis often encounters. But Freud isn't finished: He interprets other aspects of Dora's behavior as involving a repressed desire to perform fellatio, and in the process feels it necessary to defend himself against the charge of obscenity. In doing so he again— as in the *Three Essays*—deviates into a defense of homosexuality. He says that the perversion "most repellent to us," male homosexuality, was accepted by the Greeks—"so far our superiors in cultivation"; and that "this excessively repulsive and perverted phantasy of sucking at a penis has the most innocent origin" ("Fragment" 50, 52).

What's obvious, even if you dismiss all the psychoanalytic interpretation as pernicious nonsense, is that Freud does not find these activities— anal intercourse, male homosexuality, and fellatio—disgusting. What is less clear, but to me still very plausible, and still not much dependent on accepting the psychoanalytic mode, is that it is Freud who is excited by the idea of the erect penis felt beneath the clothes. As is well known, late in the analysis—on his own admission, too late—Freud "discovers" the core reason for Dora's desperation, her homosexual desire for Herr K.'s wife. What this means, then, is that Freud briskly demystifies disgust vis-à-vis fellatio and male homosexuality, while spectacularly failing to recognize it as a symptom of Dora's own homosexuality. On the contrary, he disastrously construes it as a symptom of her repressed heterosexuality. One way of looking at this would be to say that Freud's own homosexuality is allowed to surface while Dora's is repressed. His emerges at the expense of hers. But is it homosexuality exactly? Does Freud fantasize about feeling Herr K.'s erect cock beneath the clothes, perhaps even going down on him, or is he excited by the scopophilic, bisexual fantasy of imagining Dora doing it to Herr K.—or to him? At the very least, Freud is excited by the thought of the man sexually aroused by the young woman.

A few years earlier Freud encountered another young woman, eighteen-year-old Katharina, suffering from neurotic symptoms in which both disgust and the erect penis again figure prominently—at least for Freud. Actually, he encountered this "well-built girl with her unhappy look" at the top of a high mountain in the eastern Alps that he had just climbed, where she approached him, asking if he were a doctor and adding: "My nerves are bad" (*Studies* 125). Freud conducts a makeshift analysis right there, on top of the mountain. It transpires that Katharina's problems stem from a time when, aged sixteen, she witnessed her uncle having sex with her cousin. She was too young to realize what was happening but (on Freud's prompting) recalls that she must have felt disgust nevertheless. Initially neither she nor Freud can work out what was the object of this disgust. Then she recalls earlier occasions, when she was fourteen, and the same uncle made sexual advances to her. On one occasion she remembered waking up and "'feeling his body' in the bed" (130). Freud concludes—and she agrees—that the disgust she felt at seeing the uncle and her cousin together was caused by a realization that what he was doing with the cousin he had also wanted to do with her. Freud makes much of the fact that she had "felt his body" (131). Her symptoms—something is crushing her chest and she can't breathe—might suggest it was his whole body. Freud has other ideas:

> "Tell me just one thing more. You're a grown-up girl now and know all sorts of things . . ."
> "Yes, now I am."
> "Tell me just one thing. What part of his body was it that you felt that night?"
> But she gave me no more definite answer. She smiled in an embarrassed way, as though she had been found out . . . (131–32)

Even so, Freud does not leave it there; he tells his readers:

> I could imagine what the tactile sensation was which she had later learnt to interpret. Her facial expression seemed to me to be saying that I was right in my conjecture. But I could not penetrate further, and in any case I owed her a debt of gratitude for having made it so much easier for me to talk to her than

to the prudish ladies [hysterical girls? Dora?] of my city practice, who regard
whatever is natural as shameful. (*Studies* 132)

That "whatever is natural" hardly seems appropriate, especially in light
of the chilling revelation made by Freud in a footnote added in 1924: For
reasons of discretion he had distorted the original story; in reality the
man who had tried to have sex with Katharina was not her uncle but her
father (134n).

In this case, as with Dora's, Freud's concern to overcome a young woman's apparent disgust at the imagined touch of an erect penis has much
to do with his own voyeuristic fantasy investment in the same. The voyeurism that emerges so "professionally," yet seemingly involves a blindness, or at least indifference, to the respective experiences of betrayal that
must have been central to these young women's distress, must throw
doubt on the trustworthiness of the entire analytic procedure. Not only
is Dora the subject of sexual advances by the husband of the woman with
whom she is in love (Frau K.), but—we learn, from Freud—her own father
is conspiring with Herr K. in allowing those advances because he himself
is having an affair with Frau K.; the daughter is being exchanged for the
wife. It is hardly surprising, then, that Dora tries to kill herself. The betrayal of the fourteen-year-old Katharina is less intricate but even more
traumatic, in that she is the subject of sexual advances by her own father.

Freud's interpretations of sexual disgust are the occasions for great insights into the deep conflicts between human desire and human culture,
and of courageous challenges to some of that culture's inveterate prejudices. They are also the occasion for an interpretive blindness that must
throw doubt on the reliability of psychoanalysis. The two case histories
suggest, first, that this interpretive blindness derives in part from that
familiar blindness intrinsic to voyeurism wherein desire sees only because
it does not see; second, that voyeurism is probably an inescapable part of
most analytic encounters. More generally, some of the concepts central to
and indispensable for the psychoanalytic encounter seem nowhere more
unreliable than in these histories, including reversal of affect, displacement, hysteria, perhaps even the later concept of countertransference. It
has been argued that the understanding of homosexuality was indispensable for the evolution of psychoanalysis (Freud himself admitted as
much) but, by the same token, proved its stumbling block. Something
similar is true of disgust, and not only for psychoanalysis; as I suggested
earlier, not the least of its interest resides in the way it seemingly resists
the theoretical explanations it provokes.

So how do I feel about psychoanalysis? Only that I am more than ever convinced of Freud's brilliance, and that the intellectual encounter with him is inevitable, prolonged, and sometimes difficult. But I am also more distrustful than ever of having that encounter via the couch.

Notes

This is a revised version of an article that originally appeared in *Beyond Redemption: The Work of Leo Bersani*, a special issue of *OLR*.

1. *Si le grain ne meurt* was published in 1920; the following diary entry is dated February 1918, but there is some uncertainly about the exact dating of these entries.

2. On sexual attraction and repulsion in racial narratives, see Young, especially chapters 4 and 6.

3. Paglia seems to suggest that for men to experience women as disgusting is not only inevitable but reasonable. This derives from her belief that civilization is necessarily a reaction formation against nature. Female sexuality is the embodiment of nature and, as such, essentially chthonic: It is a "miasmic swamp whose prototype is the still pond of the womb." This means that feminism has been simplistic in arguing that certain pejorative female archetypes were politically motivated falsehoods by men. On the contrary, the historical repugnance toward woman has a rational basis: "Disgust is reason's proper response to the grossness of procreative nature." She also identifies disgust as integral to the aesthetic response (intrinsically a defense against nature) in the form of a rational fear of, or at, "a melting borderline" (*Sexual Personae* 12, 93).

4. Foucault has something to answer for here: "The body is the inscribed surface of events (traced by language and dissolved by ideas), the locus of a dissociated Self (adopting the illusion of a substantial unity), and a volume in perpetual disintegration. Genealogy, as an analysis of descent, is thus situated within the articulation of the body and history. Its task is to expose a body totally imprinted by history and the process of history's destruction of the body" ("Nietzsche" 148).

5. "Dirt is matter out of place": Douglas recirculated this seductive aphorism in recent times, but it has a longer history. How old exactly? Freud uses the phrase in 1908. He is trying to explain why people who repress their anal eroticism become boring—mean, obstinate, and obsessed with orderliness. Now Freud is convinced this involves sublimation, but is unsure as to how, or why, exactly: "The intrinsic necessity for this connection is not clear, of course, even to myself." But he suggests that these character traits "are reaction formations against an interest in what is unclean and disturbing and should not be part of the body." It's then that he adds: "Dirt is matter in the wrong place" ("Character" 172–73). In Freud's original

German text this phrase appears in English, in brackets, in quotation marks, and without any annotation or source. In other words, in 1908 Freud apparently regards this proposition as something like an English proverb or aphorism. It's not surprising, then, to find that Cobham Brewer records it in the 1894 edition of his *Dictionary of Phrase and Fable*. Brewer is irritated by the aphorism. He comments, dismissively and tersely, "This is not true. A diamond . . . lost on the road is matter in the wrong place, but certainly [it] is not dirt." That's all he says.

6. Segal shows the smug and self-deluding complacency of this attitude in her intelligent defense of women's heterosexual pleasure: *Straight Sex* (esp. xi, 215–16).

7. This is from Stallybrass and White's influential book *The Politics and Poetics of Transgression* (191). They arrive at this formulation through analysis of identity formation in dominant groups, especially the bourgeoisie. The "high" bourgeois subject came to define himself through the repression and exclusion of the "low" other, typically characterized in social, sexual, and racial terms. But what was excluded socially remained psychically central; bourgeois fantasy life came to be constituted by the return of what it excluded or repressed. Stallybrass and White recognize that in psychic and social life, repression and exclusion are often inseparable, and this was one reason they deployed both psychoanalytic and materialist or anthropological accounts of identity. Actually, they keep the psychoanalytic subordinate to the anthropological. But out of context, that phrase that has become so influential—"Disgust always bears the imprint of desire"—has come to be used in a primarily psychoanalytic sense even by those who would not count themselves as exclusively psychoanalytic, or who are suspicious of, or even hostile to it. Such is the enduring influence of Freud.

8. Plutarch then goes on to talk of a love affair that survives this development, but it is clear that this is the exception that testifies to the reverse being more typical—see Flacelière 56.

9. See also: "My mother had been carried to the graveyard when I was five. I scarcely remember her at all, yet she figured in my nightmares, blind with worms, her hair as dry as metal and brittle as a twig, straining to press me against her body; that body so putrescent, so sickening soft, that it opened, as I clawed and cried, into a breach so enormous as to swallow me alive" (12–13). On the representation of the feminine in this novel, see Kaplan.

10. Rupert Haselden, interviewed by Garfield in *The End of Innocence* (16).

11. Haselden later denounced such places and in terms that led others to denounce him—see the same interview with Garfield.

12. In *Three Essays* Freud says that the mental forces like disgust that resist the libido like dams are not only the product of education but, more fundamentally, are "organically determined and fixed by heredity" (177). This is his theory of so-called organic repression, a consequence of evolution, and it drives this struggle even deeper into life; that's to say, it isn't only a struggle between civilization and instinct, culture and nature, but is now somehow "inside" nature itself.

13. Remembering that for Freud these instincts are typically sublimated into highly respectable social identities and activities, consider the following not un-

typical case. A man sublimates his homosexuality into the role of a scoutmaster. When, in relation to one particular youth, the sublimation begins to break down, his reawakened homosexuality continues to be deeply influenced by the residual sublimation. The result is that intense shame about homosexual desire coexisted with intense idealization of it.

14. The problems begin when disgust is investigated as one of the key symptoms of phobia, hysteria, and neurosis. Most notably, under the pressure of repression, disgust paradoxically becomes a symptom of pleasure; repression actually "transforms a source of internal pleasure into one of internal disgust" (*Complete Letters* 281).

References

Baldwin, James. *Giovanni's Room.* 1956. London: Corgi, 1977.

Bersani, Leo. *Homos.* Cambridge: Harvard UP, 1995.

Dollimore, Jonathan. "Bisexuality and Wishful Theory." *Textual Practice* 10.3 (1996): 523–39.

Douglas, Mary. *Purity and Danger: An Analysis of the Concepts of Pollution and Taboo.* London: Routledge and Kegan Paul, 1966.

Flacelière, Robert. *Love in Ancient Greece.* 1960. Trans. James Cleugh. London: Frederick Muller, 1962.

Foucault, Michel, "Nietzsche, Genealogy, History." *Language, Counter-Memory, Practice: Selected Essays and Interviews.* Ed. and introd. D. F. Bouchard. Trans. Bouchard and Sherry Simon. Ithaca: Cornell UP, 1977. 139–64.

Freud, Sigmund. "Character and Anal Erotism." 1908. *Standard* 9:167–75.

———. *The Complete Letters of Sigmund Freud to Wilhelm Fliess, 1887–1904.* Ed. and trans. Jeffrey Moussaieff Masson. Cambridge: Harvard UP, 1985.

———. *Fragment of an Analysis of a Case of Hysteria (Dora).* 1905 (1901). *Standard* 7:1–122.

———. "The Question of Lay Analysis: Conversations with an Impartial Person." 1926 (1927). *Standard* 20:179–258.

———. *The Standard Edition of the Complete Psychological Works of Sigmund Freud.* Ed. and trans. James Strachey. 24 vols. London: Hogarth, 1953–74.

———. *Three Essays on the Theory of Sexuality.* 1905. *Standard* 7:123–245.

Freud, Sigmund, with Josef Breuer. *Studies on Hysteria.* 1893–95. *Standard* 2:1–311.

Garber, Marjorie. *Vice Versa: Bisexuality and the Eroticism of Everyday Life.* New York: Simon and Schuster, 1995.

Garfield, Simon. *The End of Innocence: Britain in the Time of AIDS.* London: Faber, 1994.

Gide, André. *The Journals of André Gide.* Vol. 2: 1914–27. Trans. Justin O'Brien. London: Secker and Warburg, 1948.

———. *If It Die.* 1920. Trans. Dorothy Bussy. Harmondsworth: Penguin, 1977.

Kaplan, Cora. "'A Cavern Opened in My Mind': The Poetics of Homosexuality and the Politics of Masculinity in James Baldwin." In *Representing Black Men*. Ed. Marcellus Blount and George P. Cunningham. New York: Routledge, 1996. 27–54.

Miller, William Ian. *The Anatomy of Disgust*. Cambridge: Harvard UP, 1997.

Paglia, Camille. *Sexual Personae: Art and Decadence from Nefertiti to Emily Dickinson*. Harmondsworth: Penguin, 1992.

Segal, Lynne. *Straight Sex: The Politics of Pleasure*. London: Virago, 1994.

Stallybrass, Peter, and Allon White. *The Politics and Poetics of Transgression*. London: Methuen 1986.

Taxi zum Klo. Dir. Frank Ripploh. 1981.

Young, Robert. *Colonial Desire: Hybridity in Theory, Culture and Race*. New York: Routledge, 1995.

20

SEXUALITY AT RISK

Psychoanalysis Metapragmatically

Elizabeth A. Povinelli

. . . .

It is the appearance of a portrait, not the immediate vision I love so much.
DAVID WOJNAROWICZ, *CLOSE TO THE KNIVES* 9–10

Disintegrations, not ruins or shrines; but decompositions, then emergences and exposures. Scattered throughout the essays, comics, and films of the deceased AIDS activist and artist David Wojnarowicz is a distrust of artifacts, a love not of forms but of the emergence of form that motion reveals; of tremblings and swellings; of sensations "just on the edge of going airborne" (*Seven* 50). His *Bildungsromane* are filled with love scenes that are uncomfortably indiscriminate as they turn with equal passion toward the gruesome and sentimental, the political and comical, the sublime and adolescent, rape and its eroticism. But this, after all, is the point. Wojnarowicz decomposes obscenity's referent by scattering it across the generic spaces of Reagan's America. The erotic plot of his texts—their ethics and desire—details the passion of itinerate becoming, rather than of sexual being. These are memoirs of the labor of survival and the risk of formal being in the seams of American cities and suburbs.

A Marxist, not Freudian, fetish organizes the movement Wojnarowicz chronicles—the misrecognition of ourselves as homosexuals and heterosexuals—when he says that these identities are merely a social relation at risk in the ceaseless generation of new social conventions in institutional and psychic constraints (see Vološinov). Thus the risings that Wojnarowicz seeks do not conceal a secret form, and do not converge toward a transcendental signified. Though "the outline of a dick" is never far away, the phallus is surprisingly absent. What emerges are the edges of intelligibility in contexts of social and personal risk, for instance, when institutions put certain persons at risk, or queers work the "violent shuttling" of meaning marking the displacement of dominant narratives of normativity (see Spivak). In the process, homo/sexuality as the site and object of desire is dispersed, but not denied.

What could seem more self-evident than that Wojnarowicz's aesthetics of the receding and the emerging, his love of a bulging on the bone of meaning, would find its nemesis in Catholicism, its "prehistorical statements," its raised wooden platforms, relics, and canons (*Close* 132)? Apparently, there is no surer outcome than that the fundamental difference between a conservative Catholicism and a homo/sexuality unvested would lead to problems of "tone," anger, and deadly intolerance (*Close* 136). Yet, as Alenka Zupančič has noted, if an ethics of difference is to have "any serious meaning," it must be situated at the level of these fundamental differences and move "from the perspective of this hostility and intolerance" (43). In the United States, the sites of homophobic hostility and intolerance often have proper names: Matthew Shepard, Billy Jack Gaither, James Dale, Aileen Wournos. And their sounds are often issued in the banter of deadly adolescent hatred, and heard on the steps of heaven's gate: "The religious types outside St. Patrick's Cathedral shouting to the men and women in the gay parade, 'You won't be here next year—you'll get AIDS and die ha ha'" (*Close* 161).

But Wojnarowicz's queer militancy finds its antithesis in all publicly sanctioned sexual relics, including those sexual identities embraced by a multicultural politics of difference. His queer embrace of the abrasive was intended not merely for the political work it did in prying open the social field to a panoply of sexual identities and practices. His was an allegiance to desire first, and to sexual form second: a general political stance toward social derangement, if not a general theory of sexuality or social generativity. And he took up a stance against the fantasies of liberal sexuality: that the voicings of sexuality are our voices; that we are the object of Christian fundamentalist intolerance; that privacy is a sanctuary in which we find rest from the provisionality of public struggle (see Berlant, "Intimacy").

Sexuality is not merely a discursive misrecognition that organizes and mediates the distribution of material, civic, and affective resources. It is also a *relief* insofar as someone finds herself in its abstraction, and in a language and community of intelligibility. This is Biddy Martin's point: Although attachment to gender and sexual forms may be a momentary allegiance, a fickle devotion passionately taken up and quickly abandoned when viewed historically, from the perspective of real-time social labor, these forms are the necessary brace of subjectivity, the compromise that feels like a commitment. This emphasis on queer provisionality brings us to the principal questions of this essay: Can a Lacanian account of desire serve as the grounds for a compelling social or political movement, or does the social embrace of desire's itinerateness—its movement away from the still life of forms—make it relevant for only a liberationist fantasy of existence without limit, separated off from other dimensions of social and psychic life (Martin 110)? How, more generally, do we understand the social and psychic conventions of form, their implications for sexual politics and queer movements, including the risks of relaxing into forms or refusing their claim on our being? And who can risk what, where? These questions core Wojnarowicz's account of being queer in America.

This essay argues that understanding the political and ethical potential of Wojnarowicz's and others' desire depends on our separating the legacy of structuralism from the logic of the psychoanalytic subject, and in replacing this legacy with a contemporary approach to metapragmatics. In this way, difference and *différance*, semantics and syntax, *langue* and grammar, are recast as virtual orders, not in the Lacanian sense of the contingent nature of language, but in the Freudian sense of a wish-fantasy (*Wunschphantasie*). Subjects are not fixed by the semantic form of sexuality, are not sutured into a (post)structure, and are not effects of having made their way through the (deferred) quiltings of the signifier. Nevertheless, liberal subjects continually construct scenes staging their imminent transfixion. They often desire a sexual artifice that is poised to pierce their being and pin them to its law. And they may wish for a structure, a ratio, a logos, a machine that works within them even if the machine itself can't quite get to its point. This essay explores the source of this wish-fantasy, its fascination, and its implications for an ethics and theory of queer politics.

A caveat: If this essay is to address some of these issues through a partial coordination of metapragmatics and the Lacanian subject, it will be on the basis of a Lacanian subject whose form stresses the obligation of the author to a proper name. We have been so busy exhuming and disciplining into form the variegated landscape of Lacan's texts that we have forgotten the specific folly of scholarly labor, a folly many of us nonetheless love for its imprudence, its vain foolery, its utter waste. Lacan's models of psychic and social life have been treated like divine texts, with us as their divinators. We have troubled ourselves with questions of heresy, of replication and violation, of proper names (Lacan) and their entailment on our obligation to his writing, thought, aspirations. Michel Foucault's engagement with psychoanalysis and psychiatry in his three volumes of *The History of Sexuality* was but a playful theoretical joust compared to how his account of the location of the author and the book disables this apostolic devotion ("Author"). Need we forget that every model we studiously labor to form provides, in its form and function, the grounds for its own undoing? And is this need to forget why we fear saying that from a historical perspective Lacan was wrong in his understanding of language and thus of the subject of language?

1. Language

Let me begin, then, with this set of questions: What are the formal orders of language and of linguistic phenomena? What is the agency and function of these orders relative to the human subject and society? Lacan was not interested in these questions. He *became* interested in them as he listened to Claude Lévi-Strauss lecture on the relevance to an analysis of culture and society of a new post-Saussurean approach to language that Roman Jakobson and his students were developing from the 1940s on. Meaning bulged when Lacan brought this emergent structural paradigm to bear on Freudian psychoanalysis. He chased its textual curvature.

Jakobson's understanding of structural linguistics was in a constant state of emergence and reformation. When Lévi-Strauss first met him in New York in 1942, Jakobson was solidifying a post-Saussurean account of linguistic structuralism, with its well-known privileging of a decontextualized synchronic account of language (*langue*)—radically divorced from speech (*parole*) and history—as the proper object of linguistic science. This approach underwent significant modifications throughout the 1950s and 1960s, as Jakobson tried to reconcile it with the semiotic system of Ferdinand de Saussure's American contemporary Charles Sanders Peirce.[1] In Peircean accounts of semiosis, no structure lies outside events of interpretation (coordination) across previously constituted fields of signification (genres, discursive fields, textualities) and of material space-time.

However, by the time Jakobson began seriously working through the implications of this Peircean understanding of semiosis for his model of structural linguistics, "structuralism" had become a brand name associated with a man, Lévi-Strauss, and a national trend, French critical theory.

Less well known is a model of textuality (metapragmatics, language in context) that emerged as scholars reworked Peircean models of semiosis against Bakhtinean models of genre and dialogics.[2] From the perspective of metapragmatics, linguistic phenomena consist of three orders: semantics, pragmatics, and metapragmatics. We start with the well-worn truth that semantic sense and value arise from grammar and syntactic structures. The post-Saussurean tradition, especially the early structuralism of Lévi-Strauss, located human culture in this order of linguistic structure rather than in linguistic events, in a system of signs radically divorced from context rather than in the principles of their use. And in this understanding of structuralism, Lacan found support (*Anlehnung*, a prop) for his understanding of the symbolic as a machine—a "structure detached from the activity of the subject"—that turns all by itself (Lacan, *Seminar* 2:47; see also 30, 41, 189; *Seminar* 7:67–68; Laplanche, *Life and Death* 15).

As Jacqueline Rose notes, however, the early work of Lacan far surpassed Lévi-Strauss's structuralism, dragging the problem of the speaking subject into the heart of social and psychoanalytic analysis. In Lacan's early work, pragmatic aspects of language defined the core displacements, dissociations, and decompositions representing the subject qua subject, exemplified in the dialectic of *I* and "me" (see Rose, "Introduction" 45–46). If the symbolic were a machine—as Deleuze would eventually say, a machine that, though blind and dumb, makes us hear and speak—the subject was the dilemma of being "thrown into" its machinery, "committed, caught up in its gears" (Lacan, *Seminar* 2:307). Speech marks the subject's situation in this machine, the temporal break ("scansion") "permitting the insertion of something which can take on meaning for a subject" (*Seminar* 2:284; also 47).

It is the fate of human beings to be thrown into some semiotic machinery. But questions remain about the nature of the machinery, its relationship to legal, economic, and social institutions, and the implication of this machinery for new forms of social agency, relationality, and community. As I noted above, Wojnarowicz and other queer theorists have stressed the social labor of discursive formations (see also Warner, "Normal"; Berlant, "Intimacy"; Bersani, *Homos*). Though the later work of Lacan underwent a shift, as Rose also notes, laying increasing stress on the "fundamental division" between language and speech and on "the effects of that division on the level of subjectivity itself," his early work repeatedly stressed simple, critical facts of the psychoanalytic relationship to linguistic subjectivity, and thus to social subjectivity: Whether as an instrument of healing, training, or exploratory depth, psychoanalysis had only a single medium, the labor of the patient's speech. This speech was always a demand for and expectation of a reply. And if psychoanalysis failed to understand the function of speech in the reply, it would dangerously posit and seek some finalization beyond the communicative exchange (see Rose, "Introduction" 46; Lacan, "Function and Field" 38, 40; also Bakhtin, "Genres"). For Wojnarowicz this finalization was the fetishization of dead labor forms such as hetero- and homosexuality (see also Berlant, "Live").

Try as he might, Lacan could not maintain these insights about subjectivity and speech within the structuralist paradigm, any more than those scholars following him can maintain them in poststructuralist accounts of performativity, iteration, and agency. A preternatural "Thing" would stand in Lacan's way. Yet his insights resemble the core displacement that metapragmatics performs on semantic and syntactic accounts, structuralist and poststructuralist, of subjectivity and textuality; namely:

1. Grammar is always projected from some instance of language use. It is only an intuition that subjects have, extrapolated from an occasion of language use, whether as a thought, speech act, or written text. Likewise, the play of signification as generated by the structure of the sign is utterly beholden to the occasion on which a subject uses that sign. Sign and grammar cannot, in this view, determine use, for they do not provide the principles by which we use texts. If grammar and the structure of the sign do not make texts or textuality, or even designate our role and place from the outside, what organizes and coheres language into interpretable forms, capable of representing social space and time?
2. If we look for the principles on which subjects base their normative, counternormative, and even nonnormative uses of language, we must turn to metapragmatic—not semantic—orders.

Metapragmatics refers to the formal ways in which linguistic signals indicate to us how to use language to produce "texts" that make sense across diverse social contexts. For our purposes here, "textuality" corresponds to Mikhail Bakhtin's notion of a speech or text genre as a "relatively stable type of utterance" ("Genres" 60; also Vološinov; Lee). The metapragmatic principles that allow us to construct genres are at root indexical. Whether within or across cultural orders, those principles construct the provisional textual scaffolding that communicates simultaneously across the contexts and co-texts of dialogue. Subjects continually express their unconscious sense of these principles in their everyday assessments of how texts hang together. For example: "To understand Pynchon's novels one has to understand their critical engagement with modernist paradigms of narrativity." Subjects also indicate how well interactional texts are hanging together ("Wow, that was the most incoherent conversation ever!"), and when they are losing their way ("I lost the plot in that last sentence"). From the perspective of metapragmatics, nothing ever achieves the status of "a text" or "a genre." We find only relative degrees of textuality. These degrees of textuality are achieved by principles of language use that draw on (what we commonly refer to as) *semantic* sense and value, but are not determined by them.

Understanding language from a metapragmatic point of view displaces the grounds of dominant discussions of sexual difference and thereby creates new ways of thinking about sexual and gender forms as subjective risks and social reliefs. Messing around with Wojnarowicz's text suggests how:

HER friend took off right away and later my friend found out that HE'D just run home, didn't bother calling the cops or nothing . . . and all these guys crowding around watching five guys beat up one GUY and none of them said or did a fuckin' thing. . . . And SHE was just lying there. . . . HIS face was just a puddle of blood. You should have seen HER afterwards, HE woke up in the hospital and found out SHE had been unconscious for about six days. (*Close* 70–71)

In their standard, heteronormative English use, third-person pronouns (*she, he, it*) convey multiple so-called semantic signals (number, person, gender) as they pragmatically index sign to context, and then both sign and context to subjects of enunciation. Each instance of pronominal use points to a context and adopts this indexical bridge (or scaffolding) to convey semantic sense and value. But if subjects are to coordinate the various orders of the world—the semiotic, social, material—they must meaningfully organize these indexical signals with higher order textual meanings.[3] For instance, pronouns do not simply function as semantic signal-clusters. They also function as metapragmatic hinges that turn unfolding interactional texts into coherent interpretable things, a relatively stable "type" that literally hangs together. To change the gender aspect of a pronoun while maintaining number and person—to switch *he* to *she*, for example, and then back again, as I have done above—seems to render the text meaningless from a semantic and pragmatic perspective, producing responses like, "Wait, hold on a second, who are we talking about now?" or "Wait, did a man or woman get beaten up?" When conservative language critics accuse feminists or queer activists of incoherence or worse, they are not wrong in this limited sense. In standard, presumptively heteronormative English, semantic and pragmatic coherence depends partly on metapragmatic compliance with conventional semantic and pragmatic signs.

We see almost immediately, though, that every level and order of language is the debris of previous instances of implicit and explicit metapragmatic discourses. And once we discover that semantic and pragmatic values can be consciously or unconsciously realigned by social actors, then we begin to see that these values are neither neutral nor extrasocietal, but are instead sites of social contestation. Queers do not lure innocent pronouns into their nasty metapragmatic work, then, perversely reordering the natural semantic values and function of pronouns in order to advance their own genres of identity. The values of these grammatical categories are the remains of previous metapragmatic practices and their now-social institutional conditions. Heteronormativity becomes commonsensical and presuppositional by leaning on the forgotten history of these metapragmatic unfoldings, now misrecognized as natural semantic rules and forms. Grammatical forms thus appear as "perfectly natural" combinations of semantic values (what could be more obvious than third-person singular pronouns signaling gender, number, and person?). Then it is "perfectly natural" for grammatical or lexical forms to organize referential and indexical use (what could be more natural than "gender" signaling sexual difference?). Finally, abiding by the grammatical forms and principles seems a "perfectly reasonable" and necessary condition for public debate and life. These "natural" histories of discourse appear as common laws, dictating form from the outside (for models of how to analyze these histories of discourse, see Silverstein and Urban).

Out of this metaconventional reflexivity arise the conditions for new formal renderings. Let's return to the above substitutions of *she* for *he*. If the substitution were intentional, we could assume either that the *she* and *he* refer to two different persons ("her" location linked to "his"), or that the second speaker had for some reason rendered the interaction uninterpretable. Or, finally, that the speaker was switching between speech genres. We might be overhearing two gay men in the Castro—or in Iowa City, for that matter—whose *commonsense* assumption is that "she" can index sex-object-choice, rather than sex-of-the-body. But if queer (and queen) pronominal use reconfigures the semantic sense and value of pronouns and, perhaps, the relationship between gender and sexuality, it does so as it leaves behind new conventions of form.[4] Indeed, when we listen to public debates, we hear the call for new forms of intimacy, relationality, and community based on specifically queer or homo culture and conventions.

But whether heteronormative or homonormative, the relative structural order of subjectivity and social life depends on subjects maintaining normative conventions. We wield the Law. And who "we" are runs into the same problems as *he, she,* and *I.* We are most conscious of the metapragmatic function of language in instances when we explicitly wield the law of genre against each other or ourselves—that is, during moments of explicit metapragmatic discourse in which we tell each other how to speak or produce social form.[5] Moments when teachers, lovers, parents, employers indicate to each other how to talk in particular types of places with particular types of people are indexical hinges, plotting contexts (this space-time) into discursive types (this genre) into subject types (this social role), and vice versa. That "we" wield the Law does not translate into an account of the voluntarist subject, a liberal phantom who by intending better, reasoning harder, textualizing properly will produce truer or more desirable and sustainable political worlds. Why it does not translate has to do with the social, textual, and psychic risks of socially mediated conventionality. Let me discuss the social and textual risks before assessing the psychic costs.

Whether implicitly or explicitly, metapragmatic frames indicate how persons should calculate and calibrate the pleasures, risks, and stakes of being or assuming a social form in a formed space. This Wojnarowicz knew well:

Five. Man on second avenue at 2:00 A.M. (N.Y.C.): "This guy I know was walking with a friend of his around West Street. They had gone into one of the bars and had a beer and after they left they were walking down the street when this car from New Jersey cruised by . . . kids come around all the time throwin' bottles and screamin' 'QUEER!' and then taking off—so this car cruised by them real slow and some kid leans out the window sayin', 'Suck my dick!' and my friend flipped him the finger and said something; all of a sudden the car slams on the brakes and five kids come piling outta the doors and start kicking the shit out of my friend . . . for the next ten minutes about a hundred guys came outta the bars and from around the corner and surrounded these five kids beating the

shit outta my friend—his friend took off right away and later my friend found
out that he'd just run home, didn't bother calling the cops or nothing . . . and
all these guys crowding around watching five guys beat up one guy and none
of them said or did a fuckin' thing." (*Close* 70–71)

A warehouse, a glory hole, a cruising strip (types of places). A sadist,
a queer, a homophobe (types of people). Pornography, literature, sacred
scripture (types of textual forms). "Hallucinations"; "national symbols of
antigay violence"; revolting, justified, understandable reactions; a threat
to ourselves as decent civil people (types and qualities of action).[6] Wojnarowicz's report from the field reveals the ordinary discursive remains of
implicit and explicit metadiscursive frames that saturate public and private life ("He started talking, you know, queer stuff, you know, and I just
didn't want no part of it"—that is, "Don't say that gay shit to me"; or,
"Don't address me as gay" [see Firestone]). But it also shows the debris of
past standardizations of space, people, and talk that makes texts meaningful in the here and now. And it suggests the formal and informal institutional forces that dictate the varying degrees of risk that different types
of people encounter when breaking frame, having the wrong body, or
just the wrong attitude about their body in the wrong space.[7]

I write *debris* to remind us that these forms (identities, genres, actions,
and their institutional supports) are not issued from the space of symbolic
Law, nor laid down in the structure of language or courts, even though a
variety of social institutions enforce particular abstracted social formations. As Foucault noted so long ago, these forms are not singular, though
they nonetheless produce singularities. In Wojnarowicz's text, cops follow the principles of normative space (who should be allowed to walk
where and in what manner), rather than the principles of normative jurisprudence (assault and battery). In so following these principles, they pull
these forms into "interactional texts," to borrow Michael Silverstein's
phrase. The social labor and implications of these negotiations can be
lightning quick or excruciatingly tedious and painful. Is this love? Or the
pleasure of ambivalence? Or manipulation for advancement? Every one
of these imagined occasions of semiotic interaction highlights a subject's
manipulation of generic fields made by other movers. Through innovative stitching, she is creating new genre types or new dimensions to older
types—degrees of acceptable difference within a type. "Sure, she's a lesbian," we now say. "She's a lipstick lesbian." We hear others ask, "Who
murdered all the real butches and femmes?"

The answer is clear. Despite the fierceness of our loyalty to its form, every generic type (lipstick, butch, femme) is under threat, at risk in every evocation. This threat, secreted into the practices of devotion, lies at the heart of Derrida's distinction between our participation in and debt to genre ("Law"). For every field gives a subject multiple points of entry (a cop may be simultaneously a law officer, father, citizen, homophile, or homophobe). And these points allow subjects to coordinate across the orders of language and modes of context, and undo these orders and modes in the process. These interactional texts are mediated in various ways, in face-to-face conversation, in print and electronic media. And these mediations affect how texts circulate, as well as the range and speed of their dissemination (for the transnational character of these disseminations, see Povinelli and Chauncey). Any genre can theoretically be plotted into any other—a love plot into a work plot, a sex plot into a math plot. Sociologically, some invaginations entail greater risks than others.

Lacan was exceptionally gifted in creating instances of nonsensical denotational text—grammatically correct though apparently meaningless phrases such as *La Femme n'existe pas* and *Il y a d'l'Un*. Such seemingly nonsensical uses of language can provide the material stuff of real-time social struggle if people are intrigued by the enigmatic alignment of syntactic sense and practical nonsense. These phrases come to have social meaning. In the first moment, the pragmatic function of a statement such as "At least one man is not" might be little more than a thin interpretive wedge driven into normative masculinity. But over time, the silent, oft-debilitating investigation of the interrogative "Are you the one?" might reconstitute the normative expectations of not only masculinity but also the social institutions regimenting, and regimented by, the genre conventions of sexuality. A grammatical category can always be inserted into a proposition, signaling an "otherwise" to any given statement regardless that no social referent of that otherwise exists *yet*.

The content of all ideological projects derives from, but isn't reducible to, these dialogical interactions. The sotto voce with which a man tells his lover that he would like to try out something he saw in a porn flick; the enlightenment bourgeois public sphere's emergence from merchant gazettes; the departure of modern psychiatry from the confessional booth; gays and lesbians hoping a millennial march might indicate their commitment to family and faith: New textualities are constantly emerging from the lamination of already preexisting texts across generic space-time, calibrating levels of commitment to these social relations, spaces, and times (see Povinelli and Chauncey). With the whisper a man turns to another; an acoustic materiality stakes the depth of his desire and of the claim he is making on the other. But the form of the request invaginates one genre to another in strange and unsettling ways. What happens when hard porn enters intimate forms, the *grosso* issued *sotto*?[8] Fundamentalists who defend the discursive purity of social and psychic life from the defiling presence of others are in one sense right. The indwelling of others will change these forms forever. Regardless of whether these values are already despoiled by relational value, they will be despoiled still further. *Travesti* and *kathoey* may become gay men; queers may become human; lesbians and gay men might be understood as having families and faith. But gay men, human beings, families, and faith will not be what they once were. What about the perspective of those who strive for inclusion, who want nothing more than to dwell within these fundamental forms of social life? The thing they desire will be gone the moment they arrive.

Before considering how the queer and homosexual subject reappears within these fields and functions of language and textuality, let me review what demands we have placed on the symbolic. First, linguistic structures, or the iteration of *différance,* are no longer the disorganizing force of social textuality or the subject. Instead, (post)structures are a fantasy about sense and value emerging from the incessant movement of language in use. Saussure himself long ago noted the phantom nature of the structure (grammar) he sought (see *Course*).[9] The provisional nature of textuality influences how we understand the function of "grammar" and the constitution of subjects, a point I will explore in more detail below.

A young girl and boy seeking to relieve themselves after a long trip on a rumbling train confront not the function and agency of grammar when they see the toilet signs LADIES and GENTLEMEN, but a use of language from which they intuit a grammar, glimpse a structure, perhaps dream of a Law into which they could relieve themselves. But Law does not assign them a fixed place and role before birth.[10] As these young people grasp the meaning of their urinary segregation, the symbolic, the Law of the Father, the Master Signifier are revealed as a wish (*Wunsch*) for an organizing stability outside themselves and for the people they know, perhaps love. Indeed, we might wonder if this wish that some nonhuman thing or agency ordered them into separate toilets were a way of loving their predicament in another form. Yet grammar's destiny—like their own—is nothing more than an unfolding virtual phenomenon tethered to historically emergent textual forms. Language—and this young pair—hang together as long as they hold it together, adhere to and enforce principles of use across linguistic orders and social contexts through means of persuasive or punitive force. From a metapragmatic perspective, the symbolic reappears as extensible and coeval sets of provisional textuality at risk from the very principles that make meaning possible. The significance of this revision may be seen in how we conceptualize the relationship of *langue* to the subject. If *langue* could speak, which it cannot, it might lament the unremitting contortions it undergoes in the hands of speaking subjects.

I can now return to the question raised above—that is, whether this emphasis on the social labor of genre, its provisionality and risk, reduces social life to a form of voluntarism, and whether it is thus a queer political commitment to a liberal and liberationist fantasy of existence without limits. I think not. But the reason stems from why I think a Lacan-inspired account of the provisional subject is necessary if we are to develop any real analysis, let alone ethics, of politics and social life. First, the conscious, intentional aspects of metapragmatics that I have discussed constitute only a small portion of what is primarily an unconscious textual process. And this "conscious operation" is itself merely a set of motivated misapprehensions of the system of textuality we are using. Unfortunately, "unconscious operation" is now typically the first phrase of a sentence that goes something like this: "Our unconscious operates us like a language." I mean something more like this: "We are using a machine whose operation we do not for the most part comprehend." That is why, in trying to remove a dangling string, we ruin the sweater, and in trying to ruin the market, we increase capital earnings. Second, the formal problems of the subject are an order of phenomena distinct from the formal properties of textuality and their circulation and dissemination. Finally, and perhaps most important for a queer ethics and politics, the institutions that enforce normative structures are themselves saturated with subjectivity's psychic provisionality.

2. The Subject

How does the subject reappear in these metapragmatic fields and functions? Those critically rethinking the problem of language and textuality through metapragmatics have tended to sidestep the formal relations between textuality and the pre- and postlinguistic subject—as, for that matter, have most Peirce-inspired accounts of semiosis and social life.

This does not mean that linguistically oriented accounts are not, and have never been, interested in the relations among language, consciousness, and the unconscious. On the contrary, the unconscious has been a central theme in American- and Prague-inspired schools of linguistic anthropology, though not centrally in Foucault's writings on discourse. Lacan's own argument that human subjects are incapable of grasping in its totality the systems they deploy stems from Lévi-Strauss's reworking of the insights of the American linguist Edward Sapir.[11]

It has been long recognized that the difference between language as a textual thing and human beings as volitional, cognitive, and affective entities is the reason that subjects misrecognize language. In the linguistic schools mentioned above, the subject's linguistic unconscious is the systematic misapprehension of the levels, orders, and phenomena of grammar she speaks, though she cannot comprehend because she cannot lift herself out of her own language by its instrumental bootstraps.[12]

However, from the perspective of metapragmatics, the unconscious is not structured like a language, if by that phrase we mean like a grammar or the play of the signifier (Lacan, *Four* 20). Metapragmatic approaches to genre deepen and complicate even as they clarify the problem of the linguistic unconscious. As Silverstein has suggested, it is not merely the denotational text (loosely, texts considered from the perspective of structure and grammar) that is misapprehended in systematic ways, but also the principles by which texts emerge, adhere, and disjoin; the ways in which the various levels of metapragmatic form (poetics, iconic indexicality) act as interpretive diagrams; and how the various levels and orders of textuality are calibrated and calibratable. This *méconnaissance* of language turns to folly all political, ethical, and social projects built on the impoverished notion of intention. Yet even from this perspective of use, if the subject could lay hold of language, her subjective interiority would not be completely accounted for.

In short, replacing the grammatical unconscious with the metapragmatic unconscious will not dislodge our habit of collapsing subjectivity into textuality, discursivity, or practice. Thus metapragmatics would not escape what Joan Copjec calls the reduction of the dynamism of the subject of language to the dynamism of discourse and practice (*Read My Desire* 1–14). All these approaches proceed as if tracking the facticity of textual practices would be sufficient to account for the subject and her relation to these orders of language. Consequently, meaning is read off practice, or practices off meaning, without regard to the subject mediating these meanings, texts, and practices. However, the Lacanian triptych of imaginary, symbolic, and real orders makes this move impossible. The Lacanian account of the unsymbolizable content of the real and imaginary negates the possibility of accounting for the subject through an accounting of semiotic forms—that is, conscious, preconscious, or unconscious; and solely through language, discourse, or textuality.

Despite bracketing the subject in its account of language and textuality, metapragmatic models presuppose a subject in a way that is compatible with the commitment and promise psychoanalysis held out to the subject, her psychic and social well-being, and her ethical and political life. Remember that unlike the structuralist legacy, metapragmatic perspectives view the semantic order of human languages as presupposing some token of language use, and thus a subject using language. They also distinguish semantic and pragmatic linguistic phenomena in every essential characteristic, even while maintaining their mutual intercalation. We should similarly distinguish between language in use and the subject using it. One of the defining phenomenological features of the subject is that she once was incapable of using language. We face, therefore, two distinct questions: How does the human subject bear the history of becoming a user of natural human languages in the context of a grammatically displaced account of semiosis? And how does this affect her stance toward social and institutional conventions?

We can still invoke what Jean Laplanche and Jean-Bertrand Pontalis long ago observed—that human beings are born into a world suffused with socially mediated textuality, which Lacan called the language of the Other ("Fantasy"). From the perspective of this prelinguistic person, the contours of social space and time emerge out of an initially uncoordinatable stream of semiotic modes and practices of coordination.[13] "The history or the legends of parents, grandparents and ancestors," a "spoken or secret discourse, going on prior to the subject's arrival," and "within which he must find his way"—the materiality of language (its acoustic nature)—is but one modality of this semiotic form, and certainly not the first that the child masters ("Fantasy" 19). In the United States, the first form is typically the misapprehended ordering of the heteronormative home:

In my dreams I crawl across freshly clipped front lawns, past statues and dogs and cars containing your guardians. I enter your houses through the smallest cracks in the bricks that keep you feeling comfortable and safe. I cross your living rooms and go up your staircases and into your bedrooms where you lie sleeping. I wake you up and tell you a story about when I was ten years old and walking around times square looking for the weight of some man to lie across me to replace the nonexistent hugs and kisses from my mom and dad. I got picked up by some guy who took me to a remote area of the waterfront in his car and proceeded to beat the shit out of me because he was so afraid of the impulses of heat stirring in his belly. I would have strangled him but my hands were too small to fit around his neck. I will wake you up and welcome you to your bad dream. (*Close* 81–82)

For Wojnarowicz, heterosexuality is not a desire but a conventionalized hierarchical recursivity that is used to arrest desire's itinerateness. There is a fine recursivity to the forms identified with this home. A private space within the public world, though only for some ("only people who are heterosexual or married or who have families" [81]); and, for the others, public space is primarily for pleasurable and abusive sex, not reason. Within this privatized space are public and private spaces; and within these private spaces are still more sacred privacies: the home and the world, the living room and bedroom, the bathroom and medicine cabinet. This house represents the material manifestation of normative concepts of space (public and private, rather than, say, ritual and nonritual) and of persons. It designates how certain subjects and pleasures are legitimately associated with specific types of spaces, and with what degree of risk and ignorance. Although the language of privacy and publicness is not in space, materiality is not inert. The difference between spatial forms and their meanings must be continually braced by acts of interpretive framing. If spatial forms are metapragmatic principles in another semiotic register, discourses must continually retranscribe these forms.

Space and time are not built up only from socially mediated semiosis; they are built into subjects. And they are built into subjects in such a way that understandings like "these are the spoken and corporeal forms allowable in this type of space" become unreflected inferences of everyday life, and thus the conditions of intelligibility and safe passage. Long before she can make such inferences, the child's body is impressed with the socially mediated semiotic forms. Strictly speaking, the earliest kernel of subjectivity—the proper name of its baptismal ritual—is our experience of a relation to socially mediated regimentation, a relation of being to provisional form. Laplanche's notion of the "enigmatic signifier" captures an aspect of this relation before a subject, induced into language, becomes a subject as such.[14]

Initially, the subject experiences the necessity of inferring principles of coordination across levels and orders of social being. Only later will arise the meaningful content of social time-space conveyed by those coordinates. And the child first experiences this factual necessity of coordination in the condition of dependent noncoordination, the experience of the risks, pleasures, or simply the corporeal facticity of not being able to navigate space or time and being subject to disciplinary acts (see Rose, *Sexuality* 172). The child bumps up against a *Gestalt* of regimented spatial and temporal scales and orders, from which she experiences a series of corporeal traumas (later interpretable as painful or pleasurable). Within the regime of language, we might say retrospectively that we have experienced the risks of being unformed in a formed world. But, initially, the child does not have the language to make sense of her experience. Instead, she bumps and bounces into her provisional grasping of the working of the social machine (Lacan, *Seminar* 2:64–76; Laplanche, *New Foundations*).

The concept of incorporation serves us nicely here.[15] For every discursive form (identity, genres) is baptized into subjective experience through bodies—space as a set of material embodiments and the bodies of specific people. As social agents (parents, teachers, daycare workers, and ritual celebrants) are mediating the tacit coordinates of social life into children, children are laminating language with the traumas and corporeal sensations they associate with the intimates who make up their lives. The signal values of linguistic forms will bear the history of their physical associations, creating what Jakobson called "individual *langue*"—a personalized linguistic code demarcated by a person's avoidance of "certain forms or certain words that are accepted by society but that seem unacceptable to him for whatever reason or to which he has an aversion." If "social *langue*" maintains the unity of a society, "individual *langue*" reflects and maintains "the unity, that is, the continuity, of the individual identity" ("Langue and Parole" 90–91; see also Lacan's discussion of "semantic evolution," in "Function and Field" 50).

Into this field of difference between "me" and these regimented forms, the child unconsciously "introjects" language, slowly inlaying her fantasies about grammar and genre: the "I and thou"; the "he, she, and it"; the "this and that." Thus, incorporated into the subject—what exposes her body to anxiety and pleasure—is social institutionality, the risk of refusing its penetration, and the feelings of mastering it.[16] All actual institutions resituate us in this subjective history when they show their teeth, explicitly or implicitly, even as they present actual threats to subjects in real time.

Unfortunately, perhaps, the symbolic is not fully introjected. Quite the contrary. To be a subject in language, the child must introject into an incorporated semiotic field the variegated fields of genre, their corporeal and material contexts, and the principles by which we map and remap them convincingly. People are not provided with one law. Indeed, cops and crowds discover that to follow one law means violating another. And as they attempt to eliminate those types of people whose very being seems to threaten their own, fundamentalists reveal the cracks in the walls upholding normative liberal (in)tolerances and expose its edifice to the sympathetic wailing of those they seek to destroy. But perhaps what makes such moments of liberal fundamentalism so unstable—truly ambivalent moments of rage and folly—is the metalingual sense that no grammar is holding us or our texts in place.

We hold ourselves in place through the interactional texts we build with and through others, and in the shadow of institutions of force. To use language effectively, all subjects must be able to operate—if not consciously understand—the principles by which texts cohere as the same principles that allow for their reformation. In short, the subject must learn to rely for survival on her provisionality within any one unfolding discursive space and her displacement across discursive spaces as her means of survival. In doing so, she places herself in the human lot: Every day, without relief from birth to death, she will remake the here and now whether she likes it or not, whether she knows it or not, in the context of institutional threat and incitement.

To be sure, these institutions might seem a welcome external brace, a resting place. While Wojnarowicz's memoir of disintegration is not on the side of form, it does not avert his eye from the psychic and social stakes of this disavowal. Indeed, *Seven Miles a Second* focuses on the pain of being outside form, not as the anguish of the insomniac, but as the torture of the awake incessantly surviving. Wojnarowicz considers relief from this knowledge-practice the privilege of heteronormativity and the death of poetics.

The stakes of the subject's relation to social form are therefore more than physical coercion stemming from an institutional outside. Moments of fundamental difference create a profound rendering, a dyshesion quaking the slumbering fault lines of semiotic subjectivity. The encounter with difference might entail merely textual alterities—discursive forms experienced as impenetrable, or, it might entail physical threat. Some human subjects, whether defined by their bodies' desires or by their bodies as such, live within these fault lines and write memoirs of disintegration. But these fault lines would rewrite the grammar books we have learned from. For instance, grammatical modality would be a register of the risks human beings face in actual, possible, and imaginable worlds. Swirling around our fundamental statements we would hear the depth charges of subjectivity.

The subject's ability to be captured within textuality is displaced at the outset, then, less because of a structural foreclosure of being in language or the inability of language structure to close, than because in using language the subject takes up the provisionality of language; this provisionality is the means of her survival and pleasure; and this provisionality is only provisionally her own. In this way, subjectivity emerges as a phenomenon entirely distinct from the orders of semiotics and discourse. And with it emerges something we might still call "desire"—a *pulsion* that is the result of semiotic subjectivity, but that is on the side neither of language nor of what language entails for gender and sexual identities, among other things, though its trace may be found in "grammatical" forms such as mood and desiderata. All social identities within this circuit of emerging and decomposing regimentation fall outside desire, and into language, discourse, and textuality. All of these identities and their normative entailments are sites of opposing forces of provisionality and desire, as well as of institutionality (generic forces such as courts of law and public opinion)—sites of fierce loyalty, in other words, whose devotional practices would do them in.

This, then, is Wojnarowicz's queer militancy: He views institutions of form as places where the incessant itinerateness of social life seems to end, so that our dream of structure arises from a nightmare of being's belabored provisionality. These institutions of form seem to be fundamental sources of the subject, insofar as they still life into form. They have different modes, scales, temporality, and might be represented as ports of call and points of departure, or calls to relax and to cease becoming. But no matter how we represent them, institutions of form provide spaces for fundamentalist dreams, for the fundamental need to sleep, to rest along the way. Perhaps if the material world could fully resist our twitches, then our provisionality in language and textuality would not matter so much. But at an abstract level we see a formal correspondence between the concreteness of our engagement with material form and our engagement with semiotic form. Our intended uses of these media produce countless unintended traces, reverberations, lines of force and forms that are exhausting, and from which we protect ourselves with institutions.

3. Jouissance

Finally, the matter of *jouissance*. Let me end by observing that nothing I have said requires a positive or negative assessment of the queer provisionality discussed here. Even relaxing into institutions of form may be represented and experienced positively or negatively, depending on the

institution and its location within larger order social formations (in homophobic societies, relaxing into homosexuality is valued differently
than is relaxing into heterosexuality). Comparing Peirce and Lacan on
this point, Teresa de Lauretis notes similarly that no transcendent value
adheres to the process by which semiosis fixes subjects: "In the general
critical discourse based on Lacanian psychoanalysis and Althusser's theory of ideology, 'suture' is bad. Peirce, on the other hand, does not say
whether the bait that provisionally joins the subject to social and ideological formations is good or bad" (*Alice* 180). The rendering of self can be
situated in countless generic forms. We have heard poets, ethnographers,
literary critics, and philosophers name but a few: rites of transition, love
and its undoings, S/M. Yet what draws de Lauretis—and Habermas—to
Peirce is the positively inflected fantasy of the final interpretant, that infinitely deferred day when all orders of semiosis are repaired, and all that
rises converges. On the way, of course, we must inspect the grounds on
which we have grown accustomed to slumbering. We must tarry with the
negative, destroying ourselves to be born again—for the better implied.
Isn't this the genre of the manifesto coordinating liberal and radical political space? Isn't the manifesto a diagram, an image, a phylogenetic fantasy mirroring the movement of the subject into semiosis, providing an
interpretive frame for each phase of the journey? We see emerging before
us a form wrapped in a form, an image within a message telling us how
to interpret it. All of these obligate us to a name, and in that name is a
genre, and in that genre, a subject who is not simply of it. In short: a
queer manifesto.

Notes

For Mlle. X

1. Outside linguistic circles, most North American scholars know Peircean semiotics primarily through the writings of Habermas on communicative action; of
Kristeva and de Lauretis on feminist and lesbian theory; and, of course, of Eco.
Peircean semiotics lent these politically and ethically informed projects a robust
model for conceptualizing how social and psychic change is mediated by the critical engagement of individuals with their material-discursive conditions (see, for
example, Peirce, "Pragmatism"; Habermas 226–27). It may well be the overtones of
Peircean pragmatics we hear in Lacan's distinction between the dual relationship
of the imaginary and the triadic structure of the symbolic, wherein a "third" (the
Peircean interpretant) makes meaning possible as it disrupts its every grounding. For

these overtones in his discussion of the Lévi-Straussean breakthrough, see Lacan, *Seminar 2*:28–31, 243; and *Seminar 3*:72; also Muller, *Beyond;* and Muller and Brent.

2. Especially vital to this developing school of thought are the works of Silverstein, especially "Shifters" and "Metapragmatic Discourse"; see also Urban, *Metaphysical Community;* and Lee, *Talking Heads.*

3. In *Sexuality in the Field of Vision,* Rose has usefully discussed how Freud and Lacan conceived this coordinating function of image and language. See also Lacan's own discussion in "Mirror Stage."

4. Thus refiguring the important debate between Copjec (*Read My Desire* 201–36) and Butler (*Bodies That Matter* 187–222) about the relationship between sexual difference and other forms of social difference. The multivocal signal capacity of pronominals is not the only normative hinge binding utterances to texts. Parallelism, for instance, functions as an indexical icon (a diagram), using formal equivalence to indicate how sequences of discourse should be interpreted, how one segment should be enfolded into another, and the whole into itself and outward into its context (see Jakobson, "Poetry of Grammar"; Silverstein, "Pragmatic 'Poetry'"). Likewise, the Bakhtinean notion of finalization seeks to explain what formal features of utterances allow for the possibility of response, of an other "assuming a responsive attitude toward it" ("Genres" 76).

5. Often these explicit statements discipline coparticipants who refuse to acknowledge these tacit interpretive structures embedded in language use, exemplified by such statements as, "Don't play games with me, girlfriend, you know exactly what this means."

6. "But trial testimony today revealed new details of the savage nature of the murder, and of Mr. Gaither's desperate attempts to resist. Jurors shook their heads in revulsion when shown large color photographs of his body, the abdomen of which had been reduced to ashes by the flaming tires placed on him after his head had been crushed by an ax handle" (Firestone).

7. Berlant and Warner separately have discussed the politics of public embodiment and abstraction in ways critical to this discussion. See Berlant, "Brands"; and Warner, "Mass Public."

8. Derrida calls this the "double chiasmatic invagination of edges" (238).

9. There is fairly widespread agreement among students of the Saussurean tradition that the synchronic axis of language is a necessary myth. But the full implications of the virtual nature of linguistic structure have yet to be acknowledged. Not only would the structure of linguistic structure (grammar or sign) need to be deferred, but structure itself (signifier and signified, grammar, *langue*) would need to be displaced.

10. As opposed to the positions sketched out in Lacan, "Agency"; and Althusser, "Freud and Lacan."

11. For evolving discussions of the linguistic unconscious, see Jakobson, "Consciousness and Unconsciousness"; Sapir, "Unconscious Patterning"; Whorf, "Grammatical Categories"; and Lacan, *Seminar 2*:127.

12. In the process of discussing the reflexive properties of language, John A. Lucy states that it is a commonplace among linguists that speakers are unaware of the complex regularities they routinely use when speaking. Speakers seem able to become aware of functions of certain of the individual forms of language, but have difficulty recognizing the place a form occupies in the systematicity of a grammar (24). A special limitation to our becoming conscious of this grammatical systematicity is the fact that the formal instrument we use to represent and describe our own linguistic system as a referential device is ultimately drawn from the same system.

13. For Lacan's understanding of the coordinating function of linguistic structure and the sign, see *Seminar* 3:183–95.

14. Drawing out Lacan's emphasis on the primacy of the signifier over the signified, Laplanche proposes the term *enigmatic signifier* to highlight the aspect of signification in which the signifier "signifies to" the addressee without "signifying what," and without the addressee knowing what (*New Foundations* 45). The prelinguistic subject we are talking about here would not, however, necessarily understand semiotic form to be addressed to anyone.

15. Especially interesting is Laplanche's understanding of the relationships among incorporation, scenario (or genre), and fantasy (*Life and Death* 207).

16. Acknowledging this level of semiotic corporeality would do away with the artificial and wholly unproductive separation and opposition of biological and social orders. Though the semiotic forms the child incorporates are of a different nature than the biological field into which they are enfolded, structured, and are structured by, the corporeal effects themselves will be indexically tied to generic tokens of the traumatic type.

References

Althusser, Louis. "Freud and Lacan." *Lenin and Philosophy, and Other Essays*. Trans. Ben Brewster. New York: Monthly Review, 1971. 189–220.

Bakhtin, M. M. "The Problem of Speech Genres." *Speech Genres and Other Late Essays*. Ed. Caryl Emerson and Michael Holquist. Austin: U of Texas P, 1986. 60–102.

Berlant, Lauren. "Intimacy: A Special Issue." *Critical Inquiry* 24.2 (1998): 281–88.

———. "Live Sex Acts: (Parental Advisory: Explicit Material)." *Feminist Studies* 21.2 (1995): 379–404.

———. "National Brands/National Body: *Imitation of Life*." In *The Phantom Public Sphere*. Ed. Bruce Robbins. Minneapolis: U of Minnesota P, 1993. 173–208.

Bersani, Leo. *Homos*. Cambridge: Harvard UP, 1995.

Butler, Judith. *Bodies That Matter: On the Discursive Limits of "Sex."* New York: Routledge, 1993.

Copjec, Joan. *Read My Desire: Lacan against the Historicists*. Cambridge: MIT P, 1994.

de Lauretis, Teresa. *Alice Doesn't: Feminism, Semiotics, Cinema*. Bloomington: Indiana UP, 1984.

Derrida, Jacques. "The Law of Genre." In *Acts of Literature*. Ed. Derek Attridge. New York: Routledge, 1992. 223–52.

Firestone, David. "Trial in Gay Killing Opens; Conspiracy of Hate Is Cited; New Details of a Crime's Savage Nature." *New York Times* (August 4, 1999): A8.

Foucault, Michel. "What Is an Author?" *Language, Counter-Memory, Practice: Selected Essays and Interviews*. Ed. Donald F. Bouchard. Trans. Bouchard and Sherry Simon. Ithaca: Cornell UP, 1977. 113–38.

Habermas, Jürgen. *Between Facts and Norms: Contributions to a Discourse Theory of Law and Democracy*. Trans. William Rehg. Cambridge: MIT P, 1996.

Jakobson, Roman. "Langue and Parole: Code and Message." In *On Language*. Ed. Linda R. Waugh and Monique Monville-Burston. Cambridge: Harvard UP, 1990. 80–109.

———. "On the Linguistic Approach to the Problem of Consciousness and the Unconscious." *Selected Writings*. 8 vols. Ed. Stephen Rudy. Berlin: Mouton, 1985. 7:148–62.

———. "Poetry of Grammar and the Grammar of Poetry." In *Verbal Art, Verbal Sign, Verbal Time*. Ed. Krystyna Pomorska and Stephen Rudy, with Brent Vine. Minneapolis: U of Minnesota P, 1985. 37–46.

Lacan, Jacques. "The Agency of the Letter in the Unconscious, or Reason Since Freud." *Écrits* 146–78.

———. *Écrits: A Selection*. Trans. Alan Sheridan. New York: Norton, 1977.

———. *The Four Fundamental Concepts of Psycho-Analysis*. 1973. Ed. Jacques-Alain Miller. Trans. Alan Sheridan. New York: Norton, 1977.

———. "The Function and Field of Speech and Language in Psychoanalysis." *Écrits* 30–113.

———. "The Mirror Stage as Formative of the Function of the I." *Écrits* 1–7.

———. *The Seminar of Jacques Lacan, Book 2: The Ego in Freud's Theory and in the Technique of Psychoanalysis, 1954–1955*. Ed. Jacques-Alain Miller. Trans. Sylvana Tomaselli. New York: Norton, 1988.

———. *The Seminar of Jacques Lacan, Book 3: The Psychoses, 1955–1956*. Ed. Jacques-Alain Miller. Trans. Russell Grigg. New York: Norton, 1993.

———. *The Seminar of Jacques Lacan, Book 7: The Ethics of Psychoanalysis, 1959–1960*. Ed. Jacques-Alain Miller. Trans. Dennis Porter. New York: Norton, 1992.

Laplanche, Jean. *Life and Death in Psychoanalysis*. 1970. Trans. Jeffrey Mehlman. Baltimore: John Hopkins UP, 1976.

———. *New Foundations for Psychoanalysis*. Trans. David Macey. Oxford: Blackwell, 1989.

Laplanche, Jean, and Jean-Bertrand Pontalis. "Fantasy and the Origins of Sexuality." 1964. In *Formations of Fantasy*. Ed. Victor Burgin, James Donald, and Cora Kaplan. New York: Routledge, 1986. 5–34.

Lee, Benjamin. *Talking Heads: Language, Metalanguage, and the Semiotics of Subjectivity*. Durham: Duke UP, 1997.

Lucy, John A. "Reflexive Language and the Human Disciplines." In *Reflexive Lan-*

guage: Reported Speech and Metapragmatics. Ed. John A. Lucy. Cambridge: Cambridge UP, 1993. 9–32.

Martin, Biddy. "Extraordinary Homosexuals and the Fear of Being Ordinary." In *Feminism Meets Queer Theory.* Ed. Elizabeth Weed and Naomi Schor. Bloomington: Indiana UP, 1997. 109–35.

Muller, John P. *Beyond the Psychoanalytic Dyad: Developmental Semiotics in Freud, Pierce, and Lacan.* London: Routledge, 1996.

Muller, John P., and Joseph Brent, eds. *Peirce, Semiotics, and Psychoanalysis.* Baltimore: John Hopkins UP, 2000.

Peirce, Charles Sanders. "Pragmatism." *Essential Peirce: Selected Philosophical Writings.* Ed. Nathan Houser and Christian Kloesel. 2 vols. Bloomington: Indiana UP, 1992. 2:398–433.

Povinelli, Elizabeth A. "The Vulva Thieves: Modal Ethics and the Colonial Archive." *The Cunning of Reason: Settler Modernities and Indigenous Politics in Multicultural Australia.* Durham: Duke UP, forthcoming.

Povinelli, Elizabeth A., and George Chauncey. "Thinking Sexuality Transnationally: An Introduction." GLQ: *A Journal of Lesbian and Gay Studies* 5.4 (1999): 439–49.

Rose, Jacqueline. "Introduction—II." In *Feminine Sexuality, Jacques Lacan and the école freudienne.* Ed. Juliet Mitchell and Jacqueline Rose. Trans. Rose. New York: Norton, 1982. 27–57.

———. *Sexuality in the Field of Vision.* London: Verso, 1986.

Sapir, Edward. "The Unconscious Patterning of Behavior in Society." *Selected Writings in Language, Culture, and Personality.* 1949. Ed. David G. Mandelbaum. Berkeley: U of California P, 1985. 544–59.

Saussure, Ferdinand de. *Course in General Linguistics.* Ed. Charles Bally and Albert Sechehaye with Albert Riedlinger. Trans. Wade Baskin. New York: McGraw-Hill, 1966.

Silverstein, Michael. "Metapragmatic Discourse and Metapragmatic Function." In *Reflexive Language: Reported Speech and Metapragmatics.* Ed. John A. Lucy. Cambridge: Cambridge UP, 1993. 33–58.

———. "On the Pragmatic 'Poetry' of Prose: Parallelism, Repetition, and Cohesive Structure in the Time Course of Dyadic Conversation." In *Meaning, Form, and Use in Context: Linguistic Applications.* Ed. Deborah Sciffrin. Cambridge: Cambridge UP, 1984. 181–99.

———. "Shifters, Linguistic Categories, and Cultural Description." In *Meaning in Anthropology.* Ed. Keith Basso and Henry A. Selby. Albuquerque: U of New Mexico P, 1976. 11–55.

Silverstein, Michael, and Greg Urban. "The Natural History of Discourse." In *Natural Histories of Discourse.* Ed. Silverstein and Urban. Chicago: U of Chicago P, 1996. 21–44.

Spivak, Gayatri. "Can the Subaltern Speak?" In *Marxism and the Interpretation of Culture.* Ed. Cary Nelson and Lawrence Grossberg. Urbana: U of Illinois P, 1988. 271–313.

Urban, Greg. *Metaphysical Community: The Interplay of the Senses and the Intellect.* Austin: U of Texas P, 1996.

Vološinov, V. N. *Marxism and the Philosophy of Language.* Trans. Ladislav Matejka and I. R. Titunik. Cambridge: Harvard UP, 1986.

Warner, Michael. "The Mass Public and the Mass Subject." In *Habermas and the Public Sphere.* Ed. Craig Calhoun. Cambridge: MIT P, 1993. 377–401.

———. "Normal and Normaller: Beyond Gay Marriage." *GLQ: A Journal of Lesbian and Gay Studies* 5.2 (1999): 119–71.

Whorf, Benjamin L. "Grammatical Categories." *Language Thought and Reality: Selected Writings of Benjamin Lee Whorf.* 1937. Ed. John B. Carroll. Cambridge: MIT P, 1956. 87–101.

Wojnarowicz, David. *Close to the Knives: A Memoir of Disintegration.* New York: Vintage, 1991.

Wojnarowicz, David, and James Romberger. *Seven Miles a Second.* New York: DC Comics, 1996.

Zupančič, Alenka. "The Subject of the Law." In *Cogito and the Unconscious.* Ed. Renata Salecl and Slavoj Žižek. Durham: Duke UP, 1998. 41–73.

21

THE FETISH OF FLUIDITY

Brad Epps

. . . .

It's a question of knowing why subjects commune [*communient*] in the same ideal. LACAN, "L'OBJET FÉTICHE," *SÉMINAIRE IV*

Unlike either the heterosexual or the homosexual, the fetishist wants to have his cake and eat it too. ELIZABETH GROSZ, "LESBIAN FETISHISM?"

In the current rush of theory, I would like to take a moment to ponder not so much what is lost in the rush as what is kept, secured, even fixed. I would like to do so, moreover, in and around homosexuality—the proverbial question, that is, of homosexuality. For I am struck by the ways in which homosexuality, recast as gayness—and recast, beyond that, as queerness— is bound up in signs of movement. How it is bent, twisted, loosened, and set adrift.[1] How it flows, with curiously increasing surety, into almost any- thing *but* a stable identity, and how it thwarts, in the very same process, any stable identity whatsoever. I am also struck by the ways in which homosex- uality, squinted ever so unstably into something else, nonetheless slips into something comfortable and quite powerful: a mode of knowledge, an ex- emplary performance, an ironic sign of privilege, a badge of honor. The queering of homosexuality, by which homosexuality is all but crossed over and out, entails some compelling and insistent moves.

One such move bears on movement itself, presented, over and again, explicitly or implicitly, as truth-value and as freedom.[2] Queer theory tends to place great stock in movement, especially when it is movement against, beyond, or away from rules and regulations, norms and conventions, borders and limits.[3] It is not, in this, alone, for a great deal of critical and theoretical work is similarly moved. It is not alone, yet queer theory, as the general effect of particular pronouncements, presents movement, fluid movement, as the liberational undoing of regulatory disciplinarity. Its own disciplinarity appears, however, to be another matter. For it is my contention that by insistently setting its sights on fluidity, by taking it as that which at once denies and affirms disciplinary power, queer theory performs a little magic of its own. To put it provocatively, even perversely, it makes fluidity a fetish.[4]

This fluidity is not that of a certain feminist "mechanics," where something feminine is maintained, almost essentially, as part of a physical reality that resists symbolic solidification, totalization, or idealization (see Irigaray 105–16). Nor is it the fluidity of a certain AIDS activism, where the ideological underpinnings of a prophylactic imperative are exposed and contested. In both cases, fluidity is understood in reference to, among other corporeal properties, blood, milk, and semen. In both cases, as well, fluidity may function as a fetish, but in ways that arguably heighten rather than diminish identificatory positions and so-called identity politics. The fluidity of queer theory partakes, perhaps, of both the aforementioned "forms" of fluidity, but it places the accent on the diminishment, or undoing, of identity. This is not to say that queer theory did not have a place in AIDS activism, but that the place it often occupied entailed the "subversive" displacement of all identities, gay and lesbian included (almost as if identity itself were the disease). The problem is that "queer" itself is hardly free from the drag of identity, that it too is consolidated as an identity, perhaps even as an identity to end all identities, with considerable *moral* charge—again, even when it impugns morality per se, strives to get beyond it. Further, as we shall see, "queer" becomes a term, if not an identity, to be protected, defended, and preserved, to be fixed, that is, as designating a lack of fixity, a generally free fluidity.

Here fluidity presumably flows beyond established channels, even more newly established channels such as feminism, and washes away essence entirely. What also goes with this flow is gender, race, age, class, and so on, all restyled as so many moving parts in a generalized performance—though rarely for a general audience—of the "human" and the "livable."[5] Along with so many things, the body is itself in trouble, rendered so discursive as to matter little if at all. Or so the story goes. Recent work in queer theory revisits, with varying degrees of anxiety, apology, and aggressiveness, the beleaguered matter of materiality, appealing to the importance of "intimate critique" and foregrounding a dialogic praxis that seems willing to reconsider almost everything but the ideological baggage and national limits of the term *queer* itself.[6] Judith Butler, from whose work I have been so allusively drawing, is paradigmatic here, a figure who casts such a long shadow that any incursion into queer theory, any speculation on it, must cite her.[7] The present work is no exception: It finds itself conditioned, perhaps even constrained, by the authority of a work that precedes and exceeds it.

This is not an idle point. Queer theory, for all its antinormative acts and pronouncements; for all its self-conscious maneuvers against proper objects and proper subjects; for all its assertions of openness and extra-academic inventiveness; for all its language of transgression, subversion, and radicality, is not free from authoritative gestures, rules, and norms of its own. And if queer theory flows, it stops short, as I have suggested, of flowing beyond itself, washing itself away, letting itself go. There is, after all, a certain amount of power and privilege here, and the maintenance and expansion of the queer, in and as queer theory, are not without benefit, economic and otherwise. This is true, of course, for any number of critical endeavors under capitalism, but with queerness it plays a bit differently. The benefit is, in a sense, an ostensible lack of benefit. I might underscore the ostensible—perhaps ostentatious—nature of this lack, which is, by the way, crucial to the psychoanalytic conception of fetishism, but for the moment I will stress the paradox of power and—in typical chiastic fashion—the power of paradox.

Lacan, as part of a compelling argument on power, introjection, and nonidentification, does not write specifically of the benefit of a lack of benefit,[8] but of the advantages of reproof, of the subject reproved. Specifically, he writes of "the dimension of the reprobate (*réprouvé*), which, as everyone knows, is not at all so narcissistically disadvantageous" (*Séminaire VIII* 398). Reproof, censure, and so on are not without benefit, paradoxical as that may seem. For Lacan, the reproof, not surprisingly, issues from the father, or the law of the father, and comes to mark, through introjection, any and every subject who contests the father and his law. The queer is presumably such a subject, but one who contests not just the father and his law, but also the regime of subjectivity, and identity, itself. Lacan is here at his most cantankerous, and what he asserts is that every contestation of authority, every move against and beyond the law, every effort to make father shit (*"faire chier père"*) is shadowed, as it were, by the signifier *father:* So much so that identity is constituted in the very resistance to identity—constituted, enriched, and benefited.

Now, admittedly, this is a frustrating state of affairs, at least for those who would seek satisfaction in the contestatory, maybe even parodic, undoing of identity per se. Butler's "hope for a coalition of sexual minorities that will transcend the simple categories of identity" ("Preface" xxvi), no less than her vaguely programmatic call to "be" "against proper objects," and her presentation of the psyche as "what resists the regularization that Foucault ascribes to normalizing discourses" (*Psychic* 86), all seem to suggest that the "proper" site of the queer, the locus from which one can be dislocated and still be a person ("Preface" xvi), is the improper. But one person's impropriety may well be the father's property. Lacan, again, is worth citing. Ridiculing the much-touted rebelliousness of certain subjects, whom he casts as "Marie-Chantal and Daddy's boy," he makes the following claim:

> The one and the other, Marie-Chantal and Daddy's boy at the wheel of his little car, would be quite simply subsumed in the world organized by the father, if it were not for the signifier father, which permits [them], if I may say so, to extricate themselves from it and to imagine making him shit and even to succeed in doing so. That is what is expressed in saying that, in the case in point, he or she introjects the paternal image. (*Séminaire VIII* 398)

It may be significant that the girl in this little story has a proper name while the boy is called, quite literally, in conjunction with the father. It may also be significant that the girl's rebellion, or resistance, takes the form of joining the Communist Party, while the boy's takes a decidedly more consumerist one. Nevertheless, sexual difference, however signified, may not be what is most at stake here. For Lacan says that the boy and girl both contend with the father, not in the flesh, but as a name—as an instance, that is, of symbolic power. More pointedly, he indicates that they can contend with him *only* through the name, the signifier, whose separation from the signified permits a realm of possibility that includes, as we have seen, making father shit.

Lacan tells this story in the course of a more involved presentation on transference, idealization (the ego ideal and the ideal ego) and the slippage of the sense of the ideal, mass analysis (including mass, or communitarian, ideals), identification, narcissism, partial objects, and so on. It is beyond the scope of this essay to follow all these threads, but I will take up one, already adumbrated in the preceding remarks on queerness and fluidity. I mean the role of authority, law, and power, "always already" enrolled in the service of (the Name of) the Father. By implicitly casting Butler in this role, by citing her as an authority—perhaps *the* authority—of queer theory, and by citing Lacan as a supplementary, curiously contestable authority in turn, I have, just possibly, performed an impertinence unpardonable for some. Impertinent, improper, perverse, I am suggesting that Butler—or, more precisely, the signifier *Butler*—sustains in the very "body" of the work that bears her name (her signature, her copyright) an authoritative image that, without being reduced to the father, nonetheless bears the mark, the shadow, of *his* name. In suggesting this, I am, I confess, courting a certain interpretative excess that risks overflowing established critical channels as well as presumed and stated critical intentions. The excess risks denying her authority by affirming it as essentially the same as his. That is not my intention, but that may be its effect.[9] My intention, for whatever it is worth, is to affirm her authority as not *essentially* different from his, as in some dogged respects akin to it. For Butler's authority, in and out of today's academy, is enviable indeed, far outstripping Lacan's authority, at least within queer theory.[10] The latter qualification is necessary, for queer theory has, as I have been arguing, its own proper subjects and authorities—typically involving the repudiation of authority and subjectivity proper—and Lacan is surely *not* one of them.

The days when Jane Gallop could celebrate Lacan for being a "prick" apparently have passed.[11] Butler draws, over and again, on Lacan, cites him as a major authority, but largely in order to outdo and redo him. Butler is "right" to do so, for Lacan undoubtedly holds on to a heteronormativity that informs, or misinforms, many of the claims he makes. Butler's reading of the lesbian phallus, for example, is a subtle, suggestive exercise in ethicopolitical critique, one that is perhaps unashamedly utopian. Her stated intention there is "simply to promote an alternative *imaginary* to a hegemonic imaginary and to show, through that assertion, the ways in which the hegemonic imaginary constitutes itself through the naturalization of an exclusionary heterosexual morphology" (*Bodies* 91). There is, of course, nothing "simple" about such a promotion, but that is not what here concerns me. What concerns me is what is left unsaid, what undergirds such an alternative promotion, and what implications its success and imagined realization might have on hegemony itself.[12] Michael Warner has expressed similar concerns, taking Butler's work to task for its penchant for metaphysics and, in the same sweep, for its assumption that "'resistance' is the thing to value, that 'norms' and 'power' are devoutly to be resisted, and that anything that resists 'the demand to inhabit a coherent identity' can be pressed into the service of this cause" (155). Hegemony, normativity, disciplinarity, and—with some provisos—power are, if not interchangeable, certainly tightly interconnected in Butler's work. One might even say that one flows into the other, but only if such fluidity is understood as precontained, consistent to the point of solidity.

This brings me back, however contrarily, to my point of provocative, perverse, paradoxical departure: the fetish of fluidity. Fluidity, I have claimed, does not have the same function in feminism and AIDS activism as it does in most academic queer theory, where it tends to be—to echo and expand Warner's criticism of Butler—metaphysical. Warner's own work, to be sure, is hardly at odds with queer theory. In fact, Warner's critique of Butler is articulated, rather explicitly, as a contribution to queer studies.[13] His unease with certain modes of queer theory stems, he notes, not from an opposition to theory per se, but from an opposition to "a procedure of decontextualization that for many people defines theory" (159n). Warner goes to great lengths to contextualize his theory, centering his discussion of norms and normativity on a discussion of gay marriage. Butler, for her part, is also increasingly concerned about contextualization, going so far as to sketch a personal history, somewhere between academicism and activism, in the latest edition of Gender Trouble. Warner's arguably more sober view of normativity, his insistence that one should not "take for granted that subversion and resistance are things to value independently of which norms they subvert or resist" (155), is itself well taken. But even as Warner claims to attend to specific norms rather than to normativity in general, a general repudiation of both informs his work. Moreover, Warner, for all his reservations and stated differences, shares Butler's investment in queer theory. He worries, for instance, about the "dequeering agenda" of Andrew Sullivan; and Butler frets, somewhat more melancholically, about "the institutional domestication of queer thinking. For normalizing the queer would be, after all, its sad finish" ("Against" 25).[14] Both, then, are concerned with maintaining, even championing, the queer, as signifier, even if such a project entails a degaying and delesbianizing agenda—even if it spells the "sad finish," for instance, of gay and lesbian studies, and even if it also seems to spell, from the perspective of a diverse array of feminists, the "sad finish" of feminism.

Butler and Warner are aware of such a reading of their work and go to varying lengths to refute it. Many critics, however, remain skeptical. Sheila Jeffreys and Biddy Martin, for example, have been at the forefront of the critique of queer theory for what they present, respectively, as the "disappearance of lesbians" and the erasure of gender. Jeffreys reproves queerness—itself given to reproofs—for not challenging "the gay male agenda that dominates the field" (461), and thereby effectively makes queerness a ruse of gay maleness. Jeffreys points to the still more uneasy status of the connection between lesbian *and* gay. Martin is arguably more nuanced, but no less incisive. Her critique points in a direction that I would like to examine more closely. For it is Martin who cautions against "defining queerness as mobile and fluid in relation to what then gets construed as stagnant and ensnaring, and as associated with a maternal, anachronistic, and putatively puritanical feminism" ("Extraordinary" 110). It is Martin who notices the significance and rhetoric of fluidity in queer proclamations of antinormativity, impropriety, and an ever-more extraordinary theatricality. For Martin, queer theory constitutes "the lure of an existence without limit, without bodies or psyches, and certainly without mothers" (132). Martin's essay, first published in 1994, obviously cannot take into consideration Butler's and others' subsequent reformulations of bodies, psyches, discursive limits, voluntarism, and idealism. Martin's argument must be contextualized, then, but it need not be dismissed. For part of what Martin held still applies, in general, today: Queerness is riddled by what she calls "an enormous fear of ordinariness or normalcy" (133), by a desire for positions always outside and beyond, for perpetually dislocated locations. Warner's essay on "beyond gay marriage" and Butler's on "against proper objects" are, as I have suggested, cases in point.[15]

Another example might be Cathy Cohen's engaging essay "Punks, Bulldaggers, and Welfare Queens," which insistently deploys signs of movement. The focus of Cohen's article, as she makes explicit, is to rethink the "disjuncture . . . between an articulated commitment to promoting an understanding of sexuality that rejects the idea of static, monolithic, bounded categories, on the one hand, and political practices structured around binary conceptions of sexuality and power, on the other hand" (441). Cohen is particularly concerned with the dichotomy between "heterosexual" and "queer," by which "homosexual" is swept back into the dustbin, or closet, of history. In this, she differs from a number of other self-professed queer theorists. Cohen is also concerned, along with this disjuncture, with the tendency on the part of many closely associated with queer theory and queer politics to reject, as she says, "any recognition of the multiple and intersecting systems of power that largely dictate our life chances" (*chances,* not *choices,* she writes; 440). This too is a point well taken, as it pushes at something monolithically queer. Yet I would draw attention to how Cohen retains the rhetoric of fluidity as vital to her ends. For alongside intersections, disjunctions, and other more emphatic images of movement, we find, in true binary fashion, stasis. There is something, just possibly, of life and death in all this, which Martin touches on as well when she writes that "the assumption of a position beyond objects—the position, for instance, of death—becomes the putative achievement or goal of queer theory" ("Extraordinary" 133).

Martin's formulation is interesting because it rehearses the assumption, within much Western thought, that movement is to stasis as life is to death. Martin positions herself, not surprisingly, on the "side" of life, which is also, for her, the "side" of objects (whether it is also the side of object-choice, object-attachment, objectivity, objectification, and so on is unclear). The other side, the "beyond," she explicitly designates as the side of death. Yet queer theory, through its various practitioners, also, not surprisingly, positions itself on the "side" of life. It does so by defining itself as continuously moving: beyond objects, sure, but also against them, and around them. It does not, *on the whole,* entertain the death drive, let alone valorize it.[16] Instead, queer theory valorizes, with admirable consistency, life and—as Butler puts it—the "livable." It does so on the level of theory and practice through a concomitant valorization of animation, dynamism, and fluidity. As Cohen puts it, "similar to queer theory, queer politics . . . first and foremost recognizes and encourages the fluidity and movement of people's sexual lives. In queer politics sexual expression is something that always entails the possibility of change, movement, redefinition, and subversive performances" (439). The overall effect of such valorizations, overdetermined by an extensive (anti)humanist tradition, is that life is all but fused to fluidity, all but permanently affixed to movement. *Always* the possibility of change, as Cohen would have it.

The question of life and death is, as I hope to show, not incidental to the question of the fetish. Having made an argument for the importance of fluidity to queer theory, I now want to fix my sights on the fetish. This is perhaps easier done than said, because the fetish appears, at first blush, to be more of the order of things than of words. It is a foot, a shoe, or an undergarment; a beauty mark, a blemish, or a wound; a graven image, a token, a charm, or an idol; a supple turn of the neck, a deceptive shine on the nose. It is a thing, but a thing more or less beside or beyond another thing: more or less, because the other "thing" tends to be God or the phallus or even labor. As Emily Apter puts it, "Fetishism records the trajectory of an *idée fixe* or *noumen* in search of its materialist twin (god to idol, alienated labor to luxury item, phallus to shoe fetish and so on)" (4). The trajectory, of course, is not so straightforward, for the "materialist twin," as that by which the *idée fixe* is granted ostensibly objective support, suggests a twin of its own. The thing "gives body to" and "brings and keeps alive" the idea, so that the fixity of the *idée fixe* comes to hinge, as it were, on something material. But the thing also searches for an idea by which it can be rendered intelligible, "make sense." The trajectory may thus also be that of a material object, fixed or not, in search of its idealist twin. The record of the trajectory presumably effected in and as fetishism is thus highly reticular, with subjects and objects, ideas and things, winding this way and that. So reticular is this trajectory that entanglement of one form or another may be almost inevitable. Naomi Schor acknowledges this when she writes that to work on the fetish, to take it as an object—and subject—of inquiry extends fetishism, with the "the writer's fetishism becom[ing] the critic's—fetishism of fetishism" (93).[17] Entanglement is such that freedom, understood as the lack of entanglement, becomes almost unthinkable—or thinkable only through paradox.

For the fetish is fraught with paradox, with what Schor deems a "double attitude" (94): It recognizes and misrecognizes, accepts and refuses, affirms and denies. As the site of all this, the fetish is a monument to a very odd (very queer?), yet very normal, forgetting. What the fetish helps us to remember and forget, at least in the Freudian tradition, is a certain devastating dismemberment: castration. And it does so, as Freud puts it, by helping the fetishist remember and forget a

> particular and quite special penis that had been extremely important in early childhood but had later been lost. That is to say, it should normally have been given up, but the fetish is precisely designed to preserve it from extinction. To put it more plainly: the fetish is a substitute for the woman's (the mother's) penis that the little boy once believed in and—for reasons familiar to us—does not want to give up. (152–53)

Freud's definition, repeatedly quoted and interrogated, has itself come to assume something like the status of an icon or auratic relic. In fact, as the post-Freudian literature suggests, the fetish can be almost anything, including a piece of paper, a work of writing, an utterance, a word. I stress this last "thing." The fluidity I have been considering—no less than the queerness to which it seems so vitally bound—is more rhetorical than material. I will nuance this statement immediately by noting that in fetishism, as fetishism, the material is fundamentally factitious, so that even the most ostensibly natural or spontaneous of things (for instance, a part, position, or property of the body) is just that: *ostensibly* natural or spontaneous.

The fetish engages a reality, then, but in a manner most mystifying. Apter presents fetishism as a discourse that "weds its own negative history as a synonym for sorcery and witchcraft (*feitiçaria*) to an outlaw strategy of dereification" (3). She likens fetishism, *as discourse,* to an "unmasking," an "exposing," an "undercutting," a "desublimating," and a "smoking out" (3). At first sight, this is curious because fetishism is perhaps primarily a masking, a concealing, and a smoking over: If it undercuts anything it is the symbolic cutting that is, for Freud, castration. For Marx, whose rendition of fetishism rivals in the strongest sense that of Freud, fetishism is associated with obfuscation, with a spurious or factitious naturalization of social relations. In *Capital,* the fetish is the religious rebaptized, if you will, as commodity, an awful displacement of God onto capital and an equally awful condensation of God in capital. I am, admittedly, articulating Marx with a Freudian vocabulary, and would do well to quote Marx himself. "A commodity is," Marx writes, "a mysterious thing, simply because in it the social character of men's labour appears to them as an objective character stamped upon the product of that labour" (72). And a few lines later: "This is the reason why the products of labour become commodities, social things whose qualities are at the same time perceptible and imperceptible by the senses" (72). Paradox, it appears, informs Marx's view of the fetish as well.

Marx, not unlike Freud, detects an oscillation in an ostensibly fixed figure, a play of surface and depth, hide-and-seek; the qualities of the commodity *cum* fetish are, remember, perceptible *and* imperceptible. Such perceptual play, quite serious in its social and psychic implications, is at the heart of Freud's understanding of the fetish as well, where the fetish is defined, first, as "a substitute for the penis" and, then, as we have seen, as "a substitute for the woman's (the mother's) penis" (152). I will not belabor the way one transcendental signifier (God) is substituted for another (penis, or in some translations, the phallus),[18] because it is the play of perception that I want to keep in the foreground. For Marx, fetishism is that by which mystery is upheld even as it moves. Fetishism marks, he says, "a definite social relation between men, that assumes, in their eyes, the fantastic form of a relation between things" (72). Marx's aim is, of course, to unveil said mystery and spoil its game. Apter's reference to dereification acquires here its critical force: The re-presentation of commodities as fetishes involves the prescription that they be *perceived* as fetishes, that is to say, that the mystery be demystified as the effect of social relations. Freud tells a similar, if more sexually sordid, story. For him, the fetish is that by which a subject—typically, even exclusively, a male subject—disavows castration (impotence, powerlessness, lack). Like Marx, he refers to the imaginary animation of an inanimate object, but stresses its termination, insufficient and illusory though it may be. According to Freud, "When the fetish is instituted some process occurs which reminds one of the stopping of memory in traumatic amnesia. . . . [T]he subject's interest comes to a halt half-way, as it were; it is as though the last impression before the uncanny and traumatic one [by which Freud means the boy's perception of the woman's sex] is retained as a fetish" (155). Freud's much-debated misogyny notwithstanding, what interests me here is the process he describes: a process of displacement and condensation, of disavowal that, through the intervention of psychoanalytic critique, entails an avowal of what is disavowed. (This avowal or unveiling is the therapeutic dimension of Freud's description.) For both Marx and Freud, the fetish is a mystery to be solved, a false mystery—as if there could be anything *but* a false mystery—but perhaps for that very reason a mystery that is hard in dying.

The preceding excursus, which brings to the fore the (de)mystifying ambivalence of the fetish while pointing, nonetheless, to its resolution or cure, is meant to be related to the digressive plays of a general and generalizable queer project. I have indicated that the fetish is a thing that is always, in some sense, factitious. I want to note now, as I gesture toward an impossible closure, how the thing that has been occupying the present work is fluidity, the signifier *fluidity*—that is to say, a matter of rhetoric. Lacan, in his examination of fetishism, drives home that this is no mean matter, declaring that language is itself material: "As soon as a real object that satisfies a real need has become an element of the symbolic object, every other object capable of satisfying a real need can take its place: above all that already symbolized but also perfectly materialized object that is speech (or the word: *la parole*)" (*Séminaire IV* 175). If the fetish is a thing, it is always in some sense a thing of language, a fact of discourse. What Apter and William Pietz present, in an important coedited volume on the subject, as the *discourse* of fetishism contends with the matter of fetishism, well, fetishistically. Apter notes how in fetishism, as cultural discourse, "a consistent displacing of reference occurs, paradoxically, as a result of so much *fixing*" (3). Pietz, for his part, pushes at the ramifications of such displacement, striving to perform a "Marxian theory of fetishism [that] may be described as a critical, materialist economy of social desire" (129). To that end, he works to lay bare the linguistic privilege that prejudices, in his eyes, the very materialism that he takes as critical to a *productive* theoretical project.

Pietz's position, in the realm of the fetish, is analogous to Donald Morton's position, in the realm of the queer (with fetishism, analogy is itself as much a problem as it is a solution). Morton, for whom queer theory is an avatar of postmodernism, criticizes both for failing to grapple convincingly with material reality. "In (post)modernism," he declares, "the subject's construction is accounted for ultimately in terms of mode of signification and not mode of production" (3). Similarly, Pietz, referring to Derrida, Baudrillard, and Lacan, among others, asserts that all these thinkers collapse the Marxian distinction between exchange value and use value (123). He is especially critical of Baudrillard's account of fetishism, where we read that "it is not the passion (whether of objects or subjects) for substances that speaks in fetishism, it is the passion for the code" (Baudrillard 100, qtd. in Pietz 124).

That passion for the code, that desire of and for language, is precisely what Lacan, as Pietz knows, also manifests. The very facticity of the fetish is called forth in language, in the history of language. It is no doubt significant that practically every essay on fetishism, mine included, has an etymological instance. The etymology of *fetish* and *fetishism* is itself, as Apter might put it, the record of a cross-cultural historical retracing, of a search for what is quite possibly an impossible origin. Etymology may itself be a fetish, but whatever the case, it makes a significant appearance in Lacan's exposition. "What we have seen at work here," Lacan observes relative to the fetish, "is a fetishized character, or fairy—it's the same word, both related to *factiso* in Portuguese, which is the historical origin of the word *fetish* and which is nothing other than the word *factitious*" (*Séminaire IV* 170). What is factitious—perhaps even facetious—is the assertion that two different words (with arguably two different origins, one in a form of saying, *fari*, the other in doing, *facere*) are the same word, as if Lacan's theory of relationality—where two are impossibly one—were gainsaid.[19]

I find fascinating the "fact" that the two words that are, we are told, the same are in English *fetish* and *fairy*.[20] Both words are also, in a further turn of the etymological screw, related to a third, *factice*, "factitious." What Lacan "does" is to "make" three words one, establishing in the process a circuit of near equivalency that mimics the circuit of fetishism with its displacements, replacements, oscillations, recursive turns, and whatnot. He accomplishes this, moreover, in the more specific context of a reading, inevitably partial, of Henri de Latouche's novel *Fragoletta*. The context is not innocent—perhaps nothing ever is in Lacan—and permits a false if phonetic play across languages, here French and English. For it might not be accidental that in the passion for the code—by which the signified is displaced ever more powerfully beyond—"fetish" is "fairy," and that it is so in and out of *Fragoletta*.[21] If there is the trace of something "faglike" in this title, something that sounds too odd to be believed, it might be because Lacan keeps Freud in mind, citing him repeatedly as his authority.

And Freud cites, as his first and most memorable example, "the most extraordinary case [of] a young man [who] had exalted a certain sort of 'shine on the nose' into a fetishistic precondition" (152). The shine on the nose is not, strictly speaking, a thing, a real, material object. But the nose is, or seems to shine forth as such, and it is to the nose that Freud comes. "The fetish, which originated from his earliest childhood, had to be understood in English, not German. The shine on the nose [in German *'Glanz auf der Nase'*]—was in reality a *'glance* at the nose.' The nose was thus the fetish, which, incidentally, he endowed at will with the luminous shine which was not perceptible to others" (152). Others, but obviously not Freud: For Freud's brilliance is such that he perceives what others do not, and he does so by shifting from an optical to a linguistic apparatus. What Freud perceives is the play of the fetish *in other words* (*Glanz* clearly resonates with "glans"). If he comes ostensibly to the thing, the nose, he does so through language. If this seems forced, factitious, so much the better: It paradoxically reinforces the fetish—defines it, that is, as something other than what it appears to be.

But what does all this have to do with fluidity and with queerness? First, it points, however extravagantly, to the discursivity of fetishism. Second, it does so by moving between and across languages, by flowing, apparently with brilliant deftness, from one tongue to another. Queerness, as I have been arguing, mobilizes a deceptively analogous rhetoric. It sets its sights on movement, fixates on fluidity, tracks down the plays of power, and does so in the name of nonnormativity and antinormativity. It does so in the name of counterauthority, counterculture, and counterpublic; in the name of an unnamed end to naming, where the name is, as the dictionary states, "a word or words by which an entity is designated and distinguished from others." This is, I admit, a bit too much, a bit unfair, for "queerness" and the "queer" continue to designate even when, as David Halperin remarks, "there is nothing in particular to which [they] necessarily refer" (62).[22] Nothing particular indeed, for not unlike the fetish as cultural discourse, "queerness" and the "queer" claim to perform a displacement of reference and a destabilization of identity in general. "Queer," as Eve Kosofsky Sedgwick takes it, "is a continuing moment, movement, motive—recurrent, eddying, *troublant*. The word 'queer' itself means *across*—it comes from the Indo-European root *-twerkw*, which also yields the German *quer* (transverse), Latin *torquere* (to twist), English *athwart*" (xii).

Sedgwick's etymological explication, invoking the authority of the dictionary and hence of a *cross*-cultural linguistic history, permits an intriguing interplay with an array of explications of the fetish, as signifier. But there may be more here than a mere passion for the code, for the heady exchange of signifiers. For what concerns Sedgwick, what prompts her etymological explication, is to make a "counterclaim against [the] obsolescence" of the "queer," a "claim that something about *queer* is inextinguishable" (xii; original emphasis). Claim or counterclaim: Nothing less than the life of a signifier—and yet ostensibly so much more—hangs here in the balance. Sedgwick, like Butler and Warner, might risk many a thing, but not something in which she, like them, seems so passionately invested. The signified is dead: Long live the signifier. In it and through it, a certain signified might make a spectral return, might be fixed as flowing forever over and beyond. If this calls to mind God, or the maternal phallus, or alienated labor, that might not be beside the point. For the beyond, the *au-delà*, is, as Lacan suggests, a powerful nonposition. The beyond informs, paradoxically, a narcissistic, specular relation that is also, in significant ways, a fetishistic relation to an object as always beyond, always lacking, and always in default.[23]

Thus, what is designated as "beyond"—beyond power, authority, law, propriety, normativity, objects, subjects, and so on—is never entirely beyond. The beyond snakes back on the here and now, reflecting itself, as Lacan claims, "not purely and simply in the ego (*le moi*) . . . but in something that is in the very bedrock of the ego, in its first forms, in its first demands (*exigences*), and, when all is said and done, on the first veil, where it projects itself in the form of the ego ideal" (*Séminaire IV* 178). Queer theory's idealist moves condition, as from the inside, an anxious, apologetic, aggressive engagement with materialism, with words, things, and bodies that matter. But whatever the emotional tenor, and whatever its faults, it is an engagement worth pursuing. Queer theory, in fine, need not be overturned or undone, as from the outside, but it need not be done as it has been. This is, I suppose, a highly involved way of saying that it might do its own undoing, might theorize its own overcoming, its own obsolescence. It might do so not in a tone of sadness and resentment, but of renewed possibility—not just in some distant future, but in a more insistent present that recognizes that words, for all their etymological interconnections and crossings, matter diversely, signify variously. The world is still too terribly divided to assume, from within the privileged confines of the "West," that words, things, and people can always flow.

Notes

Unless indicated, all translations are mine. This essay is related to a more extensive project on the politics and performances (that is, acts) of immigration in the United States, entitled "Passing Lines," forthcoming in *Passing*, ed. Linda Schlossberg and María Sánchez, NYU Press. In that piece I examine, among other things, how the persistence of juridical notions of "immutable" identity and verifiable difference gives the lie—in the "real world"—to notions of fluid movement and the "beyond."

1. I am playing here and elsewhere with the "signs" of homosexuality, gayness, and queerness. For a valorization of drift, see Hocquenghem.

2. The underlying, unexamined assumption is that the truth will set the subject free: even more, that it will undo the subjection and subjugation of subjectivity, "radically" resignify it, altogether.

3. Queer theory is generally "normaphobic." It is one thing to criticize and counter specific sociohistorical norms, but another thing, I submit, to criticize and counter normativity in general.

4. Making, doing, and their opposites are implicated in the fetish, as signifier: from the Portuguese *fetiço*, from the Latin *facticius*, from *facere* (do, make), related in turn to *fact* (*factum*) and—though rather dubiously—to *fate* (from *fatum*, "that which has been spoken"), *fay*, and *fairy*. As we shall see, such etymological moves, some more false than others, have quite intriguing repercussions.

5. The "human" and the "livable" are among Butler's central, express concerns. See the 1999 preface to her *Gender Trouble* (xxii).

6. One of my basic contentions is that *queer* does not attain internationality, let alone universality, without risk. The latter is the risk that Oscar Montero, in his "Critical Notes from a Latino Queer," underscores, stating that if "'gay' circulates in the Spanish-speaking world" in such a way that "the complexities of its imported status are impossible to edit, and something of its original celebratory mode

is lost in the translation," the "uses of 'queer' are even more circumscribed to the imperial metropolis" (162). This is a telling assessment. Montero, as a self-designated "latino queer," calls attention to the limits of these designations, writes of circumscription instead of movement and freedom, of free movement, and reminds those who might otherwise forget that "queer" is not only open to qualification—in this case "latino"—but that it is also given to some odd (dare I say queer?) normativities of its own. Queer theory, in short, should engage more rigorously the forces of (inter)nationality, study the import and implications of its ties to departments of English and American literature, and contend with the (un)-translatability of *queer* itself.

7. Butler writes the following in the 1999 preface to *Gender Trouble:* "Although I've enumerated some of the academic traditions and debates that have animated this book, it is not my purpose to offer a full apologia in these brief pages" (xvi). The sentence is intriguing: Does Butler propose to offer a "partial apologia"? Would she offer a "full apologia" if she had more pages than those of a preface? And why, indeed, does she write of an "apologia" rather than a justification, rationalization, or repositioning? Much of the preface reads as if it were a dramatized rendering of Butler's CV, a glimpse into the "person" that persists "despite the dislocation of the subject" (xvi). Is the person, or personal, a kind of humanist bedrock that "resists" the postmodern dislocation of the subject, a "real" that Butler can "personify" and "personalize" as her own? The defense—or is it an apologia?—of autobiography, *in* autobiography, is likewise curious: "That I can write in an autobiographical mode does not, I think, relocate this subject that I am, but perhaps it gives the reader solace that there is someone here (I will suspend for the moment the problem that this someone is given in language)" (xvii). It should follow that "I," as reader, will find solace in Butler's assertion of presence (suspending problems, denying relocation, and so on). "I" find not so much solace as annoyance—annoyance that "I," as reader, should be expected to expect, or even desire, solace from the author, the author's I.

8. Lacan, through Freud, does speak of the benefit of a certain psychic impoverishment, of an assumption of loss and lack, in the state of love: benefit, because what goes around comes around, and the subject is paradoxically enriched by being reduced to words. The subject's impoverishment to the point of collapse—its "radical" unsettling—permits a return, in the guise of a gift of generosity, of support ostensibly coming from beyond, from an other or others; see *Séminaire IV* 172–73.

9. If I seem willing to run this risk, articulate its contours, it is, in part, because risk has itself become a prop of an authority that would contest authority. Butler's work is rife with professions of risk, almost always "worth taking." This is not, at least not primarily, the risk of any real danger, any fleshly peril, but instead of rhetoric. One such risky instance, involving the object of the present essay, may be found in Butler's "Against Proper Objects," (1; qtd. below in note 15).

10. Envy may well haunt any critique of authority, my own included.

11. "To designate Lacan at his most stimulating and forceful," Gallop writes, "is to call him something more than just phallocentric. He is also phallo-eccentric. Or, in more pointed language, he is a prick" (36).

12. Interestingly, Butler announces, in her 1999 preface to *Gender Trouble*, that she is writing on hegemony with Ernesto Laclau and Slavoj Žižek (xviii). See Butler, Laclau, and Žižek.

13. The present critique is itself articulated as a contribution to queer studies, as part of it, even as it gestures to a letting go, in part, of the signifier *queer* by means of a *recognition* of its authority, its disciplinary implications, its linguistic, geopolitical, and cultural limits.

14. Pellegrini, without mentioning domestication, does acknowledge the "institutionalization of something called queer theory," but qualifies it, rightly, as "a *very* tenuous institutionalization." To Pellegrini's guardedly material acknowledgment of institutionalization, I cannot but contrast Butler's almost romantic refusal to let go of a putatively "undomesticated" or "wild" queerness that seems to function as the "proper" queerness.

15. In "Against Proper Objects," Butler writes the following: "For those of us who work in the interstices of the relation between queer theory and feminism (as well as other contemporary critical discourses), and who insist in continuing the important intellectual tradition of immanent critique, the risk will always take the following form: if one analyzes the heterosexist assumptions of feminist theory, one will be construed as 'anti-' or 'post-' feminist; if one analyzes the anti-feminism of some gay and lesbian theory, one will be construed as hostile to that gay and lesbian theory" (1). And, I might add, if one studies the disciplinarity and normativities of queer theory, one could well be considered "against" it too. At any rate, Butler's language is instructive: The relation between queer theory and feminism is one of tension if not, at times, hostile opposition. Movement between the two is not exactly matter of course. In the interstices of this relation, perhaps even as a constitutive aspect of it, there is an obstacle, a blockage, a point of resistance. Exactly how "mutual" this resistance and relation are remains unclear. What is clearer, I submit, is the heroic quality of Butler's language: an appeal to a particular community, to work, perseverance, tradition, and, most importantly, risk. But there is more: Something queer has happened to "queer." It has disappeared. In her rendering of the risky relation between queer theory and feminism, Butler retains only the latter. Queer theory, as such, is lost, slipped into and under gay and lesbian theory. It is as if the division were two-sided rather than multifaceted, as if gay and lesbian were a coherent unity tied, in turn, to queerness. This is not the case now, and was not even the case when Butler's reading was first published. And so the risk may take *another* form that renders relationality even more complex because it blocks any easy flow among gay, lesbian, and queer interests. Butler seems to know this, elsewhere, but she does not indicate it here. Simply put, "queer theory" is not the same as "gay and lesbian theory," "queer" not the same as "gay and lesbian." For one thing, *queer* is one word, while *gay and lesbian* is a set or sequence or cluster of words in which relationality, easy or not, is foregrounded.

Between the one and the other, the one and the more than one, a great deal is at stake.

16. Bersani's call for "the risk of self-dismissal, of *losing sight* of the self" (222), with all its mystical resonance, is not exactly "representative" of queer theory. It is precisely such representativity, such reiterability, such exemplarity, that is at issue here.

17. Schor's statement need not be taken as an endorsement of the absolute transferability of the fetish, as if one's fetish were *exactly the same* as another's. Indeed, as Tyler remarks, "the fetishist only believes in *his* fetish; what works for one fetishist will not always work for another" (247; original emphasis).

18. A great deal has been made of the relation, or nonrelation, between the penis and the phallus. The one real, the other symbolic, together they disrupt, for some, the integrity of both. Many theorists, however, hold on fast and firmly to the division, cautioning against conflating or confusing the two, against mixing them up. Others turn the terms on their purveyors. As Tyler suggestively argues, "Lacan must remain ignorant of the neurotic and psychotic dimension of fetishism if his fetish, the penis, is to 'work' as the phallus or support of patriarchal identities. To accept that the penis is only a signifier for an occluded signifier is to acknowledge that the genital organ of 'normal sexuality' is in fact the hystericized site of an inherently displaced sexuality, which is what actually follows from Lacan's description of desire as hysterical in structure, as the desire of the other" (246).

19. Lacan's theory of relationality, or nonrelationality (where relationality is understood in terms of reciprocity, correspondence, and fusion), is most supplely presented as follows: "Love is powerless (impotent: *impuissant*), albeit reciprocal, because it ignores that it is only the desire to be One, which leads us to the impossibility of establishing the relation of the two of them. The relation of which two?—the two sexes [*l'impossible d'établir la relation d'eux. La relation* d'eux *qui?*— deux *sexes*]" (*Séminaire XX* 12).

20. Strictly speaking, *fée* means "fairy," but not in the sense of "gay." Lacan's interest in etymology, translation, and something like comparative linguistics is crucial to a great deal of his work, most notably his seminar on Edgar Allan Poe's "The Purloined Letter," where he describes the word *purloin* as "anglo-français," a compound or "composed" word (39).

21. The book jacket of my edition of *Fragoletta* references Balzac discussing "*cet être inexprimable, qui n'a pas de sexe complet* [that inexpressible being who does not have a complete sex]."

22. Sounding out the differences between *gay* and *queer*, Halperin states that "queer is by definition *whatever* is at odds with the normal, the legitimate, the dominant. *There is nothing in particular to which it necessarily refers.* It is an identity without an essence. 'Queer,' then, demarcates not a positivity but a positionality vis-à-vis the normative—a positionality that is not restricted to lesbians and gay men but is in fact available to anyone who is or who feels marginalized because of his or her sexual practices" (62; original emphasis).

23. See "L'objet fétiche" in *Séminaire IV,* particularly the chapter titled "L'identification au phallus" (165–78).

References

Apter, Emily, and William Pietz, eds. *Fetishism as Cultural Discourse.* Ithaca: Cornell UP, 1993.

Baudrillard, Jean. *Pour une critique de l'économie politique du signe.* Paris: Gallimard, 1972.

Bersani, Leo. "Is the Rectum a Grave?" *October* 43 (1987): 197–222.

Butler, Judith. "Against Proper Objects." In Schor and Weed 1–30.

———. *Bodies That Matter: On the Discursive Limits of "Sex."* New York: Routledge, 1993.

———. "Preface." *Gender Trouble: Feminism and the Subversion of Identity.* 1990. New York: Routledge, 1999. vii–xxvi.

———. *The Psychic Life of Power: Theories in Subjection.* Stanford: Stanford UP, 1997.

Butler, Judith, Ernesto Laclau, and Slavoj Žižek. *Contingency, Hegemony, Universality: Contemporary Dialogues on the Left.* London: Verso, 2000.

Cohen, Cathy J. "Punks, Bulldaggers, and Welfare Queens: The Radical Potential of Queer Politics?" *GLQ: A Journal of Lesbian and Gay Studies* 3 (1997): 437–85.

Freud, Sigmund. "Fetishism." 1927. *The Standard Edition of the Complete Psychological Works of Sigmund Freud.* Ed. and trans. James Strachey. 24 vols. London: Hogarth, 1953–74. 21:149–57.

Gallop, Jane. *The Daughter's Seduction: Feminism and Psychoanalysis.* Ithaca: Cornell UP, 1982.

Grosz, Elizabeth. "Lesbian Fetishism?" *differences* 3.2 (1991): 39–54.

Halperin, David M. *Saint Foucault: Towards a Gay Hagiography.* New York: Oxford UP, 1995.

Hocquenghem, Guy. *La dérive homosexuelle.* Paris: J.-P. Delarge, 1977.

Irigaray, Luce. *Ce sexe qui n'en est pas un.* Paris: Minuit, 1977.

Jeffreys, Sheila. "The Queer Disappearance of Lesbians: Sexuality in the Academy." *Women's Studies International Forum* 17.5 (1994): 459–72.

Lacan, Jacques. *Le séminaire, livre IV: La relation d'objet, 1956–1957.* Ed. Jacques-Alain Miller. Paris: Seuil, 1994.

———. *Le séminaire, livre VIII: Le transfert, 1960–1961.* Ed. Jacques-Alain Miller. Paris: Seuil, 1991.

———. *Le séminaire, livre XX: Encore, 1972–1973.* Ed. Jacques-Alain Miller. Paris: Seuil, 1975.

———. "Le séminaire sur "La lettre volée." *Écrits I.* Paris: Seuil, 1966. 19–75.

Latouche, Henri de. *Fragoletta.* Paris: Editions Desjonquères, 1983.

Martin, Biddy. "Extraordinary Homosexuals and the Fear of Being Ordinary." In Schor and Weed 109–35.

————. "Sexualities without Genders and Other Queer Utopias." *Diacritics* 24.2–3 (1994): 104–21.

Marx, Karl. *Capital*. Vol. 1. Trans. Samuel Moore and Edward Aveling. New York: International Publishers, 1967.

Montero, Oscar. "The Signifying Queen: Critical Notes from a Latino Queer." In *Hispanisms and Homosexualities*. Ed. Sylvia Molloy and Robert McKee Irwin. Durham: Duke UP, 1998. 161–74.

Morton, Donald, ed. *The Material Queer: A LesBiGay Cultural Studies Reader*. Boulder: Westview P, 1996.

Pellegrini, Ann. "Women on Top, Boys on the Side, but Some of Us Are Brave: Blackness, Lesbianism, and the Visible." In *Race-ing Representation: Voice, History, and Sexuality*. Ed. Kostas Myrsiades and Linda Myrsiades. Lanham: Rowman and Littlefield, 1998. 247–63.

Schor, Naomi. *Bad Objects: Essays Popular and Unpopular*. Durham: Duke UP, 1995.

Schor, Naomi, and Elizabeth Weed, eds. *Feminism Meets Queer Theory*. Bloomington: Indiana UP, 1997.

Sedgwick, Eve Kosofsky. *Tendencies*. Durham: Duke UP, 1993.

Tyler, Carole-Anne. "Passing: Narcissism, Identity, and Difference." In Schor and Weed 227–65.

Warner, Michael. "Normal and Normaller: Beyond Gay Marriage." GLQ: *A Journal of Lesbian and Gay Studies* 5.2 (1999): 119–71.

22

LOVE, A QUEER FEELING

Lauren Berlant

. . . .

1. Love Is Not Love That Alteration Finds

The opening scene of Todd Haynes's *Safe* closes with an act of missionary sex between an almost featureless husband and wife—they're white, they're well-off, they speak to each other in soft voices about the weather. Amidst the unpleasant sound of sexual grunting, the camera cuts sadistically to the husband's pulsating back, framing the wife's dead eyes and the pleasureless, maternal patting motion she bestows on him as he comes. The angle of and lighting on her ivory face suggest at once a holy and an ordinary martyrdom, a *woman's* martyrdom, that well-known *figura* of marital endurance that hovers as though waiting for life to resume, a life of safety and silence, a dearth of surprise, a syncopated regularity.[1]

Yet *Safe* ends antithetically. The same woman, Carol White (Julianne Moore), who has gone through a process of therapeutic self-rescue, now looks directly at herself in a mirror and says firmly the phrase "I love you." Earlier we had heard of another woman who, through the same course of therapy, had reached the same verbal apotheosis. Then it had seemed a terrible error, the collapsing of the world into a tapped-out fetish of a phrase, a pathetic pearl of misguided optimism bound to choke the woman off from recovery. In *Safe*'s closing moments, however, we see that it's much worse than that. The fusion of "I love you" with "I love myself" is the verbal form of the bad sex we've seen, only now Carol White is in the active as well as the passive position, her skin swollen, reddened, and infected as though it were about to burst through itself. Because this scene takes place at the end of the film, we are led to think that it marks a change in the *something* from which White has been suffering. Yet this is only the logic of form. White's confused, deracinated performance of fulfillment repeats her paradoxical attachment to love as presence and, implicitly, as promise. In repeating the phrase, she embraces an impersonal structure of being that seems to secure the prospect of personal self-extension. Love marks the only name for survival that Carol White can conjure up.

It is conventional to say, and even to sing, that someone's in love with love. What does it mean to voice this view? There are historical answers to this, but first I want to address the formalism of love as its central quality, quite apart from any representation of it, and apart from any institution associated with it. Then, I will talk about love as a conventional and historical mode of attachment to form, including in queer theory, where love is a site that has perhaps not yet been queered enough. I do this on behalf of making you desire to think about incoherence as a condition of affect. By *incoherence* I do not mean to denote what the decentered, melancholic, or ambivalent subject performs, notions advanced by Leo Bersani and Judith Butler (see, respectively, *The Freudian Body* and *The Psychic Life of Power*). Nor do I raise the specter of the subject who does not know what she wants.[2] Rather, I am pointing to something smaller: a virtually rhythmic difference between the encounter with affect and the process of achieving clarity in it. This aim requires us to step back at first, to think psychoanalytically and aesthetically about what makes a form a form, and then, a form a norm.

As Roland Barthes's *A Lover's Discourse* performs so divinely, form forces us to think about repetition. And to love love—as to think thought—is to perform the very repetition that constitutes the fantasy of distinction between form and content. Even if its content is unclear, love's function is to be formally brilliant. Yet in the fantasy of love's self-love, reiteration is *always* with a difference. The detail that distinguishes the verb from the noun is deemed the main thing, the event, the matter of memory that makes one's love personal, self-referential. The stability of this detail (perhaps a particular loved one, or a smell that excites you) enables love to appear nonetheless as as an intensified relation to which you return. This return works minimally as a ground for self-recognition and, in a quite different domain, a ground for the production of social intelligibility. This points to the second resonance of love's formalism, in the problem it raises of uniqueness and convention. Repetition and uniqueness are the antithetical qualities that make up the experience of love. Conventions are what normalize repetition. The fact that these forms together involve an incoherent logic has had to be romanticized, noticed and disavowed, and aestheticized, as in the concept of *crazy love*. Meanwhile, the thing that appears to make a distinguishing mark on a love relation can be said to place the subject in history, giving the lover a template within which she can see that she is in the world of *effects*. Accordingly, the loss of the object emerges as a scar one can trace through love's *effigies*, or memory. In this sense, the beloved detail is a kind of evidence of what's personal about love.

In contrast, to seek out the shape of love's formalism is to seek out its impersonality. This has mainly involved descriptions of generic desire and death drives—the topics of Girardian structuralism and Freudian psychoanalysis (see Girard; Freud, *Beyond*). In this view, love is grazed by the historical but sustains only surface bruises. Pattern and structure are the scenes the subject personalizes with her own interior or exteriorized decoration. Yet the ideology of modern love has it that these impersonal structures of repetition are themselves pathologies that threaten the true uniqueness of one's expressive relation. This is one reason theoretical structures that describe love's aim approach it through violence and death: If the unoriginal subject is deemed not to be living, the desire to be original in love engenders a violence toward what represents the obstacles to one's control over the object. To the degree that one's own ambivalence is such an obstacle, the pleasure principle and death drive meet over one's own not-quite-dead-enough (melancholic, masochistic, sadistic) body; they beat it interminably into submission, but not defeat. At a certain distance, this struggle to murder ambivalence looks uncannily like love itself.

This intimacy of love and death means it almost makes sense that the detective novel and the love plot are so intricately related. They play with negation, crime, and death—of bodies and of optimism. And central to their capacity to absorb readers is the drama over the relation of event to narrative, evidence to closure, of the detail to the law (of genre). On the one hand, for generic satisfaction to be achieved the crime must be solved and the love fulfilled, the reader's fascination with the details of suffering and pleasure abjured.[3] On the other hand, satisfaction involves attending to more than the form that elaborates the detail into the genre, or the lover into a ground for a life narrative. It involves the lover's production of a sort of epistemic frenzy, a drive toward and aversion to knowledge. *What is the scale* of an event of attachment? *What is the difference* between this one and that one—this tone of voice, this touch, this encounter, this aversion? *Why should I believe* I can read the lover, and how well do I want to read her? *How do I know* this feeling of attachment is love and will remain so, as opposed to all of love's terrifying others, from the contingent crush to enduring hate, and—in the hardest case—ambivalence? Do we really want to know?

This rush to know *something*, but not necessarily *anything*, about the scene of intimate risk presents other kinds of problems as well, which emerge from the association of feeling with the irrational, the mad, and the undisciplined. When philosophers and humanists speak of affect these days, we tend to think of a feeling as something clear. Shame, for example, shines in queer theory as the feeling of the sexual itself (insofar as queer work tends to universalize queerness to all sexual attachment; see Sedgwick, *Epistemology;* Sedgwick and Frank; Warner). The same might be said for "shattering," Leo Bersani's translation of *jouissance* (Bersani, "Rectum"; Bersani and Dutoit, *Caravaggio's Secrets*). Do we know it when we feel it? To cite the end of *The Lady Eve*, is it "positively the same dame," this reiterated shame and shattering? A certain literalism tends to creep in when feeling is the topic of analysis, even though we know that misrecognition is central to desire's will to saturate objects. In this model the object is misrecognized, but the feeling is not. But what if, when we think about the formalism of love, we distinguish the affect from the feeling we recognize? What if the clarity of feeling were deemed itself an object of desire (Sedgwick, "A Poem")? Affect then becomes a destabilizing *punctum* with respect to which we are righted when we find for it, and for ourselves, a name and place in taxonomy.

Take ambivalence, which may well be love's backstreet partner. Ambivalence is virtually always represented as something other than itself, as a clear, well-lighted *thing:* The fetish works through disavowal; the Oedipus complex through temporality; masochism through hierarchical stability; melancholy through the ego's absorption of the lost object. From a psychoanalytic point of view, these structures are all ways of maintaining a relation to desire, despite its ruthless instability. They make history not matter. The optimistic version of this point is in the image of the ideal love that goes without saying. This means that love's plots and sound-

tracks are all archives of failure, sometimes in the tragic or the melodra-
matic mode, sometimes in fantastic overcoming—as in, for example,
happy endings. We traffic in big billboarded feeling when the topic is
love.

Yet this focus on love as form threatens to obscure something else—
its enigma. Love also maintains your access to *that feeling,* the *je ne sais
quoi:* a feeling whose restless energy could make a fetish of amor-
phousness, if that were possible. As any reader of romance knows, love
largely appeals through its incrementalism: its muddled middle, that
space of ideology and convention, fantasy and timing, that menaces
love's plot with the threat of formlessness (see Bois and Krauss). These are
some reasons why I have argued that pleasure is not always fun (Berlant,
"Compulsion"). Insofar as pleasure is an experience of self-confirmation,
repetition produces modes of intelligibility that become associated with
pleasure and so repetition becomes a mode of pleasure itself, even when
it doesn't feel good, and even when it moves through violence toward
death. For example, the agony of feeling upended by love is one of its
pleasures, whether or not it feels so, because it is deemed an incontrovert-
ible *sign* that one is in proximity to love. When our desires feel out of the
control of our intentional agency it might feel tragic or freeing, but it is
our pleasure to experience the chaos of desire to the degree that chaos is
one of its expected qualities. "This can't be love because it feels so grand,"
as the song goes. When we get to seesaw between clarities like this, it is
our pleasure to feel intelligible. It is also, I am arguing, a pleasure to appear to feel unintelligible insofar as there are conventions of confusion
that constitute evidence that we are in love's domain. Nevertheless, without the promise of clarity at root or in the end, the pleasure of not knowing can spill over into a degree of not knowing oneself that can become
intolerable. But even that drama can be a pleasure. Any impulse to find
a language for the incoherence of ordinary intensified attachment engenders very little pleasure, indeed.

Then there are the historical questions that intersect these apparent
hardwirings.[4] How did it happen—and what has it meant—that love has
been established as the core feeling of being and life, a primary feeling of
sociality from which one's history should emerge as if on a red carpet,
motored by the desire for a uniqueness expressed through convention
and a rhetoric of a safe sublimity (Berlant, "Intimacy"; Berlant and Warner)? This overlong sentence performs the perseverations of the problem
that I love. This oxymoronic structure of intimate performance sounds
like a version of the paradox that governs virtually all inquiry into mod-

ern political taxonomies—that is, of the relation between the universal and the particular. Citizenship, like love, is supposed to bridge that gap, to be the means through which people are translated into a public individuality. But that relation, as Balibar writes, is really a nonrelation at the fantasy space where the public meets the private. A site of panic, struggle, and euphemization, its delineation has become the dominant political booty of modernity. In contrast, the uniqueness and conventionality of love are not thought to express contradiction. If anything, their impossible continuity is the alibi, the mirage of social totality that enables the fractures of the social to not feel impossible, or to not be experienced.

Here I allude to Slavoj Žižek's work on the incommensurateness of Marxist and psychoanalytic renderings of the subject. He argues that the unique "I" is the positive, formal misrepresentation of the aporia between structure and agency, the social and psychic space in which the rigidified terms of meaning and value are established. Jacqueline Rose addresses the same nonplace when she argues that the posited disjoint between subjects and history, the possibility of subjectlessness, is what produces genocidal violence (*Why War?*). This suggests that the "I" is a scene for which the subject is always auditioning, a terrible fantasy of infinite and inexhaustible absorption that also terrorizes the subject with the threat of suspended animation. One's love relation with the "I" provides a comforting panic, projected onto the beloved other and the institutions that are supposed to be stable resources for one's self-elaboration. These anxieties specify the ideologeme named by modern love. Since it is the ligament of patriotism and the family, love defines governmentality in its atomic form, as a mechanism of internal monitoring through which the subject replays desire as a plebiscite on the normal. Love plots in life bear the burden of organizing personhood for others, all too frequently marking out the ground and the limit of praxis.

As a result, the singular conventionality conferred upon lovers is, against all logic, deemed not contradiction or nonsense, but the foundation of self-continuity. Queer theory has talked much about sexuality and desire, but when it comes to love, all sorts of havoc doesn't break out. Whereas the drive to attachment and to death engenders revolution, resistance, and refunctioning, the drive to love is either deemed the same as that of desire or else the opposite, the normalization of something far more sublime. What if we took love seriously as an analytic concept and a project for elaboration? What do we need to know and do in order not to repeat the usual denunciations and utopianisms, while making them objects of knowledge as well? How might such an analytic open up the intimate to the political in more critical ways? The modern subject produced by the formalism of love is exploited and expressed by the repetitions of intimate conventionality—so much so that to change the aesthetic of love, its archive of reference, inevitably animates discourses of instability from anxiety through revolution. Even when these languages produce the intimate as the conventional moral "outside" to the political, the ideological conflation of the intimate with the forms of the normal world locates power and the political in the hegemony of true feeling, a notion of right affect as a nonideological measure of truth. This idea of right affect as higher reason is central to the long history of liberalism, too, as any student of sentimental reform and imperialist empathy knows (Berlant, "Poor Eliza"). This is why any political thought that confronts overcoming structural discriminations that are experienced as visceral aversions must, as Joan Copjec writes in an analogous context, become "literate in desire" (*Read* 14). In making love matter analytically, we encounter desire in formal dress.

2. That Day They Read No More

We begin again. The paradigmatic love plot starts specifically and ends generically. A story about love's engendering in individual persons ends with marriage or something promising it, and with the presumption of reproductive acts to come, spawning future generations or sequels. *Safe* first inverts the love plot as conventionally conceived, and then it perverts its inversion. Haynes's metaformalism might speak of the futility of love's plot-bound optimism in a toxic world of capitalist pollution, privileged vainglory, and privatized ineloquent suffering. To frame this world with *I love you* is to show the tinny quality of the place where eloquence and ineloquence are said to merge through the sublimity of expressive convention, a fantasy of a sublime whose effect nonetheless is supposed to make the world beautiful, unscary, "safe." Thematics aside, though, in *Safe* the inversion and perversion of love mark an incommensurateness: "I love you" and other reiterated forms of lovemaking are extraneous to the story that the film's structure nonetheless uses love to frame, about a woman's infection by a toxic enigma, an embodied feeling she can't name. The wife's attachment to the love plot's plotness is literally the kiss of death, disabling whatever ability she has to become truly literate in that conjuncture of desire and critical analysis in which the film itself is set.

The story that *Safe* shows, about some effects of a kind of emptied-out but optimistic addiction to love, is a conventional one in the modern world, dating from the end of the Victorian period and intensified by the spread of commodity culture. There is now a metaconventionality to love, involving an insemination of the traditional love plot with a disappointed or bitter one, a melancholic one that plays out endlessly the failure of love's promise of safety, both positing and refusing the knowledge of its flimsy alliance with optimism. Vivian Gornick writes eloquently about this in *The End of the Novel of Love*. She posits a transformation from the bourgeois world, in which to have love meant to have true experience, to what she calls a postbourgeois world, in which we are no longer ruled by propriety and where love is merely sentiment, a nostalgic figure. Now, she argues, love is the very opposite of experience.

But this shift in the tone one associates especially with highbrow love does not mean that the form is losing its power to absorb us in feeling and futurity. I see something different happening to and through love in many narratives and in critical theory—something beyond the paradigm of loss that Gornick sees pervading U.S. popular culture and highbrow sensibility. However authentic and/or ironic individuals might feel when they feel the thing they call love, their attachment to it as a formal feeling that one can name, express, remember, and return to suggests its centrality. Even the most distanced or negating tone of voice toward love is a way of holding it close (see Hutcheon). This would argue for thinking about love's form not only as norm and institution, but also as an index of duration. I think about it as a kind of tattoo, a rhythm, a shape, timing. An environment of touch or sound that you make so that there is something to which you turn and return. Thinking about these qualities of love can tell us something else more general, more neutral or impersonal, about intimacy—this is why some psychologists begin with "attachment."[5]

Romantic love is the environment in which we can know what we know about attachment. Indeed, the world-image it organizes provides the only way we have of thinking about the nonpathological dimensions of the compulsion to repeat. Banal or sublime, love's function is to mark the subject's binding to the scenes to which s/he must always return. But rather than simply marking the diminution of personhood in the feeling of being overwhelmed by the opacity of big feeling, the word *love* dignifies the narratives that mark it. It holds open the possibility that, beyond all cynical knowledge and wisdom, reason and optimism might not be opposites—that there might be forms of nonviolent intimacy that will structure reliably what a life is, what fulfillment feels like, and what a text about people's lives will say. It will say "love is a condition of possibility, not the end of a story," and in so saying it turns repetition into a condition of living, and love plots into genres of realism. At least, ideally. These observations about the stabilizing function of love's narratives do not exhaust the question of the reiterated relay between the form of love and the fact of attachment. Is the love plot merely that—a mask that ornaments the tic of repetition with the fantasy of singular, authentic, and expressive plenitude?

To answer this we must return to a grizzled conceptual impasse: the tangled web that weds ideology and intimacy—or, to use a psychoanalytic translation, the conventions that bind affects to forms. The installation of romantic love as the fundamental attachment of humans has been central to the normalization of heterosexuality and femininity in consumer culture; it has become a way of expressing desires for normal life. Conversely, it also marks the rhetoric of rights, and desires for attachments beyond the possessive instrumentalities of capitalism. Because, more than anything, the desire for love congeals utopian drives to disorganize the self on behalf of better, future organizations, it bears the weight of much ideological management and pedagogy, defining the normativity of the modern self much more than "sexuality" as a category does.

Here I am not arguing with Foucault as much as I am with the use of Foucault to reconceive the modern subject mainly as an effect of pathologizing taxonomies. Foucault does not cast psychoanalysis simply as the modern science of perversion and pathology: His emphasis on normativity, the intimate, and the couple form also points to the necessity of attending to those modes of being *where pathology isn't supposed to be.* By historicizing the normativity of psychoanalytic models of love, he further particularizes the meanings of sexuality. (He does not say it quite this way, though, because in the end he is more interested in perversion and disavowal than in the working of the normal; see Canguilhem and Foucault.) One might recast Foucault here to view psychoanalysis as a science of organizing the self through the pseudo-nondiscipline of normal/formal love, a science that tracks the obstacles to love's "mature" expression. Foucauldian categories of pathogenic sexuality could then be seen as the detritus of normal love's failures to organize the subject. (The historical context of Foucault's early work is relevant here too: In rejecting "sexuality" as the site of the self's most authentic expression, he speaks against the sixties-era notion of it as the subject's authentic undisciplined drive.[6] Pleasure, for Foucault, is much more radical and uncodified.)

Foucault's work forces any historian of love to track its place in larger political struggles over the reproduction of social taxonomy, its meaning as a paradigm of false consciousness, and its antithetical meaning as a marker of alternative, noninstitutionalized attachments that circumvent the dead instrumentalities of normal family-oriented worlds. Yet even this conventional split between love as deadness and pleasure or desire as the life force once again takes for granted attachment's typical synonymy with "life." This antinomy not only disables considerations of ambivalence, aggression, and perversion where desire and pleasure are found, but negates comprehension of their sheer incoherence. One place to look for evidence of this is the emergence of the couple as a paranoid structure posed in and against the modern world. The economies of violence within which modern love is formed might clarify the traffic in erotophobia that projects that violence onto *sexuality*, as opposed to the fantasy of love's sublating achievement.

The centrality of redemptive and therapy cultures to the promise of love's formalized satisfactions means that where love provides the dominant rhetoric and form of attachment, so a discussion of pedagogy must be. Popular discourses that merge scientific expertise with a putatively general desire for better techniques of the self—as we see in talk shows, self-help books, and twelve-step semipublics—provide maps for people to clutch in their hands so that they can revisit the unzoned affective domain of which love is the pleasant and thinkable version. In these contexts love—never fully secularized—is the church of optimism for the overwhelmed. The currency that pays the price of entrance is the loss of everything except optimism.

These popular maps are also normative pedagogies that help people negotiate their clumsy groping toward "that feeling" to and from which they are driven. As goes theory, so too the sexuality classroom must be understood to be located within love's therapeutic conventions—formally, if not in content. For even when avant-garde affect theories break apart the redemptive forms of love's normative promise by focusing on the lack of fit between living and dreaming, questions of emancipation from and through sexuality inevitably arise. Moreover, in liberal culture, knowledge confers value on its object—and a nonredemptive knowledge project is a virtually impossible thought (but see the essays in Golding). The truth-value of sexuality in modern doxa about the self then produces massive anxiety around what, apart from negation, the sexuality pedagogue produces. (In *Fragment of an Analysis of a Case of Hysteria* ["Dora"], Freud predicts this resistance, arguing that it will be hard to profess about sex without being charged with having it. Foucault inhabits a similar

plane when he argues that sexuality moves from mouth to ear. Even Dear
Abby has recently said as much!)

This worry about what sex talk unleashes may be one reason for the
continued academic interest in fetishism, since fetishism provides love
an archive of fascinating details, mute forms, and crude memorabilia that
sustains captioning conversations about how longing endures in the face
of violence. The fetishist, like most feeling theorists, *believes* in the cura-
tive effects of representation. The fetishist *believes* that her intentional
gesture of loving is loving. The thought that critical representation or
analysis violates love draws a more precise portrait of what love is longing
for, because it creates mourning around an undamaged version of the
feeling, keeping it, and us, safe. Meanwhile, the history, the aggression,
the unevenness, the ambivalence—whatever is obscured by longing's
form—gets very little attention, deemed a threat to the very thing that
suffuses love's figura. Reducing the problem of living to a problem of
recognizing or making better instincts is perhaps what links feminist and
queer work to the liberalism of therapy culture. People can come to rest
in love, in the pursuit of its signs.

3. I Didn't Think This Would Happen Again

All of these modes meet up in women's culture, my particular archive, a
site of expertise about love and intimacy with its own transcripts of sublime suffering, its own conventions of evidence, affect, and ethics (Berlant, "Female Complaint" and "Poor Eliza"). The "women's culture" in-
dustry emerged in the United States during the 1830s to produce a kind
of generic feminine subject who would identify with the commodity addressed to her, seeing it as both a source of feminine identification and a
space of social critique that nonetheless protects heterosexuality. In particular, its topics constellate around the intimate. A woman must cultivate eloquence about feeling, and especially about love; she must learn
to recognize and repair the suffering generated by the cruel world; and
she must be pedagogical always, disseminating what she knows about
intimacy to her hapless public.

Different degrees of irony and critical practice are expressed by different participants in this zone of intimate publicity, but what binds these
discourses to women in particular is their self-heroized identification with
a culture of pain produced by failures of love, a constantly expanding
vault of narrative events. These aesthetic and ideological continuities

constitute the same thing as the continuity within femininity itself, established by a promise that by identifying with intimate spheres—and especially with cultivating love and language about love—women and persons generally can achieve both subjective uniqueness and a socially generic status. That is, to be in a love plot is to be made particular and generic at the same time. Love is the commodity form of subjectivity, the elastic enigmatic signifier whose potential contradictions intensify its magnetism rather than depleting it.

Like psychoanalysis and popular science, women's culture comes to love where love fails. The story of its folding likewise becomes not a site of interest or celebration but a blockage that must be dissolved or disremembered at the level of the individual, in order for happiness to be imaginable once again. (This process is usually called "sentimentality," with the marriage at the end as a figure of closure. But it must also be seen as pleasure in the formal sense: a return to a scene of impossibility with an optimism borne of a desire for optimism.) But women's culture partakes of counterhegemonic and avant-garde styles of critique too, in its insistence on dignifying a dreaming beyond conventional eloquence as a part of—and not a negation of—the real. Otherwise, in popular culture the ambivalence resolved in the plots of love gets recast as a mistake or a crime, rather than what it is—the route that the compulsion to repeat attachment takes, steaming ahead and feeding off the sublimity of aversive passions.

These ways of describing self-extension—the desire to become more than oneself, to become exchangeable, to become oriented toward a publicness that corresponds to an expanding interiority—suggest the appropriateness of naming love a queer affect. Just as we can posit that ambivalence is the thing love tries to hide when it turns into hate, aggression the thing that love tries to hide when it speaks of happiness forever, and narcissism and masochism the things that love tries to hide when we assert its other-directedness (the "you you you" aspect of love), so love queered marks an impossible desire for definition and for obfuscation, and a contradictory fear of the enigmatic and the clarified. It makes melancholia look like desire. To my mind, love is queered not when we discover it to be resistant to or more than all its known forms, but when we see that there is no world that admits how it actually works as a principle of living. This designation refracts as negativity the state of affect I have been calling *incoherence*. But whatever else it is, love is the paradigmatic form of optimism, the hope for a secured relation of cause to effect, a normative way to pursue mastery over the vicissitudes of desire.

So, it must be said at the beginning that love, more than any other topic, reveals the subject's ambivalent attachment not just to the lover, but also to knowledge. This is not a case of the will to not know, exactly— but the will to know that there's nothing shocking to know, that there will be no shock and no waste, just the consolations of the already incorporated form of the taken-for-granted. Bersani, citing Laplanche, argues inversely that this may be desire's way of signaling one's attachment to its essential enigma, which expresses itself in a multiplication of aesthetic forms as well as norms (*Caravaggio's Secrets*). This ambivalence toward the knowledge one seeks must be why critical analyses of love so often produce cynicism and mourning and rage—as, for example, in the various backlashes against feminist, queer, and sexuality studies. For where normativity is, explanation kills pleasure, interferes with the aura of inevitability that sanctions the tacit. The cultural debasement and proliferation of love's genres—talk shows, TV movies, soap operas, epics, and sagas— are also effects of the wrath that gets released when love is "explained" and relegated to some form of genetic encoding, unimaginative drive, or stupid-making instrumentality. Or, if love is explained, one is left with unbearable loneliness, with the coveted form of desire revealed as a cover story painted on a bubble. What we see here, additionally, is a figure of the desire for love as a desire for transformation without (castrating) agency. Perhaps this is what Teresa de Lauretis sees, in *Alice Doesn't*, as the mytheme of "femininity," a scene in which woman's most compelling dramatic role is to divest herself of agency, reducing her will to a gesture of its own self-annihilation. The pleasure of intelligibility that we derive from this repetition would then be a species of what Gramsci calls *passive revolution*, which involves the production of modes of consent that engender the normal world as the taken-for-granted one.

4. Absolutely Fabulous

So far, I have spoken generally of the absorption of the fantasy of love by normativity, a formative aesthetic with a large but repetitive archive. Normativity's genres are all really horror genres, threatening to fail to endorse love's contract to absorb aggression and ambivalence, whether into the happy ending or into a prior moment when the lure of that ending is confirmed before it is betrayed. Sexualities that seem to exist other than for the elaboration of the proper sign seem, in this light, like threats to the dominant genre of personhood—as Michael Warner's *The Trouble with Normal* points out with such clearheaded sense in its argument against the agendas of gay marriage politics. On the other hand, it is the pleasure of normative culture to nurture its phobias.

It is not surprising that such institutionalized and desexualized love would be the scene of many people's desire to experience at least one kind of conflict-free social belonging. What's more surprising to me is the undertheorized reappearance of love's conventionality in much of the most important work in queer theory—work that repeats the unworked-though lamination of love onto sexuality and desire that I have described as operating more generally. In the Lacanian model, desire's missed appointment with the *objet petit a* marks the disavowed impossibility of a love that is not of the law. The rest is rediscovered as a waste product of the ambivalent whiplash of *jouissance,* in which the subject ejected from love is the same one ejected from the "I" or ego. Queer theory's response to this landscape of terrifying law and normativity has been surprisingly earnest and confused. It is one thing to cough up desire's abjection: a whole other thing to counter love.

Here, briefly, are three instances of where queer theory has been—and wanted to be—in love: in Butler's *Psychic Life of Power,* Bersani and Dutoit's *Caravaggio's Secrets,* and de Lauretis's *Practice of Love.* I choose these examples because I've learned most about the perambulations of desire from them. Intricately and rigorously argued, they nonetheless hold love still as the known object around which desire travels. De Lauretis has long cast the agency-negating drama of normative femininity that I've been describing as a compulsion to repeat the incorporation of form as a specifically heteronormative, even heterosexual formation. In this, her work is echoed by Butler's recent deliberations on love and subjectification. Butler is not usually seen as a theorist of love. Yet the repetitive binding relation marked by the concept of love is central to her explanations of heterosexual melancholia and generic subjectivity. For Butler, love is the form of being that is reiterated throughout the field of the subject's activity.

The Psychic Life of Power ties love to the "passionate attachment" to the law, to dependency, and the state of being disciplined. Sexuality and its back-formation, gender, bind the subject to social norms in a constantly deferred and constantly exploited hope of recognition; this desire to be in love moves subjects to love the law. Heterosexually identifying subjects, she argues, must renounce love for their own gender, the latter of which she equates with the child's self-love. Subjects do this renunciation in order to keep alive their optimism for the law—they come to love the foreclosure that constitutes them.

This repetitive scenario raises many questions, in particular about the relations among attachment, desire, aim, and norm. What is self-love here? Loving one's own gender romantically? What concept of representation rules here, if not the long-refuted notion of homo-narcissism? What is the difference between the subject in general and the subject of heteronormativity? This version of heterosexual melancholia represents love and loss as though those categories were pre-ideological, or just obvious, because they are structures and conventions. It seems plausible to say that subjects are prepared for inequality by infantile attachment, but implausible to argue that love, desire, and libidinal attachment are different words for the same bond; that dependency and the *love* of one's subordination and the *love* of one's own gender are the same relation. *The Psychic Life of Power*'s final chapter turns to the relation of melancholia and ambivalence as the center of subjects in general, but leaves behind the question of the sexual subject: Here self-love is a relation to self, referring to nothing impersonal, like power. This too suggests how conventional is Butler's version of love, which equates attachment with its *represented* expression.

In contrast, love makes its way into *Caravaggio's Secrets* casually, as a name for fascination (38). Bersani and Dutoit contrast two models of the nonidentitarian sameness of the queered subject: an omnivorous, masochistic one and an aesthetic one. As in Butler, the subject here borrows its identity from the world—that is, the solo subject is the unit of loving, and the world is built out from that subject. But for Bersani and Dutoit, the masochistic pleasure of subordinating oneself to the law of identity (the law of form) corresponds with its antithesis, the subject's optimistic and aggressive reaching out into the world to find something of his own pleasure elsewhere, in an aesthetic of displaced form. They call this model of scavenging for being "self-incremental," because the subject reaches for form and—overwhelmed by its enigmatic construction—"metabolizes" what it can and represses the residue, becoming the secret of itself that it can't quite decipher. They suggest as well that this "nonsexual sadism"—this simultaneous submission to and incorporation of the enigmatic signifier—represses most of all the impossibility of introjection. When the subject recognizes the inevitable failure at eating its object, they argue, we discover the birth of the aesthetic, the fascination with the alterity of form, the pure pleasure of being overwhelmed and of having one's pleasures distributed across aesthetic surfaces in a way that enables surfeit without loss. The pursuit of self-relation through self-extension engenders additionally a love of one's own enigmatic condition that one experiences as a love of the knowledge of the other. This pleasure in embodied enigma is what makes Caravaggio available for a queer reading. However, the transformative outcome of this self-enfolded relation to sexual aesthetics or potentiality remains enigmatic in *Caravaggio's Secrets*.

In these models of the loving subject seeking her- or himself in the world, the presumption is that subjects make the world for themselves, and that love is fundamentally a narcissistic project, a project of inner-world building. (Bersani elsewhere imagines that these habits of incorporation might be reorganized across social spaces, breaking the paranoid fascination the couple-form engenders and thus enabling "solidarity," but it is not clear how this would happen, except by theory.) De Lauretis's *The Practice of Love*, in contrast, derives its notion of form, repetition, and the alternative possibilities of queerness from Bersani's earlier work on the centrality of fantasy and misrecognition in the formation of the subject's mobility in the scene of desire and identity (Bersani, *Freudian*). Yet for lesbians, she argues, one form of fantasy predominates, within the two-as-one of the scene of desire, and the compulsion to repeat that scene. De Lauretis argues that there is specificity to lesbian fetishism. The fetish conventionally marks castration anxiety—the traumatic loss of a sense of bodily totality for the lover who projects it onto the beloved's negatively valued corporeal difference. But lesbian desire has created its own aesthetic markers of desired and threatening "difference," because the distinctions between female lovers cannot be mapped onto sexually "different" bodies. Therefore castration, she argues, is irrelevant to lesbians. As a result, intersubjective fantasy plays a bigger part in the production of her version of lesbian love. In contrast to Freudian and heterosexual feminist theories of desire, which view love primarily as the effect of one subject's fetishized fantasies about an object of desire, de Lauretis's version of lesbian fetishism requires two lovers who fantasize together. The erotic aesthetic they generate produces an intimate boundary, a space of bodily distinction and difference, that their desire crosses and re-crosses—but not to destroy or make order from desire's unstable process. For de Lauretis, the fetishistic "perversion" of lesbian desire requires playing with form. A love liberated from repetition compulsion, a juggling with form, produces love without monuments, and therefore without destruction.

What's striking about these three paradigms of love as the ligament of sociality—the space in which the subject finds him- or herself repeatedly in fantasy and in power—is that the representational paradigms are prohibitively realist. For Bersani, shattering is represented as felt in orgasm and, later, in what he calls the terrifying and exhilarating instability of everyday subjectivity, as well as in the aesthetic form of extimate love, where one confronts and appreciates the impossibility of eating or incorporating the failed object. This model places the comforting intelligibility of conventional form at the very center of love's aesthetic sensuality. Likewise, the melancholia of Butler is felt as such, as panic, anxiety, ambivalence, and symbolization, while love is just love, an underdefined a priori–style object; and the love of de Lauretis is experienced as sexual desire in its infinite formal improvisation. In other words, in these queer zones the practice and the feeling of love replay its conventionality. Talking about "desire" is one thing: love—apparently, something else—is something that looks like itself. The mimetic ideology of its formalism remains, along with the default persistence of love as the condition of the self's continuity.

If love's function is to capture representation, to bind subjects to a world in which they feel possible, then perhaps this is not a problem. I want something other for love. The motive for this piece is to open some questions about love and its relation to formal conventions. It is to track the tacit zoning of convention as such in spaces of repetition that show love not just as a feeling one has, but also as a marker for a whole constellation of things that one wants to experience extremely. Too quickly, a picture is put on this vague cluster. Love approximates a space to which people can return, becoming as different as they can be from themselves without being traumatically shattered; it is a scene of optimism for change, for a transformational environment (Bollas, *Being* and *Shadow*). In all its domains of interpretation, love provides a rhetoric of resting, of coming to terms. To think of it as a placeholder relation, a proxy, a stand-in, a surrogate form, a starting line, we can begin to pursue the different logics of its wild syncretism. To the degree that gay and lesbian thoughts and desires threaten to impair the comfort people have learned to find in the formal inevitability of their intimate leanings, the resistance to what's *queer* about them can be read not just as a symptom of normativity in general, or as a sexual defense, but also as a fear of what will happen when those forms are separated from loving. Queer thought must take this on when it enters the political, the pedagogical—not by teaching that we are all alike and compelled to repeat our alikeness intelligibly, but by teaching some of what we've learned about love, under the surface, across the lines, around the scene, informally.

Notes

1. On the paradoxical centrality of the *figura* to the historicist text, see Shaw. On the centrality of repetitive practice to the production of intimacy, see Berlant, "Intimacy."

2. I have a queer feeling about this essay, and it isn't love. This essay is a *preliminary* part of an emergent project on affect and form (the other major part of which is about pain and trauma).

3. This thought about detection and love's epistemology came out of a conversation with Carol Clover.

4. Sedgwick argues in "Shame and Its Sisters" that we must submit to certain truths about the hardwiring of human affect. I agree and have no problem with this, especially since work on the physiology of affect argues more strenuously every day for the chemical bases of many patterns of feeling and of thought. But the affects are not a domain where words equal things, either: Why presume that the feelings we recognize are nondialectical and identical translocally and transhistorically?

5. The classic text on attachment is Bowlby's *Attachment*. For a useful summary of the ideologeme of "attachment," see Shaver, Hazan, and Bradshaw, "Love as Attachment: The Integration of Three Behavioral Systems," in Sternberg and Barnes.

6. This notion of the sexual revolution as derepression is most frequently located somewhere between the *Time* magazine version of the 1960s and the work of Marcuse (esp. *Eros and Civilization*) and of Barthes (esp. *The Pleasure of the Text*).

References

Balibar, Etienne. "Culture and Identity (Working Notes)." In *The Identity in Question*. Ed. John J. Rajchman. New York: Routledge, 1995. 173–96.

Barthes, Roland. *A Lover's Discourse*. Trans. Richard Howard. New York: Farrar, Straus and Giroux, 1978.

———. *The Pleasure of the Text*. Trans. Richard Miller. New York: Hill and Wang, 1975.

Berlant, Lauren. "The Compulsion to Repeat Femininity." In *Giving Ground: The Politics of Propinquity*. Ed. Joan Copjec and Michael Sorkin. New York: Verso, 1999. 207–32.

———. "The Female Complaint." *Social Text* 19/20 (1988): 237–59.

———. "Intimacy: A Special Issue." In *Intimacy*. Ed. Lauren Berlant. Chicago: U of Chicago P, 2000. 1–8.

———. "Poor Eliza." *American Literature* 70 (1998): 635–68.

Berlant, Lauren, and Michael Warner. "Sex in Public." In *Intimacy*. Ed. Berlant. 311–30.

Bersani, Leo. *The Freudian Body: Psychoanalysis and Art.* New York: Columbia UP, 1986.

———. "Is the Rectum a Grave?" In *AIDS: Cultural Analysis/Cultural Activism.* Ed. Douglas Crimp. Cambridge: MIT P, 1988. 197–222.

Bersani, Leo, and Ulysse Dutoit. *Caravaggio's Secrets.* Cambridge: MIT P, 1998.

Bois, Yve-Alain, and Rosalind E. Krauss, eds. *Formless: A User's Guide.* New York: Zone, 1997.

Bollas, Christopher. *Being a Character: Psychoanalysis and Self-Experience.* New York: Hill and Wang, 1994.

———. *The Shadow of the Object: Psychoanalysis of the Thought Unknown.* New York: Columbia UP, 1989.

Bowlby, John. *Attachment.* 1969. New York: Basic Books, 2000.

Butler, Judith. *The Psychic Life of Power: Theories in Subjection.* Stanford: Stanford UP, 1997.

Canguilhem, Georges, and Michel Foucault. *The Normal and the Pathological.* New York: Zone Books, 1989.

Copjec, Joan. *Read My Desire: Lacan against the Historicists.* Cambridge: MIT P, 1994.

de Lauretis, Teresa. *Alice Doesn't: Feminism, Semiotics, and Cinema.* Bloomington: Indiana UP, 1984.

———. *The Practice of Love: Lesbian Sexuality and Perverse Desire.* Bloomington: Indiana UP, 1994.

Foucault, Michel. "The History of Sexuality." *Power/Knowledge: Selected Interviews and Other Writings, 1972–1977.* New York: Pantheon, 1980. 183–93.

———. *The History of Sexuality, Volume I: An Introduction.* 1976. Trans. Robert Hurley. New York: Random House, 1978.

Freud, Sigmund. *Beyond the Pleasure Principle.* 1920. *Standard* 18:1–64.

———. "'A Child Is Being Beaten': A Contribution to the Study of the Origin of Sexual Perversions." 1919. *Standard* 17:175–204.

———. "The Economic Problem of Masochism." 1924. *Standard* 19:157–70.

———. *Fragment of an Analysis of a Case of Hysteria.* 1905. *Standard* 7:7–122.

———. "On the Universal Tendency Toward Debasement in the Sphere of Love (Contributions to the Psychology of Love II)." 1912. *Standard* 11:171–90.

———. "A Special Type of Object-Choice Made by Men (Contributions to the Psychology of Love I)." 1910. *Standard* 11:165–75.

———. *The Standard Edition of the Complete Psychological Works of Sigmund Freud.* Ed. and trans. James Strachey. 24 vols. London: Hogarth, 1953–74.

———. *Three Essays on the Theory of Sexuality.* 1905. *Standard* 7:123–243.

Girard, René. *Deceit, Desire, and the Novel: Self and Other in Literary Structure.* 1961. Trans. Yvonne Freccero. Baltimore: Johns Hopkins UP, 1976.

Golding, Sue, ed. *The Eight Technologies of Otherness.* New York: Routledge, 1997.

Gornick, Vivian. *The End of the Novel of Love.* Boston: Beacon P, 1997.

Gramsci, Antonio. *An Antonio Gramsci Reader.* Ed. David Forgacs. New York: Schocken, 1988.

Hutcheon, Linda. *Irony's Edge: The Theory and Practice of Irony.* New York: Routledge, 1995.

Laplanche, Jean. *Seduction, Translation, Drives.* Ed. John Fletcher and Martin Stanton. London: ICA, 1992.

Laplanche, Jean, and Jean-Bertrand Pontalis. "Fantasy and the Origins of Sexuality." 1964. In *Formations of Fantasy.* Ed. Victor Burgin, James Donald, and Cora Kaplan. New York: Routledge, 1986. 5–44.

Marcuse, Herbert. *Eros and Civilization.* Boston: Beacon P, 1974.

———. *An Essay on Liberation.* Boston: Beacon P, 1969.

Mitchell, Juliet, and Jacqueline Rose, eds. *Feminine Sexuality: Jacques Lacan and the école freudienne.* Trans. Rose. New York: Norton, 1982.

Rose, Jacqueline. *Why War? Psychoanalysis, Politics, and the Return to Melanie Klein.* Oxford: Blackwell, 1993.

Safe. Dir. Todd Haynes. 1995.

Sedgwick, Eve Kosofsky. *Epistemology of the Closet.* Berkeley: U of California P, 1990.

———. "A Poem Is Being Written." *Representations* 17 (1987): 110–43.

Sedgwick, Eve, and Adam Frank. *Shame and Its Sisters: A Silvan Tomkins Reader.* Durham: Duke UP, 1995.

Shaver, Philip, Cindy Hazan, and Donna Bradshaw. "Love as Attachment: The Integration of Three Behavioral Systems." In *The Psychology of Love.* Ed. Robert J. Sternberg and Michael L. Barnes. New Haven: Yale UP, 1988. 68–99.

Shaw, Harry. *Narrating Reality: Austen, Scott, Eliot.* Ithaca: Cornell UP, 1999.

Warner, Michael. *The Trouble with Normal: Sex, Politics, and the Ethics of Queer Life.* New York: Free P, 1999.

Žižek, Slavoj, ed. *Mapping Ideology.* New York: Verso, 1995.

———. *The Ticklish Subject: The Absent Centre of Political Ontology.* London: Verso, 1999.

CONTRIBUTORS

Lauren Berlant is Professor of English at the University of Chicago, and coeditor of *Critical Inquiry.* She is the author of *The Anatomy of National Fantasy: Hawthorne, Utopia, and Everyday Life* (U of Chicago P, 1991), *The Queen of America Goes to Washington City: Essays on Sex and Citizenship* (Duke UP, 1997), *The Female Complaint: The Unfinished Business of Sentimentality in American Culture* (forthcoming), and, with Laura Letinsky, *Venus Inferred* (U of Chicago P, 2000), as well as editor of *Intimacy* (U of Chicago P, 2000).

Leo Bersani was until recently the Class of 1950 Professor of French at the University of California, Berkeley. His many books include *A Future for Astyanax: Character and Desire in Literature* (Little, Brown, 1976); *Baudelaire and Freud* (U of California P, 1977); *The Death of Stéphane Mallarmé* (Cambridge UP, 1982); *The Freudian Body: Psychoanalysis and Art* (Columbia UP, 1986); *The Culture of Redemption* (Harvard UP, 1990); and *Homos* (Harvard UP, 1995). He has also coauthored, with Ulysse Dutoit, *The Forms of Violence: Narrative in Assyrian Art and Modern Culture* (Schocken, 1985); *Arts of Impoverishment: Beckett, Rothko, Resnais* (Harvard UP, 1993); *Caravaggio's Secrets* (MIT P, 1998); and, most recently, *Caravaggio* (BFI, 1999), a study of Derek Jarman's films.

Daniel L. Buccino maintains a private practice in Baltimore and is Student Coordinator in the Community Psychiatry Program at the Johns Hopkins Bayview Medical Center. He is on the faculties of the Johns Hopkins University School of Medicine as well as the Smith College and University of Maryland Schools for Social Work.

Arnold I. Davidson is Professor of Philosophy, Divinity, and the Conceptual Foundations of Science at the University of Chicago, where he is also executive editor of *Critical Inquiry.* He is the editor of Pierre Hadot's *Philosophy as a Way of Life: Spiritual Exercises from Socrates to Foucault* (Blackwell, 1995) and *Foucault and His Interlocutors* (U of Chicago P, 1997), as well as coeditor of *Questions of Evidence: Proof, Practice, and Persuasion across the Disciplines* (U of Chicago P, 1994). He is also the general editor for the English language edition of Michel Foucault's courses at the Collège de France. His forthcoming book is entitled *The Emergence of Sexuality: Historical Epistemology and the Formation of Concepts* (Harvard UP).

Tim Dean is Associate Professor of English and Interpretive Theory at the University of Illinois, Urbana-Champaign. He is the author of *Gary Snyder and the American Unconscious* (Macmillan, 1991) and *Beyond Sexuality* (U of Chicago P, 2000), as well as of numerous articles on sexuality and psychoanalysis. He is currently completing two books: *The Otherness of Art* and *Modernism and the Ethics of Impersonality.*

Jonathan Dollimore is Professor of English and Related Literature at the University of York, England. His books include *Radical Tragedy: Religion, Ideology and Power in the Drama of Shakespeare and His Contemporaries* (Harvester Wheatsheaf, 1984; Duke UP, 1993); *Sexual Dissidence: Augustine to Wilde, Freud to Foucault* (Oxford UP, 1991); and, most recently, *Death, Desire and Loss in Western Culture* (Penguin, 1998). He is also coeditor of *Political Shakespeare: New Essays in Cultural Materialism* (Manchester, 1985; Cornell UP, 1994).

Brad Epps is Professor of Romance Languages and Literatures at Harvard University. He is the author of *Significant Violence: Oppression and Resistance in the Narratives of Juan Goytisolo, 1970–1990* (Oxford UP, 1996). His new project is entitled *Daring to Write: Gay and Lesbian Literature in Spain, Latin America, and the United States.*

Michel Foucault (1926–1984) was Professor of the History of Systems of Thought at the Collège de France. Among his numerous influential works are *Madness and Civilization: A History of Insanity in the Age of Reason* (1961); *The Birth of the Clinic: An Archaeology of Medical Perception* (1963); *The Order of Things: An Archaeology of the Human Sciences* (1966); *The Archaeology of Knowledge* (1969); *Discipline and Punish: The Birth of the Prison* (1975); and three volumes of *The History of Sexuality* (1976–84). *Dits et écrits,* a four-volume collection of his writings, was published in 1994.

Lynda Hart was Professor of English at the University of Pennsylvania until her death in December 2000. She was the author of *Sam Shepard's Metaphorical Stages* (Greenwood, 1987); *Fatal Women: Lesbian Sexuality and the Mark of Aggression* (Princeton UP, 1994); and *Between the Body and the Flesh: Performing Sado-Masochism* (Columbia UP, 1998). She was also editor of *Making a Spectacle: Feminist Essays on Contemporary Women's Theatre* (U of Michigan P, 1989) and *Of All the Nerve: Deb Margolin Solo* (Cassell, 1999), as well as coeditor, with Peggy Phelan, of *Acting Out: Feminist Performances* (U of Michigan P, 1993).

Jason B. Jones, a graduate student in English at Emory University, is currently writing a dissertation entitled "Histories of the Real: Victorian Representations of Reform."

Christopher Lane is Associate Professor of English and Director of the Psychoanalytic Studies Program at Emory University. He is the author of *The Ruling Passion: British Colonial Allegory and the Paradox of Homosexual Desire* (Duke UP, 1995) and *The Burdens of Intimacy: Psychoanalysis and Victorian Masculinity* (U of Chicago P, 1999), as well as editor of *The Psychoanalysis of Race* (Columbia UP, 1998). He is currently completing a book on misanthropy in Victorian literature and culture.

H. N. Lukes is studying in the English Department at UCLA, where she is writing her dissertation, "Let's Get Lost: The Psychoanalysis of Wanderlust and Perversion in Twentieth-Century American Literature." She has published an essay in the *Oxford Literary Review* entitled "Is the Rectum *das Ding*? Bersani, Lacan, and the Ethics of Perversion."

Catherine Millot is Professor of Psychoanalysis at the University of Paris, VIII, and a practicing analyst. She is the author of *Freud antipédagogue* (Bibliothèque d'Ornicar?, 1979); *Horsexe: Essay on Transsexuality* (1983; trans. Autonomedia, 1990); *Nobodaddy: L'hystérie dans le siècle* (Hors Ligne, 1988); *La Vocation de l'écrivain* (Gallimard, 1991); and *Gide, Genet, Mishima: Intelligence de la perversion* (Gallimard, 1996).

Elizabeth A. Povinelli is Professor of Anthropology and of Social Sciences at the University of Chicago and editor of *Public Culture*. She is the author of *Labor's Lot: The Power, History, and Culture of Aboriginal Action* (U of Chicago P, 1994) and of essays in *Public Culture, diacritics, American Anthropologist,* and *Critical Inquiry*. She also coedited *Thinking Sexuality Transnationally*, a special issue of GLQ: *A Journal of Lesbian and Gay Studies*, and is currently completing a book on Aboriginal sexuality and Australian nationalism.

Ellie Ragland, Professor of English at the University of Missouri-Columbia, is founding editor of *Newsletter of the Freudian Field* and the author of several books, including *Jacques Lacan and the Philosophy of Psychoanalysis* (U of Illinois P, 1986) and *Essays on the Pleasures of Death: From Freud to Lacan* (Routledge, 1995). Her most recent collection, *Critical Essays on Jacques Lacan* (Macmillan, 1999), will be followed by a book coedited with David Metzger, *Proving Lacan* (U of Illinois P, forthcoming).

Paul Robinson is Richard W. Lyman Professor in the Humanities and of History at Stanford University. His books include *The Freudian Left: Wilhelm Reich, Géza Róheim, Herbert Marcuse* (Harper and Row, 1969; Cornell UP, 1990); *The Moderniza-*

tion of Sex: Havelock Ellis, Alfred Kinsey, William Masters and Virginia Johnson (Harper and Row, 1976; Cornell UP, 1989); *Opera and Ideas: From Mozart to Strauss* (Harper and Row, 1985; Cornell UP, 1986); and, most recently, *Gay Lives: Homosexual Autobiography from John Addington Symonds to Paul Monette* (U of Chicago P, 1999).

Judith Roof is Professor of English at Michigan State University. She is the author of *A Lure of Knowledge: Lesbian Sexuality and Theory* (Columbia UP, 1991); *Come As You Are: Sexuality and Narrative* (Columbia UP, 1996); and *Reproductions of Reproduction: Imaging Symbolic Change* (Routledge, 1996). She is also coeditor of *Feminism and Psychoanalysis* (Cornell UP, 1989); *Who Can Speak? Authority and Critical Identity* (U of Illinois P, 1995); and *Staging the Rage: The Web of Misogyny in Modern Drama* (Fairleigh Dickinson, 1998).

Joanna Ryan is a psychoanalytic psychotherapist working in London. She is the coauthor of *The Politics of Mental Handicap* (Free Association, 1980, rev. 1987) and of *Wild Desires and Mistaken Identities: Lesbianism and Psychoanalysis* (Columbia UP, 1993). She also coedited *Sex and Love: New Thoughts on Old Contradictions* (Women's P, 1983) and is the author of recent articles in *Gender and Psychoanalysis* and the collection *Who's Afraid of Feminism?* (Hamish Hamilton, 1997). She has been involved, with others, in setting up a new organization in Britain, "The Site for Contemporary Psychoanalysis," which aims to incorporate philosophy and politics into a critical approach to practice and teaching.

Ramón E. Soto-Crespo is Assistant Professor of Humanistic Studies at University of Wisconsin, Green Bay. He has held research fellowships at the University of Michigan and the University of Illinois, Urbana-Champaign, and is currently completing two books: *Imaginary Islands in Caribbean Literature and Culture* and a project tentatively entitled *Mourning Otherness: Homosexuality, Psychoanalysis, and the Praxis of Loss*.

Suzanne Yang received her M.D. from the University of California, San Francisco, in 1998 and is currently completing her residency training in psychiatry at Columbia University and the New York State Psychiatric Institute.

INDEX